On the Fiery March

Italy, Southern Europe, and the Mediterranean

Italian East Africa

On the Fiery March

Mussolini Prepares for War

G. BRUCE STRANG

International History
Erik Goldstein, William R. Keylor, and Cathal J. Nolan, Series Editors

PRAEGER

OCM 50695336

Westport, Connecticut
London

Library of Congress Cataloging-in-Publication Data

Strang, G. Bruce, 1963–
   On the fiery march : Mussolini prepares for war / G. Bruce Strang.
     p. cm. — (International history, ISSN 1527–2230)
   ISBN 0–275–97937–7(alk. paper)
   1. World War, 1939–1945—Italy. 2. Mussolini, Benito, 1883–1945. 3. Fascism—Italy. 4. Italy—
Politics and government—1914–1945. I. Title. II. Series.

   D763.I8 S755 2003
   940.54'0945—dc21   2002032984

British Library Cataloguing in Publication Data is available.

Library of Congress Catalog Card Number: 2002032984
ISBN: 0–275–97937–7
ISSN: 1527–2230

First published in 2003

Praeger Publishers, 88 Post Road West, Westport, CT 06881
An imprint of Greenwood Publishing Group, Inc.
www.praeger.com

Printed in the United States of America

The paper used in this book complies with the
Permanent Paper Standard issued by the National
Information Standards Organization (Z39.48–1984).

10 9 8 7 6 5 4 3 2 1

For Nancy

Contents

Preface

Historians have sifted through the disastrous decisions of the 1930s that plunged the world into depression and war. Historians, political scientists, and philosophers have spilled proverbial rivers of ink trying to explain the causes of World War II, surveying an ever wider array of sources and evidence. Why, then, do we need another study that attempts to explain a part of the complex, interrelated origins of that war? The answer lies in two broad categories. The first, more nebulous one is that successive generations of historians bring new perspectives to old, unchanging histories. We have the benefit of assessing past writers' works, subjecting them to critical scrutiny, and, ideally, over time improving our collective understanding of the past. The second, more tangible reason is that historians occasionally achieve greater access to historical documentation.

Such is the case with this study on Mussolini and Italian foreign policy. After a long process of restoration, the Italian Foreign Ministry Archive has restored and microfilmed the so-called *Carte Lancelotti*, a collection of papers that then Foreign Minister Raffaele Guariglia removed in September 1943 from the Foreign Ministry to safeguard from German capture as the new Italian government tried to arrange its exit from the war. These papers from Galeazzo Ciano's *Gabinetto*, the Foreign Ministry office under which Mussolini and Ciano successively centralized and tightened Fascist control of foreign policy, comprise an important collection of telegrams, notes of interviews with foreign statesmen and diplomats, and personal memoranda. In addition, scholars now have access to the *Serie Affari Politici*, copies of telegrams from embassies abroad plus the diplomatic traffic sent from the *Gabinetto* to various embassies. These archival sources supplemented by published material, particularly Ciano's diaries, which historians and archival evidence have for the most part corroborated, provide the most comprehensive documentation available on Italian policy before the Second World War.

This study also adds a substantially new interpretive cast to the historical debate. During the archival research for this project, I became increasingly convinced that Mussolini's policy had a coherent thread and paradoxical consistency amid his seemingly opportunistic maneuvers and occasionally wavering policies. His decisions were not wholly rational; he was no mere opportunist, nor was he entirely inconsistent. In searching for the appropriate methodology to use to explain Italian policy, the evidence compelled me to discard many of the tools of recent international relations history; the now conventional reference to structuralist causation cannot properly explain the decisions of a fundamentally irrational thinker. Accordingly, I have focused my explanation of Mussolini's policy on an understanding of his *mentalité*. Mussolini's ultranationalist belief system, based on a high degree of racism, militarism, and social Darwinism, led him to cast his lot with Nazi Germany in order to expand Italy's power, influence, and territory at the expense of the Western democracies of France and Great Britain.

Given this focus, I have concentrated my detailed discussion of Italian foreign policy on the period from June 1936 to September 1939. I chose to examine this period because, after the conquest of Ethiopia, Mussolini had the option to reorient his foreign policy in the light of British and French attempts to restore the Stresa Front against Germany. This choice would protect Italy against the growing might of Germany and the potential German threat to Austrian independence and to Italy's northern frontier. It would also inhibit Mussolini's ability to carry out territorial aggrandizement in Europe or Africa, as British and French statesmen aimed to preserve the status quo. A second option would be to straddle the fence, to play each side against the other, hoping to extract concessions from both in exchange for temporary Italian favor. A third choice was to link Italy to the increasing dynamism of Nazi Germany, setting Italy on a course toward eventual expansion in Africa, the Mediterranean, and the Balkans. This policy would inevitably entail confrontation with Britain and France. In addition, this monograph begins its detailed examination of Mussolini's foreign policy in June 1936 because Mussolini appointed his son-in-law, Galeazzo Ciano, to the Foreign Ministry, starting the process of Fascisticizing Italian diplomacy. Ciano, Mussolini's thoroughly loyal subordinate, was his father-in-law's stalking horse for the implementation of this initiative as well as the rapprochement with Nazi Germany.

By August 1939, Mussolini had substantially changed the orientation of Fascist foreign policy, having chosen in January to pursue a tripartite Italo-German-Japanese alliance directed against Great Britain. He hoped to reach that agreement so that he could carry out a program of expansion to displace France and Britain as the great North African colonial powers. In other words, he had chosen the third alternative. Although Mussolini chose to remain a nonbelligerent in September 1939, he did so only because Fascist Italy was woefully unprepared for a war that the Duce considered premature. Nevertheless, Mussolini had foreclosed the chance to realize a genuine rapprochement with the West, and although Mussolini's relationship with the German ally was sometimes difficult, it is not surprising that he threw Italy into the Second World War as Germany overran France. The German alliance offered Mussolini the best chance to realize his extravagant imperial dreams, and although events would conspire against his idealized, fatalistic vision of the future, Mussolini had deliberately embarked Italy on a course that carried Italy to defeat and him to a bitter, violent end.

Although this monograph is in many ways an individual accomplishment, I never could have completed it without the advice and support of many people. I owe a profound debt of gratitude to so many, though I can name only a few here.

I would like to thank colleagues Alan Cassels, Robert H. Johnston, Martin Horn, and Stephen Morewood, who read all or part of the manuscript. Their thoughtful criticisms made this a better work. Naturally, the responsibility for the text is my own. I would like to thank Alan Cassels in particular for agreeing to supervise my thesis well into his retirement. I would also like to thank Wayne Thorpe for his encouragement during my graduate years and Rob Hanks and John Schindler for the many discussions that we have had about history and politics, as well as less weighty matters.

The staff of many archives, the Archivio Storico del Ministero degli Affari Esteri, the Archivio Centrale dello Stato, the Public Record Office, the National Archives and Record Administration, and the University of Birmingham Library, provided access to important research material. I would especially like to thank Michele Abbate of the Archivio Storico for his gracious assistance during my most recent trip to Rome.

The Social Sciences and Humanities Research Council of Canada, the Ontario Graduate Scholarships Committee, and McMaster University provided vitally important funding support, and I would especially like to thank the family of Richard J. Fuller, whose generous bequest to the History Department made my archival research possible.

I owe a profound debt to members of my family: to many aunts, uncles, and cousins; to Lynn Mitchell-Pederson for showing me that it could be done; to Kent, Shawna, and especially David and Kristel, for their financial and emotional support, as well as their fellowship in Hamilton; to newfound family, Oliver, Mavis, and Bill Whitworth and Margi and Brian Hennen; to Alex Cruickshank; to my grandmothers, Eva Mitchell and the late Agnes Strang, who instilled in their children the value of education; and to George and Joyce Strang, without whom I could not have made it this far. My profound regret is that my father did not live to see this work completed.

I have saved three people for the last. I thank Robert J. Young of the University of Winnipeg for making my academic career possible. He continues to be a mentor and a friend. His graciousness and academic accomplishments inspire me to strive to achieve a higher level in my own work. I would like to express my profound thanks to my mother, Ruth Mitchell, for inspiring me to pursue this goal, for encouraging me to carry on when the path seemed bleak, and, most of all, for convincing me to keep the courage of my convictions. I could not have done it without her. Finally, I am amazed and grateful for the good fortune that Nancy Hennen shares in my life and work. Although we pursue different paths, in our own ways we both aspire to artistry.

Series Foreword

This series furthers historical writing that is genuinely international in scope and multiarchival in methodology. It publishes different types of works in the field of international history: Scholarly monographs, which elucidate important but hitherto unexplored or underexplored topics; more general works, which incorporate the results of specialized studies and present them to a wider public; and edited volumes, which bring together distinguished scholars to address salient issues in international history.

The series promotes scholarship in traditional subfields of international history such as the political, military, diplomatic, and economic relations among states. But it also welcomes studies that address topics of nonstate history and of more recent interest, such as the role of international non-governmental organizations in promoting new policies, cultural relations among societies, and the history of private international economic activity.

In short, while this series happily embraces traditional diplomatic history, it does not operate on the assumption that the state is an autonomous actor in international relations and that the job of the international historian is done solely by consulting the official records left behind by various foreign offices. Instead, it encourages scholarly work that also probes the broader forces within society that influence the formulation and execution of foreign policies, social tensions, religious and ethnic conflict, economic competition, environmental concerns, scientific and technology issues, and international cultural relations.

On the other hand, the series eschews works that concentrate exclusively on the foreign policy of any single nation. Hence, notwithstanding the central role played by the United States in international affairs since World War II, or of Great Britain in the nineteenth century, history written according to "the view from Washington" or "the view from London" does not satisfy the editors' criteria for international history, in the proper sense of that term. The books in this series do not assume a parochial perspective. In addition to reviewing the domestic context of any one country's foreign policies, they also accord appropriate consideration of the consequences of those policies abroad and the reciprocal relationships between the country of primary interest and other countries (and actors) with which it comes into contact.

The vast majority of recent publications in international history, in both book and article form, deal with the period since the end of the Second World War. The Cold War in particular has generated an impressive and constantly expanding body of historical scholarship. While this series also publishes works which treat this recent historical period, overall it takes a long view of international history. It is deeply interested in scholarship dealing with much earlier, even classical, eras of world history. The prospect of obtaining access to newly declassified documentary records (from Western governments and especially from the former members of the Warsaw Pact Organization) is an exciting one and will doubtless lead to the publication of important works that deepen our understanding of the recent past. But historians must not be dissuaded from investigating periods in the more distant past. Although most of the pertinent archives for such periods have been available for some time and have already been perused by scholars, renewed interpretations and assessments of earlier historical developments are essential to any ongoing understanding of the roots of the contemporary world.

The editors of this series hold appointments in departments of history, political science, and international relations. They are, therefore, deeply committed to an interdisciplinary approach to international history and welcome submissions from scholars in all these separate, but interrelated, disciplines. But that eclectic, humanistic approach should not be misconstrued to mean that any political science or international relations work will be of interest to the series, or its readers. Scholars from any discipline who locate their research and writing in the classical tradition of intellectual inquiry, that which examines the historical antecedents of international conflict and cooperation in order to understand contemporary affairs, are welcome to submit works for consideration. Such scholars are not interested in constructing abstract, and abstruse, theoretical models that have little relation to historical reality and possess no explanatory power for contemporary affairs, either. Instead, they share the conviction that a careful, scrupulous, deeply scholarly examination of historical evidence is a prerequisite to understanding the past, living in the present, and preparing for the future. And most fundamentally, although they may disagree on the precise meaning of this or that past event or decision, they reject the fashionable but ultimately intellectually and morally sterile assertion that historical truth is entirely relative and therefore that all interpretations of past events are equally valid, or equally squalid, as they merely reflect the whims and prejudices of individual historians. This group of scholars, the natural clientele of this series, instead believe that it is the principal obligation of scholarship to ferret out real and lasting truths. Furthermore, they believe that having done so, the results of scholarly investigation must be conveyed with clarity and precision to a more general audience, in jargon-free, unpretentious language that any intelligent reader may readily comprehend.

Erik Goldstein, William R. Keylor, and Cathal J. Nolan

Introduction

In April 1945, Mussolini's imperial dreams lay in ruins. Victorious Western allied armies advanced up the Italian peninsula, and Mussolini fled Milan hoping to postpone his day of reckoning. At dawn on 27 April, Mussolini and his entourage, including his mistress, Clara Petacci, joined a retreating German column heading for Austria. The column encountered a group of partisans, and having no stomach for a fight, agreed to turn over any Italian personnel in exchange for free passage. Mussolini was victim of yet another German betrayal. The partisans secluded him in a farmhouse near the town of Dongo. Word of Mussolini's capture reached Milan, and the self-styled Colonel Valerio (Walter Audisio), a communist member of the *Comitati di liberazione nazionale,* went to find the Duce. About a mile from the farmhouse, he lined Mussolini and Petacci up against the wall of a local villa and machine-gunned them. The following day, their bodies hung upside down at a gas station in Milan's Piazzale Loreto. Mussolini's dreams of expansion had led him to an ignominious end.

Mussolini's decision to declare war on Britain and France on 10 June 1940 was fraught with peril. Even though France lay prostrate, the British empire represented a formidable foe—one that would stretch Italian men and resources to the limit. Mussolini, his generals, and his men proved inadequate to the task, primarily owing to failures of the regime. The regime did not provide sufficient modern tanks, trucks, airplanes, or artillery pieces for modern warfare, and there was insufficient will on the part of soldiers to bring Mussolini the victories for which he thirsted. The British counterattack and victory at Beda Fomm in February 1941 doomed

Mussolini's African campaign, and it was only with a German-dominated army that he could stave off defeat there until 1943. Similarly, his folly in invading Greece in October 1940, when he thought that the Greeks were too intimidated to fight effectively, essentially ended Italy's role as an independent power. Rescuing Mussolini's hollow legions in both North Africa and in the Balkans, Hitler took his fellow dictator and the Italian war effort in tow. In July 1943, Mussolini's henchmen, including his own son-in-law, plotted to overthrow him; King Vittorio Emanuele III dismissed him in favor of Marshal Badoglio and had Mussolini arrested and imprisoned.

Given the appalling nature of the failures of Mussolini's Italy during the Second World War, why had he committed Italy to the battle on the Nazi side? Many historians have ventured answers to this question.[1] The earliest writers were harsh critics. Contemporaries of Mussolini, many had been active in the domestic resistance to Fascism. Gaetano Salvemini is the most notable. A social democrat and one of Italy's leading historians, Salvemini founded an anti-Fascist newspaper after Mussolini's rise to power. Harassed into exile in 1925, Salvemini wrote several polemics attempting to raise Western opposition to Mussolini's regime.[2] In 1953, he published *Prelude to World War II,* a polemic based in part on a prewar book; Salvemini condemned Mussolini as "an irresponsible improviser, half madman, half criminal."[3] Salvemini's interpretation dominated Italian scholarship until the 1960s, not so much owing to the accuracy of his vision but rather to his place in Italian society. His last volume appeared before the release of official documents. His stature as historian and member of Italy's political and intellectual elite reinforced his work, and, by almost casually dismissing real meaning from Mussolini's Fascism, he gave some comfort to a society that did not want to confront its expansionist, imperialist, and sometimes racialist past.[4] Nor did early international writers challenge this interpretation. British journalist Elizabeth Wiskemann also argued that for all Mussolini's bluster, he never had any clear foreign policy goals.[5] H. Stuart Hughes, in a short article on Italian diplomacy, also suggested that Mussolini did not pursue a consistently irredentist policy.[6]

These early efforts, hampered by a lack of even published documentation, did not provide an entirely convincing picture of Mussolini's foreign policy. If Mussolini were a mere propagandist and opportunist, then how could he have deeply entangled himself so deeply in the Second World War? Ennio Di Nolfo, a Professor at the University of Florence, published his *Mussolini e la politica estera italiana* in 1960.[7] Hampered by the lack of available documents for the period after 1925, he did not substantially revise the Salveminian version. Still, Di Nolfo held that, by subordinating foreign policy to domestic policy, Mussolini did have at least some concept of eventual ends.

Two modern, often acerbic British writers continued this tradition. The iconoclastic A.J.P. Taylor wrote his famous, or infamous, *The Origins of the Second World War* in 1961. Taylor, a strong anti-Fascist and antiestablishment figure, had refused to visit Italy while Mussolini ruled it. Not surprisingly, he denounced Mussolini's pretensions. "Everything about fascism was a fraud. The social peril from which it saved Italy was a fraud; the revolution by which it seized power was a fraud; the ability and policy of Mussolini were fraudulent. Fascist rule was corrupt, incompetent, empty; Mussolini himself a vain, blundering boaster without either ideas or aims."[8] Taylor's depiction allowed little room for explaining the importance for Mussolini's foreign policy; Taylor consigned Mussolini to the periphery of European affairs. In a similar manner, Denis Mack Smith has written highly entertaining, unflattering portrayals of Mussolini.[9] Mack Smith's Mussolini is a man of few convictions, without real talent, save the highly skilled use of propaganda. "He had got used to living in a cloud-cuckoo-land, where words and not facts mattered, where the army was judged by its parade ground performance rather than by anything more substantial, where wars were won not by superior munitions and by superior strategy but by knowing how much to manipulate the news so as to give the illusion of strength." Mack Smith saw Mussolini as a sawdust Caesar for whom "prestige, propaganda, and public statements were what counted; and it is hard to avoid the conclusion that this was the central message and the real soft core at the heart of Italian fascism."[10] As historical analyses, however, these views do not seem to have the power to explain Mussolini's Axis policy and his rash entry into the Second World War. These events were essentially the very antithesis of opportunism—they destroyed the Fascist regime—and a real opportunist without any central vision would not have driven Italy to this disastrous defeat.

Since the wider availability of documentation, historians have generally subjected these interpretations to a substantial revision. For the most part, scholars agree that Mussolini had a coherent foreign policy, despite the rhetoric he often employed. The difficulty now is that these interpretations differ so widely regarding Mussolini's aims. Alan Cassels's 1970 monograph, *Mussolini's Early Diplomacy,* based on published evidence, argued that the first decade of Mussolini's rule was not a decade of good behavior.[11] Mussolini flirted with a German alliance to immobilize the French army on the Rhine and openly considered foreign military adventures such as the Corfu crisis, though his cautious diplomats usually managed to rein

him in. In Cassels's view, Mussolini's foreign policy was much more consistent and not generated purely for propaganda reasons. In the early years,
he generally played a policy of equidistance between the revisionist Germany and the conservative Britain and France, though always with an eye
toward defending the Brenner frontier against German irrendentism. His
main aim was to establish Italy as a member of the four European great
powers.

Similarly, Esmonde Robertson, who published *Mussolini as Empire
Builder* in 1977, portrayed the Duce as a man who planned a foreign policy. Initially, within the strained European states system, Mussolini sought
to profit in prestige from playing a kind of role as balancer of power. If
Britain and France refused to accommodate his demands for increased
power in the Mediterranean, then he could threaten to disrupt their control
of British and French territories. His approaches to and divergences from
the European powers determined Mussolini's policy. When he failed to
profit from European tension, he turned toward African conquest, which,
despite the long military and diplomatic preparation necessary, seemed to
offer Mussolini the only spectacular success remaining.[12]

MacGregor Knox is perhaps the most important English-language
writer on Fascist foreign policy. He published *Mussolini Unleashed* in
1982, a monograph on Italian foreign policy and military adventure from
the outbreak of the Second World War to the summer of 1941. Although
denied access to the Italian Foreign Ministry files at the time, MacGregor
Knox made extensive use of Mussolini's *Carteggio Reservato,* or private
papers, as well as other archival documents. MacGregor Knox argued,
"Mussolini had a genuine foreign policy programme: the creation of an
Italian *spazio vitale* in the Mediterranean and the Middle East."[13] In his
later work, MacGregor Knox has slightly qualified and expanded his earlier views; he has argued that foreign expansion also served a role in
helping Mussolini to conquer domestic resistance to his attempts to transform the Italian political culture and people. Through military conquest,
MacGregor Knox argued, the Duce sought to radicalize Italians, creating
new Fascist men, hardened by war, and to defeat the bourgeois opponents
that remained as hangovers from the old, liberal, transformist regime.[14]

Italian scholars, however, continue to dominate the historiography of
Italian Fascism, especially the late Renzo De Felice. The longtime doyen
of the Italian historical community, his magisterial, eight-volume biography represents the most comprehensive account of Mussolini's life.[15] De
Felice and his assistants and colleagues trolled a vast array of archival
material and private papers. De Felice wrote a magnificent account of
Mussolini's political life, and De Felice has few if any equals when it

comes to explaining the internal dynamics of the Fascist party. His central argument was that Mussolini was an essentially conservative leader, avoiding grand confrontations and seeking compromise. He sought merely to survive as ruler while weakening potential competitors—leftists, industry, monarchy and army—at least until 1929. By his fourth volume, De Felice wrote of a Mussolini turned radical, attempting to change Italian society fundamentally, trying to create a third road between capitalism and communism. The Ethiopian war represented the culmination of this new dynamism and represented Mussolini's greatest victory.

De Felice's interpretation of foreign policy issues, however, is less credible.[16] In his view, Mussolini's early policy was traditional and largely cautious; the Duce sought above all a general settlement with France that would allow Italy to pursue colonial expansion while firmly establishing itself as a European great power. Mussolini pursued this goal through unusual means; he "pursued an anti-French policy in order to reach an agreement with France."[17] After the Ethiopian war, he sought a general agreement with the Western powers, which the Popular Front government in France and the seemingly uncomprehending government in Britain failed to grasp. Only when this effort at a general settlement failed did Mussolini consider playing the German card. Over time, Mussolini, primarily owing to the Spanish quicksand, increasingly failed to navigate his policy of the applying the *peso determinante,* or decisive weight, to European affairs. Despite this general line of argument, De Felice admitted that eventually the Duce would have turned against the British empire. This internal inconsistency, among others, suggests that De Felice's explanations of Mussolini's character and of his foreign policy have considerable difficulties.[18]

Renzo De Felice's disciples have presented similar yet even more extreme arguments—Rosaria Quartararo foremost among them. In her 1980 monograph *Roma tra Londra e Berlino,* she in essence removed responsibility from Mussolini's shoulders for Italian entry into the Second World War. In her view, Mussolini played a waiting game; he refused to choose between France and Britain on one hand and Germany on the other, but waited to see their policies. British failure to appreciate what Mussolini saw as legitimate claims led to a series of blunders. British statesmen such as Neville Chamberlain pushed Mussolini into the German camp through failure to arrange French concessions to Italy, planned war against an unwilling Italy, and, incredibly, forced an unwilling Mussolini into war in 1940. To be blunt, these conclusions strain credulity.[19] Not to be outdone, Donatella Bolech Cecchi also argued De Felice's concept of the *peso determinante.* For Bolech Cecchi, Mussolini wanted nothing more than an accord with Great Britain that would have recognized Italy's place in the Mediterranean. Only after Britain refused this reasonable request did Mussolini turn toward Germany, and even then, expansion such as the annexation of Albania had a purely anti-German character.[20] One can find similar arguments in Paolo Nello's biography of the Italian diplomat and Fascist heirarch Dino Grandi, *Un fedele disubbidiente.*[21] One recent Italian writer, Paola Brundu Olla, has broken somewhat from this tendency. While she still apportioned some blame to Britain and France for their lack of understanding of Mussolini's policy of *peso determinante,* she wrote that the Duce himself failed to carry out that policy effectively. In her view, Mussolini could have achieved a pact that would have created Mediterranean stability. He did not aim to do so, primarily because that policy would limit his freedom of action. Consequently, Mussolini's expansionist pursuits, trying to wean France from Britain and his moves toward Germany, were largely responsible for the catastrophe that was to come.[22]

De Felice's interpretation, though, is not entirely limited to Italy; one British author shares its essential conclusions. Richard Lamb argued that British failure to appease Mussolini, in spite of the Duce's occasional bluster, meant the cleavage of the Anglo-French-Italian Stresa Front against Hitler's revisionism. In particular, Lamb singled out Anthony Eden as the chief culprit because Eden's hostility to an Anglo-Italian agreement pushed Mussolini into Hitler's embrace. This vital miscalculation squandered the chance to create an effective front against German expansionism and helped to create the conditions that sparked the Second World War.[23] In a somewhat different vein, H. James Burgwyn's recent monograph consciously attempts to bridge the gap between MacGregor Knox and De Felice. Burgwyn argued that Mussolini had "expansionist goals that remained constant and were never forgotten," and that Mussolini, like many Italian nationalists, was a convinced social Darwinist. At the same time, Burgwyn argued that the Duce was too much "a believer in action based on expediency and day-to-day interests for any pre-ordained doctrine or fixed program to dictate his diplomacy." After the *Anschluss,* Mussolini struggled to escape "Germany's iron cage," and the Pact of Steel represented his attempt to restore Italy's balancing role between Germany and the West.[24] Unfortunately, the significant lack of archival evidence for the vital period from 1936 to 1939 weakens Burgwyn's interpretation.

Despite the variations within the debate, MacGregor Knox called recent Italian historiography the "anti-anti-fascist orthodoxy." For the sake of convenience, I shall use the rubric "De Felice school" to represent this scholarship.[25] The difficulty with the interpretations of the De Felice school is that they cannot account for substantial archival evidence that tends to contradict them. More damningly, it is very convenient for Italian scholars to write history that absolves Italians of responsibility for the origins of the Second World War and minimizes Italy's expansionist and imperialist past on which Fascism built.

This brief survey of some of the available literature suggests some lacunae in the historiography. First, the published documents do not yet cover the period from 1938 to May 1939; Italian historians are still preparing these last volumes in *I Documenti Diplomatici Italiani*. Furthermore, during the 1970s and 1980s, while other major Western archives had opened their door to scholars, the Italian Foreign Ministry Archives remained closed. With the exception of certain Italian historians who had privileged access, most researchers and writers on the period from 1936 to 1939 have not been able to use these centrally important documents. In particular, the Italian Foreign Ministry Archive has recently finished restoring and microfilming the so-called *Carte Lancellotti,* papers that Raffaele Guariglia, the Italian foreign minister, had secreted from the German military in September of 1943.[26] Accordingly, I have used these papers extensively as well as the other diplomatic documents housed in the Italian Foreign Ministry. Second, considerable debate remains regarding Mussolini's foreign policy, and the De Felice school, with its tendentious claims regarding Mussolini's decision making, seems to dominate the historiographical landscape. This study, therefore, uses original archival research to explain Mussolini's foreign policy during the period from June 1936 and the end of the Ethiopian war to the outbreak of World War II in September 1939.

Modern writing on foreign policy questions has developed beyond the hoary discipline of purely diplomatic history. Historians now tend to emphasize structural constraints in history rather than focusing purely on the diplomatic realm. We use diverse approaches, utilizing economic history, intellectual history, civil-military relations, military history, and public opinion, among other forms of inquiry. Structuralist history, however, ultimately cannot explain Italian foreign policy before the Second World War. In the case of Fascist Italy, the evidence is overwhelming that Mussolini himself controlled Italian foreign policy. Mussolini made every major decision, tightly controlled his subordinates, frequently ignored advisers, and often adopted potentially unpopular policies. He largely ignored rational military planning and economics (except at the most rudimentary level) and often did not heed public opinion, although he tried very hard to control and to shape it. His behavior, therefore, poses a problem for historians. How does one explain rationally the beliefs and actions of an irrational person? After considering the available evidence, the only available path is to seek to explain Mussolini's *mentalité*. How, specifically, did Mussolini view the world and the arena of international politics in which he operated?

The first chapter therefore provides an explanation of Mussolini's *mentalité*. It canvasses his public speeches and writings to try to determine Mussolini's thoughts about international relations. In addition, because Mussolini was something of a propagandist and a very prolific orator and writer, it is necessary to draw specific ties between Mussolini's *mentalité*, as revealed in his intellectual world, and the specific actions and policies that he implemented. By making these essential connections, one can demonstrate that Mussolini had an internally consistent *mentalité* that governed both his thought and his actions as the ruler of Italy. His *mentalité* was ultranationalist; he subordinated many elements of his ideology to a simplistic test—how did the individual or issue in question relate to the power of the state? There were five distinct yet interwoven strands to this ultranationalist worldview: anti-Bolshevik leanings; opposition to the secretive international Masonic Order; contempt for democracies; belief in white supremacy over the so-called dark nations of Africa and anti-Semitism; and social-Darwinism, which included the simplistic equation of the growth or decline and the vitality of national populations with national power, war worship, and a kind of fatalism seemingly common to messianic dictators.

Mussolini's *mentalité* governed Italian foreign policy, and from 1936 to the outbreak of the Second World War, it led the Duce to tie Italy ever more tightly to Nazi Germany. During the finale of the Ethiopian war, Mussolini decided to court Germany as a potential ally against the decadent Western democracies. He also ranged Italy against France in the Spanish Civil War while at the same time trying to drive a wedge between Britain and France. In 1937, Mussolini continued the policies begun the year before. He intensified the Spanish Civil War, courted Japan as an ally against Great Britain, and wooed Yugoslavia as a client state in the Balkans. During the first eight months of 1938, Mussolini sought to maneuver Anthony Eden's resignation as British foreign secretary and continued to work to split Britain from France. Mussolini followed an aggressive policy during the Czechoslovak crisis that culminated in the Munich agreement; he drew back from the brink of war only after realizing that a general war would unite Britain and France in a grand offensive against Italy. In the aftermath of Munich, Mussolini aimed to convert the Axis into a tripartite, Italo-German-Japanese military alliance against Britain and France, and he set the conditions under which he would feel confident in undertaking a war with the Western democracies. The Pact of Steel, signed in May 1939, drew Italy and Germany together in a strictly offensive-minded military alliance, and the two dictators contemplated war with the West when they deemed it opportune. Mussolini's subordination of foreign policy questions to the needs of social Darwinist expansion ultimately compelled him to seek out the German alliance in order to expand Italian territory at the expense of Britain and France. But his failure to understand the pace of German expansion doomed Italy to fight a major war before it was ready. In June 1940, he deliberately cast Italy into the Second World War because he thought the conditions ripe to make a long-contemplated grab for control of North Africa and the Suez Canal.

Any study such as this one has limits; no author can hope to cover every possible aspect of a topic. This study concerns itself with foreign policy; although Fascist internal politics is fascinating, Mussolini operated in a realm outside the *Primat der Innenpolitik*. I do not intend to write about broader Italian societal beliefs; although they are interesting in and of themselves, they do not specifically bear on Mussolini's decisions regarding foreign policy. Though of course his ideas developed within the context of Italian society, as a decision maker he often ignored constraints of Italian public opinion and dissenting views from within the Italian polity. He also departed from the tenets of traditional Italian nationalism in one central respect; he openly pursued policies that would pit Italy against the British empire. Still, I am not especially concerned with arguing a continuity or discontinuity thesis. Again, although this point is interesting and there is likely more continuity between Fascist and liberal Italian politics than many Italians would like to admit, this question is not central to explaining Mussolini's foreign policy. Despite these inevitable limitations, this work explains Mussolini's perilous decision to align himself as Hitler's partner in the events leading to the outbreak of the Second World War.

NOTES

1. For some useful historiographical surveys, see R. J. B. Bosworth, *The Italian Dictatorship: Problems and Perspectives in the Interpretation of Mussolini and Fascism* (London: Arnold, 1998); Stephen Corrado Azzi, "The Historiography of Fascist Foreign Policy," *Historical Journal* 36, no. 1 (March 1993): 187–203.

2. Gaetano Salvemini, *The Fascist Dictatorship in Italy* (New York: Howard Fertig, 1967); Gaetano Salvemini, *Under the Axe of Fascism* (London: Victor Gollancz, 1936); Gaetano Salvemini, *Italian Fascism* (London: Victor Gollancz, 1938).

3. Gaetano Salvemini, *Prelude to World War II* (London: Victor Gollancz, 1953).

4. Others who shared Salvemini's essential interpretation include Luigi Salvatorelli and Giovanni Mira, *Storia d'Italia nel periodo fascista* (Turin: Einaudi, 1956); Luigi Salvatorelli, *Storia del fascismo: l'Italia dal 1919 al 1945* (Rome: Edizioni di Novissima, 1952). For a brief statement on Benedetto Croce's theory that Fascism represented a parenthesis in Italian history, see C. Sprigge, "Introduction to Benedetto Croce," in *Philosophy, Poetry, History: An Anthology* (London: Oxford University Press, 1966), vii.

5. Elizabeth Wiskemann, *The Rome-Berlin Axis: A History of the Relations between Hitler and Mussolini* (London: Oxford University Press, 1949).

6. H. Stuart Hughes, "The Diplomacy of Early Italian Fascism, 1922–1932," in *The Diplomats, 1919–1030,* vol. 1, eds. Gordon A. Craig and Felix Gilbert (New York: Atheneum, Princeton, 1954), 210–33.

7. Ennio Di Nolfo, *Mussolini e la politica estera italiana, 1919–1933* (Padua: Facoltà di scienze politiche dell'Università di Padova, 1960).

8. A. J. P. Taylor, *The Origins of the Second World War* (London: Hamilton, 1961), 56. See also Alan Cassels, "Switching Partners: Italy in A. J. P. Taylor's *Origins of the Second World War,*" in *The Origins of the Second World War Reconsidered: The A. J. P. Taylor Debate after Twenty-Five Years,* ed. Gordon Martel (Boston: Allen and Unwin, 1986), 73–96.

9. Denis Mack Smith, *Mussolini's Roman Empire* (London: Penguin, 1976); Denis Mack Smith, *Mussolini* (London: Weidenfeld and Nicolson, 1981).

10. Mack Smith, *Mussolini's Roman Empire,* 252.

11. Alan Cassels, *Mussolini's Early Diplomacy* (Princeton: Princeton University Press, 1970).

12. Esmonde M. Robertson, *Mussolini as Empire Builder: Europe and Africa 1932–36* (London: MacMillan, 1977).

13. MacGregor Knox, *Mussolini Unleashed, 1939–1941: Politics and Strategy in Fascist Italy's Last War* (Cambridge, U.K.: Cambridge University Press, 1982), 256.

14. MacGregor Knox, *Common Destiny: Dictatorship, Foreign Policy, and War in Fascist Italy and Nazi Germany* (Cambridge, U.K.: Cambridge University Press, 2000). This work collects and expands on several earlier articles, including MacGregor Knox, "Conquest, Foreign and Domestic, in Fascist Italy and Nazi Germany," *Journal of Modern History* 56, no. 1 (1984): 1–57. See also MacGregor Knox, "Il fascismo e la politica estera italiana," in *La politica estera italiana (1960–1985),* eds. Richard Bosworth and Sergio Romano (Bologna: Il Mulino, 1993), 287–330. Another recent monograph, Aristotle Kallis's comparative work assessing both Nazi and Fascist ideology, also questions the early historiographical dismissal of Mussolini's alleged ideological pretensions (Aristotle A. Kallis, *Fascist Ideology: Territory and Expansionism in Italy and Germany, 1922–1945* [London: Routledge, 2000]).

15. De Felice has organized the eight volumes into four categories: *Il rivoluzionario, 1883–1920; Il fascsita, 1921–1929,* 2 vols.; *Il duce, 1929–1940,* 2 vols.; *L'alleato, 1940–1945,* 3 vols. (Turin: Einaudi, 1965–1996).

16. For a penetrating criticism of De Felice's foreign policy writing, see Mac-Gregor Knox, "The Fascist Regime, Its Foreign Policy and Its Wars: An 'Anti-Anti-Fascist' Orthodoxy?" *Contemporary European History* 4, no. 3 (1995): 347–65. For the views of a prominent scholar of Italian military history, see Giorgio Rochat, "Ancora sul 'Mussolini' di Renzo De Felice," *Italia Contemporanea* 33, no. 44 (1981): 5–10; "L'ultimo Mussolini secondo De Felice," *Italia Contemporanea* 43, no. 182 (1991): 111–19.

17. Renzo De Felice, *Mussolini il duce, II: Lo Stato Totalitario, 1936–1940* (Turin: Einaudi, 1981), 37–38.

18. Knox, "The Fascist Regime," 352–65.

19. Rosaria Quartararo, *Roma tra Londra e Berlino: La politica estera fascista dal 1930 al 1940* (Rome: Bonacci, 1980), 271–72, 413–25, 610, 616–20. See also Rosaria Quartararo, "Inghilterra e Italia: Dal Patto di Pasqua a Monaco (con un appendice sul 'canale segreto' italo-inglese)," *Storia Contemporanea* 7 (1976): 607–716.

20. Donatella Bolech Cecchi, *Non bruciare i ponti con Roma* (Milan: Giuffrè, 1986), 507–9, 513.

21. Paolo Nello, *Un fedele indisubbidiente: Dino Grandi da Palazzo Chigi al 25 luglio* (Bologna: Il Mulino, 1993), 285.

22. Paola Brundu Olla, *L'Équilibrio difficile: Gran Bretagna, Italia e Francia nel Mediterraneo, 1930–7* (Milan: Giuffrè Editore, 1980); Brundu Olla, "Il Gentleman's Agreement e la Francia (2 gennaio 1937)," in *Italia, Francia e Mediterraneo,* eds. J.B. Duroselle and Enrico Serra (Milan: Angeli, 1990), 52–70.

23. Richard Lamb, *Mussolini and the British* (London: John Murray, 1997).

24. H. James Burgwyn, *Italian Foreign Policy in the Interwar Period, 1918–1940* (Westport, Conn.: Praeger, 1997), xiii, xv.

25. For a recent effort to counter MacGregor Knox's criticisms of the orthodox Italian interpretation and to argue the essentially defensive nature of Italian policy, see Fortunato Minniti, *Fino all guerra: Strategie e conflitto nella politica di potenza di Mussolini, 1923–1940* (Naples: E.S.I., 2000). Structural problems of causality and use evidence similar to those in Quartararo's *Roma tra Londra e Berlino* undermine Minniti's conclusions. See, for example, chapter 3, note 100. The strange lack of consideration of Mussolini's expansionist thinking means that Minniti cannot accurately explain the Duce's entry into the war in spite of the strategic considerations that strongly argued against it. Nevertheless, Minniti's fairly detailed coverage of Italian military planning is welcome.

26. For a description of the unusual treatment of Italian diplomatic documents during the war, see Howard McGaw Smyth, *Secrets of the Fascist Era: How Uncle Sam Obtained Some of the Top Level Documents of Mussolini's Period* (Carbondale, Ill.: Southern Illinois University Press, 1975).

CHAPTER 1

Mussolini's Mentalité

Mussolini ultimately determined the course of Italian foreign policy. Unlike the case of Nazi Germany, where the unfortunately named intentionalist-functionalist debate rages, there is general consensus that Mussolini was the "sole unimpeachable creator...and interpreter" of the Fascist movement.[1] During the 1920s and 1930s, the Duce was responsible for making the final decision on foreign policy questions, often apparently irrationally and over the objections of his advisors. In order to understand Italian policy, therefore, one must try to understand Mussolini's mind. Methodologically, some of the instruments at hand have potential pitfalls. The word "ideology" carries with it great baggage. The Marxist appropriation of the term means that it is associated with a priori assumptions of control and hegemony. The term *mentalité* seems, therefore, to be the more appropriate. Philosophers sometimes apply the term to group consciousness, not individual consciousness. In this book, however, the term applies to Mussolini's individual view of the world and not in any way to groups.

Mussolini's *mentalité* was a set of related intellectual constructs that represented a coherent, though not necessarily rational, framework for interpreting both history and contemporary events. One can identify someone's *mentalité* while at the same recognizing that it does not have to be entirely consistent; inconsistency can be part of a worldview. Every individual has a *mentalité,* even the deranged.[2] In Mussolini's case, it consisted of both rational and irrational concepts. It is clear, though, that throughout his career he expressed the ideas of a programmatic thinker, both in public and in private. The central principle of Mussolini's *mentalité* was extreme nationalism. As early as 1909, one could see that even while ostensibly a socialist internationalist, Mussolini held nationalistic beliefs. He revered Mazzini and read with approval the writings of the nationalist Alfredo Oriani.[3] After his conversion to interventionism during the First World War, his nationalistic views rarely wavered. There are five identifiable, interrelated strands to Mussolini's ultranationalist *mentalité:* anti-Bolshevik leanings; opposition to the secretive international Masonic Order; contempt for democracies; anti-Semitism and a racialist belief in white supremacy over the so-called dark nations of Africa; and social Darwinism, which included the simplistic equation of the growth or decline and the vitality of national populations with national power, war worship, and imperialism. As a result of these views, Mussolini believed that it was necessary to expand Italy's borders and to create a new Italian empire. These beliefs also helped to select the ultimate victims, namely, the population of North Africa and the seemingly effete French and British empires.

The story of Mussolini's early life is well known. He was born in 1883 in Predappio, a small town in the Romagna region of east-central Italy. He drew his early contempt for Italy's elite from his socialist father, and while in school he soon displayed his combative nature, physically assaulting authority figures and fellow students. Despite his tendency toward violence, he graduated with a certificate to teach elementary school. After a few months, he abandoned teaching and went to Switzerland, where he earned an income through manual labor and begging, and landed for a brief time in jail. He eventually fell in with a group of socialists and found a talent for political agitation. After returning to Italy to fulfill his obligatory military training, he secured the editorship of a socialist paper in the Austrian town of Trent. His agitation led to his expulsion after only eight months, and he returned to Italy, where he rose rapidly through the ranks of the *Partito Socialista Italiana.* An extremist who advocated revolutionary social change, he was one of the leading figures of the party and edited the party organ *Avanti!* for two years prior to the outbreak of the Great War. In October 1914, he broke with the party, rejecting neutrality and advocating active intervention. During the war, he migrated from socialism to a kind of national syndicalism, and the pattern of his political thinking coalesced around certain central tenets, including an intense nationalism and opposition to Italy's transformist elite.[4] He sought to revolutionize Italian domestic life and to enable Italy to secure its place amongst the great powers of Europe. Although during the 1920s and early 1930s he appeared to some observers to be relatively quiescent, throughout his adult life, he maintained remarkably consistent and aggressive views regarding Italy's foreign policy. From his accession to dictatorial power in the mid-1920s, Mussolini displayed a persistent *mentalité,* seeking to expand Italian national power at the expense of putative enemies. Although the intended victims sometimes changed, the Duce's drive to create a new Roman Empire seldom did.[5]

Mussolini's views on Bolshevism appear eccentric to outside observers. In his political infancy, Mussolini was, of course, a revolutionary socialist. His conversion to nationalist causes during the First World War alienated his socialist brethren, and, following the war, Mussolini associated himself openly with Italian nationalistic movements. By 1921, Fascism had aligned itself against socialist and rural labor movements. In the towns, Fascist *squadristi* frequently raided the offices of leftist newspapers or trade unions and treated opponents to beatings or purging doses of castor oil. In rural areas, Fascist violence was more extreme, as the *latifondisti* employed Fascist paramilitary thugs to break peasant leagues and associations. By the time Mussolini gained power, anti-socialism was the unifying theme of the Fascist movement, and there was a virtual state of civil war between Fascist blackshirts and socialist redshirts.[6] Although for the first fifteen years of the regime Mussolini's anti-Bolshevism was primarily domestic, it did have some effect on Italian foreign relations.[7]

At times, Mussolini showed his distinct admiration for Joseph Stalin, the leader of the only avowedly socialist country. For example, he praised Stalin's realism, which made it possible for Italy to work to bring the Soviet Union back into European affairs. Both Italy and the Soviet Union were revisionist powers, and both chafed under the predominance of political power held by the "demoplutocracies" of Great Britain and France.[8] Mussolini hoped that Stalin might abandon communism in favor of a brand of authoritarianism akin to Fascism, as the Duce believed that Soviet communism was the less revolutionary movement; he thought the power of the state bureaucracy could transform the Soviet Union into some kind of Slav Fascism. The two movements had similar potential enemies in the demoplutocracies, and they shared a common belief in eradicating the power of the individual within society.[9] The two states also had trade interests. Italy built ships and planes for the Soviets in exchange for roughly one-third of Italy's oil requirements. On 2 September 1933, they signed an Italo-Soviet Pact of Friendship, Non-aggression and Neutrality, which signaled both Mussolini's regard for Stalin and Italy's need for fuel.[10] As long as Soviet influence was confined to Eastern Europe, Mussolini remained unconcerned.

Even while courting Soviet friendship and trade, however, Mussolini feared the threat of Bolshevism in Western Europe. In a 1933 interview, he said that "more than ever I detest bolshevism! Spiritually it constitutes the greatest danger which can menace our civilization.... Bolshevism remains an infection against which the West must range all its forces."[11] He feared that despite the "labyrinthine" internecine politics of the communist Third International, it posed a threat to certain countries, particularly republican Spain and France. They were "enfeebled" by the predominance of "liberalism, democracy, socialism, [and] free-masonry," and were, therefore, more likely to fall victim to the Bolshevik "asiatic peril."[12] He believed that the leftist French Popular Front government, installed on 4 June 1936, was inherently hostile to Italian Fascism, as it openly sympathized with Fascism's victims and housed the *fuorusciti,* or Italian opponents of Fascism living in exile. As Mussolini had said of the *fuorusciti,* they excited "all of the antifascist forces of democratic parliamentarism, of second and third internationalism, [and the] society of nations."[13] The Popular Front's association with the French Communist Party further alienated the Duce and appeared to establish clear ideological differences between the two governments.[14]

In Spain, Mussolini took steps to deal with what he perceived to be the increasingly dangerous and unstable Republican government. At a secret meeting held at the Palazzo Venezia on 31 March 1934, Mussolini promised a delegation of Spanish rightists that he would give them 1.5 million pesetas, 10,000 rifles, and other assorted equipment in order to organize a coup against the Republican government. The arrangement included an understanding regarding the territorial integrity of the would-be new Spain, a commercial agreement, financial aid, and immediate Italian recognition of the new government whenever it could take power. Mussolini concluded their discussion by saying that he expected the coup plotters to "strike down the republic which defined the move backward to a century and loyalty to principles exceeding those not only in France but in all the world."[15] In part, of course, Mussolini was merely hoping to install a favorable regime in place of a relatively hostile one. There was, however, also the underlying desire to create an authoritarian government that would, in his view, know how to eliminate its opponents on the political left, as Fascism had done in Italy. Mussolini's dislike of the perceived left-leaning political culture and intellectual outlook of the Western democracies predisposed him to see both weakness in and threat from the so-called demoplutocracies.

Mussolini's detestation of Freemasonry intensified his distrust of the Western democracies, and particularly of France. Domestically, Mussolini saw Freemasonry as a bulwark of the old bourgeois, liberal order, and as inherently hostile to his regime. The issue was slightly more complicated than he allowed. Many Masons supported Fascism, at least in its early days. One grand master, for example, said in 1923 that so far as Fascism had worked to defeat Bolshevism and to increase Italy's strength, Masons had supported its goals. The regime, however, had not abandoned violence after it took power, and it was destroying the accomplishments of the revolutions of 1848 and 1870. Masons deplored the returning power of clericalism. They had come to see the early dynamism of Mussolini's regime as the very antithesis of Masonic ideals.[16]

Mussolini, on his part, apparently never shared any affinity with Freemasonry. He said that his opposition to Freemasonry existed long before his entrance into national politics, and this claim is entirely in accord with his early socialist beliefs.[17] He argued that the regime needed to maintain its vigilance in order to prevent Italian Masons from coordinating their resistance to Fascism with outside organizations.[18] He believed that Masons were responsible for past disastrous Italian military defeats such as Caporetto and wanted to limit their influence on the Italian General Staff. More damningly, in Mussolini's view, Freemasons maintained their "aberrations of universal love which often annulled the love owed to the country."[19] Not only would they not abandon their other allegiances in order to give their loyalty to the regime and to the nation, they persisted in their opposition to Fascism. Any attempt to destroy their power would be risky, as Masons would no doubt be forewarned; they had "tentacles in every area."[20] In 1926, Mussolini banned Freemasonry, and many officers of the armed forces resigned their lodge memberships rather than risk a confrontation with the regime. The army and its loyalty to the monarchy comprised the greatest potential threat to Mussolini's power, and Fascism made only limited inroads into control over military matters. Mussolini went no further on this issue, as he was unwilling to risk a purge of the armed forces.[21] Mussolini accepted an uneasy accommodation with the former adherents of Freemasonry, as he had apparently forced Freemasons to declare their loyalty to the Fascist regime.

In foreign relations, Mussolini also resented the power of Freemasonry. He believed that Freemasons controlled French politics and that they were hostile to Italian Fascism. He wrote that "the opportunism of French Freemasonry is chameleon-like [*camaleontesco*]." In his view, they existed within all French governments and had been responsible for installing Louis Napoleon as emperor. "In the course of half a century, French Masonry sold itself to five different patrons to have strength, to carry out its vengeance, gains, profits, honours... all in fraternal brotherhood."[22] Masons controlled the Quai d'Orsay, and, in the words of one member of the Italian Foreign Ministry, "the demo-masonic influence behind the scenes in French politics always rendered impossible the conclusion of a durable pact" between the two governments.[23] Mussolini's advisors saw the French Radical Socialist Party as the political emanation of Masonry and further resented its association with the Socialists and Communists in the Popular Front government.[24] The result of this climate of anti-Masonic opinion was that it helped to create a barrier of mistrust between the Italian and French governments, particularly in the aftermath of the Ethiopian campaign, when the restoration of amicable relations otherwise appeared to be both desirable and possible.

Mussolini's contempt for Bolshevism and Freemasonry spilled over to the liberal elite of Western Europe. Throughout his adult life, Mussolini opposed the democratic and transformist principles of Italian democracy. Initially, he had aligned himself with socialist opponents of the regime, seeking to destroy it through Marxist revolution. The prewar failure to mobilize an effective general strike, combined with his latent nationalist leanings, ensured that at some point he would break with the internationalist *Partito Socialista Italiana.* During the First World War, Mussolini angered his socialist comrades over the question of intervention, and they expelled him from the party. Mussolini had come to believe that nationalism would supply the instrument to channel the revolutionary violence of the working class. He freely borrowed many of his ideas from the political philosophers Enrico Corradini, Wilfredo Pareto, and Friedrich Nietzsche. From Corradini, the founder of the Italian Nationalist Association, Mussolini derived the view that the virtues of the proletarian nation—unity, discipline, and social solidarity—would enable it to destroy the bourgeoisie. War would harden the proletariat and prepare it for its essential task.[25] Mussolini adopted Pareto's view that humanitarian concern impaired the elite's resolution; it merely served to limit the appropriate process of social-Darwinist selection. France and liberal Italy were "sick with excessive humanitarianism."[26] The prevalence of humanitarian sensibilities in Western liberal regimes would lead inevitably to social disintegration and decadence. Perhaps most importantly, Mussolini embraced Pareto's idea that the only way to break the otherwise inevitable cycle of the renewal of the old elites was to create a new, nonsocialist elite that was prepared to use violence to achieve its ends. In Mussolini's view, only proletarian violence would be able to shatter the democratic plutocracy.[27] Similarly, Mussolini emphasized Nietzsche's beliefs regarding the decadence of Europe's elite, as well as his worship of the martial virtues of "heroism, dynamism and faith."[28] The Duce arranged these concepts into a fatalistic view of eternal struggle among classes, races, and nations.

After World War I, Mussolini founded the inchoate Fascist movement and began an uneasy process of compromise regarding his revolutionary leftist leanings. At the Piazza San Sepolcro, the first open assembly of the

Fascist Party, Mussolini spoke of nationalist claims on Dalmatia and of revolutionary changes for the working class. Despite Mussolini's public sympathies for the working class, Fascist *squadristi,* comprised largely of veterans unhappy with Italian transformist politics, fought the Socialist working class in the cities and poor farmers in the country, the latter at the behest of Italian *latifondisti,* or wealthy landholders. Mussolini had to accept these connections to maintain control of his then unruly movement. While seemingly determined to gain power, Mussolini refused to bet *va banque,* and until 1924 he worked loosely within the bounds of parliamentary and constitutional means.

Despite his initial compromises with liberal politicians, Mussolini was contemptuous both of parliaments and of liberal democracy. He believed that Fascism represented "the clear antithesis of democracy, of plutocracy, of freemasonry, of all...the immortal principles of [17]89."[29] He saw liberal democracy as the function of transitory social conditions arising out of the nineteenth century. He detested the liberal politics of the Giolittian era; he thought that liberal Italy had betrayed the heroic principles of Mazzini and Garibaldi—men who had exemplified the spirit of the *Risorgimento.*[30] Mussolini argued that democratic forms of government were doomed to fail in the twentieth century, as they could not unify the state; individuals who refused to cooperate with liberal governments could effectively usurp power from the state and "render it powerless." Fascism aimed to overcome the "moral prostration, regional division, and personal ambition" inherent in liberalism and to instill in Italy's citizens a "moral and spiritual patrimony."[31]

In the realm of international relations, it is often difficult to determine Mussolini's attitudes toward liberal democratic regimes. On several occasions, he reached agreements with France or Britain, and he cultivated the friendship of certain statesmen who represented democratic countries, most notably Sir Austen Chamberlain. Mussolini did tend, however, to overemphasize certain characteristics of the demoplutocracies. Mussolini assumed that ostensibly democratic governments were in fact controlled by unseen machinations of certain groups, usually Jewish financiers or Masons, who were inherently hostile to Fascist principles. He was intensely interested in any indications of pacifism in democratic societies and ascribed to them importance far beyond their real effect. For example, Fascist propaganda amplified the results of an earlier debate in the Oxford Union Society in which students rejected the idea of fighting for king and country. In his own mind, Mussolini transformed this debate from the relatively insignificant event it was into an expression of the universal pacifism of British youth and refused to accept any questioning of his reasoning.[32] As he believed that pacifism was "an absurdity, or better a dangerous deformation," he assumed a dogmatic belief that democratic Britain was a declining power and that it had lost any will to defend its empire.[33] This belief, supported by the views of Dino Grandi, the Italian ambassador in London, in part underlay Mussolini's determination to continue the Ethiopian campaign despite British objections and the half-hearted imposition of sanctions. As Mussolini had often forecast, Fascist Italy's strident, forceful assertion of its rights would inevitably provoke a response form the "dead" and "decrepit" old world.[34]

Paradoxically, the Duce had long resented the power of the British empire. Mussolini thought that Britain's plutodemocratic elite sought to suffocate the dynamic Italian Fascist state. At the formation of the Fascist movement at the Piazza San Sepolcro, he had denounced the stranglehold that the British empire held over Italy's access to the sea. Great Britain controlled both the Suez Canal and the Straits of Gibraltar, in effect imprisoning Italy in the Mediterranean Sea. Italy would have to expand "economically and spiritually" in order to overcome this handicap to secure its right to dominate the Mediterranean and to seize its place in the world. Mussolini repeatedly made it clear that Italy would have to confront the plutodemocratic powers of Britain and France to accomplish this vital goal. In essence, he forecast the march to the ocean that he would eventually undertake in the late 1930s.[35] By the mid-1920s, the Duce had come to contemplate war with Britain to overthrow its domination of the Mediterranean. As he told appalled officials in 1925,

Gibraltar, Malta, Suez, Cyprus represent a chain that permits England to encircle, to imprison Italy in the Mediterranean. If another link, Albania, were added to [that chain], we would have had to break it with a war. A short war; it would not have lasted more than a few weeks, for Italy today is no longer the Italy of the days of Giolitti.[36]

Mussolini habitually repeated similar refrains. By the mid-1930s, he had established a geopolitical dogma that Italy would have to replace the demoplutocratic British and French empires as the dominant power in the Mediterranean; for the Duce, this conflict increasingly carried the cast of inevitability.[37]

In part, Mussolini's racialism gave strong impetus to his geopolitical dreams. In his view, racial differences divided the world into civilized white and uncivilized nonwhite populations, both of which he believed were potentially revolutionary. By the early 1930s, Fascist Italy had dealt effectively with the white revolutionary ideas of democracy and liberalism, but it had not yet dealt with the perceived threat from the nonwhite races. He was obsessed with demographic trends and believed that the birthrate among nonwhites outstripped that among whites by five or six times. As he once responded to his own rhetorical question, "Are Blacks and Yellows at the door? Yes, they are at the door." He believed that its black population would overwhelm the United States owing to its insufficiently developed racial consciousness and low white birthrate.[38] In Europe, nonwhite races from Africa would eventually swamp the less prolific European whites unless the latter took strong action to prevent their destruction.[39] His response was to develop a racial consciousness, which would establish "not only the sharpest differences between races, but also levels of superiority."[40] Fascist policy implemented these clear distinctions in Italy's colonial conquests.

Italian colonial policy was brutal, even by the often-dismal standards of the time. In Libya, for example, previous liberal governments had been unable to exert control over the entire territory that Italy claimed. During the First World War, Libyan rebels had driven Italians back to hold only four coastal towns. From 1921 to 1930, Italians and Eritrean levies restored control over Tripolitania through the destruction of the nomadic tribes' livestock, which constituted their main resource.[41] In Cyrenaica, the Senussi religious sect and rebels under the command of Umar al-Mukhtàr still resisted, aided by difficult terrain. By 1929, neither sporadic battles nor truce talks had pacified the resistance, and Mussolini resolved to impose total Italian control. He charged Pietro Badoglio, then Governor of Libya, and General Rodolfo Graziani to eliminate all resistance.

The resulting campaign was conducted by some 10,000 Italian troops supported by light tanks and armored cars against roughly 1,000 rebels. Unable to defeat the rebels in the field, despite the use of gas bombs, Italian commanders attempted to destroy all links between rebels and the pacified areas. Italian troops destroyed over 90,000 head of livestock and erected 270 kilometers of barbed wire fence to interdict supplies from Egypt. Beginning in June 1930, Italian troops herded roughly 100,000 Senussi into concentration camps, where at least 20,000 died. Mussolini required the execution of all those who resisted Italian conquest, and anyone suspected of association with the resistance faced execution or imprisonment. The Senussi religious order forfeited a half million acres, which the state ultimately turned over to Italian settlers. Italian soldiers eventually captured al-Mukhtàr and, in September 1931, executed him in a brutal public display before the population of one of the camps. Estimates of the total dead in the three-year campaign range from 100,000 to over

300,000.[42] Mussolini sought not only to defeat local opposition, but also to replace the local populace with an emigrant Italian one.

Italian atrocities such as the use of poison gas in the Ethiopian campaign are now well known, but the suppression of postwar rebellions proved even more brutal. Mussolini again ordered that anyone resisting Italian pacification should be shot. In one town, this punishment resulted in the execution of the entire male population over the age of eighteen and the complete destruction of the town. Mussolini urged Marshal Graziani, then Viceroy, "to initiate and systematically to conduct [a] policy of terror and extermination against rebels and populations in complicity with them. Without the policy of ten eyes for one we cannot heal this wound in good time."[43] These directives applied especially to Coptic clerics and other potential rallying points for dissent. After the attempted assassination of Graziani, Italian troops executed thousands of innocent victims. In the Amhara rebellion of late 1937, Mussolini told Graziani that "prisoners, their accomplices, and the uncertain will have to be executed" in order to carry out the "gradual liquidation" of the area's population.[44] In response to a rebellion in Gojjam, the Duce directed that the Italian military commit the "maximum use of the air force and poison gas," aiming to eliminate all those who had not proven their loyalty to the Fascist regime.[45]

In April 1937, Mussolini introduced Decree Law 880. As Italian diplomat Baron Pompeo Aloisi remarked, the "French made an appalling blunder by allowing sex between the races in Tunisia."[46] Mussolini initially intended the law to prevent the practice of *madamismo,* which usually meant the practice by white soldiers or colonial officials of maintaining nonwhite mistresses. It prescribed a penalty of one to five years imprisonment for conjugal relations between whites and colonial subjects of Italian East Africa, or with any foreigners whose customs were similar to those of Italian East Africa, either in Italy or the colonies. In addition, Italians were to establish separate living quarters, and natives were never to see Italians performing menial tasks. The law applied only to Italian citizens, as Mussolini believed that their behavior injured the prestige of the Italian race by blurring the necessary distinction between societies.[47] Another Decree Law passed in October 1938 eventually banned marriage between races.[48]

Mussolini's underlying rationale for Italy's appalling colonial behavior extended beyond the need to cow local resistance. He believed that those with black or brown skin could never acquire the moral stature or intellectual prowess of whites, even if educated in the European tradition over many generations. Arab Bedouins or Ethiopian tribesmen, by his definition inferior, could never develop an appropriate national consciousness;

their resistance, therefore, consisted only of banditry. Mussolini believed the use of gas and widespread executions were appropriate techniques for dealing with these so-called criminals. His mission was not to civilize but to displace. He hoped to export millions of Italian citizens to Ethiopia and Libya and to create entirely separate Italian societies among the ruins of the ones he had destroyed.[49] As he wrote in 1931, "the Italians of tomorrow will consider Tripoli and Benghazi as two metropolitan cities the equal of Syracuse or Cagliari."[50] Mussolini believed that Italy needed to conduct these campaigns of terror in order to rule North Africa with a proverbial rod of iron. Britain and France, weakened by plutocracy and demographic decline, would no longer be able to maintain European domination. Only a dedicated, virile Italian race, hardened by the Duce's discipline, could govern the northern rim of Africa properly and keep the black hordes at bay.

Mussolini's developing racial consciousness and antimiscegenation laws signaled the eventual implementation of anti-Semitic laws as well. Mussolini's anti-Semitism parallels some aspects of his opposition to Freemasonry. It too was often equivocal. He associated openly with and appeared to bear no personal animus toward individual Jews. He learned his early socialism from the Russian Jewess Angelica Balabanov. Margherita Sarfatti was his mistress as well as his biographer. He had Jewish officials in the early Fascist government, and there were 4,819 Jews in the ranks of the *Partito Nazionalista Fascista* by 1933. In 1930–31, the government passed legislation designed by Alfredo Rocco, the Justice Minister, which consolidated Jewish communities into one organization with legal standing; the legislation pleased both Jews and Fascists.[51] There were, however, some subtle indications of Mussolini's bias against Jews. In 1929, Mussolini refused his daughter Edda permission to marry the son of a Jewish colonel; the Duce thought such a union would be scandalous. Paradoxically, he criticized Jews who opposed mixed marriages, as he believed that they should show themselves to be "good, sincere and loyal Italians."[52]

Similarly, the Duce's views on Jews as a group contained some contradictions. Hitler's biological racism embarrassed the Duce, as it implied German superiority over Italians as well as Jews. Mussolini worked for a short time with Chaim Weizmann, the President of the World Zionist Organization, to try to moderate Hitler's anti-Semitism.[53] Mussolini did so not because of any love for Jews, but because he resented the power of an international Jewish conspiracy. In Mussolini's eyes, Jews were responsible for the Great War and the Russian Revolution, and a close connection existed between Jewish bankers and democratic governments.[54]

World finance is in the hands of the Jews. He who owns the treasury vaults of the people, directs their policies. Behind the puppets in Paris are the Rothschilds, the Warburgs, the Schiffs, the Guggenheims, all of whom have the same blood as the dominators in Petrograd.... A race does not betray itself.... Bolshevism is defended by international plutocracy.[55]

Because of the supposed power of this international conspiracy, Mussolini thought Hitler unwise to persecute Jews. "It is better to leave them alone." Nazi "anti-Semitism has already brought Hitler more enemies than is necessary."[56]

There were some subtle yet important distinctions between Hitler's and Mussolini's anti-Semitism. Whereas Hitler believed that race was determined biologically, Mussolini equated race with nation. In an address to the Third National Fascist Congress in 1921, Mussolini said that "Fascism must take up the problem of race; Fascists must concern themselves with the welfare of the race, which is what makes history. We believe in the concept of the 'nation,' which for us is an indelible, insuperable fact. We are therefore hostile to all internationalisms," including, of course, Jewish internationalism.[57] Mussolini repeatedly used newspaper articles to attack alleged Jewish subversives and thought that international Jewry underwrote the *fuorusciti* financially.[58] In the Duce's eyes, Jews were potentially disloyal and therefore a threat to the Fascist regime.

Mussolini's various military adventures sparked renewed anti-Semitic attacks in the Fascist press. Fascist propagandists blamed international Jewry for the application of sanctions in the Ethiopian war. The renegade priest Giovanni Preziosi wrote that Italy was at war with "Jewish bankers," and that Anthony Eden, the British foreign secretary, was "international Jewry's confidence man." Mussolini met with the anti-Semitic French journalist M. Batault and endorsed the latter's *Revue Hebdomadaire* articles that blamed the Ethiopian war on Judaeo-Masonic circles. Mussolini keenly resented Jewish opposition to his war of conquest. Similarly, after the outbreak of the Spanish Civil War in 1936, Mussolini again equated Judaism to Bolshevism, as Jews condemned Italian intervention and supported the Republican government, and he said that Jews were the instigators of Spanish Republicanism.[59] Opposition from international Jewry prompted Mussolini once again to question the loyalty of Italian Jews. He attacked their "ferocious exclusivism" and their "disproportionate political and economic influence." Mussolini's paper *Il Popolo d'Italia* congratulated those Jews who declared their loyalty to the regime but castigated those who refused to "forswear their closed racial circle" or who would not repudiate Zionism, which was "incompatible with fascism."[60]

Mussolini also often assessed foreign statesmen in part according to their perceived Jewishness. He detested Léon Blum, the Jewish politician and, in 1936, soon-to-be French Premier.[61] According to Italian diplomats, Blum was "a militant and observant Jew: *a fanatic of his race.*" Blum and the Popular Front would serve to increase Jewish penetration of the French government.[62] Mussolini asked his subordinates to prepare a report on the connections between the British cabinet and Jews. The report gave only Ernest Brown a clean bill of health. Viscount Halifax's niece had married a Rothschild, and Ramsay MacDonald's private secretary was Jewish. Mussolini's bête noire, Anthony Eden, was an "intimate of the Rothschilds." One of the directors of Baldwin's company was a Jew, and Jews had supported the career of Neville Chamberlain's father.[63] In the Duce's mind, even the most tenuous connection to Jews meant that these British politicians were tainted.

Eventually, Mussolini introduced a series of decree laws implementing anti-Semitic discrimination. Tellingly, the various laws, including the notorious "Defense of the Race Law," would apply only to those Jews who, in the Duce's view, had failed to prove their loyalty to the Italian state. Consequently, legislation exempted decorated or wounded war veterans, early Fascist Party members, or the families of those who had fallen in the cause of Fascism. The various decree laws prevented Jews from teaching at or attending school, banned Jews from government, the military, and the Fascist Party, limited Jewish doctors and lawyers to serving Jews, limited the size of Jewish businesses, and also stripped citizenship granted after 1 January 1919 to foreign-born Jews.[64] In all, almost 4,000 Jews lost their jobs in business, teaching, or public service. Some 4,000 Jews converted to Catholicism, and 6,000 emigrated.[65]

Given the occasionally contradictory nature of Mussolini's statements on anti-Semitism and the greater evil of Nazism and the Holocaust, it is easy to overlook Mussolini's anti-Semitism or to downplay it as mere opportunism. At the time he introduced the racial laws, most Italians assumed that the Duce passed the legislation as part of some agreement with Hitler. There is, however, no evidence to suggest any German pressure on Mussolini to introduce an anti-Semitic policy.[66] At the same time, one must allow for the possibility that Mussolini was merely imitating Nazi policy in an effort to pave the way for closer relations or an alliance between the two countries. This alleged example of Mussolini's tactical flexibility, however, is not incompatible with his other expressions of anti-Semitism and does not explain indications of Mussolini's anti-Semitism that cannot be associated in any manner with German racialism. Diplomats and confidants were under no illusions regarding Mussolini's vitri-

olic attacks on the Jews. To William Phillips, the United States ambassador, Mussolini recounted "the iniquities of the German Jews and of Jews
in general, their lack of loyalty to the country of their residence, their
intrigues and the fact that they could never assimilate with another race."
Phillips was struck by "Mussolini's apparently genuine antagonism
toward the Jews." Galeazzo Ciano, Mussolini's son-in-law and foreign
minister, wrote of several of Mussolini's outbursts against the Jews.[67] Further, the actual implementation of the racial laws closely mirrored Mussolini's nationalist and racialist *mentalité*. The laws' intended effects fell
most harshly and completely on foreign Jews, who could never be part of
the Italian race nation. Domestically, Mussolini assumed that Italian Jews
were not part of the Italian nation unless they specifically proved their loyalty to the regime and the race through either religious assimilation or
demonstration of nationalist credentials. In Mussolini's sometimes strange
reasoning, Judaism tied together the major internationalist threats to the
regime: Bolshevism, capitalist democracy, and Freemasonry, and he
intended to destroy the ability of Jews to undermine Fascist Italy's
national crusade.[68]

Unlike some other strands of Mussolini's nationalism, his social Darwinistic beliefs were not at all equivocal; social Darwinism was the most
important element of his *mentalité*. He was prone to adopt programmatic
beliefs, as his earlier acceptance of Marxist historical materialism would
suggest. After his conversion to nationalism before the First World War, he
displayed a consistent view that life consisted of fatalistic struggle and
selection. Mussolini's obsession with population demographics was a
major element of his social Darwinism. He believed that demographic
expansion was necessary lest Italy be reduced to the status of a colony.
Italy needed to increase its population from the 40 million of the mid-
1920s to 60 million by 1960. This growth was the prerequisite for Italy to
face the challenge of an expected 90 million Germans and 200 million
Slavs, plus 40 million French supplemented by 90 million colonials, and
56 million English supplemented by 450 million colonial subjects.[69] Only
a full 60 million Italians would "make the weight of their numbers and
their power felt in the history of the world."[70] He stated that "a few unin-
telligent people say: 'We are too many.' The intelligent ones reply: 'We are
too few.'" He repeatedly returned to the theme that demographic strength
underlay the economic and moral health of the nation.[71] For Mussolini,
demographic strength was a fundamental determinant of historical pro-
cesses. He detested Malthusian reasoning, which he believed was falla-
cious: "I hope that no one will hold forth to me the story of that greatest
idiocy, the most phenomenal idiocy that appears in history and responds to

the name of Malthus."[72] He argued instead his belief in "the influence of the birth rate in the life, power, and economy of the nations, demonstrated in the history of all the great peoples."[73] Mussolini made a clear and simplistic equation between demographics and a nation's power; more births meant more soldiers. Nations that saw a decline in their birthrate would inevitably see themselves overcome by their enemies and reduced to the status of colonies.[74] Mussolini tried to implement these views as policy. In 1924, he introduced penal sanctions against anyone guilty of advocating contraception. In 1926, he sponsored a nationwide campaign to double the birthrate in order to meet his population objectives.[75]

This campaign and others that followed were not especially successful, and the failures left Mussolini perplexed. He determined that the fault lay in the people of urban centers, as only the people in Rome and the largely rural areas south of Rome performed their patriotic procreative duty.[76] The birthrate in northern industrial cities such as Milan stagnated or declined, and they maintained or increased their population only by immigration from rural Italy.[77] Mussolini concluded that industrialism caused birthrates to decline. In his words:

At a given moment the city grows morbidly, pathologically, not for a virtuous goal but toward another end. The more the city increases and becomes a metropolis, the more it becomes infertile.... The city dies, the nation—without the vital lifeblood of new generations—can no longer resist—composed as it is by now of a feeble and aged people—against a younger population that will require the abandonment of its frontiers. It has happened. It can happen. It will happen again and not only between city and nation, but in an infinitely greater magnitude: the entire white race, the Western race, can be submerged by the other races of colour that multiply with a rhythm unknown to us.[78]

His solution to this perceived problem was to emphasize the development of rural over urban areas. Despite the absurdity of his views in retrospect, Mussolini exalted agriculture over industry, as only the former could give Italy the demographic strength that he deemed necessary for the creation of the new Italian empire.[79] In addition, he believed that any increase in population would increase Italian industrial productivity, by the simplistic determination that as a county's population increased, then so did its economic markets.[80] Mussolini's odd beliefs regarding productivity and demographics help to explain his failure to develop a fully modern army during the late 1930s; he apparently believed his own rhetoric that military power lay simply in the strength of 8 million bayonets. He considered the vitality of national populations and their will to power as a central element of a nation's military strength.[81]

Mussolini also applied his demographic theories to external affairs. In his view, demographic stagnation in a country signaled its political and moral decadence. He noted the failure of a British government plan to encourage people to return to the countryside. He connected this failure with Britain's declining birthrate, which he believed had recently passed that of France as the lowest in Europe. As Britain's population aged and became more pacifistic, the country's elite lost the will and the ability to defend its empire.[82] Regarding France, he believed that its fertile plains were turning into veritable deserts as the urban population fed off the land while at the same time depopulating it. Mussolini believed that the decline in French population was "absolutely horrifying," and that its demographic decline made it weak and vulnerable to the will of the apparently more dynamic Italian people.[83] Italy, with its compact living space and its vibrant population demographic, would have to expand its territory to escape the confines of its limited frontiers.[84]

The second aspect to Mussolini's social Darwinist idée fixe was his belief in the purifying virtues of war. As a young man, he seemingly lived for combat, although he did wait to be drafted by the army in the First World War. Fascism by its very nature was combative; most Fascists earned their spurs in the state of virtual civil war between the Fascist blackshirts and the Socialist redshirts. Much of Mussolini's talk of war appears almost comical. He referred to machine guns as "adorable" and often repeated the phrase "better one day as a lion than one hundred years as a lamb."[85] Underlining Fascism's putative emphasis on action rather than philosophy, the Duce said, "Words are beautiful things, but rifles, machineguns, ships, aircraft and cannon are still more beautiful."[86] Beyond the opéra bouffe, however, there were many more serious indications of the Duce's love of war. One of his diplomats wrote that Mussolini "all the time is inclined to the thought of war."[87] Mussolini had an almost mystical belief in the historical necessity of violence; he wrote that "only blood could turn the bloodstained wheels of history."[88] He believed in the essential idea of permanent struggle and saw war as ennobling because it revealed to man the nature of his ultimate commitments. "All other trials are substitutes which never really put a man in front of himself in the alternative of life and death."[89] The "Doctrine of Fascism," which appeared over Mussolini's signature in the 1932 *Enciclopedia italiana,* was rife with language that showed the Duce's worship of war. Mussolini wrote that Fascism "rejects the doctrine of pacifism which is a cloak for renunciation of struggle and cowardice in the face of sacrifice. Only war brings to the highest tension the energies of man and imprints the sign of nobility on those who have the virtue to confront it." Fascist principles understood "life as duty, moral elevation and conquest." Borrowing the language of Nietzsche, Mussolini extolled the "sanctity of heroism," which was entirely alien to those motivated by materialism.[90] Fascism, in Mussolini's view, embodied martial virtue.

More than merely reveling in struggle and violence, Mussolini hoped to use war to transform Italians into a martial race. The early Fascist movement relied on a core of veterans, the *squadristi,* to provide the necessary violence to combat socialism and peasant leagues. These soldiers, tempered by combat in the Great War, were, in Mussolini's eyes, a breed apart. Their valor and their consciousness of Italy's national power had created a new elite—the *trincerocrazia.* Mussolini hoped that their aggressive belief in action and heroic deeds would provide the example for a new generation of military conquerors.[91] He told the June 1925 Party Congress that he aimed to create a new Fascist man: "the class of warriors who are always ready to die." Among the judges, captains of industry, and governors, he aimed to carry out a methodical selection and inculcation of the ideas of imperial and martial virtues.[92] He wanted to reorient the national character and mores of Italy in order to serve his demand for expansion.[93] He gloried when labeled a militarist. He argued that "the doctrine, the nation, the people that subordinates to military necessities all the rest of material and moral life of individuals and the collectivity are militarist. All the great States that count today in the history of the world are 'militarist.'"[94] In 1934, as minister for war, he enacted a law that decreed every Italian citizen was a soldier and should be educated militarily from age eight. Fascist propaganda exalted the virtues of those youth who adopted "the masculine poetry of adventure and danger," who understood "the virtues of obedience, sacrifice, and dedication to the fatherland."[95] Fascism's wars, combined with military education for youth, he believed, would develop the martial ardor in the population necessary for Italy to take its figurative place in the sun. Mussolini's new race of hardened warriors would carry out the expansion that the Duce deemed vital for the existence of the Italian race. Italy's assertion of its right to rule the Mediterranean would be hollow unless Italy developed the military strength to seize its destiny. Mussolini's geopolitical aims called for struggle both inside and outside Italy.[96]

Mussolini's drive to create a new Fascist empire was the third aspect of his social Darwinism. From its earliest days, the Fascist movement made imperialism one of its central goals. Although Mussolini sometimes denied imperialist ambitions, in 1920, he wrote, "Our imperialism is Roman, Latin, Mediterranean. It expresses itself through a need of all the individuals and all the peoples. The Italian people necessarily must be expansionist."[97] In the 1921 electoral campaign, Mussolini demanded that Italy chase the British from the Mediterranean basin, and "imperialism" and "national expansion" were watchwords of the campaign. He believed that the imperial mission was part of Italy's inevitable rise to greatness; his goal was to create in Italians the will to empire.[98] Imperial expansion also tied in with social Darwinism. Mussolini believed expansionist nations, underpinned by their demographic strength, developed natural rights to conquer declining powers. "If we dream sometimes of being able to expand, that is an expression of an historical and imminent reality; a people that rises has rights over a people that declines. And these rights are inscribed with letters of fire in the pages of our destiny."[99] In 1926, he wrote that "everyone living, who wants to live, has imperialist tendencies, and therefore the people, who are the entire community conscious of living and the desire to live, must develop a certain will to power." He related imperialism to the moral dignity of the Italian nation and cited the need for "economic and intellectual expansion."[100]

Although imperialism was a staple of early Fascist doctrine, Mussolini emphasized its importance much more in the 1930s. He tightened the connection between national dynamism and imperialism. In the "Doctrine of Fascism," he argued that

for Fascism the tendency to empire, that is to say, the expansion of the nation, is a manifestation of vitality; its opposite . . . is a sign of decadence: people who rise or revive are imperialists, people who die are renunciationists. Fascism is a doctrine perfectly adapted to represent the tendency, the state of animation of a people such as the Italians who are rising after many centuries of abandonment or of foreign servitude. But Empire calls for discipline, co-ordination of forces, duty and sacrifice.[101]

He claimed that Italy had "historic objectives" in Asia and Africa. He intended not only to make the Mediterranean Sea an Italian *Mare Nostrum,* but also to occupy the northern half of Africa and to take Italy into the Middle East. He assumed that Italy had the moral sanction for this program of expansion owing to its superior culture and dynamic virtue.[102] He expected to make Italy the center of European civilization once more, building a third Roman Empire, compelled by the laws of history.[103] He believed that Italy had to have an outlet for his hoped-for rapid expansion in Italy's population. In his words, Italy "must therefore expand or suffocate."[104] The Duce had developed a fatalistic belief that Italy's dynamic population would be able to assert its moral force in the Mediterranean, overthrowing the "dead" and "decrepit" old world.[105]

Mussolini, therefore, established Fascist expansionism as the central motivating goal of his regime.[106] Mussolini's *mentalité* was that of a programmatic thinker. His belief system was at times simplistic and at times absurd, but it is necessary to try to understand it in order to explain Mussolini's actions. He combined several elements in his ultranationalistic *mentalité:* anti-Bolshevik, anti-Masonic, and anti-democratic beliefs, as well as crude racialism, anti-Semitism, and social Darwinism. Throughout his adult life this set of beliefs remained remarkably consistent, and he applied these beliefs in his actions in both domestic politics and in international relations. His beliefs led him to make certain assumptions about Italy's role in the world. Mussolini synthesized concepts of demographic expansion with a rudimentary understanding of geopolitics.[107] Italy needed to expand in order to seize its share of territory and raw materials and territory lest it perish. In a manner common among those who shared social Darwinistic beliefs, he was predisposed to overlook the necessary "logistical preparations for conquest of a world empire in favour of a naïve trust in a beneficent providence." He was fatalistic and often impervious to reason. He made a simplistic division of the world into declining and rising states and assumed that Fascism's vitality meant that he had destiny on his side.[108] He assumed that both Britain and France and their empires were in an inevitable state of decline, and he hoped that Fascist Italy would replace those empires with an Italian empire that would rival classical Rome at its height. He was naturally predisposed to associate Italy with revisionist Nazi Germany in order to carry out his hoped-for expansion.[109]

Still, on occasion, Mussolini could make rational calculations, and it would be foolish to assume that Italian policy carried the imprint of inevitability. Mussolini, even as a programmatic thinker, had to act in the world as it existed; he was a politician as well as an ideologue. "The programmatic thinker of a movement has to determine its goals, the politician has to strive for their attainment. Accordingly, the former is guided in his thinking by eternal truth, the latter's action depends to a greater extent on the practical realities of the moment."[110]

In the mid-1930s, the objective realities did not immediately favor the Duce's expansionist dreams. He well understood that Italy would need to confront the two great Mediterranean empires—France and Great Britain—in order to reach his ultimate goals. While Mussolini often contemplated war with the Western democracies, his economic and military advisers counseled caution. Fascist Italy had expended enormous amounts on armaments over the decade following the establishment of a dictatorship in 1926, averaging roughly 10 percent of national income and reaching a peak of 18.4 percent during the war with Ethiopia. But the high cost of the campaigns in Libya and Ethiopia, combined with Italy's weak industrial base, meant that Italy faced serious difficulties in any conflict with Britain and its vaunted Royal Navy. During the crisis surrounding the Ethiopian invasion, Admiral Domenico Cavagnari, the Navy Chief of Staff and Undersecretary, had warned Mussolini about the likelihood of defeat in a war with Britain. Cavagnari's assessment emphasized the massive British superiority in battleships of fifteen to two, with all of the Royal Navy's capital ships carrying superior armament to the two 1912-vintage Italian dreadnoughts. Similarly, Britain could deploy four times as many cruisers as could Italy. The *Regia Marina* had no aircraft carriers and an ineffective air arm, meaning that Italy could do little to threaten British control of Gibraltar and the Suez Canal. In Cavagnari's view, Italy could hope to fight little more than a desperate defensive action, while running the risk that Britain could sink Italian convoys and bombard the mainland with ease.[111] Despite Cavagnari's stark predictions, Mussolini had refused to back down from a confrontation with Britain, and Italy's temporary weakness merely served to whet the Duce's appetite. In order to defeat an Anglo-French coalition, Mussolini would need to create a stronger battleship fleet and to recruit a dynamic and powerful ally—Nazi Germany. Accordingly, Mussolini's attempts to carry out an expansionist program within the confines of an international system apparently dominated by powers seeking to maintain the status quo governed Italian foreign policy and motivated Mussolini's fatal path to war.

NOTES

1. MacGregor Knox, "Conquest, Foreign and Domestic, in Fascist Italy and Nazi Germany," *Journal of Modern History* 56, no. 1 (March 1984): 5; Kallis, *Fascist Ideology,* 97–98.

2. Eberhard Jäckl, *Hitler's Weltanshauung: A Blueprint for Power* (Middleton, Conn.: Wesleyan University Press, 1972), 14.

3. Knox, "Conquest Foreign and Domestic," 6–7, 8. Later writers saw Oriani as a precursor to the Fascist movement. See also Edoardo Susmel and Duilio Susmel (eds.), "Il Popolo d'Italia," 27 May 1909, *Opera Omnia di Benito Mussolini,* vol. 2, 128 (hereafter cited as *OO*), 36 vols. (Florence: La Fenice, 1951–63), 9 vols. (Rome: G. Volpe, 1978–80).

4. Several biographies cover Mussolini's early life. For more information, see Renzo De Felice, *Mussolini il rivoluzionario, 1883–1920* (Turin: Einaudi, 1965) and Mack Smith, *Mussolini,* among a host of others.

5. For accounts in English of Mussolini's foreign policy before 1936, see Cassels, *Mussolini's Early Diplomacy;* Robertson, *Mussolini as Empire Builder;*

Knox, *Common Destiny;* and Burgwyn, *Italian Foreign Policy in the Interwar Period.*

6. Adrian Lyttelton, *The Seizure of Power: Fascism in Italy, 1919–1929* (London: Weidenfeld and Nicolson, 1973).

7. P. V. Cannistraro and F. D. Wynot, Jr., "On the Dynamics of Anti-Communism as a Function of Fascist Foreign Policy, 1933–43," *Il Politico* 38 (1973): 647. See also Giorgio Pettracchi, *La Russia rivoluzionare nella politica italiana: Le relazioni italo-sovietiche 1917–1925* (Bari: Laterza, 1982).

8. Pier Giorgio Zunino, *L'ideologia del fascismo: Miti, credenze e valori nella stabilizazione del regime* (Bologna: Il Mulino, 1985), 341–43.

9. "Il Popolo d'Italia," 30 June 1933, *OO,* vol. 26, 12–13; Zunino, *L'ideologia del fascismo,* 340–43; Mack Smith, *Mussolini,* 171, 182.

10. Mack Smith, *Mussolini,* 182; see also Jonathan Haslam, *The Soviet Union and the Struggle for Collective Security in Europe 1933–1939* (New York: St. Martin's, 1984); J. Calvitt Clarke, *Russia and Italy against Hitler: The Bolshevik-Fascist Rapprochement of the 1930s* (Westport, Conn.: Greenwood, 1991).

11. "Intervista con Henry Massis," 26 September 1933, *OO,* vol. 44, appendix 8, 54–67.

12. Quoted in Zunino, *L'ideologia del fascismo,* 333, 341.

13. "Relazione al Gran Consiglio del Fascismo," 17 June 1926, National Archive (hereafter cited as NA), RG T586, r1122, 074455–75.

14. Robert J. Young, *In Command of France: French Foreign Policy and Civil Military Relations, 1933–1940* (Cambridge, Mass.: Harvard University Press, 1978), 135.

15. Archivio Storico del Ministero degli Affari Esteri, Carte Lancelotti, Ufficio di Coordinamento (hereafter cited ASMAE, UC) 44, Minutes of meeting among Mussolini, Italo Balbo, General Barrere, Signor Goicochea, and Dr. Olazabal, 31 March 1934; see also Massimo Mazzetti, "I contatti del governo italiano con I conspiratori militari spagnoli prima del luglio 1936," *Storia contemporanea* 10, no. 4 (December 1979): 1181–94; William Askew, "Italian Intervention in Spain: The Agreements of March 31, 1934, with the Spanish Monarchist Parties," *Journal of Modern History* 24, no. 2 (1952): 181–83.

16. "Fascism and Masonry: Interview between an Unnamed Reporter and Masonic Grand Master," 12 November 1923, NA, RG T586, r1118, 073864–8. For indications of Masonic support for the early Fascist movement, see Gianni Vannoni, "Su alcuni momenti salienti del rapporto fascismo-massoneria," *Storia contemporanea* 6, no. 4 (1975): 619–73.

17. "Discorso al Senato," 20 November 1925, *OO,* vol. 22, 13–14. For more on Mussolini's early opposition to Freemasonry, see Vannoni, "Su alcuni momenti salienti del rapporto fascismo-massoneria," 614–39.

18. "Relazione del Gran Consiglio del Fascismo," 27 June 1926, NA, RG T586, r1122, 074455–75.

19. "List of Masons for 1926," 14 June 1928, NA, RG T586, r1093, 068995–069042.

20. "Memorandum on Masonry," 17 May 1927, NA, RG T586, r1193, 069112–9.

21. Knox, "Conquest, Foreign and Domestic," 28, 32–34.

22. "Il Popolo d'Italia," 23 June 1933, *OO*, vol. 26, 4.

23. "Francia: Situazione politica nel 1935," NA, RG T586, r1291.

24. "Amedeo Landini to Galeazzo Ciano," 29 January 1936, NA, RG T586, r417, 007929–34. Landini later called Yvon Delbos, the then French foreign minister, "a jesuit mason, the worst type of mason on the zoological scale" ("Amadeo Landini to Colonel Luciano," 2 September 1937, NA, RG T586, r475, 043503–9).

25. Zeev Sternhell, with Mario Szajder and Maia Asheri, *The Birth of Fascist Ideology: From Cultural Rebellion to Political Revolution* (Princeton: Princeton University Press, 1994), 12–13; Meir Michaelis, "Italy's Mediterranean Strategy, 1935–1939," in *Britain and the Middle East in the 1930s: Security Problems, 1935–39*, eds. Michael J. Cohen and Martin Kohinsky (New York: St. Martin's, 1992), 41–42.

26. Quoted in Adrian Lyttelton, *Italian Fascisms from Pareto to Gentile* (New York: Harper and Row, 1973), 20.

27. "L'individuel et le social," 14 October 1904, *OO*, vol. 1, 73–75; "Intermezzo polemico," 25 April 1908, *OO*, vol. 1, 127–29.

28. Quoted in Adrian Lyttelton, *Italian Fascisms*, 22.

29. "Discorso al Direttorate del Partito nazionale fascista," 7 April 1926, *OO*, vol. 22, 107–10.

30. Kallis, *Fascist Ideology*, 29–31, 32–33, 36–37.

31. "Intervista con Associated Press," 1 August 1926, *OO*, vol. 22; "Il Popolo d'Italia," 6 August 1926, *OO*, vol. 22, 187–88; "Intervista con Henry Massis," 26 September 1933, *OO*, vol. 44, appendix 8.

32. Mack Smith, *Mussolini*, 194–95.

33. Quoted in Zunino, *L'ideologia del fascismo*, 345; see also Mack Smith, *Mussolini*, 194–95.

34. "Discorso di Firenze," 17 May 1930, *OO*, vol. 24, 233–36.

35. "Atto di nascita del fascismo," 23 March 1919, *OO*, vol. 12, 321–27; "Discorso inaugurale al secondo congresso dei fasci," 27 December 1919, *OO*, vol. 14, 216–20; "Via da Valona? No!," 11 June 1920, *OO*, vol. 15, 28–29; "Restare a Valona," 15 June 1920, *OO*, vol. 15, 36–37; "Discorso di Cremona," 5 September 1920, *OO*, vol. 15, 182–89. For more on the widespread dissemination of Fascist literature attacking Britain and France, see Tracy H. Koon, *Believe, Obey Fight: Political Socialization of Youth in Fascist Italy, 1922–1943* (Chapel Hill, N.C.: University of North Carolina Press, 1985), 153.

36. Quoted in Knox, *Common Destiny*, 119.

37. Knox, *Common Destiny*, 119–20; Alan Cassels, *Fascism* (Arlington Heights, Ill.: Harlan Davidson, 1975), 78.

38. "Mussolini's Preface to Ricardo Korherr, Regresso delle nascite: morte dei popoli," *OO*, vol. 23; also published in *La Gerarchia* (9 September 1928): 209–16.

39. "Il Popolo d'Italia," 5 May 1934, *OO*, vol. 26, 218–19; "Il Popolo d'Italia," 15 December 1933, *OO*, vol. 26, 122–23. Mussolini apparently borrowed much of his argument from Oswald Spengler's *Jahre der Enscheidung: Deutschland und die weltgeschichtliche Entwicklung* (Munich: C. H. Beck, 1933).

40. Quoted in Gene Bernardini, "The Origins and Development of Racial Antisemitism in Fascist Italy," *Journal of Modern History* 49, no. 3 (September 1977): 442.

41. Giorgio Rochat, "Le Guerre coloniali dell' Italia fascista," in *Le Guerre coloniali del fascismo*, ed. Angelo del Boca (Rome: Laterza, 1991), 177.

42. Angelo Del Boca, *L'africa nella coscienza degli italiani: Miti, memorie, errori, sconfitte* (Milan: Mondadori, 2002), 113; H. W. Al-Hesnawi, "Note sulla politica coloniale verso gli arabi libici," in *Le Guerre coloniali del fascismo*, ed. Angelo del Boca (Rome: Laterza, 1991), 44–45; Rochat, "Le Guerre coloniali dell' Italia fascista," 177–80; Knox, "Conquest Foreign and Domestic," 36; Mack Smith, *Mussolini's Roman Empire*, 36–40, 42.

43. Quoted in Knox, *Mussolini Unleashed*, 3–4.

44. Mussolini to Graziani, 19 January 1938, NA, RG T586, r412, 004908–9, 004907.

45. Mussolini to Graziani, 28 November 1937, *OO*, vol. 42, 199; Mussolini to di Savoia-Aosta, 29 December 1937, *OO*, vol. 42, 201–2.

46. Quoted in Esmonde Robertson, "Race as a Factor in Mussolini's Policy in Africa and Europe," *Journal of Contemporary History* 23, no. 1 (January 1988): 40.

47. Luigi Preti, "Fascist Imperialism and Racism," in *The Ax Within: Italian Fascism in Action*, ed. Roland Sarti (New York: New Viewpoints, 1974), 190.

48. Robertson, "Race as a Factor in Mussolini's Policy in Africa and Europe," 51.

49. Preti, "Fascist Imperialism and Racism," 192–93.

50. "Preface to Attilio Teruzzi, *Cirenaica verde,*" (Milano: Mondadori, 1931), *OO*, vol. 24, 326–28.

51. Alan Cassels, "Italy and the Holocaust," in *Holocaust Literature: A Handbook of Critical, Historical, and Literary Writings*, ed. Saul S. Friedman (Westport, Conn.: Greenwood Press, 1993), 382. For more on Jewish representation in the Fascist movement, see Susan Zucotti, *The Italians and the Holocaust: Persecution, Rescue, and Survival* (New York, Basic Books, 1987), 25–27.

52. Meir Michaelis, *Mussolini and the Jews: German-Italian Relations and the Jewish Question in Italy, 1922–1945* (Oxford: Clarendon Press, 1978), 33; Meir Michaelis, "The Attitude of the Fascist Regime to the Jews in Italy," *Yad Vashem Studies* 4 (1975):12, 14.

53. Michaelis, *Mussolini and the Jews*, 65–71, 75.

54. Bernardini, "The Origins and Development of Racial Antisemitism in Fascist Italy," 439.

55. Quoted in Bernardini, "The Origins and Development of Racial Antisemitism in Fascist Italy," 432; Michaelis, *Mussolini and the Jews*, 12–13.

56. Michaelis, "The Attitude of the Fascist regime to the Jews in Italy," 10; see also Mussolini a Vittorio Cerruti, 30 March 1933, *OO*, vol. 42, 36.

57. "Discorso al terzo congresso nazionale fascista," 8 November 1921, *OO*, vol. 42, 219.

58. Michaelis, *Mussolini and the Jews*, 60. Michaelis, "The Attitude of the Fascist Regime to the Jews in Italy," 16. For more on the Turin affair, where Mussolini trumped up charges against Jewish students, see Zucotti, 28–29.

59. Michaelis, *Mussolini and the Jews*, 90–92, 100–101.

60. Preti, "Fascist Imperialism and Racism," p.190.

61. "Appello agli studenti di tutti Europa," 1 February 1936, *OO*, vol. 27, 224.

62. Mussolini added the emphasis. ASMAE, Carte Lancelotti, Archivio di Gabinetto (hereafter GAB), 333, Direzione Generale Affari Politici Appunto, 29 May 1936, Servizio Storico Diplomatico Ufficio Iº Appunto, 5 June 1936.

63. 5 February 1936, NA, RG T586, r418, 008762–008765.

64. "Discorso al Gran Consiglio Fascista," 6 October 1938, NA, RG T586, r1112, 074978.

65. Cassels, "Italy and the Holocaust," 385–86.

66. Michaelis, *Mussolini and the Jews*, 189–91, and passim.

67. William Phillips to Secretary of State, 3 November 1939, NA, RG T1284, r24, file 1306; see also Galeazzo Ciano, *Ciano's Hidden Diary 1937–1938* (hereafter cited as *CHD*), ed. trans. Andreas Mayor (New York: E. P. Dutton, 1953), 6 September 1937 to 28 November 1938, passim. I have used Ciano's diaries extensively. Our increasing access to Italian archival evidence has allowed historians to compare Ciano's version of events to the documentary record. For the most part, Ciano was an accurate chronicler. Though vain, cynical, and inclined to inflate his own importance and to denigrate the abilities of certain perceived competitors, there is little reason to doubt his veracity. For a longer discussion of Ciano's diaries and their essential accuracy, see Knox, *Mussolini Unleashed*, appendix I, 291–92.

68. Bernardini, "The Origins and Development of Racial Antisemitism in Fascist Italy," 437.

69. "Discorso alla Camera dei Deputati," 1 June 1927, *OO*, vol. 22, 360–90. For a recent monograph that discusses Mussolini's fascination with demography, see Carl Ipsen, *Dictating Demography: The Problem of Population in Fascist Italy* (Cambridge, U.K.: Cambridge University Press, 1996).

70. Quoted in Knox, "Conquest Foreign and Domestic," 18–19.

71. "Discorso alla Camera dei Deputati," 1 June 1927, *OO*, vol. 22, 360–90.

72. "Discorso al Consiglio Nazionale del Partito nazionale fascista," 26 October 1933, *OO*, vol. 44, appendix 8, 70–76.

73. "234a riunione del Consiglio dei Ministri," 20 February 1928, *OO*, vol. 23,102; see also "Il governo fascista e la nazione," 4 October 1924, *OO*, vol. 21, 88–99.

74. "Discorso dell'ascensione," 26 May 1927, *OO*, vol. 22, 364–67.

75. "Discorso dell'ascensione," 26 May 1927, *OO*, vol. 22, 364–67; see also Knox, *Common Destiny*, 70–71; Ipsen, *Dictating Demography*, 67–89; Mack Smith, *Mussolini*, 160.

76. "Il Popolo d'Italia," 1 October 1933, *OO*, vol. 26, 64–65.

77. "L'azione dell' Istituto nazionale delle assicurazione," 25 November 1927, *OO*, vol. 23, 71.

78. "Mussolini's Preface to Ricardo Korherr, *Regresso delle nascite: morte dei popoli*," *OO*, vol. 23; also published in *La Gerarchia* (9 September 1928): 209–16. For more context on Mussolini's fascination with Oswald Spengler and demographic decline, see Ipsen, *Dictating Demography*, 65–68.

79. Mussolini to Giurati, 24 March 1927, *OO*, vol. 40, 298; see also Luigi Preti, *Impero fascista, africani ed ebrei* (Milan: Mursia, 1968), 69–72.

80. "Il Popolo d'Italia," 16 September 1933, *OO*, vol. 26, 52–53.

81. "Per la riforma dell'esercito," 2 April 1925, *OO*, vol. 21, 270–79.

82. Mack Smith, *Mussolini*, 194.

83. "Mussolini's Preface to Ricardo Korherr, *Regresso delle nascite: morte dei popoli*," *OO*, vol. 23; also published in *La Gerarchia* (9 September 1928): 209–16.

84. "Per essere liberi," 8 January 1921, *OO*, vol. 16, 104–6; "Discorso di Verona," 13 May 1921, *OO*, vol. 16, 334–36; "Il problema dell'emigrazione," 30 March 1923, *OO*, vol. 19, 191–93.

85. 23 May 1932, *Al Direttorio dell'Associazione nazionale combattenti*, vol. 25, 104; Mack Smith, *Mussolini*, 157–58.

86. "Discorso di Firenze," 17 May 1930, *OO*, vol. 24, 233–36.

87. Quoted in Robertson, *Mussolini as Empire Builder*, 84.

88. "Discorso al Senato," 2 April 1925, *OO*, vol. 21, 271.

89. Quoted in Lyttelton, *Italian Fascisms from Pareto to Gentile*, 12.

90. "La Dottrina del Fascismo," *OO*, vol. 34, 124.

91. Koon, *Believe, Obey Fight*, 22–23.

92. Quoted in Knox, "Conquest Foreign and Domestic," 362–63.

93. Alan Cassels, "Was There a Fascist Foreign Policy? Tradition and Novelty," *International History Review* 5, no. 2 (May 1983): 259.

94. "Constatazione," 6 September 1934, *OO*, vol. 24, 316–17.

95. Quoted in Koon, *Believe, Obey Fight*, 22; Mack Smith, *Mussolini's Roman Empire*, 63.

96. "Messagio per l'anno nono," 21 October 1930, *OO*, vol. 24, 278–85.

97. Quoted in Giorgio Rumi, *L'imperialismo fascista* (Milan: Mursia, 1974), 29.

98. "Discorso di piazza Belgioso," 3 May 1921, *OO*, vol. 16, 299–302; see also Mack Smith, *Mussolini*, 43, and Mack Smith, *Mussolini's Roman Empire*, 29.

99. "Al popolo di Venezia," 3 June 1923, *OO*, vol. 19, 233–35.

100. Quoted in Preti, *Impero fascista*, 16.

101. "La Dottrina del Fascismo," *OO*, vol. 34, 131.

102. Cassels, "Was There a Fascist Foreign Policy?", 260–61.

103. Knox, "Conquest Foreign and Domestic," 10; Mack Smith, *Mussolini's Roman Empire,* 15. For more on Mussolini's cultivation of the myth of Rome, see Romke Visser, "Fascist Doctrine and the Cult of the Romanità," *Journal of Contemporary History* 27, no. 1 (January 1992): 5–22.

104. "Intervista con Associated Press," 1 August 1926, *OO,* vol. 22, 190.

105. "Discorso di Firenze," 17 May 1930, *OO,* vol. 22, 233–36. For more on the notion of an Italian *spazio vitale* and Mussolini's rationale for expansion, see Kallis, *Fascist Ideology,* 48–51.

106. "Discorso di piazza Belgioso," 3 May 1921, *OO,* vol. 16, 299–302.

107. Knox, "Conquest Foreign and Domestic," 17.

108. Cassels, "Was There a Fascist Foreign Policy?" 262.

109. Knox, *Common Destiny,* 124–26.

110. Jäckl, *Hitler's Weltanshauung,* 14.

111. Robert Mallett, *The Italian Navy and Fascist Expansionism, 1935–1940* (London: Frank Cass, 1998), 22–31. For more detail on strategic calculations in the potential conflict over Ethiopia, see Arthur Marder, "The Royal Navy and the Ethiopian Crisis," *American Historical Review* 75, no. 5 (1970): 1327–56.

CHAPTER 2

Toward the Axis

Mussolini's invasion of Ethiopia in October 1935 seriously troubled Italy's relations with Britain and France. Mussolini had secured permission for the attack from Pierre Laval, the French foreign minister who signed the Rome Accords in January 1935, and the Duce seemingly believed that he had received at least tacit approval from the British government during the Anglo-French-Italian Stresa meetings in April that had sought to coordinate resistance against Nazi German rearmament and revisionism. Nevertheless, the British cabinet had thought that domestic public opinion demanded some kind of adherence to the collective security principles of the League of Nations. Constrained by fears of a potentially damaging Anglo-Italian military conflict and by Laval's determination not to offend Mussolini in order to maintain France's newfound alliance with Italy, British sponsorship of the halfhearted imposition of League of Nations sanctions had not stopped the Duce's triumphal conquest, and the Duce gloried in the belief that he had faced down opposition from Britain and a reluctant France. In addition, he had exploited British, French, and League opposition to rally Italian public opinion behind the regime and its war, further raising the level of mutual antagonism. By June 1936, however, Italy's victory over Ethiopia and the League collective security apparatus was ultimately assured, and given the ineffectiveness of sanctions, their end was only a matter of time. Accordingly, there was no objective reason that Mussolini could not seek a rapprochement with the Western democracies.[1] Mussolini, therefore, faced three broad choices as to the future orientation of Italian foreign policy. He could return to the Stresa

Front and cooperate with Britain and France to limit German revisionism; this choice would imply that Italy was content to maintain the status quo ante in Europe while consolidating its hold on Ethiopia. Alternatively, he could play the middle game and try to earn concessions from either Germany or the West. More dangerously, he could align Italy with Germany in an attempt to challenge the power of Britain and France.[2] An examination of Italy's relations with France, Britain, and Germany, plus Italian intervention in the Spanish Civil War and its policy in the Far East, suggests that Mussolini's policy brought Italy much closer to Germany than to the Western democracies; he aimed not to preserve the status quo but to challenge it.

On 10 June 1936, Mussolini signaled his preference to explore the possibility of an Italo-German rapprochement by appointing his son-in-law, Galeazzo Ciano di Cortelazzo, as minister of foreign affairs. Ciano was in some ways unlike most Fascist hierarchs. He was only forty-three years old and had not fought in the First World War, nor had he played a role in any of the pivotal battles that brought Mussolini to power. Ciano owed his position less to his abilities than to his father's war record and close friendship with Mussolini. Of course, Galeazzo Ciano's marriage to Mussolini's daughter Edda helped his rapid advancement.[3] His distinguishing characteristics were a taste for adventure and his unconcealed ambition. Though he admired the Nazis' strength and increasing power and prestige, Ciano was not precisely a Naziphile; he was not wedded to any particular ideology. In part owing to the apparent dynamism of Nazism, he was inclined toward friendly relations with Germany. Whatever Ciano's politics, he was ultimately Mussolini's creature; Mussolini could trust Ciano to implement his foreign policy decisions.[4] The same day, Mussolini dismissed Fulvio Suvich, the undersecretary of state at the Palazzo Chigi. Suvich had been a stalwart of Austrian independence, and he had opposed any substantive Italian alignment with Germany. Mussolini informed Suvich shortly before the latter's dismissal that he intended the following: "to break with France and with England, to leave the League of Nations, and to throw myself in the arms of Germany."[5] Suvich's continued presence was an obstacle to Mussolini's approaches to Germany, and he needed a more pliable undersecretary. Ulrich von Hassell, the German ambassador in Rome, cabled that "the re-orientation of Italy's policy toward Germany has played a part in the change of Foreign Ministers."[6] With Ciano and his new Undersecretary Giuseppe Bastianini installed in the Palazzo Chigi, the way appeared clear for a possible Italo-German rapprochement.[7]

Still, Mussolini had not publicly foreclosed any opportunities to treat with France and Britain. Instead, he and Ciano played a double game regarding the Franco-Italian military alliance and France's hoped-for Mediterranean pact, which would have various Mediterranean powers guarantee the territorial status quo ante in the Mediterranean basin. In late May and early June 1936, Suvich, Ciano, and Mussolini all had given assurances to Charles De Chambrun, the French ambassador in Rome, that Italy was prepared to cooperate with France, but that such cooperation depended on the end of sanctions at Geneva. On 16 May 1936, for example, De Chambrun had asked Suvich to clarify Italy's position regarding the Rome Accords, the four public and four secret agreements signed by Mussolini and French Foreign Minister Pierre Laval in January 1935; French diplomats were especially concerned whether or not Mussolini still considered himself part of a system to contain potential German aggression. Suvich had equivocated about Italy's precautionary troop movements toward the French border but said that there had been no change in Italy's position and that the various accords were still in effect. Suvich had warned, however, that the continuation of sanctions after the imminent end of the Ethiopian war would lead to problems with Italian public opinion and that sanctions were inconsistent with the friendly relations implied by the political accord signed the last year in Rome.[8] In early June, Mussolini had echoed these sentiments on different occasions to two distinguished French visitors, Jean-Louis Malvy, a French Senator touring Rome, and Hubert de Lagardelle, a prominent French Socialist journalist. Mussolini had emphasized that Italy was prepared to abide by the terms of the Rome Accords and to consider the Mediterranean pact, but only on the condition that Britain and France lifted sanctions.[9]

Mussolini did recognize that France was working to minimize and to end sanctions. During the Ethiopian war, while France had not maintained its end of the Rome Accords, as its long-term strategic interests required British support, successive Foreign Ministers Pierre Étienne Flandin and Joseph Paul-Boncour had "fought effectively for Italy" at Geneva.[10] They had interceded to prevent Britain from instituting an oil sanction, which would have had all but crippled Italy's military campaign. In Mussolini's view, while in London hysteria often ruled, in Paris many French politicians had greeted the Italian occupation of Addis Ababa with satisfaction, as it could presage the return of Italy to the Stresa Front against Germany.[11] On 19 June, Léon Blum, the French premier, summoned Vittorio Cerruti, the Italian ambassador in Paris, to inform him that the French Council of Ministers had decided to abolish sanctions. Although this policy would not take formal effect until the following month's meeting at Geneva, Blum hoped that this decision would lead to improved Franco-Italian relations immediately.[12] At the end of June and beginning of July 1936, Yvon Delbos, the French foreign minister, worked at Geneva to achieve the most favorable outcome for Italy possible in the circumstances. France did not take the lead there regarding the end of sanctions. It could not break openly with England, and appearing to undermine League resolutions was not in keeping with the public image of the Popular Front, but it was still clear that the end of sanctions was imminent. More importantly, Delbos did not make any specific resolution at Geneva regarding recognition of the Italian conquest of Ethiopia, which in effect worked to Italy's advantage. It meant that each member government was free of League dictates on the issue and had the option to recognize the Italian empire according to its own wishes.[13]

Nevertheless, despite France's somewhat limited attempts at accommodating Italy, Mussolini was clearly not keen on accepting any French démarches. In his view, the creation of the Popular Front government had brought to power men who were seemingly his avowed political enemies. In Léon Blum, who took office on 4 June 1936, Mussolini saw a Jew who was clearly hostile to Fascism. As Ambassador Cerruti had written from Paris, Blum was "a militant and observant Jew: *a fanatic of his race.*" Mussolini feared that Blum would increase the penetration of Jewish influence in the French government. Furthermore, Blum had long opposed Laval's policy of seeking tighter ties with Italy. He had attacked the signing of the Rome Accords as they violated the principles of disarmament and collective security through the League of Nations. He also believed in France's and Britain's close association in the League and its sanctions policy. Finally, Blum was a strong supporter of Zionism and was a member of the France-Palestine Committee and other Jewish agencies.[14] Nor did Mussolini see the new French foreign minister in a better light. Delbos was a French Mason, and, like Blum, had opposed Laval's policy of accommodation with Mussolini. Delbos had stated publicly that the failed Hoare-Laval plan had served to encourage Mussolini's intransigence over Ethiopia. As did Blum, Delbos tended to believe in the League of Nations and collective security.[15] In addition, the Popular Front's parliamentary cooperation with the French Communist Party further alienated the Duce and apparently established clear ideological differences between the two governments. In short, Blum, Delbos, and the Popular Front represented several of Mussolini's chief bêtes noires: freemasonry, socialism, communism, and internationalism in both its League of Nations and Jewish variants.[16]

Mussolini's assurances to French politicians, therefore, were insincere. He openly declared to his subordinates that he intended to draw closer to

Germany in an effort to begin isolating France. On 17 June, for example, Mussolini wrote to Dino Grandi, his ambassador in London, directing him to pursue a new policy there regarding Anglo-French relations. Grandi should aim to reorient British thinking away from a multilateral Mediterranean pact and toward a bilateral Anglo-Italian accord. He should belittle the idea that France, "nailed to the cross of the Soviets," would make an effective British partner in Mediterranean affairs. As France was too concerned about the German threat, Britain should jettison its association with the French in favor of a modus vivendi with Italy. Mussolini aimed to drive a wedge between the Western democracies in an attempt to isolate France.[17]

Italian approaches to Britain, therefore, had two compatible goals: ending sanctions and isolating France. In late May, Grandi, on instructions from Mussolini, had informed Anthony Eden, Britain's foreign secretary, that the Duce hoped to "restore confidence" in Mediterranean affairs. He would entertain any offers that the British government might make, but only after it raised sanctions. Grandi added disingenuously that Italy intended to make no difficulties for Britain in Egypt or Palestine through the use of anti-British propaganda.[18] In early June, Mussolini had directed Grandi to emphasize that Italian patience regarding the continuation of sanctions was running out. Grandi should offer several concessions to Britain. Mussolini would rein in Italy's polemical press campaign against Britain and would promise to respect the British empire and to work toward an Anglo-Italian rapprochement. In addition, Marshall Graziani, the Viceroy of Ethiopia, would allow the Sikh guard at the legation in Addis Ababa to remain, even though after the proclamation of the Italian empire it no longer had legal status. Grandi should warn Eden, however, that if His Majesty's government did not respond by lifting sanctions, Italy would withdraw from the League of Nations, and that Italian patience was rapidly running out.[19] Eden had replied that he could not open immediate conversations, as the crisis would have to be resolved through eventual League action.[20] Still, Grandi knew from conversations held with Sir Robert Vansittart, the permanent undersecretary, that most of the British cabinet had been persuaded of the need to lift sanctions as soon as possible—the only question was the matter of timing, form, and how much face Mussolini was willing to allow the British government and the League of Nations to save.[21]

Mussolini's appointment of Ciano came as a mild shock to the Foreign Office. It was somewhat disconcerting because Ciano, while Minister for Propaganda, had conducted the anti-British press campaign during the

Ethiopian war. The change appeared to have little effect on Anglo-Italian relations, however, other than removing the access of Britain's diplomats to the Duce; as Mussolini had given up the foreign minister's title, diplomats would have to deal with Ciano as a matter of protocol.[22] Despite the implications of Mussolini's appointment of Ciano, the apparent impasse broke slightly in the middle of June. After repeated urging from British diplomats, Mussolini agreed to make a gesture to the League, announcing that his minister there would read a conciliatory message to the next League Council meeting.[23] Bastianini also told Sir Eric Drummond, Britain's ambassador to Italy, that Italy was now a satisfied power and that it had no more territorial desiderata. It wished only to return to take up its part in European affairs and to reestablish cordial relations with Britain.[24] Mussolini also hinted at both his underlying motives by directing Grandi to tell British officials that ending sanctions would allow Britain "to demonstrate its courage" and help to "restore its prestige." It would also "deflect on to France the bitterness and rancour of the Italians." Mussolini also supported the idea of bilateral Anglo-Italian negotiations including the mutual respect of rights in the Mediterranean.[25] On 18 June 1936, at least in part owing to the Italian declaration to the League Council, Anthony Eden told the House of Commons that His Majesty's government no longer saw any need for continued sanctions against Italy. The effect was lessened by Eden's qualification that certain guarantees of assistance to Greece, Turkey, and Yugoslavia, replacing earlier mutual assistance agreements under Article 16 of the League Covenant, would remain for an indeterminate time after sanctions lapsed. Although the fear of the smaller powers prompted these guarantees, the implied distrust of the Duce's intentions was clear. Even though the entrance into force of the guarantees had been preceded by the withdrawal of the British home fleet from the Mediterranean, Ciano and Mussolini were chagrined.[26] Eden's announcement, therefore, removed one obstacle in the way of an Anglo-Italian rapprochement, but left others in place.

British charges of Italian espionage represented another source of tension. On 30 June 1936, Drummond met with Ciano to protest the espionage carried out by Italian Consul-General Ferrante in Malta. A British Maltese dockyard worker by the name of d'Elia had been sentenced to three years imprisonment for spying in Malta's Arsenal. D'Elia's public confession suggested that Ferrante was d'Elia's paymaster. Ciano protested that this evidence was insufficient, and refused to accept that the Consul-General should be expelled. A week later, Drummond insisted that Ferrante leave, but Ciano remained evasive, refusing to accept any responsibility for Ferrante's actions.[27] Dealing with more substantive issues on 12 July, Ciano told Drummond that Anglo-Italian relations would not return to normal until all aspects of Article 16, including the guarantees, had been removed. In response, Drummond suggested unofficially that Italian diplomats in all three of the applicable capitals declare that Italy had no intention of retaliating for the imposition of sanctions. After receiving his orders from Mussolini, Ciano did as Drummond had suggested, and, after consulting with Athens, Ankara, and Belgrade, Eden eventually declared on 22 July that the guarantees were no longer operable owing to Italy's "spontaneous" gesture.[28]

Despite the removal of these impediments to better Anglo-Italian relations, Whitehall's halting steps toward Italy ran counter to Mussolini's pursuit of closer ties with Germany. There were two issues in June and the first half of July that Germany and Italy settled: recognition of the declaration of the Italian empire and the question of Austrian foreign policy. During Italy's war in Ethiopia, Hitler had taken no steps to end the period of cold relations sparked by the 1934 murderous putsch against then Austrian Chancellor Engelbert Dollfuss. While Germany had not adhered to the League sanctions policy, it did not increase its shipments of strategic supplies to make up for the losses owing to sanctions. Germany had also continued to send arms to Ethiopia's defenders. In short, Hitler was annoyed because Mussolini refused to play the role as the Mediterranean counterbalance to France in which Hitler had cast him.[29] Nevertheless, after the end of the conflict, with Germany facing the potential repercussions of the remilitarization of the Rhineland, the offer of recognition of the Italian conquest was a gesture that was a unique opportunity for Germany. Nazi Germany did not have the difficulty of hostile public opinion and League entanglements, as did France and Britain, so recognition of Italy's conquest cost the German government nothing. Consequently, von Hassell told Ciano that Hitler was prepared to deal with the question of recognition whenever Mussolini thought the time was ripe, and that, in addition, the Führer would not expect any reciprocal gesture.[30]

The other, more important, potential obstacle was the delicate question of Austria's position between Germany and Italy. During the height of the tension with the West regarding the war in Ethiopia, Mussolini had astonished German Ambassador von Hassell by suggesting an Austro-German agreement "which would in practice bring Austria into Germany's wake, so that she could pursue no other foreign policy than one parallel with Germany. If Austria, as a formally quite independent state, were thus in practice to become a German satellite, [Mussolini] would have no objection."[31]

German officials had treated this démarche with extreme skepticism, but after repeatedly sounding Mussolini on the point, they eventually accepted this sea change in Italian policy. In response to German probing, Mussolini had also confirmed that he considered the Stresa Front "dead" and that he would take no part in action by Britain and France in the possible event of a German breach of the Locarno Treaty.[32] Hitler had eventually sent Hans Frank, a minister without portfolio, to carry a personal message to Mussolini, assuring the Duce of Hitler's sympathy regarding the Ethiopian war and the Italian struggle against both Bolshevism and the democracies.[33] Mussolini had fulfilled his promise to place pressure on the Austrian government to come to an agreement with Germany. In essence, Mussolini had implied that if Chancellor von Schuschnigg resisted German advances, then Austria would find itself isolated from all outside support.[34] Mussolini had greeted the resulting accord, signed on 11 July 1936, with great pleasure, as it removed "the only point of friction between Italy and Germany."[35] By the middle of July, therefore, Mussolini had taken substantive steps to reach a genuine rapprochement with Germany, while his relations with the West, and with France in particular, were plagued with mistrust and ill will. Events over the following three months would find Mussolini on a course of new expansion of Italian power in the Mediterranean and new conflicts with Britain and France, while at the same time he drew ever closer to the German camp.

From mid-July to the end of October, international relations in Europe were driven by two multilateral questions: the negotiations for a new Locarno, and, more importantly, the Spanish Civil War. Still, there were interesting undercurrents in bilateral relations between Italy and various powers, particularly regarding Ethiopia. Although Ciano refused to issue an ultimatum for the removal of the French and British legations, during July, Mussolini and Ciano directed Viceroy Graziani's harassment of the British and French ministers remaining in Addis Ababa. De Chambrun complained that Graziani had summoned French Minister Bodard and had berated Bodard as an "enemy of Italy." The Viceroy also prohibited French radio broadcasts, as he argued that they spread alarmist news reports.[36] Graziani interfered with the British Minister's use of the legation's telegraph route in violation of normal international protocol. A week after requiring the legation to use Italian telegraphic services, he prohibited the use of cyphers; all British traffic, therefore, would have to go en clair. Next, he arbitrarily arrested one of the British legation's interpreters. Finally, Graziani sent Italian carabinieri to enter the legation compound in order to secure the wireless.[37] In short, Mussolini and Ciano sanctioned the open harassment of Britain's and France's diplomatic representatives in order to try to close the legations. To the protests of these highly improper and extraordinary actions, Ciano merely replied churlishly that the French and British legations would have to leave.[38] These poor relations with the Western powers over Ethiopia were in sharp contrast to Italy's relations with Germany. On 25 July 1936, Ambassador von Hassell informed Ciano that Hitler had decided to change Germany's legation in Addis Ababa to a consulate.[39]

Italy also continued to work against British interests elsewhere. In August, British officials noted that Italy was then conducting espionage campaigns against Britain, particularly in Malta and Gibraltar. It was involved in supporting the Imam of Yemen in the Arabian Peninsula to try to extend Italian influence at the expense of Britain there. Italy continued its propaganda campaigns against Britain in both Egypt and Palestine, producing "mendacious and violently anti-British" propaganda; Italian agents had also distributed funds to spark Arab disturbances.[40] Unknown to Whitehall, in September, Mussolini also ordered Grandi to maintain his propaganda network established during the Ethiopian war. It published extensive numbers of books, articles, and other propaganda pieces, many of which played on Mussolini's idées fixes.[41] Regarding France, Mussolini could scarcely conceal his contempt. He said that France was "weak and old," and a "country in which cuisine had become a principle of the State." Its demographic decadence was "horrifying," as it lost some 2,000 people per week. He would not be interested in pursuing friendly relations with France until it solved its overwhelming internal problems.[42] In short, Mussolini showed no inclination to deal with either Britain or France on an amicable basis. The difference between his level of hostility to the two Western democracies was that he still hoped to compel Britain to give concessions to Italy in order to isolate France.

Italy's continuing rapprochement with Germany and estrangement from the West is apparent in the larger issues of the proposed renewal of Locarno and the Spanish Civil War. The negotiations for a new five-power agreement to replace the Treaty of Locarno had their roots in Hitler's offer following the Nazi remilitarization of the Rhineland in March 1936. With sanctions in place, however, there was no realistic prospect of any substantive meetings involving Italian representatives. With the imminent removal of sanctions at the beginning of July, Belgian, French, and British statesmen began to discuss the possibility of bringing Italy back into a system of guarantees against potential German aggression. The task was enormously difficult as, despite Hitler's offer, Germany was unlikely to participate in an arrangement that would seriously limit its freedom of action. Any reconstruction of the Stresa Front also appeared to be out of the question.[43] There were substantial differences between France and Britain as to the best way to proceed. Officials in Whitehall wanted to postpone any meetings, lest they give Italy and Germany common cause to prevent any effective result as, following the German-Austrian agreement of 11 July, an Italo-German rapprochement appeared possible. The French government wanted to push ahead, whether or not Italy decided to attend.[44]

Early soundings of the Italian attitude did not bode well. Ciano stalled for time, using the pretext that he could not foresee Italy taking part in any negotiations until sanctions and the lingering effects of Article 16 through the British guarantee to Greece, Turkey, and Yugoslavia had been removed; he said their continued presence "stigmatized" Italy.[45] More importantly, Ciano also stated that although no decision had been taken as yet, Italy would not likely take part in any talks unless German representatives were also present.[46] On 24 July, De Chambrun, speaking for the British and Belgian Chargés d'Affaires, told Ciano that Germany would receive an invitation to the proposed new round of talks and, as the Mediterranean Accords under Article 16 had lapsed, Italy had no reason to avoid new meetings.[47] The next day, von Hassell told Ciano that Germany would accept the invitation provided certain conditions were met. Germany would require parity with the other countries present and would only proceed if there were extensive diplomatic preparation for any actual conference.[48] The following week, Ciano met again with von Hassell. Ciano said that Italy was in complete accord with Germany regarding the obvious delaying tactic of the need for "careful diplomatic preparation."[49] Constantin von Neurath, the German foreign minister, told Bernardo Attolico, Italy's ambassador in Berlin, that Hitler wanted to work in "full accord with Italy." Given these tactics, von Neurath believed that they should be able to delay any meetings until late October. Both foreign ministers agreed that any new agreement should bear little relation to the old one, as any kind of mutual assistance pact, the heart of the original Locarno, would be damaging to Italy and Germany.[50] Essentially, by the end of July, Italy had established "100% accord" with Germany in response to the proposed new Locarno, as neither power wanted discussion of substantive issues at any putative conference.[51]

The Spanish Civil War, which erupted on 17 July 1936, was the other major issue that helped Germany and Italy to develop closer relations. Mussolini initially resisted intervening in the generals' rebellion against the Republican government. Despite long-standing Italian contacts with

Spanish anti-Republicans and the March 1934 agreement with a group of Spanish monarchists, he had refused Franco's initial requests for aid.[52] Franco needed to move some 15,000 troops from Spanish Morocco across the Straits to Spain. As most of the Spanish Navy had remained loyal to the Republic, he needed transport planes to do so. Franco's increasingly desperate appeals for planes accused Mussolini of "political myopia" for his failure "to save Spain from bolshevism."[53] On 23 July 1936, Cerruti informed Ciano that the French Popular Front government had decided to send twenty-five Potez 54 bombers and 20,000 bombs to the Spanish government. It was also considering requests for eight Schneider seventy-five-millimeter artillery pieces, eight Hotchkiss machine guns, and 1,000 rifles. The French government started shipping part of the order on the evening of 24 July, even though no contract had then been signed.[54] It was only in response to France's intervention that an emissary from General Mola, the chief planner of the revolt, was able to convince Mussolini to send twelve Savoia S.81 planes to Franco, although Ciano demanded cash in advance. The planes eventually left on 27 July. Although only nine actually reached Franco's forces, they were an essential factor in early Nationalist successes in the war.[55]

The discussion of any ideological component in Italy's initial intervention has been clouded by the fact that there was little threat of an actual Communist takeover in July 1936.[56] Mussolini, of course, did not place such a narrow definition on his generic use of the term "Bolshevism." He detested precisely the kind of leftism that the Spanish Republican government represented. Essentially, in Mussolini's view, it did not matter whether the particular brand of leftism was democratic, communist, socialist, or anarchist; all carried the threat of introducing Bolshevism into Spain and even beyond Spain into other countries in Western Europe. In addition, the intervention of the French Popular Front government promised the extension of French influence even further over its sister Popular Front government in Madrid. Mussolini hoped that a Nationalist victory would allow him greater leverage over France, as an unfriendly Spain would require France to guard the Pyrenees frontier and would threaten French imperial communications.[57] It is important to note, however, that Mussolini's initial decision to intervene was made independently of German influence and that it was at a very low level of involvement.

In early August, there were two new outside initiatives regarding the civil war. On 1 August, Admiral Canaris, the head of the German armed forces intelligence office, the *Abwehr,* asked his Italian counterpart, General Roatta, head of the *Servizio Informazioni Militari,* for a meeting, which took place on 4 August. Canaris said that Germany had sent four Junkers transport planes, plus one ship carrying various small arms to the insurgents. He hoped that the Italian government could satisfy Franco's urgent demand for fuel; would the Italians send a ship? The German Air Ministry also wanted to know if it could stage planes through Italian air-fields to reach Nationalist forces in Spain. Roatta reserved any decision until he could speak with Mussolini but replied three days later that Mussolini had agreed to the German requests.[58]

At another meeting later in August, Canaris and Roatta detailed the respective levels of support for Spanish Nationalists. They agreed on several issues to coordinate their support for Franco, such as consultation over sending specialists and whether or not to allow their specialists to fight in battle. Both sides pledged that they would not demand territorial concessions from Spain, though in fact Ciano hoped to gain the Balearic Islands or the concession of a permanent base there. Roatta and Canaris also discussed the advisability of creating and sustaining a fleet for Franco's forces. Perhaps most importantly, they decided to send a joint mission to Franco to determine appropriate levels of arms shipments and use of advisors to advise Franco on the war against the "reds" and to guarantee Italy's and Germany's political, economic, and military interests.[59] Ciano met with Canaris the same day and confirmed the decisions.[60] Essentially, Italian and German officials had decided to coordinate closely their involvement in the Spanish Civil War.

While Germany and Italy began a slow crescendo in their intervention, the Blum cabinet announced in early August that France had reversed its policy regarding the supply of arms to Spain and that it hoped to establish instead an international arms embargo.[61] On 3 August, De Chambrun called on Ciano to give him the French government's appeal for a nonintervention agreement in Spain. Ciano reserved his answer, as Mussolini was not then in Rome. He also lied to De Chambrun regarding the two Italian planes that had landed in French territory; Ciano disclaimed any knowledge of their mission.[62] Upon his return to Rome, Mussolini told Ciano that he should adhere in principle to the proposal. Ciano should inquire, however, whether the moral solidarity, including public demonstrations, press campaigns, monetary subscriptions, and the like would also be prohibited under any agreement. He should also ask if the French plan would cover only government aid. If so, it would allow British or French private firms to continue to supply aid to the government forces. Finally, Mussolini wanted to know whether or not there would be any kind of direct observation or control.[63]

These early communications spelled out the problem that would plague the nonintervention committee throughout its dubious existence. France wanted to prohibit Italian and German direct governmental aid to Franco while maintaining a free hand for French civilians and businesses to give a wide array of aid to the government side. Ciano insisted repeatedly that any realistic agreement would have to prohibit all foreign aid, especially the raising of money and recruiting of volunteers that already was occurring. Further, Ciano demanded that any agreement would have to include the Soviet Union, which, he argued, was already underwriting the government in Madrid.[64] In a formal counterproposal, Ciano said that Italy would participate provided any agreement banned all forms of direct and indirect aid, including arms, munitions, war matériel, and civilian planes and ships, plus public subscriptions and volunteers. Any agreement would have to include a specific definition of "indirect aid." Finally, Ciano argued that any accord would have to include Great Britain, France, Portugal, Germany, and the Soviet Union.[65]

Four days later, however, Ciano decided to accept the French proposal without insisting on all of his previous conditions. He arrived at that decision after the German government decided to accept the French proposal. Still, Ciano accepted only in order to avoid being blamed for the failure of the negotiations and to ensure continued French neutrality. Even if the Blum cabinet implemented the nonintervention agreement, Ciano believed that the perceived betrayal of the Spanish Popular Front would help to undermine Blum's government, as its radical supporters might turn against it.[66] He told his liaison with Franco that Italy would insist on the eventual acceptance of its views on subscriptions and volunteers and would wait for the other states to adhere. At that point, then Italy would reconsider its position. In the meantime, Germany and Italy both would keep supplying arms to the Spanish insurgents.[67] Accordingly, Ciano gave his formal acceptance of the proposal to De Chambrun on 29 August. At the end of August, therefore, Germany and Italy had established tight cooperation on both their intervention in Spain as well as their resistance to the resurrection of Locarno. Italy was engaged in something close to a proxy war with France in Spain, and circumstances offered Mussolini the opportunity to carry out a thorough rapprochement with Germany.[68]

In a marked contrast, Italy's confrontation with France would escalate in August as Italy struck at France's imperial communications. On 16 August, some 10,000 Republican forces landed on Majorca in an attempt to retake it from the primarily Falangist defenders. In response to a request from the local Falange leader on the island of Majorca for a military advisor, Mussolini sent Major Arconovaldo Bonaccorsi, a former Fascist *squadrista,* who would become known as Conte Rossi.[69] Mussolini's interest in the Balearic Islands lay in the fact that they straddled the main routes between France's North African colonies and its Mediterranean ports. In wartime, French planners expected to move roughly one million soldiers over those routes to metropolitan France. If Italy could interdict that troop movement, then its position in the Mediterranean would be strengthened by the considerable weakening of that of France. In sending Bonaccorsi, an adventurer who could easily be disowned, Mussolini took a small risk that could pay great dividends. Bonaccorsi arrived on Majorca on 26 August. Dressed in a black Fascist uniform and bedecked with pistols, hand grenades, and daggers, he set out to stiffen the defenses of the dispirited Nationalist forces. Owing in part to Bonaccorsi's élan, and in part to the incompetence and timidity of the Republican invaders, he was able to convince the commander of the Republican troops to evacuate the bridgehead, despite the Republican's roughly six to one superiority in troops. Undoubtedly Conte Rossi had saved Majorca, even though he never had had more than 250 Italians fighting with him.[70]

Italian possession of the Balearics eventually became an international issue. The obvious threat to France's imperial communications was too great to ignore. Further, Italian planes based in Majorca could strike any of France's Mediterranean ports.[71] Eventually, Ciano yielded to diplomatic pressure from France and Britain and declared that Italy would observe the territorial integrity of Spain.[72] Still, Ciano's assurances did not allay French fears, for their vital strategic interests were undoubtedly affected. Potentially more seriously, Bonaccorsi had reported that French citizens were among those killed in the fighting at Port Christo, meaning that Italian and French nationals were ranged in combat with each other as early as August.[73] Despite his public assurances that Italy had no intention of remaining in the Balearics after the end of the Civil War, Ciano clearly hoped to do so. He told Colonel General Göring that Italy wanted a naval base as a permanent territorial concession from Spain. If Republican forces won the war, there would be little doubt that Italy would try to maintain its control over the Balearics.[74] Italian policy aimed to diminish France's Mediterranean position.

Italy and Germany reached a modus vivendi in another area in August. German economic penetration in the Balkans worried Attolico, the Italian ambassador in Berlin. Both Italy and Germany had interests in the region, with Italy supporting Hungarian revisionism against the Trianon Treaty and sponsoring the terrorist Ustaša to destabilize Yugoslavia. The 1934

Rome Protocols established tripartite political consultation among Austria, Hungary, and Italy and also provided for economic cooperation among the three countries. Concluded as a bulwark against German economic and political influence in the Balkans, Mussolini initially believed that the agreement secured the Italian position in the Balkans, but German influence continued to grow. In light of the increased German economic interest in the Danube basin, Attolico thought that direct competition between them would be very damaging. He argued that it would be wise for Italy to work toward some kind of restoration of friendly relations with Yugoslavia in order to facilitate Italian commercial interests in the Danube basin. Mussolini concurred.[75] Constantin von Neurath responded reasonably well to Italian suggestions for economic cooperation. He suggested that Italy work toward bilateral treaties, which had worked for Germany with Bulgaria, Hungary, Yugoslavia, and even Romania. He thought that Italy could sign basic commercial agreements, which then could become treaties of preference in the future. Finally, he suggested that Italy and Germany should not attempt to delimit "geographical spheres of influence," as those would alienate the countries in the region. Instead, Germany and Italy should cooperate in negotiating agreements with third-party states.[76] Accordingly, Italy began negotiations toward a commercial agreement with Yugoslavia, which was eventually signed on 2 October 1936 and which paved the way for the later Italo-Yugoslav political accord in 1937.[77]

During September and October, Italy and Germany strengthened their ties still further. In London, where the nonintervention committee was meeting, Grandi worked closely with Joachim von Ribbentrop, the German ambassador, to scuttle any effective limits on Italian and German intervention in Spain. Grandi told the committee at its second meeting on 14 September that Italy was prepared to adhere to an arms embargo. He also ensured that any previous violations prior to the accord would be outside its scope. At a subcommittee meeting a week later, Grandi insisted that any accord would have to give equal weight to indirect intervention as it did to direct intervention. He said that the committee would have to prohibit the following: the recruitment of volunteers, whether by governments or individuals; the presence in Spain of so-called political agitators; and both public and private financial aid. Grandi was successful in convincing the subcommittee to consider indirect intervention, over Soviet objections for obvious reasons, thus ensuring that its work would proceed at a glacial pace. Throughout the month of meetings, Grandi and his Soviet counterpart repeatedly denounced the others' alleged violations.[78] More importantly, Grandi worked in virtual lockstep with von Ribbentrop in delaying the various committees' work. German and Italian policy toward the nonintervention accord was nearly identical.[79]

Given the great similarities between Italian and German policies regarding Locarno and Spain, it was not surprising that both desired a more formal arrangement. On 23 September, Hans Frank met with Mussolini at the Palazzo Venezia. Frank carried a personal message from Hitler extending an invitation to Ciano to visit Berlin. In a rambling, sometimes aimless, discussion, Frank and Mussolini noted the similarity of Italian and German views regarding several issues. The Duce offered his support for Germany's claims for the restoration of German colonies. He said that Germans, like Italians, were a people "without living space," though he fully expected that England would prove obdurate in redistributing colonial holdings; Mussolini also offered the information that Anglo-Italian relations were bad and unlikely to improve. Given France's internal disarray, Italy could find no common policy with the Popular Front government.[80]

In early October, Ciano agreed that he would go to Berlin later that month. The agenda for that conference and the secret protocol officially approved there showed the extent of German and Italian coordination of policies.[81] The protocol covered the following issues: coordination of resistance to the proposed five-power conference to renew the Locarno Treaty, recognition of Franco upon his occupation of Madrid, German recognition of Italy's conquest in Ethiopia, common attitude toward potential Italian withdrawal from the League of Nations, Italy's support for Germany's demands for colonial restoration and raw materials, and an agreement on economic cooperation in the Danube basin.[82] Ciano also wanted to make a public statement on a common attitude toward defense against communism and a declaration of the concept of Italo-German parallelism in action. Both men agreed that the war in Spain showed their common struggle against Bolshevism. That said, there were some minor differences between the powers. Though they shared a common resistance to the five-power pact, they had different tactics in mind as to how to doom any conference. Though both were making approaches to Japan, Germany had decided to negotiate a different set of agreements with Japan, while Italy was more willing to recognize Manchukuo. Finally, although Germany and Italy had agreed to cooperate at some level in economic expansion in the Danube basin, Germany did not allow any real limits on its ambitions in the region.[83]

Ciano arrived in Berlin on 20 October and met von Neurath the next day. In a wide-ranging discussion, Ciano and von Neurath covered many of the points of the protocols to be signed. In addition, they spoke of Britain's *"policy of encirclement against Italy."*[84] Ciano referred to certain documents that Mussolini had ordered turned over to the Führer that showed Britain's unfavorable intentions toward Germany. Grandi had procured the documents in London; they were a collection of reports and telegrams that discussed in frank terms the British view on the perceived Nazi expansion of power. In another anti-British vein, von Neurath emphasized that Italy should try to establish better relations with Yugoslavia, as it would have the double advantage of *"attaching Yugoslavia to the anti-communist bloc and subtracting it from the British camp."* In Ciano's discussion with Hitler three days later at Berchtesgaden, both men rubbished British policy and British statesmen. They also emphasized their common heroic defence against Bolshevism in Spain. Hyperbole aside, they essentially rehashed the various points of agreement in the secret protocol.[85]

Though Ciano and von Neurath did not negotiate any kind of strict alliance, Italy's relations with Germany were of an entirely different character than those with any other nation. Mussolini did not desire and was not pursuing a policy of equidistance; he had moved Italy into a partnership with Germany in order to expand Italian power at the risk of confrontation with the Western democracies. Mussolini thought that Italy's next war would be fought for domination of the Mediterranean and would pit Fascist Italy against Britain and France.[86] Mussolini made the orientation of Fascist foreign policy explicit in his 1 November speech in Milan that publicly announced the Rome-Berlin Axis. He denounced the League of Nations because, in Mussolini's view, it was based on the absurdity of equality among nations, which served only to confine a virile people. He condemned France for allowing sanctions to remain in force for almost two months after the occupation of Addis Ababa and for allowing an Ethiopian representative to appear at the Geneva League meetings. Regarding Yugoslavia, he noted that there was the possibility of genuine friendship between Italy and that country on the basis of spiritual, political, and economic ties. Ciano's meetings in Berlin created an "axis around which can cooperate all the European states." That said, however, Italy and Germany would fight their common enemy, Bolshevism, against which they had sacrificed much blood and won many victories. Finally, Mussolini said that democracy was the antithesis of Fascism. Turning to grand strategy, he spoke to his potential British listeners, saying that for Britain, the Mediterranean Sea was "a road, one of many roads, or rather a short cut with which the British empire reaches more rapidly its peripheral territories.... If for others the Mediterranean is a road, for us Italians it is life." Mussolini demanded that the British empire accommodate itself to Italy's parity of rights in the Mediterranean, preferably through a comprehensive bilateral agreement.[87] Mussolini's penchant for grand, sweeping phrases makes it easy to dismiss much of this speech as hyperbole.[88] What is interesting here, however, is how closely the speech represents Italy's actual policy. Mussolini stressed rapprochement with Germany and Yugoslavia, the need for extension of Italy's power and influence in the Mediterranean, a bilateral agreement with Britain that recognized Italy's growing power, and the complete exclusion of France from the equation. Mussolini's policy was in no way equidistant between Germany and the West.

While Ciano was preparing his trip to Berlin, there were two other events that would serve to alienate Mussolini even further from France: the impending retirement of De Chambrun and the increased Soviet involvement in the Spanish Civil War. De Chambrun was scheduled to retire as he reached age sixty in October 1936. The difficulty for France was that the Italians would likely demand credentials addressed to the king of Italy, emperor of Ethiopia. In diplomatic parlance, that designation could imply both de facto and de jure recognition of Italy's conquest, which the Blum government was not prepared to do; in any event, its hands were tied by its loyalty to the League Covenant. Delbos instructed De Chambrun to inform Ciano that the ambassador would leave his post at the end of October. Although De Chambrun offered to stay on, Delbos refused; if the Italians insisted on trying to achieve a backhanded recognition of the empire, then Jules Blondel, the chargé d'affaires, would represent France in Rome. Mussolini replied through Ciano that he "would prefer to see France represented by a Chargé d'Affaires, more so than to admit a new Ambassador who would be accredited only to the king." What was galling to the French government was that Italy had already accepted the credentials of the new ambassador from the United States made out only to the king of Italy.[89] Neither side would compromise, and De Chambrun left at the end of the month.[90]

More seriously, Stalin decided in September to carry out a major intervention in the Spanish Civil War. The republic faced imminent defeat, as Franco appeared to be close to occupying Madrid. Stalin decided to work on two fronts. He would send large quantities of war matériel to government-held ports, and he would recruit "an international army for use in Spain."[91] During the latter half of September, Italian intelligence sources counted some twenty-seven Soviet shipments reaching Spain. They unloaded roughly seventy-five modern fighters, more than one hundred trucks, dozens of artillery pieces, and some one hundred T26 tanks, which were then likely the best in the world, plus thousands of military advisors and thousands of tons of ammunition, rifles, explosives, and diesel and aviation fuel. Total Soviet supplies, in broad terms, equaled or exceeded those of Germany and Italy combined.[92] These weapons, plus those from France, not only helped to arm government forces, but also supplied the backbone of the war matériel to equip the International Brigades that arrived in the front lines in early November. Though there has been much myth making that the brigades consisted primarily of volunteers fighting to preserve democracy against Fascism, that claim is largely false. While there were some noncommunists in the Brigades, particularly in the forces from North America, the Comintern army allocated all command positions to Communist Party members, and the Comintern paid for most of the volunteers to reach Spain. The Comintern also provided "direction and control" through its political commissars. The International Brigades clearly saved Madrid, and with it the Republic, during several battles between 8 November 1936 and January 1937.[93] The Spanish Civil War, which had begun owing to domestic reasons, had become an international ideological struggle.

Mussolini and Ciano both reacted strongly to the increasing Bolshevization of the war. In late October, after his triumphant visit to Berlin, Ciano proposed that Italy and Germany recognize Franco immediately. He still hoped for a quick victory, as the weight of Republican reinforcements had not then been felt. In case the fall of Madrid were delayed, however, Ciano thought that both countries should establish "open relations" with the insurgent government in Burgos. Finally, he informed the German ambassador that Italy was sending two submarines to the Nationalist forces in order to try to interdict Soviet shipping. Von Neurath demurred regarding the immediate recognition of Franco, as Hitler believed that it might cause Franco to delay the occupation of Madrid, and Ciano acquiesced at that time.[94] Eventually, the Führer changed his mind, and on 18 November, Italy and Germany both agreed to recognize Franco's regime in Burgos as the official Spanish government.[95]

Also during November, the International Brigades halted the Spanish Nationalist forces' drive on Madrid. Mussolini became disenchanted with Franco's slow rate of progress, which the Duce blamed partly on the lack of offensive spirit of Franco's troops and partly on the influx of Soviet arms and the Soviet-inspired International Brigades. On 27 November, he decided to send a division of Blackshirts to fight in Spain. Before he did so, however, he wanted assurances from Franco that Nationalist Spain would conduct its future foreign policy in harmony with Italy. Mussolini demanded that Nationalist Spain promise to build certain airports and to guarantee that it would not allow French troops to cross Spanish territory. Accordingly, Italian officials prepared a text, dated 28 November, for Franco to sign. It promised further Italian military aid until such time as Franco would be able to establish a secure Nationalist order. In exchange, Franco agreed not to allow transit of enemy troops without Italy's permission, to work to eliminate Article 16 of the League Covenant, to refuse to participate in any collective measures through the League, to give preferential treatment toward Italy in supplying raw materials, and, in general, to cooperate with Italian foreign policy.[96] Officials in the Wilhelmstrasse, never keen on Hitler's intervention, saw the scope of the Italian agreement, which by its very nature precluded an equally wide-ranging German pact, as a pretext to require Italy to take the lead in Spain.[97]

Consequently, Admiral Canaris, Mussolini, Ciano, and other officials held a meeting at the Palazzo Venezia on 6 December to determine future Axis policy. Faced with the augmentation of Republican military power, Mussolini thought that it was time to prepare to send military units that would serve as a separate foreign legion, to increase the numbers of specialists and advisors, to send German and Italian instructors to train Franco's troops, and to establish a combined Italo-German general staff. In addition, he argued that Germany and Italy should take the war to sea and attempt to blockade Republican ports through aviation and submarine units. He was prepared to increase the number of Italian submarines he would give to Franco's forces from two to eight. Mussolini believed that Germany and Italy should "divide the work." Canaris agreed with the Duce's proposed course of action but said that Germany would be unlikely to send units of ground troops. Germany would, however, provide forty more Junkers bombers and 4,800 aviation specialists. Italy, for its part, would send more C.R. 32 and R.O. 37 fighters. Finally, Admiral Cavagnari torpedoed, so to speak, Mussolini's scheme to interdict shipping in Spanish territorial waters; he emphasized the difficulty of identifying ships and the likely international backlash to Italian submarine attacks.[98] Still, with the Italian decision to send *Regio Esercito* military units, Mussolini had decided to escalate Italian participation in the war to a higher level.

In addition to their ever-closer ties to Germany, Mussolini and Ciano also tried in the latter half of 1936 to reach a rapprochement with Britain's chief Asian rival, Japan. Italy had until 1936 supported the Chinese Nationalist government in its defense against both Japanese aggression and the Chinese Communist insurgency. Italian and Chinese relations had been strong up until the time of sanctions. Chiang Kai-Shek had adhered to sanctions much more strictly than Mussolini had expected, as the Chinese dictator hoped to be able to use the precedent of sanctions against the Japanese. Still, after sanctions had obviously failed, relations had returned to normal. As Mussolini had promised, the Italian military air and naval missions to the Kuomintang returned to work helping to defend the Nationalist army against the Japanese invaders and communist insurgents. Italy had also developed a strong commercial position in China.[99] Simultaneously, Britain and the United States both seemed unwilling to challenge Japanese aggression in northern China, suggesting that British power was overstrained by the confrontation with Italy. Furthermore, the Soviet Union had increased its arms shipments to the Chinese Communists; this change in policy threatened the power of the Chinese Nationalists.[100] The Japanese "intrepid resistance" in the face of opposition from the League of Nations pleased Mussolini and demonstrated the vitality of the Japanese in the face of the "old" British empire.[101] According to Giacinto Auriti, Italy's ambassador in Tokyo, despite Japanese domestic political and industrial problems, its population was fiercely patriotic and had "the need and the power to struggle and to expand." Accordingly, Japan would tie up British and Soviet resources in the Far East, which would "diminish their power and liberty of action in Europe."[102] The time seemed ripe, therefore, for Mussolini to exploit the comparative isolation of Japan.

During April through June 1936, diplomats had explored the possibilities of mutual recognition of the Italian empire and the Japanese puppet state of Manchukuo. The Japanese desire not to offend Britain and Italy's missions in China complicated the discussions, but the common interests between Italy and Japan were too great to ignore. On 19 July 1936, Ciano promised Japanese Ambassador Sugimara Yotaro that Italy would reconsider its policy, which had supplied the Chinese Nationalist army with most of its air power, as Japan's anti-Bolshevik struggle took precedence.[103] Eventually, in October, Ciano and Sugimara worked out the details of de facto recognition of the two countries' mutual conquests, plus an agreement on future de jure recognition. After the publication of the German-Japanese anti-Comintern Pact of 23 October 1936, Ciano and Japanese Foreign Minister Arita Hachirō reached agreement on the de jure recognition of the status on Manchukuo and Ethiopia.[104] In November, Ciano authorized Ambassador Auriti to pursue negotiations for a commercial accord with Japan. The accord would cover not only cultural and economic interests, but also common defense against Bolshevism. Auriti believed that the accord would pave the way for a three-way anti-Comintern Pact among Germany, Japan, and Italy.[105] The Japanese government saw these steps as primarily anti-Bolshevik in nature, as Japan's main enemy was the Soviet Union. For Mussolini and Ciano, however, the impetus for the rapprochement with Japan came primarily from European affairs. The potential bloc of Germany, Japan, and Italy would create conditions where Italy could dictate terms to a British government that feared the loss of the empire.[106]

While Mussolini arranged with Germany the massively increased Italian involvement in Spain, he continued to try to separate France from England. Several senior British diplomats, including Vansittart and Drummond, could scarcely credit that Italy would permanently side with Germany. Vansittart wrote that "if we are reasonably polite to both we needn't be afraid that they will go into partnership against us."[107] In early November, the cabinet, recognizing the need to ensure the separation of Germany and Italy, decided over Eden's objections to make a considered effort to court friendlier Anglo-Italian relations.[108] On 6 November, Drummond signed two trade accords that had been long in negotiation. Drummond also informed Ciano of the cabinet's decision to convert the legation in Addis Ababa into a consulate, thus giving the Italian government de facto recognition of the conquest of Ethiopia.[109] On 8 November, British journalist Ward Price interviewed Mussolini, and the latter mentioned a possible gentlemen's agreement. Whitehall officials seized on this unstructured format for talks to try to further develop better relations with Italy. In doing so, they specifically rejected the French formula for a wider Mediterranean pact. There were two sets of outstanding issues that neither party addressed formally in the agreement. Britain hoped that Italy would stop its propaganda campaigns in Palestine and Egypt and its intrigues in Yemen.[110] For its part, Italy hoped that Britain would grant de jure recognition of the Italian empire. Relations were too strained to make substantial headway on these issues, so the discussions evolved toward a mutual exchange of notes highlighting Italy's and Britain's respect for the status quo in the Mediterranean, though neither side made any real commitments even in this area.[111] After drawn-out negotiations, Drummond and Ciano eventually signed the essentially meaningless agreement on 2 January 1937.[112]

While these diplomatic discussions took place, however, Mussolini and Ciano continued a foreign policy hostile to the British empire. In a series of letters, Ciano and Grandi discussed present and future Anglo-Italian relations. Only Grandi's letters apparently survive, but they clearly show

Ciano's policy toward Britain. Italy and Britain were entering a "permanent conflict" over such issues as Malta irredenta and the fate of the British empire in the Mediterranean and Near East.[113] Britain feared the Axis and the resulting threat to the empire. Therefore, as Grandi congratulated Ciano:

If Italy and Germany will show England an increasingly united bloc without cracks, without dead ends, without tendencies to exploit the difficulties of the other, determined to follow a common direction and a united front to the other Powers, British policy will be constrained to come to agreements with Rome and Berlin simultaneously, accepting those conditions that Rome and Berlin together will dictate to London in order to guarantee and maintain in Europe and the world that peace which alone will permit the British Empire to maintain itself laboriously in existence.[114]

Despite the fact that, in Grandi's words, Italy had nothing to fear from Britain, the Axis would give Italy the power to extort concessions from Britain. Further, the possibility of the addition of Japan to the Axis meant the union of the three states "which are the youngest, the fiercest, the most heavily armed, and the most coldly determined to expand their power." It would create "the gravest danger that has ever threatened the British Empire in the course of its history."[115] Ciano's aims, as Grandi understood them, were not to reach genuine a rapprochement with Britain, but rather to manage through temporary agreements with Britain the advancement of Italy's power and influence in the Mediterranean.

The Anglo-Italian conversations, which led to the gentlemen's agreement, worried French officials; they correctly feared what was in reality an Italian attempt to isolate France from Britain. Delbos followed in British footsteps regarding the transformation of the French legation in Addis Ababa to a consulate, but it led to little change in Italy's attitude.[116] Ciano instructed Ambassador Cerruti to placate Alexis Léger Saint-Léger, the secretary-general at the Quai d'Orsay, in an effort to extract de jure recognition from France. Ciano said that he wanted more than mere friendly words from France, but friendly deeds; he was unimpressed with only de facto recognition.[117] At the same time, however, Italy made no gestures of reconciliation toward France. Despite Ciano's promise that Italy expected no territorial gains from the Spanish Civil War, Italian troops had established virtual sovereignty in the Balearics, which constituted a grave menace to French security. With British cooperation, Ciano had worked to reject French overtures toward a Mediterranean pact and conducted instead negotiations that deliberately excluded France.[118] By the end of

1936, Franco-Italian relations had reached a "dead end point."[119] In Mussolini's view, he had heard from France only "useless and irritating words."[120] In Ciano's view, the rapprochement with Britain was predicated on the understanding that "France remained outside" and that Italy and Germany would continue to work together to achieve "the triumph of their common ideals."[121]

The reorientation of Italian military planning further indicated the shift in Mussolini's geopolitical thinking. Early in 1936, Italian naval planners had called for a dramatically increased fleet to combat a potential Franco-British alliance. This escape fleet, designed to break out of the Mediterranean prison, would contain nine or ten battleships, up to four aircraft carriers, three dozen cruisers, and several dozen submarines. This construction could only occur, however, if the state could carry out a vast increase in Italy's industrial capability. Given the financial realities governing Fascist Italy, such grandiose plans were impossible. Already, raw material shortages had delayed the expected completion of the new *Littorio* class battleships by a year. At two general staff meetings in late 1936, the heads of the respective service ministries agreed that these shortcomings would limit the *Regia Marina* to resupplying Libya during a future war with Britain and France. Nevertheless, General Pariani, the undersecretary for war, thought that a lightning attack by motorized troops and aircraft would be able to seize the Sudan and possibly Egypt from British control. Despite the opposition of General Badoglio, the Chief of Staff, to this plan, Mussolini thought that it offered an opportunity to challenge British domination of the Mediterranean basin.[122] As the Duce had told fellow Fascist hierarch Giuseppe Bottai in October, proper preparation would allow Italy to fight a victorious war against Great Britain, achieving victory in as little as seven weeks.[123] Despite Mussolini's optimism regarding this so-called lightning war, he would find it difficult to build the resources necessary to carry out Pariani's ambitious plan.

Despite the obstacles to military success, by the end of 1936 Mussolini had changed most of the important aspects of Italian foreign policy that had existed only two years earlier. He had abandoned the Rome Accords and the Stresa Front, and he had replaced them with open hostility toward France and attempts to compel concessions from Britain. He had replaced the watch on the Brenner with tight cooperation with Germany on the central questions in European affairs. He had decreased his support for Chinese Nationalists in favor of closer ties with Japan. He cooperated with Britain where he thought it profitable, but he did so primarily in order to isolate France. Each of these changes followed from the desire to expand

Italy's power in the Mediterranean, mainly at the expense of Britain and France. In short, the belief that Mussolini followed policy of equidistance constitutes a retrospective construction based on partial evidence; it would have been unrecognizable to the architects of Italian foreign policy. Mussolini's social Darwinism seemingly compelled him to challenge the power of the apparently weak Western democracies. He would continue to do so in 1937.

NOTES

1. For a small part of the extensive English-language historiography on the Ethiopian war and its international ramifications, see G. W. Baer, *Test Case: Italy, Ethiopia and the League of Nations* (Stanford: Hoover Institution, 1976); A. J. Barker, *The Civilizing Mission: The Italo-Ethiopian War, 1935–6* (London: Cassell, 1968); Burgwyn, *Italian Foreign Policy in the Interwar Period, 1918–1940;* Robertson, *Mussolini as Empire Builder;* Daniel Waley, *British Public Opinion and the Abyssinian War, 1935–6* (London: Temple Smith, 1975); R. A. C. Parker, "Great Britain, France and the Ethiopian Crisis of 1935–1936," *English Historical Review* 89, no. 351 (1974): 293–332; Alan Cassels, "Switching Partners: Italy in A. J. P. Taylor's *Origins of the Second World War,*" in *The Origins of the Second World War Reconsidered: The A. J. P. Taylor Debate after Twenty-Five Years,* ed. Gordon Martel (Boston: Allen & Unwin, 1986), 78–80; Brian R. Sullivan, "More Than Meets the Eye: The Ethiopian War and the Origins of the Second World War," in *The Origins of the Second World War Reconsidered: A. J. P. Taylor and the Historians,* 2nd ed., ed. Gordon Martel (London: Routledge, 1999), 178–203; Arthur Marder, "The Royal Navy and the Ethiopian Crisis of 1935–36," *American Historical Review* 75, no. 5 (1970): 1327–56; G. Bruce Strang, "Imperial Dreams: The Mussolini-Laval Accords of January 1935," *Historical Journal* 44, no. 3 (September 2001): 709–809; and G. Bruce Strang, "The Spirit of Ulysses? Ideology and British Appeasement in the 1930s," in *Appeasement: Rethinking the Policy and the Policy-Makers,* ed. B. J. C. McKercher and Michael L. Roi (Cambridge, U.K.: Cambridge University Press, 2003), publication pending.

2. The now orthodox Italian school of interpretation, led by De Felice and Quartararo, contends that Mussolini chose the middle course, and that he would play the German card only "if he was not able to mend relations with the Western powers and with England in particular" (De Felice, *Mussolini il duce,* 339).

3. Felix Gilbert, "Ciano and his Ambassadors," in *The Diplomats, 1919–1939,* vol. 2, *The Thirties,* eds. Gordon A. Craig and Felix Gilbert (New York: Atheneum, 1974), 514–15. For more on Ciano's life, see Ray Moseley, *Mussolini's Shadow: The Double Life of Count Galeazzo Ciano* (New Haven: Yale University Press, 1999); Giordano Bruno Guerri, *Galeazzo Ciano: una vita* (Milan: Bompani, 1979); Orio Vergani, *Ciano: una lunga confessione* (Milan: Longanesi, 1974); and Edda Mussolini Ciano, *My Truth,* trans. Eileen Finsletter (New York: Morrow, 1977).

4. Malcolm Muggeridge, ed., *Ciano's Diplomatic Papers* (hereafter cited as *CDP*) (London: Odhams Press, 1948), xiii–xv; Mario (Luciolli) Donosti, *Mussolini e l'Europa: la politica estera fascista* (Rome: Leonardo, 1945), 43–47.

5. Quoted in De Felice, *Mussolini il duce,* 338. Paradoxically, Mussolini also said that he planned to "make the same policy with Galeazzo that he had made with [Suvich]."

6. Von Hassell to the Foreign Ministry, 18 June 1936, *Documents on German Foreign Policy* (hereafter cited as *DGFP*), ser. C, vol. 5, no. 381 (London: Her Majesty's Stationery Office, 1966), 637–39. Von Hassell believed that Ciano played a role in Suvich's dismissal (von Hassell to the Foreign Ministry, 7 January 1936, *DGFP,* ser. C, vol. 4, no. 486 [London: Her Majesty's Stationery Office, 1962], 977–78).

7. François-Poncet to Delbos, 23 June 1936, *Documents diplomatiques français* (hereafter cited as *DDF*), 2d. ser., vol. 2, no. 338 (Paris: Imprimerie Nationale, 1964), 512–13.

8. De Chambrun to Flandin, 26 May 1936, *DDF,* 2d. ser., vol. 2, no. 248, 388–89. For other examples, see "Il Capo di Stato Maggiore Generale, Badoglio, al Capo di Stato Maggiore Generale dell esercito Francese, Gamelin, 9 June 1936," *I documenti diplomatici italiani,* 8th ser., vol. 4 (hereafter cited as *DDI*), no. 223 (Rome: Istituto poligrafico e zecca dello stato, 1993), 273; Mussolini to Cerruti, 11 June 1936, *DDI,* 8th ser., vol. 4, no. 230, 282. For a translation of the records of the Mussolini-Laval conversations and a discussion of their import, see Strang, "Imperial Dreams," 799–809.

9. William Shorrock, *From Ally to Enemy: The Enigma of Fascist Italy in French Diplomacy, 1920–1940* (Kent, Ohio: Kent State University Press, 1988), 182–83.

10. For a discussion on French interwar strategic doctrine, see Young, *In Command of France,* 13–32; and Young, "La Guerre de longue durée: Some Reflections on French Strategy and Diplomacy in the 1930s," in *General Staffs and Diplomacy before the Second World War*, ed. Adrian Preston (London: Croom Helm, 1978), 41–64.

11. "Francia: situazione politica nel 1936," NA, RG T586, r1291.

12. Cerruti to Ciano, 19 June 1936, *DDI,* 8th ser., vol. 4, no. 326, 372–75.

13. Colloquio con l'ambasciatore di Francia, 24 June 1936, 29 June 1936, ASMAE, UC 84; Appunto per il Duce, 4 July 1936, ASMAE, GAB 25. Ciano used some of the documents from the UC and GAB in preparing his papers, which eventually were published as *L'Europa verso la catastrofe* (Milan: Mondadori, 1948). In all possible cases, I have used the originals, as some of the published documents are incomplete.

14. Cerruti to Mussolini, 3 June 1936, ASMAE, GAB 333 (Mussolini added the emphasis); "Servizio Storico Diplomatico—Ufficio I," 5 June 1936, NA, RG T586, r431, 016563–016614.

15. "Servizio Storico Diplomatico—Ufficio I," 5 June 1936, NA, RG T586, r431, 016563–016614. See also Paola Brundu Olla, "Il Gentlemen's Agreement e

la Francia (2 gennaio 1937)," in *Italia, Francia e Mediterraneo,* eds. J.B. Duroselle and E. Serra (Milan: Franco Angeli, 1990), 56–57. Vittorio Cerruti, the Italian Ambassador in Paris, described Delbos as a "doctrinaire without real ideas and ill-informed of foreign affairs" (Cerruti to Mussolini, 10 June 1936, *DDI,* 8th ser., vol. 4, no. 227, 276–78).

16. Servizio Storico Diplomatico, Ufficio I, Appunto, 5 June 1936, ASMAE. For Ambassador Cerruti's assessment of the new Cabinet, see Cerruti to Mussolini, 6 June 1936, ASMAE, GAB 333; see also Young, *In Command of France,* 135.

17. Mussolini to Grandi, 17 June 1936, ASMAE, GAB 25. William Shorrock argues that French Popular Front leaders willfully and unwisely ignored Italian overtures in May and June 1936 and that this flawed policy led to the eventual malaise in Franco-Italian relations (Shorrock, *From Ally to Enemy,* 182–83). But Mussolini's overtures at most aimed to convince French diplomats to remove sanctions, and Mussolini displayed no real interest at that time in a close political association with France.

18. Eden to Drummond, 28 May 1936, Public Record Office, FO 371 20411, R3122/226/22. At that time, Italy's Radio Bari was transmitting virulent anti-British propaganda supporting Arab insurrections in both Palestine and Egypt (Callum A. McDonald, "Radio Bari: Italian Wireless Propaganda in the Middle East and British Countermeasures, 1934–38," *Middle Eastern Studies* 13, no. 2 [May 1977]: 196).

19. Mussolini to Grandi, 3 June 1936, *DDI,* 8th ser., vol. 4, no. 171, 218.

20. Grandi to Mussolini, 4 June 1936, *DDI,* 8th ser., vol. 4, no. 180, 226–29.

21. Grandi to Mussolini, 3 June 1936, *DDI,* 8th ser., vol. 4, no. 170, 215–17.

22. Drummond to Eden, 13 June 1936, FO 371 20414, R3491/241/22.

23. F.O. Minute, Sir R. Vansittart, 16 June 1936, FO 371 20411, R3533/226/22.

24. Drummond to Eden, 28 June 1936, FO 371 20411, R3849/226/22.

25. Ciano to Grandi, 15 June 1936, *DDI,* 8th ser., vol. 4, no. 278, 328; Mussolini to Grandi, 17 June 1936, *DDI,* 8th ser., vol. 4, no. 300, 350.

26. Colloquio con l'ambasciatore di Gran Bretagna, 11 July 1936, ASMAE, UC 84; Drummond to Eden, 12 July 1936, FO 371 20382, R4131/294/67. Neville Chamberlain, the Chancellor of the Exchequer, had forced Eden's hand with his famous speech of 10 June 1936 before the 1900 Club at Grosvenor House, where he called the campaign by League of Nations advocates in favor of the continuation of sanctions "the very midsummer of madness" (*The Times,* 11 June 1936, 10).

27. Colloquio con L'ambasciatore di Gran Bretagna, 30 June 1936, ASMAE, UC 84, 9–10. This aspect of the meeting does not appear in the edited collection of *CDP.*

28. Ciano to Galli (Ankara), Grandi, Cerruti, Rosso (Washington), Boscarelli (Athens), Viola (Belgrade), 14 July 1936, *DDI,* 8th ser., vol. 4, no. 520, 580. For the various replies, see, in this same volume, no. 532, Boscarelli to Ciano, 15 July 1936, 595; no. 550, Viola to Ciano, 17 July 1936, 617; no. 588, Galli to Ciano, 22

July 1936, 655–56. The foreign ministers all claimed that they had no need for any guarantee in light of the Italian declaration. For the British decision, see Ingram to Eden, 23 July 1936, FO 371, 20382, R4476/294/67; Sargent Minute, 24 July 1936, FO 371, 20382, R4476/294/67; Eden to Ingram, 22 July 1936, FO 371, 20382, R4492/294/67.

29. For more detail, see Manfred Funke, *Sanktionen und Kanonen: Hitler, Mussolini und der internationale Abessienenkonflikt 1934–36* (Düsseldorf: Droste Verlag, 1971); Manfred Funke, "Le relazioni italo-tedesche al momento del conflitto etiopico e dello sanzioni della società della nazioni," *Storia contemporanea* 2, no. 3 (1971): 475–93; and Giovani Buccianti, "Hitler, Mussolini e il conflitto italo-etiopico," *Il Politico* 37 (1972): 415–28.

30. Colloquio con l'ambasciatore di Germania, 29 June 1936, ASMAE, UC 84; see also Appunto per il Duce, 18 June 1936, and 29 June 1936, ASMAE, GAB 25.

31. Quoted in von Hassell to the Foreign Ministry, 7 January 1936, *DGFP,* ser. C, vol. 4, no. 485, 974–77.

32. Von Hassell to the Foreign Ministry, 22 February 1936, *DGFP,* ser. C, vol. 4, no. 579, 1170. This declaration was especially important owing to Hitler's imminent remilitarization of the Rhineland.

33. Gerhard L. Weinberg, *The Foreign Policy of Hitler's Germany: Diplomatic Revolution in Europe 1933–36* (Chicago: The University of Chicago Press, 1970), 266–67.

34. Colloquio del Mussolini con Schuschnigg, 5 June 1936, *DDI,* 8th ser., vol. 4, no. 192, 240–43.

35. Aloisi appunto sul colloquio di Mussolini con von Hassell, 11 July 1936, ASMAE, GAB 22. For more detail, see Pietro Pastorelli, "L'Italia e l'accordo austro-tedesco dell'11 luglio 1936," *Annali dell'istituto storico italo-germanico in Trento* 15 (1989): 395–410.

36. Colloquio con l'ambasciatore di Francia, 11 July 1936, ASMAE, UC 84.

37. Drummond to Eden, 15 July 1936, FO 371 20201, J6348/3957/1. Roberts to Eden, 22 July 1936, FO 371 20201, J6529/3957/1.

38. Colloquio con l'ambasciatore di Gran Bretagna, 30 July 1936, ASMAE, UC 84. For a similar demand to the French Ambassador, see Colloquio con l'ambasciatore di Francia, 29 July 1936, ASMAE, UC 84.

39. Appunto per il Duce, 25 July 1936, ASMAE, GAB 25, Colloquio con l'ambasciatore di Germania, 25 July 1936, ASMAE, UC 84.

40. McDermott (Southern Department) Minute, 1 September 1936, FO 371 20411, R5102/226/22. See also Lawrence Pratt, *East of Malta, West of Suez: Britain's Mediterranean Crisis* (Cambridge, U.K.: Cambridge University Press, 1975), 40.

41. Grandi to Alfieri, 18 September 1936, NA, T586, r415, file 006513–8. The entire list of papers, books, subventions to journalists and publishers runs to over twenty pages.

42. Resconte del colloquio tra il duce e Ministero Frank al Palazzo Venezia, 23 September 1936, ASMAE, GAB 22.

43. Eden to the Foreign Office, 1 July 1936, FO 371 19908, C4721/4/18.

44. F.O. Memorandum, 14 July 1936, FO 371 19909, C5195/4/18; Vansittart Memorandum, 14 July 1936, FO 371 19909, C5141/4/18.

45. Drummond to Eden, 7 July 1936, FO 371 19908, C4977/4/18. Drummond was reporting the results of an unofficial conversation between the French ambassador and Ciano.

46. Colloquio con l'ambasciatore di Gran Bretagna, 11 July 1936, ASMAE, UC 84.

47. Colloquio con l'ambasciatore di Francia, e gli incaricati d'affari di Gran Bretagna e di Belgio, 24 July 1936, ASMAE, UC 84.

48. Appunto per il Duce, 25 July 1936, ASMAE, GAB 25, Colloquio con l'ambasciatore di Germania, 25 July 1936, ASMAE, UC 84.

49. He objected to one aspect of German policy. Germany wanted to accept a leadership role for Britain, as Hitler's original offer in March had established. Ciano argued that no nation should have primacy. His intercession worked, and Germany dropped that specific part of its policy (von Hassell to the Foreign Ministry, 31 July 1936, *DGFP,* ser. C, vol. 4, nos. 487, 488, 849–51, 851–52, 852n6).

50. Attolico to Ciano, 31 July 1936, *DDI,* 8th ser., vol. 4, no. 662.

51. Ciano quoted in De Chambrun to Delbos, 26 October 1936, *DDF,* 3d. ser., vol. 2, no. 256, 625–26.

52. Appunto per il Duce, 31 March 1934, ASMAE, Carte Lancelotti, Ufficio di Spagna (hereafter cited US) 1. For more information on the discussions and the level of Italian aid, see John F. Coverdale, *Italian Intervention in the Spanish Civil War* (Princeton: Princeton University Press, 1975), 50–54.

53. For the list of appeals, see Luccardi (Tangiers) to Ministero della Guerra, 20 July 1936, 21 July 1936, 23 July 1936, *DDI,* 8th ser., vol. 4, no. 570, no. 578, no. 592, 640, 647, 659–60, 663; De Rossi (Tangiers) to Ciano, 23 July 1936, *DDI,* 8th ser., vol. 4, no. 599, 664–65. Franco also sent personal representatives to Mussolini, but the Duce refused the appeals in person (Coverdale, *Italian Intervention,* 70–72).

54. Cerruti to Ciano, 23 July 1936, *DDI,* 8th ser., vol. 4, no. 598, no. 601, 664, 669–70; see also Signature illegible to De Peppo, 28 August 1936, NA, T586, r415.

55. Coverdale, *Italian Intervention,* 73–74; De Felice, *Lo Stato totalitario,* 366; see also Ciano to De Rossi, 24 July 1936, 27 July 1936, *DDI,* 8th ser., vol. 4, no. 611, no. 630. The operation was very hastily laid on. The two planes that crash landed in French Morocco had Italian markings visible through a sloppily applied coat of paint.

56. Coverdale, *Italian Intervention,* 78–79.

57. Donosti, *Mussolini e l'Europa,* 47–50.

58. Roatta to the Gabinetto, 5 August 1936, *DDI,* 8th ser., vol. 4, no. 685, 751–52, 752n1.

59. The total list of German and Italian arms to Spain as of 28 August 1936 reads as follows. Germany: twenty-six Junker bombers with equipment, fifteen

Heinkel fighters without equipment, twenty antiaircraft guns and machine guns, fifty machine guns, 8,000 rifles, various bombs and munitions, and 5,000 gas masks; and from Italy: twelve AA twenty-millimeter cannons plus 96,000 rounds, 20,000 gas masks, five armored cars plus equipment, 100,000 rounds for the mod, thirty-five machine guns, forty St. Etienne machine guns plus 40,000 rounds, twelve bombers with equipment, twenty-seven fighters with equipment, 20,000 2 kg bombs, 2,000 50, 100, or 250 kg bombs, 400 tonnes of fuel plus 300 tonnes shipped for the Reich, and eleven tonnes of oil (Proposte e richieste recate da admiriglio Canaris il 28 agosto 1936 a nome del governo tedesco, 28 August 1936, ASMAE, UC 44, US 1).

60. Colloquio tra Ciano e Canaris, 28 August 1936, *DDI,* 8th ser., vol. 4, no. 819.

61. For but two examples of the debate over Blum's decision, see David Carlton, "Eden, Blum and the Origins of Non-Intervention," *Journal of Contemporary History* 6, no. 3 (1971): 44–55; M. D. Gallagher, "Leon Blum and the Spanish Civil War," *Journal of Contemporary History* 6, no. 3 (1971): 56–64. Carlton argues that Blum determined his policy owing primarily to French domestic concerns. Gallagher takes the more traditional line that Blum subordinated French policy to that of Britain. What much of the debate ignores, however, is that France did not even remotely adhere to the nonintervention agreement until 1938, when Édouard Daladier, then Premier, closed the border. In the meantime, as Blum later acknowledged, France gave arms to Spain through a system in which it "organized arms smuggling almost officially" (Gallagher, "Leon Blum and the Spanish Civil War," 64). For more detail on the internal debate and politics of the Popular Front, see Julian Jackson, *The Popular Front in France: Defending Democracy, 1934–1938* (Cambridge, U.K.: Cambridge University Press, 1988). At the time it was negotiating the proposal, France was shipping Potez bombers to Spain (Bossi [Barcellona] to Ciano, 11 August 1936, *DDI,* 8th ser., vol. 4, no. 714, 786).

62. Colloquio con l'ambasciatore di Francia, 3 August 1936, ASMAE, UC 84.

63. Mussolini to Ciano, 5 August 1936, *DDI,* 8th ser., vol. 4, no. 683, 749–50.

64. Colloquio con l'ambasciatore di Francia, 10, 14 August 1936, ASMAE, UC 84.

65. Ciano to De Chambrun, 21 August 1936, *DDI,* 8th ser., vol. 4, no. 781, 857.

66. Ciano to Grandi, 7 September 1936, ASMAE, GAB 28. For Ciano's continued attempts to try to neutralize French intervention, see Ciano to Grandi, 17 October 1936, ASMAE, GAB 28.

67. Magistrati (Berlin) to Ciano, 24 August 1936, *DDI,* 8th ser., vol. 4, no. 793, 864–65; Ciano to De Rossi (Tangiers), 25 August 1936, *DDI,* 8th ser., vol. 4, no. 801, 872–73.

68. Magistrati to Ciano, 25 August 1936, *DDI,* 8th ser., vol. 4, no. 625, 700–702.

69. Mussolini had already made plans to send a small scale Italian air mission of nine planes and three antiaircraft batteries in exchange for 3,000,000 lire. The first planes did not arrive until 19 August (Coverdale, *Italian Intervention,* 130–33).

70. Bonaccorsi was also exceedingly brutal in carrying out reprisals in Majorca after the Italian and Nationalist victory. He executed some 3,000 Majorcans, most of whom were killed without trial. Italian authorities did not seem particularly concerned with Bonaccorsi's murderous activities (Coverdale, *Italian Intervention,* 128–29, 130–39).

71. Note de l'État-Major géneral de la Marine, 20 November 1936, *DDF,* 3d ser., vol. 2, no. 10, 11–13.

72. Corbin to Delbos, 26 November 1936, *DDF,* 3d ser., vol. 2, no. 40, 55.

73. De Rossi to Ciano, 20 August 1936, *DDI,* 8th ser., vol. 4, no. 760, 827.

74. Mackensen (Budapest) to von Neurath, 14 October 1936, *DGFP,* ser. C, vol. 4, no. 600, 1083–85.

75. Attolico to Ciano, 21 August 1936, *DDI,* 8th ser., vol. 4, no. 782, 781–82.

76. Von Neurath to von Hassell, 31 August 1936, *DGFP,* ser. C, vol. IV, no. 523, 936–42.

77. "Ufficio V, Jugoslavia, Situazione politica nel 1936," NA, T586, r1291.

78. Grandi to Ciano, 9 September 1936, 14 September 1936, 19 September 1936, 23 September 1936, ASMAE, Serie Affari Politici (hereafter cited as SAP), Spagna, B. 10.

79. Ciano to Grandi, 11 September 1936, ASMAE, GAB 28; see also, for example, Woermann (Rome) to the Foreign Ministry, 22 September 1936, *DGFP,* ser. D, vol. 3, no. 85, 93.

80. Resconto del colloquio tra il Duce e il Ministro Frank, 23 September 1936, ASMAE, GAB 22, UC 84.

81. For a copy of the protocol, see Protocolli di Berlino del 23 ottobre 1936, 23 October 1936, ASMAE, UC 44; German-Italian Protocol, 23 October 1936, *DGFP,* ser. C, vol. 5, no. 624, 1136–38.

82. During a meeting with von Hassell, Mussolini insisted on rejecting the five-power pact, as it was backed by Britain, which was "to a remarkably large extent dominated by Jewish influence" (von Hassell to von Neurath, 6 October 1936, *DGFP,* ser. C, vol. 5, no. 572, 1041–45).

83. Von Neurath Memorandum, 12 October 1936, *DGFP,* ser. C, vol. 5, no. 588, 1065; von Hassell to von Neurath, 13 October 1936, *DGFP,* ser. C, vol. 5, no. 593, 1072–73.

84. Mussolini added the emphasis. Resconte del primo colloquio Ciano-von Neurath, 21 October 1936, ASMAE, UC 2; see also von Neurath Memorandum, 21 October 1936, *DGFP,* ser. C, vol. 5, no. 618, 1125–30.

85. Mussolini added the emphasis. Colloquio del Ministro Ciano col Führer, 24 October 1936, ASMAE, UC 44, UC 84.

86. Giuseppe Bottai, *Diario 1935–1944* (Milan: Rizzoli, 1994), 31 October 1936.

87. *Discorso a Milano,* 1 November 1936, *OO,* vol. 28, 67–72.

88. Sir Robert Vansittart, for example, called the speech "flapdoodle" (Vansittart Minute, 4 November 1936, FO 371 19914, C7824/4/18).

89. De Chambrun to Delbos, 7, 9 October 1936, *DDF,* 3d. ser., vol. 2, nos. 318, 329, 476, 491; Delbos to De Chambrun, 13 October 1936, *DDF,* 3d ser., vol. 2, no. 340, 506–7.

90. William Shorrock overemphasizes the importance of the French decision. He blamed France entirely for the impasse, as Delbos ignored "all good sense." In his view, Delbos sent the Italians the signal that the foreign policy of Laval was dead by insisting on a purely technical point (Shorrock, *From Ally to Enemy,* 192). Of course, this comment raises the question that if the point were a mere technicality, why did Ciano and Mussolini insist on treating France and the United States differently? The answer is that they did want to force France to confront the question of recognition of Italy's conquest. The fault, therefore, lay at least equally with Italy, and likely more so, as the Duce did not then value good relations with a France he viewed as decadent.

91. R. Dan Richardson, *Comintern Army: The Internatinal Brigades and the Spanish Civil War* (Lexington: The University Press of Kentucky, 1982), 176.

92. Ciano to Grandi, 3 November 1936, ASMAE, SAP, Spagna B. 10; Ministero di Guerra, Commando del Corpo di Stato Maggiore, Promemoria per il Sig. Capo Ufficio S del Ministero degli Esteri, 15 November 1937, ASMAE, US 30; Major Napier (War Office) to St. C. Roberts, 23 November 1936, FO 371 20586, W16391/9549/41.

93. Richardson, *Comintern Army,* 14–15, 31, 176–78.

94. Von Hassell to von Neurath, 28, 29 October 1936, *DGFP,* ser. D, vol. 3, nos. 110, 111, 122, 122–23; von Neurath to von Hassell, 30 October 1936, *DGFP,* ser. D, vol. 3, no. 113, 123–25.

95. Weinberg, *The Foreign Policy of Hitler's Germany,* 295.

96. Von Hassell to von Neurath, 27, 28 November 1936, *DGFP,* ser. D, vol. 3, nos. 130, 133, 139–40, 143–44. For the published text of the proposed agreement, see von Hassell to von Neurath, 1 December 1936, *DGFP,* ser. D, vol. 3, no. 137.

97. Von Neurath to von Hassell, 5 December 1936, *DGFP,* ser. D, vol. 3, no. 142, 152–53. Eventually, Hitler decided not to send units of ground troops, while Italy would ultimately send thousands. See also Weinberg, *The Foreign Policy of Hitler's Germany,* 296–97.

98. Verbale della riunione a Palazzo Venezia del 6 Dicembre 1936, 6 December 1936, ASMAE, UC 44, US 1.

99. "Ufficio V, Cina 1936," NA, RG T586, r1289, 107185.

100. Valdo Ferretti, *Il Giappone e la politica estera Italiana, 1935–41* (Rome: Giuffrè Editore, 1983), 115, 119.

101. "Ufficio V, Giappone 1936," NA, RG T586, r1289, 107386.

102. Mussolini added the emphasis. Auriti to Ciano, 2 July 1936, *DDI,* 8th ser., vol. 4, no. 428, 487–91.

103. Appunto per il Duce, 19 July 1936, ASMAE, GAB 26.

104. Auriti to Ciano, 7,18, 20 November 1936, ASMAE, SAP, Giappone, B. 13. For an English language version of the anti-Comintern Pact, see German-Japanese Exchange of Notes on the Occasion of the Initialling of the Agreement

against the Communist International, 23 October 1936, *DGFP,* ser. C, vol. 5, no. 625, 1140–41.

105. Auriti to Ciano, 15 November 1936, 11 December 1936, ASMAE, SAP, Giappone, B. 13; Ciano to Auriti, 18 November 1936, 12 December 1936, ASMAE, SAP, Giappone, B. 13.

106. Ferretti, *Il Giappone e la politica estera Italiana, 1935– 41,* 128–29.

107. Vansittart Minute, 11 November 1936, FO 371 20418, R6636/341/22. One official, Lawrence Collier, on the other hand, argued that "the 'expansionist' creed of both Germany and Italy *must* force them together in opposition to us" (emphasis in original) (Collier [Northern Department] Minute, 23 December 1936, FO 371 20418, R6636/341/22; see also Sargent Minute, 11 December 1936, FO 371 20385, R7312/1167/67; Vansittart Minute, 12 December 1936, FO 371 20385, R7312/1167/67). The Admiralty also demanded that Whitehall try to wean Mussolini from the Axis, as Britain could not face war against the feared combination of Japan, Italy, and Germany (Admiralty to the Foreign Office, 21 November 1936, FO 20412, R6974/226/22).

108. Conclusions (Extract) 63 (36), 4 November 1936, FO 371 20412, R6694/226/22, CAB. 64 (36); 11 November 1936, FO 371 20412, R6794/226/22, 66 (36); 18 November 1936, FO 371 20412, R6968/226/22.

109. Drummond to Eden, 7 November 1936, FO 371 20412, R6585/226/22.

110. Lampson (Cairo) to Eden, 18 December 1936, FO 371 19979, E8029 /2617/91.

111. Drummond to Eden, 8 November 1936, FO 371 20412, R6600/226/22; Vansittart conversation with Grandi, 13 November 1936, FO 371 20412, R6813/226/22; Vansittart conversation with Grandi, 17 November 1936, FO 371 20412, R6918/22/22; Eden to Drummond, 3 December 1936, FO 371 20412, R7117/226/22; Drummond note-verbale, 21 December 1936, ASMAE, GAB 397; Ciano appunto, 31 December 1936, ASMAE, GAB 397. For more detail, see Christopher Seton-Watson, "The Anglo-Italian Gentleman's Agreement of January 1937 and Its Aftermath," in *The Fascist Challenge and the Policy of Appeasement,* eds. Wolgang Mommsen and Lother Kettenacher (London: George Allen and Unwin, 1983), 267–82.

112. Dichiarazione italo-britannica per il reciproci interessi nel mediterraneo, 2 January 1937, ASMAE, GAB 397, *DDI,* 8th ser., vol. 4, no. 5, 6–7.

113. Grandi to Ciano, 27 October 1936, ASMAE, Carte Grandi, B 40.

114. Emphasis in original. Grandi to Ciano, 6 November 1936, ASMAE, Carte Grandi, B 40. The document also appears in NA, T586, r499, file 026759–79.

115. ASMAE, Carte Grandi, B. 40, Grandi to Ciano, 23 November 1936.

116. Delbos to Blondel, 19 December 1939, *DDF,* 4th ser., vol. 2, no. 175, 285.

117. Ciano to Cerruti, 18 December 1936, ASMAE, GAB 28.

118. D.G.A.G appunto, n.d., ASMAE, GAB 303; see also Delbos to Corbin (London), 16 November 1936, *DDF,* 3d ser., vol. 2, no. 490, 771; Delbos to Corbin and Blondel, 5 December 1936, *DDF,* 4th ser., vol. 2, no. 102, 158–59.

119. "Uffico V, Francia, Situazione politica nel 1936, NA, T586, r1291.

120. Mussolini to Cerruti, 10 October 1936, ASMAE, GAB 23, GAB 303.

121. Ciano to Attolico, 22 December 1936, ASMAE, GAB 28.

122. Mallett, *The Italian Navy and Fascist Expansionism,* 56–70. For more on Italian raw material shortages, see Fortunato Minniti, "Le materie prime nella preparazione bellica dell'Italia, 1935–1943 (parte prima)," *Storia contemporanea* 27, no. 1 (1986): 19–21. For an interesting assessment of the corruption in the Fascist regime and the Italian arms industry, see Lucio Ceva e Andrea Curami, *Industria bellica anni trenta: Commesse militari, l'Ansaldo ed altri* (Milano: Franco Angeli, 1992).

123. Giuseppe Bottai (a cura di Giordano Bruno Guerri), *Diario, 1935–1944* (Milan: Rizoli, 1982), 31 October 1936, 113–14; see also Lucio Ceva, *Storia delle forze armate in Italia* (Turin: Libreria UTET, 1999), 249.

CHAPTER 3

The Spanish Imbroglio and the Strengthening of the Axis

Despite the slight hopes for an Anglo-Italian rapprochement engendered by the gentlemen's agreement, there was little progress in early 1937. The earliest and most important sticking point came from Mussolini's escalation of the Spanish Civil War, which came to full fruition in January, close on the heels of the gentlemen's agreement. By mid-February, almost 50,000 Italian ground troops had landed in Spain. Members of Blackshirt militias represented a slight majority of these troops, but the units included roughly 14,000 infantrymen and artillerymen from the *Regio Esercito,* plus some 4,000 men in supporting units. Mussolini also sent an additional 130 planes, plus bombs, artillery, machine guns, submachine guns, rifles, hand grenades, and munitions to support Italian and Spanish Nationalist units. While some of these troops were legitimate volunteers seeking some kind of adventure, most were not. The bulk of them merely happened to be members of four divisions: the Blackshirt divisions Dio lo Vuole, Fiamme Nere, and Penne Nere, and the *Regio Esercito* division "Littorio."[1] Mussolini ordered the dispatch of these troops, as he believed that "it is absolutely indispensable that Franco is victorious. In the contrary case it would be a defeat for us and Russia would be able to claim its first victory over Western Europe."[2] Mussolini had the corollary consideration that a Popular Front victory could push France ever closer toward its own version of Bolshevisation.[3] Mussolini committed Italy to a Nationalist victory in the war—at almost any cost.

Despite their commitment to Franco's victory, however, Mussolini's and Ciano's policy toward the Spanish war also worked on another track;

they heeded the necessity to pay lip service to the nonintervention committee. Accordingly, they tried to justify the flagrant Italian violation of
nonintervention by citing previous French and Soviet violations.[4] The
recent massive influx of Italian and German troops and equipment led the
Duce to believe that Italy had given Franco a clear military superiority
over Spanish government forces. In order to lessen temporarily the perceived challenge to the Western democracies and the ensuing level of
international tension, Italy and Germany intended to promise to uphold
the nonintervention agreement provided that France and especially the
Soviet Union also did so. Italy's offer was, of course, largely disingenuous because Italian tactical maneuvers in the nonintervention committee
were subordinate to Mussolini's requirement of a Nationalist victory. For
example, Grandi told the nonintervention committee that Italy would
cease shipping volunteers to France after 20 February 1937, but Mussolini intended to honor that commitment only as long as Spanish Nationalists maintained a decisive superiority in men and matériel.[5] Franco,
however, strongly resisted Italy's attempts to limit its intervention. He
argued vociferously that he would require continued provision of ammunition and other supplies. In any event, the Caudillo refused to consider
any kind of international control that would infringe on Spanish Nationalist territory.[6] Fortunately for Italy, neither France nor the Soviet Union
were committed to ensuring the application of genuine nonintervention,
and their violations of the agreement gave Ambassador Grandi considerable latitude in delaying tactics and in creating convenient anti-Bolshevik
propaganda.[7] The essential division over the withdrawal of volunteers
between Germany and Italy on one hand, and France and the Soviet
Union on the other, occurred over Soviet and Spanish government insistence that Franco's Moroccan soldiers were foreign volunteers and
should be counted among the total of Nationalists who would have to
leave Spain under any withdrawal scheme. That method of calculation
would likely ensure a government victory. Italy, Germany, and Franco
insisted that the Moroccans would not be counted under any withdrawal
scheme. If only German, Italian, and Soviet-backed volunteers withdrew,
then most observers believed that Franco's victory was assured. This
issue deadlocked the nonintervention committee for most of 1937, as neither side would concede the point.[8] Still, Mussolini hoped for either a
quick Nationalist victory or for some face-saving agreement that would
allow Italy to wind down its support for Franco, as Italy could not afford
to maintain its increased level of commitment for long. Ciano, therefore,
warned Franco that Italian aid would not last indefinitely and that Mus-

solini wanted to see a rapid and decisive Nationalist offensive in order to end the war quickly.[9]

Events surrounding the nonintervention agreement's international control schemes also demonstrated Italy's devotion to moving in lockstep with Germany. On 24 May, Spanish government aircraft bombed the Italian ship *Barletta,* which was lying in the harbor at Palma, and, five days later, bombed the German battleship *Deutschland,* which was lying in the roads of Ibiza. Both these ships were involved in implementing the nonintervention committee's control scheme; unsurprisingly, the bombings provoked a strong Axis reaction. Grandi vigorously protested the former attack, while the German government withdrew from the control scheme and from the nonintervention committee itself until it received guarantees that such events would not recur.[10] The Wilhelmstrasse took these decisions without first consulting the Italian government, and it hoped that Italy would continue to attend the nonintervention committee in Germany's absence. Mussolini, however, refused to follow a divergent course from Germany, which he feared would give the appearance of differences between the Axis partners. Consequently, Italy followed suit. After minor Anglo-French concessions, both Axis powers returned to the patrol scheme and to committee meetings. On June 18, the German cruiser *Leipzig* reported that an unknown submarine had fired four torpedoes at her, and both Italy and Germany withdrew permanently from naval patrols. This Italo-German action frustrated any possible control schemes. Italy and Germany, of course, remained in the nonintervention committee primarily to prevent France and the Soviet Union from having free rein there.[11]

In order to mollify foreign opinion, Italian officials also interceded with Spanish Nationalists to try to limit the reign of terror instituted in newly captured territories. Responding to thousands of summary executions in Seville and Malaga, Italian diplomats and soldiers urged Ciano to intercede with Franco to stop the killings. They argued that such cruelty would serve to increase resistance among Republican soldiers and in government-controlled territories and would blacken the name of Italian troops who had fought honorably. After consulting with the Duce, Ciano tried to convince Franco to moderate his troops' behavior, although to little avail.[12] Despite their concern for Italy's image, however, Mussolini and Ciano did not quail from taking harsh measures of their own. Ciano issued orders that the *Corpo Truppe Voluntarie* should subject captured "international mercenaries," especially "Italian renegades," to summary military justice.[13]

Italy's transparent attempts to court public opinion and to placate Western leaders largely failed. Léon Blum and the Popular Front government bitterly resented Mussolini's attack on a fellow leftist government. Although nominally committed to nonintervention, primarily for domestic reasons, France continued to allow war matériel and volunteers to cross the Pyrenees frontier.[14] Yvon Delbos criticized the Italian decision to continue sending volunteers to Spain, especially after Italy's broken commitment regarding the rules of nonintervention after 20 February 1937.[15] Most importantly, neither Blum nor Delbos could ignore the Italian air power stationed in the Balearics, which potentially represented a serious threat to French imperial communications. In the spring of 1937, the Popular Front government relaxed France's rather limited commitment to nonintervention even further, asking several French Ministries to coordinate increased French shipments to Spain.[16] Despite Blum's intentions, France and Italy had become embroiled in a kind of proxy war across the Pyrenees.

Italy's increased intervention in Spain also annoyed British decision makers, and it led to sharp divisions among them.[17] Several, including Sir Orme Sargent, the deputy undersecretary of state, Sir Eric Drummond, and Sir Robert Vansittart, argued that Britain had to ignore the Italian provocations. The Admiralty and the Chiefs of Staff had repeatedly called for close Anglo-Italian relations in order to lessen the strategic threats to the empire. There was no alternative, they argued, to the unpalatable job of conciliating Mussolini, however difficult that might be.[18] Others, such as Sir Miles Lampson, the British ambassador in Cairo, and, more importantly, Anthony Eden, believed that it was inopportune to try to reach any wider agreement with Mussolini until the latter had shown evidence of good will toward Britain. Eden, especially, saw Mussolini's recent policy as a personal insult. They had taken a dislike to each other after the ill-fated meeting in the summer of 1935 during which Eden could not dissuade the Duce from his plan to conquer Ethiopia. More recently, Eden bitterly resented Mussolini's invasion of Ethiopia and defiance of the League of Nations and also believed that the Duce had used the gentlemen's agreement as diplomatic cover for Italy's escalation of the Spanish Civil War, particularly since the various shipments appeared to arrive immediately following Eden's signing of the agreement on 2 January 1937. Eden unrealistically hoped to use the nonintervention committee "to call a halt" to Italy's and Germany's actions in Spain; if successful, he thought that he could return Italy to comparative respectability and develop Anglo-Italian relations sufficiently warm to enable the two powers to resume negotiations for a wider agreement.[19]

Italian policy alienated Britain and France on other fronts as well. In early 1937, Ciano carried out a major volte-face regarding relations with

Yugoslavia. Mussolini's long-held view was that Yugoslavia was an unnatural creation of the various Paris Peace Treaties. Even worse, Yugoslavia had aligned itself with France, Romania, and Czechoslovakia through the Little Entente and various agreements with France. During the Ethiopian war, Yugoslavia faithfully implemented sanctions against Italy at grave cost to its own economy. Finally, Italy had territorial claims against Yugoslavia remaining from the days of the so-called mutilated victory. Given Mussolini's hostility to Yugoslavia, he had provided varying levels of moral and logistical support for antigovernment terrorist groups, particularly the Croat extremist Ustaša, in the decade prior to 1937.[20] Italy provided most of the training and financing for the Ustaša, led by Ante Pavelić, and Mussolini allowed its terrorists refuge in Italy. After the Ustaša's complicity in the assassination of Yugoslav King Alexander and French Foreign Minister Louis Barthou in 1934, Mussolini had refused French requests to extradite Pavelić and his cohorts, though he did disarm Ustaša units and isolate Pavelić in a kind of exile on the Isle of Lipari.[21]

In December 1936, Ciano, with Mussolini's approval, undertook to reverse the course of Italo-Yugoslav relations, and negotiations with the Stoyadinović government began in January 1937. Ciano hoped to sign an Italo-Yugoslav alliance, but the Yugoslav negotiators balked. Instead, they reached a reasonably comprehensive agreement short of an alliance. Both parties secured several objectives, with Ciano making by far the more important concessions. There was, of course, the usual language regarding mutual nonaggression and friendship. Ciano also offered to relax considerably restrictions that the Italian government had placed on ethnic Slavs living in Italy. Negotiators reached an economic agreement that was to Yugoslavia's benefit, as it went a long way to restore trade lost during Yugoslavia's adherence to League sanctions against Italy.[22] Most importantly, there were two secret clauses in the agreement. One gave an Italian pledge regarding the independence of Albania, which partially placated Yugoslav concerns about Italian expansionism there. In the other clause, Ciano promised to rein in the Ustaša even further. Italian police would intern Pavelić and other Croat leaders and prevent any Croat terrorist action emanating from Italian soil.[23] In short, Italy made some serious concessions in order to achieve the agreement.

In return, Ciano won some important tactical victories over France, Britain, and even Germany. The Italo-Yugoslav agreement occurred at the same time as an outright Yugoslav rejection of a French offer for a pact of mutual assistance that would link the powers of the Little Entente. The rebuff of the French démarche by Milan Stoyadinović, the Yugoslavian prime minister and foreign minister, sent a clear signal rejecting a close association with Western security interests. As the Italo-Yugoslav agreement promised neutrality in the event of third-party conflicts, it formally ruptured the Little Entente; the terms of the two pacts were irreconcilable. Furthermore, the Yugoslav defection from the French camp meant that Czechoslovakia seemed increasingly isolated. Stoyadinović also wounded French prestige, as he failed to give Delbos prior notice of the signing as was required under the Franco-Yugoslav Treaty of 1927, and he cavalierly rejected the French suggestion that he delay the public signing of the agreement with Ciano.[24] The Italo-Yugoslav accord represented a clear setback for French policy in the Balkans and a corresponding gain for France's Italian enemy.[25]

Similarly, Ciano aimed this blow at Great Britain. Britain had maintained friendly relations with the Yugoslav Regent, Prince Paul, and had issued a guarantee of assistance to Yugoslavia in event of Italian reprisals in the aftermath of sanctions. Whitehall counted on a friendly Yugoslavia both to resist German encroachment in the Balkans and to support indirectly Britain's important Mediterranean ally, Greece. Its adherence to sanctions during the Ethiopian crisis had apparently confirmed both Yugoslavia's friendship with England and its support for the League of Nations. After the Italo-Yugoslav accord, however, Foreign Office officials could no longer make such easy assumptions regarding Yugoslavia's loyalty. In addition, the lowering of tensions with Yugoslavia allowed Italy to reorient its naval forces away from the Adriatic and toward the Mediterranean; Italy thus improved its relative power in any potential confrontation with Britain. Finally, the accord seriously damaged British prestige and influence in the Balkans. Eden concluded that the accord showed that "Italy's hostility to us is at present real, and I believe vindictive."[26] The agreement fulfilled von Neurath's October 1936 prediction that Italy could detach Yugoslavia from the Anglo-French orbit and add it to the Rome-Berlin Axis. The policy was a great success for the Italian foreign minister; as Grandi wrote to Ciano, the latter had successfully courted a country that previously had been a mercenary "in the service of England against Italy."[27]

Ciano's final aim in signing the accord with Yugoslavia was to give both countries some ability to resist and some protection from the seemingly inevitable German absorption of Austria. After the 1 June 1936 agreement with Germany, Ciano viewed the Anschluss as a foregone conclusion; the only question was when it would occur.[28] In order to protect Italy from the increase in German power and its penetration of southeast Europe, Ciano wanted to develop Yugoslavia as a counterweight. Stoyadinović feared potential German domination and resented the stinginess of Britain and France in supporting Yugoslavia with arms and economic aid, so Ciano's overture seemed opportune. Both Italy and Yugoslavia could benefit from lessening German domination of their respective economies and from the resulting benefits of increased trade.[29] In addition, Italy's preferential association with Yugoslavia allowed it to continue and even to extend its influence in the Danube basin. Italy maintained its role as the primary sponsor of Hungarian revisionism, and the accord with Yugoslavia even provided Italy with a diplomatic opening to the previously hostile Romania. Finally, as Ciano later wrote, the accord allowed Italy "to view with calmness the possibility of the Anschluss."[30] In short, the Italo-Yugoslav accord of 25 March 1937 fulfilled several goals for Italy. In part it reflected Ciano's knowledge of the extent to which Italy was becoming increasingly dependent on Germany and his desire to preserve some freedom of maneuver within the close cooperation developed within the Rome-Berlin Axis. Ciano's more important aim, however, was to weaken Anglo-French power and prestige in the Balkans and the Mediterranean and simultaneously to strengthen the Italian challenge to the Western powers. Ciano believed that Stoyadinović was a Fascist at heart and that Italy and Yugoslavia would, over time, develop economic and political arrangements that would be tantamount to an alliance.[31]

In the aftermath of this accord, Ciano also worked to develop Italy's relations with both Hungary and Romania. The latter country approached Ciano with a suggestion that Italy and Romania reach a rapprochement through an agreement analogous to the one recently signed by Italy and Yugoslavia. The offer intrigued Ciano, but he believed that Italian policy should look to Hungary first. He would encourage the Hungarian foreign minister to approach Romania in an attempt to undermine the Little Entente, which aimed primarily at resisting Hungarian revisionism. If the two Balkan powers could reach an accord, then Hungary would be able to concentrate its limited power against Czechoslovakia, a nation that Mussolini particularly despised.[32] Ciano hoped that this path would lead to a revolution in Balkan politics; in one blow, he could shatter French policy, complete the destruction of the Little Entente, and rally three Balkan powers to the Axis cause. Ultimately, his attempts failed owing to Romanian resistance to some Hungarian demands. Bucharest refused to make concessions on minority rights and Hungarian rearmament without first securing agreement among its Little Entente partners. Ion Lugusiano, the Romanian minister in Rome, said that his government feared Soviet interference and relied on Czechoslovak support. Ciano's dreams of a system of Italian diplomatic domination of the Balkans foundered on the shoals of regional, ethnic, and territorial disputes.[33]

Despite Ciano's limited competition with Germany for influence in the Balkans, the Axis continued to function well regarding several issues. In Spain, of course, both powers cooperated in supplying Nationalist forces with matériel and men. Hitler had developed somewhat different aims than Italy; above all, he wanted to see the war continue indefinitely; it helped to keep Italy loyal to the Axis and to create a level of international tension that served to divert attention from German expansionism in Central and Eastern Europe. He also hoped to be able to exploit Franco's dependence on supplies in order to develop German economic control over certain Spanish natural resources.[34] Mussolini and Ciano recognized that German officials seemed less dedicated to supporting Franco and repeatedly urged a stronger commitment of German forces, to little avail.[35] Nevertheless, despite this difference in ends, Germany cooperated fully with Italy in the nonintervention committee and in Spain itself. For example, in April, German officials sent a request to Italy regarding the shipment of German airmen and supplies to Spain across Italian territory. They hoped that Ciano would allow the transhipment and that he would create a "small logistical nucleus" to facilitate the process. He concurred, despite some objections from Italy's naval staff.[36] In London, Grandi continued to meet with von Ribbentrop every day to coordinate their activities in the nonintervention committee. Grandi described to Ciano the complete sense of trust that he had developed with his German colleagues and how they exchanged information on all aspects of the Spanish situation.[37]

In the economic sphere, Ciano also moved Italy into a closer embrace with Germany. In early March 1937, he told von Hassell that, given the challenge of the Axis to the Western powers, war was likely and could break out at any time. He argued, therefore, that Italy and Germany should strike a coordinating committee in order to achieve Axis autarky in the event of war. Ciano was particularly concerned that the two powers cooperate in exchanging each other's raw materials needs.[38] The talks proceeded sporadically through both exchanges of experts' drafts and high-level talks between the likes of Göring and Mussolini.[39] Eventually, in May, an Italo-German commission signed a secret protocol that allowed for reciprocal economic aid "in normal and abnormal times." The scope of the agreement included not only raw materials but also transport, exchange of industrial licences, and the provision of labor detachments. Though neither power was disinterested enough to allow this protocol to function at a very high level, it is indicative of Mussolini's and Ciano's growing belief that the Axis represented something more than a mere political arrangement; Italian and German decision makers both expected that their strategies would require close military and economic cooperation in the expected Axis wars to come.[40]

Ciano also tried to convince the German government to join the Rome Protocols, which had been in effect since 17 March 1934. These agreements linked Italy, Austria, and Hungary in a loose consultative arrangement regarding affairs in the Danube basin. Ciano hoped eventually to convince both Poland and Yugoslavia to join; this new group of supposedly like-minded authoritarian states would then appear to be a serious counterweight to the League of Nations and to the Little Entente. More importantly, for Mussolini, it would show the solidarity of the Axis. The Wilhelmstrasse strongly resisted this démarche, as the first proposal contained language referring to Austrian independence. Germany's adhesion to the protocols could imply its acceptance of that clause, and, for obvious reasons, Hitler was unwilling to limit his ambition of achieving the Anschluss. Eventually, German intransigence convinced Mussolini to let the initiative drop, but he was keenly disappointed by Germany's reluctance to make this public display of its commitment to Italy. Despite the failure to reach an agreement, the episode demonstrates Mussolini's desire to tighten the ties of the Axis, even at the risk of allowing the eventual absorption of Austria by the Third Reich.[41]

In marked contrast to his warm relations with Germany, Mussolini apparently sought confrontation with Britain. One important issue concerned British press coverage of the Italian defeat at Guadalajara. Italian troops suffered a disastrous setback when a numerically inferior group of the International Brigade, including Italian nationals, blunted an Italian attack and forced the *Corpo Truppo Voluntarie (C.T.V.)* into a humiliating retreat. In truth, the defeat was relatively minor. Republican soldiers had the support of Soviet-built T26 tanks, superior to anything in the Nationalist arsenal. More significantly, Franco and his generals had conspired to place the *C.T.V.* in a position where its offensive would likely fail; they sought to take the arrogant Italians down a peg, while at the same time bleeding Republican forces of their reserves. Franco deliberately delayed launching a parallel offensive that would have pinned down Republican forces.[42] Nevertheless, despite the circumstances, the "Italian Skedaddle," as former British Prime Minister David Lloyd George triumphantly labeled it, shattered the myth of Fascist Italian invincibility.

Franco's behavior and British press accounts outraged Mussolini. He wrote a major article defending his troops' actions. In particular, he argued that bad weather, Spanish Nationalist inaction, and superior numbers of Red soldiers had determined the outcome at Guadalajara. Mussolini followed foreign press coverage with ill-concealed anger; British attacks such as Lloyd George's on Italian courage and honor particularly enraged him.[43] Most significantly, Mussolini decided that it would be impossible to withdraw any troops until the perceived stain on Fascist Italy had been wiped away. Consequently, the Duce made a virtually open-ended commitment to prosecute the Spanish Civil War to its conclusion, whatever the cost to Italy.[44] This decision was certain to continue to strain Italy's relations with France and Britain.

Italy also challenged France and Britain on several other issues in the spring of 1937. The occupation of Ethiopia raised several issues that indicated that fractious nature of Italy's confrontation with France. Ciano aimed to secure both de jure recognition of Italy's conquest and French concessions. Citing French actions during the Ethiopian crisis, Italy refused to abide by the economic agreement reached in the Mussolini-Laval accords of January 1935.[45] Italian officials in Ethiopia instituted repressive measures against French businesses, causing Alexis Léger Saint-Léger, the Secretary-General of the French Foreign Ministry, to complain that Italy sought the complete expulsion of French firms from the territory. In fact, Italian officials sought to indicate their displeasure over France's attitude over sanctions, and, more constructively, to convince France to make concessions over the tariff rates on the Addis Ababa Railroad, over which most of the Italian traffic to supply its forces in Ethiopia would have to travel. In addition, the two sides differed over the status of a contingent of French troops in the town of Dire Daua, with Léger hoping to establish French rights in Ethiopia in exchange for the withdrawal of the soldiers. In spite of French concessions, Ciano continued to hold a high line, seeking to demonstrate the extent of Italy's victory over its League of Nation's foes.[46]

More seriously, Ciano tried to convince Turkish officials to strike against French colonial interests, suggesting that Turkey seize the Sanjak of Alexandretta, a small territory administered by France under its League Mandate in Syria. He argued that France would be unlikely to react given its internal divisions, its concerns in the Spanish Civil War, and, above all, its fear of the Germany *Wehrmacht*. Ciano also promised that Italy would not interfere and implied that Italy might provide more than mere support and a simple declaration of disinterest. At the same time, he ordered Italian diplomats in Ankara to circulate rumors that the French government was prepared to cede the Sanjak to Italy as part of a general Mediterranean sentiment; he hoped that this disinformation would infuriate Turkish leaders, perhaps provoking military action. His machinations did have some results, increasing the strain in relations between France and Turkey and furthering an Italo-Turkish rapprochement, but did not lead to a military confrontation. Rüstü Aras, the Turkish Foreign Minister, refused to invade the Sanjak, citing his fear of Arab, Kurdish, and Armenian guerrilla warfare if Turkey conquered the territory.[47]

Italy's relations with Britain were similarly strained. Mussolini continued to sponsor anti-British propaganda in the Middle East. Radio Bari criticized British rule in Palestine and attempted to foment and to exploit rebellion there. Italian workers disseminated propaganda, and agents supported the rebellion from within Palestine.[48] The Italian community in Egypt used cultural centers and other agencies as outlets for attacking Britain's tutelage of the nominally independent country. Italians in Egypt even formed a green shirts organization modeled on the Fascist Party. During his visit to Libya in 1937, Mussolini hypocritically named himself the Protector of Islam, with its implication that he was protecting Islam from Great Britain, despite the hundreds of thousands of Muslims that his troops had killed in Africa.[49] In Ethiopia, Marshall Graziani, the viceroy, maintained the policy of low-level harassment of British subjects and diplomats. In one case, Graziani closed the British-controlled firm of Mohamedally, blocked its bank accounts, and gave the staff two days to leave. The capricious deadline was impossible to meet, as there were no trains during that time. In another incident, Fascist Blackshirts broke into the French legation.[50] In Italy proper, Mussolini banned certain British newspapers, while Italian government-controlled newspapers and even school textbooks carried the message that Britain was a "decadent, feeble, and finished nation, and that the Roman legions would shortly destroy [it] for ever."[51] Ciano dismissed out-of-hand British protests of these activities, and, because the Fascist Party largely controlled them, Whitehall had to assume that Mussolini or Ciano had ordered these manifestations of ill will toward Britain.[52]

In violation of the Rome Understanding of 1927, which prohibited Italian alteration of the status quo in the Arabian Peninsula, Italian agents fomented unrest against Britain in Yemen and Saudi Arabia. The *Servizio Informazione Militare* directed its efforts to creating an eventual protectorate or a colony on the east bank of the Red Sea. Italian agents provided rifles, artillery, and tanks to Yemeni opponents of British influence over

Ibn Saud, the most powerful local leader.[53] At the same time, however, Ciano sought to foment rebellion against Britain in its mandate in Palestine. He arranged through Arab agents to ship arms and ammunition to the Gran Mufti of Jerusalem, who was preparing for an eventual revolt by Palestinian Muslims. To avoid interception, the Mufti's agents suggested that Italy route its shipments through the town of Jedda, under the control of Ibn Saud, who would take some of the arms as payment. Ciano hoped to be able to exploit Saudi resentment againt British suppression of Arab nationalism to establish greater Italian influence in the region. Italy, therefore, was simultaneously supplying arms to competing sides in the struggle for dominance of the Arabian Peninsula.[54] If regimes favorable to Italy were to control either Yemen or Saudi Arabia, it would allow Italy to interdict British use of the Suez Canal; this Italian policy, therefore, potentially represented a grave threat to British imperial communications.[55]

Even more seriously, Mussolini directed an expansionistic policy against Britain in Africa and the Middle East. Italian military planners oriented their preparations southward toward British possessions with the development of air bases in Southern Italy, Pantelleria, and Sicily. In Libya, Italian engineers continued to build a coastal road toward the Egyptian and Libyan border. The primary function of this road would be to support an Italian military attack toward Egypt and the Suez Canal.[56] Nor were these idle precautions; Mussolini openly contemplated war with the British in the Middle East. In February, he ordered Marshall Graziani, the viceroy in Ethiopia, to begin recruiting a Black African Army of some 300,000 troops for use against Great Britain. The Duce expected this new force to be ready for war by 1940. In the meantime, Mussolini demanded that Graziani should prepare for autarky in Italian East Africa "in times of peace and above all in times of war."[57] In addition, Mussolini ordered Italian shipyards to modernize the remaining *Andrea Doria* class battleships and to plan for construction of two new 35,000 ton *Littorio*-class ships.[58] As Mussolini and General Göring had discussed in January, an eventual fleet comprising eight German, eight Italian, and twelve Japanese battleships would create an enormous threat to the Royal Navy's nineteen capital ships, allowing Italy tremendous freedom of action in challenging British power in the Mediterranean.[59] On several fronts, therefore, Italy created and pressed deliberate political conflicts against Great Britain and its empire, while preparing for an eventual war to seize Egypt and the Suez Canal.

Dino Grandi, the Italian ambassador in London, unwittingly furthered Mussolini's confrontation with Great Britain. He wrote that these various irritants in Anglo-Italian relations were necessary in order to compel Britain to reach an agreement between the two powers. In Grandi's view, Anthony Eden, "*a vile democrat, ready to change, it seems, from black to white*," aimed to become prime minister. Eden focused his hatred on Italy and therefore constituted the central obstacle on the path to an Anglo-Italian accord, so it was necessary to outflank him in the British Cabinet and foreign policy–making elite. The closer the relations between Germany and Italy, the more that both Westminster and Whitehall would see the need for a fundamental agreement with the Fascist government in order to prevent an outright Italo-German alliance. Even though Grandi expected the then incoming Prime Minister Neville Chamberlain to be ready to reach a comprehensive settlement with Italy on its own merits, he argued that it was necessary to maintain and even to increase the pressure in London. In short, the best policy was to try to coerce British decision makers to reach an Anglo-Italian agreement.[60]

There were several problems with Grandi's interpretation. Although he was in one sense an Anglophile, he also had profound contempt for aspects of English life. In the Fascist style, he ridiculed the so-called death of the late nineteenth-century British imperial impulse, which left the empire "a lion without teeth." Fifteen years of "pacifist, anti-militarist, and anti-patriotic propaganda" had wrought its mischief on the British psyche; the ensuing "pacifist corruption" extended to all aspects of British life. Yet the defeat in Ethiopia had woken some statesmen to the need to rearm, and the governing class was at last preparing for war against Italy. Grandi's views could hardly do more to convince the Duce that the allegedly decadent Britain was a soft target, further inciting Mussolini's dreams of replacing the British empire through military conquest.[61] Even if one took Grandi's view as representing Italian policy, it failed to achieve his objectives, serving mainly to irritate Eden and to postpone an Anglo-Italian agreement.[62] Mussolini and Ciano increasingly believed that an Italian war against Britain was becoming inevitable, as it was Italy's destiny to replace what they saw as decrepit and declining empires.[63] Grandi's often-mistaken impressions of English society led the Duce to err in his own understanding of Great Britain's foreign policy.

As a result, Mussolini escalated tensions with Great Britain even further in May of 1937. He worked on two tracks. The first track consisted of particularly nasty anti-British propaganda spewed out by Radio Bari. It accused Britain of being "false and hypocritical" in its dealings with Italy, which was not surprising given the "villainy and falsehood" of British politicians.[64] An Italian Wireless Broadcasting Institute report

declared that Italy could destroy the Suez Canal in two to three hours and
Britain's Malta base in sixty minutes; Italy, therefore, held the real keys
to the Mediterranean. Simultaneously, Ciano threatened Drummond
with "something more than a press campaign" if Britain did not meet
Mussolini's demands. Whitehall officials feared possible Italian air
strikes in the Middle East.[65]

At the same time, Mussolini continued to redeploy his air strength
southward—away from Germany and toward Britain's Mediterranean
bases. Britain's air attaché in Rome concluded that this new stance signaled Mussolini's "contemplation clearly of possible hostilities."[66] Potentially more seriously for Britain, Mussolini played what he thought would
be a trump card. He strengthened the Italian garrison in Libya to constitute
two European army corps, the Twentieth and Twenty-first, totaling
roughly 60,000 men. The new troops would arrive in September 1937 after
preparatory exercises in Sicily. Two of these divisions were mechanized,
which made a potentially powerful striking force against Egypt. Because
Britain was bound by its treaty with that nominally independent country, it
could station no more than about one-tenth the strength there of Italy's
Libyan garrison. Mussolini assumed that his Libyan forces would represent an effective negotiating tool; theoretically, they would intimidate the
British government, making it more likely to accede to Italian demands.[67]
At the same time, Mussolini kept one eye focused on the possibility of a
war of expansion against the British empire. He encouraged the development of General Pariani's plan for a lightning strike on Suez. The Duce
thought that it could begin the fulfillment of his fondest dream—an
African empire spanning from the Mediterranean Sea to the Indian
Ocean.[68] The hostile nature of Mussolini's policy did not escape the attention of British soldiers and diplomats. In view of Italy's provocative
actions, the British Committee of Imperial Defence decided that Italy
would have to be considered as a potential enemy for "an indefinite
period."[69]

In mid-June, however, Mussolini and Ciano decided that the time was
ripe for a new push for the negotiations toward British de jure recognition
of the Italian empire. There were two reasons underlying the timing of this
démarche. First, the British Foreign Office asked German Foreign Minister von Neurath to pay a visit to London for a wide-ranging discussion of
mutual concerns. Despite German assurances to the contrary, Ciano
believed that Britain would try to weaken Germany's commitment to the
Axis. Accordingly, Ciano received the news with "strict coldness." He
feared that, at the very least, such a visit would allow anti-Fascists in the

West to predict the decline of the Axis. A simultaneous Italian approach to Britain regarding an Anglo-Italian rapprochement would discourage any idle talk that there were differences between the Axis partners.[70] Second, there was conflicting, even paradoxical, evidence on the state of Anglo-French relations. There were many public manifestations that Britain and France were increasingly relying on the other for imperial defense and for maintaining European peace in the face of Fascist revisionism.[71] The Italian ambassadors in London and Paris indicated that British and French military officials had undertaken staff talks to coordinate common defense policies.[72] The new Camille Chautemps cabinet in Paris was in public less ideologically ranged against Mussolini and Fascism, which implied the possibility of lowering the level of tension between Italy and Britain and France.[73] At the same time, the Palazzo Chigi had received considerable evidence of French weakness. Economic problems, especially the serious flight of capital, undermined the Popular Front's attempts at labor reform, and it appeared uncertain to Italian observers whether or not the French government would be able to secure sufficient loans to maintain solvency. As Cerruti wrote from Paris, *"The general conditions of the country continue to be characterized by the financial crisis and social disorder."*[74] This apparent French weakness implied a greater reliance on British diplomatic and financial support, but there were signs that Anglo-French relations were strained over French policy toward the Soviet Union, Spain, disarmament, and the recognition of Ethiopia, perhaps as far as to the point where it would be possible to divide the two Western powers.[75] Vittorio Cerruti, Italy's ambassador in France, thought the time opportune to approach Chautemps to lessen tension between France and Italy, but Ciano refused. He said instead that it was better that "Paris understands only that our intransigence is absolute."[76] If, however, an Italian offer of discussions could pry Britain from its French association, then any minor Italian concessions to Britain would be worthwhile. Mussolini, therefore, would try to split the Western democracies through a proposal for negotiations with Great Britain.[77]

From the Italian side, the proposed negotiations would have a strictly limited scope. As a gesture toward reconciliation, Mussolini ordered Radio Bari to abstain temporarily from any anti-British activity.[78] But Italy was prepared to go little further. It refused to modify its policy in the Arabian Peninsula or to stop expanding its forces in Libya. In his letter to Grandi ordering the ambassador to pursue negotiations with Chamberlain, Ciano argued that Italy should have to make no concessions regarding Italy's war in Spain. British statesmen should realize that Italy did not

have territorial ambitions there and that both Britain and Italy would benefit from Franco's victory, as neither power wanted a Bolshevik government in Western Europe. Italy's sole negotiating point was to achieve
Britain's de jure recognition of Italy's Ethiopian conquest. Ciano aimed to
ensure that Britain definitively admitted the defeat of its sanctions policy
and indicated that it would never interfere in Italian colonial policy
again.[79] At the same time, Grandi was told to lose no occasion to emphasize to British decision makers that they would have to choose between
France and Italy; as Grandi told Chamberlain, "an agreement between
Rome and London cannot exist alongside an agreement between London-
Paris."[80] The extremely limited nature of Italy's possible concessions,
combined with its efforts toward splitting Britain from France, belies any
suggestion that Mussolini and Ciano wanted to achieve a genuine Anglo-
Italian rapprochement; on Italy's side, the negotiations were purely self-
interested and tactical in scope. As Ciano told a young Fascist writer at the
time, he maintained contacts with Britain in order to ensure breathing
room for his policy in Spain while simultaneously keeping Anglophile elements in Italy quiescent.[81] Mussolini wanted the British cabinet to recognize the Italian empire, and he wanted to separate Britain from France;
there was no genuine comity of interests between Fascist Italy and Britain.

   This Italian offer sparked a lengthy debate in the cabinet and in Whitehall. There were two major opponents to recognition of Italy's Ethiopian
empire: Anthony Eden and Lord Cranborne, Eden's parliamentary private
secretary. The latter believed that Britain would eventually have to grant
recognition, but Cranborne wanted to ensure that "we shan't cringe before
Musso[lini]." Italian economic weakness, he believed, offered Britain the
best chance to appeal to the Fascist dictator; Italy's need for British economic assistance could eventually bring Mussolini to heel.[82] Eden
believed that British recognition of Italy's Ethiopian conquest would grant
Mussolini too great a boost in prestige. The foreign secretary hoped to tie
Mussolini more tightly in a wider-reaching Mediterranean pact. Without
this more encompassing agreement, Eden feared, Mussolini would simply
accept any British recognition as a fait accompli and return to a position of
hostility to Britain, as he had appeared to do after the gentlemen's agreement.[83] There were few Whitehall advisers, however, who accepted this
reasoning. Virtually no Foreign Office officials trusted Mussolini, but
some believed that the timing was appropriate to use the one negotiating
card that Britain still held—de jure recognition. Britain had no other issues
on which it could appeal to Italy, so it could be useful to pry as many concessions as possible from the Duce. The prospects for restoring Italy to the

Stresa Front were undoubtedly weak, but this first step toward better relations was necessary. The Chiefs of Staff's warnings regarding the tripartite threat posed by Germany, Italy, and Japan seemingly compelled Britain to seek to turn at least one of these potential enemies. The major goals on the British side were to require Italy to cease anti-British propaganda in the Middle East and in Italy, to modify its policy in the Red Sea, to withdraw its volunteers from Spain, and to remove a substantial part of the threatening garrison in Libya. The last two of these desiderata were by far the most important objectives.[84]

Even more importantly, Neville Chamberlain, the prime minister since May 1937, was determined to reach an accommodation with Italy. He approached Italy through both regular and highly irregular channels. For example, a supposed exchange of letters of mutual goodwill with Mussolini helped to clear the way for negotiations. In fact, Grandi created the appearance of a letter from Mussolini to give greater weight to Ciano's initiative of 10 June, and Chamberlain did not spot the subterfuge before replying to the Duce's letter.[85] Simultaneously, Chamberlain also set up a so-called secret channel to Italy's Foreign Ministry. He established it through Sir Joseph Ball, the Head of the Conservative Research Office. This office, which Chamberlain considered his personal fiefdom, had as its main task spying on the Labour Party. Ball was an intimate friend of Chamberlain's and maintained a close association with Britain's intelligence services. The channel to the Italian embassy in London operated through a Maltese national by the name of Adrian Dingli. Dingli, trained in Malta and Italy as a lawyer, served the Italian embassy in London as legal counsel. He was a member of the Inns of Court as well as the Carlton Club, the official club of the Conservative Party. Ball approached Dingli in early July in order to determine through unofficial channels the prospects of an accord between Britain and Italy. Over the following months, the highly unusual relationship flourished, and Dingli, Ball, and Grandi held several clandestine meetings. On one occasion, Dingli even carried messages from Ball directly to Ciano in Rome. Chamberlain often used this route to circumvent the Foreign Office, and, in particular, Anthony Eden.[86] Chamberlain, like most Foreign Office officials, believed that it was necessary to try to use the prospect of recognition to compel Mussolini to grant concessions over the series of outstanding issues creating Anglo-Italian tension.[87] Given Chamberlain's opposition and his intriguing, Cranborne's and Eden's objections were overruled, and both the British and Italian governments tacitly agreed in mid-August to begin negotiations in September, after Drummond's return to Rome. This delay would have to occur owing to Britain's need to coordinate its recognition with the League of Nations meeting scheduled for Geneva in the second week of September, as Ciano well recognized.[88]

Mussolini and Ciano had already known that their aggressive anti-British actions provoked divisions between British officials and that Chamberlain had decided to negotiate with Italy. For years, an Italian national working as a janitor in Britain's Rome embassy had been removing documents from the embassy safe at night and returning them before the next morning, although only after Italian intelligence officials had copied their contents. British diplomats remained largely oblivious to this leak, even when faced with circumstantial evidence that Ciano had used evidence obtained from British documents. Mussolini thus had excellent knowledge that his various anti-British measures encouraged Chamberlain and certain Foreign Office officials to pursue an agreement with Italy, but at the same time they profoundly discouraged Eden from negotiating seriously. The Duce's tactic of varying the level of friction while trying to weaken Eden's position was apparently working.[89]

Ultimately, however, Mussolini's push for a limited bargain to secure de jure recognition of the Ethiopian conquest did not occur as planned. Mussolini cavalierly threw away the chance for negotiations because of a new adventure in Spain. On 3 July 1937, Francisco Franco had sent a letter with his brother Nicholas to Mussolini informing the latter of large-scale Soviet shipments through the Mediterranean to Spanish government forces. He asked the Duce to intervene in order to prevent these shipments from reaching port. If not, the massive influx of matériel would imperil the Nationalist victory.[90] Two days later, at a meeting with Nicholas Franco, Mussolini agreed to institute a blockade against any shipping that Italian forces even suspected might be carrying supplies to Republican Spain. Italian *Regia Marina* submarines would provide the primary force, with secondary support coming from the Italian air units stationed in the Balearics.[91] During the month of August, Italian submarines sank several ships, and identifiably Italian airplanes also carried out several attacks. Through naval wireless intercepts, the British government knew that Italy was responsible for the attacks.[92] This provocative behavior demanded a response, and, eventually, at the end of August, the French government proposed holding a conference at the Swiss town of Nyon to deal with the issue of the allegedly unknown perpetrators of Mediterranean piracy.

The proposal gradually marshaled supporters, especially after the night of August 31 to September 1, when the Italian submarine *Iride* attacked the British destroyer *Havock,* which it had mistaken for a Spanish govern-

ment vessel. Potential British or French counterattacks against Italian submarines could spark a war, and neither the French nor British governments
were prepared to risk that outcome. The role of the Nyon conference,
therefore, was to head off continued Italian submarine attacks without
publicly naming Italy as the offending party. Even after Whitehall learned
that Ciano had ordered the attacks to cease on 4 September, the conference
went ahead as a public relations exercise.[93] Accordingly, the Western
democracies invited Italian participation at the conference. Ciano was initially prepared to accept this formal offer, but the Soviet Union interceded,
publicly accusing Italy of having carried out the attacks. Ciano, after consulting with Mussolini and the Wilhelmstrasse, refused to take part owing
to the Soviet's "sabotage" of the conference.[94] Britain and France proceeded, apparently moving forthrightly to protect shipping in the Mediterranean.[95] As Eden described British policy, "In any retreat there must be an
occasional counterattack, and the correct method to counterattack is to do
so against the weakest member of the three in overwhelming force. That is
the justification of Nyon."[96] He blunted his allegedly sharp riposte to
Italy's attacks, however, through his insistence on two cardinal points: the
conference should not allow the Soviet Union a presence in the Mediterranean, and it should not alienate Italy.[97] Seeing that Italy's refusal to
attend had not prevented the conference's decision on Mediterranean
patrols, Ciano convinced Mussolini that Italy should take on a patrol zone
under the Nyon regime, provided it had a position of parity with Britain
and France.[98] Somewhat optimistically, Ciano crowed that Italy had
earned a "fine victory. From suspected pirates to policemen of the
Mediterranean—and the Russians, whose ships we were sinking,
excluded."[99] Despite the element of bravado in this claim, it held considerable truth. Italy had prevented Soviet shipments from reaching Spain,
and the Soviet Union did not resume shipping supplies until October; the
Italian piracy, therefore, despite its limited operation, did serve to give
Franco some breathing room. Furthermore, Mussolini decided in the aftermath of Nyon to dispatch four more submarines with Italian personnel to
the Spanish Nationalists to allow them to interdict supplies closer to Spain.
He also increased the shipment of Italian planes and advisors to Spain. The
Nyon conference, therefore, did little to hamper Mussolini's drive toward
a Nationalist victory in Spain.[100]

Despite this small victory, it did have a cost. Mussolini's reckless piracy
tossed aside his chance to secure de jure recognition, at least in the short
term. His determination to win the war in Spain was, in Mussolini's eyes,
far more important than any mere agreement with Great Britain. He could

not, however, endlessly provoke Britain without some consequences. His Mediterranean adventures meant that it was impossible for Britain to bring the question of de jure recognition to the League of Nations, and so Mussolini lost the chance to secure that objective in September. The death of Drummond's half brother gave Whitehall a convenient excuse to delay the return of their ambassador, newly called Lord Perth, to Rome until after the League meeting.[101]

While Britain and Italy jousted over negotiations and piracy, Ciano tried to further Italy's influence in the Balkans and in the Far East. In August, Italy signed a commercial accord with Hungary. Italy made some relatively minor concessions regarding preferential treatment in clearing arrangements, exports, and tourism, in an effort to convince the Gömbös regime of Italian friendship toward Hungary.[102] Ciano was also successful at promoting negotiations for an agreement between the Little Entente powers and Hungary, as he subordinated any Italo-Romanian discussions to a prior Romanian agreement with Hungary. Romania, therefore, was prepared to make considerable concessions regarding removing the Trianon Treaty's limits on Hungarian arms. In addition, the three countries of the Little Entente were prepared to accept Hungary's adherence to the Kellogg Pact as constituting its guarantee of nonaggression, so Hungary assumed no new obligations toward the Little Entente. The talks broke down, however, over Hungary's insistence on generous minority rights, which the Romanian negotiators refused to grant. Still, Ciano hoped to be able to remove this roadblock, and, eventually, to bring Romania into a pro-Italian bloc with Hungary and Yugoslavia.[103] Such an arrangement would further enhance Italian power and prestige in southeast Europe and would continue the dismantling of the Little Entente begun with the Italo-Yugoslav Accord.

Even more importantly, events in the Far East gave Ciano a chance to rally Japan to an anti-Bolshevik and anti-British coalition. In early 1937, European events dominated Italian foreign policy, and the Far East was relatively quiet. Rome was concerned primarily to ensure that both Chinese Nationalists and the Japanese focused on fighting Chinese Communism and, by extension, the Soviet Union. As long as both parties maintained their anti-Communist aims, then Italy would not have to sacrifice its potential political and commercial development with either.[104] During the first six months of 1937, the Palazzo Chigi and the Gaimushō made only sporadic attempts to improve relations, as Giacinto Auriti, Italy's ambassador in Tokyo, believed that it would be necessary to establish close cultural and economic arrangements before any substantive Italo-Japanese political rapprochement would be possible.

In May, however, Hirota Kōki, the Foreign Minister in a new and more aggressive Japanese Cabinet, had spoken to Auriti on several occasions about the need to strengthen Japan's ties to Italy.[105] Ciano followed up these overtures, suggesting to Ambassador Sugimara that it would be useful for Japan and Italy to reach an anti-Comintern accord, but Sugimara demurred, citing the negative effects for Japan in its dealings with Britain and the United States.[106] In June, Captain Chiapparo, the Italian air attaché to the Chinese Nationalist government at Nanking, recommended liquidating Italy's air mission in China. He reported that the Soviet Union had dispatched some 1,800 relatively modern aircraft to the Chinese Nationalists, and the latter had established clear air superiority over Japanese forces. Given Japan's marked inferiority, it would be more profitable, Chiapparo argued, to concentrate on giving technical aid to the Japanese.[107] Eventually, Hirota dispatched a letter dated 3 July 1937 to Mussolini, carried by Hotta Masaki, Japan's new ambassador to Italy. The letter spoke of the possibility of bringing Italy into the anti-Comintern Pact. Such an accord would include a secret clause allowing for "technical collaboration in the military sphere," plus possible Japanese arms purchases from the technologically more advanced Italians. The Japanese military also wanted aid from Italian naval and air missions. In the political realm, it would help both powers in their various confrontations with the Soviet Union and Britain.[108]

A chance occurrence in the Far East gave tremendous impetus to these previously halting steps toward tighter Italo-Japanese relations. On 7 July 1937, while Hirota's letter was still in transit, Japan and the Chinese Nationalists renewed their war in northern China. A confused small-unit engagement at the Marco Polo Bridge led to wider fighting, as both the Japanese Government and Chiang Kai-Shek believed the time opportune to solve the issue of Japan's status in Manchuria and China by force.[109] Ciano initially tried to remain neutral and to act as a mediator. Neither side, however, was prepared to accept such help. Ciano had to face, therefore, the problem of Italy's air mission to the Chinese Nationalists. Even if it did not take part in combat, the mission was incompatible with Italy's declared friendship toward the Japanese government. On 17 July, Sugimara, as one of his last official acts in Rome, raised this issue with Ciano. The latter assured Sugimara that the mission was purely commercial and would not take part in combat, but that, given Italy's friendship toward Japan, it would be useful to reconsider Italian policy and the mission's continued presence in China.[110]

As Hotta delivered Hirota's letter to Ciano on 31 July, the ambassador argued even more strongly about the need for an anti-Comintern pact and military and technical cooperation. Immediately thereafter, Ciano spoke to Mussolini about Italian policy in the Far East. The Duce decided to proceed on the basis of the Japanese proposals. Ciano thought that Japan's regard for the Italian military was flattering and the economic aspects of an agreement would be useful, but the Duce's prime consideration was Italy's foreign policy and its various alliances around the world.[111] Ciano wrote to Grandi in London to sound out the latter's views on Britain's reaction to an Italo-Japanese accord. Would Italy be able to carry out talks toward Britain's de jure recognition of the Ethiopian conquest simultaneously with negotiations with Japan? Would such talks serve to alienate Britain, or would they serve to coerce Britain to come to an agreement with Italy? Both men agreed that such talks in the short term would likely damage Italy's chances of securing de jure recognition. Grandi supported the Japanese initiative but thought that it seemed prudent to move slowly until after the September meeting of the League of Nations at which Chamberlain intended to raise the question of recognition.[112]

These questions proved moot, however, as the ever-shifting political alignments in Japanese politics led the cabinet to back away from the proposed agreement. Japanese parliamentarians feared that an open agreement with Italy could drag the Japanese into a war with Great Britain.[113] Despite this rather abrupt rejection, Ciano continued to move Italian policy toward closer ties with Japan. The Chinese Nationalist government hastened these changes in Italian policy when it signed a nonaggression pact with the Soviet Union. Ciano was incensed. He denied any further Chinese requests for Italian military shipments and told Hotta that, in the future, Italy would send no more military supplies of any kind to the Chinese Nationalists. Instead, he would look very favorably on Japanese requests for aid.[114] By September, Ciano had virtually ruptured relations with Chinese Nationalists, with whom he had had such close ties only a few months before. He spoke of his confidence in Japan's imminent victory in China and in the common anti-Bolshevik struggle that they carried out: Italy in Spain and Japan in China.[115]

It is interesting to note the marked differences between Italian and German policy in the Far East. Although it was Germany that had signed an anti-Comintern pact with Japan, and not Italy, Germany lagged far behind Italy in its support for Japan. Germany's primary interest lay in protecting its economic influence in China. It supplied military advisors and war matériel to China in exchange for raw materials. Paradoxically, Germany sought Japan's friendship at the same time that it armed Japan's greatest foe.[116] After the Marco Polo Bridge incident, Germany stopped shipping supplies to China only after extremely vigorous protests by the Japanese ambassador. Germany refused to accept that Japan's war in China was an anti-Bolshevik struggle at all. Though Hitler decided that Germany would be officially neutral, it would not withdraw its military advisors, as von Neurath feared that Soviet advisors would quickly replace the departing German ones. In short, German officials believed that the Japanese war in China would serve primarily to increase Bolshevik penetration there. Germany, far from supporting its purported anti-Bolshevik ally, strongly criticized it. Germany's sole involvement was to offer to serve as a mediator if the two belligerents decided to carry out armistice talks.[117] As a result, the only serious foreign policy disagreement between Germany and Italy during 1937 occurred over Italy's far more aggressive and pro-Japanese posture in the Far East.

At the end of September, Mussolini and Ciano visited Berlin. The trip was relatively uneventful; the German government refused to sign any agreements that were not strictly anodyne. It served primarily as a public relations exercise showing the solidarity of the Axis. In von Neurath's view, Mussolini's major aim was to ensure that neither Germany nor Italy would conclude a separate agreement with either Britain or France. On the German side, von Neurath sought Mussolini's agreement to even greater German encroachment on Austrian independence; Mussolini guaranteed that he would not impede German "special interests" in the ostensibly independent country.[118] After his return, Ciano, in one of his rare moments of introspection, noted how closely he had associated Rome with Berlin.

No one can accuse me of being hostile to the pro-German policy. I initiated it myself. But should we, I wonder, regard Germany as a goal, or rather as a field for manoeuvre? The incidents of the last few days and above all Mussolini's fidelity to his political allegiance make me incline towards the first alternative. But may not events develop in such a way as to separate our two peoples once again?

We shall see. The Rome-Berlin Axis is to-day a formidable and extremely useful reality. I shall try to draw a line from Rome to Tokyo, and the system will be complete.[119]

The real effect of Mussolini's visit, however, was psychological. German officials feted Mussolini throughout, and adoring crowds showered him with applause. He lauded Germany for its support during the sanctions episode and announced with fateful words, "We shall never forget." German army maneuvers, parades, and a tour of the Krupp works in Essen convinced the Duce of the renaissance of German power. He sensed that Hitler, far from being the clownish figure that Mussolini had thought on their first meeting, represented instead a man of destiny such as Mussolini fancied himself. The Axis represented a fatalistic partnership of two men and two countries destined for glory. Though Ciano speculated that the German and Italian peoples might part ways in the future, that occurrence was unlikely after German strength beguiled Mussolini.[120]

After his return to Rome, Ciano continued to try to convince the reluctant Japanese government to reach an anti-Comintern agreement with Italy. On 3 October, he directed Auriti to determine the exact stance of the Konoe cabinet's attitudes toward negotiations with Italy. For his part, Ciano was prepared to conclude a pact on the following bases: a public anti-Bolshevik accord analogous to the German and Japanese anti-Comintern Pact and a secret protocol indicating at worst neutrality in the event of conflicts with a third party, with a codicil calling for mutual consultation and in certain cases limited technical support in the event of war.[121] After more than two weeks passed, the Japanese ambassador in Rome apologized to Ciano for the delay. He said that Japan was interested in an accord with Italy, but that Germany had raised the possibility of an Italo-German-Japanese pact. Mussolini quickly agreed, and, on 23 October, he decided to join the already existing anti-Comintern Pact, provided that Italy entered in a position of parity with the other two powers.[122]

After a brief diplomatic preparation, Italy signed on to the prior German-Japanese pact on 6 November 1937 in Rome. Mussolini and Ciano had two primary aims. The first, and most obvious, was anti-Bolshevik. The briefing notes prepared by the Palazzo Chigi emphasized that anti-Bolshevik did not necessarily mean anti-Soviet. As long as the Soviet Union did not try to expand its power, neither Mussolini nor Ciano bore it any especial ill will. In Spain and China, however, Italy and Japan, respectively, were fighting against what Mussolini saw as Soviet-sponsored movements. He was not willing to see Bolshevik expansion in Western Europe or against Italy's new Asian ally.[123] More importantly, however, Mussolini and Ciano directed the pact against Great Britain; as Ciano wrote, the tripartite accord was "anti-Communist in theory but in practice unmistakenly anti-British." He expected that the weight of the three powers would force Britain "to reconsider her position everywhere." Ciano was not merely contemplating applying pressure to Britain to concede de jure recognition. He believed that the new pact created the "most formidable political and military combination that has ever existed." The three powers were embarking on a course that could lead them to war to "break through the crust which is stifling the energy and aspirations of the young nations." The ultimate enemy of all three powers was, in both Mussolini's and Ciano's eyes, the decadent British empire.[124]

The signing of the tripartite anti-Comintern Pact provided the opportunity for a wide-ranging discussion between Hitler's emissary, von Ribbentrop, and the Duce. They expressed mutual hopes that Franco's Aragon campaign would bring a quick end to the Spanish war. If, however, some new force were to threaten to delay Franco's victory, then Mussolini was prepared to commit new *Regio Esercito* units. The major problem, in the Duce's point of view, was that Britain would come around to supporting Franco. This potential maneuver would pose two threats. First, Italy had invested many lire and lives in Franco's victory, and Italians would "want to be and have to be paid." Only if Nationalist Spain remained in the Axis orbit would that repayment occur. Second, Franco's foreign minister displayed alarmingly Anglophile tendencies. The Duce's plans needed a Spain hostile to the Western democracies, so Italy and Germany both would have to work to attach Franco ever more tightly to Fascist politics. Further, Mussolini hoped to be able to maintain the Italian air and naval bases in the Balearics as long as possible, and well beyond Franco's ultimate victory. They offered Italy the best chance to defeat France's strategy of *la guerre de longue durée;* the Duce believed that France would not be able to transport one colonial soldier past Italy's military blockade as long as it was based on Majorca. Mussolini also hoped that Franco would soon adhere to the anti-Comintern pact, with potentially serious consequences for both France's and Britain's strategic positions. Likewise, Mussolini thought that he had the measure of Britain. In the imminent war between the Axis and the West, the major Italian land war would occur in the desert. There, he argued, Italy had the advantage, as Westminster had no stomach for conscription. He boasted of having sent six divisions to Libya, which he thought would paralyze the British cabinet because, in his view, British troops in Egypt would inevitably be outnumbered and could not in any event stand up to desert conditions. In short, though the time was not then ripe for the next war, as neither Germany nor Italy had sufficiently rearmed, Mussolini fully expected that, when the time came, the Axis would have a decisive advantage in the Mediterranean theater.[125]

While Ciano secured his tripartite association, the British government renewed its attempts to lessen Italy's confrontations with the empire. On 1 October, Chamberlain approved a telegram to Perth suggesting that the ambassador approach Ciano to determine whether or not Italy was prepared to discuss the outstanding issues in the Near and Middle East and in Libya. Owing to British public opinion, Whitehall was unwilling to discuss the question of de jure recognition at that time. It offered instead a rather vague quid pro quo of exchanging limited military information in an effort to lessen tension. The next day, Britain and France also made a démarche to try to begin tripartite discussions regarding the withdrawal of Italian volunteers from Spain.[126] Ciano initially reserved judgement on the proposals, but he rejected the Anglo-French one a few days later. His primary objection was that he did not want to appear to be involved in any discussions without German delegates present. Given Ciano's reservations, the Anglo-French initiative died a quick death. The foreign minister did, however, make a moderately conciliatory response to Perth; Ciano sought the resumption of negotiations toward an Anglo-Italian agreement. He would not proceed, however, until Britain agreed to put the question of de jure recognition back into play, and, at that time, Whitehall refused to consider that concession owing to the tense political climate.[127]

Despite this dilatory renewal of negotiations, there was virtually no chance of a genuine Anglo-Italian rapprochement, for that was not Mussolini's desire. While Ciano was telling Perth that Mussolini wanted better relations, the Duce sought a new issue to create tension in Italy's relations with Britain. He decided on the question of alleged British rearmament in Egypt. When Ciano replied that these armaments existed only on paper, Mussolini admitted that he knew but that he needed a "subject for dispute at the right moment."[128] In addition, Fascist Italy continued to seek to undermine British influence in the Arabian Peninsula. During December, for example, Ciano would arrange to ship a further 10,000 rifles with ammunition and ten seventy-five-millimeter artillery pieces to Ibn Saud. Despite Italy's poor foreign exchange balance, Ciano gave half of the rifles and the artillery as a free gift in order to demonstrate Italian friendship. Given the potential confrontation over this violation of the 1927 Rome Understanding, he aimed to ensure that the Finance Ministry kept the expenses hidden from foreign eyes.[129] Mussolini also gave Ciano virtual carte blanche in waging war in Spain and in reaching an agreement with the Japanese; Mussolini no longer feared alienating the British. As he told Ciano, "Either they [Britain and France] refuse to recognize us, and we are free to act. Or they recognize us and we are equally free, because of the Fascist rule that once a thing is done it's done." In Mussolini's view, the decadent British would not react strongly, as there were two million more women than men, and twelve million subjects over the age of fifty, "the age limit for bellicosity." Britain's population, therefore, consisted of those who favored a "static" life rather than "the dynamic elements of youth." Against such weakness, Italy could afford to take a high hand.[130] In light of Mussolini's rejection of the British and French proposals, Ciano remarked that it was "enough to make one speculate about the decline of the British and French peoples. The moment will come, it has perhaps already come, when we shall stake all on the final throw."[131] Mussolini's dogmatic social Darwinism increasingly had led him to pose increasingly strong challenges to the British empire.

Faced with an apparently increasing Italian threat in the Mediterranean, Chamberlain sought to reinvigorate the drive for an Anglo-Italian rapprochement. British strategic policy could not succeed given the tripartite cabal of Italy, Germany, and Japan, and Chamberlain and most Whitehall officials hoped to subtract at least one of these powers from the list of putative enemies. It appeared that Italy might be the easiest to placate, at least as seen from London, so despite Eden's reservations, Britain would not close any path to compromise. Foreign Office officials still maintained four major goals: to remove the threat of Italian troops in Libya, to end the Italian occupation of the Balearics, to get Italian troops out of Spain, and to convince Mussolini to cease Italian propaganda in the Middle East.[132] Eden offered to meet Ciano during the forthcoming Brussels conference, during which the nine signatories of the 1922 Washington Naval Conference would seek to mediate between China and Japan. Eden hoped that he and Ciano could clear the air. Ciano was initially disposed to accept. Mussolini vetoed the idea, as he did not want to see such a meeting fail for lack of diplomatic preparation, and he resented the association of the League of Nations with the conference.[133] In London, Grandi used some rather disingenuous tactics to try to give some impetus to negotiations. He insisted that Germany was placing great pressure on Italy to sign an alliance. If that document were signed, then Italy would have no longer any need to preserve Austria as a buffer, and Austrian independence would be sacrificed on the altar of German friendship. Grandi argued that Britain needed to grant de jure recognition of Italy's Ethiopian empire and to make concessions regarding Spain immediately in order to avoid such an occurrence.[134] Grandi also used the secret channel to outmaneuver Eden. He held several conversations with Joseph Ball, arguing that the tripartite anti-Comintern pact proved the bankruptcy of Eden's foreign policy. Chamberlain, Ball said, agreed with that appreciation.[135]

Grandi fundamentally misunderstood British policy, however, despite his close contacts with Chamberlain, and he fed this misunderstanding back to Ciano. In Grandi's view, the British and French had developed a close military alliance. The Quai d'Orsay and the Popular Front were ready to attack Italy at any time, and French politicians tried to exploit

every sign of tension between Italy and Britain in order to prevent any rapprochement. Up to that point, Britain had always adhered to its alliance
with France, though it always refused at the last minute to follow France
into war. The result of this pernicious French influence was that many people in Britain saw Italy as public enemy number one. In light of this analysis, Grandi strongly supported Mussolini's attempts to extort concessions
from Britain.[136] His tactics, however, served largely to give Eden more evidence of Italian ill will toward Britain, and, therefore, to prevent Britain
from negotiating with Italy.

Despite the delays in negotiations caused by these disreputable Italian
tactics, Chamberlain would not let the chance for Anglo-Italian talks pass,
and he used the secret channel to communicate with Grandi on several
occasions. Chamberlain, through Ball, said that Britain would not place
any prior conditions upon negotiations. In addition, the prime minister
indicated his keen desire to bring about a genuine rapprochement.[137] Ciano
hoped that Grandi could meet Chamberlain officially and convince the
prime minister to override Eden's objections. Grandi was bound by diplomatic protocol to secure Eden's permission to pay an official visit to the
prime minister, and Eden, aware of Chamberlain's inclinations, refused to
grant such permission. Instead, he declared to Grandi that Italy would first
have to cease its anti-British propaganda as a goodwill gesture. Without
this precondition, Eden argued, His Majesty's government would not be
able to consider de jure recognition.[138] In short, the two countries had
reached an impasse, Britain would not start conversations without a conciliatory gesture on Mussolini's part, and Mussolini was determined that
the best path to achieving recognition of the Italian empire lay through
threatening Britain. This mutual incomprehension effectively prevented
any substantive progress for the rest of December. As a result, Ciano
thought that Italians "had better sharpen our swords."[139]

Even though Mussolini still sought a limited agreement with Britain, he
maintained his attitude of outright hostility to France. Italy and France
continued to fight their virtual proxy war in Spain, as the French government had allowed torrents of supplies and volunteers to reach Spain.[140] But
the rift went far deeper than that, as Mussolini refused to consider any kind
of reasonable discussions with France in order to end the tension. Instead,
he directed Ciano to concentrate his efforts to ensure that France would
have no part of any Anglo-Italian rapprochement. Instead, Mussolini
wanted an "attitude of strict severity in [Italy's] confrontation with
France."[141] He decided, therefore, to withdraw the Italian ambassador
from Paris both as a reprisal for the absence of a French ambassador in

Rome and to show his disdain for the French. Cerruti left his post on 31 October 1937. After Cerruti arrived back in Rome, he rather daringly criticized Mussolini's policies that had convinced the French government that Italy represented its greatest threat. Mussolini replied that the French did him "a great honour. I want to be feared and hated, rather than tolerated or protected." Bombast aside, he clearly had no interest in cultivating better relations with France.[142]

Mussolini's withdrawal from the League of Nations gave another signal of his contempt for the Western democracies. In late October, he announced to Ciano that he wanted "an unexpected" meeting of the Fascist Grand Council to declare Italy's withdrawal from the League on 18 November, the second anniversary of sanctions. Mussolini wavered over the precise details. He thought at one point that it would be sufficient to send a telegram to the "Secretary of the moth-eaten League." In the end, he decided on the full ceremony of the Grand Council, and, on 11 December he notified the League of his decision to leave.[143] Mussolini's action had the appropriate effects in the West. As the French chargé d'affaires in Rome correctly interpreted the deed, Mussolini was annoyed by the League's refusal to recognize the conquest of Ethiopia. It displayed his hostility toward France and showed his solidarity with the other bêtes noires of the League, Germany and Japan.[144]

In furthering Italy's confrontation with the Western democracies, Ciano continued to work to create a coalition of states hostile to Britain. Accordingly, Italy quickly proved its loyalty to its Japanese partner in the aftermath of the anti-Comintern agreement. The Japanese cabinet was willing, eventually, to negotiate with Chiang Kai-Shek's government to end the Manchurian war but would not do so through the intermediaries of the nine-power conference at Brussels. Japan preferred first to establish a clear military superiority over the Chinese Nationalist army before any negotiations could take place. Consequently, Ambassador Hotta asked Ciano if he would be willing to prevent the conference from taking any effective action. Mussolini and Ciano, naturally, obliged. Ciano told Auriti that Italy would simply refuse to attend the conference, which Ciano believed would scupper it.[145] Ambassador Hotta instead asked Ciano to send an Italian delegation, as Italy could better work from within the conference in "obstructing decisions hostile to Japan." The head of the Italian delegation, Count Luigi Aldrovandi-Marescotti, annoyed Mussolini by voting on 7 November to issue a second invitation to Japan to attend. Ciano quickly interceded to put Aldrovandi on the proper obscurantist track. From then on, the Italian delegation worked to prevent the member nations from carrying out any effective intervention. As Ciano noted in his diary, "Nothing could be more dangerous than to fall for this technique of collective security. If your finger gets caught in the machine you could lose your whole arm." Italy voted down a strongly worded motion condemning Japan, and the conference failed to make any headway toward ending the Sino-Japanese fighting.[146]

Ciano continued to cultivate Japanese friendship during November. On 14 November, Hotta told Ciano that the Japanese cabinet was prepared to recognize Franco's regime as the legal government of Spain. As a tacit quid pro quo, Hotta asked whether or not Italy would be willing to recognize the Japanese conquest of Manchuria. Mussolini had no objection but wanted to coordinate the recognition with Berlin. In response to the Italian query, von Neurath said that Germany was unprepared to do so, as it hoped to maintain a policy of equidistance between Nationalist China and Japan. Still, he gave Italy a free hand to determine its own path. Mussolini, who had abandoned any pretence of neutrality, decided to recognize the Japanese conquest, despite the obvious repercussions that this policy would have in Sino-Japanese relations. On 28 November, Ciano informed Hotta that Italy would act, and the Italian foreign minister made the announcement public on 12 December.[147] Another example of Italy's attempts to curry favor with Japan occurred the same day as Ciano told Hotta of the Italian decision to recognize Manchuria. The Italian consul, Alberto Perego, in yet another example of the Italian penetration of British security, had stolen the plans for the British base at Singapore. Mussolini ordered Ciano to give the Japanese ambassador a set of the plans, which he did a few days later. As he did so, Ciano declared that his next goal was to sign a military agreement with the Japanese general staff, because, in his view, "that alone [could] decide the issue with England."[148]

In late December, Mussolini directed Ciano to make the anti-British nature of Italy's policy completely clear to the Japanese ambassador. Ciano wanted Japan to moderate its behavior toward Washington but to "be rougher toward Britain." Mussolini cited two elements to his reasoning. First, Japan could drive a wedge between London and Washington in order to isolate Britain. Second, in the event of war between Japan and the United States, Italy could give little help to the Japanese effort. Against Britain, however, Italy would give Japan "the greatest possible assistance." Ciano left unspoken the fact that the reverse was true. Japanese action against the United States did not further Italian aims, whereas a Japan hostile to Britain was an important strategic pillar for Italy.[149] As Auriti understood Ciano's policy in the Far East, it was primarily directed against Britain and France. It was necessary to court Japan as "our expansion cannot continue except at the expense of these two states."[150] Just as Ciano made this initiative, however, he learned that Japan had rejected Italian hopes to act as mediator between China and Japan. Instead, the Gaimushō accepted a German offer to do so because Italian relations with China were so poor. Ciano, in a fit of pique, could only complain that Italy's relations with China were so poor precisely because Italy had gone to great lengths to be a loyal friend to Japan.[151]

Despite this Japanese rebuff, Ciano did not waver in his loyalty to the tripartite anti-Comintern Pact. In the immediate aftermath of the decision, Ciano merely tried to convince Germany to abandon its neutrality in the Sino-Japanese war. He wrote to Massimo Magistrati, his brother-in-law and counselor at the embassy in Berlin, directing him to see Göring, or perhaps von Ribbentrop or Göbbels, to demonstrate Italy's concern over Germany's "dangerous and absurd" policy in China. Ciano believed that, in effect, alleged German neutrality and its military missions there meant that Germany was making common cause with the Soviet Union in favor of China. He wanted Germany to recognize Manchuria immediately and to order its military mission to end its support for Chiang Kai-Shek's forces. As Italy had already withdrawn its military mission and recognized Japan's conquest of Manchuria, Germany's policies represented the appearance of a strong divergence between the Axis partners.[152] Despite Ciano's request, Magistrati made no immediate headway in changing Berlin's policy.

While Ciano worked to recruit allies against the Western democracies, Italian military planners contemplated the shape of a war in the Mediterranean that Mussolini increasingly viewed as inevitable. Given the orientation of Mussolini's foreign policy, they operated on the assumption that Germany and Italy would be allies in a war against Britain and France. At a meeting of the Chiefs of Staff on 2 December 1937, Pariani advocated his plan for the invasion of Egypt. Given the limited number of troops available to the defense, Pariani thought that the Suez Canal would fall easily to his mechanized forces. Marshal Badoglio remained cool to this ambitious plan and argued that it needed further study. Despite Badoglio's opposition, naval planners matched their strategy with Pariani's. In their view, the major difficulty lay in the need to defend the central Mediterranean convoy routes that would allow supplies to reach Italian forces in Libya. The *Regia Marina* would have to concentrate on defending the passage from Sicily to Africa, leaving it to ground forces and the *Regia Aeronautica* to carry the battle to the enemy.[153] Given the superior numbers of

British and French battleships, Italian strategists hoped that Ciano's diplomacy could cement a tripartite association with Germany and Japan, forcing the Royal Navy to deploy its ships outside of the Mediterranean.
Without a substantial increase in Italian naval strength or the dispersal of
the Royal Navy, Italy would likely lose any battle to keep supplies flowing
to Libya. In these circumstances, an attack on Egypt would represent a
grave risk. Though the Duce aimed to create a Mediterranean empire, Italian military weakness prevented him from launching the war necessary to
achieve his imperial dreams.[154]

Still, as 1937 drew to a close, Mussolini and Ciano had moved Italy further toward a possible confrontation with the Western powers. Italy's relations with France were so poor as to be almost nonexistent. Mussolini
bitterly resented French support for the Spanish government, and he
refused to make allowances for Italy's tremendous provocation in continuing to threaten France from the Balearics. Likewise, Mussolini directed
his foreign policy against Britain. He hoped to be able to achieve an agreement with Chamberlain regarding de jure recognition of the Italian
empire, but there was no prospect of a genuine Anglo-Italian rapprochement. Even after any agreement with Britain, he would not honor any
promises; Mussolini expected to preserve a free hand in Libya, the Middle
East, and Spain. Both Mussolini and Ciano thought that their perceived
need for Italian expansion would eventually lead to a war with Britain.
Their policy, therefore, aimed primarily to ensure that when this war
occurred Italy would fight it on the best possible terms. Italy's relations
with Germany were, in contrast, excellent. Mussolini was ready to concede an enormous German dominance in Austria, which removed the
greatest barrier of potential confrontation between the two Axis powers.
Though Germany and Italy pursued slightly different aims in Spain, they
continued to cooperate at a high level there, and both committed themselves to Franco's ultimate victory. Though they maintained a relatively
friendly competition for influence in the Balkans, on most of the important
diplomatic questions during the year, the Axis powers engaged in very
close consultation. The only serious difference of opinion between Italy
and Germany occurred over the Sino-Japanese war. Even then, it was Italy
that took by far the more aggressive posture. It deliberately ruptured its
relations with the Chinese Nationalists in order to court Japan. Italian
adhesion to the anti-Comintern Pact was, in part, anti-Bolshevik. More
importantly, however, both Mussolini and Ciano intended the pact to operate primarily against Britain. They hoped that Japan's growing power in
the Far East would fatally undermine Britain's strategic situation. In short,

during 1937, Italy moved further into the embrace of the Axis and into greater opposition to the West. In no way was Italian policy equidistant between London and Berlin.

NOTES

1. Unsigned memorandum, ASMAE, US 2. For more information see also Coverdale, *Italian Intervention in the Spanish Civil War,* 169–82.

2. Verbale della riunione a Palazzo Venezia del 14 gennaio 1937, ASMAE, US 1 (*DDI,* 8th ser., vol. 6, no. 55, 58–66).

3. Colloquio del Duce con S.E. Schuschnigg presente S.E. Ciano, 22 April 1937, ASMAE, UC 84.

4. Ciano to Grandi, Cerruti, and Attolico, 6 January 1937, ASMAE, US 24.

5. See, for example Verbale della riunione a Palazzo Venezia del 14 gennaio 1937, ASMAE, US 1 (*DDI,* 8th ser., vol. 6, no. 55, 58–66); Cerruti to Ciano, 15 March 1937, ASMAE, US 229; Ciano to Colli (Spain), 19 January 1937, ASMAE, US 24; Ciano to Grandi, 22 January 1937, *DDI,* 8th ser., vol. 6, no. 76, 95; Ciano to Grandi, 8 February 1937, *DDI,* 8th ser., vol. 6, no. 138, 175; Ciano to Drummond, 25 January 1937, *DDI,* 8th ser., vol. 6, no. 87,104–5; Ciano to Attolico, 30 January 1937, *DDI,* 8th ser., vol. 6, no. 106, 131.

6. De Ciutiis (Salamanca) to Ciano, 11 January 1937, *DDI,* 8th ser., 6, no. 35, 41; Anfuso to Ciano, 24 January 1937, *DDI,* 8th ser., vol. 6, no. 83, 101–2; Cantalupo (Salamanca) to Ciano, 17 February 1937, *DDI,* 8th ser., vol. 6, no. 171, 221; Cantalupo (Salamanca) to Ciano, 18 February 1937, *DDI,* 8th ser., vol. 6, no. 177, 228; Cantalupo (Salamanca) to Ciano, 19 February 1937, *DDI,* 8th ser., vol. 6, no. 179, 229.

7. Ciano to Grandi, 8 February 1937, ASMAE, GAB 28.

8. Grandi to Ciano, 21, 26, 29 January 1937, ASMAE, US 6; Ciano to Drummond, *DDI,* 8th ser., vol. 6, no. 87, 104–5. Italian policy fluctuated on the issue of withdrawal of volunteers. At times, Mussolini and Ciano strictly opposed it. At other times, however, they considered that it might serve to create a permanent Nationalist superiority. For example, after the Italian defeat at Guadalajara in March 1937, Mussolini considered a policy of a phased withdrawal of volunteers provided there was an equal number of Soviet advisors and International Brigade members withdrawn. Ultimately, however, he decided that Italians had to avenge Guadalajara with a decisive victory, and the momentary consideration passed (von Hassell to the Foreign Ministry, 27 March 1937, 29 March 1937, *DGFP,* ser. D, vol. 3, no. 238, 260–61, 261–62). Grandi complicated the process, when, on 27 March 1937, he contradicted his instructions and declared in the nonintervention committee that Italy would not withdraw any volunteers until after a Nationalist victory (von Hassell to von Neurath, 27 March 1937, *DGFP,* ser. D, vol. 3, no. 237, 260–61). Despite Grandi's mistake, Mussolini and Ciano decided that Italy would repatriate volunteers if Franco requested their withdrawal (Ciano to

Attolico, 20 June 1937, *DDI,* 8th ser., vol. 6, no. 769, 1011; Ciano appunto, 26 June 1937, *DDI,* 8th ser., vol. 6, no. 803, 1044–45, no. 804, 1045–46).

9. Verbale della riunione a Palazzo Venezia del 14 gennaio 1937, ASMAE, US 1 (*DDI,* 8th ser., vol. 6, no. 55, 58–66); Communicazione fatta al Generale Franco a nome del governo italiano e del gov. tedesco, 23 January 1938, ASMAE, UC 44; see also Ciano to Attolico, 18 January 1937, ASMAE, US 226 (*DDI,* 8th ser., vol. 6, no. 69, 84–85). This latter telegram reported Ciano's view of the results of the 14 January 1937 meeting with Göring.

10. Attolico to Ciano, 31 May 1937, ASMAE, US 225; Grandi to Ciano, 23 June 1937, 31 May 1937, US 6; von Neurath to von Ribbentrop, 30 May 1937, *DGFP,* ser. D, vol. 3, no. 267, no. 268, 296–97, 297; von Neurath Memoranda, 30 May 1937, *DGFP,* ser. D, vol. 3, no. 269, no. 270, 297–98, 298; Memorandum by an Official of the Foreign Minister's Secretariat, 31 May 1937, *DGFP,* ser. D, vol. 3, no. 272, 299–300.

11. Ciano to Grandi, Attolico, and Viola (Salamanca), 15 June 1937, ASMAE, US 6.

12. Ciano to Cantalupo (Salamanca), 1 March 1937, *DDI,* 8th ser., vol. 6, no. 220, 279; Cantalupo (Salamanca) to Ciano, 5 March 1937, *DDI,* 8th ser., vol. 6, no. 240, 298–99; Ciano to Cantalupo (Salamanca), 6 March 1937, *DDI,* 8th ser., vol. 6, no. 249, 305; Conti [Roatta] (Seville) to Ciano, 9 March 1937, *DDI,* 8th ser., vol. 6, no. 262, 317–20; Cantalupo (Salamanca) to Ciano, 11 March 1933, *DDI,* 8th ser., vol. 6, no. 265, 322–23; Ciano to Cantalupo, 15 March 1937, *DDI,* 8th ser., vol. 6, no. 274, 334; Cantalupo to Franco, 29 March 1937, *DDI,* 8th ser., vol. 6, no. 357, 431–33.

13. Ciano to Roatta, 6 February 1937, *DDI,* 8th ser., vol. 6, no. 132, 171.

14. Italian intelligence sources reported widespread French violations of the nonintervention agreement, including shipments of modern French antitank guns, French planes with scarcely concealed Air France colors, thousands of volunteers crossing the Pyrenees, Soviet military advisors traveling through France, plus French military aviators training volunteer pilots on French territory (Pietromarchi [Rome] to Ministero di Guerra, 22 January 1937, ASMAE, US 231; Vice Console [Tolosa] to Ciano, 16 December 1936, ASMAE, US 231; Pietromarchi to Ministero della Cultura Populara, 23 July 1937, ASMAE, US 231; Console Generale [Tolosa] to Ciano, 3 March 1937, ASMAE, US 231; Ministero degli Affari Esteri al Ministero di Guerra, 27 March 1937, ASMAE, US 231).

15. Cerruti to Ciano, 15 March 1937, 27 March 1937, ASMAE, US 229.

16. Jackson, *The Popular Front in France: Defending Democracy, 1934–1938,* 199–205.

17. For Britain's early protests over the dispatch of volunteers and Ciano's rather dismissive response, see Colloquio con l'ambasciatore di Inghilterra, 6 January 1937, ASMAE, UC 84 (*DDI,* 8th ser., vol. 6, no. 15, 18–19).

18. Sargent Minute, 15 February 1937, FO 371 21174, R863/200/22;. Vansittart Minute, 16 February 1937, FO 371 21174, R863/200/22. For a recapitulation of Admiralty and Chiefs of Staff argument and the documentary sources, see also

Sargent Minute, 1 April 1937, FO 371 21136, R2261/5/67; and Admiralty to the Foreign Office, 21 November 1936, FO 20412, R6974/226/22.

19. Diary entry, 4 January 1937, The University of Birmingham Library, Avon Papers (hereafter cited as AP) 20/1/17. Several Italian historians argue that Eden's anger over the Italian troop shipments was unreasonable. For example, Paola Brundu Olla argues that the Italian escalation did "not constitute a violation of the commitments assumed because it responded to the intentions of Eden who through his comportment had succeeded in legitimizing Mussolini in the role of defender of Spain and the Mediterranean from the threat of communism in the place of Britain" (Olla, *L'Equilibrio difficile*, 227). Simply put, it is impossible to reconcile this rather extravagant claim with Eden's attitude at the time. Even while ordering Grandi to try to create sympathy in anti-Bolshevik British circles, Ciano made the pro-German orientation of Italy's policy abundantly clear (Ciano to Grandi, 7 January 1937, *DDI,* 8th ser., vol. 6, no. 18, 22–23).

20. For more information, see James Joseph Sadkovich, *Italian Support for Croatian Separatism, 1927–1937* (Madison: University of Wisconsin Press, 1982).

21. Italy allowed Ustaša members sanctuary beginning in 1929 and trained and organized Ustaša military units beginning in 1932. Unfortunately, much of the Italian documentation on the Ustaša kept in the *Carte Lancelotti* has been destroyed by damp and rot (Instituto Generale di P. S. [Anfuso], 18 April 1941, ASMAE, UC 50).

22. Grandi to Ciano, 9 January 1937, ASMAE, Carte Grandi, B. 40, fasc. 93/3; von Hassell to the Foreign Ministry, 12 January 1937, *DGFP,* C, 6, no. 138, 282; von Hassell to the Foreign Ministry, 14 January 1937, *DGFP,* C, 6, no. 143, 294–95; de Dampierre (Belgrade) to Delbos, 23 March 1937, *DDF,* 2, 5, no. 152, 244–45. For more on the negotiations, see Ciano to Indelli (Belgrade), 15 March 1937, *DDI,* 8th ser., vol. 6, no. 279, 338–39; Ciano to Indelli (Belgrade), 15 March 1937, *DDI,* 8th ser., vol. 6, no. 293, 353–54; Ciano to Indelli (Belgrade), 18 March 1937, *DDI,* 8th ser., vol. 6, no. 294, 354–55; Indelli to Ciano, 20 March 1937, *DDI,* 8th ser., vol. 6, no. 302, 361–62.

23. Strettamente Segreto—patto segreto sull' accordo italo-iugoslavia, 25 March 1937, ASMAE, UC 49 (*DDI,* 8th ser., vol. 6, no. 340, 402–9). Mussolini commented dismissively to von Hassell that he did not mind abandoning the Ustaša, as it had accomplished nothing in the prior eight years (von Hassell to the Foreign Ministry, 25 March 1937, *DGFP,* ser. D, vol. 3, no. 236, 258–60). In a relatively rare occurrence, Mussolini actually maintained this promise for roughly two years. He reactivated the Ustaša only in 1939. See also von Plessen (Rome) to the Foreign Ministry, 23 March 1937, *DGFP,* C, 4, no. 291593–94.

24. Eden conversation with the French Ambassador, 24 March 1937, FO 371 21198, R2108/224/92; von Hassell to the Foreign Ministry, 25 March 1937, *DGFP,* C, 6, no. 291, 258–60. For Yugoslav resistance to French overtures, see Shorrock, *From Ally to Enemy,* 199–200; Weinberg, *The Foreign Policy of Hitler's Germany: Starting World War II,* 79–80.

25. Prunas (Paris) to Ciano, 3 April 1937, ASMAE, SAP—Francia, B 27; Harvey (Geneva) to Millar (London), reporting Eden's conversation with the Yugoslav Minister, 25 January 1937, FO 371 21197, R650/224/92; Jackson, *The Popular Front in France: Defending Democracy, 1934–1938,* 195; see also Shorrock, *From Ally to Enemy,* 200.

26. Eden Minute, 1 April 1937, FO 371 21158, R2258/1/22; See also Sargent Minute, 3 April 1937, FO 371 21158, R2258/1/22. For another copy, see Memorandum dictated by the Secretary of State for the guidance of the Departments concerned, 1 April 1937, FO 954/13, It/37/3.

27. Grandi to Ciano, 9 January 1937, ASMAE, Carte Grandi, B 40, fasc. 93/3; see also Memorandum by the Head of Political Division IV, 30 April 1937, *DGFP,* C, 6, no. 347, 708–14.

28. Heeren (Belgrade) to von Neurath, 8 March 1927, *DGFP,* C, 6, no. 254, 515–16; von Hassell to von Neurath, 15 March 1937, *DGFP,* C, 6, no. 274, 559–61.

29. Colloquio con il Presidente Stoyadinovitch, 26 March 1937, ASMAE, UC 84. The Yugoslav government had asked the Wilhelmstrasse for advice on the approaches from Italy and France. The response suggested the Stoyadinović regime avoid tying itself too closely to any power, but especially the French (von Ermansdorff Circular to the Foreign Ministry, 25 March 1937, *DGFP,* C, 6, no. 295, 601).

30. *CHD,* 5 December 1937, 41. The Wilhelmstrasse was well aware of Mussolini's and Ciano's views regarding the inevitability of the Anschluss and their desire to use Yugoslavia as a potential counterweight to Germany. German officials assumed correctly that both Mussolini and Ciano recognized the need for German support, and that their moves in the Balkans were not directed against Germany, but represented instead friendly competition with Germany. (Heeren [Belgrade] to von Neurath, 8 March 1937, *DGFP,* C, 6, no. 254, 515–16; von Hassell to von Neurath, 15 March 1937, *DGFP,* C, 6, no. 274, 559–61).

31. Ciano appunto, 26 March 1937, *DDI,* 8th ser., vol. 6, no. 345, 412–18.

32. Interestingly, Hungarian leaders resented Germany's attempts to focus Hungarian revisionism entirely against Czechoslovakia, as in their view, claims against Romania were at least equally important (Salata [Vienna] to Ciano, 23 January 1937, *DDI,* 8th ser., vol. 6, no. 85, 103; Vinci [Budapest] to Ciano, 1 February 1937, no. 111, *DDI,* 8th ser., vol. 6, 143–44).

33. Sola (Bucharest) to Ciano, 31 March 1937, ASMAE, SAP—Romania, B 10; Ciano to Vinci (Budapest), 21 April 1937, ASMAE, SAP—Romania, B 10; Ciano to Vinci, 20 April 1937, ASMAE, GAB 28; Ciano to Vinci (Budapest), Attolico, Sola (Bucharest), 11 May 1937, ASMAE, GAB 28; Sola (Bucharest) to Ciano, 2 February 1937, 3 February 1937, 27 March 1937, 31 March 1937, 7 April 1937, 10 May 1937, 14 May 1937, 22 May 1937, *DDI,* 8th ser., vol. 6, no. 115, no. 120, no. 350, no. 367, no. 420, no. 570, no. 592, no. 629, 147–48, 152–53, 421–22, 440–42, 516–18, 736–37, 765, 824–26; Ciano to Indelli (Belgrade), 13 April 1937, *DDI,* 8th ser., vol. 6, no. 452, 568.

34. Weinberg, *Starting World War II,* 142–44, 147–154. For the standard study on the economic dimension of Hitler's intervention in Spain, see Robert H. Whealey, *Hitler and Spain: The Nazi Role in the Spanish Civil War, 1936–1939* (Lexington, Ky.: The University Press of Kentucky, 1989).

35. See, for example, Magistrati (Berlin) to Ciano, 2 April 1937, *DDI,* 8, vol. 6, no. 389, 475;Magistrati (Berlin) to Ciano, 13 April 1937, *DDI,* 8th ser., vol. 6, no. 457, 574–75; Ciano to Attolico and Cantalupo (Salamanca), 6 April 1937, *DDI,* 8th ser., vol. 6, no. 411, 506–7; Ciano to Attolico, 9 April 1937, *DDI,* 8th ser., vol. 6, no. 431, 539.

36. Promemoria, 22 April 1937, ASMAE, US 225; Ciano to Attolico, 26 April 1937, ASMAE, US 225.

37. Grandi to Ciano, 7 July 1937, ASMAE, US 6.

38. Von Hassell to von Neurath, 5 March 1937, *DGFP,* C, 6, no. 247, 503.

39. Von Hassell to von Neurath, 25 March 1937, *DGFP,* ser. D, vol. 3, no. 236, 258–60.

40. Secret Protocol between the German and Italian Governments, 14 May 1937, *DGFP,* C, 6, no. 368, 752–55; see also The Foreign Ministry to von Plessen, 28 August 1937, *DGFP,* C, 6, no. 536,1041–42, 1042n2.

41. Von Neurath Memorandum, 7 July 1937, *DGFP,* C, 6, no. 453, 902–3; von Neurath Memorandum, 7 July 1937, *DGFP,* C, 6, no. 458, 908; von Neurath to von Hassell, 13 July 1937, *DGFP,* C, 6, no. 461, 910–11; von Hassell to von Neurath, 21 July 1937, *DGFP,* C, 6, no. 485, 948; von Hassell to von Weizsäcker, 29 July 1937, *DGFP,* C, 6, no. 499, 972–74; von Hassell to von Weizsäcker, 31 July 1937, *DGFP,* C, 6, no. 503, 986–88; von Neurath to von Weizsäcker, 29 July 1937, *DGFP,* C, 6, no. 502, 985–86. Mussolini had received several indications that Germany would not remain content with the 11 July 1936 agreement. For example, Göring had indicated in his January 1937 meetings with Mussolini that Germany could not abandon six million Germans living in Austria (Dichiarazioni del Ministro Göring nel colloquio con Mussolini del 15 gennaio 1937, *DDI,* 8th ser., vol. 6, no. 60, 71–76; see also Magistrati (Berlin) to Ciano, 1 February 1937, *DDI,* 8th ser., vol. 6, no. 113, 145–46).

42. Paul Preston, *Franco: A Biography* (London: HarperCollins, 1993), 233–36.

43. Mussolini to Ciano, 20 March 1937, *OO,* vol. 42, 183; Mussolini to Grandi, 31 March 1937, *OO,* vol. 42, 187; see also Azione di Guadalajara, n.d., ASMAE, UC 45. In a fit of pique, Mussolini signaled his displeasure by refusing to send an official Italian delegation to the coronation of King George VI (Mussolini to Ciano, 17 March 1939, *DDI,* 8th ser., vol. 6, no. 285, no. 286, 345).

44. Mussolini to Grandi, 25 March 1937, *OO,* vol. 42, 184–85; Mussolini to Vittorio Emmanuele III, 26 March 1937, *OO,* vol. 42, 185–86.

45. For an English translation and a commentary on the text of the accords, see Strang, "Imperial Dreams," 799–809.

46. Cerruti to Ciano, 16 February 1937, 27 February 1937, 6 April 1937, 17 April 1937, *DDI,* 8th ser., vol. 6, no. 167, no. 210, no. 415, no. 476, 217–18,

267–68, 510–13, 594–98; Ciano to Cerruti, 25 February 1937, 11 April 1937, *DDI,* 8th ser., vol. 6, no. 200, no. 445, 258–59561–62.

47. Ciano to De Astis (Ankara), 7 January 1937, 8 January 1937, *DDI,* 8th ser., vol. 6, no. 19, no. 25, 23, 30; Galli to Ciano, 11 January 1937, 17 January 1937, *DDI,* 8th ser., vol. 6, no. 43, no. 66, 49–51, 81–82.

48. Warner Memorandum, 13 March 1937, FO 371 20786, E1488/145/65.

49. Drummond to Eden, 19 March 1937, FO 371 21157, R1908/1/22; McDonald, "Radio Bari," 200; Pratt, *East of Malta, West of Suez: Britain's Mediterranean Crisis,* 66–67.

50. Stonehewer-Bird (Addis Ababa) to Eden, 6 March 1937, FO 371 20932, J1077/74/1; Wikely-Harrar (Addis Ababa) to Eden, 13 March 1937, FO 371 20932, J1174/74/1.

51. Drummond to Eden, 13 January 1937, FO 371 21158, R3301/1/22; Drummond to O'Malley, 21 April 1937, FO 371 21158, R2869/1/22. For more on British reactions to the barrage of Italian propaganda, see also O'Malley minute, 20 March 1937, FO 371 21158, R2376/1/22, plus the ensuing commentaries by Cadogan and Eden.

52. Drummond to Eden, 23 March 1937, FO 371 21157, R1908/1/22.

53. Unfortunately, the available Italian archival evidence on this issue is rather sketchy and certainly incomplete, but see Pariani to Ciano, 1 June 1937, ASMAE, SAP—Yemen, B 13; Ciano to Dott. Dubbiosi (Sanaa), 7 November 1937, ASMAE, SAP—Yemen, B 13.

54. Mazzolini (Jerusalem) to Ciano, 26 March 1937, *DDI,* 8th ser., vol. 6, no. 341, 409; Caruso Appunto, 7 April 1937, *DDI,* 8th ser., vol. 6, no. 421, 518–20; Ciano to Sillitti (Jedda), 14 April 1937, *DDI,* 8th ser., vol. 6, no. 459, 576; L'Ufficio di Gabinetto to Ciano, 14 April 1937, *DDI,* 8th ser., vol. 6, no. 460 576; Sillitti (Jedda) to Ciano, 14 April 1937, *DDI,* 8th ser., vol. 6, no. 463, 579–80; Ciano to Sillitti (Jedda), 29 May 1937, *DDI,* 8th ser., vol. 6, no. 657, 859; L'Ufficio III to Ciano, no date, *DDI,* 8th ser., vol. 6, no. 741, 972; Ciano to Campini (Aden), 30 June 1937, *DDI,* 8th ser., vol. 6, no. 822, 1072.

55. Lampson to Eden, 18 December 1936, FO 371 10780, E2979/872/91; Lampson to Eden, 18 February 1937, FO 371 20772, E1242/27/91; Warner Memorandum, 13 March 1937, FO 371 20786, E1488/145/65; see also Rosaria Quartararo, "L'Italia e lo Yemen. Uno studio sulla politica di espanione italiana nel Mar Rosso (1923–1937)," *Storia contemporanea* 10, no. 4/5 (October 1979): 855–56. Although Quartararo is a seemingly tireless researcher who has uncovered some excellent archival material, her conclusions about Anglo-Italian relations are often highly suspect.

56. Drummond to Eden, 2 March 1937, FO 371 21157, R1579/1/22.

57. Mussolini to Graziani, 22 February 1937, Archivio Centrale dello Stato (hereafter cited as ACS), Carte Graziani, B 72, fasc. 59.

58. Mallett, *The Italian Navy and Fascist Expansionism,* 93–94.

59. Verbale della riunione a Palazzo Venezia del 23 gennaio 1937, ASMAE, US 1; *CDP,* 80–91; see also Attolico to Ciano, 30 January 1937, *DDI,* 8th ser., vol.

6, no. 109, 132–41 (this telegram forwarded the German minutes of the conversation of 23 January).

60. Mussolini added the emphasis. Grandi to Ciano, 7 April 1937, ASMAE, Carte Grandi, B40, fasc. 93/3 (*DDI*, 8th ser., vol. 6, no. 425, 524–33). Several Italian and English-language historians have taken Grandi's words at face value as evidence that Italian policy aimed only at reaching an agreement with Great Britain and that the Rome-Berlin Axis was merely a tactical ploy to further this aim. Italy sought first British de jure recognition of its Ethiopian conquest, and second, parity of rights and prestige with Britain in the Mediterranean. Consequently, they blame British statesmen for failing to understand Italy and this Italian policy; the result of this failure was that the British government forced Italy into an ever closer arrangement with Berlin. Eventually, Italy became trapped in the Axis owing to the alleged obduracy of His Majesty's Government. See, for example, De Felice, *Mussolini, il duce, I: Gli anni del consenso,* 686–88, 706–8, 743; De Felice, *Mussolini il duce, II: Lo Stato totalitario,* 333, 339, 466; De Felice, *Mussolini l'alleato, I/1/2, L'Italia in Guerra,* 61; Quartararo, *Roma tra Londra e Berlino,* 326–518 (passim); Brundu Olla, *L'equilibrio difficile,* 227; Nello, *Un fedele indisubbidiente,* 305; MacDonald, "Radio Bari," 200. De Felice did allow at one point that "in the historical-political conception of the Duce Italy would sooner or later have turned against England," though the balance of his work attempted largely to argue that Mussolini wanted to avoid that very occurrence (De Felice, *Lo Stato totalitario,* 348). Unfortunately, the De Felice school ignores entirely the larger aims of the Duce, which included replacing first France, and, ultimately, Great Britain, as major Mediterranean powers. Mussolini and Ciano were the architects of Italian foreign policy, not Grandi; his wishes were of little consequence, and the balance of evidence weighs exceedingly strongly against these interpretations. In early 1937, Mussolini did hope to achieve the temporary goal of Britain's de jure recognition of the Italian conquest of Ethiopia. (Ciano to Grandi, 2 April 1937, *DDI,* 8th ser., vol. 6, no. 384, 466–67). More importantly, however, he sought to create the best climate possible for the expansion of Italian power at the expense of the Western democracies.

61. Appunti per il Gran Consiglio Fascista, 1 March 1937, ASMAE, Carte Grandi, B 43, fasc. 106.

62. See, for example, notes 17, 19, and 26 of this chapter. Through stolen documents, Grandi, Ciano, and Mussolini all knew of the deleterious effects that their many provocations created in London, particularly with Eden. Instead of modifying Italian policy, however, Mussolini merely focused his anger against Eden. (Pratt, *East of Malta, West of Suez: Britain's Mediterranean Crisis,* 68n13).

63. For Ciano's views in this vein, see *CHD,* 5 October 1937, 6 November 1937, 19–24 December 1937, 17–18, 28–29, 45, 48–49. For Mussolini's views, see *CHD,* 21 December 1937, 46–47 and Knox, "The Fascist Regime," 355. This brief list is by no means exhaustive; a full recounting could run to dozens of citations.

64. O'Malley to Drummond, 10 May 1937, FO 371 21158, R3160/1/22.

65. Lampson to Eden, 22 May 1937, FO 371 21159, R3795/1/22; Lampson to Eden, 21 May 1937, FO 371 21159, R3825/1/22.

66. Ingram to Eden, 20 May 1937, FO 371 21181, R3542/1920/22.

67. Mussolini to Vittorio Emmanuele, 4 October 1937, *OO,* vol. 42; Lt. Col. Arnold (War Office) to Nichols (Foreign Office), 20 May 1937, FO 371 21168, R3475/69/22; see also Vansittart's Minute, 26 May 1937, FO 371 21168, R3475/69/22. For more detail on the British defense and political relationship with Egypt, see Steven S. Morewood, "Appeasement from Strength: The Making of the Anglo-Egyptian Treaty of Friendship and Alliance of 1936," *Diplomacy & Statecraft* 7, no. 3 (1996): 530–62.

68. Mallett, *The Italian Navy and Fascist Expansionism,* 109–111, 111n36; Ceva, *Storia delle forze armate in Italia,* 249. General Pariani continued to believe in the possibility of a rapid strike against Egypt, even after the eventual formation of a British armored division there. The more cautious Marshal Badoglio, however, restrained the impetuous Pariani (Lucio Ceva, "Appunti per una storia dello Stato Maggiore generale fino alla vigilia della 'non-belligerenza.' " *Storia Contemporanea* 10, no. 2 [1976]: 233, 238).

69. O'Malley Memorandum, 15 June 1937, FO 371 21159, R3831/1/22. This note reported the contents of the Committee of Imperial Defence (C.I.D.) paper 1332-B, 1 June 1937. Within a few months, C.I.D. language had changed from "Italy cannot be counted on as a reliable friend, but in present circumstances need not be regarded as a probable enemy," to "Italy cannot be considered as a reliable friend and must for an indefinite period be regarded as a possible enemy, especially if she can count on the goodwill and potential support of Germany, or if the United Kingdom were involved in difficulties elsewhere."

70. Appunto per il Duce, 14 June 1936, ASMAE, GAB 26 (*DDI,* 8th ser., vol. 6, no. 733, 958–59); Ciano appunto per il Duce, 16 June 1936, ASMAE, GAB 30. Magistrati (Berlin) to Ciano, 13 May 1937, *DDI,* 8th ser., vol. 6, no. 590, 762–64; Attolico to Ciano, 15 May 1937, *DDI,* 8th ser., vol. 6, no. 601, 775–76; Attolico to Ciano, 15 June 1937, *DDI,* 8th ser., vol. 6, no. 735, 960–61; Attolico to Ciano, 16 June 1937, *DDI,* 8th ser., vol. 6, no. 746, 977–79; Attolico to Ciano, 16 June 1937, *DDI,* 8th ser., vol. 6, no. 748, 980.

71. Cerruti cited several speeches made at a 1 July 1937 dinner honoring Sir Eric Phipps. Blum called for tight Anglo-French relations "in the face of great danger." A week earlier, Lord Lloyd spoke in Paris of the need for greater understanding in London of French policy toward Fascist Italy (Cerruti to Ciano, 30 June 1937, 3 July 1937, ASMAE, SAP—Francia, B 27).

72. Grandi to Ciano, 24 April 1937, *DDI,* 8th ser., vol. 6, no. 506, 639–41; Cerruti to Ciano, 24 April 1937, *DDI,* 8th ser., vol. 6, no. 509, 643–44. For the actual state of Anglo-French military cooperation, see Young, *In Command of France,* 156–59.

73. Cerruti to Ciano, 23 June 1936, ASMAE, SAP—Francia, B 36; Cerruti to Ciano, 26 June 1936, US 229.

74. Mussolini added the emphasis. Cerruti to Ciano, 22 May 1937, *DDI,* 8th ser., vol. 6, no. 630, 827–30.

75. Grandi to Ciano, 21 May 1937, *DDI,* 8th ser., vol. 6, no. 622, 798–816.

76. Cerruti to Ciano, 5 July 1937, ASMAE, US 229; Ciano to Cerruti, 6 July 1937, ASMAE, US 229.

77. Ciano to Grandi, 20 June 1937, ASMAE, UC 89; Ciano to Grandi, 5 July 1937, ASMAE, GAB 28; Ciano to Grandi, 3 July 1937, ASMAE, US 227; see also von Hassell to von Neurath, 12 June 1937, *DGFP,* ser. D, vol. 3, no. 306.

78. Ciano to Grandi, 7 July 1937, ASMAE, GAB 28.

79. Ciano to Grandi, 20 June 1937, ASMAE, UC 89 (*DDI,* 8th ser., vol. 6, no. 770, 1011–12).

80. Colloquio con Chamberlain, 2 August 1937, ASMAE, US 231.

81. Coverdale, *Italian Intervention in the Spanish Civil War,* 311.

82. Cranborne to Eden, 18 August 1937, AP 20/5/20; Cranborne Minute, 30 August 1937, FO 371 21167, R5617/64/22.

83. Eden Minute, 26 August 1937, FO 371 21167, R5617/64/22; Halifax to Eden, 12 August 1937, FO 954/13, It/37/29; Eden to Halifax, 13 August 1937, FO 954/13, It/37/30.

84. Advocates of this position included Sir Maurice Hankey, the powerful cabinet secretary; Sir Orme Sargent; Sir Robert Vansittart; and Viscount Halifax, the lord president of the council, and, during August, the replacement for the vacationing Eden as foreign secretary (Hankey to Chamberlain, 19 July 1937, Prime Ministers' Series PREM 1/276; Hankey to Eden, 23 July 1937, FO 954/13, It/37/12; Sargent Minute, 27 July 1937, FO 371 21160, R5104/1/22; Halifax to Vansittart, 4 August 1937, PREM 1/276). For the clearest statements of the British position, see F.O. Minute, Record of a meeting held in the S[ecretary] of S[tate's] room on August 10th to deal with the question of de jure recognition of the Italian conquest of Abyssinia and conversations with the Italian government as proposed in the P[rime] M[inister's] letter to Sr. M[ussolini] of 27th July, FO 371 21161, R5532/1/22; and Halifax to Chamberlain, 11 August 1937, PREM 1/276.

85. Colloquio con Chamberlain, 2 August 1937, ASMAE, US 231. For a description of Dino Grandi's inventiveness in creating a first fictitious letter from Mussolini, see William C. Mills, "The Chamberlain-Grandi Conversations of July–August 1937 and the Appeasement of Italy," *International History Review* 19, no. 3 (August 1997): 594–619. Grandi also gave a further push to Anglo-Italian rapprochement by changing Chamberlain's anodyne greeting at their first official meeting after Chamberlain had assumed the Prime Ministership. Grandi reported that Chamberlain had emphasized the need to clarify Britain's relations with Italy. Although these words were not inconsistent with Chamberlain's policy, Grandi wrote in his diary that Chamberlain had not actually uttered them but had merely been polite (Grandi to Ciano, 17 June 1937, *DDI,* 8th ser., vol. 6, no. 751, 982–83, 983n1). It is important to note, however, that the impetus for this démarche came from Ciano; it was not Grandi's initiative.

86. For Grandi's description of the initiation of this secret channel, see Grandi to Ciano, 12 July 1937, ASMAE, Carte Grandi, B 66, fasc. 158/1. In 1976, Rosario Quartararo published extensive selections from the lengthy records that are now available in the Italian Foreign Ministry Archives after an extremely long delay in cataloguing (Rosaria Quartararo, "Inghilterra e Italia. Dal Patto di Pasqua a Monaco, Con un' appendice sul «canale segreto» italo-inglese," *Storia contemporanea* 7, no. 4 [December 1976]: 607–716). The document is now found in Summary of Adrian Dingli's action, n.d., ASMAE, Carte Grandi, B 66, fasc. 158/2.

87. For the best indication of Chamberlain's views regarding negotiations, see Chamberlain to Halifax, 7 August 1937, FO 954/13, It/37/20, and PREM 1/276.

88. Drummond aide-memoire to Ciano, 6 August 1937, ASMAE, SAP—Gran Bretagna, B 19 (Mussolini initialled "d'accordo" on this note); Drummond to Eden, 2 August 1937, FO 371 21160, R5280/1/22. For further evidence of the different nuances between the views of Chamberlain and Eden, see Trevor Evans, ed., 25 October 1937, *The Killearn Diaries, 1934–46: The Diplomatic and Personal Record of Lord Killearn (Sir Miles Lampson)* (London: Sidgwick and Jackson, 1972), 85–87.

89. For more detail on this issue, see David Dilks, "Flashes of Intelligence: The Foreign Office, the SIS, and Security before the Second World War," in *The Missing Dimension: Governments and Intelligence Communities in the Twentieth Century,* eds. David Dilks and Christopher Andrew (Chicago: University of Illinois Press, 1984), 101–24; David Dilks, ed., "Appeasement and 'Intelligence,'" in *Retreat from Power, Volume I, 1906–1939* (London: MacMillan, 1981), 136–69, especially 136–39 and 150–55; and Mario Toscano, *Designs in Diplomacy* (Baltimore: The Johns Hopkins Press, 1970), 409, 412–13. Incidentally, the Italo-Yugoslav accord had provided Britain with the best chance to prevent Italy from stealing British documents. Ronald Campbell, the able British Minister in Belgrade, reported that Prince Paul believed that the Italians had penetrated British security. He asked Campbell to keep his communications both secure and confidential and not to allow the Foreign Office to send them to the Rome Embassy. The Foreign Office blithely continued to send documents to Rome, however, and the Italians used the written record of some of Prince Paul's rather indiscreet comments to secure additional concessions from the Stoyadinović government. Campbell reported that the Italians had broken British security, but, with one exception, Foreign Office officials refused to believe the evidence. Amazingly, one less than vigorous official argued that it was not worth the expense to bring in an outside investigator, as the diplomatic cyphers were, in his view, entirely safe and the Rome Embassy well knew how to handle sensitive documentation (Campbell to the Foreign Office, 10 March 1937, FO 371 21198, R187/224/92; O'Malley Minute, 11 March 1937, FO 371 21198, R187/224/92; Norton Minutes, 16 March 1937, 19 March 1937, FO 371 21198, R187/224/92; Campbell to the Foreign Office, 11 March 1937, FO 371 21198, R1688/224/92). Interestingly, an Italian spy with a diplomatic cover as a consular official in Paris reported in July

1937 that British agents had cracked Italian military and diplomatic cyphers. This claim was partially correct, but the Italian military apparently took little action to remedy the situation (Landini [Paris] to Luciano [Rome], 22 July 1937, NA, T586, r416, file 008738–40).

90. Franco to Mussolini, 3 August 1937, ASMAE, UC 46.

91. Processo Verbale, Riunione a Palazzo Venezia, 5 August 1937, ASMAE, UC 46; see also Ciano to Attolico, 6 August 1937, ASMAE, UC 46; and Colloquio tra il Capo di Gabinetto ed il Sottocapo di Stato Maggiore della Marina spagnola, 7 August 1937, US 2. There is considerable evidence to suggest that Italian submarines previously had torpedoed ships in the Mediterranean. One report mentions that Italian submarines had launched twenty-seven torpedoes by mid-February 1937 (Contributo della Regia Marina alle operazioni in Spagna, 18 February 1937, ASMAE, US 1; see also Contributo della Regia Marina alle operazioni O.M.S. dal 1 dicembre 1936 al 19 gennaio 1937, ACS, Segretaria Particolare del Duce, Carteggio Riservato, 72/463/R-6). Another file contains a letter sent to Ciano and forwarded from Ciano to Mussolini, suggesting that intelligence sources knew the rendezvous of a Soviet destroyer with a cargo ship carrying twenty-five tanks, thirty artillery pieces, four aircraft, and 200 Soviet military advisors. The Spanish Nationalist Embassy had asked the Italian government to order Italian submarines to torpedo the destroyer. The letter asked for special permission to carry out the attack, as Mussolini had previously ordered Italian submarines to suspend such attacks. Unfortunately, that file does not contain Mussolini's response to the request. (Appunto per S.E. Il Ministro, 18 March 1937, ASMAE, US 233). Another document implies that Mussolini had ordered the cessation of attacks on 18 February 1937 (Promemoria, 25 March 1937, US 19). For more information on Mussolini's orders for submarine attacks, see Franco Bargoni, *L'impegno navale italiano durante la guerra civile spagnola* (Rome: Ufficio Storico della Marina Militare, 1992), 209, 280–314.

92. Ismay (War Office) to Chamberlain, 18 August 1937, PREM 1/360; Meeting of Ministers, 17 August 1937, FO 371 21357, W15727/23/41.

93. For more on the origins of the conference, and, especially, the intelligence aspects, see Dilks, "Appeasement and 'Intelligence,'" 144–45; and Vice Admiral Sir P. Gretton, "The Nyon Conference—The Naval Aspect," *European History Review* 90 (1975): 103–12. The German Foreign Ministry informed the Italians that Britain had broken Italian naval cyphers, but Ciano appears to have taken no action in this regard (von Neurath to von Hassell, 12 September 1937, *DGFP*, ser. D, vol. 3, no. 418, 433).

94. *CHD*, 6 September 1937, 8 September 1937, 9–10.

95. For more detail on the Nyon conference, see Pratt, *East of Malta, West of Suez: Britain's Mediterranean Crisis,* 89–92; William C. Mills, "The Nyon Conference: Neville Chamberlain, Anthony Eden, and the Appeasement of Italy in 1937," *International History Review* 15, no. 1 (February 1993): 1–22.

96. Note by the Secretary of State at Geneva, 14 September 1937, AP 13/1/58M.

97. Eden to Chamberlain, 14 September 1937, PREM 1/360; Eden to the King, 23 September 1937, AP 13/1/58P. For more evidence of the British government's desire to prevent the Soviet Union from securing a role in naval patrols, see Grandi to Ciano, 30 January 1937, *DDI,* 8th ser., vol. 6, no. 103, 128–29.

98. Ciano to Grandi, Cerruti, and Viola (Salamanca), 19 September 1937, ASMAE, GAB 28.

99. *CHD,* 21 September 1937, 15.

100. Appunto per Sua Eccelenza il Ministro, 9 October 1937, ASMAE, US 2; Ciano to Viola, date missing, ASMAE, GAB 30; von Bülow-Schwante Memorandum, 2 October 1937, *DGFP,* D, 1, no. 2. The reaction of De Felice school historians to the Nyon Conference demonstrates some of the severe methodological weaknesses of the master and his adherents. Fortunato Minniti, for example, quoted De Felice that this minor setback represented "the blackest days for the regime since the time of the Matteoti crisis." Minniti argues, therefore, that the legitimate Italian fear of an Anglo-French attack made the dispatch of new troops to Libya and new aircraft to the Balearics entirely appropriate, "proportionate countermeasures." He did not, however, provide any direct evidence for this claim and confused the sequence and causality (Minniti, *Fino alla guerra,* 156; De Felice, *Lo Stato totalitario,* 430–44). De Felice did refer to a document that Ciano sent to Grandi dated 18 September 1937. This communication mentioned that Mussolini had decided to send three divisions to Libya in response to the crisis, but in reality that decision had been taken in April and aimed to intimidate the British and French governments. The letter also directly contradicts Minniti's assertion that the reinforcement of the Balearics was a precautionary measure against an Anglo-French attack. Ciano clearly wrote that the dispatch of planes to Majorca aimed to shift the burden of interdiction of neutral shipping to Republican Spain from submarine piracy on the open seas to less illegitimate aerial attacks in Spanish territorial waters. Ciano also said that Italian planes would conduct terror bombings of Spanish cities (Ciano to Grandi, 18 September 1937, ASMAE, UC 53; "389ᵃ Riunione del Consiglio dei Ministri," 10 April 1937, *OO,* vol. 28, 157–58). French intelligence information on the reinforcement of Libya also clearly contradicts Minniti's argument, correctly establishing that the Council of Ministers made the decision on 10 April 1937 (Daladier to Delbos, 4 October 1937, *DDF,* 2, 7, no. 17, 34–36).

101. Appunto per il Duce, 27 August 1937, ASMAE, GAB 26; Grandi to Ciano, 31 August 1937, ASMAE, SAP—Gran Bretagna, B 26. For the calculated use of Perth's family situation to delay having to treat with Italy, see Sargent to Perth, 28 August 1937, FO 371 21161, R5928/1/22; Perth to Sargent, 30 August 1937, FO 371 21161, R5928/1/22; Sargent Minute, 6 September 1937, FO 371 21161, R5928/1/22; Vansittart Minute, 7 September 1937, FO 371 21161, R5928/1/22.

102. Ciano to Vinci (Budapest), 2 August 1937, ASMAE, SAP—Ungheria, B 19.

103. Sola (Bucharest) to Ciano, 31 August 1937, ASMAE, SAP—Ungheria, B 19; Ciano to Attolico, Vinci (Budapest), and Sola (Bucharest), 11 September 1937, ASMAE, SAP—Ungheria, B 19; Bova Scoppa (Geneva) to Ciano, 17, 23 September 1937, ASMAE, SAP—Ungheria, B 19; Capece (Bucharest) to Ciano, 20 October 1937, ASMAE, SAP—Ungheria, B 19; von Hassell to von Neurath, 2 September 1937, *DGFP,* C, 6, no. 543, 1048–49.

104. Valdo Ferretti, "La politica estera italiana e il Giappone imperiale (gennaio 1934–giugno 1937," *Storia contemporanea* 10, no. 4/5 (October 1979): 921.

105. Auriti to Ciano, 5, 25 May 1937, ASMAE, SAP—Giappone, B 18; Auriti to Ciano, 3 June 1937, *DDI,* 8th ser., vol. 6, no. 689, 892–95; Auriti to Ciano, 7 June 1937, *DDI,* 8th ser., vol. 6, no. 702, 917.

106. Von Hassell to von Neurath, 26 May 1937, *DGFP,* C, 6, no. 38, 739–40.

107. Chiapparo to Ministero dell' Aeronautica and Ministero degli Affari Esteri, 6 June 1937, ASMAE, SAP, Giappone, B 18.

108. Hirota to Ciano, 3 July 1937, delivered 31 July 1937, ASMAE, UC 53, UC 84, GAB 26; *CDP,* 130–31.

109. For more on the various military and economic issues, as well as public opinion considerations, see Akira Iriye, *The Origins of World War II in Asia and the Pacific* (London: Longmans, 1987), 41–42; and Ferretti, *Il Giappone e la politica estera italiana, 1935–41,* 145–46.

110. Appunto per il Duce, ASMAE, GAB 26; Colloquio con l'ambasciatore di Giappone, 19 July 1936, ASMAE, UC 84. For more detail, see Michael R. Godley, "Fascismo e nazionalismo cinese, 1931–1938. Note preliminari allo studio dei rapporti italo-cinese durante il periodo fascista," *Storia contemporanea* 4, no. 4 (December 1973): 772–73.

111. For Mussolini's interest in Japanese imperialism and its search for raw materials, see his markings on Cora to Ciano, 5 May 1937, *DDI,* 8th ser., vol. 6, no. 555, 713–17.

112. Ciano to Grandi, 2 August 1937, ASMAE, UC 53; Grandi to Ciano, 5 August 1937, ASMAE, UC 53.

113. Ferretti, *Il Giappone e la politica estera italiana, 1935–41,* 166; see also Il Capitano di Vascello to Ciano, 30 September 1937, ASMAE, SAP—Giappone, B 18. For Auriti's perceptions of the complicated relationship between the Japanese parliament, the Gaimushō, and the various factions of the military, see Auriti to Ciano, 3 July 1937, ASMAE, SAP—Giappone, B 18.

114. Ciano to Consulato Shanghai, 26 August 1937, ASMAE, SAP—Cina, B 61; *CHD,* 23 August 1937, 27 August 1937, 3, 5.

115. *CHD,* 16 September 1937, 13.

116. Trautmann (Nanking) to von Neurath, 27 January 1937, *DGFP,* C, 6, no. 162, 341–50.

117. Dirksen (Tokyo) to von Neurath, 217 July 1937, *DGFP,* D, 1, no. 469, 740; von Neurath to Dirksen (Tokyo), 28 July 1937, *DGFP,* D, 1, no. 472, 742–44; von Neurath Memorandum, 17 August 1937, *DGFP,* D, 1, no. 4789, 750.

118. Von Hassell to von Weizsäcker, 1 October 1937, *DGFP,* C, 6, no. 568, 1086–89; von Neurath to all German Diplomatic Missions in Europe and to the Consulate General at Geneva, 30 September 1937, *DGFP,* D, 1, no. 1, 1–2.

119. *CHD,* 29 September 1937, 16.

120. Weinberg, *Starting World War II,* 281–83. Weinberg based his argument on part on Filippo Anfuso's memoirs. Though Anfuso's memoirs, like so many of those written by Italian participants in the events of the 1930s and 1940s are often tendentious, there is little reason to disbelieve Anfuso's argument; it did nothing to exonerate Anfuso in the eyes of an anti-Fascist postwar public (Filippo Anfuso, *Roma. Berlin. Salò. [1936–1945]* [Bologna: Capelli, 1957], 39–77). Mussolini's former mistress held a similar perception (Philip Cannistraro and Brian R. Sullivan, *Il Duce's Other Woman* [New York: Morrow, 1993], 504).

121. Ciano to Auriti, 3 October 1937, ASMAE, GAB 28.

122. *CHD,* 22 October 1937, 23–24. Appunto per il Duce, 20 October 1937, ASMAE, UC 53; Colloquio con l'ambasciatore di Giappone, 23 October 1937, ASMAE, UC 53.

123. L'accordo-italo-nippo-tedesco contro l'internazionale communista, 6 November 1937, ASMAE, SAP—Giappone, B 17, Ufficio no. 5, Segreto, N. 50. For a published English language version, see Protocol, 6 November 1937, *DGFP,* D, 1, no. 17, 26–27.

124. Mussolini to Vittorio Emmanuele, 4 October 1937, *OO,* vol. 42; *CHD,* 1 November 1937, 2 November 1937, 6 November 1937, 27, 28–29.

125. Colloquio Duce—Ciano—von Ribbentrop, 6 November 1937, ASMAE, UC 84; See also ASMAE, UC 46, though this copy is missing five pages.

126. Appunto per il Duce, 2 October 1937, ASMAE, GAB 26; Eden to Perth, 1 October 1937, FO 371 20781, E5804/872/91.

127. *CHD,* 9 October 1937, 15 October 1937, 19, 21.

128. Quoted in *CHD,* 2 September 1937, 78.

129. Ciano to Silliti (Gedda), 12 December 1937, ASMAE, GAB 202; Silliti (Gedda) to Ciano, 16 December 1937, ASMAE, GAB 202; Ciano to Thaon di Revel, 20 May 1938, ASMAE, GAB 202; Thaon di Revel to Ciano, 26 June 1938, ASMAE, GAB 202.

130. Quoted in *CHD,* 2 September 1937, 3 September 1937, 7–8, 8–9.

131. *CHD,* 14 October 1937, 20–s1.

132. Nichols Memorandum, 25 October 1937, FO 371 21162, R7339/1/22; Rendel Minute, 28 October 1937, FO 371 20819, E6462/22/31; Kelly (Cairo) to Eden, 27 October 1937, FO 371 20819, R6569/22/31. For an example of Eden's objections, see Cranborne Minute, Eden Minute, 16 November 1937, FO 371 21162, R7536/1/22; Lampson, 27 November 1937, FO 371 21163, R8100/1/22.

133. *CHD,* 28 October 1937, 29 October 1937, 11 November 1937, 12 November 1937, 25–26, 26, 31.

134. Leeper Minute, 6 November 1937, FO 371 21162, R7419/1/22.

135. Grandi to Ciano, 9 November 1937, ASMAE, Carte Grandi, B 40, fasc. 93/3.

136. Grandi to Ciano, 11 November 1937, ASMAE, UC 53.

137. Grandi to Ciano, 16 November 1937, ASMAE, Carte Grandi, B 66, fasc. 158/1, B. 40, fasc. 93/3.

138. Ciano to Grandi, 4 December 1937, ASMAE, Carte Grandi, B 66, fasc. 158/1, ASMAE, GAB 28; Eden conversation with Grandi, 2 December 1937, FO 371 21163, R799/1/22.

139. *CHD,* 24 December 1937, 48–49.

140. Ciano to Cerruti, 6 August 1937, ASMAE, US 229.

141. Ciano to Grandi, 17 October 1937, ASMAE, GAB 28.

142. Quoted in *CHD,* 11 October 1937, 12 October 1937, 31 October 1937, 17 November 1937, 19, 19–20, 27, 34.

143. Quoted in *CHD,* 25 October 1937, 22 November 1937, 24 November 1937, 25 November 1937, 24–25, 36, 36–37, 37, 11 December 1937, 43.

144. Blondel to Delbos, 9 December 1937, *DDF,* 2, 7, no. 326, 645–46.

145. Appunto per il Duce, Ciano to Auriti, 7 November 1937, ASMAE, GAB 26.

146. *CHD,* 7 November 1937, 12 November 1937, 14 November 1937, 16 November 1937, 29, 31, 32, 33. For more detail, see Ferretti, *Il Giappone e la politica estera italiana, 1935–41,* 192–99.

147. *CHD,* 14 November 1937, 25 November 1937, 26 November 1937, 28 November 1937, 32, 37, 37–38, 38–39; von Weizsäcker Memorandum, 20 November 1937, *DGFP,* D, 1, no. 523, 784–85; von Neurath Memorandum, 22 November 1937, *DGFP,* D, 1, no. 524, 785–86; Auriti to Ciano, 28, 30, November 1937, ASMAE, SAP—Giappone, B 17.

148. *CHD,* 28 November 1937, 1 December 1937, 38–39.

149. *CHD,* 25 December 1937, 49.

150. Auriti to Ciano, 22 November 1937, ASMAE, SAP—Giappone, B 17.

151. *CHD,* 26 December 1937, 49–50.

152. Ciano to Magistrati, 21 December 1937, ASMAE, UC 3. For more detail on Italy's withdrawal of its military mission in China, see Godley, "Fascismo e nazionalismo cinese, 1931–1938," 776, and Ferretti, *Il Giappone e la politica estera italiana, 1935–41,* 208–9.

153. Mallett, *The Italian Navy and Fascist Expansionism,* 109–10.

154. Mallett, *The Italian Navy and Fascist Expansionism,* 107–13; Ceva, *Storia delle forze armate in Italia,* 249–50.

CHAPTER 4

The Easter Accord and the Flourishing of the Axis

In early 1938, Mussolini and Ciano faced the threat of German annexation of Austria, as Hitler exploited Austrian Nazi agitation to further his pursuit of the Anschluss. He had outlined his desire to annex Austria the previous November in the infamous Hossbach memorandum, and thereafter German officials had repeatedly stressed that some form of German action against Austria was imminent. In an effort to accelerate potential action, Hitler's minister in Vienna, Franz von Papen, had arranged a meeting between Austrian Chancellor Kurt von Schuschnigg and the Führer to be held some time around the end of January. In preparing maneuvering room for this meeting, von Schuschnigg carried out two bold moves. He directed Austrian police to raid the Vienna headquarters of the Austrian National Socialists and arrested several Nazi members. Simultaneously, von Schuschnigg negotiated with Arthur Seyss-Inquart, whom the chancellor believed was both a less radical member of the party, and whatever his Fascist leanings, loyal to Austria. If von Schuschnigg could make an arrangement with Seyss-Inquart before meeting Hitler, then he could present a relatively calm domestic front, having alternately smashed extreme elements of the Austrian Nazis and brought others into the comparative fold of respectability. This plan was fatally flawed. Seyss-Inquart was not loyal to Austria, and he betrayed von Schuschnigg's proposed concessions to Hitler. Extraneous domestic German matters delayed the meeting between the two leaders, but when von Schuschnigg showed up at Berchtesgaden on 12 February, he faced a far different situation than he expected. Hitler demanded a set of concessions based on those that von Schuschnigg

had already given to Seyss-Inquart and created an aura of military ultimatum by summoning several senior military generals. Hitler's threats
worked, and von Schuschnigg capitulated, agreeing to implement Hitler's
demands within three days.[1]

Hitler's brinksmanship did not especially worry either Mussolini or
Ciano. As reports came in, they learned that Seyss-Inquart would control
the public security forces and the Austrian government would legalize the
Nazi Party and grant amnesty to certain of its members. Pellegrino Ghigi,
the Italian minister in Vienna, reported that the Austrian chancellor had
made these concessions in the face of Hitler's threats. With the Austrian
police under Nazi control, the initiative lay entirely in Hitler's hands. In
essence, Ghigi argued, von Schuschnigg had capitulated.[2] Ciano thought
that these events signaled the Nazification of Austria. Mussolini concurred.
The abrupt German move and the lack of notification did annoy Mussolini,
but he had long since forfeited control of the situation. As Ciano noted,
"The Anschluss is inevitable, the only thing to do is to delay the inevitable."[3]
Despite his private annoyance at Hitler's tactics, Mussolini supported the
deal in public. He issued "Informazione Diplomatica 15," an official declaration of Italian policy. He rejected the current opinion that von
Schuschnigg's concessions represented a defeat for Italy. They were
instead, he argued, a natural outgrowth of German, Italian, and Austrian
relations as established by the 11 July 1936 agreement that Italy had
approved. He condemned the "absurd" suggestions emanating from France
that Austria could do anything other than cooperate with Germany.[4]

Hitler did not stop there, and the following month he carried out another
of his foreign policy coups; he accomplished the Anschluss. In his efforts
to maintain Austrian independence, Chancellor Kurt von Schuschnigg had
made yet another critical error. At a meeting at Innsbruck on 9 March, he
announced a plebiscite to occur four days hence. Every Austrian voter
would have the chance to determine whether or not Austria would maintain its independence. Fully confident of victory, von Schuschnigg failed
to consider that Hitler would not allow a plebiscite to thwart his expansionist ambitions. On 11 March, the Führer sent a special envoy to deliver
his response to the Austrian government. This ultimatum called for the
immediate dismissal of von Schuschnigg's government and its replacement by a Seyss-Inquart administration, plus the cancellation of the
plebiscite. If von Schuschnigg failed to yield, then the *Wehrmacht* would
invade. The Austrian military had taken only minor steps to prevent any
attack, so von Schuschnigg appealed to foreign governments to help him
stave off Hitler's threatened attack.[5]

The Austrian chancellor's appeals to Mussolini fell on deaf ears. Two weeks before, Mussolini had determined Italian policy if faced with this eventuality. A memorandum dated 27 February and signed by Mussolini laid out the strategic situation that required Italian acquiescence in the Anschluss. The first consideration was that Mussolini preferred Austria to be independent. The same conditions that had previously guided Italian policy still existed. It was better to avoid having the weight of 70 million Germans on Italy's northern border, and an independent Austria would help to prevent German irredentism in the Alto Adige. Despite Mussolini's preference, however, Austria was undeniably a German state, and any attempt to steer a course independent of Germany could provoke Hitler to hasten the Anschluss. Moreover, Italian interest in Austrian independence was worth neither a war in its defense nor "still less the revolution of our political position in our relations with Germany." Mussolini would not sacrifice the Axis and his revisionist goals in order to defend Austria. Accordingly, the best that he could do was to ensure that the Anschluss did not appear to be an Italian defeat and at the same time try not to provoke a hostile Germany on Italy's northern frontier. Well before the Anschluss, therefore, Mussolini had determined that Italy would rather meekly accept this accretion of German power.[6]

Mussolini had limited forewarning of the Anschluss. On 5 March, Attolico had sent a report from the air attaché at the Berlin Embassy. Colonel Teucci reported recent discussions with Hermann Göring and State Secretary Erhard Milch. In their view, Austria had become an entirely German issue. The Führer had decided, they said, that any interference by other countries would lead to war. Attolico concluded that Hitler believed that he had carte blanche to deal with Austria on his own terms and timetable.[7] Mussolini learned of von Schuschnigg's planned plebiscite on 7 March. The Austrian minister in Rome had no direct access to Mussolini, as the Duce no longer held the official portfolio of minister of foreign affairs. Consequently, von Schuschnigg ordered his military attaché in Rome, Colonel Emilio Liebitzky, to see Mussolini in the latter's official capacity as minister of war. Liebitzky informed the Duce of von Schuschnigg's planned plebiscite. Mussolini, confident of Göring's assurances of January and September 1937 that Germany would not move against Austria without first informing the Duce, was not overly worried. He cautioned against the radical step that von Schuschnigg planned and gave no commitment of support.[8]

On 10 and 11 March, Mussolini and Ciano learned of the escalating danger of the situation. As Ciano noted in his diary, the plebiscite bomb was exploding in von Schuschnigg's hands. Reports flowed in about German military preparations for an invasion of Austria, but Mussolini took no steps to preserve Austrian independence. With von Schuschnigg's resignation at 6:00 P.M., Ciano concluded that Austria had ceased to exist.[9] At 9:00 that evening, the Prince of Hesse asked to see Ciano. Both men went to see the Duce at the Palazzo Venezia. Hesse bore a letter from the Führer explaining recent events. Hitler cited von Schuschnigg's plebiscite plan as a direct violation of the German-Austrian accord of 1936. More importantly, Hitler gave Mussolini a solemn and precise declaration guaranteeing the Brenner frontier and an assurance of German support in future Italian endeavors. When Hesse informed the Führer of Mussolini's acquiescence, Hitler asked his messenger to tell Mussolini, "I will never forget this."[10] Through official channels the next day, Magistrati confirmed the preceding language, but in even more effusive terms. "The Führer and Nazi Germany will never forget what il Duce has done this day." Hitler further promised to prevent any problems raised by the ethnic German residents of the Alto Adige.[11]

Hitler's assurances both belied and indicated the extent to which the Anschluss represented a serious setback for Italy. At the Fascist Grand Council on 12 March, the day that Hitler's troops carried out their occupation, the Fascist hierarch Italo Balbo criticized Hitler's policy. Mussolini quickly squelched this incipient opposition.[12] He tried to put the best face on the Anschluss; he wrote to Hitler assuring the German dictator that "my attitude is determined by the friendship between our two countries as consecrated in the Axis." In a speech two days later to the rubber-stamp Chamber of Deputies, Mussolini sought to minimize the importance of Hitler's coup. Mussolini spoke of the long decline in Austrian power. The rise of Hitler had led to Mussolini's temporary flirtation with the Stresa Front, but British and French hostility had prevented any genuine cooperation between Fascist Italy and the West. Accordingly, Mussolini had agreed at the April 1937 meeting in Venice that Austrian independence would be a fundamental concession to the Axis and that Austrians would have to maintain their own independence in future. Mussolini trumpeted the "categorical" guarantee from Hitler regarding the immutability of the Brenner frontier. With considerable bragadoccio, he said that "for we Fascists frontiers, all frontiers, are sacred. We don't discuss them: we defend them." Finally, the Duce condemned the false hopes of international communism and the Western democracies that the Anschluss would break Axis solidarity; such hopes, he argued, were "simply puerile." Axis policy, he concluded, was both united and parallel.[13] Though this speech contained a certain amount of bravado, it represented elements of continuing Italian policy. Ciano summed up the unpleasant realities in his diary in the immediate aftermath.

To-day all is calm again. The fatal event has reached its conclusion. It has not been pleasant for us—far from it. But one day the world will realize that all this was inevitable. The Duce says that one ambiguity has been removed from the map of Europe. And he enumerates three others still in existence, which will, in his opinion, one after the other and in the following order, have to go the same way: Czechoslovakia, Switzerland, and Belgium.

Mussolini apparently failed to understand the extent to which these hypothetical changes would increase relative German strength within the Axis at the expense of Italy. Ciano concluded that "German friendship is a fatality, oppressive perhaps, but very real."[14] Mussolini's perceived need for German friendship had led him to sacrifice Austrian independence, for years a cardinal element of Italian policy, on the altar of Axis solidarity.

Mussolini's actions during the Anschluss demonstrated the extent to which he had estranged himself from the Western democracies and tied himself to the rising power of Nazi Germany. Both the British and French governments had made last-ditch attempts to coordinate policy with Italy during the crisis. On 11 March, Jules Blondel, the French chargé d'affaires, had phoned Ciano to request an urgent meeting. Blondel said that he had received instructions from his government to ask Italy to join an Anglo-French appeal to von Schuschnigg to resist Hitler's ultimatum. Ciano had emphatically and rudely rejected this démarche, saying that he and Mussolini did not "intend to associate ourselves with France and England in regard to Austria." Ciano had cited French support for sanctions and its nonrecognition of Ethiopia as preventing any cooperation in resisting the Anschluss. He had argued that if Blondel had nothing more to say, then he might as well not bother appearing. Given this sharp rebuff, Perth had thought it inopportune to follow his orders to seek a meeting with Mussolini. He had interceded to have these orders canceled and had not pursued the Austrian question at his meeting with Ciano on 12 March.[15] Despite the ongoing Anglo-Italian negotiations, therefore, there was no realistic prospect of resurrecting the Stresa Front in defense of Austria. Mussolini's faithfulness to the Axis and his acquiescence in the Anschluss had made any French or British intervention futile.

Still, despite Mussolini's commitment to the Axis and his break with West, the Anschluss did require some relatively minor adjustments in Italian policy, primarily in the Danube basin. At the beginning of 1938, Ciano had continued his attempt to create tighter relations between the Rome Protocol powers of Hungary, Austria, and Italy in advance of an imminent meeting in Budapest. He had sent a draft agreement to both Rome Protocol governments regarding tighter adherence by both Vienna and Budapest to the principles of the Axis and the anti-Comintern Pact. This démarche reflected Mussolini's concern that both governments failed to be sufficiently grateful for Italian friendship. Though both Austria and Hungary feared German encroachment in the Balkans, neither would align themselves too tightly to Mussolini's Italy, as neither wanted to foreclose their relations with the West. The Austrian foreign minister wanted a firm declaration of Italian support for continued independence in the face of Germany, an assurance that Ciano could not give. The Hungarian Foreign Minister Kálmán de Kánya hoped for Italian support of Hungarian revisionism regarding the substantial Magyar minority populations in Rumania and Yugoslavia. Ciano refused, as he did not want to alienate Prime Minister Stoyadinović of Yugoslavia. Ciano used Italy's diplomatic muscle to secure an anodyne agreement, but he concluded that the Rome Protocols had become "impotent."[16] The Anschluss effectively dissolved the Rome Protocols, signaling the need for a renewed Italian diplomatic initiative in the Balkans.

Ciano reassured himself that Italo-Yugoslav relations remained strong. In a 13 March meeting with Bosko Cristić, the Yugoslav minister in Rome, Ciano had recalled his past meetings with Stoyadinović in which he had stated that the Italo-Yugoslav pact of March 1937 foresaw increased German power after the Anschluss. Italy's horizontal axis with Yugoslavia would help to counterbalance German domination of the official vertical Axis. Ciano informed Cristić that after an appropriate time, Italy and Yugoslavia would have to reinforce their previous agreement, though tighter relations with Yugoslavia would of course be subordinate to those of Germany.[17]

Against the backdrop of the Anschluss, negotiations toward a second Anglo-Italian agreement speeded up in large measure owing to developments in the Austrian question. Mussolini and Ciano had continued to hope for an agreement with Britain, though still on their own disingenuous terms of the previous autumn. The Anglo-Italian deadlock started to break in early January 1938. Perth saw Ciano on 3 January to indicate Britain's reconsideration of the Italian demand for de jure recognition of the Ethiopian conquest. Such discussion represented an advance over the British position after the Nyon affair, which had excluded the possibility of such recognition.[18] Perth's careful words reflected the division within the British cabinet. Chamberlain hoped to be able to reach an agreement that would neither grant recognition without conditions nor appear to be a corrupt bargain. He wanted instead a spirit of general reconciliation that would settle outstanding issues. Senior Foreign Office officials generally agreed with Chamberlain's view regarding the necessity of granting de jure recognition. It was necessary to gain some concessions for this one card that Britain still held. Eden disagreed, however, arguing that Mussolini was a "complete gangster and his pledged word mean[t] nothing."[19]

In order to outmaneuver Eden and the foreign secretary's resistance to his policy, Chamberlain continued to work through his secret channel to Grandi. On 10 January, Chamberlain's representative, Sir Joseph Ball, contacted Dingli, conveying a sense of great urgency. Ball informed the intermediary that if the Italians would agree to open conversations in London, then Ball could guarantee that Chamberlain would override Eden's objections. Such discussions would have no preconditions and would have the widest possible latitude. In essence, this démarche conceded the bulk of Italian demands, with the sole exception that Mussolini and Ciano both had maintained their insistence that any talks would have to occur in Rome. Dingli duly informed Guido Crolla, the chargé d'affaires in the London Embassy. Crolla, however, did not know where Ambassador Grandi could be found, and he did not want to telephone Rome; he understood that the embassy's phone calls were monitored by British intelligence, and he could not let the secret channel be compromised. Eventually (and ironically) Crolla tracked Grandi to the Hotel Eden in Rome and arranged to send a cipher telegram to Grandi's attention at the Foreign Ministry. In order to give greater impetus to the démarche, Ball confirmed to Dingli on 14 January that his proposal came from Chamberlain himself. After his return to London, Grandi attempted first to arrange to see Chamberlain alone. Foiled once more by the demands of protocol, Grandi tried to arrange a meeting with both Eden and Chamberlain together. Ball assisted this endeavor, having Chamberlain approve a draft note for Grandi to submit to Eden. The foreign secretary skillfully thwarted this attempt at an end run and summoned Grandi instead for a face-to-face meeting.[20]

At his unwanted meeting with Eden on 19 January, Grandi found a cold reception, with the foreign secretary emphasizing the difficulty of talks that would consider de jure recognition of the Italian empire. Afterward, Grandi wrote to Ciano that, owing in part to Eden's obduracy, negotiations with Britain offered an unusual opportunity. Grandi had believed for several months that Eden's anti-Italian attitudes betrayed an attempt to usurp Chamberlain's prime ministership. Eden needed to prevent an Anglo-Italian rapprochement in order to maintain standing with a left-leaning block in Parliament that would form the basis for a new government. Accordingly, an Italian policy of seeking an agreement while maintaining diplomatic and strategic pressure in other ways would outflank Eden. In particular, Grandi argued, the presence of the otherwise needlessly large Libyan garrison created great fear for the safety of Egypt in the British general staff. This perceived need for an agreement would compel Chamberlain to reach a settlement on relatively favorable terms for Italy—both to preserve Britain's Mediterranean position and to diminish Eden's political influence.[21]

While Grandi plotted against Eden, the British cabinet debated whether or not to pursue discussions with Italy. President Roosevelt's appeal to diminish world tension by establishing agreed principles of international law and order had complicated this debate. The President's vague plan had four main points: to establish essential principles of international behavior, to limit armaments, to allow equal access of the world's population to raw materials, and to determine the rights and duties of governments in time of war. In addition, Roosevelt had raised the potentially difficult issue of the alleged inequities of the Versailles treaty and had spoken of the traditional freedom from European involvement of the United States. He had sent this rather uninspiring and likely quixotic proposal first to the British government to secure its approval. In Eden's temporary absence, Chamberlain had dealt with this proposal without referring it first to his foreign secretary, as protocol normally demanded. The prime minister feared that this proposal would prevent the opening of Anglo-Italian talks—either it would offend the dictators with its implicit criticism of their bad behavior or would take precedence over direct talks with Italy. Sir Ronald Lindsay, the British ambassador in Washington, while supporting the President's initiative, confirmed that Roosevelt would not insist on carrying through his démarche if Chamberlain decided to pursue direct Anglo-Italian talks. Eden disagreed with Chamberlain's thinking and actions. He thought that the need for Anglo-American cooperation outweighed any agreement with Mussolini. By 20 January, Chamberlain decided on a compromise; he would pursue talks with Italy while at the same time offering qualified support for Roosevelt's plan in an effort not to alienate Roosevelt. He still thought that plan would prove futile, but he too did not want to alienate American opinion. Given lukewarm British support and changed conditions owing to German government restructuring, Roosevelt eventually dropped the plan, clearing the field for Chamberlain's preferred policy. The episode, however, had signaled a clear breach between Chamberlain and Eden.[22]

In the aftermath of Eden's 19 January meeting with Grandi, Chamberlain expressed his frustration at the slow pace of discussions. Still working through Joseph Ball and Adrian Dingli, Chamberlain assured the Italian ambassador that he still intended to meet with Grandi as soon as Eden returned from the League Meeting at Geneva. If Grandi thought that conditions were so desperate that he needed an immediate meeting with Chamberlain, then the prime minister would gladly oblige, despite the consequences of this obvious usurpation of Eden's position. Chamberlain preferred to wait, however, because he thought it wiser to secure the foreign secretary's approval rather than to provoke an incident that might lead Eden to resign. Chamberlain asked Grandi to "hold the fort" for the near future. Grandi concurred, though he chafed at the delay. Chamberlain later promised to arrange the meeting as soon as possible after Eden's return on 30 January 1938.[23]

After Eden's return, he summoned Grandi, but the meeting covered only technical matters arising from the torpedoing of a British ship, the *Endymion*.[24] On 5 February, Grandi submitted Ciano's agreement with Eden's request for tighter Mediterranean patrols under the Nyon agreement. This apparent Italian concession, which Ciano brushed off as "simply a waste of time," somewhat mollified Eden's anti-Italian rancor. More importantly, in Grandi's view, recent German rebuffs of Eden's attempts at a rapprochement were proving a frustration. Consequently, Eden discussed at that meeting possible conditions for opening Anglo-Italian talks.[25] The next day, Grandi and Eden discussed once more possible recognition of the empire. Eden cordially suggested that both he and the prime minister shared the same policy and would consider de jure recognition of the Ethiopian context as part of any negotiations. He referred to Spain and Italy's continuing participation in the Spanish Civil War as the primary outstanding issue between Britain and Italy. Eden expected to be able to reach an accommodation with Italy provided that Mussolini was willing to make concessions regarding nonintervention. Despite the primacy of the Spanish issue, however, Eden also mentioned other issues remaining from the gentlemen's agreement of 2 January 1937. Grandi replied that he thought that none of these issues would prove difficult.[26] A few days later, Dingli and Ball communicated Chamberlain's express desire that Grandi should help to smooth conclusion of any talks by convincing Mussolini to reduce tensions in Spain. This information convinced Grandi that the imminent negotiations essentially would trade British recognition of the Ethiopian conquest for Italian concessions in Spain.[27]

On 8 February, Grandi spoke once more with Eden. Eden raised Italian-sponsored anti-British propaganda as another of the important elements of the tension between the two countries. Grandi refused to consider this issue as a precondition for any negotiations, as the British government had suggested in the past. He further denied that Italian propaganda caused any tension between Italy and Britain; rather disingenuously, Grandi argued that this propaganda barrage merely reflected the already existing tension. Eden replied to Grandi's claims by stating that he merely wanted the Italian ambassador to know that the cessation of propaganda would have to be an important element of the talks, not a precondition. This exchange of views further narrowed the number of outstanding issues.[28]

The same day, Ciano cabled Mussolini's formal approval for Grandi to inform Eden that the Italian government was ready to initiate talks at any time. Mussolini's minimum conditions were that any discussions would have to be general, cover all outstanding issues, and definitively recognize the Italian conquest of Ethiopia. The negotiations would have to take place in Rome. Ciano further instructed Grandi that he should present this démarche in such a manner to convince Eden that Italy was not at all anxious to reach an accord at any price; in Ciano's words, the Fascist government was "not ready to throw ourselves at the first offer." Ciano also wrote that he ascribed Eden's apparent change of heart entirely to German snubs of British approaches; in particular, he believed that the appointment of Joachim von Ribbentrop as German foreign minister indicated a clear rebuff of British efforts to appease Germany. Eden, failing to weaken the Axis in Germany, was trying the same gambit on the Italian end. Ciano, however, was unwilling to allow that maneuver to succeed.[29] In his diary, he noted that he would remain loyal to the Axis; he believed that any Anglo-Italian agreement would carry few onerous Italian commitments.[30]

As potential negotiations inched forward in London, Lady Ivy Chamberlain, the widow of Sir Austen Chamberlain, unwittingly furthered the tension between Eden and Neville Chamberlain. She and her husband had met Mussolini on several occasions during Sir Austen's tenure as foreign secretary. She was sympathetic to Italian Fascism and admired Mussolini. On 1 February 1938, she met Mussolini at Ciano's initiative. Mussolini inquired as to whether or not she had received a letter from Neville Chamberlain, and if so, whether he could see it. This letter, almost certainly opened and read by Italian intelligence authorities, stated that the British prime minister expected to have negotiations well in hand by the end of February. Lady Chamberlain also told Mussolini that the cabinet was coming round to the idea of formal recognition of the Italian empire. Mussolini readily encouraged this view. He dictated a five-point memorandum that Lady Chamberlain would send to her brother-in-law, indicating the Duce's desire for a comprehensive agreement.[31] Eden learned of this informal diplomacy roughly a week later and sent a note to Neville Chamberlain protesting this end run around his department. The foreign secretary argued, in retrospect correctly, that Lady Chamberlain's actions helped to create the view in Mussolini's mind that he could ignore any conditions that Eden might impose for the opening of conversations and could divide Eden and Chamberlain over the question. Eden asked the prime minister to instruct Lady Chamberlain not to see Mussolini in future. Chamberlain complied but thought that she had caused little harm. He also wrote to Eden that Britain "should not appear so reticent that we do not want to open conversations at all."[32] Unquestionably, however, Lady Chamberlain's diplomacy helped to further the divide between prime minister and foreign secretary by undermining the latter's authority.

In February, Hitler's increasing threat to Austrian independence gave added impetus to Italian efforts to sign an accord with Britain. To that point, Grandi had shown much greater urgency in pushing for talks than the reticent Ciano. The need to counterbalance Germany's moves toward Austria pushed Ciano to speak to Mussolini regarding the Anglo-Italian conversations. After securing Mussolini's approval, Ciano cabled Grandi to say that he considered all of the issues between the two countries initially explored. With the exception of the withdrawal of volunteers and the recognition of belligerency rights for Franco in Spain, currently under consideration through the nonintervention process, Ciano was ready to open negotiations on Eden's already proposed conditions.[33] He also informed Perth of his orders to Grandi, referring obliquely to "certain future happenings."[34] The following day, Ciano spelled out the reasons for his new urgency. German plans for the Anschluss were well in hand, he wrote to Grandi, and could occur at any time. When the Germans eventually would act, Germany's massive population on Italy's northern border would potentially foreclose the option of dealing with Great Britain. In that eventuality, world opinion might see an Italian rapprochement with Britain as "going to Canossa" under German pressure. "It is not that the Duce is more anxious today than yesterday to seize the hand of the English," Ciano wrote, but after the Anschluss, "we would have to orient our policy definitively in a clear, open, immutable sense of hostility to the Western Powers." In short, the proposed agreement with Britain was a tactical device to secure maneuvering room and to resist the increasing tide of German strength within the bounds of the Axis partnership. Securing

Britain's recognition of Italy's Ethiopian conquest was a goal in its own right, but any Anglo-Italian agreement would not reorient Italian policy away from the Axis or from its expansionist aims.[35]

Hilter's ultimatum to Austria had also increased Chamberlain's urgency to open negotiations for an Anglo-Italian Accord. Chamberlain, and European diplomats generally, believed that this arrangement was the only possible hope for Italy, and by extension the other powers, to preserve Austrian independence.[36] Consequently, Chamberlain arranged through Ball and Dingli to hold, at long last, the face-to-face meeting between the prime minister and Grandi. Eden resisted this move, arguing that he had not been able to clarify the Italian position regarding Spain. Further, he did not like "'now or never' threats." Chamberlain reacted angrily, accusing Eden of missing "chance after chance" to secure an agreement with Italy. Still, Eden refused to commit to negotiations "until we have time to go into all of the implications." Eden summoned Grandi, but the ambassador demurred, waiting for the hoped-for meeting where the prime minister would also be present. Chamberlain intervened through his secret channel and finally arranged a three-party meeting for the morning of 18 February 1938.[37]

This momentous discussion met certain of its participants' expectations. In Grandi's lengthy, almost gleeful report, he wrote to Ciano of his personal triumph. Chamberlain had begun by pushing hard to determine the Italian government's attitude toward events in Austria. Grandi refused to be drawn, as per Ciano's instructions. To Chamberlain's charge that Mussolini and Hitler had had a secret agreement regarding Austria, Grandi counterattacked. The Anglo-French sanctions policy had ruptured the Stresa Front and had made Mussolini's policy of defending Austria much more difficult, but Mussolini had not as yet made any agreement with Germany. In the future, however, the Duce's attitude would depend on that of His Majesty's government. British hostility to Italy had prevented any agreement that would have allowed Mussolini greater latitude in defending Austrian independence. Only the immediate initiation of negotiations in Rome leading to British recognition of the Italian empire could ensure that Italy did not throw itself into Hitler's embrace. This discourse emphasized the division between Eden and Chamberlain. The foreign secretary replied that, in current conditions, Britain could not undertake any negotiations that would lead to recognition of Italian sovereignty over Ethiopia. After Grandi delivered a long speech complaining of British hostility toward Italy in Spain, Chamberlain intervened. He was fired by the pressing need to reach accommodation with one of Britain's potential enemies in order to remove some of the strategic and economic pressure owing to the Fascist challenge. Accordingly, he contradicted Eden and declared that Britain was ready to begin negotiations that would include formal British recognition of the empire, plus a general accord between Italy and Great Britain. The morning conversation finished with Eden demanding an a priori quid pro quo in Spain; Mussolini would have to agree to a withdrawal program under the auspices of the nonintervention committee. Chamberlain notably failed to pick up on Eden's proposal. With that, the talks broke off for lunch and consultations between Chamberlain and his foreign minister.[38]

The talks resumed at 3:00 P.M. that afternoon between Chamberlain and Grandi, with Eden's absence signaling to Grandi the growing chasm between the two British ministers. According to Grandi's narrative, Chamberlain openly contradicted his foreign minister's view on withdrawal of volunteers of that morning. Chamberlain wanted an immediate declaration that talks would begin without preconditions, but that Italy would have to be prepared to address the withdrawal of volunteers during any negotiations—an important caveat that would allow conversations to begin in the immediate future. Grandi rejected this sally, arguing that his government could not accept this plan owing to the taint of Soviet and French membership of the nonintervention committee. If that point represented British policy, then Mussolini would think that Chamberlain had little interest in reaching an accord. At that stage, the meeting broke up, with the essential question of the repatriation of Italian volunteers as the only significant outstanding question, though the location of the negotiations was still a side issue. Chamberlain arranged to meet Grandi three days hence to give the cabinet's formal reply. Grandi characterized Chamberlain's and Eden's behavior in the morning as "two enemies" with a "combative attitude." Afterward, Grandi met Ball in a taxi, and Ball conveyed Chamberlain's personal thanks for the meeting. In addition, Chamberlain sent a message to Grandi through Ball and Dingli asking the Italian ambassador to try to ensure that his government meet Chamberlain's requirements as much as possible during the negotiations. In his lengthy, official report of the day's events, Grandi further defined his theory that Eden's stance reflected an attempt to unseat Chamberlain as prime minister. In Grandi's view, Eden was "an implacable enemy of Fascism and of Italy." The foreign secretary sought to exploit his disagreement with Chamberlain over negotiations with Italy to appeal to British public opinion. "Eden has the man in the street with him," Grandi argued, "or rather the historic wild beast trapped inside a large part of the British people, the left, anti-fascists and French

Masonry, that see in him the head of a future British Popular Front."[39] Grandi believed that the long-hoped-for showdown between Chamberlain and Eden was at hand.

Against this background of Italian intrigue, Eden and Chamberlain continued their disagreement at a cabinet meeting the next day, held on a Saturday in a highly unusual break with tradition. The two British protagonists laid out their differences for the cabinet. Chamberlain argued that the cabinet's general policy called for better relations with both Italy and Germany, while in fact relations with both countries appeared to be worsening. Military weakness and the burden of rearmament compelled an agreement with Italy. Mussolini distrusted British rearmament, but Hitler's recent maneuvers in Austria must have annoyed Mussolini, who was looking to end his relative isolation. Eden disagreed with this appreciation. He wanted proof of Mussolini's change of heart, if it had occurred at all, for Eden did not think that it had. Mussolini had replied to sanctions with the declaration of the Rome-Berlin Axis, the gentlemen's agreement with the dispatch of troops to Spain, and, Eden suspected, had already cut a deal with Hitler over Austria. Grandi's recent moves represented little more than blackmail. In this situation, Eden argued, granting de jure recognition of the Italian empire represented surrender, and he would not do so without prior, substantive gestures of good will. With only minor exceptions, the cabinet supported Chamberlain's view, even to the point of opening negotiations without receiving assurances from Grandi regarding the necessity for eventual withdrawal of volunteers. Eden said that he would not be able to carry forward that policy and suggested that the cabinet find another foreign minister to do so. With that ultimatum, the cabinet adjourned until 3:00 P.M. on Sunday, while in the meantime a special cabinet committee sought to bridge the gap between Chamberlain and Eden, although to no avail.[40]

In the meantime, Grandi sent his report of the previous day's meeting to Ciano and sparked both considerable elation and some panic in the Italian foreign minister and in Mussolini himself. Perth had called on Ciano the same day to protest forcefully Italian border violations in East Africa. At the end of December 1937, Captain R. C. R. Whalley had discovered an Italian garrison at Kangilamoru, some twenty-five miles across the Sudanese border. The Italian officer in charge, Captain Vigna, consulted his superiors only to receive orders prohibiting his withdrawal. Similarly, an Italian garrison had violated the Kenyan border.[41] In light of Grandi's news, Ciano believed that Perth's strong protest, normally handled at a lower level, signaled Eden's desperate attempt to derail conversations.

Ciano concluded, therefore, that Chamberlain had been victorious in the internecine struggle. Grandi's report confirmed that view.

With victory in sight, however, Mussolini and Ciano lost their nerve. News of Eden's resignation during the cabinet meetings on 20 February sparked fears that the situation might lead to war. Grandi's previous misrepresentations of Eden's power and ambitions within the cabinet misled his superiors; Ciano believed that Eden could both form a cabinet and lead a crusade against the dictators. Accordingly, he decided to support Chamberlain as much as possible in order to prevent the formation of a hostile cabinet. Ciano dampened the gloating in the Fascist press at Eden's downfall. More importantly, he granted a major concession to Chamberlain. In a telephone call to London during the night of 20–21 February, Ciano instructed Grandi to concede Chamberlain's demands regarding the necessity for negotiating the withdrawal of volunteers from Spain as part of the implementation of any agreement. This seemingly minor change, an unnecessary effort to prop up Chamberlain's position in the cabinet, eventually would lead to the several-months delay in entrance into force of the resulting Easter Accord.[42]

At long last, on 21 February, the parties agreed on the opening of negotiations. Grandi met Chamberlain to deliver Ciano's concession regarding the acceptance of the principle of the withdrawal of Italian volunteers. Chamberlain insisted that this point was an essential aspect of any agreement. He would make any agreement contingent not only on withdrawal of Italian volunteers, but also on the basis that Mussolini would dispatch no more troops. With that issue settled, Grandi and Chamberlain agreed that they would announce the opening of negotiations. Grandi assured Chamberlain that British policy would give Mussolini much greater leverage in dealing with Germany over the Austrian question and submitted his government's formal approval of negotiations at 4:00 that afternoon.[43] Grandi wrote that the resignations of Eden and Cranborne did not seem to be sparking a Parliamentary rebellion and that Chamberlain should survive any no-confidence vote with a large majority. The way forward to an agreement seemed clear.[44]

The tortuous road to the opening of conversations demonstrates the serious gulf between Italian and British aims. Chamberlain hoped that an eventual Anglo-Italian agreement could bolster Mussolini's stand against the Anschluss and could perhaps wean Italy from its tight relations with its German Axis partner. Against a variety of issues, including Italy's large Libyan garrison, Italian involvement in Spain, anti-British propaganda, and Italian moves in the Middle East, Britain had only one arrow in its proverbial quiver—de jure recognition of Mussolini's Ethiopian conquest. Once given, the cabinet could not retract this concession. Still, facing the constellation of Italy, Germany, and Japan, the Chamberlain government hoped to be able to separate at least one of these potential enemies. The proof of Mussolini's sincere desire for Anglo-Italian amity would come in his faithfulness to the intentions declared during the maneuvering to secure negotiations. If he resisted the Anschluss, ceased anti-British propaganda, decreased the Libyan garrison, lessened his effort in Spain, and respected the Mediterranean status quo ante, then one could reasonably suppose that Mussolini desired only parity with Britain and to use Italy's position between Germany and Britain as the *peso determinante*—the decisive weight. Unfortunately, a series of other issues concurrent with and following these diplomatic preparations for negotiations betrayed Mussolini's real intentions.

Even while negotiating the commencement of talks with Britain, however, Mussolini and Ciano continued to work against British interests in the Far East, the Red Sea, and the Mediterranean. Ciano's dealings with a shipment of armored cars to his former Chinese Nationalist associates provide one tragicomic example of Italian enmity toward Britain. Given his rapid and unceremonious rupturing of relations with the Chinese Nationalist government during 1937, Ciano found himself in a potentially embarrassing position. The *Ischia,* an Italian registered ship, was carrying fifty Italian armored cars bound for the Chinese Nationalist army. Ciano gave its position to the Japanese government so that it could intercept the shipment, preventing the Italian government from delivering arms to be used against its putative ally. The Japanese military, fearing international complications from this sort of piracy, demurred. Ciano noted that Mussolini, who intended "to make of the Japanese military allies against Great Britain," would not contemplate the presumed affront of arming Japan's enemy, and demanded that his foreign minister prevent the *Ischia's* arrival. Mussolini approved of Ciano's plan simply to have the ship run aground on the island of Hainan, but the *Ischia's* owners protested, wisely citing the potential blow to the prestige of Italian seamanship. Faced with the Japanese refusal to board or to sink the *Ischia,* and having received Japanese permission to land the arms shipment, Ciano had to content himself with the thought that fifty armored cars would hardly turn the tide of battle. The next day, Ciano dispatched the Marchese Giacomo Paulucci de Carboli to Japan as the head of the Fascist Party's mission in Tokyo. Ciano thought that Paulucci, a staunch opponent of the League of Nations and an Anglophobe, would get on well with like-minded Japanese leaders.[45]

In a more serious vein, Ciano held a dinner at the Villa Madama to honor Baron Okura, the Japanese military attaché in Rome. Ciano spoke of the common bond between the Japanese military and the Italian government. Both countries resented British tutelage, and both hoped for eventual gains at the expense of the British empire. Accordingly, Ciano thought the time opportune to sign a bilateral Italo-Japanese agreement covering benevolent neutrality in time of war and a tighter cooperation between the two countries. Ciano, citing the lesser enthusiasm of the Gaimushō to European entanglements, hoped to work through the Japanese military to achieve this goal. Okura refused to be drawn on this informal proposal, as he had no authority to pursue it. Eventually, after it circulated through Japan's diplomatic corps in Europe, the Japanese ambassador in Berlin submitted this démarche to his government, and it later formed the basis for the newly shuffled Konoe cabinet's response to Italy in May.[46]

Mussolini's policy in the Middle East also threatened British interests. Early in January, Ciano had dispatched Count Serafino Mazzolini as the Italian minister to the nominally independent government of Egypt. Mazzolini's duty was to study ways to use the Italian community in Egypt in the event of war with Great Britain. Ciano wanted Mazzolini to prepare groups to foment rebellion and to carry out military sabotage in the Suez Canal zone. Fearing possible British interception of cables from Egypt, Ciano wanted Mazzolini to report only in person. Obviously, if the British intelligence services learned of this hostile mission, it could rupture Anglo-Italian relations.[47] Simultaneously, the Italian mission in Sanaa in Yemen, allegedly there to improve Yemeni sanitation, negotiated with anti-British local forces led by Sheik Ali el Hamdani for a major shipment of weapons, including four batteries of medium artillery and 10,000 rifles. This shipment was part of the mission's objective of "orienting and developing Yemeni internal politics" toward a tighter association with Italy. Ciano hoped that, if successful, the Italian mission might be able to create an Italian protectorate or friendly government. This association would both undermine the British position with Ibn Saud in the Arabian Peninsula to the North and establish Italian bases on both sides of the Red Sea, thus allowing Italy to dominate one exit of the Suez Canal. This mission represented a potentially serious threat to British imperial communications.[48]

In addition, Mussolini's forces pursued victory in Spain with a reckless disregard for British concerns. As the new year began, Italian planes participated in the bombing of Barcelona, which had little aim other than terrorizing the civilian population.[49] Italian planes based in Majorca continued to bomb neutral shipping, and an unidentified submarine had torpedoed the *Endymion,* a British registered vessel.[50] The land campaign went less well. Spanish government forces had counterattacked near Teruel, forcing Franco's army to retreat. The situation worried Berti, the Italian commander in Spain, as well as Ciano. This successful attack appeared to show superior morale and generalship on the part of the Red forces. Mussolini remained sanguine, however, and thought that this set-back was merely temporary.[51] The success of the counterattack did high-light the need for a continued effort on the part of Italian troops. It would not be advisable in the short run to lessen the Italian commitment. Fur-thermore, the need for more effective command structure led to tight diplomatic cooperation between the German and Italian governments.[52] Though Republican forces were unable to exploit their victory, Mussolini sent a dispatch to Franco complaining that Teruel had prevented the Nationalist side from carrying forward their planned offensive. If Franco planned to renew the offensive, then Mussolini would only be too happy to commit his forces. If Franco maintained a dilatory tempo, then the Duce would have to consider withdrawing some of his volunteers. Mussolini hoped that this threat would encourage Franco to quicken the pace of the war.[53]

As the diplomatic intrigue regarding the Anglo-Italian negotiations reached its height, Mussolini continued to push for a greater intensifica-tion of the Spanish Civil War. In the first half of February, Franco recom-menced his offensive toward Teruel and ended any serious threat of a Red breakthrough. Franco replied to Mussolini's earlier letter with a litany of excuses for the delays in his offensive. He wrote that he was in accord with Mussolini's ideas for greater dynamism in the attack and asked for new shipments of antitank guns, machine guns, and artillery to support this effort.[54] Ciano replied on Mussolini's behalf, promising to fulfill some of Franco's arms requests. He also suggested that the Duce was considering the withdrawal of some troops from Spain. This action, Ciano argued, was independent of any scheme under the auspices of the nonintervention committee, but he thought that it would have useful repercussions in the negotiations with Great Britain.[55]

With Eden's resignation on 20 February, combined with Hitler's recent truculent speeches, Mussolini once more urged Franco to seize the initia-tive. The political left throughout Europe was in a panic, Mussolini argued, and the time was ripe for a fatal strike against the Republican army. Furthermore, the Duce insisted that Franco make greater use of Ital-ian forces in delivering a knockout blow; he could not stand to let his Italian heroes sit idle.[56] The Caudillo replied through Count Guido Viola, the Italian ambassador in Salamanca, with an account designed to smooth Mussolini's ruffled feathers. Franco had merely kept the Italian *Corpo Truppe Voluntarie* as a strategic reserve to prevent any government attack on the Madrid front. He did not want to squander these troops on insignificant battles; he preferred to save them for vital attacks. Franco also wrote that he understood the current opportunity and that he had called up a new class of recruits for training.[57] Still, Mussolini chafed at the slow progress in Spain and felt humiliated by the inertia of Italian forces there. In a fit of pique, he even suggested to Ciano that he withdraw all of the Italian ground forces. In the meantime, he ordered the *Regia Aeronautica* on the Balearics to take part in every action in order to cover up the passivity of the *C.T.V.*[58]

Finally, against the background of the diplomatic maneuvers in London, Mussolini sought to build a navy capable of dominating the central Mediterranean. On 1 January 1938, Mussolini had approved the construction of two new *Littorio*-class battleships, *Roma* and *Impero*. He thought that they would form the backbone of the Italian fleet, securing the sea lane to Libya that would allow Italian mechanized forces in Africa sufficient supplies to attack Egypt successfully. Eventually, the Duce hoped that his eight battleships would enable Italy to defeat Britain and France in the coming war, giving the *Regia Marina* "access to the vast ocean outside the encircled Mediterranean."[59] In reaching this decision, however, Mussolini had ignored reports that raw material shortages and industrial deficiencies had already delayed the production of the first two battleships in the class. Even contemplating the availability of eight capital ships by 1942, Italian planners were far less ambitious than was the Duce. Nevertheless, they forecast that the core of eight battleships would allow the *Regia Marina* to deploy sufficient strength in the central Mediterranean to counter the combined power of the British and French navies.[60]

These military and diplomatic policies indicate that Mussolini had little intention of reaching any genuine rapprochement with Britain. While one might allow that Mussolini's desire for a quick end to the war in Spain would help to restore a measure of international stability, he certainly would accept only victory on his terms—a victory that he assumed would tilt the balance of power away from Great Britain and toward Italy. Combined with his moves in the Middle and Far East and his increased military preparations, it is clear that he sought conflict, not cooperation. As Lord Perth met Ciano in Rome before returning to London to receive instructions for the imminent negotiations, Ciano already began to cavil regarding his promises of the previous weekend. Given the ease with which Chamberlain had subdued Eden in their struggle within the cabinet, Ciano no longer meant to uphold his pledge regarding the withdrawal of volunteers. He told Perth that the issue should not be a part of the discussions in Rome. Instead, the nonintervention committee should work to resolve the question of volunteers. Otherwise, the two diplomats only vaguely explored the possible scope of the negotiations that would resume with Perth's return the following week.[61]

At long last, the formal negotiations commenced in Rome on 8 March. Perth carried with him not only his government's instructions but also a message from Viscount Halifax, the new foreign secretary, to Ciano. This personal letter expressed Halifax's hopes for renewed Anglo-Italian friendship. Perth's extensive agenda for the talks, however, indicated how far estranged the two powers had become. The thorniest issue was Spain. Chamberlain had recently made an official declaration in the House of Commons linking the de jure recognition of the Italian empire to the "substantial withdrawal" of Italian volunteers. Ciano protested that this plan was different from what had been agreed in London. He had accepted only the declared British withdrawal formula, he argued, and would not base the entire agreement on meeting any set conditions. Meeting those conditions was also not entirely under his control; all parties would have to work through the nonintervention committee. He placed three questions to Perth on this issue. First, what precisely did the British government mean by concrete progress regarding the withdrawal of volunteers? Second, what would happen if an agreement preceded the solution of the Spanish problem? Third, when and how would the British government raise the issue of de jure recognition at the League of Nations? Perth replied that he would have to seek clarification of the first question. To the second, he suggested that any agreement would simply be suspended until a satisfactory solution could be found. Finally, the British government would deal with the question of recognition at the next League meeting in May.[62] These conditions perturbed Ciano; they would require a considerable period of good behavior in Italian foreign policy before the parties could implement any agreement, and therefore, would tie his hands to a far greater extent than he had previously supposed.

In addition to these pressing issues, Perth carried a long list of desiderata that indicated the extent of Italian provocations. The two parties would confirm their gentlemen's agreement of the previous January. Ciano had no objection to this soporific measure. He did object, however, to Perth's request that other Mediterranean powers could announce their adherence to points four and five of the gentlemen's agreement of the previous January but promised that he would consult Mussolini. In practice, of course, Ciano was unalterably opposed to allowing countries such as France or Greece to associate themselves with an Anglo-Italian understanding. More importantly, Perth heavily emphasized one of the cabinet's cardinal goals; Mussolini would have to reduce his garrison in Libya. He also called for the cessation of action by Italian agents in Egypt. He further wanted an exception made regarding the status quo provisions of any agreement to allow changes in the administration of both Palestine and Syria. He expected Ciano to repeat past Italian assurances on maintaining the status quo ante in Arabia. There were some other relatively minor matters. On all of the serious issues at stake, Ciano displayed the utmost reserve.[63] This laundry list of British government demands underlined the gulf between Britain and Italy in their Mediterranean dealings. For British strategic concerns in the long term, the questions of Italy's Libyan garrison and its intrigues in the Red Sea represented the most important of these conditions.[64]

On 12 March, Ciano repeated his protests against British plans to subordinate any Anglo-Italian agreement to the issue of the withdrawal of Italian volunteers and to the workings of the nonintervention committee. Perth agreed and replied that his government was currently exploring that very issue. Ciano wanted to know what the British term "substantial progress" would mean. Perth, in the absence of official instructions, had to say that he would provide an explanation as soon as possible.[65] On 15 March, Perth had three major items on his agenda. The British government wanted the removal of all Italian forces from the Balearic Islands. Ciano replied disingenuously that Italy had no ground forces on the islands, requiring Perth to specify that he meant the Italian air forces there. Ciano refused to consider the request, as it had appeared neither in the nonintervention committee nor its proposal for withdrawal of volunteers. Perth dropped the subject. Second, both parties agreed to confirm the gentlemen's agreement, and, at Mussolini's insistence, to drop any mention of asking other parties to associate themselves with any declarations regarding maintaining the status quo. Third, and most importantly, Perth asked the Italian government to withdraw one of the two Italian corps comprising the Libyan garrison. Ciano demurred, citing the need to consult the Duce.[66] These two meetings established the essential matters for negotiation. The British government aimed to reduce Italian forces in Libya and to lessen the impact of Italy's intervention in Spain. On the Italian side, Ciano wanted to make as few commitments as possible in order to secure British recognition of the Italian empire.

As the weeks passed, Perth and Ciano gradually removed these sticking points, and an agreement began to cohere. Gradually, Mussolini made minor concessions in the negotiations. He agreed to reduce the Libyan garrison, removing the substantial part of one of the two European corps, but would make only a symbolic withdrawal of some 3,000 to 4,000 men during the negotiations. Italy would withdraw some 1,000 men every week until reaching peacetime levels. Unknown to the British negotiators, however, the Duce ordered that the withdrawal should concentrate on repatriating the oldest men and the ones most needed in industry or in agriculture. Italy would withdraw none of the equipment for its mechanized units, thus ensuring that it would quickly be able to return its cadres to wartime levels.[67] The negotiators agreed that the agreement would enter into force only after substantial progress in Spain and that the British promise to recognize the Italian empire would be tied to progress in Spain through an official exchange of letters. The British foreign secretary would, however, open the possibility of other countries recognizing the Italian conquest by placing the issue before the League of Nations Council in early May. Italy would cease its propaganda in the Middle East through its Radio Bari broadcasts. Mussolini and Ciano refused to compromise on the evacuation of the Balearics, on British attempts to have Franco bound by the declaration on the maintenance of the Mediterranean status quo, and on any association of France with the agreements. Perth and Ciano signed the agreement on Easter Sunday, 16 April 1938, coincidentally Halifax's birthday.[68] Mussolini achieved his primary goal, British de jure recognition of his conquest of Ethiopia, though he had to accept Ciano's earlier concession that this event would not occur until after the good-faith withdrawal of some Italian volunteers. In the Duce's view, the agreement signaled Italy's decisive defeat of Britain and its League of Nations–sponsored sanctions, and it definitively closed the Ethiopian war. Ciano gloated that Mussolini had faced down the powerful British empire and forced it to accept the parity of Italy as a Mediterranean power. For him, too, the Easter Accord signaled the real end of the Ethiopian war.[69] As for Chamberlain's hopes that he could remove Italy from the list of potential enemies, that would depend on Mussolini's willingness to honor the spirit and substance of the agreement.

As the main points of the Easter Accord were being settled near the end of March 1938, however, Mussolini gave a bellicose speech in Rome to the rubber-stamp Senate. He trumpeted many of the major themes of his ideological fixations. Fate had blessed Italy with strong natural defensive boundaries and profound demographic strength. The metropolitan population in Italy exceeded 44 million in 1938 and would grow to more than 50 million within ten years. Demographic power, Mussolini emphasized, underlay military power. It was a simplistic equation; without men one could create no battalions, but with many men, one could create great armies. Mussolini spoke of mobilizing 8 million soldiers, of whom 5 million would be frontline material. Accordingly, the Duce dismissed claims from foreigners that his wars in Africa and Spain had depleted Italy's military strength. Instead, it had forged battle-ready veterans, "hundreds of thousands who had marched, fought, and suffered while making war." Furthermore, infantry would always be the queen of battle, as mechanization could only go so far. Finally, the Duce emphasized the completion and then current construction of modern battleships and submarines as defining Italian naval power. Construction of airplanes, he said, continued at a high rate. Finally, Mussolini spoke of the dynamic military consciousness that he was inculcating in the Italian people. Even allowing for elements of Fascist Party politics in this speech, Mussolini did seem to believe his own rhetoric, as it was in complete accord with his long-standing beliefs. Mussolini believed that he was preparing Italy for the decisive battles to come.[70]

Despite his bombast, Mussolini's closest flirtation with restoring less fractious relations with France occurred in the immediate aftermath of the Easter Accord. Throughout the negotiations with Britain, Mussolini and Ciano had consistently rejected any French association with those discussions.[71] Successive French cabinets had tried to avoid strictly bilateral Anglo-Italian talks, concluding for the most part correctly that the British government would not take into account French security concerns. Halifax's curt response rejecting an earlier démarche indicated that the discussions aimed only at an Anglo-Italian understanding; the French government would have to look after its own interests.[72] In the first week of March, French Foreign Minister Delbos tried again. He prepared a list of French strategic and diplomatic issues, including the legal standing of Italian subjects in Tunisia, the Italian occupation of the Balearic Islands, Corsica, and the status quo in the Mediterranean. He gave these desiderata to the British ambassador and said that he hoped Halifax would agree that they would be discussed *à trois,* with France joining the ongoing bilateral negotiations. Perth cabled from Rome that Mussolini would undoubtedly refuse this proposal and that it would wreck any chance of a successful agreement. Halifax sent another dismissive suggestion that the French government approach Ciano directly.[73] Despite French overtures to Italy, Mussolini and Ciano refused to include France in direct negotiations.[74] Privately, Ciano emphasized that the Anglo-Italian negotiations "were destined to accentuate French isolation and in consequence to weaken all of the system or systems of a collective character in which France had placed its hopes." Naturally, given this objective, he continued to rule out of hand any French participation in the negotiations.[75]

Still, despite Mussolini's anti-French animus, there were some improvements in Franco-Italian relations in April. A lengthy set of economic negotiations reached fruition in the spring. The major issue at stake was a clearing exchange agreement that France and Italy had reached in 1936. Trade between the two countries had been balanced through the clearing exchange. The terms represented a small concession on the part of the French government, as they increased Italian exports, thus allowing Italy to pay part of its commercial debt to France. But the agreement limited overall Italian exports, for they had to pass through the strict controls of the clearing system. During the new round of negotiations, Mussolini and Ciano demanded that France cancel the clearing exchange. The new accord, signed in April 1938, represented another set of French concessions. It abolished the clearing system as of 1939, allowed an immediate increase of Italian exports to France, and arranged for a percentage of the new trade to go to debt repayment, while permitting new Italian purchases of French goods. The agreement annoyed French business leaders who disliked its limits on their investment in Italy. Nevertheless, the Popular Front government thought that these concessions could lead to a Franco-Italian rapprochement.[76] Ciano recognized the importance of this French concession but ensured that the communiqué would not convey "any note of exaggerated political optimism."[77]

As the economic negotiations continued in the first part of April, the new Blum cabinet, with Joseph Paul-Boncour as its foreign minister, also decided to approach Italy for permission to join the Anglo-Italian discussions. Paul-Boncour spoke to Renato Prunas, the chargé d'affaires, at the Italian Embassy in Paris on 8 and 9 April. The French foreign minister wanted to repair the breach in France's relations with Italy. Specifically, he hoped to send a mission to Rome in order to participate in the negotiations between Perth and Ciano. Paul-Boncour said that he hoped to discuss several questions, including the eventual end of Italian intervention in the Spanish Civil War, Djibuti, and the Libyan garrison. Prunas, having already received instructions from Ciano on this point, put forward several roadblocks and said that he replied to this French initiative with "palpable distance and coldness."[78]

On 10 April, the Popular Front era ended with Blum's resignation, and Édouard Daladier became prime minister with Georges Bonnet as his foreign minister. Bonnet had long supported friendly relations with Mussolini's Italy and continued to work to develop Paul-Boncour's ideas. On 15 April, he instructed Jules Blondel, the chargé d'affaires in Rome, to approach Ciano with an official request for negotiations to lead to France's joining the Anglo-Italian accord.[79] Blondel saw Ciano the next day to carry out his instructions.[80] Ciano thought that this move represented French blackmail; either Italy would have to negotiate or France would scuttle British efforts at the League of Nations to achieve de jure recognition of the empire. Nevertheless, he agreed to place this démarche before Mussolini. Mussolini agreed, but on strictly limited terms. As Ciano noted in his diary, the Duce wanted to receive the French proposal but would not allow any discussions to weaken the Axis. Any agreement would have to wait at least until after Hitler's visit to Rome in early May. Further, any Franco-Italian discussions would send an unmistakable message that the Spanish Republican government was thoroughly isolated.[81]

Ciano was cordial to Blondel. The French chargé d'affaires gave Ciano the list of French desiderata on 22 April. This twelve-point memorandum contained several rather minor issues: declarations on the maintenance of the status quo, the Libya garrison, the French mandate in Syria, cessation of propaganda, Italian adherence to the 1936 Mediterranean Naval Treaty, rights in Ethiopia and Somalia, the Djibuti railroad, and other issues left over from the Mussolini-Laval accords of 1935.[82] An Italian promise regarding Italian disinterest in Spanish territory and the eventual withdrawal of volunteers and a discussion of relative rights in Tunisia based on the 1935 accord represented the two most important elements of this proposal. Ciano was somewhat encouraging to Blondel but said that any further discussion would have to wait until after Hitler's visit. Without Ciano's knowledge, however, Mussolini had categorically rejected the fundamental elements of the French proposal. He would not give any similar guarantee to France as he had to Great Britain regarding Spain, nor would he negotiate the Tunisian question on the basis of the French proposals. Given the Duce's reaction, there was no possibility of reaching agreement on the substance of the outstanding issues.[83] Despite Mussolini's rejection of a genuine rapprochement, Ciano continued the negotiations with Blondel until after Hitler's visit in early May, encouraging French statesmen's hopes for a pact.[84]

Why, then, did Mussolini continue these hopeless discussions with his longstanding bête noire—the French government? The answer lies in the state of Italo-German relations in the wake of the Anschluss. In early April, Ciano had mentioned to Mussolini the need to quiet irredentism amongst ethnic Germans in the South Tyrol. He cited agitation calling for the frontier to move southward at Italy's expense. In Ciano's view, such talk could "blow the Axis sky high." He even raised the possibility of a population exchange. Despite repeated assurances by German diplomats that Hitler did not support this irredentism, unrest did not diminish. On 16 April, demonstrations at Lasa included the use of firearms. Neither Mussolini nor Ciano could tolerate these signs of dissent. Ciano urged Mussolini to send a sharp note to Göring, and he also sought active intervention from the German government to quell the unrest. Magistrati saw Göring, but the latter did not fully seize the extremity of Italian anger. His vague response satisfied neither Mussolini nor Ciano. Mussolini was prepared to go a long way to make concessions on language and culture to assuage ethnic German anger but would not consider territorial revision. At the height of the dispute, Mussolini lamented that German actions "will compel me to swallow the bitterest pill of my life. I mean the French pill."[85] By the time Hitler visited Italy on 5 May, there had been no definitive solution to this pressing issue.

Despite the potential seriousness of South Tyrolese irredentism, there was no substantive break in Italo-German relations prior to Hitler's visit. Ciano drafted a clumsy friendship pact, which he called an alliance, that Mussolini approved. Ciano expected that his anodyne phrases would tighten the Axis partnership without preventing the entrance into force of the Anglo-Italian agreement, which would finally grant official British recognition of Mussolini's Ethiopian conquest.[86] When Hitler and his entourage arrived, however, Ciano was somewhat surprised to receive a proposal for a full-blown alliance from von Ribbentrop.[87] There is no convincing evidence to indicate whether or not Hitler knew of his foreign minister's alliance proposal, as Hitler apparently did not mention it to Mussolini or Ciano. The German foreign minister did not push his proposal very hard in the face of Ciano's reticence. Hitler, however, was certainly accommodating on the major issue of Italian concern. At a major speech at a 7 May banquet at the Palazzo Venezia, he declared in clear terms the permanent inviolability of the natural frontier on the Brenner. In discussions with the Duce, Hitler promised to rein in South Tyrolese irredentism, while Mussolini undertook to give greater cultural and linguistic rights to that minority. As for the respective alliance proposals, Ciano resisted tying Italy to a formal agreement that could foreclose future British recognition of the Ethiopian conquest if it became public, while German diplomats considered Ciano's hastily prepared friendship pact a harsher rebuff than either Ciano or Mussolini would ever have intended.

Still, despite respective Italian and German differences over the exact nature of the Axis relationship, Hitler's visit was a great success. He allayed Mussolini's fears about the Alto Adige and the Brenner frontier and was tentatively able to explore the Italian attitude toward Germany's interest in action against Czechoslovakia. As Hitler left Italy, Mussolini told him, "Henceforth no force will be able to separate us."[88]

As Hitler's visit ended, therefore, Mussolini faced a clear choice. On one hand, he had a recently signed agreement with Great Britain and knew from Grandi and intelligence reports that Prime Minister Neville Chamberlain desperately desired strong relations with Italy. The French government had also requested a pact analogous to the Anglo-Italian accord, although Mussolini had not yet explored the cost of reaching an agreement with the Daladier cabinet. The path was clear for Mussolini to restore relations with the West at any of several levels up to and including restoring the Stresa Front. On the other hand, Adolf Hitler's Germany sought an alliance that would formalize the Axis, though leaving some room for adventures by each individual country. In short, if Mussolini ever intended to play the role of the decisive weight, the arbiter of European affairs between Nazi Germany and the Western democracies, then conditions could hardly have been better. Suitors approached from both sides; which path would the Duce choose?

Mussolini made his answer to this question clear in the immediate aftermath of Hitler's visit. Since the end of March, Ciano had been considering annexing Albania. The Anschluss, while disquieting for Italy, also threatened Yugoslavia. He mused that Stoyadinović's need for Italian friendship might mean that the Yugoslavian prime minister would be prepared to sacrifice Albania's independence in order to secure an Italo-Yugoslav alliance. Mussolini later agreed, saying that he was prepared to face a war, "as long as we get Albania."[89] Ciano's tour of Albania, preceding Hitler's visit to Italy, had represented a kind of reconnaissance mission; Mussolini and Ciano needed better information to determine whether or not their project was desirable or feasible. Upon his return, Ciano submitted a report that encouraged Mussolini's expansionist desire. Albania had excellent agricultural potential, Ciano wrote, and had very extensive deposits of coal, though no one had yet completed a full list of Albania's potential mineral wealth. On the strategic side, there were several advantages. In the wake of the Anschluss, German economic, cultural, and political tentacles would reach into the former Austrian sphere of influence. A firm warning from Italy and subsequent annexation of Albania would prevent any further German penetration there. In addition, Italian control of Albania would turn the Adriatic Sea into an Italian lake. The *Regia Marina* would be able to divert resources there to bring greater pressure on the British and French navies. Finally, annexation of Albania would bring serious pressure to bear on the Yugoslav government, perhaps increasing its reliance on Italy. King Zog's army was entirely ineffective, so Italian forces would easily overcome it. In short, Ciano heartily recommended annexation, drawing parallels between modern Italy and the days of the Caesars. Significantly, Mussolini heavily marked several passages where Ciano wrote in favor of annexation.[90]

On 10 May, Mussolini and Ciano discussed the report. Mussolini agreed wholeheartedly with its conclusions. He thought that May 1939 would be the most opportune timing, allowing one year for diplomatic and military preparations. Most importantly, Great Britain and France would undoubtedly disapprove of Italian annexation plans, so Mussolini would first need to secure a pact with Germany. Though vitally necessary in order to provide the necessary diplomatic and military cover for Italy's expansion, that pact, of course, would have to wait until after British de jure recognition of the Italian empire went into effect.[91] Mussolini's cavalier disregard for maintenance of the Mediterranean status quo indicated that his pledged word in the Easter Accord counted for little in the Duce's mind.

Ciano implemented the first stages of Italian planning immediately. He spoke to Francesco Jacomoni, the Italian minister in Tirana, regarding public works projects, charities, economic development, sporting events, and political organizations that would raise the Italian profile in Albania and prepare the ground for the takeover. Mussolini directed Ciano to give a stern hands-off warning to the German government, which Ciano did later in May. In May and June, Jacomoni commenced this plan, spending money on roads, sports exchanges, theater, radio, cinema, and a sports stadium. The Fascist government sent a stream of advisors to work in the fields of industry, commerce, and aviation. Ciano also dispatched Fascist Senator Natale Prampolini to work on plans for land reclamation, one of Mussolini's pet ideas. In May and June, therefore, Mussolini and his underlings had set in train the annexation of Albania that occurred in 1939. As little as a month after signing the Anglo-Italian agreement, Mussolini planned to violate its central tenet in order to carry out his plans for expansion.[92]

Similarly, the Duce deliberately ruptured Italy's relations with France in the immediate aftermath of Hitler's visit. He finally corrected Ciano's belief that Italy would sign a Franco-Italian accord. Mussolini would not consider the fundamental elements of the French proposals, despite their similarity to those in the Easter Accord. He had held out the possibility of such an accord long enough, however, so that French politicians had supported British moves at the League of Nations to allow individual League members to grant de jure recognition of the Italian conquest of Ethiopia. Consequently, the Duce no longer needed to consort with his Gallic enemy. After Bonnet and Halifax opened the door for League members to grant de jure recognition of the Italian empire on 12 May, Mussolini quickly cast aside any thought of even a surface appearance of a rapprochement with France. Despite the Duce's transparent intransigence, Ciano blamed the Quai d'Orsay for frustrating his recent moves. On his way to Genoa, where Mussolini would make a major speech on 14 May, the Duce was increasingly anti-French. He told Ciano that France was "a nation ruined by alcohol, syphilis, and journalism."[93] At Genoa, Mussolini departed from his prepared text and delivered a bellicose anti-French speech. The Anglo-French sanctions policy had rendered the Stresa Front forever "dead and buried." Though conversations with France continued, Mussolini thought that they would not likely be successful, as in Spain, France had ranged itself on the opposite side of the barricade to Fascist Italy. Significantly, Mussolini gave markedly better treatment to Britain, signaling a return to attempts to split the Western democracies.[94] Mussolini's distaste for all things French deepened over the remainder of May. According to Renato Prunas, the Italian chargé d'affaires in Paris, French Foreign Minister Bonnet gave every indication that he would be willing to make major sacrifices in order to reach a rapprochement with Italy. Bonnet was markedly decreasing French aid to the Barcelona government, putting the final nail in the coffin of Republican hopes for stalemate, never mind victory.[95] Despite Bonnet's efforts to normalize relations, Mussolini decided to intensify a propaganda barrage against France. He wanted the Fascist Party to create "a wave of Gallophobia in order to liberate the Italians from their last remaining slavery and servility towards Paris." As the Duce launched his campaign, Ciano mused about seizing Corsica from France.[96] In short, Mussolini spurned French advances to improve relations and instead deliberately provoked a breakdown in negotiations and the worsening of Franco-Italian relations.[97]

Ciano also rejected British suggestions that Italy reach a rapprochement with France. Having concluded their own agreement, British officials no longer feared that French talks might create difficulties for the Anglo-Italian negotiations. Ciano made it clear, however, that Italy precluded any similar agreement with France. He informed Perth that Mussolini's Genoa speech signaled a clear distinction in Italy's attitude toward France and

Great Britain, respectively. He cited continuing French support for Republican Spain, plus supposedly unreasonable French requests during the abortive negotiations as preventing any rapprochement.[98] French officials believed that Mussolini's and Ciano's actions had become transparent. Mussolini had merely held out the possibility of a Franco-Italian accord until after France had supported British management of the recognition issue at the League of Nations. Once Halifax and Bonnet had removed the League prohibition against de jure recognition of the Ethiopian conquest on 12 May, Mussolini had deliberately sabotaged relations with France. Ambassador Phipps reported that Alexis Léger Saint-Léger, the secretary general of the Quai d'Orsay, had implemented a policy of appearing as reasonable and tractable as possible to Italy. Léger had little doubt that Italy would not respond positively, but he expected that Mussolini's intransigence would show that he aimed to split France from Great Britain. Foreign Minister Bonnet also spoke along these lines; he had worked hard to achieve a rapprochement with Italy but had faced frequent rebuffs. As a last ditch effort to show French goodwill, the Daladier government decided to close the frontier with Spain, cutting off the Barcelona government from its supply lifeline.[99] The French government officially closed the frontier to personnel and military shipments on 13 April, but despite this removal of the self-declared Italian objection to better Franco-Italian relations, Bonnet and Léger were unable to make any headway. Despite repeated British attempts to start stalled Franco-Italian talks, Ciano refused to discuss substantive issues with France until after the Chamberlain cabinet first ratified the Easter Accord. When Perth strongly urged Ciano to open talks with France, for example, the British ambassador indicated French willingness to make concessions, but Ciano categorically refused to follow up this démarche.[100]

While Italy's relations with Germany, Great Britain, and France dominated Italian foreign policy during April, May, and June, other issues were also important. In early March, while the negotiations with Perth were underway, Mussolini had reassured Franco that those discussions would not affect his commitment to Franco's victory. He would not withdraw any troops until Nationalist victory was assured, and he would continue Italian support at the highest level consistent with economic and international restraints, despite any promises given to the British government.[101] Nationalist successes in first halting the Republican attack near Teruel and the eventual reoccupation of that city temporarily restored Mussolini's equanimity, as did Franco's commitment of the *C.T.V.* in the Aragon campaign. Ciano believed that victory could be imminent. At the same time, however, he cited unnamed sources that suggested that Britain and France both intended to send men and matériel to aid the Republican side. Ciano did not think these rumors true, but if they were, then Italy would dispatch large-scale units in an "open manner" to battle against the Western democracies.[102] Even though Blondel categorically denied that any French intervention would occur, Ciano did not want a premature war with France, so he arranged with the German government to create a buffer zone of fifty miles from the French border that neither Italian nor German troops would violate. Given the current nature of operations, however, it would be some time before Franco could ensure that the *C.T.V.* would operate solely outside the buffer zone.[103]

Nationalist advances intensified in the first half of April. Mussolini and Ciano hoped that this campaign could decisively rout Republican resistance. Mussolini ignored Franco's wishes to avoid the bombing of civilian areas and ordered renewed terror bombing of cities. On 9 April, Ciano dispatched 300 officers to reinforce the *C.T.V.,* as he admitted, "in defiance of all agreements." Ciano gloated that his negotiations with England and the prospective talks with France had isolated the Barcelona government.[104] In the last week of April, Ciano tried to determine the level of French support for the Republican forces. He had conflicting reports that supplies were either increasing or diminishing. It was important to know which, as the "duration of the war depends on the measure of reinforcement that the Reds receive from France."[105] As Daladier and Bonnet assumed control in April, French supplies to Spain began to dwindle. By the end of April, Mussolini vacillated regarding the continued presence and use of Italian volunteers in Spain. He wanted at least some to remain as evidence of Fascist Italy's commitment to Franco but wanted them held only as a reserve. He thought that a nonintervention agreement would allow him to repatriate some troops, allowing the entrance into force of the Easter Accord. Two weeks later, however, after Hitler's visit, he wanted the *C.T.V.* to take part in new offensives.[106] By mid-May, the Duce looked forward to an imminent attack that he hoped would finally end the civil war.

Also in mid-May, the Hungarian government sought to clarify the nature of Italian policy in the Balkans. Frédéric de Villani, the Hungarian minister in Rome, told Ciano that the Horthy regime wanted to sign a secret pact with Italy that would provide for some element of consultation plus an Italian guarantee in the event of unprovoked Yugoslav aggression against Hungary. Ciano resisted this proposal, musing that supposedly secret pacts could often become public at inconvenient times. Mussolini too was skeptical. He wanted an a priori Hungarian withdrawal from the

League of Nations before he would consider any agreement. Still, Mussolini allowed that, in the event of an unprovoked offensive by Belgrade, however unlikely that may have been, then Italy would invade Yugoslavia. If the Hungarian government attacked Czechoslovakia along with Germany, then Mussolini would disinterest himself. Ciano informed Villani of the Duce's response and emphasized Mussolini's insistence that Hungary leave the League of Nations. Further, he suggested that Hungary attempt to reach a rapprochement with Romania in order to ensure the isolation of France and Czechoslovakia in the Balkans. Both Mussolini and Ciano hoped to splinter the Little Entente.[107]

While Mussolini tilted Italian policy further toward the Axis and away from the West, the first indications of Hitler's plans to destroy Czechoslovakia took shape. Mussolini's initial part in the destruction of Czechoslovakia was entirely unwitting. In April, as Hitler had plotted against Czechoslovakia, he indicated to his aides that Italian support was essential. It was possible that the victory in Ethiopia and the likely eventual one in Spain had either drained Italy or satisfied Mussolini's ambitions. If that were so, then Germany would not have the strategic and military strength to attack Czechoslovakia. If, however, Mussolini's aims were more ambitious, then he would require German acquiescence and support to proceed in the face of likely British and French opposition. If Hitler were able to exploit Mussolini's ambitious nature, then Italy would become more tightly tied to German coat tails. In an attack on Czechoslovakia, the threat of Italian intervention, Hitler believed, would deter France from entering a war in defense of Prague. Even if the French government did declare war, however, Hitler believed that the Italian presence on the Alpine frontier, combined with Italian naval and land threats against France's North African colonies, would relieve enough pressure to allow the *Wehrmacht* the time necessary to regroup after its inevitable victory over Czechoslovakia. Given this set of circumstances, Hitler thought that an Italo-German alliance was an essential element of Germany's political and military strategy. After his visit to Italy in May and his initial probing there, Hitler convinced himself that Mussolini's aggressive nature and expansionistic goals would mean that Italy would fall in line with his plans for Czech destruction.[108]

Mussolini was not unwilling to fill the role in which Hitler had cast him. In the latter half of May, rumors of German aggression abounded. The Czechoslovak army mobilized, and Mussolini offered Hitler his unqualified support. Italy had no direct interest in the issue, but Mussolini declared solemnly to Ciano that Italy would "immediately enter the strug-

gle by the side of the Germans" in the event of war.[109] Ciano informed the
German government that Italy would support its Axis partner whatever its
plans, and he offered to issue a public communiqué to that effect. The following day, he asked to be informed of Hitler's exact aims. Mussolini did
not care whether Hitler planned to destroy Czechoslovakia or simply to
achieve regional autonomy for the Sudeten Germans. He merely wanted to
concert Italian aims with those of Germany to avoid working at cross-
purposes. If the German government wanted an Italian semiofficial Informazione Diplomatica issued, then the Mussolini and Ciano would need to
know how to couch their support. The crisis died down without further
incident, however, and Hitler declined the Italian offer of an official statement. The German ambassador, von Mackensen, misled Ciano about the
true and aggressive nature of German policy; he said that the Führer
sought only concessions regarding local autonomy for Sudeten Germans.
Thus mollified, Ciano temporarily ceased his probing to determine Hitler's
intentions. Mussolini's display of Italian support, however, encouraged
Hitler's belief about Italian loyalty to the cause of Czechoslovakia's
destruction.[110] It also reflected Mussolini's readiness to overturn the European status quo as well as the Mediterranean one.

Similarly, Mussolini violated the spirit and letter of the Easter Accord in
the Mediterranean and the Middle East. While negotiating the agreement,
Mussolini and Ciano had become worried about the possible effects of the
Easter Accord on Arab and Islamic opinion. Both men well knew that the
Arab world focused its attention on the possibility that Britain might create a Jewish state in the region. Such an action would inevitably inflame
Arab opinion. In response to a British request that Italy promise not to
interfere in Palestinian affairs, Mussolini had sought to ensure that Britain
would guarantee to develop Palestine only according to the principles of
its territorial mandate—that is, preparing Palestine for eventual independence. If Britain were to affirm such principles, then Italy would be able to
portray itself as the one country able to guarantee Arab freedom and
Islamic dynamism against British colonial domination. British officials,
however, had refused to agree to make any such declaration, arguing that
they could not provide any guarantees as long as the government was
awaiting the Peel report to present new policy options. Eventually, realizing that he could not seize this advantage, Mussolini had ordered his negotiators to yield the point.[111] Furthermore, at British insistence, Italy had
agreed that both countries would pledge to respect the independence of
Saudi Arabia and Yemen and to foreswear the attempt to seek political
advantage in the Arabian Peninsula. Despite the anodyne nature of this

declaration, Italian officials had feared that its nature—a bargain between two colonial powers—might provoke a backlash in Arab circles that would threaten Italy's increased influence in East Africa and the Middle East. In the aftermath of the agreement, Ciano had launched diplomatic barrage throughout the Islamic world, seeking to portray the language in the agreement as an Italian initiative designed to limit British imperial penetration and control over Islam, to protect the sovereignty of already-independent Arab states, and to work toward the independence of those territories under British and French mandates.[112] His diplomatic initiative met with only mixed success but does indicate the extent to which Italian policy continued to oppose British interests and sought to create problems in the British empire.[113]

Mussolini's forward policy in Spain also indicated his lack of commitment to the principles of the Anglo-Italian agreement. Shortly before the May crisis of the possible German coup against Czechoslovakia, Halifax had summoned Grandi to protest the dispatch of six new Italian planes to Palma. Members of the British navy had seen their arrival, so there was little use for Grandi to deny this violation of Mussolini's promises. Instead, Grandi cited French violations of the nonintervention agreement as a pretext for this Italian shipment. Halifax took note of Grandi's objections, saying that prior French violations meant that the British government was making only an unofficial protest. Nonetheless, Halifax insisted that such obvious Italian violations created difficulty for Chamberlain and the cabinet both with the public at large and within Parliament. Grandi received this information with ill grace, blaming the French government for trying to scuttle the Easter Accord through its continued support for the Barcelona government.[114]

Since February, however, Mussolini had become far less concerned with Chamberlain's difficulties. Mussolini's Genoa speech and his obvious violations of the nonintervention agreement had given Anthony Eden powerful ammunition to attack Chamberlain. Although Mussolini thought that Eden's return to power would no longer threaten Italy, Chamberlain was the lesser of two evils, and he ordered Ciano to placate the British prime minister and to smooth any feathers that the Genoa speech might have ruffled. Ciano's speech in Milan on 2 June did publicly paper over some of the cracks in Anglo-Italian relations, though it did nothing substantive to change Italian policy.[115]

The next day, Perth met Ciano to thank him for his speech but also to protest Italian participation in the bombing of civilian populations in Spain. The British ambassador cited previous Italian intervention with

Franco in preventing Nationalist raids on Barcelona. Considering that Mussolini had ordered these terror-bombing campaigns, Ciano knew that he had to reject Perth's request. Once more, he blamed the excesses on France's reinforcement of the Republican side, though he allowed that he would consult with Mussolini. More importantly, Ciano told Perth that Mussolini had given explicit instructions to draw Perth's attention to the need for immediate implementation of the Easter Accord. Disingenuously, Ciano said that Italy had fulfilled all of its pledges, citing the withdrawal of some 8,000 troops from Libya, the cessation of anti-British propaganda, and the Italian acceptance of new proposals for the eventual withdrawal of volunteers from Spain. The eventual withdrawal of troops was tied to the workings of the nonintervention committee, and Italy could not hasten its work; therefore, Ciano argued, Italy had met its obligations.[116] Perth replied that he personally accepted Ciano's view and hoped that the cabinet would implement the agreement. Perth relayed Ciano's words to the Foreign Office, amazingly adding that Italy had behaved with "scrupulous honesty towards us."[117] The same day, however, Mussolini betrayed the real face of Italy's alleged commitment to the Easter Accord. He decided to send 2,000 troops to Spain. To try to avoid detection, these soldiers would travel in small groups and would wear mufti. Six days later, Mussolini decided to increase the number of reinforcements to 4,000 during June and July.[118]

British failure to implement the Easter Accord on demand, combined with the Chamberlain government's continued association with France, brought Mussolini's patience to an end. On 20 June, Perth carried the Chamberlain government's reply to Ciano's demands of 3 June. In order to settle the Spanish imbroglio and to allow the entrance into force of the Easter Accord, the cabinet suggested three possible solutions: execution of the nonintervention committee plan, unilateral withdrawal of Italian volunteers, or a cease-fire between Franco's Nationalists and the Barcelona government. Mussolini directed Ciano to reject these proposals. Franco had established a clear superiority over the Republican forces, and, combined with Daladier's closing of the Pyrenees frontier, a Nationalist victory seemed assured. Mussolini would not throw away his hard-earned military and propaganda victory. In rejecting this initiative, Ciano told Perth that Mussolini would not stop until the final defeat of Communism in Spain. Mussolini confirmed Ciano's language; the foreign minister had noted in his diary that Mussolini "absolutely refuses to compromise—we shall not modify our policy towards Franco in the smallest degree and the agreement with London shall come into force when God pleases. If indeed it ever will."[119]

Similarly, the Duce expressed his impatience with British protests over the bombing of British shipping. In the last week of June, Chamberlain used the secret channel to convey the difficult position in which such attacks placed him. Chamberlain directed Sir Joseph Ball to contact Grandi, informing the Italian ambassador that the continuing attacks by Italian planes flown by Italian pilots could lead to a schism in the Conservative Party. Chamberlain could not continue to defend the Easter Accord in the face of such willful Italian assaults. Ball pleaded with Grandi to intercede to stop the attacks. Grandi, faithful to the idea of Anglo-Italian amity, tried to do so.[120] Simultaneously, Halifax worked through normal diplomatic channels to try to achieve the same goal. Perth called on Ciano on 28 June to protest both the attacks and the triumphalism of the Italian press that exalted the supposedly glorious deeds of Italian pilots. Ciano claimed falsely that such attacks were under local control, and that, in any event, ships in port were fair game for Nationalist pilots.[121] Ciano informed Mussolini of the damage that these attacks were causing to Anglo-Italian relations, but Grandi's and Perth's intercessions sparked Mussolini's ire. He refused to stop the bombing campaign and was annoyed at these signs of British pressure. He contemplated refusing Perth access to the Palazzo Chigi. Mussolini declared that he did not care if these attacks led to Chamberlain's ouster; he would simply deal with any successor.[122]

He prepared a diplomatically offensive memorandum that would reject categorically recent British proposals. He refused to consider a unilateral withdrawal of volunteers from Spain, even though that would allow the entrance into force of the Easter Accord. Despite the inevitable delay in its implementation, he declared that he would not resume negotiations with France until after the Easter Accord went into effect. He would not consider any possibility of a peace settlement in Spain. Ciano had to intercede with the Duce to change the wording of the draft, as Mussolini had repeatedly used the word "absurd" to indicate British policies. Though Ciano still valued good Anglo-Italian relations, his chief did not. Mussolini insisted that until the Chamberlain cabinet implemented the agreement, he would preserve complete freedom of action. In particular, he would continue to send reinforcements to Spain—he sent 600 artillerymen on 1 July—and he would suspend his withdrawal of the second corps of the Libyan garrison. Ciano concluded that Mussolini was deliberately precipitating an "almost inevitable" crisis in relations with Britain.[123]

Ciano faithfully followed Mussolini's wishes at a meeting with Perth on 2 July. Until the accord was implemented, Ciano stated, Mussolini would stop withdrawal of the Libyan garrison and would retain complete freedom of action. Ciano also threatened to publish documents exchanged at the last meeting with Perth before the signing of the accord. The publication of these documents, which both parties had intended to be kept secret, would unavoidably enrage both British public opinion and the French government. Perth replied that his government had fulfilled its obligations to that point, especially regarding the League of Nations and the recognition issue. Furthermore, Mussolini had pledged to withdraw the Libyan garrison at the time the accord was signed. To renege on that commitment would violate his word. The essence of Perth's reply was that Mussolini's reaction put in doubt eventual implementation of the accord.[124]

After the meeting, Perth sought instructions. He ascribed Mussolini's outrageous behavior to a possible fit of temper or, alternatively, to his need to implement the accord in order to restore breathing room within the Axis. Bizarrely, he suggested that the Foreign Office secure an official request from the French government for the implementation of the accord. This maneuver would supposedly allow the cabinet to ignore the provision of the withdrawal of Italian volunteers. Perth expected that once implemented, the Anglo-Italian agreement would push Mussolini to reach a similar agreement with France. This rationale strained credulity, and not surprisingly several members of the Foreign Office dismissed it; they thought that Mussolini's actions aimed to split Britain from France through rather transparent blackmail.[125] Given this consensus, Sir Alexander Cadogan, the permanent undersecretary at the Foreign Office, prepared a strong rejection of Mussolini's demands. He instructed Perth to say that His Majesty's government regretted the delay caused by the question of the withdrawal of volunteers, but it would not relax the cabinet's policy. After all, the accord that Ciano had signed expressly included that central element. He wanted Perth to inform Ciano that Mussolini's decision not to negotiate with France was a blow; if the Easter Accord entered into force while Franco-Italian relations were bad, then it would appear that Mussolini merely aimed to drive a wedge between the two Western democracies. Finally, Cadogan said that publication of documents including confidential information and reinforcement of Libya would be "unfortunate." This term was thinly veiled diplomatic language that such action would scupper the Easter Accords.[126] In short, Halifax and his Foreign Office staff completely rejected Mussolini's ill-mannered blackmail. Perth followed his instruction on 11 July. Ciano was relatively quiet during this meeting and merely accepted Perth's reply, despite its failure to kowtow in the face of Mussolini's bluster. Mussolini was clearly unhappy with the

British reaction, but he could do little other than to await further developments in Spain.[127] Still, his failure to intimidate Chamberlain, combined with foreign reactions to Mussolini's racial policies, raised his ire; "I will do anything I can to sever relations with France and England—nothing can come from that quarter except putridity [pourriture]."[128] Tellingly, Mussolini ordered General Pariani to reinforce the Italian Corps in Libya, allowing the Duce to raise the threat that he posed to Britain and France.[129] The other major result of this flurry was to signal the failure of Chamberlain's hopes of a genuine rapprochement. In the affair's immediate aftermath, the Chiefs of Staff noted gloomily that they still had to rank Italy among Britain's potential enemies.[130]

While Mussolini's provocations damaged Italy's relations with Britain, Ciano worked to solidify Italy's relations in the Balkans and the Far East. In mid-April, Bosko Cristić, the Yugoslav minister in Rome, had informed Ciano of Prime Minister Stoyadinović's attitude in the event of a German attack against Czechoslovakia. Stoyadinović intended to harmonize Yugoslav policy with that of Italy. Despite his country's obligations as a member of the Little Entente, Stoyadinović had little stomach for military action, particularly if that meant fighting on the side of France against the Axis. During an official visit to Venice in mid-June, Stoyadinović confirmed this attitude. He would not resist any German moves, though he certainly did not want to see the Reich adding another three million citizens to the dominant power in Europe. He was more concerned, however, that Hungary might seize the initiative in an attack. That aggression, Stoyadinović argued, would oblige him to uphold his commitment to defend Czechoslovakia. Ciano assured his guest that Hungary had no intention of provoking any crisis. Despite his promised acquiescence in the event of German moves against Czechoslovakia, Stoyadinović feared German domination of the Balkans. Though both Italy and Yugoslavia needed friendly relations with Germany, he hoped to be able to rely on a close partnership with Italy to resist German economic and political might. Ciano's account of the conversation painted a picture of almost fawning servility on Stoyadinović's part. The prime minister said that his relationship with Mussolini's Italy was tighter than a mere alliance and that he expected his policy to conform to that of Italy.[131] Mussolini's and Ciano's efforts to earn Yugoslavia's trust had apparently paid off.

One month later, Mussolini received a Hungarian delegation that included Béla Imrédy, the prime minister, and Kálmán de Kánya, the foreign minister. After brief discussions on internal politics and economic ties, de Kánya raised the Czechoslovak question. It had become obvious, he said, that Hitler would force a solution sometime in the near future. Hungary would never initiate hostilities but would instead join the conflict after it had begun. Hungarian diplomats would soon try to determine the Yugoslav attitude toward this issue. In the meantime, however, de Kánya hoped to receive an Italian guarantee against a possible Yugoslav attack. Without such a guarantee, Hungary would be unable to press forward its claims. Ciano informed de Kánya and Imrédy of Stoyadinović's assurances of the preceding month; as long as Hungary did not carry out a unilateral attack, then Yugoslavia would stand aside. Though both Hungarian statesmen distrusted Stoyadinović's word, Mussolini and Ciano believed that they had squared matters; Yugoslavia would leave its Czechoslovak Little Entente partner to its fate. Accordingly, Mussolini urged his guests to act decisively when the time came. He also informed de Kánya and Imrédy that he was willing to risk war in support of Hitler's plans, including the possibility of war with France. The Hungarian visit disappointed Mussolini; he thought Imrédy the ruler of a moribund regime and de Kánya a relic of Habsburg vintage.[132] Nonetheless, joint Italo-Hungarian military discussions later in July showed more promise. Jenö Rátz, the Hungarian minister of defense, discussed potential strategy in the potential conflict over Czechoslovakia as well as Italian arms shipments.[133] Mussolini and Ciano had helped to prepare the way for a German attack on Czechoslovakia and had been able to weaken France by splitting that country's Little Entente allies.

A new démarche from Japan represented the other important development in Italian foreign policy during the early summer of 1938. As far back as March, Mussolini had tried to tighten the relationship between the two anti-Comintern signatories. He had dispatched a letter to Prime Minister Konoe Fumimaro, citing the common aspirations of the two countries that had bound them in a pact against "the dissolute ideologies that infect the sacred patrimony of humanity."[134] On a more serious vein, his Fascist Party mission to Japan under Paulucci de Carboli sought to develop Italo-Japanese political and economic ties. During April, both Mussolini and Ciano had rejected any kind of concrete agreement in order not to place unnecessary obstacles in the way of the Anglo-Italian negotiations.[135] Opposition from the Gaimushō and elements within the Byzantine Japanese government also had blocked any substantive development, but on 31 May, the Japanese military attaché in Rome approached Ciano to suggest the signing of a secret pact. Ugaki Kazunari, the newly appointed Japanese foreign minister, was more sympathetic to the West and hoping to achieve some compromise settlement of the war in China. He hoped to create an Italo-German-Japanese political bloc in order to put pressure on Britain and the Soviet Union to modify their support for China. At the same time, Konoe appointed Lt. Gen. Itagaki Seishirō as war minister. Itagaki believed that Japanese military successes would reduce Anglo-American and Soviet influence in China and that German and Italian support would help to achieve this goal.[136] Ciano naturally was receptive to these views, noting that "one sees from the historical point of view that Italy and Japan will have to march side by side for a long time." Mussolini echoed his subordinate's view; he no longer seemed to fear offending British sensibilities. On 6 June, Ciano arranged with Admiral Cavagnari, the undersecretary for the navy, to send a mission headed by Admiral De Courten to Japan. Ciano needed a representative to arrange the military pact that would inevitably accompany any political agreement. The same day, he instructed Ambassador Auriti to proceed with plans for a secret protocol to contain three clauses: benevolent neutrality in the event that either party was at war, political consultations, and military and technical cooperation. These discussions proceeded sporadically, however, as members of the Japanese Navy and the Gaimushō feared alienating Great Britain and its naval power. More importantly, they did not want to become involved in a European war over Czechoslovakia. By July, the preliminary stage had been set for the continuing evolution of the negotiations that would proceed later in the year.[137] Mussolini continued to try to recruit potential allies for a confrontation with Britain and France.

Mussolini's overtures to Japan did not conceal the fact the Axis and European affairs were the central considerations of his foreign policy during the summer of 1938. Although the Duce had resisted signing an open alliance at his meeting with Hitler in May, diplomats from both countries conducted sporadic talks to determine a possible pact that would accurately indicate the virtual alliance that existed between Italy and Germany. At the end of June, von Ribbentrop, on his own initiative, proposed a military alliance. Mussolini and Ciano were no longer opposed, as relations with Britain were so poor that Mussolini had temporarily lost hope of the implementation of the Anglo-Italian agreement. Mussolini wanted von Ribbentrop and Ciano to meet at Como to discuss the matter, but at the same time, the Duce thought that he needed time to prepare Italian public opinion for a German alliance. The German foreign minister sent his intermediary, the Prince of Hesse, to Italy in early July. Although the Prince carried a message that von Ribbentrop was anxious for an alliance, he preferred to have Ciano come to the Nuremberg Party rally in September rather than to visit Como for what would be a lower profile meeting. Ciano did not want to go to Nuremberg, however, as Mussolini had by then recovered some hope for British implementation of the Easter Accord, and that required a delay in signing an open alliance with Germany until after official recognition of the Ethiopian conquest.[138] Though these exploratory conversations had not reached fruition by the end of July, Mussolini still felt able to give an open commitment of support for German aspirations in Czechoslovakia. In the context of anxious international concern over German pressure on the Beneš government, Attolico, the Italian ambassador in Berlin, informed German Foreign Minister von Ribbentrop that the Duce would "support German policy to the full." If France were to mobilize, then so would Italy. If France attacked Germany, then Italy would attack France. In Mussolini's eyes, "Germany and Italy were so closely linked together that their relationship was tantamount to an alliance." Mussolini hinted at the possible conclusion of a formal agreement, containing the usual soporifics of eternal friendship, but more importantly, including staff conversations and mutual declarations of diplomatic and military support in the case of outside interference.[139]

During June and July, therefore, Mussolini's attempted blackmail of Great Britain had temporarily poisoned relations between those two countries. He had failed to secure implementation of the Easter Accord and had also failed to split Britain from France. Mussolini's contempt for the French government had ruptured relations with that country. He had alienated himself and Italy from the Western democracies. At the same time, Mussolini had cleared the way in the Balkans for an eventual German attack on Czechoslovakia, and, to varying degrees, had brought both Yugoslavia and Hungary into the Italian camp. Ciano's 1937 volte-face in jettisoning Italian support for Nationalist China had begun to pay off, and Mussolini looked forward to a possible anti-British military and political pact with Japan. He also contemplated a stronger public declaration of Axis solidarity, including the possibility of a formal alliance. Mussolini and Ciano had essentially prepared the ground for a possible three-way alliance against the West, and Mussolini had given virtual carte blanche to Germany in its efforts to destroy Czechoslovakia. The Chamberlain cabinet's refusal to implement the Easter Accord represented the only snag in these plans. Mussolini still had a vague hope of achieving formal British recognition of his conquest of Ethiopia. But Mussolini's reliance on Germany and his estrangement from the West had grown substantially over the first months of 1938.

NOTES

1. Weinberg, *Starting World War II,* 287–93. For more detail, see Jürgen Gehl, *Austria, Germany and the Anschluss, 1931–1938* (London: Oxford University Press, 1963).

2. Ghigi to Ciano, 13 February 1938, 14 February 1938, 16 February 1938, ASMAE, UC 57.

3. *CHD,* 11 February 1938, 13 February 1938, 14 February 1938, 15 February 1938, 73–75.

4. "Informazione Diplomatica #15," *Popolo d'Italia,* 18 February 1938, *OO,* vol. 29, 495–96.

5. For more detailed coverage of Hitler's and von Schuschnigg's beliefs and actions, see Weinberg, *Starting World War II,* 294–99.

6. Appunto, autographo del Duce, 27 February 1938, ASMAE, UC 57.

7. Attolico to Ciano, 5 March 1938, ASMAE, UC 57.

8. Col. Emilio Liebitsky appunto, 7 March 1938, ASMAE, UC 57.

9. *CHD,* 10 March 1938, 11 March 1938, 86–87.

10. Führer to il Duce, 11 March 1928, ASMAE, UC 87; *CHD,* 12 March 1938, 87–88.

11. Magistrati to Ciano, 12 March 1938, ASMAE, UC 4. Hitler sent another letter some two weeks later confirming his eternal friendship and his ideological solidarity with the Duce (Führer to il Duce, 25 March 1938, ASMAE, UC 87).

12. *CHD,* 12 March 1938, 87–88.

13. "Discorso sull'Anschluss, Camera dei deputati," 16 March 1938, *OO,* vol. 29, 67–71.

14. *CHD,* 13 March 1938, 88.

15. Ciano to Attolico, 11 March 1938, ASMAE, GAB 29; *CHD,* 11 March 1938, 87; Colloquio con l'ambasciatore di Gran Bretagna, 12 March 1938, ASMAE, UC 84. The published version exists in *CDP,* Conversation with the British Ambassador, 12 March 1938, 194–95. This evidence directly contradicts Shorrock's claim that French Foreign Minister Delbos's "absolute distaste for dealing directly with Italy" effectively sacrificed Austrian independence. Shorrock's sole reliance on French sources betrayed him (Shorrock, *From Ally to Enemy,* 218). Certain French diplomats did hope that a French démarche could increase Italian support for Austria, but their opinion was obviously unfounded.

16. *CHD,* 2 January 1938, 4 January 1938, 5 January 1938, 8 January 1938, 10–14 January 1938, 58–59, 63–65; *CDP,* Conversation of the Duce with Count Bethelen, 5 January 1938, 158–59.

17. *CHD,* 13 March 1938, 24 March 1938, 89, 93.

18. Colloquio con l'ambasciatore di Gran Bretagna, ASMAE, UC 84. A copy exists in ASMAE, SAP—G.B., B 17 and *CHD,* 58–59. For the published version, see *CDP,* 3 January 1938, 158.

19. Chamberlain to Eden, 7 January 1938, PREM 1/276. Chamberlain to Eden, 13 January 1938, AP 13/1/49Z; Cadogan to Eden, 12 January 1938, FO 954/13,

It/38/1; Eden to Chamberlain, 9 January 1938, AP 13/1/49W. For further information on the highly detailed debate within the foreign policy establishment, see also Sargent Minute, 31 December 1937, FO 371 22395, R249/7/22; Eden to Chamberlain, 9 January 1938, FO 371 22395, R306/7/22.

20. Crolla Note, 10 January 1938, ASMAE, Carte Grandi, B 66, 158/1; Handwritten addition, 14 January 1938, ASMAE, Carte Grandi, B 66, 158/1; Summary of Adrian Dingli's Action, n.d., ASMAE, Carte Grandi, B 66, 158/2.

21. Grandi to Ciano, 20 January 1938, ASMAE, Carte Grandi, B 40, fasc. 93/4; see also Grandi to Ciano, 20 January 1938, SAP—Gran Bretagna, B 25. For Eden's impressions of the 19 January meeting, see Eden to Perth, 19 January 1938, FO 371 22402, R662/23/22.

22. Lindsay to Eden, 11 January 1938, 14 January 1938, 16 January 1938, 17 January 1938, 20 January 1938, 25 February 1938, PREM 1/259; Chamberlain to Lindsay, 13 January 1938, PREM 1/259; Eden to Chamberlain, 17 January 1938, PREM 1/259; Eden to Lindsay, 21 January 1938, PREM 1/259; Diary entries, 14 January 1938, 17 January 1938, AP 20/1/18; Eden Minute, 17 January 1938, AP 13/1/45F; Eden to Lindsay, 22 January 1938, AP 13/1/45G; Eden to Lindsay, 25 January 1938, AP 13/1/45H; Full record of 19 January 1938 FP (17th) mtg from the notes of Mrs. Scott, AP 20/6/38. For more detail on this plan and the British government's reaction, see Ritchie Ovendale, 'Appeasement' and the English Speaking World: Britain, the United States, the Dominions, and the Policy of 'Appeasement', 1937–1939 (Cardiff: University of Wales Press, 1975), 84–98.

23. Summary of Adrian Dingli's Action, n.d., ASMAE, Carte Grandi, B 66, fasc. 158/2.

24. For more on this attack, see Questione Spagnola dal marzo 1937 al febbraio 1938, 31 January 1938 to 6 February 1938, ASMAE, US 2.

25. Grandi to Ciano, 5 February 1938, ASMAE, GAB 398, SAP—Gran Bretagna, B 24; CHD, 4 February 1938, 69–70; Eden to Perth, 5 February 1938, FO 371 22402, R1058/23/22.

26. Eden to Ciano, 6 February 1938, ASMAE, GAB 398, SAP—Gran Bretagna, B 24.

27. Summary of Adrian Dingli's Action, n.d., ASMAE, Carte Grandi, B. 66, fasc. 158/2.

28. Grandi to Ciano, 8 February 1938, ASMAE, GAB 398, SAP—Gran Bretagna, B 24.

29. Ciano to Grandi, 8 February 1938, ASMAE, GAB 398, SAP—Gran Bretagna, B 24. See also CHD, 5 February 1938, 70.

30. Ciano insisted that the conversations take place in Rome. He thought that Grandi was trying to position himself as "the Man who made peace with England." Ciano thought that only Mussolini could assume that role. It is also likely, however, that Ciano did not want to see a competing Fascist heirarch scoring a major policy coup. Negotiations in Rome would inevitably be under Ciano's and Mussolini's control (CHD, 7–9 February 1938, 71–72, 12 February 1938, 74).

31. *CHD,* 1 February 1938, 68; Perth to Alexander Cadogan (personal), 6 February 1938, FO 371 22402, R1069, R1071/23/22.

32. Eden to Chamberlain, Chamberlain to Eden, 8 February 1938, PREM 1/276. Privately, Chamberlain placed great store in Ivy's dealings with Ciano. In a diary entry under the date 19 February 1938, but, based on internal evidence, likely written on 27 February 1938, Chamberlain wrote that his letter to Ivy had had a "magical" effect, convincing Mussolini and Ciano both of the Prime Minister's sincerity (Diary entry, 19 February 1938, Neville Chamberlain Papers [hereafter cited as NC] 2/24A).

33. Ciano to Grandi, 15 February 1938, ASMAE, GAB 29, 398, UC 89, SAP—Gran Bretagna, B 24.

34. Perth understood that Ciano referred to the possibility of an imminent Anschluss (Perth to Eden, 17 February 1938, FO 371 22403, R1441/23/22).

35. Ciano to Grandi, 16 February 1938, ASMAE, GAB 398, UC 89.

36. See, for example, Perth's report on the views of diplomats in Rome: Perth to Eden, 16 February 1938, PREM 1/276; Ingram Minute, 19 February 1938, FO 371 22403, R1550/23/22.

37. Summary of Adrian Dingli's Action, n.d., ASMAE, Carte Grandi, B 66, fasc. 158/2. Grandi to Ciano, 19 February 1938, ASMAE, GAB 398, UC 89; Diary entry, 17 February 1938, Avon, AP 20/1/18; Eden to Chamberlain, 18 February 1938, PREM 1/276.

38. Grandi to Ciano, 19 February 1938, ASMAE, UC 89. The British record, which Eden prepared, indicated none of the divisiveness that Grandi portrayed. For the published record, see Ingram to Perth, 21 February 1938, *Documents on British Foreign Policy* (hereafter cited *DBFP),* 2d ser., vol. 19 (London: His Majesty's Stationery Office, 1948–1984), 946–51.

39. Grandi to Ciano, 19 February 1938, ASMAE, GAB 398, UC 89; Ingram to Perth, 21 February 1938, *DBFP,* 2d ser., vol. 19, no. 573, 946–51; Summary of Adrian Dingli's Action, n.d., ASMAE, Carte Grandi, B 66, fasc. 158/2.

40. CAB 23/92 6(38), 19 February 1938, 7(38) & 8(38), 20 February 1938, plus Hankey Minute of Meeting of Ministers, 20 February 1938; Elizabeth Scott to Eden, notes of 19 February 1938 Cabinet meeting, 27 July 1972, AP 20/6/31; Notes in Cabinet, 19 February 1938, AP 13/1/64G; Diary entry, 19 February 1938, NC 2/24A. For more on Eden's resignation, see David Carlton, *Anthony Eden: A Biography* (London: A. Lane, 1981); A. R. Peters, *Anthony Eden at the Foreign Office, 1931–1938* (New York: St. Martin's, 1986); and Robert Mallett, "Fascist Foreign Policy and Official Italian Views of Anthony Eden in the 1930s," *Historical Journal* 43, no. 1 (2000): 157–87. For Anthony Eden's battles with historians over the memory of his political record, see Peter Beck, "Politicians versus Historians: Lord Avon's Appeasement Battle against 'Lamentably Appeasement-Minded' Historians," *Twentieth Century British History,* 9, no. 3 (1998): 396–419.

41. Colloquio con l'ambasciatore di Gran Bretagna, 19 February 1938, ASMAE, UC 84.

42. *CHD,* 19–21 February, 77–79; Grandi to Ciano, 21 February 1938, ASMAE, GAB 398, SAP—Gran Bretagna, B 24; Aide-Mémoire, 21 February 1938, ASMAE, GAB 398, SAP—Gran Bretagna, B 24; Ciano to Segretaria del Duce, 20 February 1938, ASMAE, GAB 398; Grandi to Chamberlain, 21 February 1938, PREM 1/360; Chamberlain conversation with the Italian Ambassador, 21 February 1938, FO 371 22403, R1610/23/22.

43. Grandi to Ciano, 21 February 1938, ASMAE, GAB 398, SAP—Gran Bretagna, B 24; Grandi to Chamberlain, 21 February 1938, PREM 1/360; Chamberlain conversation with the Italian Ambassador, 21 February 1938, FO 371 22403, R1610/23/22.

44. Grandi to Ciano, 22 February 1938, ASMAE, GAB 398.

45. *CHD,* 1–4 January 1938, 57–60.

46. Ferretti, *Il Giappone e la politica estera italiana, 1935–41,* 213–14.

47. *CHD,* 3 January 1938, 58–59.

48. Ciano to Ministero dell'Africa Italiana, 17 February 1938, NA, RG T586, r412, 004966–7; see also chapter 3, 19.

49. *CHD,* 1 January 1938, 57–58.

50. Questione Spagnola dal marzo 1937 al febbraio 1938, 31 January 1938 to 6 February 1938, ASMAE, US 2.

51. Pariani Promemoria, 14 January 1938, ASMAE, US 2; *CHD,* 14 January 1938, 64–55.

52. Pariani Promemoria, 14 January 1938, ASMAE, US 2; Magistrati to Ciano, 3, 5, 8 January 1938, ASMAE, UC 46.

53. Mussolini to Franco, 2 February 1938, ASMAE, UC 46.

54. Franco to il Duce, 16 February 1938, ASMAE, UC 46.

55. Ciano to Viola, 20 February 1938, ASMAE, UC 46.

56. Mussolini to Franco, 22 February 1938, ASMAE, UC 46; *CHD,* 22 February 1938, 23 February 1938, 79–80.

57. Viola to Ciano, 24 February 1938, ASMAE, UC 46.

58. Ciano to Viola, 26 February 1938, ASMAE, UC 46; *CHD,* 26 February 1938, 81.

59. Quoted in Mallett, *The Italian Navy and Fascist Expansionism,* 111n38.

60. Mallett, *The Italian Navy and Fascist Expansionism,* 109–11. Similarly, Ciano considered war with the Western democracies as inevitable, and he consulted with General Pariani about plans for a lightning war against Egypt and an attack against the British fleet. Ciano suggested that staff talks with the Germans would help to make these plans workable (*CHD,* 14 February 1938, 74–75).

61. Ciano Appunto, 22 March 1938, ASMAE, GAB 398; Perth to Halifax, 22 February 1938, FO 371 22403, R1701/23/22. For the published version of the Italian record, see *CDP,* Conversation with the British Ambassador, 22 February 1938, 186–87.

62. Colloquio con l'ambasciatore di Gran Bretagna, 8 March 1938, ASMAE, GAB 398, UC 84; see also *CDP,* Conversation with the British Ambassador, 8 March 1938, 187–93.

63. Colloquio con l'ambasciatore di Gran Bretagna, 8 March 1938, ASMAE, GAB 398, UC 84.

64. Lampson (Cairo) to Halifax, 7 March 1938, FO 371 21938, J112/5/16; Halifax to Lampson, 31 March 1938, FO 371 21938, J112/5/16.

65. Ciano Appunto, 12 March 1938, ASMAE, GAB 398, SAP—Etiopia, Fondo di Guerra, B 166; Perth to Halifax, 12 March 1938, FO 371 22406, R2408 and 2514/23/22; *CDP,* Conversation with the British Ambassador, 12 March 1938.

66. Ciano Appunto, 12 March 1938, ASMAE, GAB 398, SAP—Etiopia, Fondo di Guerra, B 166; Ciano to Attolico, 3 April 1938, ASMAE, SAP—Etiopia, Fondo di Guerra, B 166; Draft Reaffirmation of the Mediterranean Declaration of January 2, 1937, and the exchange of notes of December 31, 1936, and the extension of the status quo portion of the declaration to France. Mussolini heavily marked the word "no" in the margin (Perth to Halifax, 15 March 1938, FO 371 22406, R2685 and 2733/23/22; *CDP,* Conversation with the British Ambassador, 16 March 1938).

67. Ciano to Attolico, 21 March 1938, ASMAE, SAP—Etiopia, Fondo di Guerra, B 166; Pariani to Balbo, 30 March 1938, ASMAE, SAP—Etiopia, Fondo di Guerra, B 166; Pariani to Ciano, 31 March 1938, ASMAE, SAP—Etiopia, Fondo di Guerra, B 166.

68. The extensive files on the Italian negotiating positions appear in ASMAE, SAP—Etiopia, Fondo di Guerra, B 166. I am extremely grateful to Alberto Bianco of the University of Toulouse for informing me of the location of these papers. The British files are found in Perth to Halifax, various dates, 19 March to 9 April 1938, FO 371 22406, 22407, 22408, passim: see also, however, *CHD,* 23 March 1938, 26–29 March 1938, 2 April 1938, 3 April 1938, 5 April 1938, 6 April 1938, 8 April 1938, 10 April 1938, 13 April 1938, 14 April 1938, 93–102; and ASMAE, UC 84, passim. For the British Foreign Office debate on the importance of tying the entrance into force of the accord to specific Italian performance, see Perth to Halifax, 22 March 1938, FO 371 22640, W3710/83/41; Cadogan Minute, 23 March 1938, FO 371 22640, W3710/83/41; Halifax to Perth, 25 March 1938, FO 371 22640, W3710/83/41. For Italian assurances that this delay would not prejudice relations, see, for example, Halifax to Perth, 22 March 1938, FO 371 22407, R3102/23/22, reporting a conversation between Grandi and the British Foreign Secretary. For Mussolini's letter thanking Perth and Chamberlain for their efforts to reach the accord, see Mussolini to Chamberlain, 17 April 1938, *OO,* vol. 29, 411. For Chamberlain's views, see Chamberlain to Ida Chamberlain, 16 April 1938, NC 18/1/1047.

69. See for example, *CHD,* 13 April 1938, 14 April 1938, 100–101. Of course, Italian troops would continue to fight an ultimately unwinnable battle to establish occupation of the entire country. (Brian R. Sullivan, "The Italian-Ethiopian War, October 1935–November 1941: Causes, Conduct, and Consequences," in *Great Powers and Little Wars: The Limits of Power,* ed. A. Hamish Ion [Westport, Conn.: Greenwood, 1993], 167–201).

70. "Discorso al Senato," 30 March 1939, *OO*, vol. 20, 74–82.

71. Ciano Appunto, 12 March 1938, ASMAE, GAB 398, SAP—Etiopia, Fondo di Guerra, B 166; Ciano to Attolico, 3 April 1938, ASMAE, SAP—Etiopia, Fondo di Guerra, B 166; see notes 61–62 and 64 in chapter 3 for the Italian refusal of French participation at the opening of the tortuous road to the Easter Accord in 1937.

72. See, for example, Cranborne to Foreign Office, 28 January 1938, FO 371 22402, R852/23/22; Phipps to Halifax, 24 February 1938, FO 371 22403, R1696/23/22; Halifax to Phipps, 23 February 1938, FO 371 22403, R1696/23/22.

73. Phipps to Halifax, 5 March 1938, FO 371 22405, R2117/23/22; Perth to Halifax, 7 March 1938, FO 371 22405, R2188/23/22; Halifax to Phipps, 10 March 1938, FO 371 22405, R2188/23/22.

74. Prunas to Ciano, initialled by Mussolini, 2 March 1938, ASMAE, SAP—Francia, B 33.

75. Ciano to Attolico, 17 March 1938, ASMAE, UC 4; Ciano to Attolico, 3 April 1938, ASMAE, GAB 29. The short-lived Blum cabinet reopened the Pyrenees frontier on 17 March 1938, which did little to endear France to Mussolini and Ciano (Martin Thomas, *Britain, France, and Appeasement: Anglo-French Relations in the Popular Front Era* [Oxford: Berg, 1996], 220).

76. Gordon Dutter, "Doing Business with the Fascists: French Economic Relations under the Popular Front Government," *French History* 4, no. 2 (June 1990): 199–223.

77. *CHD,* 14 April 1938, 100–101.

78. Prunas to Ciano, 7 April 1938, 9 April 1938 x2, ASMAE, SAP—Francia, B 33. In the second dispatch on 9 April, Prunas referred directly to these instructions, which did not appear in this file.

79. Bonnet to Blondel and Cambon (London), 15 April 1938, *DDF,* 2d ser., vol. 9, no. 183, 378–79.

80. Promemoria consegnato da Blondel il 16 aprile 1938, ASMAE, UC 61.

81. *CHD,* 16 April 1938, 19 April 1938, 101–2, 103–4.

82. For a published English translation of the Italian records of the meetings in Rome, see Strang, "Imperial Dreams," 799–809.

83. Promemoria consegnato da Blondel il 22 aprile 1938, ASMAE, UC 61. Mussolini circled and heavily marked the sections on Spain and Tunisia on this copy. In a later copy, he scrawled an emphatic "no" in the margins regarding the points on Spain and adherence to the Naval Treaty (Promemoria consegnato da Blondel 2 maggio 1938, ASMAE, UC 61; *CHD,* 22 April 1938, 105).

84. Even Ciano continued to hope for an agreement in the first two weeks of May. On 2 May, he noted that he would "shortly" be making a pact with France. As late as 12 May, Ciano believed that an agreement with France would help to facilitate de jure recognition of the empire. Mussolini overruled his subordinate, finally informing Ciano of his objections (*CHD,* 2 May 1938, 12 May 1938, 111–12, 115).

85. Quoted in *CHD,* 23 April 1938, 105–6. *CHD,* 3 April 1938, 17 April 1938, 18 April 1938, 24 April 1938, 96, 102–3, 105–6; Attolico to Ciano, 21 April 1938,

ASMAE, UC 90. For more information, see Toscano, *Alto-Adige-South Tyrol,* 37–41, and Weinberg, *Starting World War II,* 304–8.

86. *CHD,* 1 May 1938, 111.

87. For a discussion and the text of von Ribbentrop's plans, see Donald Cameron Watt, "An Earlier Model for the Pact of Steel: The Draft Treaties Exchanged between Germany and Italy during Hitler's visit to Rome in May 1938," *International Affairs* 3, no. 2 (April 1957): 185–97.

88. Quoted in *CHD,* 9 May 1938, 112; *CHD,* 3–9 May 1938, 112–14; see also Toscano, *Alto Adige-Sud Tyrol,* 41; Toscano, *The Origins of the Pact of Steel* (Baltimore: John Hopkins University Press, 1967), 10–23; Weinberg, *Starting World War II,* 308–9.

89. Quoted in *CHD,* 30 April 1938, 107; *CHD,* 26 March 1938, 94.

90. Appunto per il Duce: Viaggio in Albania, 2 May 1938, ASMAE, UC 55, UC 90.

91. *CHD,* 10 May 1938, 114.

92. *CHD,* 10 May 1938, 17 May 1938, 19 May 1938, 13 June 1938, 18 June 1938, 21 June 1938, 114, 117, 117–18, 127, 128, 129, 132; Jacomoni to Ciano, 6 June 1936, ASMAE, UC 55; Appunto del M. Jacomoni: Questione Urgenti," n.d. (internal evidence suggests mid-June 1938), ASMAE, UC 55; Jacomoni Appunto sulla situazione dell'Albania, 13 June 1938, ASMAE, UC 55.

93. Quoted in *CHD,* 13 May 1938, 115–16. *CHD,* 12 May 1938, 115.

94. "Il Discorso di Genova," 14 May 1938, *OO,* vol. 29, 99–102.

95. Colloquio Prunas-Bonnet, Prunas to Ciano, 23 May 1938, ASMAE, UC 61.

96. Quoted in *CHD,* 3 June 1938, 124–25. *CHD,* 17 May 1938, 19 May 1938, 20 May 1938, 24 May 1938, 30 May 1938, 6 June 1938, 117, 117–18, 118, 120–21, 122–23, 125–26.

97. Quartararo blamed clumsy French diplomacy for the failure of the Franco-Italian discussions (Quartararo, *Roma tra Londra e Berlino,* 395–97). In her view, Rome actually initiated these approaches. Mussolini, she argued, intended to create "a solid Anglo-French-Italian front against Germany." This move would restore Italy's position as the decisive weight. For Quartararo, only the extensive and extreme list of French desiderata prevented any progress and provoked Mussolini's backlash. Ciano directly contradicted this view in several diary entries (*CHD,* 10–14 May 1938, 114–16). Significantly, Quartararo cited only French sources indicating their hopes for a possible rapprochement. In short, she provided no direct evidence of any sort to bolster her strained conclusion. William Shorrock also overemphasized the possibility of a genuine Franco-Italian rapprochement. He blamed Léger Saint-Léger, the French Secretary-General at the Foreign Ministry, who distrusted any of Mussolini's promises for almost deliberately sabotaging any discussions, 227. The extensive list of proposals had no bearing on Mussolini's refusal to reach an accord with France. He rejected the core aspect of the French approach—the Spanish question. Tellingly, Shorrock, too, relied on French sources.

98. Ciano appunto per il Duce, 18 May 1938, ASMAE, UC 61, also UC 84; *CHD,* 18 May 1938, 117; Colloquio con l'ambasciatore di Gran Bretagna, 3 June 1938, ASMAE, UC 84; see also *CDP,* Conversation with the British Ambassador, 3 June 1938; and *CHD,* 3 June 1938, 124–25, 210–12.

99. Phipps to Halifax, 16 June 1936, FO 371 22427, R5705/240/22; see also Phipps's recognition of Mussolini's strategy, 21 June 1938, FO 371 22427 R5738/240/22. Cadogan displayed his lack of sensitivity for French concerns, writing that refereeing this Franco-Italian dispute was "like trying to keep the peace between two operatic stars" (Cadogan Minute, 24 June 1938, R5705/240/22).

100. Ciano appunto per il Duce, 28 June 1938, ASMAE, UC 61; Prunas to Ciano, 18, 22 June 1936, ASMAE, US 229; Halifax Memorandum of conversation with Grandi, 17 June 1836, FO 371 22412, R5586/23/22.

101. Mussolini to Franco, 5 March 1938, ASMAE, UC 46.

102. Ciano to Attolico, 16, 19 March 1938, ASMAE, UC 46; *CHD,* 16 March 1938, 89–90; see also von Ribbentrop Memorandum for the Führer, 17 March 1938, *DGFP,* ser. D, vol. 3, no. 547, 621–22. Ambassador Phipps provided one hint of a possible source for these rumors. He wrote that his Dutch colleague had asked French General Pétain whether or not France intended to dispatch two French divisions to Spain. Pétain allegedly indicated that it would do so. But Phipps believed that General Staff Officers had threatened to resign in that case, thus preventing Paul-Boncour from acting (Phipps to Halifax, 7 April 1938, FO 371, W4579/83/41; see also W3971 and W3424 in the same file, both Phipps to Halifax, 25 and 16 March 1938, respectively).

103. Ciano to Grandi, Prunas, Attolico, Viola, 4 April 1938, ASMAE, US 229; Attolico to Ciano, 25 March 1938, ASMAE, US 225; Magistrati to Ciano, 31 March 1938, US 225; Ciano to Attolico, 30 March 1938, 1 April 1938, US 225; Viola to Ciano, 8 April 1938, US 225. Ciano to Viola, 12 April 1938, US 225.

104. *CHD,* 2 April 1938, 5 April 1938, 6 April 1938, 8 April 1938, 9 April 1938, 15 April 1938, 96, 97, 97–98, 99, 99, 101.

105. Ciano to the Consuls General of Marseilles and Toulouse, 23 April 1938, ASMAE, US 231. Ciano to Grandi, 30 April 1938, ASMAE, US 233.

106. *CHD,* 30 April 1938, 13 May 1938, 107, 115–16.

107. *CHD,* 16 May 1938, 17 May 1938, 20 May 1938, 23 May 1938, 24 May 1938, 116, 117, 118, 120, 131.

108. Date unknown, notes made by the Führer's Adjutant (Schmundt) on Observations made by the Führer on the Contemporary Strategic Situation, *DGFP,* ser. D, vol. 2, no. 32, 238–39. Based on internal evidence, Schmundt likely made this note sometime in April. For more on the likely date and the context in which Schmundt wrote this document, see Weinberg, *Starting World War II,* 337–40.

109. *CHD,* 26 May 1938, 121.

110. Von Mackensen to von Ribbentrop, 29 May 1938, *DGFP,* ser. D, vol. 2, no. 220, 356–57; von Mackensen to von Ribbentrop, 1 June 1938, *DGFP,* ser. D,

vol. 2, no. 229, 373; *CHD,* 27 May 1938, 28 May 1938, 31 May 1938, 121–23. British Intelligence information suggested that, during the meetings at the beginning of May, Mussolini had given Hitler virtual carte blanche in dealing with Czechoslovakia, provided that Hitler handled the matter without a general European war (Perth to Jebb, 16 June 1938, FO 371, R5700/43/22, entire).

111. Appunto, 15 March 1938, ASMAE, SAP—Etiopia, Fondo di Guerra, B 166. Appunto, 28 March 1938, ASMAE, SAP—Etiopia, Fondo di Guerra, B 166. Mussolini heavily marked the sections on Palestine.

112. Ciano to Silliti (Gedda), Ciano to Passera (Sanaa), 17 April 1938, ASMAE, SAP—Etiopia, Fondo di Guerra, B 166; Ciano to Consulati in Gerusalem, Beirut, Algeri, Rabat, Tengeri, Tunisi, Aleppo, Damascus, Casablanca, Tetuan, 19 April 1938, ASMAE, SAP—Etiopia, Fondo di Guerra, B 166; Ciano to Silliti (Gedda), Quaroni (Kabul), Passera (Sanaa), Consulati in Gerusalem, Beirut, Algeri, Rabat, Tengeri, Tunisi, Aleppo, Damascus, Casablanca, Tetuan, 21 April 1938, ASMAE, SAP—Etiopia, Fondo di Guerra, B 166.

113. Mazzolini (Gerusalem) to Ciano, 21, 26 April 1938, ASMAE, SAP—Etiopia, Fondo di Guerra, B 166; Quaroni (Kabul) to Ciano, 9 May 1938, ASMAE, SAP—Etiopia, Fondo di Guerra, B 166; Appunto, 29 April 1938, ASMAE, SAP—Etiopia, Fondo di Guerra, B 166.

114. Grandi to Ciano, 18 May 1938, ASMAE, US 231. This shipment of Italian aircraft stemmed in part from attempts to meet Franco's previous request for reinforcement of Nationalist airpower (Ciano to Ministero Aeronautica, 18 March 1938, ASMAE, US 20). On French supplies to Spain during April 1938, see Pietromarchi to Ministero di Guerra, Servizio Informazione Militare, Attolico, Grandi, Viola, 23 May 1938, ASMAE, US 231; see also Viola Appunto, 25 May 1938, US 232, on French resupply of a Red Brigade (seventy-second brigade of the forty-third division) isolated against the French border.

115. Ciano appunto per il Duce, 18 May 1938, ASMAE, UC 61, UC 84; *CHD,* 20 May 1938, 24 May 1938, 118, 120–21.

116. For the Italian acceptance of the British-sponsored plan, which was to trade eventual proportional withdrawal of volunteers for granting of belligerency rights to Franco's Nationalist army in Spain, see Ciano to Grandi, 21 May 1938, ASMAE, US 6; Ciano to Attolico, 25 May 1938, ASMAE, US 6; Grandi to Ciano, 1 June 1938, ASMAE, US 6; Grandi to Ciano, 27, 31 May 1938, ASMAE, US 7. For British estimates on the partial withdrawal of Italy's garrison in Libya, see Consul in Tripoli to Halifax, plus Nichols and Halifax minutes, 9 May 1938, 13 May 1938, 16 May 1938, respectively, FO 371 22430, R4738/263/22.

117. Colloquio con l'ambasciatore di Gran Bretagna, 3 June 1938, ASMAE, UC 84; see also *CDP,* Conversation with the British Ambassador, 3 June 1938, and *CHD,* 3 June 1938, 124–25. For Perth's views of the meeting, see Perth to Halifax, 3 June 1938, 4 June 1938, FO 371 22412, R5297/23/22. For Perth's credulity in the face of Ciano's disinformation, see Perth to Ingram, 4 June 1938, FO 371 22412, R5343/23/22.

118. *CHD,* 3 June 1938, 9 June 1938, 124–25, 126–27; see also von Mack-ensen to the Foreign Ministry, 9 June 1938, *DGFP,* ser. D, vol. 3, no. 599, 683–84.

119. Quoted in *CHD,* 22 June 1938, 129; Colloquio con l'ambasciatore di Gran Bretagna, 20 June 1938, ASMAE, UC 85; see also Ciano to Attolico, 6 June 1938, ASMAE, US 225.

120. Grandi to Ciano, 25 June 1938, 26 June 1938, ASMAE, SAP—Gran Bre-tagna, B 26.

121. Colloquio con l'ambasciatore di Gran Bretagna, 28 June 1938, ASMAE, UC 61, SAP—Gran Bretagna, B 26.

122. *CHD,* 20–21 June 1938, 28–29 June 1938, 129–30, 132–33.

123. For an extracted copy of this memorandum, see Estratto del promemoria redatto del Duce e consegnato da S.E. il ministro a Lord Perth in occasione del 2 luglio 1938, ASMAE, UC 61; *CHD,* 27–31 June 1938, 1 July 1938, 131–34.

124. Colloquio con l'ambasciatore di Gran Bretagna, 2 July 1938, ASMAE, UC 85. Estratto del pro-memoria redatto del Duce e consegnato da S.E. il ministro a Lord Perth in occasione del 2 luglio 1938, ASMAE, UC 61. Copies of both Ciano's account of the meeting and the memorandum for Perth exist in US 231. For Perth's account, see Perth to Halifax, 2 July 1938, FO 371 22413, R5663/23/22, R5978/23/22, R5979/23/22.

125. Perth to Halifax, 5 July 1938, FO 371 22413, R6020/23/22; Perth to Ingram, 8 July 1938, FO 371 22413, R6171/23/22; Ingram and Strang Minutes, 12 July 1938, FO 371 22413, R6171/23/22; Sargent Minute, 14 July 1938, FO 371 22413, R6171/23/22; Perth to Halifax, 8 July 1938, FO 371 22413, R6186/23/22.

126. Cadogan to Perth, 8 July 1938, FO 371 22413, R5979/23/22; Halifax to Perth, 9 July 1938, FO 371 22413, R5979/23/22; see also Halifax to Perth, 9 July 1938, PREM 1/276.

127. Colloquio con l'ambasciatore di Gran Bretagna, 11 July 1938, ASMAE, UC 85, UC 61, US 231; *CHD,* 12 July 1938, 135–36.

128. Quoted in *CHD,* 17 July 1928, 137–38.

129. Reynolds M. Salerno, "The French Navy and the Appeasement of Italy," *English Historical Review* 112, no. 1 (February 1997): 66–104.

130. C.I.D. Paper 475-C, 20 July 1938, FO 371 22438, R6795/899/22.

131. Ciano Appunto per il Duce, 18 June 1938, ASMAE, UC 49; *CHD,* 15 April 1938, 16–18 June 1938, 101, 128–29. For the published version, see *CDP,* Conversation with the Yugoslav Prime Minister, Stoyadinovich, 18 June 1938.

132. Colloquio a Palazzo Venezia tra Il Duce, Ciano, Imrédy e de Kánya, 18 July 1938, ASMAE, UC 49, UC 85; *CHD,* 17–20 July 1938, 137–38. For more on Hungarian diplomatic considerations, see Magda Ádám, "The Munich Crisis and Hungary: The Fall of the Versailles Settlement in Central Europe," *Diplomacy & Statecraft* 10, no. 2/3 (1999): 91–92.

133. Conversazioni militari italo-hungarese, 25, 26, 27 July 1938 (document dated 30 July 1938), ASMAE, UC 58.

134. Mussolini to Prince Fumimaro Konoe (Mussolini used the standard European ordering of names rather than the Japanese system), 19 March 1938, *OO,* vol. 29, 410.

135. Ciano to Auriti, 9 April 1938, ASMAE, UC 53.

136. For solid and brief coverage of Japanese politics and strategy, see Akira Iriye, *The Origins of the Second World War in Asia and the Pacific* (London: Longmans, 1987); Toscano, *Origins of the Pact of Steel,* passim.

137. Ciano to Auriti, 6 June 1936, ASMAE, UC 53; Auriti to Ciano, 24 June 1938, ASMAE, UC 53; *CHD,* 31 May 1938, 1 June 1938, 6 June 1938, 21 June 1938, 123, 124, 125–26, 129; see also Ferretti, *Il Giappone e la politica estera italiana, 1935–41,* 213–18.

138. *CHD,* 27 June 1938, 2 July 1938, 11 July 1938, 15 July 1938, 17 July 1938, July 1938, 131–32, 134, 135, 136–37, 138–39. For further discussion, see Toscano, *The Origins of the Pact of Steel,* 27–39.

139. Von Ribbentrop Memorandum, 4 August 1938, *DGFP,* ser. D, vol. 2, no. 334, 533–34.

CHAPTER 5

The Czech Crisis and the March to the Sea

In addition to his accelerating the radicalization of Italian foreign policy, Mussolini had also undertaken steps to radicalize domestic mores and attitudes. In April 1938, Mussolini had directed the Council of Ministers to create the Institute for Human Reclamation and the Development *(Ortogenesi)* of Race. He wanted this institute to study the demographic potential of the nation and the psychological and physical development of races. He planned to develop Italians' harmony of body and spirit and to correct their imperfections and anomalies. In addition, he directed the members of the institute to study racial questions, especially the question of biological determination. At the same time, he ordered the council to pass a decree law expediting the settlement of 1,800 Italian families in Libya by the end of October. It encouraged the settlers to begin land redistribution along European lines and to establish small businesses.[1]

In July, he renewed his racialist and anti-Jewish tirades. He spoke to Ciano of his plans for a third wave to transform the Italian people that the Duce would launch in October. He would institute concentration camps to allow for stricter treatment of those members of the bourgeoisie who still looked toward London and Paris for cultural and political inspiration. The campaign would begin with "a bonfire of Jewish, Masonic, and pro-French literature" and would include a ban on publication of Jewish writers. His goal, he explained, was to make the Italian populace "hard, relentless, and hateful—in fact, masters."[2] A few days later, a group of scholars, allegedly under the aegis of the Ministero della Cultura Populare, issued a statement on the racial question. Mussolini confided to Ciano that he had written most of it himself. Similarly, Achille Starace issued a series of anti-Semitic screeds that Mussolini also claimed as his own. Mussolini's central idea in this campaign was to create a racial consciousness in the Italian people. He feared that their lack of racial preparedness underlay the problems of revolts against Italian suzerainty in the Amhara; in the Duce's mind, Italians were as yet too weak to rule with an iron fist. Accordingly, the supposed scholars' statement claimed that a pure Italian race existed, of Aryan stock, which held the patrimony of the great Italian nation. Jews, who were by definition of non-European origin, emphatically did not belong to the Italian race nation. Miscegenation between Italians and non-Europeans threatened the purity of Italian blood; the new reality of racial consciousness would have to end this hybridization of the Italian race. Italian newspapers and Fascist Party orders disseminated this campaign.[3]

At the beginning of August, Mussolini took initial steps in the persecution of Jews. A 1 August decree prohibited Jewish students from attending school for the 1938–39 scholastic year. A few days later, Mussolini issued "Informazione Diplomatica #18" on the racial issue. He argued speciously that his racial policy dated from 1919 and the formation of Fascism. The conquest of the empire had brought the racial problem to the forefront. Eventually, Italy would send millions of men to Libya and Ethiopia, and these men would need an appropriate "omnipresent racial consciousness." Otherwise, they would create a "bastard race, neither European nor African," which would "foment disintegration and revolt." In Italy itself, Mussolini cited the need for discriminatory measures against Jews. Jews maintained their racial solidarity and, owing to their internationalist impulses, their refusal to recognize state borders. Given the paramount position of the state in Mussolini's *mentalité,* he thought that their outlook alienated Jews from the Italian race. Hence, in Mussolini's eyes, there was an historical "equation" between the corruption of "Judaism, bolshevism, and masonism." Only those Jews who renounced their religion and its internationalist connections or otherwise proved their loyalty to Fascism could hope to become accepted in the Fascist state.[4] In keeping with this public statement for the international community, Mussolini privately told Ciano to recall all Jews serving in the diplomatic corps. It was inappropriate for Jews to represent the Italian people.[5] Mussolini's racial consciousness highlighted the nature of his challenge to the West. Although his anti-Semitism and racism had a different nature than did Hitler's, it was clear that Mussolini sought to align the policies of the two Fascist regimes more closely. Furthermore, Mussolini's expansionistic designs underlay his discriminatory initiatives in the empire. He believed that if he could harden the Italian race, then his military would have the élan vital to defeat the Western democracies.

Despite Mussolini's increasing extremism in domestic policy and his annoyance with Britain, however, he still hoped to secure British recognition of his victory in Ethiopia. Accordingly, on 26 July 1938, when Chamberlain made a statement on Spain to the House of Commons that the accord would be implemented only after "Spain ceased to be a menace to the peace of Europe," Ciano ordered Guido Crolla, the London Embassy's chargé d'affaires, to determine Chamberlain's precise meaning. Ciano wanted to know if the prime minister meant that withdrawal of volunteers was a sufficient condition to allow the Anglo-Italian agreement's implementation or if he had raised an additional barrier.[6] Crolla tried to see Chamberlain, but the prime minister was at his weekend retreat at Chequers, so Halifax informed Crolla that there had in fact been no change in British policy. However, given the previous condition of the nonintervention proposal, Halifax explained, the cabinet's condition on withdrawal technically meant that implementation could not occur until the withdrawal of the last Italian volunteer. In order to establish a more reasonable condition, he said that he would accept substantial withdrawal as had been established in the nonintervention committee earlier that year. Upon Chamberlain's return, he confirmed to Crolla that his words to the House had been uttered during the heat of the debate. He slightly amended Halifax's terms, privately indicating that he would accept the "partial or substantial" withdrawal of volunteers as sufficient to implement the agreement. This change represented an important concession; no longer would Mussolini have to retire the entire *C.T.V.* in order to achieve de jure recognition.[7] On instructions, Crolla indicated that Mussolini understood this clarification of British policy.[8]

The same day as Chamberlain informed Crolla of the modification of his policy, however, Halifax finally reached the breaking point in the face of repeated Italian violations of the nonintervention agreement and the terms of the Easter Accord. He observed that the French government had closed its frontier for some seven weeks, and even Franco accepted that the French supply of volunteers and matériel had stopped. Still, Italy continued to send aircraft and men at rates higher than those strictly necessary to replace losses. He argued that Ciano knew of this activity and had not been entirely truthful in speaking to Perth on this issue. These actions, Halifax said, threatened the nonintervention agreement and, more significantly, implementation of the Easter Accord. Finally, the foreign secretary warned that continued Italian violation of its commitments could provoke the French government to reopen the frontier, with the result of extending the war.[9] Having consulted with Mussolini, Ciano rejected this warning. At a meeting with Perth on 20 August, he replied that no one denied that Italian forces fought in Spain. They needed replacements of men and matériel. The *C.T.V.* could not fight armed only with olive branches. He cited alleged French arms shipments as creating the need for continued Italian ones and denied that he had sent any new troops. Ciano knew that London would recognize the transparency of his deceit, but there was little that he could do in the face of the objective evidence but to issue denials. He also realized that his evasions would hardly help Italy's relations with Great Britain. Though Mussolini did want to receive the benefit of recognition from the Easter Accord, he certainly did not intend to adhere to its conditions.[10] Halifax limited himself to ordering Perth to indicate the British government's disbelief, as it had compelling evidence that disproved Ciano's claims.[11]

During August, however, Mussolini did begin to implement changes that would meet British government conditions. Franco had established a clear superiority of forces, but a Republican counteroffensive had derailed his attacks toward Valencia, thus creating a renewed stalemate. Mussolini once more despaired of immediate victory and decided to break the stalemate. In a meeting with General Mario Berti, the Commander of the *C.T.V.,* Mussolini said that his actions would depend on Franco. If the Caudillo were prepared to release Italian volunteers, then Mussolini would withdraw them, though he would not subjugate his heroes to the "humiliating formalities" of the nonintervention protocols; he would withdraw his heroes with honor. If, however, Franco wanted Italian troops to remain, then Mussolini would dispatch 10,000 replacements and reinforcements. He wanted Franco to use the *C.T.V.* in battle rather than keeping it idle. If, in response, France reopened the frontier, he would commit one or more divisions as necessary.[12] In short, Mussolini was prepared to shred the Anglo-Italian agreement in order to achieve his victory.

Berti took Mussolini's proposal to Franco. The Caudillo did not want to receive new divisions, which would serve both to provoke France and to shift some of the glory of victory from Spanish Nationalist shoulders to Italian ones. He said that he would, however, accept replacements. After a long discussion on 21 August, Mussolini decided to reduce the overall number of troops in Spain. He would concentrate the *Twenty-third March* and *Littorio* divisions into a nine-battalion division, composed of the best of the remaining troops, and withdraw the others. He would also leave in place the combined Italo-Spanish Arrow division and his specialist troops and aircraft. This plan would allow him to repatriate between 10,000 and 15,000 troops. This "substantial and unilateral" withdrawal of volunteers, he argued, would place Britain in a difficult position. Either the Chamberlain cabinet would have to implement the Easter Accord or renounce it. If the cabinet let it lapse, then Mussolini, freed from the need to account in any way for British sympathies, would immediately sign a military alliance with Germany.[13]

In the last week of August, Ambassador Viola cabled from Spain that Republican forces had regained the initiative, and their morale was increasing while that of the Nationalist troops declined. Viola suggested withdrawing all of the Italian infantry, despite Franco's preference for retaining one division. Mussolini fulminated that Franco had let another opportunity for victory slip through his hands.[14] He concurred with Viola's suggestion, since he had learned that it could take up to five months to reorganize the *C.T.V.* into one division; he therefore decided to repatriate all Italian infantry unless Franco objected strenuously. This decision did not please Franco, but he could do nothing except express his displeasure and seek to postpone any withdrawal. Mussolini, stung by Franco's apparent impression that the Duce was letting down the Nationalist side, decided to return to his original decision; he would leave one Italian division in place. Franco concurred, and Berti implemented the Duce's orders. With this decision made, Mussolini announced to Ciano that Italy would march with Franco to the end.[15] With the withdrawal of some 10,000 infantry determined, Ciano dispatched a note to London to determine Chamberlain's exact policy. He requested a precise definition of the term "substantial withdrawal" in order to implement the agreement.[16] This question landed in the midst of the increasing tension surrounding the Czechoslovak crisis and sparked strong differences of opinion among the Foreign Office officials. In the face of conflicting estimates of Mussolini's fealty to the Axis, the British government gave no immediate reply, and in the interim, German pressure on Czechoslovakia eventually overtook Ciano's démarche.[17]

In the meantime, while Mussolini and Ciano contemplated the necessary withdrawal to implement the Easter Accord, however, they continued to carry out a policy hostile to the West. At the end of July and in early August, the French government made attempts to reinvigorate the failed conversations with Ciano. According to Renato Prunas, the chargé d'affaires in the Paris Embassy, a "friend of Foreign Minister Bonnet" insistently asked why the talks had broken down. This unnamed envoy assured

Prunas that Bonnet was very anxious to make concessions in order to win Italian approval. Bonnet resorted to this unofficial démarche because he could not risk a formal Italian rejection of his approaches. If French journalists learned of an Italian rebuff, it would seriously embarrass the Daladier cabinet and perhaps even provoke a political crisis. But Bonnet would be willing to proceed through normal channels if the Duce wanted to renew contact.[18] A few days later, Jules Blondel, the French chargé in Rome, made a similar approach to Ciano, who had been away from his post owing to illness. Ciano responded noncommittally, as Mussolini had no interest in a rapprochement with France.[19]

Similarly, Mussolini and Ciano worked against British interests in the Red Sea while at the same time they sought implementation of the accord that was to prevent such actions. In February 1938, the Italian mission to Yemen had requested shipments of arms and ammunition. At that time, the Ministry of War had denied permission, as the wars in Ethiopia and Spain had significantly depleted its own stocks. General Pariani, the Italian Army Chief of Staff, however, thought that it would be wise to send a shipment for political and strategic reasons. A significant Italian presence in Yemen would apply pressure to British imperial communications, as Italy could potentially create land, air, and naval bases astride Britain's imperial communications through the Suez Canal.[20] In August, Ciano returned to this earlier proposal and decided to send four batteries of artillery, two antiaircraft weapons, 10,000 rifles, and ammunition and other supplies. In the context of the weakly armed Arabian Peninsula, these weapons represented an important contribution to Yemeni strength. In addition, Ciano dispatched military advisors to train Yemeni troops.[21] This shipment represented a direct violation of Mussolini's pledges in the Easter Accord, and Mussolini's policy in Yemen aimed to strike directly at British interests.

Most importantly, of course, Mussolini worked against Western interests in his support for German claims against Czechoslovakia. In August, Italian sources began reporting that Hitler was preparing to destroy Czechoslovakia. Admiral Canaris, the German intelligence chief, informed Efisio Marras, the Italian military attaché in Berlin, that German military leaders opposed any attack. Hitler believed that any war could be contained to Central Europe, but Canaris thought that reasoning faulty. France would surely defend Czechoslovakia, and Germany would be isolated save for Italian support. Canaris hoped that Mussolini would intervene with Hitler in order to prevent any attack.[22] Apparently Canaris was unaware that Mussolini had already offered Italian support for a German assault. Colonel Badini, the Assistant military attaché, echoed some of Canaris's information. His sources suggested that the German general staff were convinced Hitler would invade Czechoslovakia at the end of September.[23]

These intelligence reports had a common message, but Ciano hoped to receive more concrete information from the German government. He ordered Attolico to approach von Ribbentrop to determine German aims. Ciano wanted Attolico to say that Italy needed to know German intentions in order to enable "us to take measures in time on our Western frontier." Ciano expected that this "communication will have a considerable effect on the Germans as it indicates just how far we are prepared to go." Ciano noted that Mussolini had decided on action. If Hitler's war was not contained and France entered the fray, then there would be no alternative but for Italy "to fall in beside Germany immediately, with all our resources."[24] Attolico spoke to von Ribbentrop, but the German foreign minister was noncommittal at first, and Mussolini directed Ciano and Attolico to try again.[25] This repeated probing had the unintentional effect in Berlin of indicating that Italy was somewhat lukewarm about war over Czechoslovakia.[26] Significantly, Ambassador Attolico did not share Mussolini's readiness to enter a war. He went so far as to suggest a mild criticism of Mussolini's policy. It was essential, Attolico argued, for Mussolini to clear the air. Attolico thought, mistakenly, that the lack of information from Germany, combined with insufficient Italian vigor in determining German aims, had created the impression that Italy was fully behind any German action. Attolico said that this erroneous policy could involve Italy in war along the lines of the Great War. Further, he suggested that the *Kriegsmarine* was too weak to contain substantial elements of the Royal Navy, so the full weight of British seapower would fall on Italian forces. Mussolini, of course, did not share Attolico's view. Still, although for different reasons, both Mussolini and Attolico wanted to know Hitler's precise intentions and his expectations of Italy.[27]

On 1 September, Attolico was able to deliver Ciano's letter that said that Italy "was prepared to take measures of a military character." The German foreign minister, given a further indication of Italian support, was more forthcoming. He repeatedly declared that Hitler intended to destroy Czechoslovakia through an invasion but that the attack would not occur for a month.[28] Despite the clarity of von Ribbentrop's statements, however, Ciano refused to believe his ambassador's report. Attolico's lack of enthusiasm for war clouded Ciano's judgement. Over the following week, Ciano still hoped for a clearer indication from Germany of Hitler's plans. Eventually, the Prince of Hesse carried a message from the Führer to Ciano. After thanking the Italians for their support, however, Hesse misled Ciano about Hitler's intentions, stating that Hitler would attack Czechoslovakia only if provoked. On the other hand, Attolico continued to provide accurate information from Berlin that Mussolini and Ciano continued to discount.[29]

At the Nuremberg rallies on 10 September, Field Marshal Göring recommended a meeting between the leaders of both countries to occur sometime between 10 and 25 September. Attolico suggested that there would be lower expectations of this meeting if General Pariani represented the Italian government instead of Mussolini or Ciano, and Mussolini accepted this reasoning. He apparently failed at that time to understand the real implications of Göring's suggestion. Hitler wanted to arrange the details of Italian military and diplomatic action. Ciano recognized the importance of this proposal in light of the pervasive atmosphere of war, but Mussolini seemed unconcerned, preferring to take his already scheduled tour of the northern provinces.[30]

Even though Mussolini did not yet grasp Hitler's intentions, he gave strong public diplomatic support for German revisionism. On 9 September, Mussolini had issued "Informazione Diplomatica #19." This document indicated Italy's complete solidarity with the Axis, declaring that Italy was ready for any eventuality. Mussolini supported Sudeten German leader Konrad Henlein's Karlsbad program, which called for a plebiscite that could lead to extensive Czechoslovak territorial concessions to Germany. Finally, Mussolini denounced the pernicious French leftist Pierre Cot and the evil of Soviet Bolshevism that contaminated the Prague government.[31] In "Informazione Diplomatica #20," released on 14 September after consultation with Berlin, Mussolini condemned Czechoslovakia, the "paradoxical creature of the diplomacy of Versailles." He empathized with the array of ethnic groups subordinated by Czech domination. He declared that there were two possible solutions: Sudeten German self-determination or war.[32] The next day, Mussolini published his "Letter to Runciman," the British mediator between the Czech government and its minorities. Mussolini returned to a pet theme; Czechoslovakia was not a true state based on racial homogeneity. It was instead an "artificial state" of diverse races and centrifugal forces. Mussolini demanded a plebiscite not only for Sudeten Germans, but also for all subject nationalities. Bohemia, the Duce wrote, should be reduced to the ethnic "borders traced by God."[33] As of that date, Mussolini's public demands far outstripped those of Hitler.

Mussolini's triumphalist promotion of German demands helped to escalate war tension. Similarly, Ciano indicated to various diplomats in Rome that Italy would likely fight alongside Germany, though he left some room for doubt. Ciano gave an unequivocal declaration to von Mackensen that Italy would remain at Germany's side in any eventuality. He suggested that Hitler give a clearer indication of German policy so that Mussolini could better coordinate his policy with Hitler's. Most importantly, Mussolini planned to make a major speech at Trieste on 18 September. What would Hitler like Mussolini to say?[34] Mussolini confirmed to Ciano that a military solution to German claims would be necessary, and the Duce declared his policy. If Great Britain did not go to war, then Mussolini would remain neutral. If Great Britain did declare war, making the struggle an ideological battle between democracy and Fascism, then Mussolini would fight. He left unsaid that this policy would give every possible latitude for the British government to avoid supporting its fellow democratic regime in France.[35]

At Trieste, Mussolini continued to heighten European tension in support of German demands. He said that Italians would not shirk their duty but would shoulder it in full; the Axis, which Mussolini claimed included Poland and Hungary, was absolutely solid. The only peaceful solution would require a plebiscite for all national groups in Czechoslovakia. Once more, Mussolini's public demands were more extreme than Hitler's. Mussolini accused Moscow of trying to involve Britain in an unnecessary war. Mussolini wanted Neville Chamberlain to declare that if President Beneš resisted a plebiscite, then Britain would disinterest itself. In that case, the Duce argued, no other countries would resort to war. In the meantime, though, any delay could ignite a war. Mussolini said that he foresaw a peaceful solution, but that if war came, it would be limited to south-central Europe.[36] In his continuing tour of the Northeast, Mussolini's speeches became increasingly bellicose. On 20 September, he tried to whip Italians into a war fever. Fascism was committed to battle, and peace was not sufficient to balance Italian sacrifices during the Great War. Mussolini trumpeted that Italy had taken Libya and Ethiopia and overturned the old diplomatic order and was strong in the air and on the sea and land and powerful in spirit. A cold-blooded, hardened warrior caste led the military, tempered by twenty years of battle and revolution, and Mussolini had created an "Italy hardened, Italy strong-willed, Italy warlike." Mussolini declared that "Italy today is a people on the fiery march."[37] Three days later, Mussolini denounced his French enemies across the Alps for clinging to a dead ideology. "They don't understand us and are too stupid to be dangerous."[38] Mussolini's truculent, bellicose speeches signaled both his loyalty to his Axis partner and his reckless disregard for any moderation of the war fever, or fears, that pervaded Europe. As Chamberlain met Hitler at Bad Godesberg on 22 September, Attolico informed the Foreign Ministry that the Prince of Hesse would carry an important message from Hitler to Mussolini. In the meantime, Chamberlain failed to dissuade Hitler, Czechoslovak, French, and British forces began to mobilize, and Ciano learned from Attolico that Hitler demanded cession of territory to begin 1 October.[39]

While Mussolini helped to whip up war hysteria, Ciano worked to further German aims in the Balkans. He encouraged Hungarian and Polish claims against Czechoslovakia. At the end of August, Miklós Horthy, the Hungarian regent, had visited Berlin for high-level talks with Adolf Hitler. Hungarian diplomats had recently finished negotiating the Bled agreement, signed on 23 August. This arrangement, concluded with members of the Little Entente, exchanged concessions allowing Hungarian rearmament and minority rights in Little Entente countries for a Hungarian renunciation of the use of force. This last compromise ran directly counter to Hitler's expectations of the role that Hungary would play in his plans to liquidate Czechoslovakia. In a meeting with the Führer, Jenö Rátz, the Hungarian defense minister, stated in clear terms that Hungary could carry out no offensive operations, as its military was woefully unprepared after years of restrictions under the Trianon Treaty; it could play no aggressive role. The Hungarian delegation further insisted that a German attack would certainly provoke a general war that would have potentially catastrophic results for Hungary.[40] Prime Minister Béla Imrédy and Foreign Minister de Kánya shared these sentiments with Attolico, adding that Hungary would take no action until absolutely certain of Yugoslav neutrality.[41] Yet, as the crisis escalated at the end of September, Ciano sought to keep Hungarian and even Polish claims to the forefront. In order to ensure Yugoslav neutrality, Mussolini supported Hungary's plans to take no military action until after a German attack. He insisted, however, that Hungarian demands form a central part of any settlement and that the Hungarian government should provoke ethnic confrontations to keep its claims at the forefront. Ciano made the need for an integral solution for all of the subject minorities clear in a meeting with the British ambassador.[42] Even more seriously, faced with rumors of potential Soviet air support for Czechoslovakia, Mussolini agreed to dispatch Italian fighters to Hungarian airfields near Miskolo. Italian airmen wearing Hungarian uniforms would pilot these planes. This action could potentially have led to direct Italo-Soviet confrontation in the skies above Budapest.[43] Mussolini and Ciano once again had taken actions that could seriously inflame the imminent crisis.

On 23 September, amid reports that Hitler could attack as soon as the next day, Ciano informed von Mackensen that Italian military preparations had been completed. This statement was certainly not true but could only give the impression of continued Italian support for German military action.[44] The next day, Ciano received confirmation that Hitler had fixed the date of 1 October for the cession of territory. Attolico cabled that General Keitel, the chief of German armed forces high command, had informed Italy's military attaché that if Czechoslovak concessions were not forthcoming, then Germany would quickly crush the Czech army.[45] On 25 September, Hesse arrived with Hitler's message of vague appreciation for Italian support. While Hesse and Ciano drove to meet the Duce at Schio, Ciano repeated Mussolini's prior decision that Italy would enter the war immediately after Britain did. Hesse gave Ciano the rather stale news that Hitler would seek to invade Czechoslovakia by 1 October. Mussolini thought that the Western democracies would not march to war, but if they did, then Mussolini confirmed Ciano's earlier words; Italy would enter the war immediately after Britain did. He made this promise conditional on British entry, Mussolini said, only in order to avoid giving the British government a pretext for war.[46]

Upon Ciano's return to Rome the next day, he and Admiral Cavagnari went to the *Ministero della Marina* to discuss Italy's war potential with the general staff. The *Regia Marina* would have a tough task defending against the combined Anglo-French navies, so Japanese participation in the war would be essential to divert the Royal Navy in particular, but Japanese support, of course, was not forthcoming. Conditions for war, therefore, were not promising. Italy's two serviceable battleships, the *Conte di Cavour* and the *Giulio Cesare,* would face as many as twelve British and French battleships. The naval staff hoped to control the central Mediterranean through the use of mines to cover the Sicilian Channel, while light units such as submarines and motor-torpedo boats carried out a kind of guerrilla warfare against the superior Anglo-French fleets. Naval planners also hoped to be able to support the army's attack toward the Suez Canal, but, given the likely lack of air support in the eastern Mediterranean basin, that offensive represented a grave risk. Without the support of allies to divert Anglo-French resources from the Mediterranean, Italy faced almost certain defeat in a battle for control of the Mediterranean.[47]

Despite the grim prospects in the event of war, Mussolini took no steps to try to avert it. Instead, he decided on a more thorough mobilization; he would send reinforcements to Libya, which would be the only possible theatre of offensive operations for the *Regio Esercito.* General Pariani spoke idly of the need for a lightning war and thought that Italy should use poison gas. On 27 September, Mussolini ordered the undersecretaries of the air, navy and war ministries to mobilize enough troops to defend the Alpine frontier in the event of an initial French attack. Mussolini was unsure whether Britain and France would declare war, and if they did, what their tactics would be. He hoped that Germany and Italy could avoid a major war. In any event, he thought it wise for Ciano and Italian generals to meet their German counterparts to determine Axis war strategy. This meeting, which Hitler had approved, would occur at Munich on 29 September 1938. In the meantime, Hitler advanced the deadline for his ultimatum to 2:00 P.M. on 28 September. As night fell on 27 September, both Mussolini and Ciano thought that war was imminent the following day.[48]

Why did Mussolini rush to the barricades to commit Italy to battle, especially when Italy had no fundamental interests at stake? In part, Mussolini simply detested Czechoslovakia; it was a mongrel state, a creation of Versailles diplomacy, representing the worst elements of multiethnic bourgeois democracy and French international diplomacy. A charter member of the Little Entente, Czechoslovakia resisted Hungarian revisionism, long one of the Duce's goals. Czech military and political ties to France extended French influence into the Danube valley and interfered with Italian efforts to develop its competing interests there. Germany's liquidation of Czechoslovakia would allow Italy some greater freedom in extending its own influence in the Balkans, though at the cost of increased German competition. In addition, President Beneš supported precisely the kind of internationalism that Mussolini despised. More directly, Czechoslovakia had supported the League in its sanctions policy against Italy, with Beneš having chaired the meeting where sanctions had been imposed.[49] Czechoslovakia had also annoyed Mussolini through its support for Ethiopian rebels. Italian intelligence agents had reported that a French ship under Greek flags carried Czech arms to French Somalia. From there, the arms shipment traveled across the Djibouti frontier and into rebel hands.[50] Ciano had protested in the strongest terms, suggesting to his minister in Prague that the Czechs should keep their rifles there, as "it could be that they will need them shortly!"[51] Mussolini's contempt for bourgeois democratic states meant that he would revel in Czechoslovakia's destruction.

In addition, Mussolini needed to extend support to Germany in order to secure reciprocal German support for his own plans in Albania. Part of the Duce's strategic calculations for his annexation project required German intimidation of Yugoslavia, France, and Britain. His repeated indications of Italian fealty to the Axis and to revisionism, he hoped, would strengthen

the Axis and ensure that he would be able to face down the West in Albania and elsewhere in the Mediterranean. In the context of Mussolini's
beliefs about the decadence and demographic weakness of France and
Britain, he thought that his virtual carte blanche to Hitler's planned war
carried little risk. Recent information indicated that in Britain almost one-
quarter of the population was over the age of fifty; for Mussolini, that lack
of vitality meant that Britain's imperial splendor was inevitably fading.
The Duce had heavily underlined a section of a British peer's comments
on British birthrates and death rates where the writer forecast a population
decline from 40,000,000 to 4,000,000 in a hundred years if current trends
continued.[52] Mussolini assumed until very late in September that this
demographic problem and the weakness shown by Chamberlain's visits to
Berchtesgaden and Bad Godesberg meant that Britain would not go to war.
After both Britain and France began mobilizing, however, he needed to
reconsider his support in light of the very bleak strategic situation.

The *Wehrmacht,* naturally, would be tied down in the campaign against
Czechoslovakia. It would leave only token forces in the West to face the
French army. These deployments would mean that both Britain and France
could employ their ground forces almost exclusively against Italy in the
initial stages of the war. Similarly, the combined Anglo-French navies
could concentrate in the Mediterranean basin. Far from driving a wedge
between Britain and France, as Mussolini had tried to do over the last two
years, the Czechoslovak crisis appeared to be solidifying an alliance.
Accordingly, the Italian armed forces would be on the defensive in every
potential theatre of war, without significant German or Japanese support.[53]
Apparent Anglo-French cohesion suggested strongly that Mussolini avoid
war at the end of September 1938.

Similarly, the situation in Spain also indicated that Mussolini rein in his
war fever. In the atmosphere of impending war in the last week of September, Franco faced a difficult choice. The Spanish Republican government staked its last chance for survival on a general war over
Czechoslovakia. If France and Britain went to war, then the Negrín government planned to declare war immediately on Germany and Italy. Since
the international community recognized the Negrín regime as the legitimate government of Spain, both Britain and France presumably would be
obliged to accept Republican Spain as an ally. Franco feared that these circumstances could lead to a French occupation of Spanish Morocco, the
Balearics, and even Catalonia. Franco learned from his intelligence
sources, however, that if he remained neutral in this potential wider conflict, then neither Britain nor France would intervene.[54] Further, in the case

of a general war, Nationalist Spain could count on no significant support from its Axis associates. Not surprisingly, therefore, Franco declared to the representatives of the Western democracies that he would remain neutral in the imminent conflict.[55] Franco's decision initially disgusted Ciano. He wrote that Italy's war dead would "turn in their graves." He briefly considered ordering the evacuation of the *Corpo Truppe Voluntarie*. After Mussolini and Ciano discussed the matter on 26 September, however, they decided that Franco's neutrality was both inevitable and reasonable and that they would leave the *C.T.V.* in place.[56]

Mussolini's Spanish imbroglio, therefore, also suggested that the Duce draw back from going to war. Despite his pessimism regarding Franco's chances for immediate victory, the balance of forces in Spain suggested that, eventually, Franco would win. Nationalist troops outnumbered the Republic's by nearly a two to one margin, and Italian and German support gave Franco's army a clear technical advantage. At the time of Munich, Italy still had more than 40,000 men in Spain, plus roughly one hundred light tanks, 600 artillery pieces, and 250 planes. Italy had spent almost six billion lire (over sixty million pounds sterling at the official exchange rate). Over the course of the war, Italy had sent more than 700 aircraft.[57] Mussolini could not expect to recoup this extraordinary commitment in money, men, and arms unless and until Franco achieved final victory. A premature Italian war with France over Czechoslovakia threatened that victory. The Daladier cabinet potentially could take a series of steps, from reopening the frontier to volunteers and matériel to an outright invasion of Spain to defeat Franco and his Axis allies. Given Italy's bloody, expensive, and lengthy intervention, it made little sense to risk this catastrophic defeat, especially when a peaceful settlement of the Czechoslovak crisis would doom the Republican government. If Mussolini avoided war, he could maintain the hope that Italy could save its army in Spain, recoup its investment, and eventually establish a strong ally hostile to France on the Pyrenees frontier.

Italy's complicated relationship with Japan was the final issue that drew Mussolini back from the brink of war. As the Munich crisis reached its height during the last half of September, Mussolini learned that the Japanese government had decided to proceed with either a tripartite alliance or a bilateral alliance with Italy. Within a few weeks, Italy could expect to sign some manner of formal military alliance.[58] Despite the prospects of achieving this foreign policy coup, however, Mussolini could count on no meaningful Japanese military support against the British empire in the event of war over Czechoslovakia. Only if he were able to avoid a general

European conflict could he secure Japan as an ally in the eventual campaign against the Western democracies. For Mussolini, it made little sense
to cast aside this major diplomatic and strategic advantage in order to fight
a war in 1938 in which Italy held no direct interest. This complex arrangement of considerations suggested that Italian participation in a war over
Czechoslovakia carried the risk of catastrophic defeat in both the political
and strategic arenas. It is not surprising that, even given Mussolini's profound desire for a confrontation with the Western democracies, he chose
not to go to war in September 1938.

On 28 September, as is well known, Mussolini received official démarches
from both the British and American governments asking him to intercede
with Hitler to postpone his ultimatum.[59] Perth met Ciano at 10:00 that
morning to present Chamberlain's official request for Mussolini's intercession. Typically, Ciano interceded with Perth to squelch a rumored
French proposal along the same lines. He argued that any French association with attempts to save the peace would doom the initiative.[60] Ciano
hurriedly traveled from the Palazzo Chigi to meet the Duce at the Palazzo
Venezia. At 11:00, Mussolini seized this opportunity to prevent an immediate war and telephoned Attolico in Berlin. Attolico's instructions read:
"Go immediately to the Führer, and, on the premise that in any case I will
be at his side, tell him that I suggest a postponement of twenty-four hours
in the initiation of hostilities." Having thus once more committed Italy to
war at Hitler's discretion, Mussolini hoped that Hitler would accept
Chamberlain's proposal for a four-power conference to arrange the cession of Czech territory. Hitler accepted Mussolini's proposal, provided
that the Duce would attend the meeting personally. Mussolini confided to
Ciano, "As you see...I am only moderately happy, because though perhaps at a heavy price, we could have liquidated France and Great Britain
for ever. We now have overwhelming proof of this." On their way to
Munich, Mussolini condemned British policy. According to the Duce:

In a country where animals are adored to the point of making cemeteries and hospi-
tals and houses for them, and legacies are bequeathed to parrots, you can be sure that
decadence has set in. Besides other reasons apart, it is also a result of the composition of the English people. Four million surplus women. Four million sexually
unsatisfied women, artificially creating a host of problems in order to excite or
appease their senses. Not being able to embrace one man, they embrace humanity.[61]

Mussolini's churlishness aside, his fondness for population demographics
suggests that he genuinely believed that this drivel passed for serious
analysis. He had apparently already forgotten the pessimistic apprecia-

tions of his subordinates when contemplating the prospect of war with the so-called decadent British empire.

Ciano and Mussolini met Hitler at the frontier. The discussion centered on Hitler's desire to dismantle Czechoslovakia in order to free up divisions for a future campaign against France. The Führer told Ciano, "The time will come in which together we will have to battle against the Western Powers. Better that this occur while the Duce and I are at the head of our two countries, young and full of energy, and while we have the more powerful armies." Mussolini supported Hitler's demand that the Czechs be prohibited from attending the conference.[62] Senior German Foreign Office officials had prepared a draft text of an agreement, which Hitler had approved. Attolico obtained a copy of the draft through unusual channels and gave it to Mussolini. The Duce presented it at the conference as if it were an Italian proposal and it formed the agenda for the Munich conference.[63]

At the conference itself, Mussolini pushed forward Polish and Hungarian claims, though the other participants showed little interest in dealing with these demands, and he supported Hitler's views on the need for a quick solution. Ciano noted that the Duce also snubbed Neville Chamberlain when he tried to extend his thanks for Mussolini's intercession with Hitler. Mussolini refused to meet privately with the prime minister, as the Duce did not want to offend Hitler, and he also thought that protocol would require a similar meeting with Daladier, which Mussolini refused to contemplate. Instead, he invited Chamberlain to Rome. While Mussolini's relations with Hitler were very cordial, the Duce still refused to negotiate alliance terms with von Ribbentrop, as the time was still not ripe.[64] As he returned to Rome, Italian crowds en route cheered Mussolini as the savior of European peace, but he resented this display of Italians' lack of martial vigor; he wanted to be feared for his military victories, not lauded for his peacemaking.[65]

With the Czech crisis resolved peacefully and to the advantage of the Axis, Mussolini and Ciano returned to their medium-term goal of the implementation of the Easter Accord. Mussolini had told Chamberlain at Munich that Italy would shortly withdraw 10,000 volunteers from Spain and had given a polite but noncommittal hearing to Chamberlain's proposal of a four-power pact regarding Spain.[66] Back in Rome, Ciano summoned Perth and told the British ambassador that, as Communism appeared to be in retreat in Spain, Mussolini had decided to withdraw 10,000 volunteers. Typically, he paired this news with a veiled threat that if the British cabinet did not implement the Anglo-Italian accord by the time of the Fascist Grand Council meeting a few days later, then Italy would choose to "take up a different line." Perth understood that Ciano meant signing a military alliance with Germany. Furthermore, Mussolini ruled out any consideration of a renewed pact of four until the agreement entered into force.[67] Perth reserved his response until he could consult his government. The next day, he returned and questioned subtly the sincerity of Mussolini's commitment. Perth asked Ciano whether or not Mussolini would promise not to send any more soldiers, pilots, or airplanes to Spain. Ciano replied that Mussolini would certainly not bind his hands regarding the possible future need for reinforcing Italian ground forces. Ciano cited the British diplomatic note of 20 June 1938, arguing that Italy had met the specified conditions. In short, Mussolini and Ciano had rendered the entire withdrawal of volunteers a largely moot point; the British cabinet could not expect the Italian government to observe any of its past, largely unfulfilled promises regarding nonintervention in Spain.[68]

Despite the apparent hollowness of Mussolini's commitment to the principles of the Easter Accord, Perth argued that its implementation was of vital importance. He believed that if the accord were implemented, then Mussolini would work toward general pacification of European tension. If not, however, Mussolini might opt for a military alliance with Germany. Perth believed that the Duce clearly preferred to conclude the pact with Great Britain.[69] Perth's assessment reflected views within the Foreign Office and Westminster. On one hand, by formally recognizing the Italian conquest of Ethiopia, the accord could restore Mussolini's freedom of maneuver within the Axis and reduce the constant pressure he presumably faced from Berlin. It would bind Mussolini to limit his anti-British intrigues in the Middle East and would further the spirit of reconciliation begun at Munich. It would also serve as a kind of reward for Mussolini's behavior at Munich. On the other hand, the accord's implementation would give evidence of British weakness in the face of Mussolini's thinly veiled threats and would alarm the French government and leftist opinion within Britain. After an internal debate, Halifax cabled Perth that the cabinet would eventually implement the accord, as the potential benefits outweighed the presumed risks. Nevertheless, Halifax sought guarantees from the Duce that no more Italian volunteers would reach Spain. Nor would he meet Mussolini's hurried timetable; the decision would have to be taken up in cabinet and Parliament and would not occur before the beginning of November.[70] Perth delivered this verdict, and Mussolini's initial response was to reject this delay out of hand, but he eventually agreed, especially as he had no intention of granting any concessions limiting the future dispatch of volunteers to Spain. Perth's words satisfied Ciano that the cabinet would implement the accord some time in November, and over the following week, the Italian foreign minister refused all British requests for assurances regarding an embargo on future shipments of planes, pilots, or ground forces.[71] Mussolini had rendered any hopes that the accord would lead to a genuine Anglo-Italian rapprochement almost fanciful. Significantly, he had managed at long last to arrange an Anglo-Italian condominium that excluded French participation.

In the same vein, Mussolini's anti-French leanings led him to reject Daladier's and Bonnet's diplomatic attempts to reach a parallel rapprochement. On 4 October 1938, Renato Prunas, the chargé d'affaires in Paris, cabled that the Daladier government had decided to send an ambassador to Rome.[72] After consulting Rome, Bonnet decided to shift André François-Poncet from Berlin to Rome and to carry out a wide-ranging shuffle of the French diplomatic corps. Daladier indicated to Prunas that these moves signaled a strong French desire to improve relations with Italy. Mussolini and Ciano were largely unmoved, though they were pleased that the French government had capitulated to Italy's demands for recognition of the empire, especially without having to grant any quid pro quo.[73]

After Ciano eventually gave his approval of François-Poncet's appointment, Daladier tried to follow this opening through a semiofficial source—Anatole De Monzie, the Italophile minister of public works. De Monzie had an extensive conversation with Prunas, stating that Daladier would be happy to meet with Mussolini at a time and place of the latter's choosing. Daladier would potentially be prepared to offer concessions but would have to know of Mussolini's requests in advance. De Monzie said that Daladier hoped for "a decisive and rapid improvement of Italo-French relations." Mussolini scrawled a flat rejection *(niente)* in the margin of Prunas's report, and Ciano ordered Prunas to let the démarche lie.[74] Instead, Mussolini said a few days later, "An insurmountable abyss must be dug between us and them."[75] In a speech to the National Council of the Fascist Party, Mussolini trumpeted that Fascism would have to destroy the bourgeois spirit. As the Italian bourgeoisie still looked to Britain and France for inspiration, the Axis would have to destroy those plutodemocratic powers in order to end this domestic infestation. The combined demographic power of Germany and Italy gave the Axis a decisive superiority over the decadent French people, and therefore the Duce did not fear war with France.[76] Mussolini's temporary accord with Great Britain clearly did not extend to France and had little effect on his long-term goals.

Mussolini also did not hesitate to violate any post-Munich spirit of international reconciliation in his Balkan policy. In early October, Ciano resisted Hungarian requests for Italian support against the rump Czechoslovak state. He believed that Italy had more in common with the quasi-Fascist Stoyadinović regime than with the old-school Hungarian leaders. Further, he thought that Hungarian policy traditionally leaned toward Germany rather than Italy, and that von Ribbentrop could use Hungarian demands against Czechoslovakia as a stalking horse for extending German influence toward the Adriatic Sea. Ciano convinced Mussolini that Yugoslavia was the more important client. Still, Ciano promised that if the Czech government attacked Budapest, then Italy would dispatch the already mustered 100 planes that Italy had offered before Munich.[77] Mussolini could not abandon entirely his public support for Hungarian revisionism; on 4 October, he issued an "Informazione Diplomatica" calling for direct negotiations between Prague and Budapest in order to remove one million ethnic Magyars from Czech rule.[78]

The following week, Mussolini decided to push Hungarian claims more strongly. Lieutenant-Colonel Szabó, the Hungarian military attaché in Rome, had told the Duce of Hungarian plans to begin mobilizing on the Slovak frontier on 13 October. Mussolini directed Ciano to put pressure on the new Prague government to cede all territory with a majority Magyar population and to press for a joint Hungarian-Polish border in the sub-Carpathian Ukraine. Negotiations broke down between Hungarian and Czech diplomats on 14 October, and war appeared imminent. Mussolini and Ciano met with Foreign Minister de Kánya and Count István Csáky, chef de cabinet of the Hungarian Foreign Ministry. Csáky and de Kánya wanted a conference to arbitrate a territorial award to Hungary. In a telephone call to von Ribbentrop, however, Ciano could not overcome the German foreign minister's opposition to Hungarian demands. After Hungary's failure to participate in Hitler's planned war at the end of September, the Führer preferred to support his new Slovak client state rather than the allegedly treacherous Hungarians. In the face of German opposition, the Hungarian government backed down, leaving Ciano to complain bitterly about Germany having overridden Italian concerns. Although both Mussolini and Ciano bridled at the German actions, Mussolini temporarily changed his policy to match Germany's.[79]

On 20 October, von Ribbentrop phoned Ciano to say that he had arranged a territorial plan with representatives from Slovakia and Ruthenia. The German foreign minister wanted Ciano to recommend its acceptance to de Kánya. Significantly, von Ribbentrop would not provide details, and Ciano suspected a German betrayal of Hungarian interests. Accordingly, Mussolini refused to bring pressure against Budapest. Ciano's suspicions were justified; von Ribbentrop proposed to remove five towns from the Hungarian list of demands. Though de Kánya was willing to compromise on part of these desiderata, he again requested formal arbitration by both Italy and Germany. Once again, von Ribbentrop rejected this idea. Tension between Hungary and Germany had reached an acute stage. Ciano and Mussolini rudely debated von Ribbentrop's failings, including the Duce's description of von Ribbentrop's tiny brain. Nonetheless, despite the German foreign minister's dictatorial actions, Mussolini would not fully support Hungarian demands in the face of German opposition.[80]

The German foreign minister arrived in Italy for a meeting at the Palazzo Venezia on 27 October. Mussolini and von Ribbentrop decided that Italy and Germany would serve as arbiters of the territorial dispute between the semiautonomous Slovak government and Hungary. Over the following week, German and Italian delegations in Vienna pushed their respective clients' positions in often frank and disputatious discussions. Ciano argued that the arbitration award would underline the extent to which Anglo-French influence in the region had collapsed. Ciano was able to induce the German representatives, including a petulant von Ribbentrop and Hermann Göring, to accept a compromise slightly favorable to the Hungarian side. The Vienna Award settled a frontier that included the towns of Kassa, Ungvar, and Munkacs, plus some other disputed territories in Hungary. Ciano crowed that the unpreparedness of the German delegation allowed him greater freedom of movement than he had expected. The frontier drawn in Vienna pleased the Hungarian government and earned Ciano considerable prestige for his intercession in the face of German hostility to Hungarian aims.[81]

The Vienna Award, however, did not finally settle Hungarian revisionism. On 11 November, Minister Villani told Ciano that ethnic unrest in Ruthenia would require Hungarian military action to unite the territory with Hungary. Ciano cautioned against any such move. He thought that Hitler would surely oppose it, and Italy could find itself in the position of having to require Hungary to honor its acceptance of the Vienna award. The Hungarian government was unmoved by this advice, and Villani returned a week later to reemphasize the need for military action within twenty-four hours. Ciano repeated his objections; he refused to give any indication to Germany that Italy was playing a double game. He insisted that Hungary abide by the terms arranged in Vienna. Ciano appeared to sense no real impending crisis and left for a hunting holiday near Turin. In Ciano's absence, Hungarian Military Attaché Lt.-Col. Makó Laszló saw Mussolini to secure the Duce's support for Hungarian military action.[82] Laszló misled the Duce, declaring that the German government had already authorized Hungary's punitive action, when in fact Berlin had informed the Imrédy government in direct terms to observe the terms of the Vienna award. In addition to offering his diplomatic support, Mussolini arranged to dispatch ninety-six fighter planes. Filippo Anfuso, Ciano's chef de cabinet, phoned Ciano to indicate that a crisis was brewing. Ciano determined von Ribbentrop's actual attitude and learned of the extent of the Hungarian deception. Berlin then sent an official communiqué to the Imrédy cabinet demanding an immediate halt to any plans for invasion. Ciano gave similar instructions to both the Hungarian Minister Villani and to Lieutenant-Colonel Szabó. Ciano tried to cover for the Duce's actions as best he could; he argued that Mussolini had intended these planes for defensive purposes only, and that Italian support was predicated on the belief that Hitler had given his blessing to the Hungarian cause.[83] In the end, Mussolini's impetuous commitment to war did not cause any lasting damage to Italy, other than embarrassment at the ease with which the Duce had been gulled by Hungarian dishonesty. The Imrédy cabinet fared less well; it fell on 23 November.

Even in the midst of Italo-German tension over Hungarian claims on Slovakia, Hitler had decided that the time was ripe to sign a tripartite alliance with Japan and Italy. He had dispatched von Ribbentrop to Rome to secure Mussolini's adherence. In a 23 October telephone call to Ciano to announce his mission, von Ribbentrop had kept hidden his real aim, and Ciano had reacted petulantly to what he called von Ribbentrop's *coups de téléphone.*" The German foreign minister arrived for a two-day visit on the evening of 27 October. Before his meeting with his German counterpart, Ciano had already learned from the Japanese military and naval attachés of plans for a tripartite alliance roughly analogous to the one von Ribbentrop had presented at Munich.[84] Not knowing that his thunder had been stolen, von Ribbentrop presented Hitler's case. The Führer had resisted signing any alliance in the past because it could have provoked greater Western rearmament and made Chamberlain's and Daladier's positions untenable. Now that the West had awoken to the increasing tide of Axis power, there was no longer any reason to fear those repercussions. Even though both Britain and France were rearming, their weakness at Munich indicated that the Axis had achieved an overwhelming lead in arms production. In addition, von Ribbentrop argued, the initiative for the alliance proposal had come from the Japanese government, indicating that it would be possible to outflank those in the Gaimushō who wanted an Anglo-Japanese accord.[85] Ciano was in no hurry to agree to this German initiative. Von Ribbentrop's vainglorious and unspecific references to war with unnamed enemies worried the Italian foreign minister, and he still hoped to keep the door open to the eventual implementation of the Easter Accord that Perth had indicated would come the following month. Ciano thought that an Italo-German alliance existed already in practice; its conclusion would merely serve to alienate other countries and to make the Axis look even more aggressive.[86]

The next day, the two foreign ministers met Mussolini at the Palazzo Venezia. Ciano had already informed Mussolini of his personal stance, and the Duce agreed, though for different reasons. Mussolini wanted more time to guide public opinion on the need for what many Italians, particularly in the senior ranks of the *Regio Esercito,* would see as an unpopular alliance, and he too did not want to foreclose the possibility of the implementation of the Easter Accord. Accordingly, though Mussolini accepted the alliance in principle, he insisted that it should be delayed. During the meeting, von Ribbentrop expounded the Führer's reasons for concluding an alliance, speaking on the same lines as he had indicated to Ciano the previous day. Mussolini agreed that within the next few years a war with Britain and France was inevitable. A "historical trend" had created an "irreparable breach" between the Axis and the Western democracies. Consequently, Mussolini wanted a strictly offensive alliance.

We have no need for a purely defensive alliance. There is no need because no one thinks of attacking the totalitarian States. We want instead to create an alliance to change the map of the world. For this we will need to fix our objectives and our conquests: for our part we know already where we must go.[87]

In the meantime, however, the Duce thought that the existing ideological solidarity and practical arrangements between Germany and Italy meant that the Axis performed as a virtual alliance. The meeting ended with von Ribbentrop's insistence that the Mediterranean would become an Italian sea and that Germany would work to that end. Mussolini recognized that he had disappointed his German partner, and he dispatched Ciano that evening to assuage von Ribbentrop's apparent dismay. Ciano emphasized that, despite the Duce's tactical decision for postponement, Italian solidarity to the Axis was absolute. The next morning, Mussolini presented von Ribbentrop with a summary of his reasoning for delaying the signature of a formal alliance.[88] Despite Mussolini's rebuff of von Ribbentrop's démarche, the meetings had shown the essential agreement between the aims of the two Fascist powers. Both intended to carry out wars of expansion in the future. The real difference between the two was of tactics and short-term relative power. Mussolini could not yet contemplate victorious war against the combined Anglo-French armies. He needed both to split the Western democracies politically and to modernize his own forces. Though Mussolini's stated domestic reasons for postponing the alliance were undoubtedly valid, within a few short weeks he would ignore them entirely in embarking Italy on its path to destruction.

Mussolini's temporary delay did not, however, fundamentally damage Axis solidarity, despite approaches from Great Britain designed to ease strained Anglo-Italian relations. On 7 November, in the aftermath of the Vienna Award, Perth had informed Ciano that his government would finally implement the Easter Accord on 16 November 1938—some seven months after the initial signing. Ciano had reassured his German partners that Britain's final recognition of Italy's conquest of Ethiopia would not alter German-Italian relations.[89] After the signing ceremony in Rome, Mussolini complimented his foreign minister on his achievement, but dismissed the importance of the Accord. As Ciano recorded Mussolini's attitude, "'All this is very important,' he said, 'but it does not alter our policy. In Europe the Axis remains fundamental. In the Mediterranean we will collaborate with the English as long as we can. France remains outside— our claims on her have now been defined.'" Mussolini had come to regret his invitation to Chamberlain extended at Munich, but at Ciano's behest, reluctantly agreed to accept the idea of a visit in January. The foreign minister thought there would a "psychological value" to this Anglo-Italian summit, but did not expect much in the way of practical results.[90]

Chamberlain's moves to secure a rapprochement with Italy did not sway the Duce. With the Anglo-Italian agreement in hand, Mussolini moved to highlight the differences in Italian policy toward the two Western democracies, both domestically and internationally. Internally, he continued to increase his discriminatory measures against Jews. In early September, the rubber-stamp Council of Ministers had passed a set of decree laws stripping citizenship from foreign-born Jews and prohibiting foreign Jews from establishing residence in Italian possessions. Those who chose not to leave within six months would be expelled. The council also banned Jews from holding professorships at universities and expelled Jewish students from schools. The decree law removed Jews' membership in all academies and associations of arts and sciences and established a six-week termination date for employment of Jewish teachers.[91]

In October, Mussolini had introduced his plans for a wider ranging set of anti-Semitic laws in a speech to the Fascist Grand Council. He based his harangue on the idea that the development of the Italian empire required the development of an appropriate racial consciousness. Accordingly, he would ban marriages between Italians and Jews or Italians and members of non-Aryan races, between civil servants and any foreigners, and would pass measures prohibiting the lessening of white prestige in the empire. Jewish internationalism, which was inherently opposed to Fascism, Mussolini thundered, made these measures necessary; "World Judaism—especially after the abolition of Masonry—has been the animator of anti-Fascism in every camp."[92]

In keeping with his ideological convictions, however, Mussolini did somewhat qualify his anti-Semitism. While he defined Jews in part biologically—one was Jewish because of birth and not because one practiced the religion—the Duce did allow exceptions. If a given Jew had proven loyalty to the Fascist regime and to the Italian people, then he or she would be exempt from the decree laws' applications. These exceptions applied in several cases: to the families of those who had died in the Great War, Libya, Ethiopia, or Spain; to those who had volunteered in the four wars; to the families of those who had fallen or who were wounded in the Fascist cause; those who had joined the Fascist Party during its struggle from 1919 to 1922 and in the latter half of 1924; and those who had performed acts of exceptional merit recognized through a special commission. A race tribunal considered equivocal cases. In essence, Mussolini divided Jews into simple categories—those who had proven their loyalty to the state and those who by nature of their birth were perforce anti-Fascist and therefore anti-Italian.[93] The Council of Ministers approved these racialist policies in early November.[94] At the same time, it passed Mussolini's Defence of the Race laws. Mussolini had told the National Council of the Fascist Party that Italians were of pure Aryan, Mediterranean stock. Despite their racial purity, Italians had not developed their racial consciousness.[95] Mussolini blamed the continued revolts in the Amhara region of Ethiopia not on his own murderous brutality but rather on this lack of racial and imperial will. The various decree laws created separate zones in the Italian empire, with a separate "indigenous quarter," and banned miscegenation, as well as implementing the anti-Semitic discrimination that Mussolini had spelled out in October.[96] The Duce believed that these racialist policies were required in order to create a hardened Italian people who would have the martial vigor necessary to seize and to rule his new empire.

Mussolini's expansionist dreams continued to lead him toward the German camp. Three initiatives between the Italian and German Axis partners in November highlighted Mussolini's essential solidarity to the Axis. In early November, despite Mussolini's refusal of a formal alliance with Germany, General Pariani, the Italian undersecretary of state for war, continued to push for staff talks aimed at increasing military cooperation between the Axis powers. The rush to coordinate policy in the planned but ultimately canceled meeting of military and diplomatic leaders at Munich clearly demonstrated the need for some form of integrated military planning. German military officials instructed Colonel von Rintelin, their military attaché in Rome, to proceed slowly, echoing Mussolini's words regarding the alliance: agreement in principle but with a delay in the conclusion of an actual agreement.[97] More profitably, Ciano signed a cultural agreement with Germany. He noted that this arrangement was more substantial than the usual soporifics; the agreement dealt with educational issues and exchanges of officials. Both parties thought that these ties would help to create greater public acceptance of the Axis domestically, as well as cementing what Ciano called a "a true Axis atmosphere."[98]

Less happily for Mussolini and Ciano, von Ribbentrop also worked toward a Franco-German accord similar to the Anglo-German declaration for future consultation signed at Munich. Mussolini's detestation of France's government had shattered any possibility of rapprochement between the two Latin sisters, so Mussolini could hardly relish the possibility of a German initiative to reach agreement outside the bounds of Axis solidarity. He reconciled himself to the eventuality, directing Attolico in Berlin to intercede with von Ribbentrop to wait until after Chamberlain and Halifax visited Paris later in the month. Mussolini wanted to learn more clearly the lines of French policy in the aftermath of Munich. On 8 November, Attolico accordingly informed Ernst von Weizsäcker, state secretary at the Wilhelmstrasse. Later that day, Mussolini directed Attolico to try to ensure that von Ribbentrop followed the extremely loose arrangement of the Anglo-German agreement signed at Munich. German diplomats had already given the French government a document that called for joint consultation, von Weizsäcker informed Attolico, but he said that he would discuss the issue with von Ribbentrop. When informed of Mussolini's views, von Ribbentrop agreed to the requested delay and also to try to water down the clause calling for consultation. The Wilhelmstrasse eventually set the signing ceremony for 6 December and gave Attolico a copy of the declaration's text.[99] Despite von Ribbentrop's attempts to assuage Mussolini's concerns, the Duce did not entirely believe that the eventual Franco-German declaration would be the anodyne exercise that it was. Neither Hitler nor von Ribbentrop intended to be bound by promises made to the French government; they issued the declaration only for its propaganda value.

Despite the Franco-German accord that would be signed in Paris and the appearance of a possible split in Axis solidarity, Mussolini continued to reject French overtures for a rapprochement. Before the new French Ambassador André François-Poncet's arrival in Rome, he had tried to indicate the Daladier government's desire to repair the breach with Italy. In a meeting with Renato Prunas, the French chargé d'affaires, he suggested that France's recognition of Italy's Ethiopian conquest, which had carried no conditions, indicated the sincere desire of Frenchmen to restore a four-power collaborative arrangement to put an end to international anarchy.[100] Unfortunately for the French ambassador, his mission was doomed to failure, as Mussolini did not share that goal. Shortly before François-Poncet's arrival, Mussolini had told Ciano that he disliked François-Poncet intensely and, more cryptically, that the Duce would "help him break his head."[101] At the same time, the Duce ordered Fascist hierarch Achille Starace to prepare a propaganda campaign agitating for the so-called return of Tunisia and Nice. On 8 November 1938, Mussolini outlined his future plans for France. The plans fell into two categories. The first set was more immediate, and Italy might arrange them through negotiation. Mussolini wanted a condominium arrangement to give Italy virtual exclusivity of rights in the French colony of Tunisia; Ciano later noted that Mussolini wanted Italians to be the only "living force of the white race" in Tunisia. This increase of Italian control would represent a marked change from the negotiated Mussolini-Laval agreement of 1935. Similarly, Mussolini wanted control of the Djibuti railroad, vital for the continued existence and supply of Italian East Africa, and a condominium arrangement for control of the Djibuti port and surrounding areas. Increased representation on the Suez Canal Board and the lowering of tariffs for shipping were the final elements of this first stage of desiderata. In the longer term, and possible only through a victorious war against France, Mussolini wanted to extend Italian territory on its northwest frontier to the Var River, completing the ring of the Alps, and to control Corsica as a directly ruled Italian province. Obviously, the French government would never voluntarily cede these territories, and the Duce knew that these dreams would eventually lead to war with France. He was not, however, speaking of a precisely determined set of perfect plans; the timing for these adventures would depend on circumstance. It might be one year or ten, but the Duce warned Ciano that "we must never lose sight of this goal."[102]

In the short term, however, Mussolini and Ciano concentrated on the first set of demands. Accordingly, Ciano informed Grandi of the demands regarding Tunis, Djibuti, and the Suez Canal. He wanted Grandi to influence the British government toward applying pressure on France to make these concessions.[103] In order to carry out the longer-term preparations, Mussolini wanted the repatriation of Italians living in France or in French protectorates. Both Mussolini and Ciano feared French reprisals against Italians in the foreseeable collision between the two empires and wanted to ensure that they could be offered appropriate protection in the event of war. In addition, Mussolini hoped that he could score a considerable propaganda coup by repatriating potential soldiers to swell his legions of 8 million bayonets. Mussolini approved offers of pensions and subsidies to those who were willing to repatriate themselves. Despite the eventual outlay of substantial amounts of lire, however, only some 50,000 Italian expatriates would take up the Duce's offer.[104]

Mussolini and Ciano gave other indications of their disdain for France. In his memoirs, Raffaele Guariglia, the new Italian ambassador to France, recorded the obligatory meeting with Ciano where traditionally the foreign minister would give his ambassador detailed instructions. In this case, Ciano said that Guariglia should do nothing.[105] Another signal occurred at a meeting on 29 November, when Mussolini rejected outright François-Poncet's overtures for a return to a four-power pact; the French left, the Duce complained, had already ruined the first four-power arrangement, and he would not take part in similar plans again. He argued that the Spanish Civil War had poisoned Italian relations with France, and he rudely left behind a speechless François-Poncet.[106]

Against this background of anti-French rancor and inchoate war planning, Mussolini spoke to the Fascist Grand Council the same day. Mussolini repeated his plans that he had earlier outlined to Ciano, emphasizing especially the need for Tunisia, Corsica, and an expanded Alpine frontier to secure Italy's position in the Mediterranean. Once Chamberlain and Halifax had finished their visit to Paris at the end of November, Mussolini moved deliberately to try to intimidate the Daladier government. He imagined, largely incorrectly, that the Anglo-French talks had established a virtual alliance between the two countries.[107] In the face of his apparent failure to separate the two powers, Mussolini launched a two-pronged policy. He directed Ambassador Attolico to inform von Ribbentrop that Italy was ready to sign a military alliance with Germany. Mussolini was able to make this potentially public commitment as the British government had ratified the Easter Accord; the Duce no longer seemed to fear alienating the Chamberlain cabinet.[108] Attolico did not pursue this suggestion vigorously; he replied that von Ribbentrop was not immediately available. Attolico believed from his own sources that Mussolini was misinformed regarding the supposed Anglo-French alliance. When Mussolini learned that Britain had given little in the way of commitments to France, the immediate impetus for an alliance had passed. With a renewed belief that he could continue to wean Britain from France, Mussolini returned to that campaign.[109] He and an apparently unwitting Ciano carried out a coup de théâtre designed to achieve several goals: to intimidate the Daladier government into making concessions, to try once more to separate Britain and France, and to make public the long-range goals of Mussolini's irredentism.

Ciano delivered a major speech to the Fascist Chamber of Deputies on 30 November 1938. He had invited both François-Poncet and Perth to attend, lending a darker character to the subsequent events. Ciano's speech, preapproved by the Duce, consisted of a long ode praising Italian victories in Ethiopia and Spain.[110] Ciano stressed his hopes for an accord with Great Britain, albeit one based on "absolute parity," whether "moral, political, or military." When Ciano reached the climax of his oration, he declared the Fascist government's intention "to defend the legitimate interests and aspirations of the Italian people." At that moment, deputies rose to their feet, calling for the annexation of "Tunis, Nice, Corsica, Savoy." Outside, demonstrators paraded through the streets echoing the chant. Mussolini and Ciano refused to intervene to stop the deputies' antics. With François-Poncet and Perth in attendance, such passivity lent an official aura to the obviously prearranged outburst.[111] Afterward, Mussolini said to Ciano, "That is the way to pose a problem and to set a people in motion."[112] He hoped to intimidate the Daladier Government, compelling it to make frantic concessions, but the Duce miscalculated.

Unsurprisingly, this display of Italian irredentism touched off angry reactions in Paris and throughout France. Against a background of anti-Italian demonstrations, Bonnet declared in the French Chamber of Deputies that France would not cede an acre of territory. He summoned Guariglia the next day to protest the demonstrations inside and outside the chamber. The French foreign minister particularly noted Mussolini's and Ciano's refusal to quiet the protests. Guariglia reported that the incident had seriously damaged relations with France and in particular, that it had heightened the suspicions of the French General Staff that Fascist Italy aimed to seize Tunisia. He feared that it would prompt greater determination to resist Italian revisionism.[113] In addition, on instructions François-Poncet delivered an official protest to Ciano on 2 December. He asked pointedly whether or not the demonstration in the chamber, held in the presence of the Italian head of government, represented official Italian policy. François-Poncet reminded Ciano of the 1935 Mussolini-Laval accords and asked whether or not Ciano thought that they were still in force. Ciano responded that his speech represented the sole guide to Italian policy, as the demonstration had been spontaneous. Ciano refused to be drawn on the question of the Mussolini-Laval accords, responding only that he would have to review the question. He argued that that agreement rested on a basis of sound mutual relations, which France had violated with its opposition to Italy's Ethiopian war.[114] Pleased by French diplomatic hysteria, Mussolini and Ciano fleshed out their plans. In their view, the demonstrations meant that Italians would understand that the Axis had specifically Italian objectives—not merely German ones. Fascist Italy would not renounce its longer-term claims against France, even though they would require a major war. Instead, in the near future, Mussolini planned to denounce the 1935 Mussolini-Laval accords and to put forward his first round of claims regarding Tunis, Djibuti, and a share in the Suez Canal. As Mussolini would note a week later, "The time for [hostilities] has not yet come."[115]

When von Ribbentrop signed his anodyne accord with France, Mussolini moved to ensure that Western diplomats and statesmen did not interpret the event as showing any cracks in Axis solidarity. He issued an official "Informazione Diplomatica" to publicize his interpretation of the event. Germany, he wrote, had informed and consulted with Italy throughout the negotiations leading to the pact. He himself had received a copy of the text as early as October. In short, Italy approved of the German move. That said, however, he trumpeted that Italians did not believe "in perpetual peace or eternal crystallization of special interests or situations." He emphasized that French policy was hostile to Italian Fascism, and "rife with the residual spirit of Versailles." He concluded by insisting that French leaders should not delude themselves that they could drive a wedge between Italy and Germany.[116]

Ciano continued to prepare the ground for the repudiation of the Mussolini-Laval accords, and the Chamberlain cabinet's flaccid response unwittingly convinced Mussolini to maintain this policy. On 4 December, Ambassador Perth did request a clarification from Ciano of the demonstrations of 30 November, but he announced the same day that Chamberlain and Halifax had chosen to visit Rome from 11 to 14 January. Although Chamberlain undoubtedly believed that he could best moderate Mussolini's behavior through this type of contact, the announcement undermined any British criticism of Mussolini's irrendentist antics.[117] More seriously, in response to a question, Chamberlain announced in the House of Commons on 12 December that Great Britain had no specific military obligations to defend France in the event of an Italian attack through any pact or accord. Instead, he asserted weakly that Britain intended to maintain the Mediterranean status quo ante. Though Chamberlain worried that Mussolini's public salvos against France could derail renewed appeasement, he assumed that the Italian dictator wanted the Chamberlain-Halifax visit to occur and would stop short of "any extreme measures." Chamberlain apparently did not realize, however, the extent to which his lack of support for France encouraged Mussolini's extremism.[118]

Mussolini, attempting to widen the apparent gulf between British and French policy, ordered Ciano to denounce the Mussolini-Laval accords. On 17 December, Ciano informed Ambassador François-Poncet that Mussolini considered that the accords were no longer in force. Ciano argued that both sides had not ratified them, and, besides, the accord assumed amicable relations as a precondition. Ciano complained that French policy during the Ethiopian crisis had broken that trust. Still, Ciano did not entirely close the door on possible negotiations. He left François-Poncet with vague hints of possible avenues to pursue in order to lessen tension. In doing so, however, Ciano had no realistic agenda in mind. He aimed only to ensure that France could not interfere with Chamberlain's visit to Rome.[119] François-Poncet eventually attempted to show that France had implemented the accord in good faith, but Ciano, unsurprisingly, would not be moved. He called the French attempt a "bland contradiction" of the Italian case. He did not bother to respond.[120]

Italian military planning reflected the heightened tension with Britain and France. In December 1938, naval staff planners discussed a series of issues. On one hand, they hoped to be able to extend the threat that Italian aircraft and light surface forces posed to Great Britain. In East Africa, they proposed that Italian forces could strike at Aden and Djibuti to secure naval bases on the Red Sea. Italian submarines and motor-torpedo boats could interdict British communication through the Suez Canal, threatening supplies to British forces in Egypt. At the same time, however, naval staffers, along with Marshal Badoglio, the Armed Forces Chief of Staff, argued that the proposed attack against Egypt by Italian forces based in Libya was too risky. Instead, they thought that planning should begin for a combined forces assault on Malta, as British aircraft and fleet units based there could interfere with Italy's supply of its Libyan colony. Given the likely determination of any British defense of Malta, including the deployment of Royal Navy capital ships, such an attack would require Italy's full complement of eight battleships planned for completion in 1942. This round of operational planning led Mussolini to abandon his cherished plan for a strike against Egypt, at least in the short run. Nevertheless, the naval staff's strategic appreciation reinforced Mussolini's determination to secure allies that would be able to divert British and French forces from the Mediterranean theatre.[121]

In keeping with his long-term goal, Mussolini continued to tighten his ties with Germany and Japan. Since Munich, Japanese diplomats and soldiers had continued their debate about an alliance with Italy and possibly Germany. The war in China had proceeded well, with Japanese troops capturing ever more territory. At the same time, however, no hope existed for either an immediate victory or a negotiated settlement that would satisfy Japanese territorial demands. Arita Hachirō, newly reappointed foreign minister by Prime Minister Konoe, refused to consider any apparent climb down from Japan's maximalist demands. On 3 November, Konoe declared a "new order for ensuring stability in East Asia." This aim implicitly rejected the so-called Washington system that had regulated Chinese affairs and the status quo in the Pacific region since 1922. It clearly indicated that Japan was bent on diminishing American and British influence in East Asia. Arita further emphasized this aim in a strong response to an American note of protest over Japanese violations of American rights in China. In essence, Arita claimed that the old system of treaties and accepted principles was dead. This challenge to Anglo-American power required support from other revisionist powers—especially Germany and Italy. But while some Navy commanders continued to push for an alliance with Italy directed against Great Britain, Army strategists wanted a pact with Germany, primarily directed against the Soviet Union and its intervention both in China and on the borders of Manchukuo.[122] In mid-November, naval officers approached Giorgio Giorgis, the Italian naval attaché, to present a draft Italo-Japanese alliance proposal. The pact considered at least benevolent neutrality in case of war, plus military, political and economic cooperation. The draft also considered possible espionage exchanges, mutual protection of shipping, and even reciprocal shipbuilding.[123] At the same time, the Gaimushō planned to send a new ambassador to conclude some kind of pact with the Axis powers.[124] Mussolini, still not wanting to alienate Great Britain totally, did not immediately follow up on these proposals.

On 15 December, after the demonstration in the Chamber of Deputies
and the ensuing rancorous quarrel with France, Mussolini met General
Ōshima, the Japanese ambassador to Berlin, at the Palazzo Venezia.
Ōshima was an ardent supporter of a triple alliance. He talked of smashing
the Soviet Union into a number of small states, and of evicting Britain
from China and from the Pacific region in general. Mussolini, for his part,
cautioned that he would not reach a decision until mid-January at the earliest; in effect, the Duce wanted to wait to see what would come of Chamberlain's visit to Rome.[125] At the same time, Commander Giorgis, the
Naval Attaché in Tokyo, worked toward a separate Italo-Japanese pact.[126]

While Giorgis negotiated with Japanese officials in Tokyo, Italian and
German military leaders continued low-level informal discussions on
armaments and technical military matters. The discussions proceeded ami-
cably with common understanding of the eventual military confrontation
that the Fascist states would face. In Mussolini's view, it was necessary to
maintain strict cooperation with the German technocrats.[127] On 23 December, Mussolini decided to strengthen these talks, abandoning Giorgis's
separate negotiations, and instead seeking a tripartite alliance, which
offered a more powerful range of forces against both France, and eventually, Great Britain.[128]

Mussolini took a short Christmas vacation and returned to Rome on 31
December. That morning, Ciano met Shiratori Toshio, the new Japanese
ambassador, for the first time in the latter's new post. Ciano found Shiratori
to be "outspoken and energetic" and recognized his support for an alliance.
Shiratori warned that many senior military and diplomatic leaders in Japan
wanted a rapprochement with the West, so that alliance negotiations would
not be easy. In the evening, Mussolini summoned Ciano to the Palazzo
Venezia. Mussolini said that he had decided to proceed with von Ribbentrop's proposal to turn the anti-Comintern Pact into an alliance. He believed
that a conflict with France and Britain was becoming increasingly
inevitable. He needed to forge the alliance with Germany and Japan, and
not only to line up the necessary forces for that conflict. The alliance also
could intimidate the Chamberlain cabinet into abandoning France in order
to look after the empire, therefore further isolating France. Finally, a tripartite alliance would provide Mussolini with the diplomatic muscle necessary
to ensure the unopposed occupation of Albania. Mussolini thought that it
would be best to sign the agreement in the last ten days of January.[129]

Ciano drafted an astonishingly open and honest letter to von Ribbentrop
to indicate the Duce's decision. He explained Mussolini's two-tiered
claims against France. The first set included the familiar demands for

accommodation of Italians living in Tunisia, a free port at Djibuti, and the use of the Djibuti–Addis Ababa Railroad, plus Italian participation in the administration of the Suez Canal. Ciano assured von Ribbentrop that Italy would achieve these demands through diplomatic means, though Italy would not take the formal diplomatic initiative. Ciano did not specify the second set of demands, writing that they were "of a historical nature and refer to territory which belongs to Italy geographically, ethnographically, and strategically," which Italy would deal with in "a definitive way." Ciano referred, of course, to Mussolini's earlier stated claims on Corsica and French Alpine territory. He also wrote that Mussolini had changed his mind regarding an Italo-German alliance owing to an allegedly solid alliance between Britain and France, the warlike tendencies in the French government, and the preparations in the United States to supply the Western democracies with war matériel. Mussolini wanted Italy, Germany, and Japan welded into a system, with Yugoslavia, Hungary, and Romania within their sphere of influence. Perhaps, most importantly, Ciano wrote that this combination of forces would enable "Germany and Italy to work completely undisturbed for a long period of time." Ciano also spoke briefly with von Ribbentrop by phone, explaining the Duce's decision in favor of an alliance. Ciano met with Attolico, who was in Rome, and provided his ambassador with instructions to carry the letter back to Berlin.[130]

Although Ciano had been more candid than was often the case, some curious elements exist in his letter. Mussolini and Ciano both had to know that no Anglo-French alliance existed, as they had read British dispatches stolen from Britain's Rome Embassy safe. Further, there was a contradiction between Ciano's claim that Italy's sour relations with France did not influence the Duce's decision and the later statement blaming warlike tendencies in French circles for Mussolini's attitude. More importantly, Ciano's letter and the subsequent phone call to von Ribbentrop demonstrated both sides' belief that a tripartite alliance would be easy to arrange, despite Shiratori's warning. Finally, Mussolini intended to take no further initiative toward reaching his diplomatic claims against France, seemingly preferring to let relations with Paris fester, and although Mussolini needed an eventual war with the West, he did not intend to fight until he had had greater chance to prepare. Most significantly, however, was the fact that if von Ribbentrop and Mussolini wanted an alliance directed against Russia and not the Western democracies, then Japan would have been ready to sign immediately; it was only the Axis partners' determination to direct the alliance against Britain and France that would prevent the signing of the tripartite alliance during 1939.

Attolico duly took Ciano's letter to von Ribbentrop, who was naturally pleased by its contents. Attolico, however, slightly exceeded his instructions in presenting the letter. Ciano had spoken of a tentative proposal for repatriation to Germany of South Tyrolese German activists, as well as a change in the Italo-German clearing account, which required Italian payment for a portion of German exports in foreign currencies. Though Ciano hoped for some kind of German concessions on these issues, he did not see them as essential prerequisites of the alliance. Attolico's presentation of the letter implied that these conditions were necessary requirements before Ciano would sign any pact.[131] Still, von Ribbentrop was willing to make some movement on these issues given the larger questions at stake. He committed himself to repatriate some South Tyrolese Germans immediately, though a larger transfer would have to wait until Germany had conquered further *Lebensraum*. Given the scarcity of foreign currency reserves in both Italy and Germany, the economic question proved more intractable. Eventually, after some difficult negotiations, the two sides reached a compromise that called for reductions in Italian payments and the eventual abolition of the clearing system—the major Italian goal—plus a German promise to pursue tighter economic coordination.[132]

These minor disputes between partners did not hide the essential agreement of ends between the two regimes. The German foreign minister told Attolico that he fully understood Mussolini's position. He promised to respect Italian rights in the Balkans and repeated Hitler's promise that the South Tyrol question was forever settled. He dispatched a draft treaty to Ciano that he hoped would serve as the basis for the tripartite alliance. He also repeated that he expected to sign an alliance quickly, inviting Ciano to Berlin on 28 January 1939. Most significantly, both sides understood that an alliance with Japan was inherently directed against Britain and France. As von Ribbentrop wrote, "Everything you write to me as to the reasons for this decision is accepted here with full comprehension and full agreement." Ciano could hardly understand these words to mean anything other than that von Ribbentrop understood Mussolini's territorial aims and the Duce's desire that Germany and Italy should be able to work "undisturbed for a long period of time." Still, Mussolini's qualifications about the timing for an eventual war with the West did not change the fact he had committed Italy to an alliance with Germany that meant that he could no longer entirely control that decision.[133]

Despite the confidence of the two foreign ministers that they would sign an alliance that month, there were some indications that the Japanese government was in no rush to sign. In particular, some army strategists and

Gaimushō officials did not believe that they could confront a wider coalition including Great Britain while Japan was still fighting in China and facing a hostile Soviet Union on the Manchukuo border. Ambassador Shiratori hinted at this lack of political will in a meeting with Ciano in early January. Shiratori, who strongly supported the alliance, warned that Foreign Minister Arita was lukewarm, though his stance would only delay its signing and not prevent it altogether.[134] General Ōshima in Berlin also warned of the opposition of old school diplomats in the Gaimushō.[135] Later in January, a constitutional crisis precipitated a new government in Tokyo, which further called into question the possibility of Japanese adherence to the alliance. Foreign Minister Arita remained in office, and although he was a partisan of a triple alliance, he refused to sign such an agreement if Germany and Italy intended to direct it at any country other than the Soviet Union.[136] By the last week of January, Ciano and von Ribbentrop knew that it would be impossible to sign any alliance by their hoped-for date of 28 January. In early February, when Mussolini finally understood the depth of opposition to the alliance in Japanese circles, he told Ciano that he would need to sign a bilateral alliance with Germany in order to face down Britain and France.[137] As the delay would lengthen through February, Mussolini would eventually begin pushing for Italo-German staff talks to begin to coordinate Axis military plans against the two Western democracies.[138]

The attempt to reach an alliance with Germany did not mean that Mussolini planned to lessen Italy's influence in the Balkans. Consequently, he continued his friendly competition with Germany for influence in Budapest. In November, the Hungarian ambassador in Berlin had approached von Ribbentrop about joining the anti-Comintern Pact. The German foreign minister approved of the idea in principle but thought that Hungary should first prove its loyalty by withdrawing from the League of Nations. He asked Attolico to approach Ciano to determine Mussolini's attitude.[139] Mussolini and Ciano essentially concurred. When Ciano visited Budapest in December, he sought to subordinate Hungarian policy to that of Italy. In Ciano's view, Prime Minister Imrédy and Foreign Minister Csáky largely agreed to do so. They assured Ciano that Hungary would leave the League of Nations in May, citing as an excuse the issue of treatment of minorities in Romania and Yugoslavia. That decision cleared the way for Hungary's eventual accession to the anti-Comintern Pact. Further, the Hungarians promised to pursue a rapprochement with Yugoslavia. Ciano was pleased to assist in any way possible, as a solid Italo-Yugoslav-Hungarian bloc would strengthen Italian influence and power in the

Danube basin. At the same time, however, Ciano walked a diplomatic tightrope; he did not want to alienate Germany but wanted to develop Italy's sphere of influence at the expense of his future German ally. He promised the Hungarian leaders that Italy would never allow Germany to dominate Hungary.[140] Ciano returned to the issue of Hungarian accession to the anti-Comintern Pact during the last half of December. He particularly wanted to see a Hungarian declaration by 10 January for "political reasons"—obviously a reference to the Chamberlain-Halifax visit that would start the next day. Csáky promised to make a declaration on 12 January, as Chamberlain and Halifax were in Rome, and subsequently did so.[141] It is important to note the care that Ciano took to position Italy as Hungary's protector, while at the same time ensuring that he did not damage his relations with Germany, and the lengths he took to intimidate Chamberlain by the timing of the Hungarian announcement to join the anti-Comintern Pact.

While Mussolini threatened Western Europe through his alliance diplomacy, his troops continued to serve in the Spanish Civil War. In a long and bloody campaign along the Ebro River in October, Franco had bled his opponents white while repeatedly allowing the opportunity for decisive victory to pass by. After crushing Republican forces during the Ebro offensive, Franco next turned his eyes toward Catalonia, which contained most of the remaining enemy war industry. He had a decisive advantage in men and matériel, with large numbers of Spanish and Italian reserves, plus new shipments of German arms. Still, Franco dithered, postponing the offensive until, after Italian urgings, he relented and scheduled the attack to begin on 23 December. Mussolini and the new Commander of the *C.T.V.,* General Gastone Gambarra, had arranged with Franco that Italian troops would be in the vanguard of the attack. When the offensive began, the *C.T.V.* quickly outpaced the Spanish Nationalists, opening as much as a thirty-mile gap between them. This *guerra celere* both pleased and annoyed Mussolini and Ciano. On one hand, they reveled in the feat of Italian arms; on the other, they railed against Franco's slow pace, and thought that the Caudillo might allow the chance for victory to slip away yet again. The Duce decided to leave his troops in place but to indicate to Franco once more the need for an immediate victory. Mussolini also revived the idea of a joint démarche with German military officials to appoint a unified commander of troops in Spain. General Keitel rather sharply rebuffed this effort, declaring that Franco was the unified commander and that there could be no other.[142] Mussolini had little choice but to accept this response. As Republican forces crumbled, rumors abounded that France might intervene. Ciano recklessly informed London and Berlin that if that intervention occurred, then Italy would send new regular divisions to fight French forces in Spain, possibly sparking a European war.[143] In the event, French politicians had little intention of carrying out such an intervention in the face of profound opposition within France's military leadership.

In this atmosphere of tension with France, Mussolini again outlined his expectations for future conquests at the expense of his Latin neighbor. The triple alliance with Germany and Japan represented the centerpiece of his foreign policy. He also spoke with Ciano of the need to establish a strong alliance with Franco after the end of the civil war: this alliance and the one with Germany would allow him to settle accounts with France. Mussolini again stated that he had no claims against metropolitan France outside the ring of the Alps, though he would move the frontier to the Var. His plans for Corsica included "autonomy, independence, annexation," and for Tunisia "minority settlement for Italians, autonomy for the Bey, Italian protectorate." In addition, he repeated his intention to claim a free port in Djibuti and control of the Djibuti-Addis Ababa railroad, as well as his intention to annex Albania.[144]

While these negotiations played out, Mussolini's decision in favor of the tripartite alliance did not mean that he entirely breached relations with the Western powers. He received Chamberlain's official visit in the middle of January. There was little that Chamberlain and Halifax could do to revive dismal Anglo-Italian relations, as Mussolini had already cast his lot with Hitler. Still, the unknowing British statesmen tried their best to bring the Duce around to their vision of peace. Chamberlain thought that Mussolini might serve as an arbiter with England in settling German grievances, reach a rapprochement with France, and even serve a role in bringing about general disarmament. Before this general appeasement would occur, however, Chamberlain believed that Mussolini would have to abandon the kind of theatrics of the 30 November 1938 demonstrations and return to the classic Italian role of a decisive weight in the European balance of power.[145] During the visit, Mussolini and Ciano charmed Chamberlain, and the prime minister left thinking that he had "achieved all [he] expected to get and more." His trip, he thought, had "strengthened the chances of peace."[146]

The actual conversations, however, were anodyne, and the results fell far short of Chamberlain's lofty ambitions. Mussolini spoke strictly along the lines of a prepared draft. He promised that he had only peaceful intentions and that he would follow the guidelines of the Easter Accord strictly.

He said that the Axis represented the fundamental element of his policy but that the Axis did not have to be exclusive. Mussolini also indicated that he would be prepared to consider arms limitation talks. At the same time, he did not disguise the self-evident rift between Italy and France, asserting that French resistance to his anti-Bolshevik crusade in Spain was the major bone of contention. Obviously, he did not confide his eventual territorial ambitions to Chamberlain. Mussolini refused to consider any application of the latest nonintervention plan for Spain, preferring to wait for Franco's seemingly inevitable victory. Chamberlain, for his part, did not openly dispute Mussolini's language, most of which, of course, was pure deceit. In the second meeting, Chamberlain raised the issue of the vast rate of German rearmament and the rumors of various German coups, hoping that Mussolini could help assuage British concerns. For his part, Mussolini largely defended Germany, arguing that Germans had every right to feel endangered by the Bolshevik peril from the East. The meeting ended with the usual soporifics of mutual good will, and Chamberlain, as he left the country, dispatched a glowing letter thanking Mussolini for the visit.[147]

In reality, Mussolini's policy decisions had rendered the meetings useless before they had occurred. Ciano described the conversation as "tired," and he thought there had been little resonance in the desultory talk. Mussolini agreed. Afterward, Ciano recorded the Duce's words: "These men are not made of the same stuff . . . as the Francis Drakes and the other magnificent adventurers who created the empire. These, after all, are the tired sons of a long line of rich men and they will lose their empire." Ciano thought that the visit showed the effectiveness of the triple alliance, since "having in our hands such an instrument we could get whatever we want. The British do not want to fight. They try to draw back as slowly as possible, but they do not want to fight." He concluded that the visit had accomplished nothing, and he duly informed von Mackensen of the results.[148] In short, Mussolini did not alter his plans for the triple alliance and eventual war with Britain and France.

Though he expected an eventual war, Mussolini did not want it to occur immediately, and in the latter part of January, the French government offered him a chance to achieve a genuine rapprochement. Daladier and Bonnet decided to send a French banker, Paul Baudouin, to hold discussions with Ciano. Baudouin had negotiated the sale of shares in the Djibuti-Addis Ababa railroad following the Mussolini-Laval accords and had contacts within the Italian business community. One such contact, Vincenzo Fagiuoli, met with Baudouin. The evidence differs regarding the impetus for the meeting, with Baudouin's testimony recalling that Fagiuoli

initiated the contact with a telegram in which he suggested that Ciano
wanted to clarify Italy's relations with France. The Italian records, including diplomatic traffic and Ciano's diary, imply that the initiative came
from the French side, with Baudouin undertaking the mission under Daladier's and Bonnet's direction.[149] Whatever its genesis, the initial Italian
reports of the démarche suggested that French leaders adamantly refused
to consider territorial concessions but were willing to consider the three
main nonterritorial demands that Mussolini and Ciano had hinted at publicly: a condominium arrangement in Tunisia, a free port and partial control over the Djibuti–Addis Ababa railroad, and increased representation
on the Suez Canal Board. Baudouin eventually met with Ciano on 2 and 3
February and delivered precisely that message. After the first meeting,
Ciano assumed that there were two alternatives. The first was to insist on
Mussolini's maximalist program, which would immediately mean war.
He advised the Duce to take up the second, which was to take up Baudouin's initiative and to postpone Mussolini's territorial claims for a more
opportune time. Mussolini agreed but said that he would not negotiate
with a banker—he wanted François-Poncet to make an official request.
More seriously, if the Duce publicly accepted the French proposal, then it
would appear that he had only limited Italian demands against France;
this tactic would make it more difficult to justify territorial revision in the
future.[150] Mussolini's decision doomed the French démarche, as no
French government could risk such an approach. If it became known to
French journalists that a French cabinet was negotiating concessions after
the outrageous Italian display of 30 November, then the government
would surely fall. Still, Mussolini and Ciano were not unhappy to await
further French moves, as, whatever concessions might appear, they fully
intended to attack France to conquer Mussolini's desiderata whenever the
time seemed opportune.

While relations with Germany and the West, and to a lesser extent
Japan, dominated Italian policy after Munich, Mussolini and Ciano had
not abandoned their plans for annexing Albania. During October, Jacomoni
had reported from Durazzo that preparations had reached an advanced
stage. Land reclamation projects continued to develop, and King Zog
protested that Italian control had extended to every aspect of Albanian life.
Ciano worried that increasing Albanian recognition of Italian control
might spark some resistance. He toyed with the idea of assassinating Zog
to spark the attack, even meeting once with an unnamed potential assassin.
By 6 December, Italian plans had virtually reached fruition, and Mussolini
scheduled the attack for the spring. He boasted to Ciano that he did not

fear any reaction from Britain, France, or Greece. He was concerned about Yugoslavia, but only insofar as Italy's invasion could push Stoyadinović toward tighter relations with Germany and therefore weaken his friendship with Italy.[151]

To try to arrange Yugoslav compliance with Mussolini's plans, Ciano visited Yugoslavia to sound out Stoyadinović regarding the occupation and a possible Italo-Yugoslav partition of Albania. The two met at Belje and shared a hunting expedition. Their 19 January 1939 meeting started with a discussion of internal matters, but Ciano quickly broached the major international issues. Stoyadinović spoke of his plans to make a de facto renunciation of the League of Nations; the Yugoslav delegation would leave without fanfare in May and would not return. He also talked of Yugoslav adhesion to the anti-Comintern Pact and the possibility of a Yugoslav-Hungarian rapprochement. If Hungary would not bring forward territorial claims, then Stoyadinović thought that he could certainly complete an Italo-Yugoslav-Hungarian bloc in the Danubian basin. Having thus discussed the general lines of Stoyadinović's policy, Ciano turned to the Albanian question. Ciano spoke of King Zog's alleged provocations and the need for Italian action. Ciano assured Stoyadinović that Mussolini would not act without prior Yugoslav approval. Stoyadinović, initially uneasy at the mention of Albania, replied that he saw two possible options: replacing Zog or partitioning Albania between Yugoslavia and Italy. Ciano agreed that they would not consider the details at the moment but would leave it for discussion between special envoys. Ciano finished by recounting the advantages of such a partition for Yugoslavia, including Italian support for an eventual Yugoslav occupation of the Greek territory of Salonika. Ciano understood from this conversation that he had secured Stoyadinović's approval for the Italian annexation of Albania.[152]

Ciano also met Prince Paul, the Yugoslav, regent two days later. At Stoyadinović's suggestion, Ciano raised the issue of Albania's allegedly intolerable behavior and the need for Italy to rectify the situation. The Yugoslav head of state told Ciano that he thought that Yugoslavia already had enough ethnic Albanians but that he fully supported Stoyadinović. Ciano understood these words to mean that Prince Paul had also acquiesced in an eventual Italian annexation.[153] In response to Ciano's visit, however, Prince Paul told Sir Ronald Campbell, the British ambassador in Belgrade, that he intended to replace Stoyadinović, in part because Prince Paul feared the Italian annexation of Albania; he thought that an increased Italian presence would in essence create the encirclement of Yugoslavia.[154]

On Ciano's return to Italy, he told a pleased Mussolini of the apparent success of his mission, not knowing how badly it would backfire.[155] Prince Paul was already uneasy about Stoyadinović's highly risky foreign policy and its association with Italy and Germany. A constitutional crisis also brewed in Yugoslavia, with Croat parliamentarians calling for greater representation in light of their electoral strength in the December 1938 elections. Prince Paul negotiated secretly with a delegation led by Vladko Maček and eventually agreed to the Croat's demand to replace Stoyadinović.[156] Mussolini greeted the news of Stoyadinović's fall with regret. He thought that Prince Paul had carried out an anti-Fascist coup. Ciano recommended to the Duce that they push forward the plans for the invasion of Albania, and Mussolini agreed, even if it were to be carried in the face of direct Yugoslav opposition. They set the date for Easter week.[157]

By the beginning of February 1939, therefore, Mussolini had decided on the main lines of future Italian policy. He made these plans clear in a major policy announcement to the Fascist Grand Council. Mussolini called his speech "The March to the Sea" and announced that it represented "a password to future generations."[158] One historian has called it "a sort of Mussolinian *Mein Kampf*."[159] It represents the kind of geopolitical thinking that Mussolini had developed over his adult lifetime and indicates clearly his intention to create a great Roman Empire in Africa. It is worth quoting a substantial portion of the text.[160]

This speech is written down because it must remain in the acts of the Grand Council as it documents the orientation of Italian foreign policy in the short term, the long term, and the very long term. Its premise is the following: states are more or less independent according to their maritime position. Those states that possess ocean coasts or have free access to oceans are independent; states are semi-independent that cannot communicate freely with the ocean or who are closed in internal seas; states are dependent that are absolutely continental or do not have outlets on oceans nor on seas.

Italy belongs to the second category of States. Italy is bathed by a landlocked sea that communicates with the oceans through the Suez Canal. Artificial communication that can easily be blocked with improvized means through the Strait of Gibraltar, dominated by the cannons of G[reat] B[ritain].

Italy therefore does not have free communication with the oceans; Italy therefore is really a prisoner of the Mediterranean and the more populous and powerful Italy becomes the more it will suffer its imprisonment.

The bars of this prison are Corsica, Tunisia, Malta, Cyprus; the sentinals of this prison are Gibraltar and Suez. Corsica is a pistol pointed at the heart of Italy. Tunisia at Sicily; while Malta and Cyprus constitute a threat to our entire position in the Central and Western Mediterranean. Greece, Turkey and Egypt are always ready to range themselves with Britain to complete absolutely the political-military encirclement of Italy. Greece, Turkey, and Egypt must be considered virtual enemies of Italy and its expansion. From this situation, the objective geographical rigor of which leaps to one's eyes, and which tormented even before our regime those who saw beyond immediate political expediency, one can draw the following conclusions:

1. The goal of Italian policy, which cannot and does not have continental objectives of European territory, except Albania, is in the first place to break the bars of the prison.

2. Having broken the bars, Italian policy cannot have other than one watchword: to march to the ocean.

Which ocean? The Indian Ocean, through the Sudan, Libya, and Ethiopia, or the Atlantic through French North Africa.

Whether in the first or second hypothesis, we will find ourselves faced with Franco-English opposition. To face the solution of this problem without having assured support on the continent is absurd. The policy of the Rome-Berlin Axis responds therefore to an historical necessity of fundamental order.

Mussolini went on to assure his listeners that the 30 November 1938 demonstration in the chamber meant that the Axis had specifically Italian goals as well as German ones. He repeated once more the nature of his claims against France. He would move the frontier to complete the ring of the Alps but would not take Savoy proper. He would work to control Corsica through three stages: autonomy, independence, and annexation. He would substitute an Italian protectorate over Tunisia for the French one.

Mussolini also said that there were three alternative policies. The first would be to await more profitable times and not to push these claims immediately. He rejected this choice, because as a Fascist he could not endure the diplomatic defeat that he would suffer in the eyes of the world. The second course was to negotiate the immediate questions of the status of Italians in Tunisia, the Djibuti railroad and port, and Suez Canal Board representation. He declared that this solution would not be ideal, though it would satisfy some Italians because it would avoid further complications. The third course would be to present the maximum demands, which would force France either to capitulate or to resort to war. Mussolini contemplated a possible war, one that would consist of air and naval battles more than a ground war, as he believed that the defensive lines in the Alps were too strong for either side to overcome. He was certain of German support for this war. Current conditions were not yet ripe, though, as Italy needed to rearm and to complete Mussolini's plans for autarky. Accordingly, he planned to delay the war against Britain and France until 1942. That delay would allow him to reequip the artillery of the *Regio Esercito,* to complete the squadron of eight battleships, to pacify the empire and to create an army of black soldiers, to further Italian autarky, to fortify foreign currency reserves through the world exposition in Rome, and to repatriate the largest possible number of Italians from France and the world. These steps, he argued, were necessary before Italy could face war with Britain and France.[161]

The March to the Sea speech established the main lines of Italian policy. Mussolini completely rejected any long-term accommodation with Britain and France. Ultimately, he aimed to shatter their empires and to establish a new Roman Empire in their place. The Axis was a fundamental element, as he needed German support both to intimidate and eventually to defeat France and Britain. Similarly, he expected that Japan would join a tripartite alliance, increasing the array of forces facing the Western democracies. Still, he would not exclude the possibility of an interim settlement with France, though any concessions would not ultimately shorten his list of territories to be conquered. Similarly, he would not exclude further attempts to court favor in London, as it would be advantageous to split England from France. He would not, however, postpone plans to annex Albania or to prepare for further aggression; at its heart, he intended to gut the Anglo-Italian Accord of any meaning. He expected the Spanish Civil War to end soon and a grateful Francisco Franco to join the tripartite alliance to complete the encirclement of France. Essentially, Mussolini had deliberately ruptured his ties to the West in favor of an alliance with Germany, and he was prepared to wage war in order to achieve his territorial demands. Though the timing of Mussolini's war would await the development of further events, Mussolini had already decided to commit Italy to the fray.

NOTES

1. "400ᵃ Riunione dei Consiglio dei Ministri," 23 April 1938, *OO,* vol. 29.

2. Quoted in *CHD,* 10 July 1938, 134–35.

3. *CHD,* 14 July 1938, 15 July 1938, 17 July 1938, 24 July 1938, 26 July 1938, 30 July 1938, 136, 137, 137–38, 140, 140, 141; see also British reports summarizing this racial barrage in Perth to Halifax, 16 July 1938, 22 July 1938, 27 July 1938, FO 371 22442, R6343/6343/22, R6523/6343/22, R6615/6343/22.

4. "Informazione Diplomatica #18," *Popolo d'Italia,* 6 August 1938, *OO,* vol. 29, 497–98; see also Charles to Halifax, 6 August 1938, FO 371 22442, R6832/6343/22.

5. *CHD*, 8 August 1938, 141.

6. Ciano to Crolla, 28 July 1938, ASMAE, US 231; Ciano to Crolla, 28 July 1938, ASMAE, SAP—Gran Bretagna, B 24; Ciano appunto per il Duce, 29 July 1938, ASMAE, SAP—Gran Bretagna, B 24; *CHD*, 28 August 1938, 140–41.

7. Crolla to Ciano, 29 July 1938, 3 August 1938, ASMAE, US 231; Crolla to Ciano, 3 August 1938, ASMAE, SAP—Gran Bretagna, B 24. For the British record, see Sig. Crolla conversation with Viscount Halifax, 29 August 1938, FO 371 22651, W102283/83/41; Perth to Halifax, 29 July 1938, W10285/83/41; Syers to Royar-Miller, 4 August 1938, W10559/83/41; Perth to Halifax, 29 July 1938, PREM 1/276; Halifax to Noel-Charles, 5 August 1938, PREM 1/276. Chamberlain's comment on partial withdrawal did not appear in the British record, nor did Mussolini behave as if he had learned of it. There is no hard evidence to suggest why Mussolini failed to clarify this point at the time. On speculation only, it is possible that he did not want to force the issue, as Halifax had indicated a slightly different attitude, and there was little point in creating a breach over questions of numbers when the eventual withdrawal of volunteers was still at some unspecified time in the future.

8. Anfuso to Crolla, 6 August 1938, ASMAE, US 231; Crolla to Chamberlain, 10 August 1938, PREM 1/276.

9. Crolla to Ciano, 6 August 1938, ASMAE, SAP—Gran Bretagna, B 24, US 231; Promemoria, n.d., seen by Mussolini, ASMAE, SAP—Gran Bretagna, B 24, US 231.

10. Ciano Appunto per il Duce, 20 August 1938, ASMAE, SAP—Gran Bretagna, B 24, UC 85, US 231. For the published version, see *CDP*, Conversation with the British Chargé d'Affaires, 20 August 1938, 230–31; see also *CHD*, 19 August 1938, 20 August 1938, 144–45.

11. Ciano Appunto, 30 August 1938, ASMAE, SAP—Gran Bretagna, B 24.

12. *CHD*, 12 August 1938, 143.

13. 20 August 1938, Berti to Rome, il Duce to Berti, ASMAE, UC 46; *CHD*, 21 August 1938, 145.

14. Franco nota per l'ambasciatore d'Italia, 23 August 1938, ASMAE, UC 46; *CHD*, 14 August 1938, 26 August 1938, 29 August 1938, 31 August 1938, 146–47, 147–48, 149.

15. Mussolini to Berti, 3, 7, 8, 9 September 1938, ASMAE, UC 46; Berti to Mussolini, 6, 8 September 1938, ASMAE, UC 46; *CHD*, 2 September 1938, 3 September 1938, 7 September 1938, 9 September 1938, 11 September 1938, 149–50, 150, 152–53, 154.

16. Ciano to London, n.d., ASMAE, GAB 30. Internal evidence suggests that Ciano sent this telegram in the first week of September.

17. Cadogan Minutes, 7 September 1938, 12 September 1938, FO 371 22413, R7543/23/22; Roberts Minute, 12 September 1938, FO 371 22413, R7671/23/22; Noble Memorandum and Ingram and Cadogan Minutes, all 13 September 1938, FO 371 22413, R7672/23/22; Ingram Minute, 14 September 1938, FO 371 22413, R7672/23/22; Cadogan Minute, 14 September 1938, FO 371 22413,

R7672/23/22; Halifax to Noel-Charles, 15 September 1938, plus minutes of 15 and 16 September 1938 Foreign Office meetings, FO 371 22413, R7672/23/22. The outcome of these meetings was that the Cabinet would have to determine whether or not to respond to Ciano's request (Ingram Minute, 14 September 1938, FO 371 22414, R7673/23/22; Halifax to Perth, 18 September 1938, FO 371 22414, R7706/23/22).

18. Prunas to Ciano, 30 July 1938, ASMAE, SAP—Francia, B 33.

19. *CHD*, 9 August 1938, 142.

20. Ciano to Ministero di Africa Italiana, 7 April 1938, NA, RG T586, r412, 004955.

21. Pariani to Ciano, 9 April 1938, ASMAE, SAP–Yemen, B 16; Ciano to Passera, 22 August 1938, ASMAE, SAP–Yemen, B 16; Bastianini to Passera, 22 September 1938, ASMAE, SAP–Yemen, B 16; Signature illegible to Passera, 24 September 1938, ASMAE, SAP–Yemen, B 16.

22. Attolico to Rome, 9 August 1938, ASMAE, UC 5.

23. Attolico to Rome, 18 August 1938, ASMAE, UC 5; see also, for example, Berti to Ministero di Guerra, 11 August 1938, ASMAE, US 225, and *CHD*, 19 August 1938, 144–45.

24. *CHD*, 20 August 1938, 145.

25. Von Ribbentrop Memorandum, 27 August 1938, *DGFP*, ser. D, vol. 2, no. 401, 651; *CHD*, 26 August 1938, 30 August 1938, 146–47, 148–49.

26. Weinberg, *Starting World War II*, 413; von Ribbentrop Memorandum, 23 August 1938, *DGFP*, ser. D, vol. 2, no. 384, 611–12; von Ribbentrop Memorandum, 27 August 1938, *DGFP*, ser. D, vol. 2, no. 401, 651; von Weizsäcker Memorandum, 30 August 1938, no. 409, 662–63; von Weizsäcker Memorandum, 31 August 1938, no. 414, 670.

27. Attolico to Mussolini, 30 August 1938, 31 August 1938, ASMAE, UC 5. Mussolini heavily emphasized the section in the 31 August report on German and British naval considerations.

28. Ciano to Attolico, 1 September 1938, ASMAE, UC 5.

29. Attolico to Ciano, 9 September 1938, ASMAE, UC 5; *CHD*, 2, 5–7 September 1938, 148–49, 151–53.

30. Attolico to Ciano, 10 September 1938 (two correspondences), ASMAE, UC 5; *CHD*, 12 September 1938, 13 September 1938, 154–55.

31. "Informazione Diplomatica #19," *Popolo d'Italia*, 9 September 1938, *OO*, vol. 29, 488–89.

32. "Informazione #20," *Popolo d'Italia*, 14 September 1938, *OO*, vol. 29, 499–500.

33. "Lettera a Runciman," *Popolo d'Italia*, 15 September 1938, *OO*, vol. 29, 141–43.

34. Von Mackensen to von Ribbentrop, 15 September 1938, *DGFP*, ser. D, vol. 2, no. 494, 804–5; Woermann Minute, 16 September 1983, *DGFP*, ser. D, vol. 2, no. 495, 806.

35. *CHD*, 17 September 1938, 157.

36. "Discorso di Trieste," 18 September 1938, *OO*, vol. 29, 144–47.

37. "Al Popolo di Udine," 20 September 1938, *Popolo d'Italia*, 21 September 1938, *OO*, vol. 29, 152–53.

38. "Al popolo di Belluno," 24 September 1938, *Popolo d'Italia*, 25 September 1938, *OO*, vol. 29, 159–60.

39. Attolico to Ciano, 23 September 1938, ASMAE, UC 89.

40. For more detailed coverage on this state visit, see Thomas L. Sakmyster, "The Hungarian State Visit to Germany of August 1938: Some New Evidence on Hungary's Pre-Munich Policy," *Canadian Slavic Studies* 3, no. 4 (winter 1969): 677–91.

41. Attolico to Ciano, 27 August 1938, ASMAE, UC 58.

42. Appunto per il Duce, 22 September 1938, ASMAE, UC 5; see also *CDP*, 22 September 1938, 234–35; *CHD*, 19 September 1938, 20 September 1938, 22 September 1938, 158, 158–59, 159–60.

43. Reparti dell'Aeronautica Italiana in Ungheria, 24 September 1938, ASMAE, UC 58.

44. Von Mackensen to von Ribbentrop, 23 September 1938, *DGFP*, ser. D, vol. 2, no. 577, 894; *CHD*, 23 September 1938, 160.

45. Attolico to Ciano, 24 September 1938, ASMAE, UC 5.

46. *CHD*, 25 September 1938, 161–62.

47. Mallett, *The Italian Navy and Fascist Expansionism*, 115–20; see also Williamson Murray, "Munich 1938: The Military Confrontation," *Journal of Strategic Studies* 2, no. 3 (1979): 282–302.

48. *CHD*, 25–27 September, 162–63.

49. For more detail on Mussolini's relations with Czechoslovakia, see Francesco Leoncini, "Italia e Cecoslovakia, 1919–1939," *Rivista di Studi Politici Internazionali* 45 (1979): 357–72.

50. Addis Abeba to Ministero dell'Africa Italiana, 9 April 1938, NA, RG T586, r412, 004932; Lt. Col. Valfrè di Bonzo (Prague) to Servizio Informazione Militare, 4 February 1938, NA, RG T586, r412, 004932.

51. Ciano to Prague, 10 April 1938, ASMAE, GAB 29.

52. "Popolo d'Italia," 30 January 1938, *OO*, vol. 29, 51–52; Crolla to Ciano, 17 August 1938, ASMAE, SAP—Gran Bretagna, B 24.

53. Attolico to Mussolini, 30 August 1938, 31 August 1938, ASMAE, UC 5. For the difficulty of offensive action for the *Regio Esercito*, see Brian R. Sullivan, "The Italian Armed Forces, 1918–1940," in *Military Effectiveness*, vol. 2, *The Interwar Period*, eds. Alan R. Millett and Williamson Murray (Boston: Unwin Hyman, 1988), 169–70, 182–83.

54. Viola to Ciano, 17 September 1938, ASMAE, US 229. This telegram reported an official communiqué from the Spanish Minister for Foreign Affairs, noting that the French government would occupy Catalonia and Spanish Morocco in the event of war. For further indications that France might invade Spain, see Pariani to Ciano, 6 September 1938, ASMAE, GAB 368.

55. Attolico to Ciano, 26 September 1938, ASMAE, US 226; see also Johannes Bernhardt Memorandum, 26 September 1938, *DGFP*, ser. D, vol. 3, no. 665, 748;

von Stohrer to the Foreign Ministry, 28 September 1938, *DGFP,* ser. D, vol. 3, no. 666, 749–50.

56. *CHD,* 26 September 1938, 162–63.

57. Final Report of the Ufficio Spagna, 1939, n.d., ASMAE, US 1; see also Coverdale, *Italian Intervention in the Spanish Civil War,* 367–68, 392–93.

58. Auriti to Ciano, 15, 26, 29 September 1938, ASMAE, UC 53; see also Toscano, *The Origins of the Pact of Steel,* 41–42.

59. For more on these parallel proposals, see, among others, Weinberg, *Starting World War II,* 444–45, especially notes 308 and 311. Quartararo argues that Grandi was entirely responsible for Chamberlain's initiative, but her evidence is thin. According to British records, it is possible that Grandi spoke to Chamberlain at an "opportune time." If Grandi did so, no compelling evidence apparently exists of that démarche (Rosario Quartataro, "Inghiltera e Italia. Dal Patto di Pasqua a Monaco," *Storia Contemporanea* 7, no. 4 [December 1976]: 640; Quartataro, *Roma tra Londra e Berlino,* 399). The first British dispatch to Perth to ask for Mussolini's intercession left London on the evening of 27 September.

60. *CHD,* 28 September 1938, 165–66.

61. Quoted in *CHD,* 28 September 1938, 165–66; Cronica della giornate 28, 29, 30 September 1938, ASMAE, UC 89; see also "Prima telefonata ad Attolico," 28 September 1938, *OO,* vol. 29, 165, and "Seconda telefonata ad Attolico," 28 September 1938, *OO,* vol. 29, 165.

62. Cronica della giornate, 28, 29, 30 September 1938, ASMAE, UC 89; *CHD,* 29–30 September 1938, 166–68. Ciano's diary contains a slightly shorter and different version of Hitler's words than the original record.

63. For more on this process, see Attolico to Ciano, 4 October 1938, ASMAE, UC 5; *DGFP,* ser. D, vol. 2, no. 670, 1005n10.

64. Cronica della giornate, 28, 29, 30 September 1938, ASMAE, UC 5; *CHD,* 29–30 September 1938, 166–68. Note that Chamberlain, in contrast to Ciano's diary, described Mussolini's attitude as friendly. Neville Chamberlain to Hilda Chamberlain, 2 October 1938, NC 18/1/1070.

65. Alan Cassels, "Fascist Italy and Mediation in the Munich and Danzig Crises (September 1938 and August 1939)," in *Diplomazia e storia delle relazioni internazionali,* eds. Alessandro Migliazza e Enrico Decleva (eds.) (Milano: Giuffrè Editore, 1991), 433, 433n23.

66. Neville Chamberlain to Hilda Chamberlain, 2 October 1938, NC 18/1/1070.

67. Perth to Halifax, 3 October 1938, FO 371 22414, R7949/23/22; see also Perth to Halifax, 4 October 1938, FO 371 22414, R7941/23/22; *CHD,* 2 October 1938, 3 October 1938, 172–73.

68. *CHD,* 4 October 1938, 173; Perth to Halifax, 4 October 1938, FO 371 22414, R7941/23/22.

69. Perth to Halifax, 4 October 1938, FO 371 22414, R7950/23/22.

70. Perth to Halifax, 4 October 1938, FO 371 22414, R7966/23/22; Halifax to Perth, 5 October 1938, CAB 23 1(38).

71. *CHD,* 5–7 October 1938, 174–75; Perth to Halifax, 6 October 1938, FO 371 22414, R8037/23/22; Cadogan Minute, 7 October 1938, FO 371 22414, R8084/23/22; Perth to Halifax, 7 October 1938, FO 371 22414, R8084/23/22; Halifax to Perth, 12 October 1938, FO 371 22414, R8300/23/22; Perth to Halifax, 15 October 1938, FO 371 22414, R8300/23/22; Cadogan Minute, 19 October 1938, FO 371 22414, R8300/23/22; see also Neville Chamberlain to Ida Chamberlain, 9 October 1938, NC 18/1/1071.

72. Prunas to Ciano, 4 October 1938, ASMAE, UC 61; Blondel to Bonnet, *DDF,* 2d ser., vol. 11, no. 521, 760–62; *CHD,* 3 October 1938, 172–73.

73. 12 October 1938, ASMAE, SAP—Francia, B 33; *CHD,* 4 October 1938, 173.

74. Prunas to Ciano, 19 October 1938, ASMAE, UC 61, SAP—Francia, B 33; Ciano to Prunas, 23 October 1938, ASMAE, UC 61.

75. Quoted in *CHD,* 31 October 1938, 187.

76. "Al Consiglio Nazionale del P.N.F.," 25 October 1938, *OO,* vol. 29, 185–96.

77. *CHD,* 3–5 October 1938, 172–74.

78. "Informazione Diplomatica no. 21," 4 October 1938, *OO,* vol. 29, 500.

79. Ciano to Grandi, Attolico, Prunas, 14 October 1938, ASMAE, GAB 29; *CHD,* 8 October 1938, 10 October 1938, 12–15 October 1938, 175, 175–76, 176–78; Attolico Communiqué, 14 October 1938, *DGFP,* ser. D, vol. 4, no. 60, 68–69; Attolico Communiqué, 14 October 1938, *DGFP,* ser. D, vol. 4, no. 64, 78–79.

80. Ciano Appunto (recording telephone call with von Ribbentrop), 22 October 1938, ASMAE, GAB 27; Appunto per il Duce, 23 October 1938, ASMAE, GAB 27; *CHD,* 20–24 October 1938, 180–83; Altenburg Memorandum, 21 October 1938, *DGFP,* ser. D, vol. 4, no. 80, 98–99.

81. Vinci to Ciano, 5, 7, 8 November 1938, ASMAE, UC 89; *CHD,* 18–31 October 1938, 2–4 November 1938, 185–90; Memorandum on the Conference of the Four Foreign Ministers in the Belvedere Palace on November 2, 1938, *DGFP,* ser. D, vol. 4, no. 99, 118–27.

82. Ciano recorded in his diary that Lt.-Col. Vitez Szabó made the démarche. Mussolini's memorandum indicated differently. Attolico's report to the German foreign minister also mentioned Szabó's name (Mussolini promemoria, 19 November 1938, ASMAE, UC 58; *CHD,* 20 October 1938, 196–97; Mussolini to Attolico, 20 November 1938, *DGFP,* ser. D, vol. 4, no. 129, 157).

83. Mussolini promemoria, 19 November 1938, ASMAE, UC 58; Mussolini appunto, 20 November 1938, ASMAE, UC 58; Attolico to Ciano, 20 November 1938, ASMAE, UC 58; Mussolini to Attolico, 20 November 1938, ASMAE, UC 58; Vinci to Ciano, 20, 21 November 1938, ASMAE, UC 58; Ciano to Attolico, 21 November 1938, ASMAE, UC 58; *CHD,* 11 November 1938, 18–21 November 1938, 193, 196–97. The following are from *DGFP,* ser. D, vol. 4: von Ribbentrop Memorandum, 20 November 1938, no. 128, 156–57; von Ribbentrop Memorandum, 21 November 1938, no. 131, 158–59; Mussolini to Attolico, 20

November 1938, no. 129, 157; Ermannsdorff to von Ribbentrop, 20 November 1938, no. 130, 157–58; von Ribbentrop to Ermannsdorff, 21 November 1938, no. 132, 159; Ermannsdorff to von Ribbentrop, 21 November 1938, no. 133, 161. For more on Hungarian policy, see Ádám, "The Munich Crisis and Hungary," 106–15.

84. Though Ciano saw these alliance proposals as similar, the second called for much tighter and explicit commitments. It appears that Ciano, who did not plan to sign any alliance in the short term, did not pay very close heed to its terms. For an explicit comparison of the two proposals, see Toscano, *The Origins of the Pact of Steel*, 49–52.

85. Schmidt Memorandum, 28 October 1938, *DGFP*, ser. D, vol. 4, no. 400; *CHD*, 28 October 1938, 185–86.

86. *CHD*, 27–28 October 1938, 184–86.

87. Verbale del colloquio a Palazzo Venezia fra il Duce, von Ribbentrop, e il Ministro Ciano, 28 October 1938, ASMAE, UC 53, 85.

88. Verbale del colloquio a Palazzo Venezia fra il Duce, von Ribbentrop, e il Ministro Ciano, 28 October 1938, ASMAE, UC 53, 85; Schmidt Memorandum, *DGFP*, ser. D, vol. 4, no. 400, 515–20; *CHD*, 28–29 October 1938, 185–87.

89. *CHD*, 7 November 1938, 191; von Mackensen to von Ribbentrop, 7 November 1938, *DGFP*, ser. D, vol. 4, no. 404, 522–23; see also von Ribbentrop Memorandum, 18 November 1938, *DGFP*, ser. D, vol. 4, no. 407, 524–25.

90. Quoted in *CHD*, 16 November 1938, 195.

91. "403ª Riunione del Consiglio dei Ministri," 1 September 1938, and "404ª Riunione del Consiglio dei Ministri," 2 September 1938, *OO*, vol. 29, 130–35, 135–36; *CHD*, 1 September 1938, 4 September 1938, 5 September 1938, 149, 150–51, 151.

92. "175ª Riunione Gran Consiglio del Fascismo," 6 October 1938, NA, RG T586, r1112, 074978. For a published version, see *OO*, vol. 29, 167–170.

93. "175ª Riunione Gran Consiglio del Fascismo," 6 October 1938, NA, RG T586, r1112, 074978.

94. "405ª Riunione del Consiglio dei Ministri," 7 November 1938, "406ª Riunione del Consiglio dei Ministri," 9 November 1938, "407ª Riunione del Consiglio dei Ministri," 10 November 1938, *OO*, vol. 29, 205–7, 210.

95. "Al Consiglio Nazionale del P.N.F.," 25 October 1938, *OO*, vol. 29, 185–96.

96. "405ª Riunione del Consiglio dei Ministri," 7 November 1938, "406ª Riunione del Consiglio dei Ministri," 9 November 1938, "407ª Riunione del Consiglio dei Ministri," 10 November 1938, *OO*, vol. 29, 205–7, 210.

97. Von Mackensen to von Ribbentrop, 5 November 1938, *DGFP*, ser. D, vol. 4, no. 402, 521; Woermann Memorandum, 7 November 1938, *DGFP*, ser. D, vol. 4, no. 403, 522; von Mackensen Memorandum, 8 November 1938, *DGFP*, ser. D, vol. 4, 523–24.

98. Quoted in *CHD*, 17 November 1938, 23 November 1938, 195–96, 197–98; Walter Hewel Memorandum, 8 November 1938, *DGFP*, ser. D, vol. 4, no. 405, 523.

99. Von Weizsäcker Memorandum, 8 November 1938, *DGFP,* ser. D, vol. 4, no. 348, 349, 447–48, 448–49; von Weizsäcker to von Welczek (Paris), 8 November 1938, *DGFP,* ser. D, vol. 4, no. 350, 449; von Ribbentrop to von Welczek, 21 November 1938, *DGFP,* ser. D, vol. 4, no. 358, 458–59; Woermann Memorandum, 25 November 1938, *DGFP,* ser. D, vol. 4, no. 363, 463.

100. Prunas to Ciano, 5 November 1938, ASMAE, UC 61, SAP—Francia, B 34.

101. Quoted in *CHD,* 5 November 1938, 190.

102. Quoted in *CHD,* 8 November 1938, 191–92; Ciano Appunto, 9, 14 November 1938, ASMAE, UC 61, UC 85; *CHD,* 5 November 1938, 8–10 November 1938, 14 November 1938, 190, 191–93, 194.

103. Ciano to Grandi, 14 November 1938, ASMAE, UC 61, UC 85.

104. *CHD,* 10 November 1938, 14 November 1938, 17 November 1938, 192–93, 194, 195–96.

105. Raffaele Guariglia, *Ricordi 1922–1946* (Naples: E.S.I., 1950), 351. Mussolini also refused to meet with Guariglia before the Ambassador took up his new post.

106. *CHD,* 29 November 1938, 200–201.

107. Guariglia to Ciano, 25 November 1938, ASMAE, US 229. Guariglia's report that Chamberlain and Halifax had agreed to a much larger British continental commitment and greater military cooperation and coordination of military production likely helped to create Mussolini's misperceptions. See also Del Balzo (Rome) to Grandi and Attolico, 29 November 1938, ASMAE, US 229. For the British record of the talks, see CAB paper CP 269, 24 November 1938, FO 371 22428, R9704/240/22. The Foreign Office eventually sent this paper to Rome, where the *Servizio Informazione Militare* almost certainly stole it from the embassy safe, thus correcting Mussolini's misunderstanding.

108. Ciano to Attolico, 24 November 1938, ASMAE, UC 6.

109. Attolico to Ciano, 24, 25 November 1938, ASMAE, UC 6.

110. *CHD,* 23 November 1938, 26 November 1938, 197, 199. Ciano finished writing the speech on 23 November, and Mussolini gave his approval on 26 November.

111. For the text of Ciano's speech, see Discorso pronunciato da S. E. Ciano, Ministro per gli Affari Esteri, Camera dei Deputati, 30 November 1938, ASMAE, GAB 345. For a small selection of published accounts, see Shorrock, *From Ally to Enemy,* 240–41; De Felice, *Lo Stato Totalitario,* 559–61; Donatella Bolech Cecchi, *Non bruciare I ponti con Londra e Berlino* (Milan: A. Giuffrè, 1986), 18–21. For one account of the extensive organization of the demonstration by a member of the Rome University Fascist Organisation, see Perth to Halifax, 2 December 1938, FO 371 22428, R9745/240/22. Ciano noted in his diary that the outburst in the chamber was entirely spontaneous, and he repeated his belief on several subsequent occasions to various diplomats. It seems likely that even the callow Ciano would not have deliberately lied to himself. The most compelling explanation is that Mussolini and the Fascist

Party Secretary Achille Starace had arranged the incident without Ciano's knowledge.

112. Quoted in *CHD,* 30 November 1938, 200–201.

113. Guariglia to Ciano, 1 December 1938, ASMAE, GAB 345, SAP—Francia, B 34.

114. Ciano to Mussolini, 2 December 1938, ASMAE, SAP—Francia, B 33, UC 85.

115. *CHD,* 2 December 1938, 201–2. Writers of the De Felice school have ignored important evidence regarding the nature of Mussolini's policy and his intentions regarding the 30 November 1938 demonstration. De Felice canvassed three possible explanations. The first was that the Duce aimed to create tension similar to that during the Czech crisis, hoping to prompt a four-power conference to deal with Italian demands. The second was that Mussolini wanted to scupper in advance any possible Franco-German rapprochement when von Ribbentrop visited Paris. De Felice preferred the third explanation—that the events' organizer, Starace, in an "excess of zeal and without knowing Mussolini's political programme," had added demands for Savoy and Corsica that his superior had no intention of claiming (De Felice, *Lo Stato Totalitario,* 560–62). This argument breaks down in light of Mussolini's professed desire to control Corsica and to seize French territory to the Var River line, and his evident satisfaction at the results of the demonstration. It is hairsplitting to argue that because the chants did not specify the precise territory that Mussolini intended to seize from his French enemy that the incident had little significance. Quartararo argued that the events of November did not signify that Mussolini had decided to join the German camp; instead, in her view, they were not inconsistent with the Duce's "realistic and highly flexible" foreign policy (Quartararo, *Roma tra Londra e Berlino,* 401). This view is sustainable only when one ignores the evidence of Mussolini's plan to proceed in two stages and his earlier decision in favor of a tripartite alliance with Berlin and Tokyo. For further evidence of Italian plans to subvert and ultimately to replace French control of Corsica and Tunisia, see "L'azione riservata svolta dal regime per l'italianitá della Corsica, L'azione svolta localmente dal regime a sostegno delle nostre posizioni in Tunisia, Relazioni per il Gran Consiglio del Fascismo," 4 February 1939, ASMAE, UC 61.

116. "Informazione Diplomatica #25," *Popolo d'Italia,* 9 December 1938, *OO,* vol. 19, 503.

117. Perth to Halifax, 4 December 1938, FO 371 22428, R9627/240/22; Neville Chamberlain to Ida Chamberlain, 4 December 1938, NC 18/1/1078; Chamberlain clearly did not understand Mussolini's attempt to split the perceived Anglo-French alliance; see also *CHD,* 3 December 1938, 4 December 1938, 202.

118. Neville Chamberlain to Hilda Chamberlain, 11 December 1938, NC 18/1/1079.

119. Ciano to François-Poncet, 17 December 1938, ASMAE, UC 61; *CHD,* 17 December 1938, 206.

120. François-Poncet to Ciano, 26 December 1936, ASMAE, UC 61, SAP—Francia, B 33; *CHD,* 26 December 1936, 209. Ciano also refused to consider entreaties from Guariglia in Paris about the need to calm virtually unanimous French hostility toward Italy arising from Mussolini's policy (Guariglia to Ciano, 28 December 1938, ASMAE, UC 61). Had Mussolini merely intended to secure some cooperation regarding Tunisia, Djibuti, and the Suez Canal Board, as Quartararo and others have argued (see n105), Mussolini certainly could have directed Ciano to pursue that goal, but the Duce chose not to do so.

121. Mallett, *The Italian Navy and Fascist Expansionism,* 131–37.

122. Iriye, *Origins of the Second World War in Asia and the Pacific,* 67–68. For a cogent Italian explanation of the Byzantine Japanese politics, see Addetto Navale Tokio a il Sottosegretario di Stato, Ministero della Marina, 10 October 1938, ASMAE, UC 53. Mussolini heavily marked a passage on the anti-British potential of the Japanese navy.

123. The draft proposal does not apparently appear in the Italian files, but a copy does exist in the Gaimushō files for the period (Ferretti, *Il Giappone e la politica estera italiana, 1935–41,* 224–25).

124. The Gaimushō dispatched Shiratori Toshio, who many observers thought should have been Foreign Minister in Arita's place. Shiratori was a strong believer in a tripartite alliance but a realist regarding the difficulties of reaching any accord (Addetto Navale Tokio a il Sottosegretario di Stato, Ministero della Marina, 16 November 1938, ASMAE, UC 53).

125. *CHD,* 15 December 1938, 205.

126. Toscano, *The Origins of the Pact of Steel,* 99–100n63.

127. Magistrati to Ciano, 17 December 1938, ASMAE, UC 4; General Keitel to von Ribbentrop, 30 November 1938, *DGFP,* ser. D, vol. 4, no. 411, 529–32.

128. *CHD,* 23 December 1938, 208.

129. Hugh Gibson, ed., *The Ciano Diaries, 1939–1943* (hereafter cited as *CD*), 1 January 1939, (Garden City, NY: Doubleday, 1946), 3.

130. Ciano's handwritten draft is found in Ciano to von Ribbentrop, 2 January 1938, ASMAE, GAB 29. Copies exist in ASMAE, UC 85, *UC* 71. A published translation appears in *CDP,* 258–59. For a somewhat different published translation, see Ciano to von Ribbentrop, 2 January 1938, *DGFP,* ser. D, vol. 4, no. 421, 106–9; see also *CD,* 2 January 1938, 3–4.

131. Attolico to Ciano, 5 January 1939, ASMAE, UC 71.

132. One can best trace the course of the discussions through *DGFP,* ser. D, vol. 4, no. 414, no. 418, no. 419, no. 420, no. 428, no. 429, no. 431, no. 432, no. 433, no. 436, no. 437, no. 438, no. 442, no. 445. For the gist of the agreement, see Clodius & von Mackensen to von Ribbentrop, 3 February 1939, *DGFP,* ser. D, vol. 4, no. 446, 574–75, and for the text of the agreement, see German-Italian Commercial Agreement, 13 February 1939, *DGFP,* ser. D, vol. 4, no. 451, 580–82.

133. Attolico to Ciano, 5, 6, 10 January 1939, ASMAE, UC 71; von Ribbentrop to Ciano, 9 January 1939, ASMAE, UC 71; see also von Ribbentrop to Ciano, 9 January 1939, *DGFP,* ser. D, vol. 4, no. 426; von Ribbentrop Memorandum, 10

January 1939, and Enclosure, Ciano to von Ribbentrop, *DGFP,* ser. D, vol. 4, no. 427, 550–52; *CD,* 4 January 1939, 5 January 1939, 7 January 1939, 5, 6, 7.

134. *CD,* 7 January 1939, 7.

135. Attolico to Ciano, 6 January 1939, 9 January 1939, ASMAE, UC 71.

136. Attolico to Ciano, 21 January 1939, 25 January 1939, ASMAE, UC 71. For more on the discussions and factions within the Japanese government, see Ōhata Tokushirō , "The Anti-Comintern Pact, 1935–1939," in *Deterrent Diplomacy: Japan, Germany, and the USSR, 1935–1940,* ed. James William Morley (New York: Columbia University Press, 1976), 79–81.

137. Attolico to Ciano, 6 February 1939, ASMAE, UC 71; *CD,* 8 February 1939, 24–25.

138. Von Weizsäcker Memorandum, 27 February 1939, *DGFP,* ser. D, vol. 4, no. 454, 584; von Ribbentrop Memorandum, 28 February 1939, *DGFP,* ser. D, vol. 4, no. 455, 584–85; von Weizsäcker to von Mackensen, 5 March 1939, *DGFP,* ser. D, vol. 4, no. 456, 585; von Weizsäcker to von Mackensen, 10 March 1939, *DGFP,* ser. D, vol. 4, no. 459, 588.

139. Von Ribbentrop Memorandum, 28 November 1938, *DGFP,* ser. D, vol. 4, no. 408, 526.

140. *CHD,* 18 December 1938, 19 December 1938, 206–7, 207; Ermannsdorff (Budapest) to von Ribbentrop, 20 December 1938, *DGFP,* ser. D, vol. 5, no. 265, no. 266, 355, 356.

141. Von Weizsäcker Memorandum, 28 December 1938, 30 December 1938, *DGFP,* ser. D, vol. 5, no. 267, no. 268. Ermannsdorff to von Ribbentrop, 4 January 1939, *DGFP,* ser. D, vol. 5, no. 269, 359.

142. *CHD,* 25 November 1938, 23–25 December 1938, 28 December 1938, 31 December 1938, 188–89, 208–9, 209, 210; von Mackensen Memorandum, 29 December 1938, *DGFP,* ser. D, vol. 3, no. 494, 543–44; von Weizsäcker Memorandum, 2 January 1938, *DGFP,* ser. D, vol. 3, no. 495, 544–45; von Mackensen Memorandum, 5 January 1938, *DGFP,* ser. D, vol. 3, no. 497, 547–58.

143. *CD,* 5 January 1939, 6.

144. *CD,* 8 January 1939, 8.

145. Neville Chamberlain to Ida Chamberlain, 8 January 1939, NC 18/1/1081. For the official memorandum on British aims for the visit, see Draft Memorandum for Cabinet, 20 December 1938, FO 371 22417, R10223/23/22. For more detail on Chamberlain's aims and actions, see also Paul Stafford, "The Chamberlain-Halifax Visit to Rome: A Reappraisal," *English Historical Review* 98, no. 1 (1983): 61–100.

146. Neville Chamberlain to Hilda Chamberlain, 15 January 1939, NC 18/1/1082; Neville Chamberlain to King George VI, 17 January 1939, PREM 1/327. In this context, Quartararo's claim that Chamberlain left Rome determined to prepare for war against Italy seems particularly farfetched (Quartararo, *Roma tra Londra e Berlino,* 424).

147. Dichiarazioni a Chamberlain (draft), n.d., ASMAE, UC 61; Primo colloquio col Signor Chamberlain, 11 January 1939, UC 61, 85; Secondo colloquio col

Signor Chamberlain, 12 January 1939, UC 61, 85. For the published translation, see *CDP,* Conversation between the Duce and Chamberlain, 11 January 1939, 12 January 1939, 259–66.

148. *CD,* 11 January 1939, 12 January 1939, 13 January 1939, 9–11. It is difficult to see how historians of the De Felice school such as Rosaria Quartararo can maintain their argument that Mussolini had not cast his lot with the Axis in light of this evidence. In this case, Quartararo argues that, for Mussolini, good relations with England were the fundamental element of his foreign policy, and he hoped to create an Anglo-French-Italian bloc against Germany. In her view, it was only Chamberlain's alleged refusal to moderate French intransigence that pushed Mussolini toward the Axis. Significantly, she argues against the abundant evidence to the contrary that Mussolini decided on an alliance with Germany only after Chamberlain's visit. She did not, however, provide any direct evidence to support her contention regarding Mussolini's intentions. She also ignored the lengthy campaign that Chamberlain conducted from February to June to try to convince Daladier to grant concessions to Italy (Quartararo, *Roma tra Londra e Berlino,* 413–25). For a similar contention, albeit one that adheres more closely to accurate chronology, see De Felice, *Lo Stato totalitario,* 568–69. These arguments are simply unsustainable given the evidence of Mussolini's wider goals and his determination before Chamberlain's visit to forge a tripartite alliance against France and Great Britain.

149. According to Ciano's diary and the Italian records, the initial contact was made in person in France, not by telegram. Baudouin suggested otherwise. Guariglia reported from Paris that Baudouin and Fagiuoli had met, suggesting that the French report is perhaps inaccurate, though Guariglia may have been reporting a meeting subsequent to an initial telegram. Similarly, Fagiuoli said to Ciano that Bonnet and Daladier had charged Baudouin with the mission and had initiated it. For a useful summary of the French evidence, see Shorrock, *From Ally to Enemy,* 252–55. See also Paul Baudouin, "Un voyage à Rome (fevrier 1939)," *Revue des deux mondes* (1 May 1962): 69–85; *CD,* 28 January 1939, 17–18; Guariglia to Ciano, 25 January 1939, ASMAE, UC 61.

150. Guariglia to Ciano, 25 January 1939, ASMAE, UC 61; *CD,* 28 January 1939, 2 February 1939, 3 February 1939, 17–18, 20, 21. For Ciano's quite accurate description of the meeting to von Mackensen, see von Mackensen to von Ribbentrop, 4 February 1939, *DGFP,* ser. D, vol. 4, no. 447, 575–76.

151. *CHD,* 10 October 1938, 11 October 1938, 13 October 1938, 16 October 1938, 19 October 1938, 22 October 1938, 27 October 1938, 14 November 1938, 28 November 1938, 1 December 1938, 3 December 1938, 5 December 1938, 6 December 1938, 142, 142, 176–77, 178–79, 179–80, 180, 184–85, 194, 199–200, 201, 202, 202–3, 203; *CD,* 15 January 1939, 12.

152. Resconto del viaggio di S.E. Ciano in Jugoslavia a colloquio con Presidente Stoyadinovitch, 18–23 January 1939, ASMAE, UC 85. For the published version, see *CDP,* 267–73.

153. Resconto del viaggio di S.E. Ciano in Jugoslavia a colloquio con Presidente Stoyadinovitch, 18–23 January 1939, ASMAE, UC 85.

154. Campbell to Halifax, 19, 21 January 1939, FO 371 23738, R1079, R1080/111/67. Campbell also warned strongly of the possibility of an Italian coup.

155. *CD,* 24 January 1939, 15.

156. For a brief description of the internal crisis, see Joseph Rothschild, *East Central Europe between the Two World Wars* (Seattle: University of Washington Press, 1974), 257–58.

157. *CD,* 5 February 1939, 6 February 1939, 23, 24–25.

158. *CD,* 4 January 1939, 22.

159. Knox, *Mussolini Unleashed,* 39.

160. "Relazione per il Gran Consiglio," NA, RG T586, r4405, 000039–46. This document represents the text of Mussolini's speech. A published version exists in *OO,* vol. 37, 151–57, which differs slightly in a couple of places.

161. "Relazione per il Gran Consiglio," NA, RG T586, r4405, 000039–46 (*OO,* vol. 37, 151–57).

CHAPTER 6

The Pact of Steel

Mussolini's imperial dreams compelled him to tighten the Axis relationship. Faced with apparently increasing Anglo-French solidarity, he believed that he needed a military alliance with Germany to provide diplomatic cover for his Albanian coup as well as support in the event of war with France over Italy's territorial claims. The inclusion of Japan in a tripartite alliance would also serve to intimidate both France and Britain owing to the potential threat to their colonies in the Far East. Mussolini and Ciano had hoped to sign a tripartite alliance in January, but the new Hiranuma cabinet had refused to follow the Duce's timetable. Though it agreed in principle with the idea of an Italo-German-Japanese alliance, the majority of the Japanese Council of Five Ministers preferred an alliance directed solely against the Soviet Union, Japan's foe in Manchuria and China. Japanese leaders, therefore, had sent a counterproposal on 2 February, simultaneously sending a commission to support Ambassadors Ōshima and Shiratori in Berlin. The commission, consisting of Consul General Ito of the Gaimushō, Lieutenant-Colonel Tatsumi of the Japanese General Staff, and Rear-Admiral Abe of the Ministry of the Navy, would also serve to limit the ability of Ōshima and Shiratori to exceed or ignore their instructions in pursuit of the alliance. The commission eventually reached Berlin at the end of February.[1] In the meantime, however, Japanese reticence and von Ribbentrop's unfulfilled promises annoyed the Duce. Reports indicated that the Hiranuma cabinet planned to move deliberately and with great caution in discussing an alliance with the Axis powers. In early February, in the absence of a completed tripartite pact,

Mussolini began considering an immediate alliance with Germany. Mussolini thought that this arrangement could serve to counterbalance tighter Anglo-French cooperation while not entirely alienating Britain.[2]

By the time the Japanese delegation arrived in Brindisi on 25 February on its way to Berlin, Mussolini had begun to pursue a bilateral agreement with Germany. On Mussolini's orders, Ciano instructed Attolico to approach von Ribbentrop to propose an Italo-German alliance in light of Japanese delays. Owing to von Ribbentrop's brief illness, Attolico could not carry out his orders until 28 February. Attolico asked for information of the status of the negotiations with Japan and received the reply that there was little new. Attolico argued that Japan had developed diverse interests from Italy and Germany, so that an immediate alliance was preferable to waiting for Japanese agreement. Italy and Germany would inevitably have tighter ties between their ground forces than with Japan; therefore staff talks would not prejudice a later tripartite alliance.[3] German officials, however, feared that Italy's provocation of France might spark a war that would draw Germany into a premature general conflict. In addition, an optimistic report from the German Embassy in Tokyo and encouragement from General Ōshima led von Ribbentrop to believe that an alliance agreement was imminent. As he did not want separate talks with Italy to prejudice the tripartite negotiations, von Ribbentrop reserved his reply to the Duce's initiative.[4]

The arrival of the Japanese delegation in Berlin clarified the Japanese position; the Japanese government would conclude an alliance only if its application were limited to the case of war with the Soviet Union. Although this position hardly could have been clearer, von Ribbentrop still hoped that pressure from Ōshima could sway the government in Tokyo. Attolico and Magistrati, however, were more realistic. When he saw the Führer on the evening of 2 March, Attolico raised Mussolini's idea of Italo-German staff talks in advance of any accord with Japan. Hitler replied that he was "completely in agreement."[5] Ciano had just returned to Rome from his trip to Poland and considered the issue with Mussolini the next day. Ciano noted that Mussolini increasingly preferred a bilateral alliance and resented Japanese delays. The Duce thought that an alliance with Japan, far from intimidating the British and American governments, might instead provoke the United States to align itself with Britain and France. A bilateral alliance would serve to give Mussolini the confidence to annex Albania—his next major territorial ambition.[6]

Still, despite the evidence of Japanese intentions, von Ribbentrop clung to the view that he would be able to negotiate a tripartite alliance within a few weeks. He phoned Ciano on 4 March to indicate that Ōshima's and Shiratori's strong support for an alliance would overcome Tokyo's objections. Both ambassadors had threatened to resign if the Hiranuma cabinet did not acquiesce to German demands. He preferred to await that development rather than to proceed with a bilateral alliance, which might delay a tripartite one.[7] Again, Attolico's understanding of the situation was much more accurate than was von Ribbentrop's. Attolico had listened carefully to Ambassador Shiratori's explanations of Japanese policy. Shiratori had said that in Japan the anti-Comintern pact represented a genuinely anti-Soviet agreement, despite the Italian and German views that Britain was its primary target. Accordingly, he argued that it would be necessary to detail the precise obligations of each party in the event of different possible scenarios; this precision would overcome the fears of the Hiranuma cabinet of the open-ended commitment that von Ribbentrop had demanded that the Japanese leaders accept. Such an approach would eventually succeed, Shiratori argued, but would take time to negotiate. Attolico and von Ribbentrop discussed the Japanese position, but the German foreign minister insisted that he would not compromise; Japan would have to accept that an alliance would apply against both Britain and France. Attolico and von Ribbentrop agreed that the latter would tell Ōshima of this demand and would indicate that if the Japanese did not accept the alliance on these terms, then Italy and Germany would proceed with a bilateral alliance. As well, Attolico reported that von Ribbentrop finally agreed that it was time to begin staff talks with Italy, although only after Attolico repeatedly insisted. Attolico argued that Hitler had already approved the idea and von Ribbentrop eventually relented, despite the fears of his officials that Italy might draw Germany into a premature war with France; von Ribbentrop said that he would discuss the details with Ciano.[8]

After discussions with Hitler and with General Keitel, von Ribbentrop informed Attolico on 9 March that conversations could begin immediately. In internal discussions, Keitel indicated that he thought the conversations should occur in two stages. The first would last several months, consisting primarily of the two sides taking stock of available equipment and formations. Only after this initial stage and the conclusion of a Japanese alliance would the conversations proceed to a discussion of military objectives. In a separate telegram to the German Embassy in Rome, Secretary of State von Weizsäcker emphasized to von Mackensen that Germany had "no intention of giving the other side full insight into our operational intentions," especially advance warning regarding the occupation of Prague or the true state of relations with Poland. Keitel would initiate the contact through the German military attaché in Rome.[9] Attolico sent notice to Ciano, who informed the Duce. The German decision pleased Mussolini, who was still ignorant of the imminent occupation of Prague. Attolico's report emphasized Hitler's loyalty to the Axis and determination to march side-by-side with Italy. Mussolini and Ciano decided that the conversations should begin immediately and suggested Innsbruck as a convenient meeting place.[10] On instructions, Attolico phoned the German chancellery, telling Walter Hewel, the chief of von Ribbentrop's personal staff, of the Duce's decision. Mussolini wanted the opening of the conversations published in order to regain the diplomatic initiative that he thought Britain and France had seized with their public plans for rearmament. Hewel informed von Ribbentrop, who gave his approval.[11] The initiation of staff conversations appeared to settle Mussolini's immediate need for a military alliance.

Italy's economic relations with Germany also seemed to confirm Mussolini's optimism regarding the Axis partnership. Italy had had increasing difficulty raising the foreign currency necessary to pay for German goods beyond those traded through the clearing exchange set in past commercial protocols. Italian negotiators wanted the requirement for foreign currency payments dropped. German representatives, with von Ribbentrop's support, refused to do so, citing Germany's shortage of foreign currency. Both Hitler and Mussolini became involved in the negotiations, and despite von Ribbentrop's stubbornness, both sides eventually compromised. The resulting commercial agreement, signed in Rome on 13 February, also included lists of cooperative purchases and decisions on transport issues.[12] Most importantly, it helped to settle some differences between the two sides generated by their sometimes-incompatible economic interests.

German economic interest in the Balkans offered another example of the delicate nature of the Axis partnership. In early February, Ciano had protested vigorously about rumors that Germany was hoping to exploit Albanian oil deposits. Ciano told von Mackensen that Albania was virtually an Italian province and that the Italian people demanded a profit from Italy's investments in Albania. A perceived German encroachment on Italy's interests would make it difficult for Mussolini to be able to increase the popularity of the Axis. In short, Ciano wanted Germany to stay out of Italy's Mediterranean sphere of influence. The next day, von Weizsäcker expressed to Attolico his surprise at Ciano's attitude, though he admitted that a representative of King Zog had in fact approached Germany regarding developing Albanian petroleum deposits. Nevertheless, in light of the

Italian response, Germany would take no further initiative in the matter.[13] Hitler's willingness to placate Italian sensibilities on these secondary issues went a long way to strengthen Mussolini's devotion to the Axis.

Given the strength of Axis solidarity, Hitler's coup against Prague came as a considerable shock in Rome. On 11 March, signs of Slovak unrest signaled the impending crisis, but German reassurance seemingly calmed Ciano's worries. Mussolini himself said two days later that he was entirely unconcerned.[14] This attitude represented almost willful blindness on Mussolini's part, as Count Csáky, the Hungarian foreign minister, had warned the Italians of Hitler's plans to occupy Czechoslovakia and had indicated that Hitler had asked for Hungarian support.[15] On 14 March, von Ribbentrop finally informed Ciano that Germany intended to annex Bohemia and Moravia and to make Slovakia a client state. The invasion on 15 March cast a temporary pall over the Axis, as it struck at the heart of the relationship; Hitler had carried out another coup without consulting Mussolini. The destruction of the Czechoslovakia created at the Munich conference dealt a blow to Mussolini's prestige, and it alienated the Italian public, which saw once again Germany profiting from the Axis while Italy did not. Hitler had also violated his pledged word at Munich that he only wanted to reunite ethnic Germans with the Reich.[16] If Mussolini ever hoped to play the role of the *peso determinante* in European affairs, then the betrayal inherent in the German occupation of Prague offered him the perfect opportunity to restore Italy's relations with the West.

Hitler's attempt to placate Mussolini by sending the Prince of Hesse with a message thanking the Duce for his understanding did not work very well. Hesse told Mussolini and Ciano that Hitler had acted because Germany could no longer tolerate Czech mistreatment of Germans and because the Czechoslovak government would neither abandon its ties with the Soviet Union nor demobilize its forces. Though Mussolini expressed his thanks to Hesse, afterward the Duce complained gloomily to Ciano that he could not publicize this information. He said, "Italians would laugh at me; every time Hitler occupies a country he sends me a message."[17] Nevertheless, Mussolini believed that he had little choice but to accept the fait accompli. Ciano disagreed with Mussolini's loyalty to the Axis. He argued that Hitler had broken his word and questioned whether or not Italy would be able to rely on the Führer's future assurances. Ciano thought that Italy should restore its freedom of action, but Mussolini would not be swayed. The Duce understood that it would be difficult for Italy to reverse Germany's expansion. More importantly, however, he knew that he could only pursue his own expansionist goals through the alliance with Germany. With that in mind, Mussolini thought that it might be time to provoke demonstrations that would trigger Italy's occupation of Albania.[18] Ciano seized on Mussolini's response and ordered Francesco Jacomoni, the Italian minister in Albania, to proceed with the agreed plans for annexation. The scheme called for Jacomoni's agents to create disorder that would serve as a pretext for Italy to send the fleet, air force, and landing parties into action. Jacomoni would reject any protests or diplomatic responses from King Zog. Unfortunately for Ciano, Mussolini equivocated, and Ciano had to call off the plans in an undignified hurry the following day.[19]

By 17 March, Mussolini had partially adopted Ciano's anti-German rhetoric. In addition to the occupation of Prague, Mussolini reacted to rumors of German influence in Croatia. Mussolini feared that Croat leader Vladko Maček would declare independence, followed by a request for German protection. The Duce briefly flirted with the idea of a rapprochement with Britain and France; he thought that German encroachment on Italy's sphere of influence would force him to break the Axis. Despite his previous anti-German rhetoric, Ciano advised the mercurial Mussolini to approach the Germans first to find out whether or not the rumors had any substance. Ciano spoke to Ambassador von Mackensen the same day, saying that Mussolini entirely approved of Hitler's occupation of Prague. Ciano admitted that it had come as a shock to the Italian public, but he thought that Mussolini would be able to control the situation. More seriously, he cited the rumors about German influence over Maček and declared that Croatia was part of Italy's Mediterranean zone; if Hitler did not recognize Italian preeminence then Italy would have to reconsider its Axis policy. The German ambassador protested that Ciano referred only to rumors and had no solid information; von Mackensen thought that Hitler had no intention of taking any action regarding Croatia. Nevertheless, he promised to relay Ciano's concern to the Wilhelmstrasse.[20]

While awaiting a reply, Mussolini swung wildly between support for Germany and anger at Hitler's actions. On 18 March, Mussolini published an article in the *Giornale d'Italia*, arguing that President Beneš's attempts to control ethnic minorities had provoked Hitler's attack. Beneš had also flirted with the Western democracies and intended to spread Anglo-French influence in the Balkans. In Mussolini's view, Hitler's action was entirely justified, and Czechoslovakia's end proved the danger inherent in the existence of multiethnic states.[21] Privately, however, Mussolini was less sanguine. The next day, he told Ciano that it was impossible to present the idea of an alliance with Germany to the Italian people. Hitler had proved himself treacherous, and Germany's moves against Croatia were provoking a crisis. Mussolini even considered sending troops to the Venetian border to be able to attack Croatia in event of a pro-German declaration of independence.[22] Attolico added fuel to the flames in a courageous report from Berlin. He charged that Germany had violated Italy's trust by overthrowing the Munich agreement and the subsequent arbitrations that Italy had helped to negotiate. The German attack therefore represented a grave blow to Italian prestige. He suggested that Mussolini take steps to clarify the mutual obligations for consultation and to ensure that both parties understood the equality of rights within the Axis.[23]

Despite Ciano's and Attolico's concerns about the Axis partnership, German attempts to assuage the Duce's wounded pride were ultimately successful. On 20 March, von Mackensen brought von Ribbentrop's reply to Ciano's questions about Croatia. The German foreign minister indicated that Germany had no direct interest in Croatia and reaffirmed that Italy would have sole control over Axis policy in the Mediterranean, the Adriatic, and adjacent areas.[24] That evening, a reassured Duce told Ciano that Italy would not change its Axis policy; "after all, we are not prostitutes."[25] The following day, Mussolini made a bellicose speech to the Fascist Grand Council, attacking Britain and France for trying to arrange a democratic bloc against the Axis. He condemned France for its intransigence in resisting peaceful revision of the Versailles Treaty and for its jealousy of Italy's colonial conquests. He complained that Jews, Freemasons, and Bolsheviks had provoked Hitler's occupation of Prague; in light of this agitation, Fascist Italy had approved of the German occupation. He concluded by saying that Italy was committed to Axis solidarity, even to the point of war.[26] At the same time, German officials communicated that German-Italian staff talks could begin at any time.[27]

Mussolini, Ciano, and Attolico met in Rome on 22 March to consider Italian policy in the aftermath of Prague. Attolico had returned for consultations, but to forestall potential speculation from the foreign press, Italian diplomats circulated the fiction that he returned for the celebrations of the twentieth anniversary of the founding of the Fascist movement. Attolico brought news of a long meeting that he had held with Hitler on the afternoon of 20 March. During the wide-ranging discussion, Hitler had reaffirmed his absolute solidarity with Italy and had discussed the respective military balance between the Western democracies and the Axis. In the Führer's view, the main difficulty lay in British naval superiority; if war occurred in the near future, the Royal Navy would be able to cut German overseas communications and Italian supply lines to Libya. Nevertheless, in two years time, Germany would have launched two new battleships and would help to divide the British fleet between the North Sea and the Mediterranean. Accordingly, Hitler thought that a general war would be opportune in as little as two years time. Hitler inquired about Italy's demands against France, and Attolico replied that the immediate demands did not include territorial claims, but centered on adjustments in Franco-Italian colonial arrangements regarding the familiar list of Tunis, Djibuti, and Suez. The atmosphere of the discussion had been cordial and cleared the air, though Attolico's description of Italy's quarrel with France apparently had not reassured Hitler that Italy had no immediate plans for a war with France. Hitler's expression of support for Italian demands against France, however, had further calmed the waters disturbed by his occupation of Prague.[28]

Attolico relayed Hitler's views to Mussolini and Ciano, though he also presented a forceful argument that German arrogance and "power mania" required greater definition of reciprocal Axis obligations. Mussolini agreed and said that "in order to continue the policy of the Axis it is necessary to fix the objectives of our respective policies, to establish zones of influence and of action for Italy and Germany, and to insist on Germany reabsorbing the non-Italian residents of the Alto Adige." He also decided to send a letter to Hitler to tell the Führer that the precipitate nature of the German occupation of Prague had damaged Mussolini's prestige, as the Duce had not had time to prepare Italian public opinion.[29] Hitler instead took the initiative and sent a letter to Mussolini to commemorate the twentieth anniversary of the founding of the *Fasci di Combattimento*. The letter was a paean of praise for the Duce's stalwart anti-Bolshevism; Hitler thought that future generations would forever link Mussolini's name to the regeneration of Europe in the twentieth century. Most importantly, it identified the common objectives of German and Italian expansion and the solidarity needed for both parties to be united to face the ill will of the Western democracies.[30]

This letter coincided with von Ribbentrop's instruction to German diplomats in the Balkans and Mediterranean that Italy's position was predominant and that they could take no initiative with minority communities without his written consent. He took this measure to assuage Italian fears of German encroachment in Italy's zone of influence and to ensure the continued solidarity of the Axis.[31] German Foreign Ministry officials also intervened with the Ministry of Economics to ensure that Germany would fulfill its quotas of coal deliveries, which had fallen in arrears.[32] Most significantly, Colonel von Rintelin, the German military attaché in Rome, had met with General Pariani on 22 March to discuss the date for staff talks at Innsbruck.[33]

The German diplomatic offensive succeeded in papering over any cracks in Mussolini's devotion to the Axis. The Duce wrote a brief memorandum for Ciano to guide his son-in-law in planning for the alliance with Germany:

Questions to be discussed with von Ribbentrop:

a) objectives, in area and time, of German policy;

b) economic position of Italy in the Danube Basin and the Balkans;

c) Italo-French, Italo-Yugoslav, and Italo-Albanian relations;

d) elimination of the Germans from the Alto Adige;

e) the tripartite military alliance;

f) Italo-German economic relations.[34]

Mussolini clearly intended to proceed with the alliance with Germany, with or without eventual Japanese participation. He thought it necessary to learn the fundamental elements of Hitler's foreign policy planning as a basic point of departure, and he also wanted to define more precisely mutual spheres of influence, both diplomatic and economic. After the shock of Hitler's occupation of Prague, these aims were sound policy. Having covered the nature of Italian rights in the alliance, Mussolini directed Ciano to indicate the scope of Italian claims against France, Yugoslavia, and Albania. Removal of ethnic Germans from the Alto Adige would provide evidence of Hitler's loyalty to the Axis. Finally, having prepared the ground for the alliance, Ciano and von Ribbentrop would be able to discuss the alliance itself, as well as greater economic cooperation to ensure its proper functioning. German diplomatic skill, combined with the Duce's overreaching expansionist grasp, had settled a crisis in Axis relations.

Unwitting of the precise nature of Axis policy, British and French leaders hoped to exploit Hitler's occupation of Bohemia and Moravia to drive a wedge between Germany and Italy. After his visit to Rome, Neville Chamberlain had hoped for an improvement in Anglo-Italian relations, but he did not realize how completely his personal diplomacy had failed. In reality, Mussolini had ensured that relations deteriorated. Italy's rancorous press war against France spilled over against Britain, particularly after Chamberlain's public pronouncement on 6 February that Britain would be bound to defend France in the event of unprovoked aggression. A *Giornale d'Italia* article had threatened war with France unless the Daladier government conceded Italian demands on Djibuti, Tunisia, Corsica, and Nice. Whitehall officials insisted that Perth ask Ciano to disavow this article, as its semiofficial origins appeared to threaten war against Britain, which would not stand aside if Italy attacked France. Ciano refused to do so, leading Viscount Halifax to conclude that the press attacks represented official Italian policy. On orders, Perth told Ciano upon the latter's return from Poland that his attitude was "regretful," but Foreign Office officials were almost unanimous in criticizing Perth's "lack of backbone" in delivering the protest. Halifax approached Grandi, but the ambassador spoke in soporifics and provided only weak excuses for Italian press attacks.[35]

More seriously, the Italian increase in its Libya garrison again threatened the British position in Egypt. Ciano rejected Perth's protests and complained that French troop concentrations in Tunisia required an Italian response. Since Italy had approximately twice the number of soldiers in Libya than France had in Tunisia, Ciano's response carried little weight.[36] The Italian military also had recalled several classes of conscripts. Although in the short run, the need to retrain these troops would weaken the effectiveness of the *Regio Esercito*, in the long run Italy would maximize the number of trained recruits that it could mobilize for war.[37] Further Italian press attacks, including several in Mussolini's own *Il Popolo d'Italia,* accused Britain of supplying arms to "international criminals" and of "wishing to suffocate the totalitarian states militarily and economically."[38] The combination of these issues seemed to show that Mussolini and Ciano had little interest in maintaining good relations with Britain.

After Hitler occupied Prague, however, Chamberlain sent a letter to Mussolini. Chamberlain wrote that Hitler had violated his word by annexing a predominantly non-German territory. This move prompted concern that Hitler might attempt to occupy other countries. If he attempted to do so, Chamberlain argued, then another war would be inevitable; most Europeans wanted to avoid another conflict. He said that he understood that the Axis represented the core of Italian foreign policy, but he hoped that Mussolini would use whatever influence the Italian leader might have to alleviate European tension.[39] As some Foreign Office officials feared, Chamberlain's letter backfired. The lack of any warning about Britain's commitment to defend France and the Mediterranean status quo, combined with lack of precision regarding positive steps toward reconciliation undermined Chamberlain's effort.[40] The Duce told Ciano that the letter merely encouraged further risks, as it showed the "inertia" of the Western democracies. Accordingly, Mussolini rekindled the preparations for the attack on Albania.[41] When Mussolini delivered his reply to Chamberlain at the beginning of April, he included largely empty phrases. The Duce did, however, mention the poor state of relations with France and insisted that Fascist Italy would not take any diplomatic initiative until its "rights have been recognized."[42]

Mussolini's fractious and bellicose relationship with France served to prevent any serious chance of a rapprochement after Prague. Two main issues divided them. First, although the Spanish Civil War was drawing to a close, it retained the potential to destabilize Italo-French relations. The Nationalist offensive in Catalonia, spearheaded by Italian troops, conquered Barcelona in February, sounding the death knell of the Spanish Republic. With the loss of its major remaining war industries, the Spanish government could not hope to defend Madrid. General Gambarra, the Commander of the *C.T.V.*, who had returned to Rome for consultations with the Duce, promised a speedy victory. Mussolini and Ciano were ecstatic about the imminent end of the long war.[43] Nevertheless, the near collapse of the Republic meant that Mussolini wanted to secure the fruits of victory. Rumors circulated that France, at the behest of Jews and Freemasons, would extend further aid to Republican forces in order to force Franco to reach a negotiated solution. Even if unsuccessful, this ploy would in theory serve to tie down forces of the totalitarian countries and thus serve the interests of the international conspirators. Mussolini strongly resented what he saw as French attempts to prevent Fascist Italy's great victory over Bolshevism and democracy.[44]

Mussolini also hoped to be able to ensure that Franco joined the Axis camp and resisted the entreaties of the British and French governments to establish friendly diplomatic relations. On 25 February 1939, General Francisco Jordana, Franco's foreign minister, and Léon Bérard, a French senator, had signed an agreement, essentially conceding French de jure recognition of Franco's government and commitments of cooperation on several issues. Daladier's government, despite strong opposition in the French Chamber of Deputies, hoped to dissuade Franco from becoming irrevocably attached to the Axis powers. Franco himself blamed France for its alleged support of international Communism and Freemasonry, so despite this official rapprochement, relations remained extremely strained. Primarily, they consisted of brusque Nationalist demands for the return of gold reserves, war matériel, and political refugees.[45] Though the Duce understood that Spain was exhausted after the long war, he expected to see Franco's symbolic adherence to the anti-Comintern pact that would give an indication that the Spanish Nationalists intended to join the Axis, at least on a diplomatic plane. Though Franco was willing to join the pact, he wanted to delay publication of the fact until after the end of the war; he hoped to avoid the possibility of increasing French reluctance to meet his demands or to withhold diplomatic recognition. Ciano and von Ribbentrop agreed, and Franco secretly agreed to the pact.[46] Mussolini and Ciano anticipated that Franco would eventually join a military alliance, and the Duce reveled in the belief that Italian victories at Malaga and Barcelona had laid "the foundations of the Roman Mediterranean Empire."[47]

After the fall of Barcelona, the Spanish Nationalist army regrouped for the decisive attack against Madrid. The final offensive began shortly after Hitler's occupation of Prague. Madrid fell on 28 March, and by the end of the month Franco's troops had mopped up the remnants of Republican troops. On the day Madrid fell, Mussolini made a speech to a crowd from the balcony of the Palazzo Venezia. He trumpeted that Franco's victory spelled doom for the enemies of Fascism, and the Duce celebrated his defeat of Bolshevism. The jubilation of the crowd excited Mussolini, and he published an article the next day paying homage to the "warlike and Fascist" Italian spirit.[48] General Jordana had officially signed the anti-Comintern pact on March 27, charting a course of friendship toward the Axis. In a conversation with General Gambarra, Franco had said that Nationalist Spain would have to remain neutral for several years, as he needed time to rebuild his army. Still, he hoped that both Italy and Germany would help to retrain his troops, and he reassured Gambarra that Spain would not align itself with Britain and France.[49] The end of the war potentially ended a source of conflict with France and could have opened the door to a rapprochement with the Daladier government, but Mussolini refused to seize the opportunity.

Second, the Baudouin mission to Rome in February had foundered on the shoals of Mussolini's refusal to limit his demands. While Ciano had planned to follow up this contact, Mussolini was less willing. Instead, the Duce had ranted that he would level French cities in a campaign of wholesale destruction.[50] Later in February, Bonnet had approached Ambassador Guariglia to try to limit mutual press attacks. This measure of good faith, Bonnet argued, would prepare the ground for "the solution of other problems." Bonnet also assured Guariglia that French troop shipments to Tunisia were simply a reaction to the increased Italian garrison in Libya. France would send no more troops provided that Italy refrained from doing so. Mussolini had also received intelligence reports from Paris that the French general staff was strongly opposed to the idea of war with Italy and wanted to lessen tension to avoid the possibility of any conflict.[51] After Hitler's occupation of Prague, Ciano again had wanted to follow up these indications of French willingness to make concessions. Vincenzo Fagiuoli told Ciano that, according to his intermediary Baudouin, France was willing to make concessions to lessen Franco-Italian tension. Ciano, annoyed at Hitler's move on Prague, considered a rapprochement with the West but would only pursue one if he received special consideration. He sent Fagiuoli to Paris to meet with Baudouin. Ciano thought that he could persuade Mussolini to allude to the core of the immediate Italian demands—Tunis, Djibuti, and Suez—in the public speech planned for 26 March, signaling the Duce's willingness to reach a modus vivendi. At the same time, Pierre Laval, former premier and foreign minister, approached Guariglia to say that Daladier desired immediate talks with Italy. Laval would serve as a go-between. Ciano refused to use Laval as an intermediary and instructed Guariglia to reject this initiative; if Daladier wanted discussions, Ciano wrote, he should approach Italy through normal diplomatic channels. Daladier also gave a letter to Baudouin for Ciano. In it, Daladier expressed that he was willing to open negotiations the following week. In the meantime, however, he wanted the Italian press to tone down its anti-French attacks, and he promised that he would do his best to control the French press. Daladier also asked that Ciano intercede with Mussolini to soften rhetoric about the Rome-Berlin Axis. In exchange, Daladier would concede all of Italy's demands regarding Djibuti and would agree to grant some concessions on the status of Tunisia until public opinion would allow the negotiation of a new accord to replace the Mussolini-Laval agreement that Ciano had denounced. Ciano found the French response "disappointing."[52]

Mussolini's speech to the Fascist Grand Council on 21 March reaffirmed his commitment to the Axis and appeared to signal that the Duce had closed the door on these diplomatic maneuvers.[53] His public speech of 26 March, delivered in the Olympic Stadium to Fascist *squadristi*, further hardened the Italian position. He saluted Italy's victory over Bolshevism in Spain, won by a "disciplined, warlike, imperial" people, and attacked pacifism, and, paradoxically, the war psychology of the West. Mussolini said that he considered "perpetual peace as a catastrophe for human civilization." Nevertheless, he thought that Italy and Europe needed a period of peace for a few years. Still, he condemned those who tried to break the Axis, which was foolhardy, for the Axis represented not just relations between two states but between two revolutions and two compatible views of European civilization. He spoke of the barricades that France had erected between the two Latin sisters, which the Nationalist victory in Spain would bring down, and mentioned the three demands that Italy had against France: Tunis, Djibuti, and Suez. France could continue to refuse to discuss these issues, but Italy would continue its course of rearmament and would make the Mediterranean a "*spazio vitale*."[54] This speech obviously failed to meet the suggestions that Daladier had made regarding the opening of negotiations. Mussolini had deliberately rejected the possibility of a rapprochement with France. In response, Daladier delivered a speech on 29 March; observers widely interpreted it as a hardening of the French position. Mussolini told Ciano, "So much the better: it was just what I desired."[55] Sir Noel Charles, the British chargé d'affaires in Rome, approached Ciano on his own initiative to enquire whether or not Italy would accept an unofficial approach from the French government. Ciano reserved his decision to consult with Mussolini. At the same time, Bonnet approached Guariglia through a French journalist who served as an intermediary. Bonnet insisted that France and Italy needed to open talks immediately. Again, Mussolini expressly rejected this démarche; he insisted that any approach would have to come through the French Embassy in Rome.[56] French government officials were certainly willing to discuss concessions to Italy, but Mussolini's insistence that the approach come officially through diplomatic channels was an impossible condition to meet. In light of scurrilous Italian press attacks and past leaked negotiations, and colored by the noisy demonstration of 30 November 1938, French politicians could not risk a public rebuff. The Duce's intransigence had prevented any serious possibility of a rapprochement with the West.[57]

With a German commitment to arrange a bilateral military alliance, Mussolini believed the time ripe to launch the invasion of Albania. Plans had matured since Mussolini's and Ciano's decision in May 1938 to prepare for annexation. Jacomoni had established contacts with tribal chieftains who would betray King Zog, and Ciano had even subverted General Zoff Sereggi, the Albanian minister in Rome, with bribes of cash and promised honors. Nevertheless, Ciano feared the potential reaction from Yugoslavia and Britain; Italian occupation threatened to outflank Yugoslavia's southern border, to overthrow the Mediterranean status quo, and to turn the Adriatic into an Italian *Mare Nostrum*. By stationing divisions in Albania, Italy would be able to threaten both Greece and Yugoslavia and would be able to redeploy Italian naval forces from patrolling the Adriatic. The Italian threat to Greece ultimately could prevent Britain from including that country in its eastern Mediterranean war plans. Mussolini and Ciano recognized these benefits, and there was no reason to believe that other observers would fail to understand the importance of the issue. Nevertheless, Ciano expected that the imminent birth of

Zog's first child would prevent the King from resisting an Italian invasion, and Chamberlain's letter of 20 March had calmed Mussolini's fears of British intervention. Ciano also hoped to weaken foreign responses by muddying the waters. He sent Colonel Mario de Ferraris, an Italian intelligence agent, to carry a proposed pact for an Italo-Albanian defense alliance, a guarantee of Albanian independence, and Italian financial assistance, but the pact also included clauses for Italian use of Albanian ports and airfields. This last element of the proposal obviously would infringe Albanian sovereignty; King Zog knew that his acceptance of the accord would cost Albanian its independence, and he would likely lose his throne. He replied to Ciano's proposal with skilful dissimulation. Zog agreed with de Ferraris's proposals, leaving it to his ministers to raise objections. Albanian negotiators eventually accepted all of the clauses save the crucial one calling for Italian use of Albania territory. Ciano had hoped that he could carry off the coup peacefully through Zog's acceptance of the de facto ultimatum, but King Zog's refusal to bend led the Duce on 2 April to give the order for the occupation to proceed. In the confused situation, Sereggi resigned, Jacomoni told Italian subjects in Albania to prepare to leave the country while his staff began to burn legation ciphers and documents, and Ciano ordered Italian telegraph operators to mangle coded communications between Britain's legation in Tirana and London, thus preventing British diplomats in Albania from communicating with the Foreign Office.[58]

As per his instructions, on 4 April Jacomoni ratcheted up the level of tension by threatening invasion if Zog did not acquiesce in signing the accord. Mussolini ordered the ultimatum for Zog's acceptance to expire at noon on Thursday, 6 April, with landings scheduled to commence at 4:30 A.M. the following day, Good Friday. On 6 April, Ciano issued the official orders to General Guzzoni to begin the invasion. Italian troops landed at Durazzo and three other ports as scheduled, albeit amid scattered gunfire and considerable confusion caused by poor leadership and command control. Three hours after the landings, an excited Ciano flew to Durazzo, reveling in the beautiful view of the Italian fleet arrayed in the harbor. In a last-ditch effort to postpone the inevitable, Zog offered to reach a negotiated solution, and Guzzoni annoyed both the Duce and Ciano by delaying his march on Tirana while discussing terms with Albanian representatives. An angry Mussolini ordered Guzzoni to restart the occupation immediately. Italian troops reached Tirana on 8 April, to the relief of a beleaguered Jacomoni, and Ciano arrived in the city shortly thereafter to view the results of the coup he had inspired. King Zog fled into exile in Greece.[59] In an effort to limit foreign opprobrium, Ciano created a puppet government under the alleged control of Albanian national Shefkhet Beg Verlaçi, though on 15 April the Fascist Grand Council declared Vittorio Emanuele III the King of Albania. For the time being, Ciano encouraged the Duce to allow Albania to keep open its foreign ministries and legations and to maintain the fiction of an independent military, but in June, given the apparently weak foreign reaction to the occupation, Fascist Italy would unceremoniously abolish these last remnants of Albanian independence.[60]

Characteristically, Mussolini ignored reports of chaos and inadequate preparation in the military maneuvers that signaled the inadequacy of the *Regio Esercito*. Instead, the apparent lack of resistance to the occupation, German diplomatic support, and the lack of strong foreign opposition excited and pleased the Duce.[61] On 4 April, Ambassador von Mackensen had inquired about rumors of increased Italian activity in Albania. Ciano had told him that Zog had broken the treaty negotiations, and Mussolini was considering whether or not to send warships to protect Italian nationals. Less dishonestly, Ciano also said that Mussolini was considering making Albania an Italian protectorate. In his report to Berlin, von Mackensen had said that Ciano's manner indicated that events were developing more rapidly than Ciano had expected. The next day, von Ribbentrop had given Attolico carte blanche for any action in Albania, apparently confirming once more German willingness to allocate Italian primacy in the Mediterranean. On 6 April, Attolico had telephoned the Wilhelmstrasse to say that Italian troops would land on Good Friday. Later that day, von Mackensen had seen Ciano, and, on instructions, indicated German approval for the occupation.[62]

Yugoslavia represented the greatest potential threat to the Italian occupation of Albania. It shared a common border with both Albania and Italy, and could perhaps serve as a rallying point for British or French opposition. Ciano's personal diplomacy with Prime Minister Stoyadinović had collapsed when Prince Paul dismissed the would-be Fascist dictator in February. Dragiša Cvetković, the new premier, was loyal to Prince Paul and less committed to the Italo-Yugoslav accord than had been Stoyadinović. Mussolini had drawn back from the invasion of Albania in mid-March primarily owing to the fear that it might allow Hitler to exploit Croat separatism to Germany's advantage. At the same time, Ciano had consorted with representatives from Croatia who wanted to discuss Italian support for Croatian separatism. Ciano had received two emissaries, one of whom, the Marquis of Bombelles, may have been a Yugoslav spy. Fortunately for Italo-Yugoslav relations, Ciano maintained an initial position of reserve with Bombelles, who served as a go-between with Ante Pavelić and claimed to be an intimate of Maček's. At that moment, Ciano did not then want to provoke Yugoslavia; the conversation had the nature merely of establishing a connection.[63] The other contact, Amedeo Carnelutti, was a confidant of Maček's. Carnelutti told Ciano that Maček was anti-German but would fall in with Germany if Italy rebuffed Croat approaches. Ciano said that Croats should negotiate with Belgrade to secure concessions, but if that failed, then Croatia should declare independence and appeal for Italian aid. Ciano spoke of the possibility of establishing a Croat-Italian customs union. Mussolini ordered Ciano to pursue these contacts; the fall of the quasi-fascist Stoyadinović had led the Duce to return to attempts to weaken Yugoslavia.[64]

Despite Mussolini's worries about the Yugoslav attitude toward the Italian invasion of Albania, the Yugoslav government remained passive throughout the potential crisis. On 6 April, as the Italian fleet assembled, Bosko Cristić, the Yugoslav minister in Rome, asked for an interview with Ciano. Ciano feared that Cristić would announce a change in his government's policy. Instead, Cristić merely asked about Italy's worrisome actions in Albania. Ciano explained that Italy would occupy four ports and would then spread control throughout the country. He also repeated the fiction that Italy would respect the nominal independence of Albania. He believed that he had mollified Cristić's concerns, though Ciano noted to his Chef de Cabinet Anfuso that the Yugoslav minister had looked very unhappy about the developing situation.[65] In the end, Yugoslavia, with German soldiers stationed on its northern border and Italian ones in the west and the south, could do little but acquiesce.[66]

Similarly, the British government found itself in a difficult position. Albania did not represent a direct vital interest, but the occupation still would have unpleasant repercussions. The invasion occurred after considerable speculation within the Foreign Office as whether or not Mussolini would act. By 4 April, the concentration of Italian naval forces became obvious, sparking comment in the British press that Italy was about to threaten the Mediterranean status quo, thus violating the Easter Accord. Ciano had ordered that his diplomats in Britain and France should try to explain that the invasion represented an Italian attempt to resist German hegemony in the Balkans, but this duplicity would fool few contemporary observers.[67] On 6 April, Anfuso phoned London to ask Guido Crolla, the chargé d'affaires, to explain further to Viscount Halifax that Albania was an exclusively Italian interest and to ask for a British reply to press speculation. Halifax was busy with an official visit from Colonel Beck, the Polish foreign minister, so Crolla had to leave the message with Sir Orme Sargent. The next day, as the invasion progressed, Halifax replied that Great Britain rejected the Italian interpretation and that Great Britain would not disinterest itself. On orders from Mussolini, Crolla returned to see Halifax, presenting the Italian case once more and complaining about British press coverage. Halifax lost his patience at this display of Italian hubris and indicated his displeasure at Italy's resort to force. Italy's action had enraged British public opinion and was helping to create the impression that force was the only arbiter in Europe. Crolla replied that Italy could take lessons from Great Britain in the use of gunboat diplomacy. Halifax concluded the fractious meeting by suggesting that Mussolini could withdraw his troops from Spain now that the war had ended as a gesture of good faith that would help to calm British public opinion.[68]

After this acerbic exchange, Halifax assembled a meeting of cabinet ministers at Number 10 Downing Street to discuss possible reactions. The foreign secretary suggested that there were four possible options: enquiry, protest, threats, and action. In this instance, Halifax thought that the inaction of Yugoslavia in particular meant that Britain could take no effective direct action. He also thought that Mussolini might have decided to invade as a response to the British guarantee to Poland on 31 March, so protests or threats would likely be futile. The best policy in Halifax's view was to pursue closer relations with Turkey and Greece to ensure their resistance to future Italian moves, possibly issuing guarantees to bring them inside a new eastern Mediterranean security front.[69] Italy's attack on Albania had sparked the British cabinet to pursue security pacts in the eastern Mediterranean to resist further Italian aggression.

For his part, Mussolini directed Crolla to speak with Halifax once more, insisting that the occupation of Albania had been carried out in a pacific manner, that Italy was organizing a withdrawal of the *C.T.V.* from Spain, and that a crisis in Anglo-Italian relations would be deplorable. Ciano also wanted Crolla to reassure Halifax that the Greek government had accepted that Italy had no plans for invasion.[70] Still, rumors of an Italian strike against Corfu, reminiscent of Mussolini's earlier episode in 1923, sparked Halifax to interrogate Crolla regarding Mussolini's aims.[71] Crolla denied that Mussolini had any intentions of a strike at Corfu, and Halifax decided that it was worth waiting to see whether or not Mussolini kept any of these promises.[72] Similar conversations occurred in Rome, although Perth uncharacteristically wrote that he had used tough language with Ciano, leaving the foreign minister "red in the face." Perth also secured assurances from Ciano that Italy would withdraw all of its planes and pilots from the Balearic Islands.[73] Ciano found the British reaction quite muted and thought that British politicians made their protests primarily to placate domestic public opinion. He thought that he and Mussolini had successfully gulled the potential opposition.[74]

Both Italian leaders, however, were ignorant of the real British reaction. Despite the comparatively muted protests, the aggressive nature of Italian policy did provoke a response. The foreign policy committee decided on 10 and 11 April to issue a guarantee to Greece, and, under intense French pressure, agreed to extend one to Romania, while making a concerted effort to bring Turkey into an eastern Mediterranean security arrangement. Greece accepted its guarantee, although it refused in the first instance to join in guaranteeing other countries' independence. In Turkey, the Inönü government cited constitutional difficulties, and, more seriously, concerns about its own security in the absence of a British guarantee. Nevertheless, on 13 April both Chamberlain and Daladier issued public statements in their respective parliamentary chambers guaranteeing Greece and Romania against aggression.[75] Although the issuing of guarantees would in the end be significantly less than an ironclad, interlocking security system against Axis aggression, it did signal that the patience of the Western democracies with Axis aggression was eroding. Chamberlain wrote to his sister, "Musso [lini] has behaved like a sneak and a cad." Chamberlain thought the invasion showed Mussolini's "complete cynicism." The prime minister had reached the conclusion that "any chance of future rapprochement with Italy has been blocked by Musso just as Hitler has blocked any German rapprochement."[76] Mussolini's decision to invade Albania may have brought potential gains in Italy's strategic situation but at the cost of further alienating the Chamberlain cabinet and furthering the division of Europe into two competing blocks. By the middle of April, a British strategic appreciation listed Italy amongst Britain's likely enemies. British planners also shifted the emphasis in war planning to concentrate the British fleet in the eastern Mediterranean at the expense of the commitment to the Far East, a clear signal that resistance to Axis aggression had assumed a higher priority after Mussolini's attack.[77]

With the Western democracies rallying possible allies, Mussolini's expansionist aims would require him to rely on his would-be German ally more than ever. As the *Regio Esercito* was assembling its invasion force for Albania, General Pariani and General Keitel met in Innsbruck on 5 April to discuss preliminary plans for a bilateral military alliance. The discussions were cordial, but each side brought an element of duplicity to the talks. Pariani concealed Italian plans for the imminent invasion of Albania, a kind of tit-for-tat for Hitler's silence regarding the occupation of Prague. For his part, Keitel concealed rather more. He did not share with Pariani German plans for war with Poland (although even Keitel did not then know the full extent of Hitler's intentions). The German general also concealed the Führer's limits on talks with the Italian military. Hitler wanted to avoid detailed discussion of military and political objectives and military strategy and operations planning. Hitler had told Keitel that he feared the Francophile tendencies of some of the Italian Generals and the Imperial Court might lead to leaks of vital information. Nevertheless, he expected Keitel to make it clear to the Italian delegation that Germany would march with Italy to the end.[78] Despite the dissimulation and appearance of mutual distrust, therefore, the conversations served to demonstrate the closeness of the aims of the two Fascist regimes.

Keitel delivered Hitler's promise that Germany would fight alongside Italy in every case of war. Pariani replied that if the tense relations with France sparked a war, then Italy would not ask Germany to intervene directly but would ask only for military supplies. German military planners thought that war between Italy and France could ignite a general war, something that they hoped to avoid; Keitel consequently observed that he thought it unlikely that Britain would abandon its French ally in time of war. After discussing the case of a limited war with France, Pariani returned the Duce's assurance that in the event of a general conflict, Italy would march with its German ally. The two men asserted the inevitability of war with the Western democracies; the central question was when would the time be ripe? Both generals agreed that their rearmament efforts would reach a peak in perhaps as little as a year's time, though it might perhaps take as long as two or three years. Of course, they would have to leave that decision to their political masters. To prepare to face the possibility of economic warfare, they both agreed that the Axis would have to dominate the Balkans economically and politically in combination with their potential allies. Similarly, they both agreed that Italy and Germany should cooperate economically as well as militarily. Keitel also spoke of plans to withdraw German troops from Spain, and he addressed questions of Italo-German assistance to the Franco regime. Finally, Keitel and Pariani considered the proper form to implement plans for economic cooperation. On the second day, the two generals considered questions of defense against attack as well as the need for improved rail transport between Germany and Italy.[79]

On his way back to Rome, Pariani traveled with Colonel von Rintelin, the German military attaché to Rome, with whom he was considerably more forthcoming. Pariani admitted that he agreed with Keitel's view that a Franco-Italian war would not be localized but told von Rintelin that the Duce had required him to assert Italian independence; the Duce wanted to maintain the right to fight France without German approval. Pariani also said, however, that Italy had no plans for an immediate war with France, rendering the question moot. In his view, war with France would occur primarily in North Africa, as the Alpine frontier would be unassailable on both sides. He agreed with Keitel's view that war should not occur for two to three years, suggesting that no pressing need for operational planning existed and that the two general staffs should concentrate on defense for the time being. Finally, Pariani espoused his general theory of warfare. He thought armored warfare and artillery alone would not be enough to break the Maginot line. Accordingly, he thought that the German military should explore the use of mass attacks with poison gas.[80]

From the Italian perspective, two issues stood out from the talks. Efisio Marras, the Italian military attaché in Berlin, noted the extraordinary strain of rearmament on the German economy. He assumed that at some point, Germany would reach a point of economic and military preparation where Hitler would either have to force the decisive conflict or see his country face economic collapse.[81] No evidence exists that Mussolini, Ciano, or Pariani understood the implications of this report. The second is that both Italy and Germany were unprepared for war in the immediate future. Keitel insisted that Germany and Italy would have separate spheres of operations, thus indicating Italian preponderance in the Balkans, but, once again, no one defined this limit precisely, and the German intention that the Axis dominate the Balkans economically implied that Germany would not entirely respect Mussolini's Mediterranean *Mare Nostrum*.[82] Again, Italian officials showed no sign that they recognized these implications. Still, despite Hitler's orders to limit the exchange of information, Keitel and Pariani had in fact strayed into discussing political matters, setting the stage for the furtherance of the alliance in at least the appearance of mutual respect and understanding.

A week after the initiation of military talks, Field Marshal Hermann Göring traveled to Rome to meet the Duce. Ostensibly, the trip was unofficial and followed on Göring's visit to see his personal physician in San Marino. Göring traveled on Hitler's orders, however, and bore a message for Mussolini. He arrived in Rome during a time of high diplomatic tension following Mussolini's invasion of Albania and the Anglo-French guarantees to Greece and Romania. Göring opened the conversation by bringing Hitler's congratulations for the Italian occupation of Albania. The

Führer thought that it increased Axis power and would bring strategic benefits for Italy. The field marshal then turned to the substantive reasons for the meeting. He explained in very thorough terms that Germany would forego all interest in Yugoslavia and that Italian interest there would be paramount. Germany would seek only to safeguard its normal economic interests. Germany would direct any contact from nationalist minorities to Italy. Germany and Italy, he argued, would ensure that Yugoslavia could not return to its pre-1937 pro-French stance; the Axis would insist on benevolent Yugoslav neutrality in the event of war. In a similar vein, Göring told his hosts that Germany did not intend to exclude Italy in its economic relations in southeast Europe. Hitler promised to consult Italy before undertaking any initiatives; he wanted the Duce to know that Germany would not assert any exclusive claim to the region. Göring also raised the occupation of Bohemia and Moravia. He said that Germany's destruction of Czechoslovakia represented a considerable victory for the Axis and defeat for the west, as it had subtracted an enormous military potential from the encirclement of Germany. Czechoslovak industry also added to Germany's economic and military potential. He tacitly apologized for the short warning given to Italy, saying that events had developed with extraordinary rapidity and that the operation had been laid on in haste.[83]

Göring turned next to the potentially thorny issue of when Germany would be ready for a major war. He pointed out that Germany was still commissioning its two newest battleships and would not launch two more under construction until the following year. The Luftwaffe would have to regroup, reequipping its bomber squadrons with the new Ju 88 that was not yet in production. In his view, the military situation would be optimal in nine months to a year. He also indicated that German planning assumed that Britain and France would certainly fight together in the envisioned war, in effect challenging the oft-expressed Italian view that war with France could be localized. Still, despite Anglo-French unity, the combined power of the Axis would be sufficient to win a general war. This first meeting closed with Mussolini's questioning Göring's views on the role that Yugoslavia might play in a future conflict.[84]

The Axis politicians held two meetings on the second day: one at the War Ministry and one at the Palazzo Venezia. The discussions began with a dismissive exchange regarding Franklin Delano Roosevelt's quixotic request for German and Italian guarantees not to attack certain named countries. Göring thought that Roosevelt might be developing "an incipient mental disease." Turning to more serious business, Göring asked Mussolini whether or not Britain and France would stand together in the event of a general war. Mussolini temporarily abandoned his previous position that a war with France could be localized, admitting that Britain and France had apparently established a real alliance. After raising the subject of strained relations between Poland and Germany, Göring broached the idea of a rapprochement with the Soviet Union. Stalin's most recent speech to the Conference of the Communist Party signaled Soviet estrangement from the capitalist powers; it might therefore be possible to isolate Poland from any military or diplomatic support. Mussolini welcomed the idea, saying that recent Soviet diplomatic activity in Italy also suggested the possibility of a rapprochement. After discussing the likely difficulties of reaching an understanding with Stalin, Mussolini returned to the question of the appropriate timing for the inevitable war with the Western democracies. Göring replied that in 1942 and 1943 the ratio of German to British naval strength would be much better than it was at present, and French rearmament would continue to be hampered by manpower shortages. Mussolini agreed with Göring's appreciation; he stated that he thought Italy and Germany should wait two to three years before fighting a general war. The conversation included a discussion of Spain, with Ciano asserting falsely that Italy had a secret treaty with Spain allowing Italian airbases in the Balearics and on the Spanish mainland. Mussolini informed Göring of Italian attempts to create fifth columns in the Arab world to undermine British control of the Middle East, including supplying money for arms purchases.[85]

Mussolini's question to Göring about the most likely areas for the outbreak of a war in the near future was the last major new element in the conversation. The field marshal replied "Poland and Tunisia." Mussolini reaffirmed that Italy would not attack France during the next two to three years, leaving Poland as the next trouble spot. Göring qualified his view that Poland would reach a crisis point only if the Poles mistreated the German minority. He said that Hitler had told Göring personally that he "was not planning anything against Poland." The conversation closed with a recapitulation of the points agreed.[86] Ciano noted in his diary that his only major concern was the fear that Göring's language regarding Poland sounded suspiciously similar to that used against Austria and Czechoslovakia in the past. Both Mussolini and Ciano thought that Poland would fight if pressed. Still, though Göring spoke of war, Ciano thought that Hitler had at least left open the possibility of peace.[87]

Göring's visit significantly advanced the prospect of an alliance. His repeated emphasis that Hitler would acknowledge Italian primacy in

Yugoslavia diminished Mussolini's fears of German encroachment in an area the Duce called his own preserve and held out the prospect that the Axis powers would be able to intimidate Yugoslavia into following a pro-Axis foreign policy. Göring's insistence that Germany was not ready for an immediate war, conveyed partly to restrain Mussolini from involving Germany in a premature war with France, accorded with Mussolini's view. Although they believed that war with Britain and France was inevitable, they both agreed that a general war in the near future would be inopportune; both countries needed time to complete their military preparations. These issues represented the core of what would become the Pact of Steel. One misunderstood issue, however, created a grave threat for Italy. Hitler did not consider that his attack on Poland would spark a general war; he thought that he could cow any opposition from Britain and France. Despite this issue, however, the discussion in Rome had also laid the foundation for the crisis that Mussolini would face in August.

As Göring and Mussolini discussed the future course of the Axis in Rome, German and Italian diplomats considered how to react to Anglo-French guarantees to Poland, Romania, and Greece. In this case, senior officials rather than their political masters seemed to drive the process. Whereas von Ribbentrop had told Ambassador Attolico on 14 April that the British guarantees had little more than propaganda value, his subordinate von Weizsäcker wanted to begin a diplomatic offensive against the countries receiving the guarantees. He thought that Italy and Germany should demand to know whether or not Greece and Romania had been anything more than passive recipients of the guarantees. If they had had foreknowledge of Anglo-French planning, then von Weizsäcker thought that the Axis should treat them as hostile powers carrying out a policy of encirclement. Attolico thought this advice extreme, especially in light of Italy's public guarantee that it would not attack Greece. Attolico phoned Rome to speak to Ciano, who asked for Mussolini's decision. The Duce decided that von Weizsäcker's approach would be inexpedient, as Italy had already exchanged views with Greece on the matter. Mussolini said that Germany should perhaps wait until Romanian Foreign Minister Gafencu's visit to Berlin to dress him down.[88]

By 18 April, von Ribbentrop had adopted his subordinate's language. Attolico described the German foreign minister as "very agitated" by events: the Anglo-French guarantees, the lack of progress in the negotiations with Japan, and especially with Poland. Attolico wrote that von Ribbentrop claimed "anti-German sentiment in Poland increases day by day." Attolico questioned von Ribbentrop's sanguine claim that Britain and France would stand aside while Germany crushed Poland. Attolico concluded, "The Führer wants a European war." Under the baleful influence of von Ribbentrop, Hitler "could be capable of inducing himself to attempt a strike on Poland in the supposition that neither France nor England would intervene." Attolico strongly urged Ciano to take the initiative to determine Hitler's plans, as an attack on Poland would automatically imperil Italy.[89] Ciano spoke to Mussolini on 20 April, after the Duce's speech dismissing Roosevelt's call for Axis guarantees of nonaggression. They concurred that a German attack on Poland would start a general war. Mussolini would have to prepare public opinion for the possibility. For his part, Ciano planned to hasten his already proposed meeting with von Ribbentrop, originally scheduled to assuage the Nazi foreign minister's anger at Göring's trip to Rome.[90] Attolico cabled that the situation seemed "relatively less acute" than it had appeared previously, though he thought it unlikely in the long run that Poland could ever provide enough concessions to satisfy Hitler. After exchanges of proposed schedules, Ciano and von Ribbentrop agreed to meet in Como on 6 and 7 May.[91]

While relations with Germany dominated Italian foreign policy during the latter part of April, Ciano also held meetings with leaders of Hungary and Yugoslavia. Prime Minister Pál Teleki and Foreign Minister István Csáky of Hungary traveled to Rome for meetings from 18 to 20 April. Ciano thought the meetings lacked serious content. He liked Teleki but despised Csáky, whom he called a "physical and spiritual weakling who wishes to assume heroic airs." At the last meeting, Mussolini laid out his views of the course Hungarian foreign policy should follow. While Italy and Germany desired some years of peace, Hungary should continue to follow the Axis lead. No one wanted to see Yugoslavia partitioned, at least not in the immediate future, but if it occurred, then Italy's interest in Croatia would be paramount. Hungary should watch and wait regarding Slovakia and not take any initiative contrary to German interests and without German approval.[92] In essence, little changed as a result of these discussions.

Two days later, on 22 April, Ciano met Aleksandar Cincar-Marković, the Yugoslav foreign minister, in Venice. Ciano liked Cincar-Marković and found him "reasonable and understanding." The Yugoslav foreign minister said that he understood Italy's reasons for occupying Albania and thanked Ciano for not sending large numbers of troops to the northern Albanian border. Ciano assured his guest that Italy had no territorial claims against Kosovo. Cincar-Marković and Ciano discussed

Yugoslavia's relationship to the Axis. Yugoslavia would not join the anti-Comintern pact, primarily owing to the ramifications for internal policy, but Cincar-Marković did not entirely rule out the possibility of eventual Yugoslav adhesion. In the meantime, Yugoslavia would follow the general lines of Axis policy, primarily gravitating toward Italy. He promised to try to improve Yugoslavia's relations with Hungary while maintaining its traditional association with Romania. Ciano left the discussions pleased by evidence that Yugoslavia, despite the fall of Stoyadinović, was broadly sympathetic to Axis policy. In particular, Cincar-Marković's insistence that Yugoslavia would not accept a guarantee from Britain or France seemed to show some degree of Yugoslav loyalty to the Axis.[93]

As Ciano prepared to meet von Ribbentrop in Como, the eventual nature of Japan's relationship to the Axis was less easy to determine. In a long memorandum, Eugen Ott, the German ambassador in Tokyo, had described the difficult nature of the Japanese internal policy debate regarding a military alliance with the Axis. The need for an alliance grew out of Japan's invasion of China. The war in China, despite crushing Japanese military victories, showed no signs of an immediate end. Japanese attempts to rebuild conquered areas had foundered on the shoals of Chinese resistance to Japanese rule, and General Chiang Kai-Shek, the Chinese Nationalist leader, had an enormous countryside in which to conduct fighting withdrawals and strategic retreats. Army senior staff and the public both seemed to demand an immediate victory, but that policy would require a massive increase in Japanese military expenditures and would bring international complications. An alliance with Germany and Italy specifically directed against Britain and France, senior army commanders argued, would intimidate both Britain and the United States and would serve to deprive Chiang of Anglo-American financial support that allowed his resistance to continue. Opposition to this view centered on Navy commanders, court circles, and the financial community. They argued that an alliance directed against the West would antagonize the United States. Japan's lack of raw materials made her dependent on foreign trade; deliberate provocation of the United States could lead to a long-rumored trade embargo that could suffocate the Japanese economy. An alliance against the Western powers could also unite the Anglo-American fleets to oppose Japanese expansion, and naval commanders feared that the imperial navy could not successfully fight against both fleets at the same time. Naval commanders and financial circles, therefore, wanted an alliance directed solely against the Soviet Union. This policy, they believed, would intimidate Stalin, causing him to abandon his support for Chinese resistance and to lessen the possibility of Soviet intervention in Manchuria. In short, the difference of opinion lay in the perceived effects of the alliance so that there seemed to be little possibility of conducting an entirely rational debate on the relative merits. Both sides relied on inference and speculation in making their case, so it was possible that the dispute could drag on interminably.[94]

The Council of Five Ministers, the Japanese inner circle of the cabinet, contained a majority of members who favored an alliance solely directed against the Soviet Union. Foreign Minister Arita, in particular, was a stalwart opponent of an anti-Western alliance. General Itagaki Seishirō, the army minister, was the most ardent supporter of an alliance directed against Britain and France. He received support from Ambassadors Ōshima and Shiratori, both of whom often objected to the instructions that they received from Arita. During March and April, the internal battle raged over the orientation of Japanese alliance politics. On 18 April, Ambassador Giacinto Auriti cabled from Tokyo that Japan was unable to reach a compromise that would allow the immediate acceptance of an alliance with the Axis.[95] The following week, Attolico in Berlin learned from his sources that Japan would present a counterproposal that excluded the possibility of war with the Western powers and would consider military assistance to the Axis only in the event of war with the Soviet Union.[96] Ciano noted in his diary that this news did not disappoint Mussolini. The Duce had come to believe that the inclusion of Japan might be a hindrance; it might provoke the United States to provide economic and even military support for Great Britain and France.[97]

At the end of April, rumors circulated that the Japanese government would accept von Ribbentrop's conditions, but they proved unfounded.[98] The German foreign minister maintained his insistence that the Japanese pact would be useful to Germany and Italy only if it covered the case of war with the Western democracies. Although von Ribbentrop was willing to reassure the Japanese government that neither Italy nor Germany contemplated war for many years, this promise did not assuage fears of Anglo-American economic retaliation.[99] By the time that von Ribbentrop and Ciano were to meet, the Japanese cabinet had become deadlocked. Arita Hachirō, the foreign minister, summoned Ambassadors Auriti and Ott in succession to give them the cabinet's decision. Arita gave them a copy of a letter drafted by Prime Minister Hiranuma Kiichirō that saluted the dynamism of Nazi Germany and Fascist Italy and expressed Japanese solidarity in trying to establish a new moral order for the world. Despite this common objective, he wrote, the Japanese cabinet was concerned that it would not be able to give Germany and Italy proper support as long as its forces remained bogged down in China. It could only consider a defensive alliance applied against the Soviet Union, therefore, though if the Axis became involved in war with another party then Japan would offer all of the economic, political, and even military assistance it could muster. In the near term, however, Japan would not be able to provide any military assistance. Hiranuma reaffirmed the bonds of a "moral and spiritual nature" that tied Japan to the Axis powers. Arita weakened the sense of ideological solidarity inherent in the letter with his attitude of obvious annoyance as he conveyed its contents to Ott and Auriti.[100] It appeared that Japan would not accept von Ribbentrop's minimum conditions for the alliance at any time in the near future. In early May, von Ribbentrop had implied to Attolico that if Japan did not agree to a tripartite alliance then Germany would be prepared to sign a concrete military alliance with Italy, leaving an opening for Japan to join later.[101] As Ciano prepared to travel to meet the German foreign minister, it appeared certain that the two Axis powers would discuss the conclusion of a bilateral alliance.[102]

Mussolini wrote a detailed memorandum for Ciano's discussion with von Ribbentrop.

It is my firm opinion that the two European powers of the Axis require a period of peace of no less than three years. Only from 1943 on will a military effort have its best chance for victory. Italy requires a period of peace for the following reasons:

a) to organize Libya and Albania militarily and to pacify Ethiopia, which should produce an army of one half million men;

b) to complete the construction and modernization of six battleships currently underway;

c) to replace all of our medium and heavy caliber artillery;

d) to press ahead towards realization of the plans for autarchy that would render impossible any attempt of a blockade by the democracies;

e) to hold the Exposition of 1942 that, in addition to documenting the accomplishments of the first two decades of the Regime, will provide us with hard currency reserves;

f) to complete the repatriation of Italians from France, a very serious problem of a military and moral nature;

g) to complete the transfer of many war industries from the Po valley to southern Italy, a process that is already under way;

h) to further strengthen the relations not only between the Axis government, but also between the two peoples, which would be aided by an amelioration of relations between the Church and Nazism, an amelioration that is also greatly desired by the Vatican.

For all these reasons, Fascist Italy does not desire to precipitate prematurely a general European war, although convinced that it is inevitable.[103]

The memorandum also presented a survey of Italy's relations with other countries. Mussolini described relations with Britain as "formal rather than friendly and productive," despite the Anglo-Italian accord. He wrote that Italy was in no hurry to settle its demands against France and repeated that Italy would not ask for German support in the event of a limited war with France. He thought that Germany and Italy should help with Spanish reconstruction and should work to bring Spain into any alliance. The Duce asserted that Yugoslavia would be within Italy's sphere of interest. He also accepted the idea of a rapprochement with the Soviet Union, but only to a limited extent. He thought it reasonable to prevent Stalin from joining with the democratic bloc but did not think it advisable to offend other potential allies by too close an association with Bolshevik Russia. Mussolini said that he would accept either a bilateral or tripartite alliance depending on Tokyo's attitude. He also noted that the alliance should function almost automatically even if Italy or Germany attacked a third party; the Duce was not interested in a defensive alliance or one encumbered by detailed conditions for its operation. Mussolini wanted the Alto Adige situation resolved to avoid the possibility of provoking incidents that the enemies of the Axis could exploit. In the economic realm, he wanted Ciano to raise the issue of German deliveries of coal and machinery. The Duce concluded with a statement on the general lines of Axis policy: "Speak of peace and prepare for war."[104] In a discussion with Ciano before the latter left, Mussolini emphasized the memorandum's first point; Italy would need a period of peace to build its military strength.[105]

This detailed memorandum laid out the cardinal elements of the Duce's policy. He emphasized the immediate need for peace given the glaring weaknesses of the Italian military, weakened by years of combat, and prevented from rearming with modern weaponry by Mussolini's expenditures on the wars in Abyssinia and Spain. Even the *Regia Marina*, the best-equipped service, would face severe hurdles in a general war before the launch of its new battleships. Though war with the Western democracies may have been inevitable, Fascist Italy was unprepared in 1939 to fight one. His plans called for the Axis domination of the Balkans that would strengthen Italy economically and undermine the power of the democratic bloc. Most significantly, however, the Duce insisted on an extremely tight alliance without the usual provisions for its operation only in the event of a defensive war. Mussolini had often repeated that the Axis had no need for a defensive alliance, as no one would dare attack Italy or Germany. Though he expected to delay the outbreak of a general war, he clearly hoped to profit from Axis strength in the meantime, and the Duce certainly meant what he said about the inevitability of eventual war with France and Britain.

The equivalent document prepared in the German Foreign Ministry to guide von Ribbentrop in the discussions contained some interesting features. It carried a discussion of Italian war planning. Pariani had told Keitel that Italy wanted a quick success in order to avoid a *guerre de longue durée* and that he intended to seek this success in the Balkans and in North Africa. German war planners considered this approach entirely illogical, as in their view, decisive success could only come with a victory over France. German planners also recognized the inadequacy of the Brenner Pass for Italo-German trade during wartime, especially coal deliveries, which already had fallen in arrears in 1939. The German draft memorandum limited German interest only in Croatia, not all of Yugoslavia as Göring had implied in his first meeting with Mussolini in Rome in mid-April. This lack of precision signaled the divergence of views regarding potential spheres of interest with which Italy and Germany would enter the alliance. Most importantly, the draft memorandum called for Italy to work to isolate Poland and argued that "Italy must be prepared for a conflict between Germany and Poland;" von Ribbentrop's behavior on this issue would create one of the most profound elements of misunderstanding between the would-be alliance partners.[106] The German foreign minister also brought with him two draft alliance proposals, written by Friedrich Gaus, the director of the German Legal Department. Both called for an alliance strictly limited to a defensive war, in part in order to limit Italy's ability to draw Germany into a premature war with France. The German drafts also called for the alliance to be kept secret, presumably to facilitate the eventual adhesion of Japan to a tripartite pact. During the meeting in Italy, Mussolini's eagerness for an offensive military alliance would lead von Ribbentrop to keep both alliance proposals to himself.

At the last minute, Mussolini ordered the location for the meeting of foreign ministers changed to Milan. Reports in the French press about anti-German demonstrations in that city aroused the Duce's ire. He wanted to refute these rumors about the alleged lack of Axis solidarity. The discussions proved wide ranging, touching upon all of the issues that the Duce had raised in his memorandum, plus some new issues that he had not considered.

The meeting opened with Ciano informing von Ribbentrop point-by-point of the contents of Mussolini's memorandum, emphasizing especially the need for a period of peace, but also the need for an offensive alliance. Ciano said that if relations with France continued in the current state of tension then Italy would have to resort to war, if only to garner respect. Italy would fight France alone, requiring only supplies of matériel but no forces from Germany. Nevertheless, Ciano insisted that the Duce would not provoke France at the moment. Ciano indicated Mussolini's views on the Balkans, particularly the belief that the occupation of Albania had brought Greece entirely under Italy's sway. Ciano also expressed Mussolini's expectation that Germany would absorb 10,000 former Austrians living in the Alto Adige. The Italian foreign minister raised the issue of German coal deliveries as well as shipments of machinery to allow Italy to manufacture advanced artillery. Ciano closed his presentation of Mussolini's view with the Duce's words: "Speak of peace and prepare for war."[107]

For his part, von Ribbentrop expressed his substantial agreement with the Italian position, with only relatively minor reservations. He opened his reply to Ciano by rejecting the recent initiative from the Pope for a conference to discuss German claims against Poland. Hitler did not like conferences, and the Anglo-French-Polish bloc would outnumber Germany and Italy. Hitler would thank the Vatican for its effort but would not accept its mediation. Next, von Ribbentrop raised what would become the most important area of misunderstanding between the two alliance members: Poland. In a long discourse, von Ribbentrop could not resist some anti-Polish rhetoric, though his language was less bombastic than usual. He did say that the *Wehrmacht* could crush Polish forces within a couple of weeks, but on the whole he sought to reassure Ciano that no immediate crisis threatened the peace. Despite his caution, von Ribbentrop did assert his belief that France and England would eventually weary of the tension surrounding the issue; "it is certain," he concluded, "that within a few months not one Frenchman nor a single Englishman will go to war for Poland." He reconfirmed, however, that Germany would "allow the matter to mature" without provoking the Poles, while holding German forces ready should Poland make any aggressive moves.[108] Significantly, von Ribbentrop's language left Ciano under the impression that Germany did not plan a war in the near future; the German foreign minister had chosen not to disturb Mussolini's pursuit of an alliance by raising the possibly contentious issue of Hitler's plan for war against Poland.

The conversation continued with further references to the allegedly peaceful nature of Nazi policy. According to von Ribbentrop, Germany also needed time to prepare for the inevitable war with the Western democracies. Though he insisted that Germany could defend itself if attacked, it needed four to five years to ready its fleet for war with Britain. The recent conquests of Czechoslovakia and Albania significantly strengthened the Axis, he argued, and in a few years time Germany would be able to wage a war of long duration. In that vein, von Ribbentrop insisted that an Italian war with France would not be localized; Great Britain would certainly help to defend its ally. In essence, he repeated the long-held view of German officials that an Italian war with France would spark a premature general war. He stated his agreement with the Duce's views regarding Spain, Yugoslavia, and the Balkans, though once again, neither side specified a precise demarcation of spheres of interest in the Balkans. The German foreign minister indicated that he agreed that discretion would be required in approaching the Soviet Union, but he used stronger language about the need to prevent the possibility of Stalin's association with the Western democracies. On another issue of great importance to Mussolini, von Ribbentrop gave strong assurances that Germany would work to repatriate ethnic Germans from the Alto Adige. Italian and German diplomats would make further contact in order "to find a concrete solution to the problem." Finally, von Ribbentrop turned to the issue of the military alliance. He lied to Ciano, saying that he had not brought a draft but would send one as soon as it was prepared. He thought that it would be appropriate to sign the agreement in Berlin in a solemn ceremony to indicate the pact's importance. Having not abandoned his cherished world policy to bring Japan in to a tripartite alliance, von Ribbentrop expressed his gratitude that Mussolini would accept an agreement that would allow for Japan's eventual adhesion.[109]

This conversation raised several interesting issues. Mussolini's desire for a pact that would cover wars of aggression was much stronger than was von Ribbentrop's. The Duce's ardor for the alliance caused von Ribbentrop to withhold the less-binding draft proposals that he had brought with him to Milan. In response to von Ribbentrop's declarations about Germany's demands against Poland, Ciano had replied that Italy had no direct interest in the issue, though he would serve as a mediator should Germany wish it. Strikingly, Ciano also said that neither he nor the Duce had any views on whether or not Britain and France would intervene if Germany attacked Poland. Combined with Mussolini's omission of any mention of Poland in his draft memorandum, it gave von Ribbentrop the impression that neither Mussolini nor Ciano had much interest in the issue. Accordingly, von Ribbentrop had not seen fit to present to Ciano the real nature of

Hitler's plans for Poland. Ciano took von Ribbentrop's language to signal that Hitler had slowed down the pace of German aggression and that Italy would be able to count on Mussolini's hoped-for period of peace.[110] It appears that von Ribbentrop believed that he was not actually misleading his Italian counterpart; he had promised not to provoke a general war, and both he and Hitler assumed that neither Britain nor France would resist a German attack on Poland. Ciano had even confirmed that neither he nor Mussolini had any strongly held belief about the potential Western reaction. Ciano's words represent a stunning failure to appreciate the significance of the alliance and of German policy. The eventual divergence of views on this issue in August represented the greatest misunderstanding between the two alliance signatories. It was also significant that neither party had precisely specified its understanding of their respective spheres of interest in the Balkans, nor had they exchanged any written documents on any of the most vital elements that would form the core of the alliance.

Despite what was left unsaid, the conversations had covered a wide range of issues and apparently had shown agreement on all of the major and even minor issues. When Mussolini phoned Ciano on the evening of 6 May to find out the results of the talks, Ciano reported the satisfactory results. Having secured German understanding on all of the issues that he wanted, Mussolini declared himself ready to sign a bilateral alliance. He later asked that both parties immediately publicize the decision to sign an alliance. Ciano knew that von Ribbentrop preferred to wait for Japan's agreement to join, but when von Ribbentrop consulted the Führer, Hitler gave his unqualified approval. Both sides issued public statements to the press. Astonishingly, Ciano decided to let the German Foreign Ministry prepare a draft alliance proposal and left the initiative in von Ribbentrop's hands. Uncharacteristically, Ciano was even charitable to his German counterpart. During a reception at the Villa d'Este with the cream of Lombard society present, Ciano thought that von Ribbentrop had scored a personal success.[111] When Ciano returned to Rome, Mussolini announced himself well pleased by the prospect of an alliance.

The alliance would advance the Duce's foreign policy in several respects. His long campaign to drive a wedge between Britain and France had obviously failed. His press attacks on both countries, the rancorous display in the chamber on 30 November, Germany's occupation of Prague, and the invasion of Albania had wedded the two countries into virtual military allies. Mussolini's superior troop strength in Libya made him confident of winning a showdown against Great Britain, despite the superiority of the Royal Navy. He also believed that Italy could effectively challenge

France in North Africa. Against both powers together, however, Italy would be at a decisive disadvantage, outnumbered in the air and especially at sea. The alliance with Germany would give him greater leverage to continue to insist that France meet his first stage of colonial demands while allowing him the economic and military support to allow him to reequip and reinforce Italian military forces. Italian preparation for a European war trailed all of the other major powers, and the massive army the Duce had mobilized in 1935 had relied on equipment largely becoming obsolete by the standards of 1939. His wars in Abyssinia and Spain not only had squandered valuable military hardware, they had seriously depleted the hard currency reserves necessary to pay for a new military expansion. Mussolini's alliance with Germany, he thought, would tie him to the most dynamic power in Europe and would allow him to maintain the diplomatic initiative while carrying out the military preparation necessary to secure his long-term conquests.[112] The Duce's desire to create a new Mediterranean empire caused him to lead Italy ever more tightly into Hitler's embrace.

While Ciano returned to Rome to receive the Duce's congratulations, von Ribbentrop traveled to Berchtesgaden to join a conference to discuss Germany's approach to the Soviet Union. In Berlin, a worried Ambassador Ōshima approached von Weizsäcker to find out the nature of the agreement reached in Milan. In particular, he seemed desperate to learn whether or not the proposed bilateral alliance would have more far-reaching commitments than the draft treaty with Japan. If so, Ōshima argued, it would seriously damage the prospects of a tripartite alliance. The German secretary of state replied that he assumed that Ōshima would continue to work energetically to reach an agreement but also that it was natural given the geographic position of Italy and Germany to reply to the encirclement policy of the Western democracies with a tighter agreement.[113] Upon von Ribbentrop's return to Berlin, Ōshima took up the issue with the German foreign minister. The announcement of the bilateral alliance, Ōshima argued, had had a negative effect on Japanese public opinion and had even sparked press attacks on the Axis. In light of the continued deadlock in the Council of Five Ministers, he said that the Japanese position still called for a primarily defensive alliance oriented against the Soviet Union.[114]

Despite these reservations, von Ribbentrop did not want to abandon entirely his long-cherished dream of bringing Japan into a world alliance. He proposed that Italy and Japan make another attempt to associate Japan with the Pact of Steel. The plan would be for Japan to initial the earlier draft of the tripartite alliance at the same time as Germany and Italy signed the Pact of Steel. The tripartite alliance would include a clause that would indicate that the bilateral alliance between Italy and Germany would override the tripartite one when it called for less rigorous obligations between the Axis partners. When signing, Ambassador Ōshima would state verbally that Japan would be unable to fulfill its military obligations and that these obligations would be the subject of future conversations. Finally, the Japanese government would be allowed to mislead third parties by stating that the pact was a defensive alliance and that it was primarily directed against the Soviet Union. This attempt to reach a compromise agreement annoyed Ciano, then in Florence. He thought that the Japanese government was unlikely to accept this proposal after its months of dithering and also was concerned that the pact would weaken the Italo-German alliance. Still, despite his objections, Ciano did not want to prevent von Ribbentrop's démarche and suggested that the Duce approve the initiative.[115] Immediately upon receiving Italian approval, von Ribbentrop sent his proposal to Tokyo, along with some strongly worded indications that patience in Rome and Berlin was wearing thin.[116] Though Japanese officials in Tokyo promised to reply by the time that Germany and Italy would sign their alliance, the Council of Ministers would not accept von Ribbentrop's proposal without changes. The Japanese decision meant that Germany and Italy would proceed with signing the Pact of Steel, leaving open the question as to whether or not Japan would ever join the alliance. Japanese reticence had led Mussolini to shelve his dream of welding Germany, Japan, and Italy into a powerful tripartite alliance directed against the British empire.[117]

While von Ribbentrop and Japanese diplomats tried to keep alive the idea of the tripartite alliance, Mussolini anxiously awaited conclusion of the bilateral pact. The week after Ciano's meeting in Milan, he began asking Ambassadors Attolico and von Mackensen for news of the German draft. Responding to a question from von Mackensen, Ciano said that his only concern about the proposed draft was that it included the word "alliance" in the text and that the wording should "be as full as possible."[118] The next day, Attolico saw von Weizsäcker to inquire about the delay. He received the reply that von Ribbentrop and Gaus were still away from Berlin, and the Foreign Ministry would not be able to prepare a draft until their return. On his own initiative, Attolico spoke about the need for a defensive treaty, mutual demarcation of the two countries' vital interests, and language on the inviolability of the Brenner frontier, but Attolico's political superiors had already indicated that their interests lay elsewhere.[119] Upon his return, Gaus hurriedly prepared a draft and gave it to

Attolico later that day. Gaus told Attolico that he had based the draft on the content of the foreign ministers' discussion in Milan. The Italian ambassador raised the issue of the Brenner frontier and a reference to Italian and German spheres of interest, saying that they represented Mussolini's views, not his own. Gaus replied that he thought that paragraph 2 of the preamble adequately addressed these issues, and he refused to amend the draft before submitting for Ciano's approval.[120]

Still in Florence, Ciano wrote that the alliance proposal "contains some real dynamite." Nevertheless, he and Mussolini wanted some minor changes. Where the German draft referred to the two countries' working toward the "realization of their eternal rights to life, Mussolini and Ciano preferred the more aggressive resolution "to secure their living space." They also wanted Article VII to limit the duration to ten years. Otherwise, the proposed draft met with Mussolini's approval. Attolico met with Gaus, and the German Foreign Ministry readily accepted these two minor changes.[121] Ciano insisted that the signing ceremony not take place on 24 May, the anniversary of Italy's entry into the First World War. Although the parallel between Mussolini's expansionism and the "sacred egoism" of Italy's liberal regime bore some similarities, Ciano did not want to associate his grand treaty with the alleged venality of prewar Italian transformist politicians.[122]

Ciano traveled to Berlin on 20 May for the signing ceremony, Mussolini having issued his formal approval three days earlier. The day after Ciano's arrival, he met with von Ribbentrop at the Wilhelmstrasse. The German foreign minister reaffirmed that Germany had no intention of launching a general war for three years and argued in favor of continuing negotiations to bring Japan into the alliance. Ciano showed von Ribbentrop original Turkish documents that an Italian intelligence service had intercepted; they allegedly showed Turkish hostility to Germany. Ciano said that Italy could take no further initiative with Turkey to settle their tense relations other than reconfirming that Italy had no plans to attack that country. Ciano also talked of Italian policy in Yugoslavia, indicating that Italy would not seek to break apart the country but would exploit Croat nationalism if it seemed opportune. If Yugoslav policy showed sympathy to the Western democracies, then Fascist Italy would reconsider its position. Ciano also spoke with Hitler and thought the German Führer showed himself to be in a less aggressive mood. Göring's jealousy at the Italian decision to award von Ribbentrop the Collar of the Annunziata, making him a so-called cousin of the Italian Royal Family, was the major bone of contention during Ciano's visit to Berlin. Ciano had to promise to try to arrange for Göring to receive one in order to assuage the field marshal's anger. On behalf of their governments, the two foreign ministers signed the Pact of Steel on 22 May, binding the two countries in an extraordinary close military alliance geared toward aggressive expansion of their power. When Ciano returned to Rome, Mussolini expressed his appreciation and satisfaction at the conclusion of the alliance.[123]

The pact obviously had serious omissions. Mussolini had never interested himself in precise clarification of the terms of the treaty. He assumed that the ground covered during the meeting between Ciano and von Ribbentrop at Milan had adequately determined the main lines of Axis policy. Nevertheless, it is puzzling that Mussolini trusted Hitler so much, especially after German betrayals of Axis solidarity and the obligation to consult Italy leading up to the Anschluss and the occupation of Prague. Similarly, Ciano was severely delinquent in entrusting the drafting of the treaty entirely to von Ribbentrop and the German Legal Department. The German draft ignored basic elements of those discussions, failing to mention the inviolability of the Brenner frontier, and, most importantly, neglecting the central principle that neither party would provoke a general war for at least three years. Notwithstanding the astonishing naiveté displayed by Mussolini and Ciano, the Pact of Steel represented the culmination of three years of Mussolini's foreign policy planning. The Duce believed that he had secured the ability to carry forward a policy of expansion in the Mediterranean—a policy that would inevitably mean war between Fascist Italy and the Western powers.[124] His social Darwinist–inspired dream of the dynamic expansion of Italy's African empire had led Mussolini to sacrifice the independence of Italian foreign policy on the altar of the alliance with Germany. Although he hoped that he would have three years to prepare to fight the climactic battle for supremacy in the Mediterranean, he had largely surrendered to others the ability to control that decision.

NOTES

1. For more detail on the composition and aims of the commission, see the editor's note in *DGFP,* ser. D, vol. 6, 81–83, and Iriye, *Origins of the Second World War in Asia and the Pacific,* 68–89. For a more detailed examination in English on the long history of the negotiation of the Pact of Steel, see Toscano, *The Origins of the Pact of Steel,* passim. Though his conclusions deal too lightly with the ideological nature of Italian policy, his work covers the long story impressively, including extensive reprinting of otherwise unpublished documentation.

2. Attolico to Ciano, 6 February 1939, ASMAE, UC 71; *CD,* 8 February 1939, 23–23.

3. Ciano to Attolico, 23 February 1939, ASMAE, UC 71; Attolico to Ciano, 28 February 1939, ASMAE, UC 71; see also Weizsäcker Memorandum, 27 February 1939, *DGFP,* ser. D, vol. 4, no. 454, 584.

4. Von Ribbentrop Memorandum, 28 February 1939, *DGFP,* ser. D, vol. 4, no. 455, 584–85.

5. Attolico to Ciano, 2 March 1939, ASMAE, UC 71. For more on the Japanese position, see Ōhata, 85–87.

6. *CD,* 3 March 1939, 37–38.

7. *CD,* 4 March 1939, 38–39; von Ribbentrop Memorandum, 4 March 1939, *DGFP,* ser. D, vol. 3, no. 752, 861–62. For more detail on the German position, see Weinberg, *Starting World War II,* 510–13.

8. Attolico to Ciano, 4 March 1939, ASMAE, UC 71.

9. Von Weizsäcker to von Mackensen, 10 March 1939, *DGFP,* ser. D, vol. 4, no. 459, 588: von Weizsäcker to von Mackensen, 11 March 1939, *DGFP,* ser. D, vol. 4, no. 459, no. 460, 589.

10. Attolico to Ciano, 9 March 1939, ASMAE; *CD,* 10 March 1939, 42.

11. Hewel Memorandum, 11 March 1939, *DGFP,* ser. D, vol. 4, no. 461, 589–90.

12. German-Italian Commercial Agreement, Third Secret Protocol, 13 February 1939, *DGFP,* ser. D, vol. 4, no. 451, 580–82; *CD,* 13 February 1939, 28–29. For more on Italy's parlous financial state, see Franco Catalano, *L'economia italiana di guerra: La politica economico-finanziaria del fascismo dalla guerra d'Etiopia alla caduta del regime, 1935–1943* (Milan: Istituto Nazionale per la Storia del Movimento di Liberazione, 1969), 25–28.

13. Von Mackensen to von Ribbentrop, 10 February 1939, *DGFP,* ser. D, vol. 4, no. 449, 578–79; von Weizsäcker to von Mackensen, 11 February 1939, *DGFP,* ser. D, vol. 4, no. 450, 579–80; *CD,* 10 February 1939, 11 February 1939, 26, 27.

14. *CD,* 11 March 1939, 13 March 1939, 23–24, 43–44; Hewel Memorandum, 11 March 1939, *DGFP,* ser. D, vol. 4, no. 187, 234.

15. Pro-memoria, read by Mussolini, 12 March 1939, ASMAE, UC 58.

16. *CD,* 14 March 1939, 15 March 1939, 44, 44–46.

17. Quoted in *CD,* 15 March 1939, 44–46. For Hesse's summary of the conversation, see von Mackensen to von Ribbentrop, 15 March 1939, *DGFP*, ser. D, vol. 6, no. 463, 590.

18. *CD,* 15 March 1939, 16 March 1939, 44–46, 46–48.

19. Ciano to Jacomoni, 15, 16 March 1939, ASMAE, GAB 29; *CD,* 15 March 1939, 16 March 1939, 44–46, 46–48.

20. Ciano appunto, 17 March 1939, ASMAE, UC 85; *CD,* 17 March 1939, 48–49; von Mackensen to von Ribbentrop, 17 March 1939, *DGFP,* ser. D, vol. 6, no. 15, 15–16. In his report, von Mackensen said that Ciano's language and manner were almost tortuous in raising the Croat issue and that he was cordial

throughout the discussion. Ciano's diary contains much more vigorous language than Ciano apparently used with von Mackensen.

21. "Il Giornale d'Italia," 18 March 1939, *OO,* vol. 29, 246–48.

22. *CD,* 19 March 1939, 50–51.

23. Attolico to Ciano, 18 March 1939, ASMAE, UC 6.

24. Von Ribbentrop to Ciano, Ciano appunto, 20 March 1939, ASMAE, UC 85, UC 6; *CD,* 20 March 1939, 51–52; von Mackensen to von Ribbentrop, 20 March 1939, *DGFP,* ser. D, vol. 6, no. 45, 48–49; von Ribbentrop to Ciano, 20 March 1939, *DGFP,* ser. D, vol. 6, no. 55, 63–64; see also Attolico to Ciano, 27 March 1939, ASMAE, UC 6, for a further denial from von Ribbentrop of any German interest in Croatia. Ciano later sent a letter to von Ribbentrop that the assurances were completely satisfactory (Ciano to von Ribbentrop, 24 March 1939, ASMAE, UC 85). For more on the German desire to placate Italian sensibilities, see Weinberg, *Starting World War II,* 563–66.

25. Quoted in *CD,* 20 March 1939, 51–52.

26. "184ª Riunione del Gran Consiglio del Fascismo," 21 March 1939, *OO,* vol. 29, 248–49; see also von Mackensen's report on this speech, von Mackensen Memorandum, 24 March 1939, *DGFP,* ser. D, vol. 6, no. 86, 102–6; *CD,* 21 March 1939, 52–53.

27. Von Weizsäcker Memorandum, 21 March 1939, *DGFP,* ser. D, vol. 6, no. 57, 66–67.

28. Attolico did not prepare formal minutes, as he left immediately after the meeting for Rome. German officials later consulted Attolico to settle any lacunae in his recollection of the minutes (Schmidt Memorandum, 20 March 1939, *DGFP,* ser. D, vol. 6, no. 52, 57–62; von Mackensen to Erich Kordt, 24 March 1939, *DGFP,* ser. D, vol. 6, no. 87, 106–8, and enclosed von Mackensen Memorandum, 24 March 1939, 107–8).

29. Quoted in *CD,* 22 March 1939, 53–54.

30. Hitler to Mussolini, 25 March 1939, *DGFP,* ser. D, vol. 6, no. 100, 119–120.

31. Von Ribbentrop Circular, 25 March 1939, *DGFP,* ser. D, vol. 6, no. 94, 113–14.

32. Von Weizsäcker Memorandum, 8 March 1939, *DGFP,* ser. D, vol. 6, no. 457, 585–86; von Weizsäcker Memoranda, 19, 21 March 1939, *DGFP,* ser. D, vol. 6, no. 44, no. 62, 47–48, 73.

33. Von Rintelen to Keitel, 23 March 1939, *DGFP,* ser. D, vol. 6, no. 2, appendix 1, 1109.

34. Notes in Mussolini's handwriting for discussion with von Ribbentrop, 29 March 1939, ASMAE, UC 7.

35. Vansittart Minute, 13 February 1939, FO 371 23793, R1089/7/22; Halifax Minute, 18 February 1939, FO 371 23793, R1089/7/22; Halifax to Perth, 15 February 1939, FO 371 23793, R1089/7/22; Perth to Halifax, 19 February 1939, FO 371 23793, R1174/7/22; Cadogan Minute, 21 February 1939, FO 371 23793, R1175/7/22; Halifax Minute, 22 February 1939, FO 371 23793, R1175/7/22; Hal-

ifax to Perth, 25 February 1939, FO 371 23793, R1175/7/22; Perth to Halifax, 5 March 1939, FO 371 23793, R1486/7/22; Sargent Minute, 7 March 1939, FO 371 23793, R1486/7/22; Cadogan Minute, 8 March 1939, FO 371 23793, R1486/7/22; Halifax Minute, 9 March 1939, FO 371 23793, R1486/7/22; Halifax Memorandum, 13 March 1939, FO 371 23793, R1692/7/22.

36. *CD,* 5 February 1939, 13 February 1939, 22–23, 28; see also FO Minute, 15 March 1939, FO 371 23784, R1722/1/22, for concerns about the increasing garrison in Libya. According to British estimates, the garrison reached approximately 96,000 by early March (Noble Minute, 7 March 1939, FO 371 23793, R1052/7/22; Perth to Halifax, 16 March 1939, FO 371 23793, R1796/7/22).

37. Perth to Halifax, Noble Minute, 2 March 1939, FO 371 28816, 1446/399/22; Halifax Minute, 4 March 1939, FO 371 28816, 1446/399/22.

38. FO Minute, 15 March 1939, FO 372 23784, R1722/1/22.

39. Chamberlain to Mussolini, 20 March 1939, PREM 1/327. For the published text, see *DBFP*, 3d ser., vol. 4, no. 448, 402–3.

40. Cadogan to Wilson, 19 March 1939, PREM 1/327.

41. *CD,* 23 March 1939, 54.

42. Mussolini to Chamberlain, 1 April 1939, PREM 1/327 (also FO 371 22967, C3858/15/18).

43. *CD,* 21 February 1939, 22 February 1939, 23 February 1939, 32–33, 33–34, 34.

44. Bodini to Ciano and Mussolini, 14 February 1939, ASMAE, US 229; Visconti Prasca to Servizio Informazioni Militare (initialled by Mussolini), 15 February 1939, ASMAE, US 229; Unsigned appunto (initialled by Mussolini), 16 February 1939, ASMAE, US 229.

45. For Franco's attitude, see Preston, *General Staffs and Diplomacy before the Second World War,* 333, and Glyn Stone, "Britain, France and the Spanish Problem, 1936–39," in *Decisions and Diplomacy: Essays in Twentieth-Century International History,* eds. Dick Richardson and Glyn Stone (London: Routledge, 1995), 143–44; also see Mameli (Lisbon) to Ciano, 19 February 1939, 9 March 1939, ASMAE, SAP—Francia, B 42; Viola to Ciano, 2 March 1939, ASMAE, SAP—Francia, B 42; Pietromarchi to Mussolini, 2 March 1939, ASMAE, US 230.

46. Von Stohrer (Madrid) to von Ribbentrop, 5, 17, 20 February 1939, *DGFP,* ser. D, vol. 3, no. 726, no. 738, no. 741, 831, 841–42, 852; von Weizsäcker to von Ribbentrop, 22 February 1939, *DGFP,* ser. D, vol. 3, no. 742, 852; von Stohrer to von Ribbentrop, 1 March 1939, 4 March 1939, *DGFP,* ser. D, vol. 3, no. 749, no. 781, 857–88, 891–92; von Ribbentrop Memorandum, 4 March 1939, *DGFP,* ser. D, vol. 3, no. 752, 861–62; Schwendemann Memorandum, 17 March 1939, *DGFP,* ser. D, vol. 3, no. 758, 870–71; *CD,* 20 February 1939, 21 February 1939, 22 February 1939, 32, 32–33, 33–34.

47. Quoted in *CD,* 22 February 1939, 33–34; see also von Plessen Memorandum, 24 February 1939, *DGFP,* ser. D, vol. 3, no. 744, 853–54.

48. "Per la liberazione di Madrid," 28 March 1939, *OO,* vol. 29; *Il Popolo d'Italia,* 29 March 1939, *OO,* vol. 29, 254; *CD,* 26 March 1939, 56.

49. Von Stohrer to von Ribbentrop, 13 March 1939, 27 March 1939, *DGFP,* ser. D, vol. 3, 865–66, 880; Funck Memorandum, 20 March 1939, *DGFP,* ser. D, vol. 3, no. 763, 874–76.

50. *CD,* 6 February 1939, 14 February 1939, 19 February 1939, 23–24, 29, 31–32.

51. Guariglia to Ciano, 22 February 1939, ASMAE, US 229; see also Phipps to Halifax, 1 March 1939, FO 371 23793, R1388/7/22; Landini to Luciano, 8 March 1939, NA, RG T586, 043630–4.

52. Guariglia to Ciano, Ciano to Guariglia, 20 March 1939, ASMAE, UC 61; Nota consegnata alle ore 16:30 di ieri dal Presidente Daladier al Sig. Baudouin, 21 March 1939, ASMAE, UC 61; *CD,* 18 March 1939, 19 March 1939, 20 March 1939, 49–50, 50–51, 51–52.

53. "184ª Riunione del Gran Consiglio del Fascismo," 21 March 1939, *OO,* vol. 29, 248–49.

54. "Alla vecchia guardia," 26 March 1939, *OO,* vol. 29, 249–53.

55. Quoted in *CD,* 30 March 1939, 58–59.

56. Guariglia to Ciano, Mussolini Minute, 1 April 1939, ASMAE, UC 61; Perth to Halifax, 31 March 1939, FO 371 23794, R2251/7/22. Halifax also supplied some subtle pressure for French concessions. He asked Ambassador Phipps in Paris to approach Daladier about the issue. Halifax suggested that French diplomats enquire about Italian requirements for a settlement through unofficial channels without necessarily committing to recognize them; he well understood that that the Daladier cabinet could not risk a public rebuff from Mussolini. Daladier promised to leave the door open in his speech on 29 March, to no avail (Halifax to Phipps, FO 371 23794, R2080/7/22; Phipps to Halifax, 28 March 1939, FO 371 23794, R2081/7/22).

57. For more detail on the French position, see Shorrock, *From Ally to Enemy,* 256–62. Although Shorrock places too much emphasis on the perceptions of certain French officials who argued that Mussolini sought negotiations to reach a modus vivendi, his work on French sources is otherwise sound.

58. Progetto di Accordi fra L'Italia e L'Albania, 24 March 1939, ASMAE, UC 90; Jacomoni to Ciano, 28 March 1939, ASMAE, UC 90; *CD,* 23–25 March 1939, 28–31 March 1939, 1 April 1939, 2 April 1939, 54–56, 57–60, 60–63.

59. Jacomoni to Ciano (two correspondences), 4 April 1939, ASMAE, UC 90; Ciano to Jacomoni, 4 April 1939, ASMAE, UC 90; Mussolini to Jacomoni, 5 April 1939, ASMAE, UC 90; Jacomoni to Ciano x3, 6 April 1939, ASMAE, UC 90; Mussolini to Guzzoni, 7 April 1939, ASMAE, UC 90; Jacomoni to Ciano, 8 April 1939, ASMAE, UC 90; Ciano to Guzzoni, 6 April 1939, ASMAE, GAB 29; *CD,* 5 April 1939, 7 April 1939, 8 April 1939, 63–64, 64–66, 66–67. For information on Italian military planning for the invasion, see Minniti, *Fino alla guerra,* 182–87.

60. Jacomoni to Ciano, 12 April 1939, ASMAE, UC 90; Ciano appunto, 15 April 1939, ASMAE, UC 90; *CD,* 12 April 1939, 13 April 1939, 15 April 1939, 16 April 1939, 25 May 1939, 29 May 1939, 68–69, 69–70, 70, 70–71, 92–93, 95, 99; Ciano to all diplomatic representatives, 4 June 1939, *DDI,* 8th ser., vol. 7, no. 105, 88.

61. *CD,* 9 April 1939, 67; see also Grandi to Mussolini, 7 April 1939, NA, RG T586, r449, 026903–9. In this sycophantic letter, Grandi congratulated the Duce for his success. Among the fawning phrases, Grandi nevertheless displayed a reasonable understanding of the rationale for the operation.

62. Attolico to Rome, 5 April 1939, ASMAE, UC 90; von Mackensen to von Ribbentrop, 4 April 1939, *DGFP,* ser. D, vol. 6, no. 150, 187–88; von Ribbentrop to von Mackensen, 5 April 1939, *DGFP,* ser. D, vol. 6, no. 158, 194; von Weizsäcker Memorandum, 6 April 1939, *DGFP,* ser. D, vol. 6, no. 170, 207; von Mackensen to von Ribbentrop, 7 April 1939, *DGFP,* ser. D, vol. 6, no. 171, 207–9.

63. Bombelles to Pavelić, 3 March 1939, ASMAE, GAB 445; *CD,* 9 March 1939, 30 March 1939, 5 April 1939, 41–42, 58–60, 63–64.

64. Gobbi (Zagreb) to Ciano, 11 March 1939, ASMAE, UC 49; Ciano to Indelli, 14 March 1939, 19 March 1939, ASMAE, UC 49; Indelli to Ciano, 19 March 1939, ASMAE, UC 49; Indelli to Ciano, 15 March 1939, ASMAE, GAB 440; *CD,* 20 March 1939, 21 March 1939, 51–52, 52–53.

65. Colloquio col Ministero di Yugoslavia, 7 April 1939, ASMAE, UC 85; *CD,* 6 April 1939, 64.

66. Campbell to Halifax, 9 April 1939, FO 371 23712, R2493/1335/90.

67. Ciano to Guariglia and Crolla, 3 April 1939, ASMAE, GAB 29. Ciano did fool some historians who have accepted this claim at face value. See for example, Shorrock, *From Ally to Enemy,* 264. Shorrock is seriously in error in claiming that Ciano's telegrams to Guariglia and Grandi indicated that "Mussolini had made no irrevocable commitment to the Axis." Ciano obviously intended this misdirection to make the Italian invasion more palatable to the West. His attempts to ensure utmost secrecy merely show that he did not want Hitler to learn of his deception, which might have cast doubt on Italian loyalty to the Axis.

68. Crolla to Ciano, 4 April 1939, ASMAE, UC 90; Anfuso to Crolla, 5 April 1939, ASMAE, UC 90; Crolla to Ciano, 6 April 1939, ASMAE, UC 90; Colloquio Crolla-Halifax, 7 April 1939, ASMAE, UC 90; Crolla to Ciano, 8 April 1939, ASMAE, UC 90; Halifax conversation with Crolla, 7 April 1939, FO 371 23711, R2397/1335/90; Italian Chargé conversation with Viscount Halifax, 8 April 1939, 9 April 1939, 9 April 1939, 10 April 1939, FO 371 23785, R2501/1/22, R2502/1/22, R2525/1/22, R2559/1/22.

69. Notes on the meeting of Ministers at Number 10 Downing Street, 8 April 1939, FO 371 23712, R2564/1335/90.

70. Ciano to Viola, 9 April 1939, ASMAE, GAB 29 and Ciano to Crolla, 9 April 1939, ASMAE, GAB 29.

71. Ciano to Crolla, 9 April 1939, ASMAE, UC 90; Crolla to Ciano, 9 April 1939, ASMAE, UC 90; Ciano to Crolla, 9 April 1939, ASMAE, UC 90; Crolla to Ciano, 10 April 1939, ASMAE, UC 90.

72. Halifax Minute, 9 April 1939, FO 371 24118, W6033/5/41.

73. Perth to Halifax, 9 April 1939, FO 371 23712, R2489/1335/90.

74. *CD,* 9 April 1939, 10 April 1939, 67, 67–68.

75. CID, Notes of a meeting of ministers, 10 April 1939, FO 371 23982, W5991/105/80; 10 April 1939, CAB 27/624 FP 36 (42), 11 April 1939, CAB 27/624 FP 36 (41); Halifax to Phipps, 11 April 1939, FO 371 23741, R2645/661/67; Phipps to Halifax, 12 April 1939, FO 371 23741, R2646/661/67; Phipps to Halifax, 13 April 1939, FO 371 23741, R2745/661/67; Halifax to Knatchbull-Hugessen (Ankara), 11 April 1939, FO 371 23741, R2647/661/67; Knatchbull-Hugessen to Halifax, 13 April 1939, FO 371 23741, R2695/661/67; Halifax to Waterlow, 12 April 1939, FO 371 23741, R2648/661/67; Waterlow to Halifax, 12 April 1939, FO 371 23741, R2679.

76. Neville Chamberlain to Hilda Chamberlain, 15 April 1939, NC 18/1/1094.

77. CID Notes of a meeting of ministers, 10 April 1939, FO 371 23982, W5991/108/50; CID, S.A.C., 6th meeting, 17 April 1939, FO 371 23743, R3989/661/67.

78. Keitel Directive, 22 March 1939, *DGFP,* ser. D, vol. 6, no. 1, appendix 1, 1107–8, no. 3; Neubauer Memorandum, n.d., *DGFP,* ser. D, vol. 6, no. 3, appendix 1, 1110–2.

79. Verbale Riassuntivo del colloquio tra il Generale Pariani ed il Generale Keitel, 5–6 April 1939, ASMAE, UC 4; Neubauer Memorandum, n.d., *DGFP,* ser. D, vol. 6, no. 3, 1110–2. For more detail on Italian information on the strength and composition of the Wehrmacht, see Marras to Mussolini, n.d., ASMAE, UC 4.

80. Von Rintelin to Keitel, 24 April 1939, *DGFP,* ser. D, vol. 6, appendix 1, no. 5, 1113–14.

81. Marras to Mussolini, n.d., ASMAE, UC 4.

82. Verbale Riassuntivo del colloquio tra il Generale Pariani ed il Generale Keitel, 5–6 April 1939, ASMAE, UC 4.

83. Unsigned Memorandum, 15 April 1939, *DGFP,* ser. D, vol. 6, , no. 205, 248–53; *CD,* 15 April 1939, 70.

84. Unsigned Memorandum, 15 April 1939, *DGFP,* ser. D, vol. 6, , no. 205, 248–53; *CD,* 15 April 1939, 70.

85. Unsigned Memorandum, 16 April 1939, *DGFP,* ser. D, vol. 6, no. 211, 258–63; *CD,* 16 April 1939, 70–71.

86. Unsigned Memorandum, 16 April 1939, ser. D, vol. 6, no. 211, 258–63.

87. *CD,* 16 April 1939, 70–71.

88. Attolico to Ciano (two correspondences), 14 April 1939, ASMAE, UC 7; von Weizsäcker to von Mackensen, 15 April 1939, *DGFP,* ser. D, vol. 6, no. 203, 247.

89. Attolico to Ciano, 18 April 1939, ASMAE, UC 7.

90. *CD,* 20 April 1939, 73–74.

91. Attolico to Ciano, 22 April 1939, 1 May 1939, ASMAE, UC 7; *CD,* 25 April 1939, 78.

92. *CD,* 18–20 April 1939, 73–74.

93. *CD,* 22 April 1939, 75–76.

94. Ott to von Ribbentrop, 14 March 1939, *DGFP,* ser. D, vol. 4, no. 549, 703–10.

95. Auriti to Ciano, 18 April 1939, ASMAE, UC 71.

96. Attolico to Ciano, 25 April 1939, ASMAE, UC 71.

97. *CD,* 25 April 1939, 77.

98. Ott to von Ribbentrop, 27 April 1939, *DGFP,* ser. D, vol. 6, no. 275, 346; von Weizsäcker to Ott, 28 April 1939, *DGFP,* ser. D, vol. 6, no. 285, 360; Ott to von Ribbentrop, 30 April 1939, *DGFP,* ser. D, vol. 6, no. 298, 381–82; *CD,* 28 April 1939, 78–79. For more on von Ribbentrop's attempts to convince the Japanese leadership to accept an alliance directed against the West, see Weinberg, *Starting World War II,* 565–67.

99. Von Ribbentrop to Ott, 1, 2 May 1939, *DGFP,* ser. D, vol. 6, no. 304, no. 307, 396–97, 399.

100. Auriti to Ciano, 4, 5 May 1939, ASMAE, UC 71. *CD,* 5 May 1939, 83; Ott to von Ribbentrop, 4 May 1939, *DGFP,* ser. D, vol. 6, no. 326, 420–22.

101. Attolico to Ciano, 2, 4 May 1939, ASMAE, UC 7.

102. Attolico to Ciano, 4 May 1939, ASMAE, UC 7.

103. Notes for discussion with von Ribbentrop, 4 May 1939, ASMAE, UC 7.

104. Notes for discussion with von Ribbentrop, 4 May 1939, ASMAE, UC 7.

105. *CD,* 4 May 1939, 82–83.

106. Editor's Note, Draft aide-memoire, 4 May 1939, *DGFP,* ser. D, vol. 6, 444–49.

107. Colloquio con il Ministero degli affari esteri tedesco von Ribbentrop, 6–7 May 1939, ASMAE, UC 85. For the German record of the conversations, see Unsigned Memorandum, 18 May 1939, *DGFP,* ser. D, vol. 6, no. 341, 450–52.

108. Colloquio con il Ministero degli affari esteri tedesco von Ribbentrop, 6–7 May 1939, ASMAE, UC 85. Unsigned Memorandum, 18 May 1939, *DGFP,* ser. D, vol. 6, no. 341, 450–52.

109. Colloquio con il Ministero degli affari esteri tedesco von Ribbentrop, 6–7 May 1939, ASMAE, UC 85; Unsigned Memorandum, 18 May 1939, *DGFP,* ser. D, vol. 6, no. 341, 450–52.

110. *CD,* 5 May 1939, 6 May 1939, 7 May 1939, 83, 83, 83–84.

111. *CD,* 6 May 1939, 7 May 1939, 83, 83–84. In his prison cell at Verona, Ciano would later write that the Duce had reached the decision to sign the alliance "suddenly," in response to foreign press reports that diminished Mussolini's prestige. Ciano continued, "So 'The Pact of Steel' was born. A decision that has had such a sinister influence upon the entire life and future of the Italian people is due entirely to the spiteful reaction of a dictator to the irresponsible and valueless utterances of foreign journalists" (*CD,* 23 December 1943, 556–60). While Ciano's state of mind at the time is understandable, his recollection of the meeting and the discussions surrounding the alliance is not accurate. Mussolini had pursued the alliance for weeks; it was not a sudden inspiration.

112. Not surprisingly, De Felice argued that Mussolini agreed to sign the alliance only because of the policy of encirclement signaled by the Anglo-French guarantee and the discussions that would lead to the 12 May 1939 Anglo-Turkish defence agreement (De Felice, *Lo Stato Totalitario,* 624–25). De Felice minimized Mussolini's role in deciding in favor of the alliance. This view, however, is unsustainable given the evidence of Mussolini's involvement and his declared views of the alliance's objectives.

113. Von Weizsäcker Memorandum, 8 May 1939, *DGFP,* ser. D, vol. 6, no. 345, 455–56.

114. Attolico to Rome, 13 May 1939, ASMAE, UC 71.

115. Ciano to Mussolini, 14 May 1939, ASMAE, UC 71.

116. Von Ribbentrop to Ott, 15 May 1939, *DGFP,* ser. D, vol. 6, no. 382, 494–96; von Weizsäcker to Ott, 15 May 1939, *DGFP,* ser. D, vol. 6, no. 383, 496–500.

117. Ott to von Ribbentrop, 17, 20 May 1939, *DGFP,* ser. D, vol. 6, no. 400, no. 410, 522–23, 541–42.

118. Von Mackensen to von Ribbentrop, 12 May 1939, *DGFP,* ser. D, vol. 6, no. 369, 478.

119. Von Weizsäcker Memorandum, 12 May 1939, *DGFP,* ser. D, vol. 6, no. 370, 479.

120. Gaus Memorandum, 12 May 1939, *DGFP,* ser. D, vol. 6, no. 371, 479–81.

121. *CD,* 13 May 1939, 87; Gaus Memorandum, 15 May 1939, *DGFP,* ser. D, vol. 6, no. 386, 503–4.

122. *CD,* 14 May 1939, 17 May 1939, 87, 88–89.

123. *CD,* 21 May 1939, 24 May 1939, 90, 91–92.

124. For Grandi's view that the Pact of Steel would allow Mussolini greater freedom to work with London, see Grandi to Ciano, 20 May 1939, ASMAE, Carte Grandi, B 40, fasc. 93/3. The alliance, Grandi argued, struck at the foundations of Britain's foreign policy. It would therefore induce Britain to be conciliatory to Italy to try to separate Mussolini from his Axis partner. Grandi misunderstood the genesis of the alliance and Mussolini's objectives; the Duce would make no approaches to London, indicating that he had no intention of following Grandi's advice.

CHAPTER 7

War or Peace

Mussolini expected to profit from the lengthy period of peace while preparing for eventual war, but Hitler had other ideas. The divergent views became apparent, at least in retrospect, immediately after the signing of the Pact of Steel. In a radio interview reprinted in the *Giornale d'Italia,* von Ribbentrop said, "the two nations will march together, always ready to extend a hand to a friend, but firmly resolved to guarantee and to ensure their vital rights together." He avoided the word "peace" in sharp contrast to Ciano's tack. The Italian foreign minister emphasized the pacific intentions of Italian foreign policy.

Above all, Italy desires to continue her labours and her civilizing mission. There are no problems in Europe that cannot be resolved with good will and justice nor are there reasons to justify a war which, inevitably, would not remain European but would become universal.[1]

Of course, Ciano's words left a great deal unsaid. Italian policy would be peaceful insofar as Mussolini planned to avoid a general war but would still seek expansion of Italian power in Greece and Yugoslavia and an interim colonial settlement with France. Though his ultimate Darwinist conflict for European and African supremacy would be delayed, the Duce still expected to fight smaller battles to better position Fascist Italy for the inevitable war with the West.

Hitler, however, had greater ambitions in the short run; he planned to invade Poland. As soon as Ciano left Berlin to return to receive Mussolini's fulsome praise, Hitler summoned his generals to the Reichs Chancellery to outline his objectives. He expounded on the need to expand German *Lebensraum* at the expense of Poland. In order to secure vital economic and political objectives, Hitler argued, the *Wehrmacht* would have to conquer Germany's hereditary Polish enemy. If Britain and France were to intervene, then he could not guarantee a quick victory, so German foreign policy would seek to isolate Poland. The Führer thought that he would either be able to exploit Japanese enmity for the Soviet Union to neutralize the threat from the Red Army or would be able to reach an economic and political modus vivendi with Stalin. Having isolated Poland from receiving direct aid, Hitler assumed that both Britain and France would stand aside rather than fight an unwinnable war. Above all, Hitler demanded that his generals maintain absolute secrecy about his plans for Poland, even with Germany's Italian ally.[2] Although Mussolini thought that he had secured time to ready Italian armed forces, that issue would depend on whether or not Britain and France would uphold their guarantee to Poland, making the coming conflict a general war.

Despite Hitler's duplicity regarding his plans for a localized war, in the week following the signing of the alliance the two foreign ministers began to establish the military contacts called for by the Pact of Steel. For von Ribbentrop, the primary concern lay in ensuring that he and Ciano would remain in tight control of the work of the various commissions. The German proposal called for continued contacts between respective members of the German and Italian service ministries and an economic commission to consider coordination of war economies, but these contacts would be subordinate to a coordination committee.[3] Air force generals would meet late in May and Naval commanders had set meetings for June in Friedrichshafen.[4] The immediate major Italian concern in the economic realm was to ensure that Germany met its promised coal deliveries. Throughout 1939 German shipments had lagged behind schedule, in some cases leaving Italian factories idle while waiting for raw materials.[5] The nature of the political and military agreements regarding each country's separate spheres of interest ensured that they would not need detailed operational cooperation, effectively providing cover for Hitler's war plans against Poland, and the staff and economic talks occurred with little vital information exchanged.

Mussolini, however, was not concerned about these details of interallied cooperation; he preferred to work on the plane of grand strategy. Realizing that the alliance potentially committed Italy to war at any time, he hoped to ensure that Hitler shared his conception of the future course of events.

Accordingly, Mussolini sent a letter to the Führer to outline his views. He opened by reasserting that "the war between the plutocratic and therefore selfishly conservative nations and the densely populated and poor nations is inevitable. One must prepare in light of this situation." Although Mussolini's belief in the coming social Darwinist struggle had not waned, he was most concerned to ensure that Italy had time to prepare for battle. Consequently, he included the lengthy list of reasons for delaying the outbreak of a general war that Ciano had presented to von Ribbentrop at Milan. While preparing for this climactic war, Germany and Italy should try to weaken the spirit of their enemies by supporting pacifist and separatist groups in the west as well as inciting colonial unrest. Turning to the strategic situation, Mussolini thought that Britain and France were walled in, virtually immune to attack by land forces on their metropolitan area. Germany and Italy should prepare to fight a defensive war on the Alps, the Rhine, and in Libya. Only in Eastern and southeastern Europe would the Axis be able to take the offensive, subjugating or intimidating Poland and the Balkans. Italy would also attack British and French colonies from East Africa with a massive army that the Duce planned to create. Because Britain and France expected to fight a war based on economic blockade and attrition, Italy and Germany would need the *spazio vitale* of the Balkans to procure necessary food and raw materials to fuel their war effort. In the Duce's view, a so-called lightning occupation of the Balkans immediately after the start of the war would minimize the effects of the Anglo-French blockade and would subtract Greece, Rumania, and Turkey from the list of potential allies for the West. Mussolini concluded his appreciation by indicating that Italy could provide greater numbers of men than its war industries could support, while Germany could supply more matériel than men; the Duce thought, therefore, that the two countries should increase coordination to exploit their strengths. Through this letter, Mussolini wanted to ensure that both Germany and Italy would pursue common objectives in the three years necessary to marshal and to reequip their forces for the climactic battle with Britain and France.[6]

Mussolini sent this message to the Führer through General Ugo Cavallero, the undersecretary of state for war. Ciano wrote to von Ribbentrop to ensure that Cavallero received a proper welcome.[7] Upon his arrival in Berlin, Cavallero delivered Mussolini's message to von Ribbentrop, who promised to give it to the Führer. On 6 June, von Ribbentrop indicated that Hitler had read the letter and was "generally in agreement." The Führer hoped to speak with Mussolini to discuss future Axis policy and asked if Mussolini would agree to meet him at an unspecified date at the Brenner

Pass. Hitler had expressed a desire to visit Florence but thought that the oppressive summer heat would prevent such a journey until October at the earliest.[8] After considerable discussion, the two Foreign Ministries would eventually arrange the meeting of the two leaders for the beginning of August.[9]

As Cavallero traveled to Berlin, Mussolini outlined his more immediate foreign policy objectives to Ciano. The Duce directed Ciano to work toward including both Spain and Hungary in the military alliance. The inclusion of Hungary would increase Italian power in the Balkans and could potentially add another front for Yugoslav soldiers to defend. The addition of Spain would add another front for France on the Pyrenees and would seriously undermine British and French imperial communications. Also in that vein, Mussolini thought it opportune after the conclusion of the bilateral alliance to bring in Japan as well. He had returned to his earlier view that Japan would serve to divide and weaken Anglo-French naval forces. He also wanted to secure the association of Bulgaria with the Axis. This move would further isolate Yugoslavia and would diminish the capacity of Romania to threaten Hungary. Finally, he told Ciano that it had become necessary to clarify the Yugoslav position. Yugoslavia would either have to declare its fealty to Axis policy or face destabilization and perhaps an invasion by the *Regio Esercito*.[10] These moves would increase Italy's ability to threaten Anglo-French interests and its capability for carrying out a decisive attack against Yugoslavia in the event of premature war with the Western democracies.

Despite Mussolini's plans, his directive turned out to be a counsel of perfection. It proved difficult to clarify the Yugoslav position. Earlier in May, Prince Paul, the Yugoslav Regent had visited Rome, meeting with Mussolini and Ciano at the Palazzo Venezia. The conversations had raised few new issues. It proved impossible to secure a Yugoslav commitment to withdraw formally from the League of Nations as a symbol of loyalty to the Axis. In Ciano's view, the only sign of optimism arose from the renewed discussion of a Turkish presence in Balkan politics. It aroused traditional fears of Ottoman domination, sparking contacts between Bulgaria, Romania, and Yugoslavia to resist potential strengthening of Turkish influence in the region. Ciano hoped to be able to exploit those fears in order to push Yugoslav foreign policy to cleave more tightly to the Axis line.[11] The inability to determine the precise nature of Yugoslav policy led Ciano to approach the Wilhelmstrasse. While he was in Berlin to sign the Pact of Steel, Ciano had already indicated that he thought Yugoslavia's foreign policy was "not entirely above reproach." At the end of May, he asked Hitler and von Ribbentrop to apply diplomatic pressure during Prince Paul's upcoming visit to Berlin. Ciano hoped that German pressure would lead definitive clarification where he and the Duce had failed.[12]

Given the equivocal nature of Italo-Yugoslav relations, Ciano continued his intrigue with his Croat contacts. In discussions in mid-May with Maček's envoy Carnelutti, Ciano had indicated that the lack of Yugoslav commitment to the Axis meant that Italy was prepared to help a Croat insurrection. They hatched a plan in which Maček would refuse to reach an agreement with the Serb-dominated government. Italy would provide a loan of 20 million dinars to support the separatist movement, and within six months, Maček would declare independence followed by a request for Italian intervention. Croatia would become a state federated with Italy, with considerable local autonomy, but backed by the presence of Italian soldiers. On 26 May, Ciano and Carnelutti signed a memorandum incorporating the elements of the scheme. Ciano began the arrangements for Italy's payment through a Swiss bank. He also contemplated organizing Kosovar Albanians to strike against Yugoslavia; he thought that they could create a "dagger pointed at the side of Belgrade." Mussolini was slightly more cautious than Ciano, however, and wanted Maček to countersign the plan. Ciano dispatched the agreed memorandum to Zagreb, but Maček refused to sign it, saying that he had resumed negotiations with the Cvetković government. Despite this apparent rebuff, both Mussolini and Ciano ultimately hoped to be able to exploit ethnic tension to shatter Yugoslavia.[13]

In addition, Mussolini hoped to recruit Bulgaria as an ally in the Balkans. Bulgaria had territorial claims against Romania, Greece, and Yugoslavia and also feared and resented Turkish influence in the Balkans. These potential enemies meant that a Bulgarian-Italian partnership made natural sense, but despite Mussolini's expectation that Bulgarian revisionism would drive its leaders into the Axis embrace it proved hard to secure a tight association. Tsar Boris III, the skilled and authoritarian Bulgarian monarch, had dismissed the long-standing Velchev-Georgiev technocratic and social-reforming administration in 1935. He had reoriented Bulgarian foreign and economic policy toward the Rome-Berlin Axis, but the terms of the Neuilly Treaty of November 1919 had prevented substantial Bulgarian armament, sharply limiting its ability to carry out any openly revisionist action. In March 1938, Boris had allowed strictly controlled elections to the parliament, the Sûbranie, and civilian ministers nominally resumed direction of Bulgarian politics. Georgi Kyoseivanov, the new prime minister and foreign minister, largely followed Boris's pro-Axis line, though within severe limits. In particular, Greece, Romania, Turkey, and Yugoslavia had signed the Balkan Entente largely in order to coordinate common defense against Bulgaria, indicating the narrow bounds in which Bulgarian leaders could work to revise their frontiers.[14]

Rumors of possible Bulgarian flirtation with British and French efforts to guarantee Rumania had led Mussolini to make pointed inquiries in Sofia. Bulgaria resisted Western advances but similarly would not align itself definitively with the Axis. At the end of May, Ciano had a long conversation with the Bulgarian minister in Rome. Ciano said that Bulgaria's geopolitical position would make it difficult to maintain a position of neutrality, and that Bulgaria should join the Axis. Facing the reply that Bulgarian military weakness hindered its foreign policy, Ciano promised that Germany and Italy would make good its deficiencies in armaments. Ciano also directed Giuseppe Talamo, the Italian minister in Sofia, to put diplomatic pressure on the Bulgarian government to indicate its alignment with the Axis, after which it would receive generous arms supplies. Ciano wanted Talamo to issue a warning that Italy would not tolerate any Bulgarian association with Anglo-French security arrangements. The main thrust of Italian policy was to convince Tsar Boris that Bulgaria "must clearly decide to march with the Axis Powers who will be able to assure the territorial revisions to which it aspires."[15]

Kyoseivanov seemed broadly sympathetic to the Axis and resisted the approaches of Turkey and Great Britain to join the Balkan Pact, rejecting offers for mediation and even arbitration to resolve Bulgaria's claim to the Dobrudja territory it had lost to Rumania in 1919. Joining the Balkan Pact would mean general acceptance of the status quo, and neither Boris nor Kyoseivanov were likely to limit their revisionism by too close an association with the satisfied powers. Still, Kyoseivanov's friendship for the Axis did not immediately translate into military power. Bulgaria faced a strong Turkish military presence in Thrace and substantial Romanian forces in the Dobrudja. Kyoseivanov's attempts to reach a rapprochement with Yugoslavia to limit Bulgaria's potential enemies and to weaken its foes had not borne fruit. Given the weakness of the strategic situation, Tsar Boris and Kyoseivanov were unwilling to make any public declarations of solidarity with the Axis, though they would pursue German and Italian arms to increase Bulgaria's freedom of maneuver.[16] In spite of Bulgaria's sympathies for Fascist Italy, therefore, Mussolini could only hope that time would improve Italy's strategic position in Bulgaria.

The association of the Turkish government with Western security plans also threatened Italy's position in the Balkans. Ismet Inönü, president since the death of Atatürk in November 1938, had agreed to participate in the Anglo-French guarantee to Romania in April, although with some reservations. Inönü and Sükrü Saracoğlu, the foreign minister, hoped to bolster Romanian resistance to German economic and political domination, while at the same time putting pressure on Bulgaria to reach an accord over the disputed Dobrudja territory. If Turkish diplomacy could persuade Tsar Boris to reject Axis overtures, then it would secure Romania's southern flank, making its position in the face of potential German and Hungarian aggression significantly stronger. Mussolini and Ciano both strongly resented Ankara's association with Britain, and they both dispatched angry protests to Saracoğlu. Ciano spoke of Turkey's participation in the encirclement of the Axis, but he especially feared the effect of Turkish pressure on Bulgaria. Ciano issued thinly veiled threats to denounce the 1928 Italo-Turkish Treaty of Friendship, but this attempt at coercion proved hollow, and Saracoğlu resisted Ciano's bluster. By the end of June, the Turkish government reached an interim agreement with France that called for mutual military assistance and French territorial concessions in Syria.[17] These actions suggested that Turkey had joined the Anglo-French camp, and its opposition to Axis expansionism weakened Italian influence in the region. Mussolini's plans for Italian hegemony in the Balkans had run into serious roadblocks erected by the ethnic, nationalist, and military concerns of the Balkan powers.

Ciano was also unable to get any decisive commitment from Spain. Although Italo-Spanish relations were extremely cordial, there was little prospect of an immediate alliance. Serrano Suñer, Franco's brother-in-law and minister of the interior, made an official visit to Rome in the first week of June. Ciano welcomed Suñer at Naples, along with members of the combined Spanish-Italian Arrow division returning from Spain, although Mussolini refused to attend because the King would be there. Suñer was an advocate of the Axis, and Franco's withdrawal from the League of Nations and bellicose anti-British and anti-French speeches celebrating the end of the war indicated that the Caudillo's sympathies clearly lay with Rome and Berlin. In the lengthy discussions with Mussolini and Ciano, Suñer told Ciano that Nationalist Spain would always be faithful to Fascist Italy; the bonds forged during the civil war gave the two countries a common anti-Western and anti-Bolshevik destiny. Suñer said that he personally hated France and that Spanish youth dreamt "of pushing Britain into the sea." Despite this orientation, the civil war had exhausted Spain, and it needed a long period of restoration before Franco could consider further warfare. Although Franco wanted an alliance with Italy, he would have to wait before he could commit himself, as he could not afford to entirely alienate France and Great Britain before modernizing Spain's armed forces. Although relations between Franco's Spain and Italy were very friendly, Franco's court included those who rejected the Axis. Suñer warned Ciano of the attitude of General Kindelán and asked Ciano to have Italian secret police follow his rival during Kindelán's visit to Italy. Ciano interceded with Suñer to replace Ambassador Pedro Garcia Conde, as Ciano detested the ambassador's monarchist sympathies.[18] Even though Suñer's visit showed the obvious ties between Franco's Spain and nationalist Italy, Mussolini and Ciano had to content themselves with the thought that their involvement in the Spanish Civil War would pay off at some unspecified time in the future. They could expect little military assistance if events conspired to ignite a general war before 1942.

It proved similarly difficult to secure the tripartite alliance with Japan. The Japanese Council of Five Ministers had reached a compromise proposal in an effort to meet von Ribbentrop's insistence on a binding alliance that would apply in the event of war with Great Britain and France. The compromise proposal, however, called for Japanese entry in an Axis war with Britain and France to be dependent on circumstances. This limitation obviously did not meet the German position. Ambassador Ōshima had refused to follow his instructions to present it to the German government, but the Japanese cabinet remained deadlocked over the issue.[19] After the signing of the Pact of Steel and Mussolini's agreement to a German effort at a rapprochement with the Soviet Union, von Ribbentrop had asked the Japanese government for its approval for an approach to Stalin to prevent the possible conclusion of an Anglo-French-Soviet pact. Ambassador Ōshima, however, strongly warned against this move; after consulting with Tokyo, he said that it would alienate the Japanese army faction that was the strongest supporter of the tripartite alliance. Attolico also suggested that von Ribbentrop use caution. He explained to the German foreign minister that any approach to the Soviet Union that did not succeed would serve only to push Moscow closer to Britain and France. Attolico thought it wiser to continue the German initiative for improved commercial and political relations, despite the temporary obstacles that Commissar Molotov had raised.[20]

The heated battle in Japanese internal politics continued, pitting Foreign Minister Arita, Navy commanders, and financiers, who feared Anglo-American economic retaliation, against General Itagaki and his Japanese army supporters, who wanted the tripartite alliance directed against Britain and France. The central remaining issue was whether or not Japan would enter a war against the Western democracies automatically. Arita and his supporters wanted to maintain their freedom of maneuver, arguing that as long as Japan was fighting in China it would be folly to engage in a war that might bring economic reprisals from the United States government. In the event of war with the Soviet Union, Japan would enter the fray immediately. In the event of war with the West, however, Arita settled on a formula that would allow Japan to determine its attitude depending on circumstances. On Itagaki's insistence, Arita promised that the Japanese government would base this decision on the interests of the alliance as a whole rather than direct Japanese interest.[21] By mid-June, this compromise formed the core of a new set of Japanese proposals. Ōshima told von Ribbentrop, "Japan is now firmly decided to conclude the pact." The Council of Five Ministers had changed its position to include the possibility of war even if the Soviet Union were not involved, and it was willing to make this determination public. In essence, Japan would sign the alliance draft the Wilhelmstrasse had prepared but would exchange diplomatic notes indicating that Japan would declare war only if circumstances made its entry favorable to the alliance signatories. According to Arita and his supporters, Japanese participation in a war might be harmful to the interests of the Axis. In such a situation, Japan's entry into war would not be automatic and the alliance partners should consult on the best course of action. Despite the apparent compromise, it still appeared as if the Japanese government had substantial reservations about the alliance and that Japan would enter into a war against Britain and France only in exceptional circumstances. This position did not meet von Ribbentrop's demands; he refused to exchange letters that could become public if leaked by Japanese opponents of an alliance directed against the West, thus robbing Germany of its ability to deter the Western democracies. He demanded that Japan entirely meet the German position—an alliance "without reservations and limitations."[22]

The German rejection of the Japanese proposal required the Council of Five Ministers to reconsider its position. Japanese army, navy, and Gaimushō officials contacted Axis diplomats to indicate their displeasure at von Ribbentrop's intransigence. According to several sources, the Council of Five Ministers thought that it had met the major German concerns, and various officials had expressed their shock at von Ribbentrop's behavior. In their view, Japan had gone a long way to meet German demands, and yet the German foreign minister refused to understand the serious difficulties facing Japan. Members of the Council worried that if they proceeded any further they might not be able to secure the approval of the entire cabinet. Every time Japan made concessions, Japanese officials charged, von Ribbentrop sought to push them further. Above all, Japan sought to avoid a direct confrontation with the United States, but without an exchange of notes limiting Japan's exposure, government ministers could not risk Anglo-American economic retaliation. By the end of June, the tripartite alliance had met another roadblock.[23]

Mussolini, unlike von Ribbentrop, wavered on the issue. In late May and early June, he had returned to the view that the alliance with Japan would help Italy's strategic position, but the Japanese counterproposal in mid-June called into question the Duce's assessment. When Attolico sent a dispatch describing the Japanese position, he raised some uncomfortable implications that von Ribbentrop had refused to consider. Japanese equivocations owing to its position in China, he argued, would create different obligations for the alliance partners, with Germany and Italy making far tighter commitments than would Japan. More seriously, the alliance could involve Italy in a premature war over some Far Eastern complication. As Attolico argued, "In the case, for example, that today would be signed the tripartite Pact of alliance and that tomorrow war would break out between Russia and Japan for the fish of the Sakhalin Islands or over Manchuria, both Italy and Germany would be obliged to enter immediately in war at [Japan's] side." In particular, if such a war involved Britain and France, it was entirely possible that the Anglo-French military would take a defensive posture in the Far East and direct their offensive entirely against Italy. As Mussolini understood it, the tripartite alliance could create the very conditions that he most wanted to avoid—war with a united Britain and France while Italy was still unprepared for battle.[24] The Duce's ardor for a tripartite alliance partially cooled, though he still allowed von Ribbentrop to control the pace of the negotiations.

Although Ciano had difficulty recruiting allies for the Duce's struggle against the West, Mussolini refused to make any substantial diplomatic moves toward London or Paris to create breathing room for Italian rearmament. The announcement of the introduction of peacetime national service in England did not make much of an impression in Rome, although Mussolini resented continued signs of a policy of encirclement of the Axis. In early May, as he prepared to meet von Ribbentrop in Milan, Ciano had noted that British policy showed "formal friendship" toward Italy, but was in fact hostile.[25] Mussolini's bellicose speeches, such as one at Turin on 14 May, struck Sir Percy Loraine, the new British ambassador in Rome, as akin to "the highwayman's pistol." In Loraine's view, Mussolini expected the Western democracies to hand over territory, spheres of influence, and raw materials in exchange for freedom from attack by the Axis.[26] Several Foreign Office officials had criticized Loraine's pessimism about Mussolini's attitude. For example, Sir Orme Sargent, the assistant undersecretary of state, returned to the position that France should approach Italy to offer concessions. This largesse, Sargent argued, could wean Mussolini from the Axis.[27]

Even the signing of the Pact of Steel did not change this attitude. In response to a parliamentary question, Chamberlain had stated that the Pact did not represent a change in the status quo of the Mediterranean and was not, therefore, a violation of the Anglo-Italian Agreement.[28] In spite of the generally conciliatory British position, the announcement on 12 May 1939 of the intention to reach an Anglo-Turkish defense agreement aroused the Duce's ire. The agreement stemmed from the British reaction to Mussolini's invasion of Albania, but the Duce had never understood the dual nature of Britain's reaction to his adventure: conciliatory in tone but firm in creating a defensive front against future Italian aggression.[29] At the end of May, Mussolini decided to make his annoyance known to Loraine. In their first meeting since Loraine took up his post, normally a ceremonial occasion, Mussolini attacked British policy in a deliberate attempt to provoke the British ambassador. Using Ciano as an interpreter, the Duce sharply questioned whether or not the Anglo-Italian Agreement had any value, since British guarantees represented a policy of encirclement of the Axis. Loraine expressed his shock at Mussolini's attitude as his government had allowed the agreement to stand despite the Italian invasion of Albania and the alteration of the Mediterranean status quo. British discussions with Turkey over defense arrangements did not alter the status quo, and Britain's negotiations with the Soviet Union did not affect the Mediterranean at all. Mussolini shot back that Britain's encirclement of Italy's German ally constituted an encirclement of Italy as well. The Anglo-French guarantee to Poland made Polish leaders intransigent and prevented a worthwhile response to Hitler's "moderate" proposals; Great Britain was pushing Europe to the brink of war. Mussolini also called the guarantee to Romania "absurd," though Ciano did not translate that comment. Finally, the Duce asked if Great Britain intended to loose communism on the world. Loraine protested sharply, concluding that he regretted that Mussolini's point of view had become so far removed from that of His Majesty's Government. Loraine's departure occurred in an icy silence.[30]

Ciano noted afterward that Mussolini's apparent fit of pique was calculated. The Duce had already drafted a memorandum calling for Axis domination of the Balkans and Central Europe. He thought that the Chamberlain cabinet should understand that Fascist Italy was clearly in the Axis camp. Ciano noted that Mussolini's attitude meant that the Easter Accord was dead and that the Chamberlain government might die with it.[31] Loraine responded to Mussolini's boorish tactic by changing his views on Anglo-Italian relations. Previously he had thought that London needed to keep open every possible avenue to Rome. After the confrontation with the Duce, however, Loraine thought that the only argument Mussolini would heed was that of "the visibility of overwhelming physical force."[32] Mussolini's provocation also required a reevaluation of policy in Whitehall. Halifax immediately approved Loraine's improvised language defending British policy to Mussolini. After a meeting of all of the top Foreign Office advisers on 1 June, officials prepared a draft response that Chamberlain ultimately approved. The aide-memoire expressed surprise at Mussolini's questioning of the value of the accord. As long as the Italian government placed value in retaining the accord, so would Britain. The British government, however, noted that its surprise was all the greater owing to its acceptance of Italy's alteration of the status quo in Albania. British guarantees to Greece and Romania sought to maintain the peace, which was the rationale for the Easter Accord. His Majesty's Government, therefore, had not changed its attitude as Mussolini charged.[33]

Loraine asked to present the response directly to Mussolini, but Ciano said that the Duce was unavailable, so Loraine left the communiqué with Ciano on 8 June. Ciano truculently said that it did not answer Mussolini's concerns. Loraine replied that it directly answered the question that Mussolini had asked. Ciano denounced British encirclement of the Axis, but Loraine countered, saying that British negotiations with Turkey concerned only direct defense interests and could not be considered hostile to Italy.[34] In London, Halifax informed Grandi of the nature of the British response to Mussolini's attack. Grandi tried to defend his leader's Albanian action as an anti-German move, but met with little success. According to Halifax's notes on the meeting, the Italian ambassador complained that Mussolini's actions had placed Grandi in a difficult position.[35] By mid-June, Mussolini had switched the focus of Italian propaganda attacks from France to Britain. The press campaign especially emphasized British impotence and loss of prestige over the Tientsin standoff in the Far East.[36] Angry British press responses signaled the strained relations caused by the Duce's idiosyncratic Axis diplomacy that had once again calculatedly provoked confrontation with the British government.[37]

Mussolini's anti-British actions and rhetoric did not end Whitehall's attempts to have France appease Italy. French approaches to Mussolini in

March had failed owing to Mussolini's refusal to moderate anti-French propaganda and his refusal to make a formal approach to Paris that could serve to limit the nature of Italian demands against France. Although the Duce hoped to secure concessions regarding the Addis Ababa-Djibuti railway, a free port in Djibuti, Suez Canal Directorships, and the status of Tunisia, these issues represented only the first stage of his claims against France. Mussolini, of course, intended ultimately to seize French territory to the Var River, Corsica, and Tunisia, though Western politicians and officials did not know the entire scope of Mussolini's desiderata. Still, Mussolini refused to make any initiative to discuss even the first stage of his demands against France. He expected the French government to make a formal diplomatic approach to determine Italy's demands, something that Daladier was determined to avoid—at least until Mussolini showed some evidence of good faith. The Duce's intransigence meant that Ciano had rejected every French approach through unofficial channels.

Still, since mid-April, British Foreign Office officials, stymied in their attempts to appease either Italy or Germany, had seized on the idea of Mussolini's public demands against France for a French démarche to wean Italy from the Axis. In April, Halifax had instructed Sir Eric Phipps, the British ambassador in Paris, to approach Daladier to ask for concessions to Italy. Halifax was diffident in his approach, not wanting to alienate France by pressing too hard, though Chamberlain was more forthright, wanting French ministers to do "their share" of fence-mending with Italy.[38] While Foreign Minister Bonnet had welcomed the British suggestions, Prime Minister Daladier had not. He told Phipps that France had made several overtures to Italy and Mussolini had rejected them. In Daladier's view, Mussolini had entirely thrown in his lot with Hitler, and France could not afford to show signs of weakness. Not only would an offer to Mussolini anger French public opinion, it would weaken France's position in the Muslim world of North Africa.[39] Through diplomatic channels, Daladier indicated his puzzlement over the British attitude. On instructions, Charles Corbin, the French ambassador in London, informed Halifax that any French concessions to Mussolini would simply lead to greater claims against France.[40] Daladier's understanding of Mussolini's attitude and tactics was entirely correct, but it did not dissuade his British counterparts from pursuing their goal of French concessions to appease Italy.

Despite his views of Mussolini, however, Daladier was prepared to offer concessions, provided he could convince Italy to make a formal request and provided he could be sure that the diplomatic terrain was prepared ahead of any public discussions; Daladier could not afford a public rebuff from Mussolini. At the end of April, Ambassador François-Poncet had approached Ciano to indicate French preparedness to resume the interrupted Baudouin negotiations on the same terms as they had previously discussed; at some point, Italy would have to make a public proposal that France would then be able to accept. Ciano asked whether or not he could deem François-Poncet's approach as official, one of Mussolini's minimum demands. François-Poncet said that it was. Still, Mussolini rejected this approach, saying he would not treat with France until after he had signed the alliance with Germany.[41] British government pressure on France continued, especially during Halifax's meeting with Daladier in Geneva near the end of May, but Daladier did not change his view.[42]

After he had decided in favor of the alliance with Germany on the evening of 6 May, Mussolini had briefly considered discussing his interim demands against France, but he decided not to pursue the issue because Daladier's language in a public speech was not sufficiently placatory.[43] Mussolini also rejected further unofficial approaches. Roberto Suster, a journalist with the Stefani agency, told Ciano's Chef de Cabinet Anfuso of one such approach. Suster said that the Chief of Foreign Minister Bonnet's cabinet had asked him to carry a message that France was willing to discuss concessions to Italy. Bonnet's assistant, Monsieur Bressy, had said that France would even be prepared to make a public approach provided that it knew the precise nature of Italian demands on Tunisia. Anfuso consulted with Mussolini, who refused to take up the initiative.[44] Anatole de Monzie, the Italophile minister of public works, made a similar advance in early June. He told an Italian confidante that France would be prepared to meet all of Mussolini's public demands, though he admitted that Tunisia would be a difficult issue. In addition, de Monzie's contact wrote, the French minister also promised that France would help Italy to secure its *spazio vitale,* helping Italy to carry out a "spiritual penetration" of the Balkans. France could also help Italy gain greater access to Romanian and even Iraqi oil. Again, Mussolini did not take up the offer.[45] Even after the signing of the Pact of Steel, French and British diplomats did not cease their attempts to wean Mussolini from the Axis through French concessions, and British pressure on Daladier would continue throughout the summer. In light of Mussolini's rejections of these overtures, however, Western diplomats could make little headway toward appeasement of Fascist Italy.[46]

Mussolini's devotion to the alliance with Germany did not mean that the Axis partnership was entirely untroubled. Two issues served as a kind of superficial barometer of the Axis relationship: military planning and the repatriation of Germans from the Alto Adige. From the Italian perspective, the military talks seemed to proceed smoothly. Meetings at the end of May between the air staffs had been productive. Generals Erhard Milch, Göring's deputy in the Luftwaffe, and Giuseppe Valle, undersecretary of state for the *Regia Aeronautica,* had agreed to broad exchanges of information, including numbers of aircraft, production, training methods, and intelligence reports on Anglo-French and other potentially allied air forces regarding types of aircraft and possible bombing targets. They delineated zones of operation over France and considered basing squadrons in each other's territory to maximize the combat effectiveness of their aircraft. Both sides agreed that exchanging officers would help to integrate the two air forces, and they also agreed to exchange units for maneuvers and training. The two generals thought it wise to establish a commission of experts to explore the possibility of standardizing fuel and ammunition types as well as coordination on issues of communication and meteorological information. The talks were cordial and had laid the groundwork for extensive cooperation.[47] Unbeknownst to the Italian delegation, however, the German generals had far exceeded their instructions. Göring interceded afterward, limiting tremendously the flow of information and cooperation. According to the new restrictions, Luftwaffe officers could not share any information regarding technical developments such as the new Ju 88 bomber, and Italian pilots were not to fly the plane at any time. Göring ordered that the Luftwaffe should be extremely dilatory in establishing liaison with its Italian counterparts and should limit contacts to exchange of visits. The new orders more closely reflected Hitler's desire not to risk the leak of German war plans to Italy or military secrets to the West, but they also prevented effective cooperation between the two air forces.[48]

Naval Staff conversations occurred in Friedrichshafen in June. The formal exchange of views began with a long meeting between Admirals Erich Raeder, chief of the German Naval Staff, and Domenico Cavagnari, undersecretary of state for the *Regia Marina.* Cavagnari outlined the central Italian naval plans in the event of a war with the West. The navy's prime mission would be to safeguard the supply line to Libya. It would defend a north-south corridor based on southern Italy, Sicily, Sardinia, and Libya. Cavagnari stated that Italy was outnumbered in battleships and could expect Germany to divert only a limited part of the Royal Navy. The French Air Force could threaten Spanish control of the Balearics, and the Turkish air force could threaten the Dodecanese Islands, preventing their use as offensive bases, though Cavagnari thought these outposts were well

enough defended to repel any attack. Given the small numbers of battleships and the range of forces arrayed against Italy, only Italy's powerful
submarine fleet would be able to carry out offensive operations, at least
until commissioning of Italy's six new or refitted battleships. Outside the
Mediterranean, Italy was building a new base at Kismayu in Italian Soma-
liland to support operations in the Indian Ocean, and Cavagnari hoped to
be able to base as many as twenty-four submarines and three cruisers there
to threaten British imperial communications south of the Suez Canal. Italy
would also station ten submarines in the Red Sea and eight in the Persian
Gulf. Cavagnari expected that Italy would be able to send eight battleships
and 144 submarines to sea by 1942. The two admirals also discussed other
issues, such as exchanges of officers for fleet exercises, sharing of intelligence on Anglo-French naval forces, and possible Italian use of German
ships for mine-laying operations in the Sicilian Channel. Raeder strongly
disagreed with the Italian position; he wanted Italian units to attack the
western Mediterranean, serving to pin down the French navy and forcing
France to send convoys from North Africa to France via the Atlantic route,
vulnerable to German submarines.[49] Informal discussions held by Italian
naval officers outside of the main meeting between Raeder and Cavagnari
proved interesting. Admirals Luigi Sansonetti and Raffaele De Courten
emphasized to their German counterparts that the Italian forces would be
hard pressed in North Africa. French forces in Tunisia would no doubt
launch an offensive against Libya's Western frontier. Depending on the
level of Turkish assistance to Great Britain, the Italian officers thought that
it might prove impossible even to carry out an offensive against Egypt.
Nevertheless, Sansonetti and De Courten felt reasonably confident about
Italy's ability to defend its Mediterranean position. German Admiral Otto
Schniewind, however, was less optimistic. He thought that France could
overwhelm Libya and that Italian plans merely to fight a defensive battle
against the French Navy would allow France to divert forces to face Germany in the Atlantic. At any rate, German officials did not hold a high
level of respect for the ability of Italy to carry out decisive operations in
the event of a general war in the near future.[50]

Despite these German suspicions of Italian capability, from the Italian
side, the conversations among the service branches had appeared to establish solid initial contacts with German commanders. General Cavallero's
mission to Germany also apparently furthered the ties between the two
militaries. Cavallero believed that he had established excellent contacts
with the German High Command and found the preparations for the
staffing of the commissions called for in the Pact of Steel to be satisfac-

tory, in spite of the fact that the commissions would not even meet for the first time until the latter part of July.[51] Only one senior Italian diplomat appeared to notice the lack of German commitment to genuine military cooperation. Bernardo Attolico thought that the Germans had put insufficient effort into the establishment of the various commissions to oversee military cooperation. Attolico wanted to see far greater political direction given to the discussions, which up to that point had consisted of generalities. He thought that it would be wise to postpone the meeting of various commissions until Mussolini met with Hitler to create a stronger political understanding of the future course of Axis military planning. Mussolini and Ciano, however, did not immediately recognize the nature of German stalling tactics.[52]

Discussions over the repatriation of Germans living in the Alto Adige also provided a sense of cooperation between the two allies. In April, Mussolini had raised again the idea of the removal of former Austrian citizens living in the Alto Adige. Their campaign of passive resistance to Italian destruction of their ethnic and linguistic identity annoyed the Duce. He asked Germany to extend a ban on shipment of recordings with South Tyrolese songs and complained of the distribution of anti-Italian leaflets. In light of the difficulty of assimilating this group, Mussolini wanted Germany to repatriate them, though Italy would defray the costs by paying compensation for property. As these ethnic Germans were technically Italian nationals, Mussolini hoped that Hitler would make an official proposal. Hitler knew that for Mussolini this issue represented a touchstone for the health of the Axis relationship. Consequently, his diplomats responded encouragingly, though many were skeptical about a complete resettlement. Nevertheless, the Führer ordered SS leader Heinrich Himmler to take charge of the planning for the resettlement, although he undertook few immediate initiatives.[53]

In June, an incident during a parade in Bolzano led to the arrest of *Ortsgruppenleiter* Kaufmann, a local Nazi party leader. Ciano, mortified at the thought of how Western propaganda could exploit the situation, secured the Duce's permission to have the official released. Hitler, however, exploded in rage at Kaufmann's possible provocation of Mussolini and asked Ciano to return the hapless official to Germany, where Hitler had him interned in a concentration camp. Ciano thought this gesture "elegant."[54] The furor added impetus to the discussions for repatriation. A commission met in Berlin to coordinate joint action. Himmler expressed the need for "a rapid and concrete solution" that would start within a week, concentrating initially on resettling the "politically undesirable." The

Reich would establish an official German Repatriation and Emigration Office in Bolzano and four other towns. Italy would pay a generous rate of compensation and would prepare legislation to exempt those who were leaving from military service. Ultimately, the commission envisaged transferring tens of thousands of ethnic Germans in 1940.[55] The proverbial fly in the ointment for Ciano was that Hitler would not allow publication of these measures. The Führer cited hostile international press coverage of the issue, though he appeared in fact to want to delay the possible ramifications on nationalist domestic opinion at least until after his invasion of Poland.[56] Despite Hitler's refusal to allow the publication of the details of repatriation, his determination to placate Italian sensibilities had satisfied Mussolini that the Axis remained united and strong.

The apparent signs of German cooperation, however, partially concealed the real divergence of views over the issue that would dominate European politics over the summer—Hitler's imminent war with Poland. By the end of June, Italian diplomats began to receive stronger signals of Hitler's determination to provoke a crisis with Poland. Attolico reported that Hitler was in a violently anti-Polish mood and that a speech delivered by Field Marshal Göring in Danzig reflected the Führer's attitude. In Attolico's view, Nazi activity had created an atmosphere of "black pessimism in the diplomatic corps." Attolico thought it vital for Mussolini to meet Hitler in the first week of August lest Hitler provoke a premature conflict.[57] Pietro Arone, the Italian ambassador in Warsaw, reported truckloads of heavily armed German so-called volunteers arriving in Danzig from East Prussia. Given Polish declarations that Danzig was a vital interest, German violations of Danzig's international status could spark a violent confrontation.[58] Attolico also reported that Johannes von Welczek, the German ambassador in Paris, had told Foreign Minister Bonnet that Germany would be ready to destroy Poland in the last half of August and that if Great Britain intervened, Germany would destroy its empire. According to Attolico's sources, von Welczek had spoken on von Ribbentrop's direct instructions, lending an official confirmation to an apparent German plan to confront Poland. In Attolico's view, the situation was one of "evident instability if not downright danger;" the diplomatic community was becoming desperate.[59]

Ciano wrote back to Attolico to instruct him to see von Ribbentrop. In light of the international situation, Ciano said that it was of central importance "to be informed with all possible precision of German intentions in relation to the Danzig problem." Ciano sought to ensure that Attolico's questions did not have the tone of an official request for consultation under the Pact of Steel. At the same time, however, Ciano said that Mussolini needed to know Germany's precise schedule. Only if the Duce were properly informed could he make Italy's "military and moral preparations."[60] Attolico was delayed in carry out his instructions, as von Ribbentrop was indisposed.[61] In the meantime, Mussolini drafted a proposal for a plebiscite in Danzig. Entirely misunderstanding Hitler's ultimate objective—to provoke war with Poland—Mussolini thought that the international community could avert a crisis by allowing Danzig's citizens to show the unequivocally German nature of the city. In Mussolini's view, international supervision would ensure the de facto incorporation of Danzig into the Reich. If the Polish government rejected the plan, then its refusal would strengthen Germany's position.[62] Despite the state of alarm in Berlin, Ciano was largely unconcerned. Recovering from the death of his father, Ciano had come to believe that the lack of communication from Hitler signaled that no immediate crisis threatened.[63]

Attolico finally saw von Ribbentrop on 6 July during a luncheon for the visiting Bulgarian Premier Kyoseivanov. Attolico told the German foreign minister that Ciano was preparing to leave on a trip to Spain and had asked to know what Germany had planned. In a long conversation, von Ribbentrop asserted what would become a common mantra. Germany had no plans for a coup against Danzig, although it was involved in a war of nerves. Nevertheless, if war came, then Germany would crush Poland. The Poles would receive no aid from Britain and France. Approaches to the Soviet Union were bearing fruit, and commercial negotiations would begin shortly, thus isolating Poland. If France intervened, it could not attack effectively across the Siegfried defensive line on Germany's western border, and the Luftwaffe would flatten Paris. Great Britain would not march to defend Poland because it did not want to lose its empire. The threat from Japan would paralyze the United States. Attolico called this diatribe "von Ribbentrop's fantasy." He interrupted, saying that Mussolini and Hitler had both agreed that they did not want war. "Almost as if waking from a dream," von Ribbentrop replied that Germany did not want an immediate war and that Poland would simply acquiesce. Attolico and von Ribbentrop debated at length the possibility of a general war erupting from German action. Attolico repeatedly insisted that such a war could not remain localized, while von Ribbentrop said it would be. Attolico could not change von Ribbentrop's mind, which was, in Attolico's words, ruled by a sense of Germany's "axiomatic invincibility," whether war came in six weeks or six months. On 7 July, von Ribbentrop phoned Attolico, essentially covering the same ground he had the day previously. Attolico also reported that Germany was sending SS and Nazi *squadristi* to Danzig, and if Poland used force to evict them, then the *Wehrmacht* would attack. Even with these military preparations, Attolico believed that it was unlikely that the crisis would erupt in the immediate future, but he returned to the oft-discussed idea of a meeting between Hitler and Mussolini to clear the air and to renew their mutual commitment to avoiding war until 1942. Hitler agreed with Attolico's recommendation, suggesting a 4 August meeting at the Brenner frontier.[64]

Ciano did not share Attolico's concern. Assuming that Attolico had panicked, Ciano thought that a meeting in August would be inopportune. He would prefer a date sometime near the end of September. The delay would give both sides time to prepare the diplomatic terrain in order to make such a meeting productive.[65] Ciano's sanguine reaction annoyed Attolico, who thought his foreign minister entirely misunderstood Hitler's attitude. In Ciano's absence during his trip to Spain, Attolico sent a long letter to Filippo Anfuso, Ciano's chef de cabinet. Attolico surveyed Hitler's reaction to Mussolini's letter at the end of May. The Führer's response then had been to express his general agreement but also to suggest a meeting with Mussolini. Attolico argued that Hitler had wanted to discuss with his ally the issues that could spark a general war and that he needed to do so before any irrevocable decisions had been made. After hectoring Ciano for a formal response, Ciano had said that the end of September would be sufficient. The dilatory reply, Attolico argued, had created a bad impression, but all signs indicated that Germany was preparing at a fever pitch for action by the middle of August. By 15 August, Hitler would make his final political decision. By the time Hitler chose to break off talks with Poland, Mussolini would no longer be able to divert the Führer from a course that German "national honour" compelled him to take. Furthermore, Attolico argued that all of the leading Nazi party members had reached the conclusion that Britain and France would not fight, so in that sense Hitler would not even think that he was violating his pledge to Mussolini by provoking a war with Poland. In Ciano's absence, Attolico begged Anfuso to give his letter to the Duce so that Mussolini could provide instructions before Attolico's next meeting with von Ribbentrop.[66] Anfuso tracked down Ciano in Spain and asked him whether or not he should give Attolico's letter to Mussolini. Ciano approved, and Mussolini agreed to meet Hitler at the Brenner on 4 August.[67] Attolico continued to deal with the widespread rumors of war as he traveled to Munich, where he spoke with Hitler. The Italian ambassador urged Hitler not to make any final decisions until after the planned meeting with Mussolini.[68]

While Attolico worked to arrange a meeting between Mussolini and Hitler, Ciano made his official visit to Spain. Ciano was able to assure himself that a rumored rapprochement between Spain and the Western democracies was not in fact underway.[69] His trip culminated in a long and friendly discussion with Franco, where Ciano delivered Mussolini's message of friendship and camaraderie.[70] In their lengthy conversation, Franco promised to align Spanish foreign policy with that of the Axis but said that the need for major rearmament would prevent too complete an association in the near future. In particular, Franco said that he wanted to build four modern battleships of the *Vittorio Veneto* class. The purchase would not only strengthen the Spanish fleet but would establish closer cooperation between the Spanish and Italian navies. Franco expressed his intention to carry out a substantial transformation of society modeled on Mussolini's Fascist regime. Ciano reached the conclusion that "Franco is completely dominated by Mussolini's personality.[71] Still, even though Franco had obviously charmed Ciano and convinced the Italian foreign minister of Spanish loyalty to the Axis, Fascist Italy could hope for little concrete military assistance from Franco's Spain for at least five years.[72] It looked increasingly unlikely that either country would have that long to prepare for war.

Ciano's trip to Spain had been a pleasant interlude, but immediately on his return he had to turn to the central question of German relations with Poland. He summoned Massimo Magistrati, his brother-in-law and the counselor of the Italian Embassy in Berlin, to Rome to consult about the Duce's planned meeting at the Brenner. Ciano believed that Attolico had been infected by an epidemic of fear, and he wanted to know Magistrati's assessment of the situation. Ciano said that he planned to have Mussolini promote the idea of an international peace conference. Britain and France either would have to negotiate German and Italian demands or they would refuse to attend; in either case, the Axis would gain the diplomatic initiative and would strengthen their case for concessions. Magistrati agreed with Ciano's appreciation of Attolico's behavior and thought that Ciano's proposal had merit, though he was concerned that Hitler might interpret it as an attempt to evade Italy's obligations under the Pact of Steel. Ciano discussed the issue with Mussolini, and they agreed to go ahead with the scheme provided that von Ribbentrop approved and provided that Hitler had not already made the decision to go war.[73] Ciano, having had his suspicions of Attolico's behavior evidently confirmed, decided that Magistrati should accompany Attolico to any important meetings; Ciano no longer trusted his ambassador, the very observer who had been supplying the Foreign Ministry with the most accurate information.

Mussolini gave Magistrati written instructions to carry to von Ribbentrop regarding Italy's agenda for the Mussolini-Hitler conversation. Attolico met Magistrati, and on 25 July they took Mussolini's message to Fuschl, von Ribbentrop's lakeside country house expropriated from its former owner, whom the Gestapo had executed. Mussolini's note began by committing Italy to war at Hitler's discretion;

If the Führer thinks that we truly have reached the opportune moment for a war then Italy is disposed to agree one hundred percent. If Germany is forced to mobilize then Italy will do the same, intending to maintain fully its commitments with all its forces. This is, as I have already said, clear.[74]

Nevertheless, despite Mussolini's commitment to fight, he thought that Hitler should be aware of the Duce's belief that neither France nor Great Britain would stand aside if Germany invaded Poland. The moment for war, therefore, was not opportune for the Axis. Mussolini cited the inability to breach French border defenses, the lack of Italian battleships, and, especially, the need to allow Spain time to rebuild its armed forces. In addition, Mussolini argued that public opinion in the West seemed to be oriented toward war with Germany. In this instance, no possibility of strategic surprise existed. It would be better to wait until French and British public opinion relaxed and the objective conditions for war would be better. Accordingly, Mussolini thought the time ripe for the Axis to initiate the idea of the international conference to settle European questions. His scheme called for the exclusion of the Soviet Union, the United States, and Japan, as these were intercontinental powers. Only the European countries of Great Britain, France, Germany, Italy, Poland, and Spain (to counterbalance Poland) would attend. Such a proposal would place both France and Great Britain on the horns of a dilemma. Both countries had substantial pacifist elements that would want to see the conference succeed. In this situation, the Axis could secure substantial concessions at the negotiating table while continuing their military preparation. In particular, Mussolini thought that Italy could make progress on economic issues. Whatever occurred, the Axis partners would not be bound by any agreements and could resort to force when the time seemed opportune. However, if the democracies rejected the proposed conference, then "the responsibility for future events would fall entirely on the shoulders of the governments of France and England." Germany and Italy could use force at their convenience. In either case, Mussolini argued, the Axis would hold the diplomatic initiative. The note concluded that Mussolini would put forward this argument to the Führer in their meeting at the Brenner, but only if Hitler had not already decided on a war that would invoke the military alliance provisions of the Pact of Steel. Although Mussolini clearly intended that this information should help to prevent an immediate war, his confirmation of Italy's readiness and its loyalty to the Axis alliance confirmed Hitler's belief that he could count on Mussolini's Italy in the event of war with Britain and France.[75]

For his part, von Ribbentrop resisted the idea of a conference. He replied that Hitler did not want an immediate war. Repeating his earlier language to Attolico, he said that at most Germany was involved in a war of nerves with Poland. Showing signs of weakness through a conference proposal would undermine Germany's position. The opposition, von Ribbentrop said, was cracking. Britain had capitulated in its standoff over Tientsin, and the neutrality legislation prevented the involvement of the United States. German diplomacy would soon isolate Poland. Furthermore, the Führer was unlikely to be willing to sit at a conference table with Polish representatives, as their rejection of his previous overtures had enraged him. The international Jewish-Masonic press would prevent substantial concessions and would place blame for failure on the Axis, so it would be better to act directly and decisively. Attolico and Magistrati had carried with them a draft communiqué for release after Mussolini's meeting with Hitler. It spoke of the reaffirmation of German and Italian friendship and their mutual desire for peace despite the encirclement policy of the West, but von Ribbentrop refused to consider releasing it. Attolico concluded that he could not rule out the possibility of an imminent German war with Poland; the war of nerves would eventually erupt into a general war unless someone intervened decisively.[76]

Hitler's absence at the Wagner Festival in Bayreuth delayed a definitive response until von Ribbentrop could consult the Führer. Hitler eventually rejected Mussolini's proposal, saying that Munich had been a torment and that he detested conferences. Hitler's opposition forced Mussolini and Ciano to reconsider their options. German assurances about the desire to avoid war had hit their mark, and Ciano thought a meeting between Mussolini and Hitler was no longer necessary. Ciano issued instructions to Attolico to secure the meeting's postponement until the international situation became clarified.[77] Attolico and von Ribbentrop met again on 28 July. The German foreign minister explained that Hitler had wanted to meet Mussolini in order to discuss international issues. If Poland provoked an attack, then Hitler would have to react. In the event that the war was not localized, then Italy and Germany would need to coordinate common action. Hitler, therefore, had wanted to determine Mussolini's view. In light of von Ribbentrop's assurances that no immediate war threatened, Attolico replied according to Ciano's instructions—the meeting should be postponed. Hitler agreed. In subsequent discussions, Hitler and von Ribbentrop said that they understood Ciano's desire for a delay, but that a postponement of seven to ten days would suffice. Attolico wrote to Ciano that this response signaled extreme danger for Italy. In Attolico's view, Hitler wanted desperately to punish the Poles, and both Hitler and von Ribbentrop believed that a war could remain localized. In this situation, their continued desire to speak to Mussolini suggested two possibilities. Either Mussolini's recent proposal for a conference had caused the Führer to rethink his plans for war or Hitler perhaps merely expected to discuss international relations to harmonize Axis views. Attolico thought it far more likely, however, that Hitler's repeated denunciations of Poland meant that he had already decided on war and that he planned to crush Poland. Attolico also raised von Ribbentrop's fantastic "indifference to a war of ten years duration." These signs all pointed to an imminent conflict. If Mussolini did not meet with Hitler, then the Führer would be free to commit Italy to a general war.[78]

Ciano remained sanguine despite the rejection of Mussolini's proposed conference and the many signs of an approaching crisis. He still thought Attolico's reports alarmist. Magistrati confirmed this attitude in a letter in the first week of August. He argued that Italy should not pursue von Ribbentrop for a clarification of the German position but should wait for German consultation under the terms of the Pact of Steel.[79] Nevertheless, reports continued to arrive at the Palazzo Chigi detailing widespread German military preparations.[80] Ciano grew increasingly uneasy about this evidence. He spoke to Mussolini on 6 August, seeking the Duce's assessment of Italy's position. In a lengthy discussion, they agreed that if war came then they would have to fight, "if only to save [Italy's] 'honour.'"[81] In the prevailing circumstances, however, war was unfavorable. Gold reserves and stocks of strategic metals were almost depleted, and Fascist Italy's military and economic preparations were nowhere near complete.[82] Both men agreed that they should try to avoid an immediate conflict. Ciano raised the idea of a meeting between the two foreign ministers to clear the air, while postponing the Hitler-Mussolini discussions until after the conclusion of the Anglo-French-Soviet Treaty negotiations. After considering the proposal overnight, Mussolini agreed. Attolico secured von Ribbentrop's approval, and they scheduled Ciano to travel to arrive in Salzburg on 11 August.[83]

The need to prevent a premature conflict had become more pressing in light of evidence that Britain and France were prepared to wage war over the issue of German demands against Poland. In late June, Guido Crolla, the Italian chargé d'affaires in London, had reported that he had learned from his sources that the British government planned to resist any further aggression in Europe. The Conservative Party had suspended preparations for a fall election owing to the crisis brewing over Danzig and the evident German military movements.[84] In early July, Chamberlain sent Loraine to deliver an aide-mémoire to Mussolini, drawing the Duce's attention to the Danzig situation. Germany was sending paramilitary troops to Danzig disguised as tourists; a coup against Danzig would mean war, as the cabinet had a duty to carry out its declared obligation to Poland, as had France. Germany could not take over Danzig without provoking a war into which Italy would inevitably be drawn. The only possible route to avoiding war would be a clear German declaration that it harbored no hostile intentions toward Poland. Chamberlain held out an olive branch seeking a negotiated solution but said that he believed it had become necessary to give this warning to Mussolini in order to avert a catastrophe.[85] Mussolini counterattacked. He accused the Poles of profiting from the destruction of Czechoslovakia and said that Danzig was an indisputably German city. More seriously, he said that Loraine should "tell Chamberlain that if England is ready to fight in defense of Poland, Italy will take up arms with her ally Germany."[86] The Duce also drafted a memorandum for Ciano to use to respond further to Chamberlain's message. It placed the blame for the situation squarely on Polish shoulders. Polish delusions and war psychosis threatened the peace, but if Britain took up arms with Poland, then Italy would fight alongside Germany.[87] Mussolini also ratcheted up Italian anti-British propaganda threatening the British empire, including launching territorial claims against Malta and supporting Spanish claims against Gibraltar. At the same time, Mussolini withdrew the Anglophile Grandi as ambassador to the court of St. James. As the Italian government had not announced the move beforehand, diplomats correctly interpreted it as an anti-British snub.[88] Chamberlain's attempt at deterrent diplomacy had apparently failed dismally.

At the same time, however, persistent British attempts to convince Italian diplomats of its determination to resist Axis aggression did have some success. Sir Nevile Henderson, the British ambassador in Berlin, persuaded Attolico that public opinion in Britain would compel its government to defend Poland. In Henderson's view, Chamberlain had lost control of his cabinet, which had reached the conclusion that it would have to resist German attempts to dominate Europe.[89] The Italian Embassy in London also submitted reports of increasingly tight Anglo-French military cooperation to resist not only German aggression but also possible Italian moves in the Mediterranean.[90] More seriously still, documents stolen from the British Embassy in Rome had verified Anglo-French determination to prevent German hegemony in Europe. If Germany invaded Poland, then Britain and France would surely fight.[91] In Rome, Loraine concluded that Mussolini's behavior signaled that Italy no longer valued its long-standing friendship with Great Britain. Halifax inquired as to whether or not Britain could approach Mussolini regarding a settlement of the Italian claims against Djibuti and Suez, a guarantee of the Brenner frontier, and a loan to Italy. Loraine thought it unlikely that this bribe could wean Mussolini from the Axis. The British ambassador could see little prospect of Mussolini foreswearing the threat of aggression and the use of military force.[92] The path to peaceful resolution of the Mediterranean status quo seemed blocked, but signs of British resolution had brought home the likelihood that further Axis aggression would lead to a general war.

Similarly, French government officials convinced Mussolini and Ciano that France would be prepared to go to war to resist further Axis expansion. Foreign Minister Bonnet, certainly no hard-liner, held open the prospect of discussions of Franco-Italian relations but firmly told Ambassador Guariglia that France would honor its commitment to Poland.[93] Italian military attachés in Paris understood that Anglo-French forces would launch a devastating attack against Italy in the event that Germany provoked a war against Poland. French naval officers seemed very optimistic about war with Italy. Anglo-French naval superiority, combined with the British military agreement with Turkey, made the timing for war more opportune for the West. If Italy supported its German ally, then it would face attacks against its colonies and metropolitan areas.[94] Both Ciano and Mussolini had come to believe that a localized war was extremely unlikely.

The Axis partners had made little headway in securing the alliance with Japan, further weakening Italy's position in the event of war. Throughout the summer, the Japanese Council of Five Ministers had continued to dispute the exact wording of the alliance with Germany and Italy. The Tientsin confrontation with Britain had delayed the conclusion of this internal debate, as some Japanese leaders wanted to see the outcome before determining Japan's diplomatic orientation. At the same time, however, the prospect of a breach between Tokyo and London held out the prospect that the Axis partners would be able to entice Japan to join. The escalating war in Manchuria, where Japanese and Soviet forces faced off in the summer of 1939, complicated Japan's position. By the last half of

July 1939, the Japanese Kwantung Army fought increasingly large battles against the Red Army. Japanese Naval commanders, who would be forced to bear the brunt of an armed conflict against an Anglo-American coalition, still resisted any definitive alignment that would call for Japan to assume an open-ended commitment. The Roosevelt administration had dealt a severe blow to Japanese interests by refusing to renew a commercial accord, signaling growing resistance to Japanese expansionism in Washington. This combination of threats led Foreign Minister Arita to move cautiously, ignoring the signs of a growing rapprochement between Germany and the Soviet Union.[95] By the beginning of August, extensive internal negotiations between army and navy subordinates had hammered out yet another compromise formula. Rumors circulated that General Itagaki and his confederates, Ambassadors Ōshima and Shiratori, would resign if the council did not conclude the tripartite alliance immediately. At a meeting held on 10 August, Itagaki was unable to persuade his cabinet colleagues to modify Japan's last proposal. He told the Italian ambassador that he planned to resign, triggering a cabinet crisis. Little prospect remained for the early conclusion of a tripartite military alliance.[96] Ciano knew, therefore, that Italy could expect little help in diverting Anglo-French naval forces from the Mediterranean to the Far East.

Similarly, Mussolini and Ciano could take little comfort from the array of forces in the Balkans. Hungary had shown itself to be an unsteady ally. During the summer, Hungarian diplomats had approached the British and Turkish governments to intercede regarding Romania's treatment of its Hungarian minority. As Foreign Minister Csáky explained his initiative, he hoped to prevent a scheme whereby London would convince Bucharest to settle Bulgarian claims against the Dobrudja territory. This cession would pave the way for Bulgaria to join the Balkan Pact, helping to resist further border revision in the region. A skeptical Ciano rudely rejected this line of reasoning; he viewed the Hungarian action as a sign of bad faith.[97] Although Ciano approved of a Hungarian approach to German to establish military and economic cooperation in the event of war, the lack of a parallel approach to Italy caused some disquiet, as did the Hungarian acquisition of German aircraft. Hungary seemed to be slipping further into Germany's orbit.[98] Most damagingly, Prime Minister Teleki sent parallel notes to Mussolini and Hitler to declare Hungarian willingness to follow Axis foreign policy in the event of a European war. He thought it wise to pursue tripartite discussions to coordinate Hungarian military plans with those of Germany and Italy. Teleki weakened this declaration by including a caveat; Hungary would not declare war against Poland.[99] Demonstrating

some stunning hypocrisy, Ciano said that this letter had created a disastrous impression in Rome. It seemed as if Hungary sought to evade the
most obvious consequence of its declared intent in seeking an alliance.
Though Foreign Minister Csáky would respond to German and Italian
anger by asking that Ciano and von Ribbentrop considered it as if the letters had never been sent, neither Rome nor Berlin could maintain any illusions that Hungary would go to war over the Danzig crisis.[100]

Nor could Italy count on significant support from Bulgaria. The Kyoseivanov administration had resisted attempts from Balkan Pact members
to enlist Bulgaria in exchange for mediation over its territorial claims
against Romania. Bulgarian membership in the Balkan Pact would imply
its general acceptance of the status quo. With territorial claims against
Greece and Yugoslavia in addition to those against Romania, no prominent
Bulgarian politician would accept the perpetual limitation of Bulgaria's
frontiers.[101] Nevertheless, Bulgaria lacked the military strength to be able
to take offensive action in the summer of 1939. Potentially facing the combined armed forces of Greece, Romania, Yugoslavia, and Turkey, Bulgaria
needed substantial commitments of German and Italian arms supplies and
economic aid simply to be able to defend its borders if attacked. Kyoseivanov hoped that Hungarian pressure could neutralize Romania, and he
also had attempted to reach some kind of accommodation with Yugoslavia
in order to reduce its number of enemies, but that initiative had not by then
borne fruit. Turkey's long-rumored association in an Anglo-French security pact obviously boded ill for Bulgarian revisionism, and Bulgaria could
do little to prevent the Turkish arms buildup in Thrace. The Turkish military threat obviously curtailed Sofia's ability to carry out an aggressive
policy. Prime Minister Kyoseivanov had traveled to Berlin in July, and the
visit seemingly demonstrated his allegiance to overall Axis aims. Hitler
and von Ribbentrop promised to help Bulgaria to reequip its forces, and
Kyoseivanov hoped to secure similar Italian support.[102] Ciano arranged an
official Bulgarian visit to Rome in September, though events would prevent Kyoseivanov from making the journey. Given Bulgaria's inferior military capability, however, Ciano knew that he could count on no
meaningful support from Sofia in the imminent crisis.

The stance of the Yugoslav government also gave Ciano little reason for
optimism. Relations with Italy were correct but had deteriorated since
Prime Minister Stoyadinović's fall from power earlier in 1939. In June, the
two countries had signed a deal for a large sale of Italian arms to
Yugoslavia. The arms purchases, Ciano hoped, would help to tie
Yugoslavia more firmly to the coattails of the Axis, and, at the same time,

develop much needed trade to help Italy's foreign currency reserves.[103] The apparently cordial relationship, however, only superficially concealed the tension between the two countries. Ciano continued to foster ethnic tension in Croatia and Kosovo. The Italian-sponsored Kosovar secessionist movement was in its infancy, however, and Croat leader Vladko Maček showed little sign of accepting Italian control of Croat irredentism. During the summer, negotiations between Maček and the Serb-dominated Cvetković cabinet showed signs of reaching an accord that would settle certain long-standing Croat demands. For Ciano, this development was displeasing because it threatened to weaken the Croatian separatist movement. The Yugoslav military also had heavily reinforced its borders with Albania and Italy, thus raising a further obstacle to Italian adventurism.[104] Italy's invasion of Albania had aroused tremendous suspicion in Belgrade, and Ciano expected that Yugoslavia would maintain a position of heavily armed neutrality in the event that war erupted in the summer of 1939.

This constellation of forces suggested that Italy's strategic situation was far from ideal. The delay in reaching a tripartite alliance, the concentration of German forces in the East, the apparent strength of Germany's Western fortifications, and the signs of unity between Paris and London all implied that Anglo-French military planners would make the Mediterranean the first battlefield. Given the prevailing balance of military power, the *Regio Esercito* and *Regia Marina* could only hope to defend against an expected British and French onslaught. Mussolini's attempts to drive a wedge between London and Paris had failed utterly, and the alliance with Germany had not provided the military and industrial strength for Mussolini to pursue his imperial dreams in the face of determined Western opposition.[105] Italy had friends but no sure allies in the Balkans and would have a difficult time carrying out offensive operations. As Ciano left for Salzburg, therefore, he knew that he had to prevent the outbreak of a premature general war that could have disastrous consequences for Italy.

Although the situation seemed bleak, a determined and oddly jubilant Ciano, accompanied by a delegation of Italian diplomats and journalists, arrived in Salzburg on the morning of 11 August to confront von Ribbentrop. Their German hosts conveyed them to Schloss Fuschl, where an informally attired von Ribbentrop hosted a luncheon that turned icy after he let slip Germany's intention to provoke a war with Poland. After the largely silent repast, the two foreign ministers repaired to the salon for a long conversation. As was their wont, it consisted not of a genuine exchange of views but rather of a dialogue of the deaf conducted in an extremely tense atmosphere. For his part, von Ribbentrop insisted that war was inevitable; Polish provocations, including the alleged castration of ethnic Germans, had offended Hitler's honor. He mouthed the now axiomatic refrain; Germany had intimidated its foes and they would not react. The war would not become general. If Britain and France did declare war, they would not be able to harm the Axis, and Germany and Italy would win the resulting conflict. He also insisted that the Soviet Union would not intervene owing to the successful German overtures under discussion in Moscow. German strength and diplomacy had neutralized all other countries. The time was ripe, von Ribbentrop argued, for Germany to march with utmost determination. Ciano bitterly contradicted von Ribbentrop's blithe assurances. He showed the German foreign minister information on the poor state of the Italian economy and the military and repeatedly insisted that Britain and France would both fight. Ciano's arguments were in vain; the only concession that he could secure was an admission from von Ribbentrop that Germany had changed its position regarding the advisability of a two- to three-year waiting period before fighting a general war. Even then, however, von Ribbentrop refused to be drawn on Hitler's immediate plans, saying only that events were proceeding rapidly. Ciano understood that von Ribbentrop would resist every attempt to reach a peaceful solution.[106]

That evening, Ciano held a fruitless discussion with Italian diplomats. They agreed that Italy should remain neutral but failed to develop any ideas as to how Ciano should persuade Hitler to abandon his drive to war. The following morning, Ciano traveled to Berchtesgaden and Hitler's villa, the infamous Eagle's Nest. After another dismal luncheon, Ciano met with Hitler, von Ribbentrop, and an interpreter. Little had changed. Hitler outlined Germany's impregnable strategic position. No power would be able to breach its fortifications. The *Wehrmacht* had a massive superiority over the Polish military, which was especially weak in its artillery, antitank weaponry, and the air. After defeating the Poles, Hitler would turn 100 divisions to the West to prepare to destroy France in the inevitable war with the Western democracies. For various reasons, real and imagined, Hitler was determined to smash Poland some time before 15 October, when wet weather would hamper operations. He reassured Ciano that Britain and France would never fight on Poland's behalf and that German diplomacy in Moscow would isolate the Poles. Hitler therefore urged that Italy should seize the opportunity to attack Dalmatia and Croatia.[107]

Ciano tried to dispute the Führer's version of events but was lacking the energy that he had expended with von Ribbentrop the previous day. Ciano stated that Hitler had promised a two- to three-year delay before a general war. Though the Duce would stand beside Germany in the crisis, Italy needed time in order to prepare its military. Hitler interrupted, saying that Polish provocation had changed the German timetable and that the war would remain localized. Accordingly, Germany would not need Italy to resort to force. Ciano noted Hitler's attitude but continued his argument, raising several ideas that Mussolini had noted in the past. Italy needed to replace its artillery, to finish its battleship fleet, to replenish its stocks of raw materials, to restore its currency balances, and to relocate its industry. Without time, Italy would be woefully unprepared for battle. In these circumstances, Ciano thought it wise to issue a communiqué that would hold out at least the chance for a negotiated solution. Hitler reserved judgement, and given the late hour, thought that they should continue the conversation the following day.[108]

After another late night of ineffectual consultations with his entourage, Ciano returned to Berchtesgaden on 13 August to finish his desultory discussion with the Führer. Hitler asked Ciano if he had anything to say. A deflated Ciano replied that he awaited Hitler's decisions. The Führer stated that he had determined that the two parties should issue no formal communiqué, leaving their hands free to reach any decision. He repeated the necessity of reaching a totalitarian solution to the Polish problem. Germany needed to seize its living space just as Italy would establish its domination of the Mediterranean. The Western democracies would limit their response to mouthing words of protest over a German attack; they would not march to defend Poland. Ciano sought only to learn when the attack would begin. Hitler responded that he had not yet fixed the date, but that the *Wehrmacht* would march before the end of August. Hitler finished by saluting the Duce and promising to stay at Mussolini's side come what may. Ciano took his leave.[109] Hitler's discourse led Ciano to several unpalatable conclusions. Hitler's will to war was implacable, even if France and Britain intervened. Italy could do nothing to deflect the Führer from his course. Even when confronted with Italian military weakness, he seemed content to know that Italy could potentially tie down French and British forces. Ciano left Berchtesgaden determined that Italy should remain neutral in the coming conflict, though Mussolini would of course be the final arbiter of that decision. Ciano noted in his diary that he was "completely disgusted by the Germans, with their leader, with their way of doing things. They have betrayed us and lied to us."[110]

In addition to his inability to dissuade Hitler from seeking war, Ciano also lost a battle with Hitler and von Ribbentrop over the official communiqué regarding the discussions. The Italian draft had asserted the two ministers' "perfect identity of views," including the common desire of both parties to resist the encirclement of the Western democracies. It also confirmed their will to reach peaceful, negotiated solutions to European problems. Ciano had contended that even in the current circumstances his language could have a useful tactical advantage in soothing Western pacifist opinion, but to no avail. Obviously, the communiqué's tone entirely failed to convey von Ribbentrop's warlike attitude. The German foreign minister argued lamely that it would merely show sign of Axis irresolution. He proposed instead that the bulletin should emphasize Axis resolve to meet any crisis. Immediately after Ciano's departure for Rome, von Ribbentrop released an official communiqué that indicated the "extraordinary amity and cordiality" of the meeting and the "absolute unanimity" of both partners in their desire to deal with the Polish crisis. The German press release apparently committed Italy publicly to follow Hitler's march to war.[111] It further hammered home the fact that Ciano had wholly failed in his mission. Hitler had broken his promises to Mussolini; the Führer's insistence on a premature war threatened to involve Fascist Italy in a conflict against the combined forces of France and Great Britain. Mussolini's imperial dreams had landed Italy in a forbidding quagmire. Ciano was determined to extricate Italy from the trap of the Duce's making.

Ciano and Attolico agreed on a course of action. Attolico thought that Italy should try to secure a legalistic exit from the obligation of the Pact of Steel. He suggested that Mussolini send the Führer an official démarche, saying that the Axis should hold a conference to reach a pacific solution. Attolico recognized that this proposal would not work, but he wanted to receive a written refusal. Italy could also make a formal approach to Poland. At the same time, Italian diplomats should carry the message to Hitler that all indications pointed to an Anglo-French intervention after Germany's attack on Poland. They should ask von Ribbentrop for direct proof that the Western democracies would not intervene—evidence that would be impossible to gather. After preparing this diplomatic terrain, Italy could insist on its view that Germany had committed to a two- to three-year delay before fighting a war against Britain and France. If Hitler insisted on provoking a general war, then it would be incumbent on Nazi Germany to make good all "Italian deficiencies in arms and that this would have to occur *before* Italian entry into the war."[112] After consulting with Mussolini, Ciano instructed Attolico to proceed with this plan, while at the same time insisting that Germany could receive all its stated demands through negotiation.[113] Attolico readied himself to travel to Germany, preparatory to meeting von Ribbentrop or Hitler.

In Rome, Ciano continued his campaign to convince Mussolini to opt for neutrality. Ciano tried to play on the Duce's emotions, arguing that Hitler and von Ribbentrop had betrayed Mussolini's trust by their premature rush to war. Ciano begged Fascist Party Secretary Achille Starace not to hide the level of anti-German public sentiment in the Italian countryside. The foreign minister also accused Hitler of reducing Mussolini to a role of playing second fiddle in the Axis. Ultimately, a resurgent Nazi Germany would threaten Mussolini's position in Italy as well. In light of German actions, Ciano argued that Mussolini should abandon his fealty to the Axis. Mussolini's initial reaction was to say that he could not change sides. After two days of hectoring, however, the Duce equivocated. He agreed that Italy's weak military position prevented him from participating in a wider conflict. Nevertheless, he still allowed the possibility that Britain and France would stand aside, and he did not want to forego the chance to expand Italy's borders in the short term. If the West did not declare war, then Italy would attack Yugoslavia, and Mussolini ordered the creation of an ad hoc army under General Graziani for the purpose.[114] To further the Duce's planned Yugoslav campaign, Ciano hastened preparations for Croat terrorist attacks against Yugoslavia. Fascist Italy would supply Ante Pavelić's Ustaša with one million Swiss francs, arms and explosives to spark a Croat insurrection. After a Croat uprising, Italy would intervene, allowing Pavelić to establish a quasi-independent state, with its foreign policy controlled from Rome.[115]

Mussolini continued to vacillate before Attolico's departure from Rome. He decided that Fascist Italy would declare war even if Britain and France made the conflict general. His lust for war temporarily overcame objections from his less bellicose advisors; only by joining the struggle could Fascist Italy hope to seize a new Mediterranean empire. Ciano fought strenuously against this new position and succeeded in having the Duce amend his instructions; Attolico would inform the Germans of Mussolini's decision only in response to a direct question regarding Italy's attitude.[116] On 18 August Attolico and Magistrati journeyed to Schloss Fuschl to present Mussolini's new instructions. Attolico relayed the Duce's verbal message to von Ribbentrop; the conflict would not remain localized and would become a war of long duration. Italy was in no condition to fight such a campaign. Italy would certainly need massive coal and oil shipments from Germany, and the Brenner frontier was insufficient to carry wartime supplies. This declaration did not sway von Ribbentrop. He replied to Attolico with the familiar refrain—Britain and France would not fight, and even if they did march, the Axis would surely defeat them. After Germany liqui-

dated Poland, it would turn its forces Westward. If France bombed northern Italy, then the Luftwaffe would take defensive measures and it would
also pulverize France. Germany would be able to provide Italy with ample
supplies of oil from Romania and the Soviet Union. Finally, von Ribbentrop played his trump card; he announced that he would shortly conclude
not only a commercial agreement with Stalin but would sign a comprehensive political agreement as well. With this coup in hand, von Ribbentrop was certain that the West would capitulate and that Poland would be
completely isolated. Even faced with a direct statement that Mussolini differed entirely in his appreciation of the international situation, von
Ribbentrop refused to budge.[117] Attolico had failed to change the German
decision for war; at best, Attolico had been able to take a small step toward
preparing the ground for Italy's renunciation of its alliance obligation.
Attolico saw von Ribbentrop the following day, but he made no more
headway. Despite the fundamental disagreement regarding the future
course of the expected war, von Ribbentrop said that the German decision
was irrevocable. Nazi Germany would be able to defeat Poland and protect
Italy if necessary. Under Soviet and German pressure, Eastern Europe
would have little choice but to supply Germany and Italy with whatever
resources they needed to fight a drawn out war.[118] In the face of von
Ribbentrop's obstinacy, Mussolini's objections proved futile.

Italy's poor military preparations left Mussolini in a quandary. He
earnestly coveted the opportunity to support his German ally and to march
to the sound of battle. His social Darwinist dreams seemingly compelled
him to join the coming struggle, but the strategic situation argued against
it. Contrary to the rosy predictions of Hitler and von Ribbentrop, Italian
military experts did not expect Germany's planned invasion to proceed
easily. For example, General Mario Roatta, the military attaché in Berlin,
submitted a report on German military capabilities. Basing his view in part
on information supplied by the German Intelligence Chief Admiral
Canaris, Roatta questioned the confident predictions of a triumphal two- to
three-week campaign against Poland. Even though Germany had developed a highly efficient mechanized army, it would be hard pressed against
tough Polish resistance. More seriously, the *Wehrmacht* had no effective
contingency plans for a French attack in the West. Whatever the prospects
for the Polish campaign, Roatta argued that the coming conflict would last
for years, making economic considerations paramount and therefore
weakening Axis likelihood of long-term success.[119]

The Italian military situation was much worse than that of its German
ally. Mussolini's foreign policy decisions had seriously undermined the

ability of the services to prepare for war. In 1936, military spending had accounted for an astonishing 18.4 percent of Italy's Gross National Product. Although that astronomical proportion had declined slightly after the end of the Ethiopian War, by 1939, military spending still accounted for almost 40 percent of Italy's government expenditures. In real terms, Italian spending far surpassed that of France, a country with a significantly larger economy. But this Herculean effort to rearm had had poor results. Almost two-thirds of the military budget expended between 1935 and 1939 had gone to pay for the wars in Ethiopia and Spain. Little remained to modernize all three service branches to improve the fighting ability of frontline units. Although Fascist Italy had devoted enormous resources to military expenditures, almost bankrupting the state, the armed forces faced severe shortages of fundamental equipment and strategic resources. In particular, Italy suffered perpetual shortages of coal and steel. In 1938, Italian industry had produced only one million metric tons of high grade coal, while importing another 12.1 million tons. France, Italy's putative main enemy, had produced 47.6 million tons. Italy produced less than half as much steel as did France, while British production quintupled Italy's. This shortage of heavy industry had severely hampered Italian production of armor plate for tanks and ships. Italy was also seriously short of petroleum. Estimates pegged the services' wartime operational requirements at eight million tons per year, but Italian stockpiles held only a little more than two million tons, while Italian production and trade could acquire less than two million tons per year. The grave financial crisis indicated that Fascist Italy would face serious difficulty in making good these critical shortages.[120]

In many ways, the *Regia Marina* had fared the best of the services, as the Duce expected that it would carry the brunt of the fighting against France or Britain in the Mediterranean. Between 1926 and 1934, Fascist Italy had replaced or modernized much of its fleet and had increased its tonnage by almost 50 percent. Mussolini had ordered the construction of four battleships. Nominally listed at 35,000 tons in order to comply with the Washington Naval Treaty, these modern designs actually displaced 42,000 tons; they would give Italy a strong core of capital ships with which to challenge the French, and perhaps, British navies. Italian naval strategists, however, faced the prospect of war with considerable alarm. As Admiral Cavagnari had told Admiral Raeder at Friedrichshafen in June, the Italian navy had founded its plans for Italian expansion on the completion of eight modern battleships by 1942, plus the completion of bases to allow motor-torpedo boats and submarines to harass British imperial com-

munications in the Red Sea and Indian Ocean. As of August 1939, however, none of these plans had reached fruition. Italy had only two modernized battleships ready for sea, so its main fleet would be unable to take the
offensive against either Britain or France in any part of the Mediterranean.
In the Eastern Mediterranean, the uncertain attitude of Turkey and Greece
meant that Italy would be hard-pressed to defend the Dodecanese Islands.
The main battle fleet had no adequate bases; Genoa lay too close to French
bombers and most of the new facilities at Taranto were still under construction, years from completion. The main strength of Italy's fleet would
strain to defend the supply line to Libya against the threat of Anglo-French
naval action that could cut off Italian forces there. Only Italy's submarines
could hope to carry the battle to Italy's enemies, although it was uncertain
how successful they would be given the lack of forward bases. Nevertheless, *Regia Marina* commanders prepared eighty-seven submarines to sor-
tie in the event of war, and they planned the mining of the passage of the
Sicilian Channel. Italy's naval staff planned to fight a largely defensive
war, hoping to stave off defeat in detail, but having little prospect for
effective action to defeat France and Britain in the first years of war.[121]

The plight of the *Regia Aeronautica* was worse. In 1935, Fascist Italy
had had one of the largest air forces in the world, but by 1939 it had fallen
behind its potential enemies. Undergunned biplanes such as the Fiat Cr. 32
and the Cr. 42 comprised the bulk of Italy's fighter squadrons. Extremely
maneuverable, they had served adequately in Spain, but their slow speed
meant that they could not provide escort for Italy's medium bombers, and
the newest Soviet Ilyushin fighters had outclassed them. The *Regia Aeronautica* had only begun to receive its first shipments of metal-hulled
monoplane fighters, the Fiat G. 50 and the Macchi M.C. 200; it had only
some 260 frontline fighter aircraft, although even they were inferior to the
newer British fighters. In addition, Italian pilots had had relatively little
opportunity to train with the new planes or to implement more suitable tactics. Italy's bomber force was also in disarray. Italian planners had long
based their strategic doctrine on Douhet's theories of mass bombing, but
Italian industry proved unable to produce a heavy bomber suitable to the
task. Italian medium bombers had weak engines, requiring trimotor
designs that would have limited effectiveness in carrying out their missions. Italian tacticians had begun to compensate for the complete divergence between their aircraft and their theoretical missions, developing
ground attack and dive-bombing techniques. In the summer of 1939,
however, the poor quality of Italian aircraft in comparison with their
Anglo-French enemies, combined with the lack of aviation fuel, would

necessitate an entirely defensive posture. The *Regia Aeronautica* would be unable to contribute to any major offensive action designed to win a war with the West.[122]

The situation for the *Regio Esercito* was even more dire than for its sister services. It tended to train its conscripts poorly, and given the lack of widespread automotive skills in Italian society, was unable to develop the infrastructure to support a large armored force. Despite the construction of more than 2,500 tanks, Italy's armored divisions were extremely weak. Most tanks were of 1920s vintage or were designed primarily for colonial warfare. The *Regio Esercito* had equipped the bulk of the armored divisions with L3 tanks, a small 3.5 ton vehicle carrying either one or two machine guns. Although the army had requested a main battle tank from the Fiat-Ansaldo conglomerate in 1936, it had received only a few dozen by the summer of 1939. The M11/39 was far inferior to the tanks it would face in battle with France or Great Britain, especially as it mounted its small cannon in the hull and not in the turret. Furthermore, the lack of petroleum meant that Italy's armored striking force, which the Duce hoped would bear the brunt of the fighting in an attack against Yugoslavia, had sufficient fuel supplies only to advance from its peacetime laagers to the Italo-Yugoslav border. Italy's other divisions were largely compelled to march to battle, as most had neither trucks for transport nor motorized artillery. Italian artillery was mostly of World War I vintage, and the anti-tank weaponry was entirely inadequate to defend infantry or armor against the tanks of another major power.[123] It seemed highly unlikely, therefore, that the *Regio Esercito* could carry off an offensive against British or French colonies, never mind metropolitan France. Mussolini already had abandoned his plans for a lightning attack against Egypt, although he hoped to be able to strike at Yugoslavia if circumstances permitted. Italy's forces in the eastern Mediterranean, in East Africa, and perhaps in Libya faced the prospect of defeat in detail, while Italy could do little to carry the battle to the enemy.[124] Given the inability of Italy's forces to conduct any kind of offensive in the early months of war, Ciano knew Fascist Italy's economy would collapse long before anyone could expect the weight of German arms to rescue the Duce from the combined assault of the superior Anglo-French forces. These desperate circumstances compelled Ciano to pursue neutrality. In his view, Mussolini's burning desire to enter the fray would be ruinous for Italy.[125]

Despite the seemingly grim situation, the Duce still equivocated about Italian entry into the war. He tended to discount warnings of the severe financial crisis; he trusted that fate and the discipline instilled by Fascism would allow Italy to weather the storm. Nevertheless, Mussolini worried about both the combined might of the British and French navies and German retaliation if Italy did not honor its alliance commitment. He even contemplated the possibility that Hitler would cancel the invasion of Poland to attack Italy if the Duce reneged on the obligations assumed in the Pact of Steel. Still, it was possible that Britain and France would not march, and Mussolini hoped to be able to carry out a parallel Italian attack if the war remained localized. To Ciano, the Duce appeared "nervous and disturbed."[126] After considerable discussion, Ciano thought that he had convinced Mussolini that Italy had only one option—to remain neutral. Despite the Duce's obvious unease, Ciano felt confident enough in the policy of neutrality to travel to Albania to conduct a brief inspection tour and to receive the Collar of the Annunziata, his official reward for the invasion of Albania. In Durazzo, however, he received an urgent message from Anfuso, begging Ciano to return to Rome immediately. Ciano flew his own aircraft to Rome, arriving in time for a pivotal meeting on the evening of 20 August.[127]

After receiving news of von Ribbentrop's rejection of the latest Italian proposal, Mussolini's bellicose nature led him to decide that Italy could follow no other course than to support its German ally—whatever the cost. He could not face the prospect of the world press ridiculing Italian unpreparedness and perceived cowardice, nor could he bring himself to stand aside in the struggle against the plutodemocratic empires. Consequently, Mussolini planned to send Attolico as an emissary carrying a promise to stand beside Italy's German ally in any eventuality. Despite the grim news from his military advisers, the Duce had decided that Italy had to fight whatever the perceived strategic imbalance and whatever the risk. He would trust to providence and the élan that Fascism had instilled in Italian soldiers to bring him victory. That evening, Mussolini, Ciano, and Attolico held a conference, with Ciano trying hard to sway the Duce from his course. Ciano brought forward the idea of another draft proposal for Mussolini's cherished conference to settle European problems. Not even the prospect of acquiring French territory without bloodshed—and concomitant risk—cooled the Duce's martial ardor. Ciano and Attolico left the Palazzo Venezia without persuading the obdurate Mussolini to change his mind, though Ciano did succeed in securing a day's delay in sending any official communication to Hitler.[128]

The following morning, Ciano continued to beseech the Duce to change his mind. He had received strong warning the previous day that Italy could not expect a localized war. On 17 August, Ambassador Loraine had spoken to Ciano of Great Britain's determination to resist German hegemony. On a personal basis, Loraine had added, "if the crisis comes, we will fight."[129] On 20 August, Loraine returned to say that Halifax had whole-heartedly endorsed Loraine's unofficial declaration. Halifax had instructed Loraine to deliver a clear yet tactful warning to Ciano.

On what may be the eve of such a disaster it is of vital importance that no room for doubt should exist anywhere that if the disaster does overtake Europe, and if Italy considers it her duty to range herself alongside her German ally, then Great Britain and Italy, in spite of long traditions of friendship in the past, will find themselves opposed in war. If war once started in such circumstances it would be a dangerous illusion to believe that it would be brought to an early conclusion by the defeat of Poland.[130]

Loraine balanced this language with a request to Mussolini to intervene with Hitler in order to settle the crisis peacefully. Ciano clearly understood Halifax's warning; if war came, Italy would face an Anglo-French offen-sive and the likelihood of a protracted war. Italy would find itself in dire straits if that occurred.[131]

Accordingly, Ciano returned to his crusade for Italian neutrality. He argued heatedly that Hitler had betrayed the alliance with his drive to pro-voke a premature war while leaving Italy in ignorance of his objectives. Ciano even begged Mussolini to tear up the Pact of Steel and to lead an anti-German crusade. The Duce naturally refused. Mussolini approved the idea of a further meeting between Ciano and von Ribbentrop, but the Ger-man foreign minister said that he was unavailable owing to the negotia-tions then underway in Moscow.[132] That evening, Ciano showed Mussolini an extensive memorandum drafted by Leonardo Vitetti, the Director Gen-eral of the Political Affairs Department. It highlighted several occasions on which German statesmen had made solemn declarations regarding the two- to three-year period before launching a general war, as well as British declarations of the certainty of Western intervention in the event of a Ger-man attack on Poland. In this situation, it seemed certain that Anglo-French military operations would concentrate primarily against Italy, which would therefore represent a point of weakness for the Axis. Hitler and von Ribbentrop had rejected repeated Italian attempts to pursue a negotiated solution, meaning that Germany alone was determining the course of alliance policy. Vitetti reached the conclusion that Italy had the right to make its own decision regarding peace or war, and that Mus-solini's idea for a European conference held considerable merit.[133] Mus-solini accepted a small part of the inherent logic of Vitetti's and Ciano's positions; Germany unquestionably had taken Italy in tow during the crisis, and Mussolini thought he should reassert Italy's right to make its own decisions within the alliance framework.[134]

With Ciano's guidance, Mussolini sent a letter to Hitler, laying out four possible outcomes to the crisis and indicating the Italian course of action in each eventuality.

1) If Germany attacks Poland and the conflict remains localized, we will give Germany the support that it requests.

2) If Poland and allies attack Germany we will intervene on the side of Germany.

3) If Germany attacks Poland and France and Britain counter-attack Germany we will not take the initiative of offensive operations, given the actual condition of our military preparations, repeatedly communicated to the Führer and to von Ribbentrop.

4) If negotiations fail because of the intransigence of others and Germany intends to resolve the dispute with force, then we will intervene on Germany's side.[135]

Mussolini concluded his letter with a now familiar call for a European conference to settle the imminent crisis as well as other outstanding territorial claims and economic issues. In Ciano's view, the only contingency of significance was the third; Italy would not intervene if Germany attacked Poland directly. Ciano believed that he had won an important victory. Late in the evening, von Ribbentrop phoned to say that he would be unable to meet Ciano until after returning from Moscow, where he would sign a new pact with the Soviets. Mussolini decided to postpone a meeting between the two foreign ministers until after the new situation became clearer. Mussolini and Ciano plotted to attack Croatia and Dalmatia in the event that Britain and France did not intervene now that their proposed alliance with the Soviet Union had definitively failed.[136]

The Nazi-Soviet Pact initially did appear to hold out the prospect of an immediate solution to the crisis. If Britain and France could not provide any aid to Poland, would they intervene? All indications showed that, if anything, the British government seemed more determined to fight for Poland after the conclusion of the pact than before. In Berlin, British Embassy staff had already begun burning documents preparatory to departing the capital.[137] The new situation carried great peril for Italy. The Nazi-Soviet Pact had alienated Japan. The Hiranuma cabinet eventually submitted its resignation after Germany's betrayal of the anti-Comintern

Pact left Japan bereft of allies. Although Rome might profit from greater Japanese reliance on Italian friendship in the long run, in the immediate future Japan would certainly not participate in a war begun in Europe. Britain and France therefore would face a vastly decreased threat in the Far East to divert their forces.[138] The agreement with Moscow also put Germany in a seemingly unassailable military position. If Italy entered the conflict, then Britain and France would have only one viable option—to attack Italy and its colonies. In short, an Italian declaration of war would serve to threaten Italy while undermining the Axis military effort. Mussolini would better serve the alliance by waiting until he could find an opportune moment to attack. Italy would in time become a useful German ally, especially after Germany provided the raw materials necessary to rebuild the Italian armed forces. Mussolini found this advice compelling and dispatched Attolico to Berlin to carry his decision that Italy would not join the fray in the event that Germany attacked Poland.[139]

Mussolini remained in a warlike mood, speaking of the battles to be won and the movements of armies, but he continued to equivocate about Italy's position. After von Ribbentrop's return from Moscow, he repeatedly tried to telephone Ciano to coordinate the beginning of the invasion that Hitler had moved forward to 26 August. In spite of the indications of the lack of Italian enthusiasm for his plans, Hitler fully expected that Italy would provide the military support required by the Pact of Steel, especially after the Nazi-Soviet Pact had so improved German military prospects. Ciano was away briefing the King on 24 August, so von Ribbentrop could not reach him. Eventually, von Ribbentrop spoke to Ciano at 1:00 A.M. on 25 August. The German foreign minister was evasive about the true situation, though he spoke of Polish provocations pushing the situation to a breaking point. Ciano spoke to Mussolini the following morning. Initially, Mussolini ordered Ciano to draft instructions for Attolico on the prospective course of action; if the conflict remained localized, then Italy would give Germany every political and military aid requested. If, however, the Western democracies intervened, then Italy would not initiate hostilities. Italian forces would only be able to pin down as many French and British units as possible. After issuing these instructions, however, Mussolini again changed his mind, determining that Italy would have to intervene in order to keep faith with its German ally. Ciano had a long conversation with the Duce, and Mussolini temporarily acquiesced in light of Italy's strategic weakness. Ciano returned to the Palazzo Chigi, only to have Mussolini issue another summons. Mussolini had made yet another about-face, deciding that Italy could not risk German reprisals; Italy would have to enter the war immediately. While he and Ciano debated the issue, Ciano had to cancel Attolico's instructions. Attolico received this note while sitting in Hitler's antechamber; Attolico had to explain that he no longer had the instructions that had led him to request the audience in the first place.[140]

In the afternoon, a message from Hitler to Mussolini arrived. It contained a vague and inaccurate explanation of the Nazi-Soviet Pact as well as discussion of the benefits that the agreement would bring for the Axis alliance, particularly in intimidating the countries of Eastern Europe. It also asked for Italian understanding of the German position regarding Poland.[141] The message changed nothing, but news of German troop movements and the knowledge that Britain had concluded a military alliance with Poland placed more pressure on Mussolini to decide on a definitive course of action. The Chamberlain cabinet would hardly conclude an alliance only to break it immediately, so its signature presented certain proof that the war would not remain localized. At Ciano's urging, Mussolini at last reached a decision. Mussolini obviously craved to be able to join in the coming battle. Italian prestige demanded it. Only through the crucible of war could the Duce mold the Italian people into a brutal, ascendant race. Only through victorious battle could he forge a new Roman Empire. The decisive element, however, was that a heavy-hearted Mussolini finally had to accept that Italy could not face a general war. He had hoped to be able to complete the reconstruction of his battleship fleet to counter British and French naval superiority, to attract a Japanese ally against Britain, and to separate the two Western allies, but he had not yet achieved these goals. In light of these military and diplomatic failures, the coming conflict was premature, and the military and strategic situation was too unfavorable. The Duce had to choose an extraordinarily bitter alternative to his triumphant march to victory.

Having swallowed his pride, the Duce sent Attolico a response to carry directly to Hitler. Mussolini approved of the signature of the Nazi-Soviet Pact and generally agreed with the Führer's appreciation of the agreement's effects in Eastern Europe. Consequently, Attolico informed Hitler that Italy would not "take the *initiative* in military operations given the *actual* state of Italian military preparations, repeatedly and promptly told to you, Führer, and to Herr von Ribbentrop." Still, the militaristic Mussolini could not entirely forego the chance for battle, so he included conditions that could lead to Italian participation in a general war. If Germany would make good Italian military deficiencies so that Italy could withstand an attack from the combined Anglo-French armies, then Fascist Italy would join the conflict. In the interim, the Italian military would tie down as many Anglo-French forces as possible. Even at the eleventh hour, the Duce could not abandon his hope to be able to throw Italy into the fray.[142] Nevertheless, Mussolini's message shocked Hitler. By rejecting an immediate declaration of war, the Duce was refusing to play the role as obedient ally that Hitler had cast. Faced with certain resistance from the Western democracies and seemingly abandoned by his trusted ally, Hitler hurriedly called off the attack.[143] That evening, General Roatta phoned a vastly relieved Ciano to say that Hitler had stopped the invasion.[144] Ironically, the bellicose Duce once again, however unwittingly, had played the role of peacemaker.

Later on the evening of 25 August, Hitler tried to repair the situation. He sent a note to Mussolini through von Mackensen to try to determine the supplies that Italy would need in order to enter the war and when it would need them. The German ambassador hurried to the Palazzo Venezia, where he, Mussolini, and Ciano spoke that evening. Mussolini said that he understood Hitler's desire to crush the Poles, though perhaps they could have reached a negotiated solution. The Duce reiterated his belief that a general war would be preferable only in three years' time, though he promised that Italy would stand beside Germany and would support it with all its available resources. In response to von Mackensen's probing regarding the urgent military supplies that Italy required, Mussolini replied that he needed antiaircraft batteries to protect northern Italian cities and military units, as well as raw materials. The Duce said that he would supply the complete list the following day.[145] As von Mackensen and Ciano took their leave from Mussolini, the ambassador added that he opposed war and suggested that Ciano make the list of supplies as long and detailed as possible.[146]

Throughout the following day, German officials made repeated requests to see the list of requirements.[147] On 26 August, Mussolini called a meeting of the Chiefs of Staff. Ciano and Antonio Benni, the minister of communications and a prominent industrialist, also attended. Together, they prepared a list of the minimum supplies that Italy would need in order to fight a twelve-month general war. As Ciano noted in his diary, the list was "enough to kill a bull—if a bull could read."[148] In the first year alone, it called for Germany to deliver six million tons of coal in addition to Italy's regular quota, two million tons of steel, seven million tons of petroleum, one million tons of timber, plus lesser amounts of copper, sodium nitrate, potassium salts, colophony, rubber, toluol, turpentine, lead, tin, nickel, molybdenum, tungsten, zirconium, and titanium. In addition, Italy required the immediate delivery of 150 batteries of ninety-millimeter antiaircraft guns plus ammunition. Mussolini added that if any possibility of a negotiated solution remained then he would be happy to mediate. In delivering the Duce's message, Attolico departed from his instructions, informing von Ribbentrop that Germany would have to fulfill the entire list of Italian requirements before Italian entry into the war rather than just the antiaircraft batteries Mussolini had actually specified. Although Ciano quickly rectified the error, it became obvious to Hitler that Mussolini would not join the coming battle. It would be impossible to deliver Italy's petroleum requirements, and although Hitler promised to meet the demand for coal, it was unrealistic to think that Germany could ship sufficient supplies through the bottleneck of the Brenner Pass. As it was, Germany already had had to suspend the vast majority of its coal shipments to Italy for fear of French naval action. Above all, Hitler and von Ribbentrop hoped that Mussolini would keep his decision to remain neutral confidential, thus requiring Britain and France to divert forces to defend against potential Italian attacks. Though Hitler wrote that he understood Italy's position, Mussolini's actions left the Führer disheartened. Mussolini's reply indicated his sense of betrayal for having reneged on his alliance commitment: "I leave it to you to imagine my state of mind in finding myself compelled by forces beyond my control not to afford you real solidarity at the moment of action."[149] Ciano noted in his diary that Mussolini had "had to confront the hard truth. And this, for the Duce, is a great blow." For Mussolini, Fascist Italy's failure to join the struggle represented a betrayal of his very nature. For his part, Ciano thought that his own energetic pursuit of neutrality had saved Italy from tragedy.[150]

Hitler wrote to the Duce on 27 August to release Italy from its alliance obligation to declare war. He asked only that Italy continue its military preparations in order to apply pressure on Britain and France, to send Italian agricultural and industrial workers to Germany, and to keep the decision for nonintervention secret as long as possible. In addition, von Ribbentrop asked that Fascist Italy maintain an appropriate pro-German attitude in its propaganda. Nazi leaders hoped to maintain at least the myth of Axis solidarity. Mussolini granted these requests. Having decided on neutrality, Mussolini seemed determined to salvage as much pride and prestige as he could. He promised Hitler that Italy would tie down forces on France's alpine frontier. Italy would also send reinforcements to Libya to create a greater potential threat to Egypt or Tunisia. Mussolini assured Hitler that "the world will not know the attitude of Italy before the outbreak of war, and will know instead that Italy has concentrated its forces on the frontiers of the great democracies."[151]

Although Mussolini sought to demonstrate his continued devotion to the Axis, Ciano received a further indication that his German ally might be acting in bad faith. On 25 August, Hitler had spoken to Sir Nevile Henderson, the British ambassador in Berlin. The Führer had presented an offer of an alliance with Britain, to be arranged after the settlement of Germany's dispute with Poland. This agreement would include German support for continued existence of the British empire, a promise to limit German claims for colonial restoration, and a guarantee that Germany would present no further territorial demands in the West. The alternative, Hitler argued, was a war in circumstances unfavorable to Britain. Obviously, the Führer hoped to dangle this bait in front of the cabinet in an attempt to discourage it from supporting Poland. As in the Rhineland crisis of 1936, Hitler had no intention to follow through with these proposals once they had served to beguile British statesmen. The cabinet did not take Hitler's offer very seriously. British politicians clearly understood that Hitler's proposal would require them to stand aside while he dismembered Poland, and only then would any discussions on lessening Anglo-German tension take place. They assumed that it was a rather transparent attempt to isolate Poland. Hitler's ploy, however, offered an opportunity for Whitehall to try to drive a wedge between Rome and Berlin. Loraine brought the proposal to Ciano's attention on 27 August. The promise to respect the British empire left little room for Italy to pursue its own Mediterranean conquests. Not surprisingly, an indignant Ciano, entirely in the dark about Hitler's real intentions, wondered how deeply committed the Führer remained to the principles of mutual expansion that had shaped the Pact of Steel.[152]

Whatever Ciano's personal misgivings about the alliance with Germany, however, Mussolini maintained his devotion to the Axis. Nevertheless, he hoped to find a way out of the ignominy of showing Italian military weakness. Having decided not to initiate offensive operations, he thought that a negotiated solution could prevent the outbreak of war, secure territorial gains for Italy and Germany, and restore the Axis timetable for war two to three years hence. Hitler's measured response to Italian neutrality offered hope that the Axis remained strong, and the possibility remained open that Mussolini could intercede as he had before Munich. At Ciano's urging, Mussolini dispatched a personal message for the Führer. In the Duce's view, negotiations could still accomplish Hitler's goals: acquiring Danzig and part of the corridor and settling the minority question in Poland. The propaganda victory would allow Hitler to maintain his string of foreign policy successes. A general conference could also address Italy's claims against France, colonial restoration, redistribution of raw materials, and, strangely, arms limitation. Hitler told Attolico that Britain had made approaches about some form of negotiated agreement. The Führer would only consider discussing terms of settlement directly with a Polish plenipotentiary; he would not participate in a general conference. Moreover, Hitler stated that he was skeptical about the idea that war could be averted.[153]

By 30 August, the atmosphere of impending war escalated once more. Ciano had come to believe that Hitler would not accept a negotiated solution. News of Poland's general mobilization signaled that the conflict could break out at any time. Mussolini was convinced that Germany would invade Poland as early as the following day. He ordered the Italian armed forces to carry out a substantial mobilization. Disheartened by his decision to remain neutral, Mussolini wanted to be able to issue a propaganda barrage about Italian military preparedness in the event that a negotiated solution was found, and he ordered civilian war measures such as adoption of blackout procedures. Ciano thought that the Duce's plan carried great risk. If the British and French governments believed that Italy was preparing for war, they could launch a preemptive strike against Italy or its colonies.[154]

The situation seemed increasingly desperate the next morning. At 9:00 A.M., Attolico telephoned to say that war could break out within a few hours.[155] Ciano traveled to the Palazzo Venezia to see Mussolini. They decided to phone Viscount Halifax in London, hoping that the prospect of a peaceful settlement would prove enticing for the Chamberlain-led cabinet. The minimum condition, Ciano argued, was that Poland would have to cede Danzig; otherwise, Hitler would resort to war. Halifax urged Ciano to put pressure on Hitler in Berlin to agree to direct talks between Berlin and Warsaw. Halifax phoned later to say that Britain could not agree to the Italian proposal; any settlement would have to leave Polish territory essentially intact. Consulting with Ciano, Mussolini raised the idea of a conference for 5 September that would discuss the settlement of all of the clauses of the Versailles Treaties that still disturbed the peace. Mussolini still nurtured a faint hope that Italy could profit from the crisis. Ciano supported the idea, but only because he knew that Hitler would reject it and that Hitler's rejection would establish a clear difference between the Italian and German positions. In Berlin, Attolico pursued the line of direct negotiations between Germany and Poland. Hitler dashed these faint hopes later that afternoon; he told Attolico that Polish intransigence prevented any possibility of a peaceful settlement. Still, Ciano discussed the idea of a conference with Ambassadors Loraine and François-Poncet, keeping a channel open to London and Paris. At 8:20 P.M., Ciano learned that Britain had cut its communication lines with Italy, the logical result of Mussolini's boisterous public adoption of war measures. Ciano feared that Britain and France, expecting an Italian declaration of war, might launch an attack rather than wait for Italy to clarify its position. Ciano proposed to the Duce that he should make a calculated indiscretion; he would tell Loraine that Italy would never attack Britain or France. Mussolini approved of this scheme, and Ciano summoned Loraine. Ciano's news pleased Loraine, and Mussolini lifted the blackout orders, lowering the level of tension in both Rome and London.[156]

Mussolini's German ally proved less tractable. Hitler rejected the idea of further negotiation with the Poles; he said he would launch his devastating offensive overnight. Magistrati phoned at midnight to say that German papers would carry news of the attack in the next editions. On the morning of 1 September, Ciano learned that the German invasion had begun. Ciano went to the Palazzo Venezia to meet Mussolini. The Duce maintained his commitment not to go to war. He directed that Attolico secure a formal commitment from Hitler releasing Italy from its obligation to go to war as Germany's ally. Mussolini wanted to avoid the public appearance of betrayal. Hitler sent a response through Ambassador von Mackensen stating, "In these conditions it is not necessary to involve the Italian military." Hitler added his thanks for the Duce's support in the common cause of Fascism and Nazism. Hitler included this expression of public thanks to Italy in a speech to the *Reichstag* during the morning, and, more importantly, said that Germany would not need Italian military support during its war with Poland. Ciano received Ambassadors Loraine and François-Poncet, who said that neither Great Britain nor France would launch an unprovoked attack on Italy. At 3:00 P.M., Mussolini announced Italy's position to the Council of Ministers in Rome. He still could not bring himself to declare official Italian neutrality, but he did say that Italy would not take the initiative in military operations. He publicly broadcast Hitler's message releasing Italy from its military obligations.[157]

Ciano, secure in the belief that he had saved Italy from the immediate tragedy, turned to efforts to save the wider peace. He still maintained a faint hope that some form of negotiated settlement could result in gains for the Axis. The last, quixotic effort occurred owing to a fundamental misunderstanding. Ciano had mentioned Mussolini's idea for a conference to discuss issues stemming from the Versailles Treaty to both Ambassadors Loraine and François-Poncet. On 1 September, the French Council of

Ministers accepted Mussolini's proposal, as it appeared to be the last diplomatic channel to pursue. While Viscount Halifax was potentially willing to discuss terms of settlement, he refused to place any pressure on Warsaw. On the contrary, he demanded that Hitler would have to agree to a complete withdrawal of German forces from Poland before any further conversations could take place. Halifax clearly thought this eventuality unlikely, but he preferred to leave the door open. In Paris, Foreign Minister Georges Bonnet desperately sought to avoid a military confrontation, and he was willing to undertake discussions if Hitler would agree to a ceasefire that would leave German troops in place. In agreeing to Italy's proposal for a conference on that basis, Bonnet did not inform Rome that he did not even have the complete support of his own Premier, never mind agreement from Halifax. On Mussolini's instructions, Attolico tried to see von Ribbentrop, but the German foreign minister was unavailable. Attolico informed von Weizsäcker that Italian diplomats had secured French agreement for a conference within two to three days, provided that an armistice prevented further combat. The armies would remain temporarily in place. Attolico argued that such a conference would certainly have a favorable outcome for Germany. Ciano initially was surprised that Hitler would consider the idea. That evening, however, Halifax telephoned Ciano, making it clear that the minimum British condition would require a complete German withdrawal, and Ciano knew that Hitler would never agree to that demand. Consequently, Ciano let the discussions for Mussolini's conference lapse.[158] The impossibility of halting the war became entirely apparent on the morning of 3 September. As of 11:00 A.M., the British ultimatum expired, and as of 5:00 P.M., so did the French one. Britain and France were at war with Germany. Ciano received a note from Hitler for the Duce, saying that Germany could not consider accepting a withdrawal dictated by Great Britain, especially in light of the tremendous advances that the *Wehrmacht* had made; in the Führer's view, Polish resistance would collapse shortly. Hitler also argued that Britain and France would in any event eventually have closed the gap between their military capability and Germany's, so war in these circumstances was opportune. The time for harsh action had arrived. The note concluded with Hitler's belief that the two Fascist regimes would march together one day to meet their common destiny.[159] Although Italy had managed initially to avoid the premature war that Hitler had willed, Mussolini's nature would not allow him to remain on the sidelines indefinitely. Ciano's efforts to evade the conflict would ultimately founder on the shoals of the Duce's driving, social Darwinist ambition to rule the Mediterranean.

NOTES

1. Both quoted in Toscano, *The Origins of the Pact of Steel,* 368, from *Giornale d'Italia,* 23 May 1939.

2. Schmundt Minute, 23 May 1939, *DGFP,* ser. D, vol. 6, no. 433, 574–80. For more detail on Hitler's foreign policy in the summer of 1938, see Weinberg, *Starting World War II,* 557–95.

3. Attolico to Ciano, 26 May 1939, 27 May 1939, 31 May 1939, *DDI,* 8th ser., vol. 12, no. 33, no. 47, no. 72, 22, 31–32, 60.

4. Raeder to Cavagnari, 17 May 1939, *DGFP,* ser. D, vol. 6, appendix 1, no. 7, 1116; Löwisch to Keitel, 1 June 1939, *DGFP,* ser. D, vol. 6, appendix 1, no. 9, 1117–9.

5. Giannini to Ciano, 26 May 1939, *DDI,* 8th ser., vol. 12, no. 29, 20; von Weizsäcker Memoranda, 19 March 1939, 21 March 1939, 7 April 1939, *DGFP,* ser. D, vol. 6, no. 44, no. 62, no. 174, 47–48, 73, 210–11; Clodius to von Mackensen, 8 April 1939, *DGFP,* ser. D, vol. 6, no. 175, 211; von Mackensen to von Ribbentrop, 10 May 1939, *DGFP,* ser. D, vol. 6, no. 360, 470–71; Clodius Memorandum, n.d., *DGFP,* ser. D, vol. 6, no. 360, 557–58.

6. Note del Duce per il Fuehrer, 30 May 1939, ASMAE, UC 87, UC 7 (*DDI,* 8th ser., vol. 12, no. 59, 49–50).

7. Ciano to Attolico, 31 May 1939, *DDI,* 8th ser., vol. 12, no. 65, 56; Ciano to von Ribbentrop, 31 May 1939, *DDI,* 8th ser., vol. 12, no. 71, 59; Ciano to von Ribbentrop, 31 May 1939, *DGFP,* ser. D, vol. 6, no. 459, 617–18; Mussolini Memorandum for the Führer, 30 May 1939, *DGFP,* ser. D, vol. 6, 618–620.

8. Cavallero to Ciano, 3 June 1939, *DDI,* 8th ser., vol. 12, no. 84–85; Attolico to Ciano, 5, 6 June 1939, *DDI,* 8th ser., vol. 12, no. 114, no. 130, 94, 112.

9. Von Weizsäcker Memorandum, 19 June 1939, *DGFP,* ser. D, vol. 6, no. 546, 749–50. Anfuso to Ciano, 14 July 1939, ASMAE, UC 8. In his memoirs, von Weizsäcker claimed that Hitler made no reply to this letter and that there had been no indication of a three- to four-year period of peace in the terms of the treaty. His memory failed on the first point. On the second, it is certainly true that the desire for a peaceful policy did not appear in the treaty, but von Weizsäcker also failed to mention the repeated discussions before the conclusion of the treaty on precisely that point (Ernst von Weizsäcker, *Erinnerungen* [Munich: Paul List, 1950], 185).

10. *CD,* 31 May 1939, 96–97.

11. *CD,* 10–13 May 1939, 15 May 1939, 18 May 1939, 85–87, 87–88, 89.

12. Erich Kordt Memorandum, 23 May 1939, *DGFP,* ser. D, vol. 6, no. 431, 571; von Mackensen to von Ribbentrop, 31 May 1939, *DGFP,* ser. D, vol. 6, no. 45, 613.

13. Ciano Appunto, 26 May 1939, ASMAE, UC 49. Bombelles to Anfuso, 29 May 1939, ASMAE, UC 49; Carnelutti to Anfuso, 30 May 1939, ASMAE, UC 49; *CD,* 18 May 1939, 24 May 1939, 26 May 1939, 31 May 1939, 89, 91–92, 93, 96–97. For Bombelles's perceptions of Croat and Serb policy, see Bombelles to Ciano, 7 May 1939, 14 May 1939, ASMAE, GAB 440, both initialled by Mus-

solini. Mussolini marked passages indicating that Maček aimed for Croat independence and arguing that Serb Generals loyal to the Black Hand would ensure
that the Yugoslav state would ultimately orient itself with Britain and France and
against the Axis.

14. For more on Bulgarian politics during the interwar period, see Rothschild,
East Central Europe between the Two World Wars, 348–53.

15. Ciano appunto, ASMAE, UC 85, 30 May 1939; Ciano to Talamo, 30 May
1939, *DDI,* 8th ser., vol. 12, 50; *CD,* 12 May 1939, 29 May 1939, 20 June 1939,
86–87, 95, 105.

16. De Peppo to Ciano, 13 June 1939, *DDI,* 8th ser., vol. 12, no. 217, 187–88;
Talamo to Ciano, 13 June 1939, *DDI,* 8th ser., vol. 12, no. 214, 185–86.

17. Ciano to De Peppo (Ankara), 10 April 1939, ASMAE, UC 53; Mussolini
to De Peppo, 12 April 1939, ASMAE, UC 53; De Peppo to Ciano, 10 June 1939
(two correspondences), 20 June 1939, *DDI,* 8th ser., vol. 12, no. 178, no. 179, no.
289, 158, 159, 238–41; Ciano to De Peppo, 15 June 1939, *DDI,* 8th ser., vol. 12,
no. 235, 202–3; Guariglia to Ciano, 25 June 1939, *DDI,* 8th ser., vol. 12, no. 351,
282. For Turkish qualifications of its military obligations in support of the Anglo-
French guarantee to Romania, see Halifax to Knatchbull-Hugessen (Ankara), 26
April 1939, FO 371 23742, R3325/661/67 and Memorandum for Cabinet, 9 May
1939, FO 371 23742, R3858/661/67.

18. Ciano to Viola, 1 June 1939, *DDI,* 8th ser., vol. 12, no. 76, 62; *CD,* 1 June
1939, 5 June 1939, 9 June 1939, 10 June 1939, 12 June 1939, 13 June 1939, 97,
99–100, 101–2, 102, 103, 103–4; von Mackensen to von Ribbentrop, 8 June 1939,
DGFP, ser. D, vol. 6, no. 494, 665; von Mackensen to von Weizsäcker, 10 June
1939, *DGFP,* ser. D, vol. 6, no. 506, 695–97; von Mackensen to von Ribbentrop,
DGFP, ser. D, vol. 6, no. 525, 723–25. For British estimates on the Spanish position, see Roberts Memorandum, 17 April 1939, FO 371 23983, W6272/108/50.
Roberts concluded that owing to its war weariness, Spain would maintain a wait-
and-see attitude of neutrality favorable to the Axis, holding out for the eventual
possibility of seizing Gibraltar. For Franco's attitude, see Preston, *General Staffs
and Diplomacy before the Second World War,* 328–34.

19. Auriti to Ciano, 26 May 1939, ASMAE, UC 71; Auriti to Ciano, 25 May
1939, 26 May 1939, *DDI,* 8th ser., vol. 12, no. 14, no. 32, 13, 21; Giorgis to Mussolini, 27 May 1939, *DDI,* 8th ser., vol. 12, no. 14, no. 49, 34–41; Ott to von
Ribbentrop, 17 May 1939, 23 May 1939, *DGFP,* ser. D, vol. 6, no. 400, no. 427,
522–23; 564–65.

20. Attolico to Ciano, 27 May 1939, 29 May 1939, ASMAE, UC 71 (*DDI,* 8th
ser., vol. 12, no. 48, no. 53, 32–34, 44–46).

21. Auriti to Ciano, 5 June 1939, 6 June 1939, ASMAE, UC 71 (*DDI,* 8th ser.,
vol. 12, no. 111, no. 126, 93, 110–11);. Attolico to Ciano, 29 May 1939, *DDI,* 8th
ser., vol. 12, no. 53, 44–46; Auriti to Ciano, 5 June 1939, *DDI,* 8th ser., vol. 12,
no. 110, 92–93; Ott to von Ribbentrop, 27 May 1939, 3 June 1939, *DGFP,* ser. D,
vol. 6, no. 444, no. 467, 594–95, 629; von Ribbentrop to Ott, 28 May 1939,
DGFP, ser. D, vol. 6, no. 447, 599–600.

22. Attolico to Ciano, 16 June 1939, ASMAE, UC 71 (*DDI,* 8th ser., vol. 12, no. 254, 211–17); Attolico to Ciano, 15 June 1939, *DDI,* 8th ser., vol. 12, no. 203; von Weizsäcker Memorandum, 16 June 1939, *DGFP,* ser. D, vol. 6, no. 535, 734; von Ribbentrop to Ott, 17 June 1939, *DGFP,* ser. D, vol. 6, no. 538, 737–40.

23. Auriti to Ciano, 21 June 1939 (two correspondences), 22 June 1939, ASMAE, UC 71; Auriti to Ciano, 19 June 1939, 21 June 1939, 22 June 1939, *DDI,* 8th ser., vol. 12, no. 274, no. 294, no. 303, 229, 246, 251; Ott to von Ribbentrop, 20 June 1939, *DGFP,* ser. D, vol. 6, no. 538, 750–51.

24. Attolico to Ciano, 16 June 1939, ASMAE, UC 71. Mussolini underlined this passage.

25. *CD,* 3 May 1939, 82.

26. Loraine to Halifax, 16 May 1939, FO 371 23797, R4103/9/22. For the text of the Duce's speech, see "Discorso a Torino," 14 May 1939 and "Il Popolo d'Italia," 15 May 1939, *OO,* vol. 29, 272–75.

27. Sargent Minute, 19 May 1939, FO 371 23797, R4103/9/22; see also Noble Minute, 17 May 1939, FO 371 23797, R4103/9/22.

28. Grandi to Ciano, 25 May 1939, *DDI,* 8th ser., vol. 12, 13–14.

29. CID Notes of a meeting of ministers, 10 April 1939, FO 371 23982, W5991/105/80 and 10 April 1939, CAB 27/624 FP 36 (41), 11 April 1939, CAB 27/624 FP 36 (42). For the British strategic appreciation on Turkey, Greece and the Eastern Mediterranean, see 31 March 1939, CAB 55/15, C.O.S. 383.

30. *CD,* 25 May 1939, 27 May 1939, 92–93, 93–94; Loraine to Halifax, 27 May 1939, FO 371 23785, R4399/1/22. Loraine's account and Ciano's differ slightly, with Loraine's giving a slightly more flattering portrayal of his performance while Ciano lauded Mussolini's. Ciano did agree that Loraine presented a stout defense. For an assessment of Loraine's tenure in Rome, see Gordon Waterfield, *Professional Diplomat: Sir Percy Loraine of Kinharle Bt., 1880–1961* (London: John Murray, 1973), 228–78.

31. *CD,* 27 May 1939, 93–94. Ciano related the nature of Mussolini's meetings with Loraine to the German Ambassador (*CD,* 30 May 1939, 95–96; von Mackensen to von Ribbentrop, 31 May 1939, *DGFP,* ser. D, vol. 6, no. 456, 613–14).

32. Loraine to Halifax, 27 May 1939, FO 371 23785, R4400/1/22.

33. Halifax to Loraine, 4 June 1939, FO 371 23785, R4399/1/22.

34. Loraine aide-memoire, 8 June 1939, ASMAE, SAP—Gran Bretagna, B 35; *CD,* 8 June 1939, 101; Halifax to Loraine, 4 June 1939, FO 371 23785, R4399/1/22. Loraine to Halifax, 8 June 1939, FO 371 23785, R4746/1/22. Ciano provided a summary of the British response to von Mackensen (von Mackensen to von Ribbentrop, 10 June 1939, *DGFP,* ser. D, vol. 6, no. 505, 694–95).

35. Halifax Memorandum, 6 June 1939, FO 371 23785, R4685/1/22.

36. Loraine to Halifax, 21 June 1939, 24 June 1939, FO 371 23785, R5063/1/22 and FO 371 23785, R5168/1/22. The Tientsin crisis occurred over the issue of the small British extraterritorial concession in the northern Chinese city of Tientsin, garrisoned by a single battalion of British infantry. The Japanese had

several divisions of soldiers in the area, giving Japan a decisive edge in the event of a military confrontation. Japanese army officials thought that the economic aid routed through the British concession helped substantially to support Chiang Kai-Shek's forces. On 14 June 1939, Japanese troops blockaded Tientsin over a convoluted question of treatment of alleged terrorists. Japanese and British negotiators reached a tentative framework for an agreement on 24 July. For more information, see, for example, Watt, *How War Came,* 349–59, and Iriye, *Origins of the Second World War in Asia and the Pacific,* 76–77.

37. Ciano to Crolla, 19 June 1939, *DDI,* 8th ser., vol. 12, no. 279, no. 280, 231–33.

38. Halifax to Phipps, 20 April 1939, FO 371 23794, R3077/7/22. 21 April 1939, CAB 23/98, 18 (39). For more on Anglo-French relations, see Young, *In Command of France,* 230–32, and passim.

39. Phipps to Halifax, 22 April 1939, FO 371 23795, R3166/7/22; Halifax Memorandum, 26 April 1939, FO 371 23795, R3323/7/22, .

40. Halifax Memorandum, 26 April 1939, FO 371 23795, R3323/7/22.

41. *CD,* 25 April 1939, 77, 77–78.

42. Phipps to Halifax, 27 April 1939, FO 371 23795, R3350/7/22; Phipps to Halifax, 1 May 1939, FO 371 23795, R3498/7/22; Phipps to Halifax, 5 May 1939, FO 371 23795, R3675/7/22; Halifax Memorandum, 8 May 1939, FO 371 23795, R3788/7/22; U.K. Delegation (Geneva), 22 May 1939, FO 371 23795, R4278/7/22.

43. On instructions, François-Poncet made a specific request to Ciano to submit a written list of Italian demands (Bonnet to François-Poncet, 3 May 1939, *DDF,* 2d ser., vol. 16, no. 21, 46–47; François-Poncet to Bonnet, 4 May 1939, *DDF,* 2d ser., vol. 16, no. 43, 105–6; Bonnet Note, 5 May 1939, *DDF,* 2d ser., vol. 16, no. 76, 150–52; see also *CD,* 10 May 1939, 12 May 1939, 85, 86).

44. Anfuso appunto, 18 May 1939, ASMAE, UC 61; Signed by Mussolini, 19 May 1939, ASMAE, UC 61; Anfuso to Suster, 22 May 1939, ASMAE, UC 61.

45. Rocca to Guarneri, 26 May 1939, ASMAE, UC 61; Signed by Mussolini, 2 June 1939, ASMAE, UC 61. William Shorrock strongly criticized Daladier for the alleged failure to make a timely approach to Mussolini. Shorrock argued that had Daladier made a determined effort to reach an accommodation with Mussolini in the immediate aftermath of Hitler's occupation of Prague it stood a good chance of success. He also charged that Daladier's failure to do so effectively drove Mussolini into the alliance with Hitler, as Mussolini had learned that he had no other friend in Europe (Shorrock, *From Ally to Enemy,* 267–69). This view is seriously in error. It ignores entirely Mussolini's long-term territorial demands against France that no French government could ever meet, and it does not adequately account for the repeated efforts that the French government made to establish a sound basis for talks, especially in the immediate aftermath of Hitler's occupation of Prague. Mussolini deliberately chose to ignore several French initiatives, as he did not want a premature settlement with France that could prejudice his greater and longer-term historical objectives.

46. Wilson to Chamberlain, 5 June 1939, PREM 1/329; Notes of a meeting, 12 June 1939, 13 June 1939, PREM 1/329; Phipps to Chamberlain, 13 June 1939, PREM 1/329; Chamberlain to Phipps, 14 June 1939, PREM 1/329; Phipps to Chamberlain, 22 June 1939, 7 July 1939. PREM 1/329; see also Ingram Minute (including amended drafts by Cadogan and Vansittart), 13 June 1939, FO 371 23795, R4872/7/22; Phipps to Halifax, 7 July 1939, FO 371 23795, R5613/7/22; Halifax to Phipps, 17 July 1939, FO 371 23795, R5613/7/22. For yet another attempt to restore discussions with Italy, see Guariglia to Ciano, 6 June 1939, *DDI*, 8th ser., vol. 12, no. 128, 111.

47. Löwisch to Keitel, 1 June 1939, *DGFP,* ser. D, vol. 6, appendix 1, no. 9, 117–19.

48. Mössel Memorandum, 12 June 1939, *DGFP,* ser. D, vol. 6, appendix I, no. 10, 1119.

49. Unsigned Memorandum, 20–21 June 1939, *DGFP,* ser. D, vol. 6, appendix I, no. 12, 1121–13. Cavagnari's report was a reasonably accurate portrayal of Italian naval and military plans in the "Direttive per l'azione delle forze armate dell'Impero in caso di improvviso conflitto." For further details, see Mallet, *The Italian Navy and Fascist Expansion 1935–1940,* 133–35, 140–45.

50. Fricke Memorandum, 21 June 1939, *DGFP,* ser. D, vol. 6, appendix I, no. 13, 1124–25.

51. See especially Cavallero to Ciano, 25 June 1939, *DDI,* 8th ser., vol. 12, no. 349, 278–79, but also von Ribbentrop to Ciano, 9 June 1939, *DDI,* 8th ser., vol. 12, no. 171, 149–50; Cavallero to Ciano, 10, 12 June 1939, 161, 174, *DDI,* 8th ser., vol. 12, no. 182, 199; Attolico to Ciano, 11, 12 June 1939, *DDI,* 8th ser., vol. 12, no. 186, no. 200, 166, 174–75. For more on the context of these meetings, see Lucio Ceva, "Altre notizie sulle conversazioni militari italo-tedesche alla vigilia della seconda guerra mondiale (aprile-giugno 1939)," *Il Risorgimento* 30, no. 3 (1978): 151–82; and Gerhard Schreiber, "Political and Military Developments in the Mediterranean Area, 1939–40," in *Germany and the Second World War. Volume III: The Mediterranean, South-east Europe and North Africa, 1939–1941,* eds. Wilhelm Diest et al. (Oxford, U.K.: Clarendon, 1995), 9–10.

52. Attolico to Ciano, 1 July 1939, *DDI,* 8th ser., vol. 12, no. 428, 328–30.

53. Von Weizsäcker Memorandum, 1 April 1939, *DGFP,* ser. D, vol. 6, no. 143, 179; Heinburg Memorandum, 5 April 1939, *DGFP,* ser. D, vol. 6, no. 163, 198–200. For reference to otherwise unpublished documents from the Himmler papers, see Conrad F. Latour, *Südtirol und die Asche Berlin-Rom, 1938–1945* (Stuttgart: Deutsche Verlags-Anstalt, 1962), 31–37.

54. *CD,* 17 April 1939, 20 April 1939, 105–6, 106; Attolico to Ciano, 24 June 1939, *DDI,* 8th ser., vol. 12, no. 328, 266.

55. *CD,* 21 June 1939, 23 June 1939, 3 July 1939, 6 July 1939, 106, 106–7, 113–14, 114–15; Attolico to Ciano, 24 June 1939, 4 July 1939, 5 July 1939, 5 July 1939, *DDI,* 8th ser., vol. 12, no. 334, no. 454, no. 475, no. 474, 269–70, 345, 359, 359; Woermann to von Mackensen, 24 June 1939, *DGFP,* ser. D, vol. 6, no. 562, 778–79.

56. Attolico to Ciano, 7 July 1939, *DDI,* 8th ser., vol. 12, no. 493, 373; Siegfried Memorandum, 6 July 1939, *DGFP,* ser. D, vol. 6, no. 624, 866; Attolico to von Ribbentrop, 7 July 1939, *DGFP,* ser. D, vol. 6, no. 631, 878–79; von Weizsäcker to von Mackensen and the Consul General Milan, 10 July 1939, *DGFP,* ser. D, vol. 6, no. 643, 889–90.

57. Attolico to Ciano, 23 June 1939, *DDI,* 8th ser., vol. 12, no. 323, 263–64. For a description of Göring's speech, see Arone (Warsaw) to Ciano, 23 June 1939, *DDI,* 8th ser., vol. 12, no. 324, 264.

58. Arone to Ciano, 28 June 1939, 30 June 1939, *DDI,* 8th ser., vol. 12, no. 384, no. 415, 302–21.

59. Attolico to Ciano, 26 June 1939, ASMAE, UC 8 (*DDI,* 8th ser., vol. 12, no. 367, 291); Attolico to Ciano, 28 June 1939, ASMAE, UC 8.

60. Ciano to Attolico, 2 July 1939, ASMAE, UC 8 (*DDI,* 8th ser., vol. 12, no. 432, 332).

61. Attolico to Ciano, 4 July 1939, 5 July 1939, *DDI,* 8th ser., vol. 12, no. 466, no. 474, 353, 359.

62. Mussolini appunto, 3 July 1939, ASMAE, UC 8 (*DDI,* 8th ser., vol. 12, no. 443, 338). Unattributable autograph, 3 July 1939, *DDI,* 8th ser., vol. 12, no. 444, 338–39.

63. *CD,* 3 July 1939, 4 July 1939, 5 July 1939, 113–14, 114, 114.

64. Attolico to Ciano, 7 July 1939 (two correspondences), ASMAE, UC 8 (*DDI,* 8th ser., vol. 12, no. 495, no. 503, 377, 378–81). For Attolico's phone call, see Attolico to Ciano, 7 July 1939, *DDI,* 8th ser., vol. 12, no. 504, 381; Attolico to Ciano, 7 July 1939, *DDI,* 8th ser., vol. 12, no. 495, 379.

65. *Ciano to Attolico,* 9 July 1939, ASMAE, UC 8 (*DDI,* 8th ser., vol. 12, no. 518, 389).

66. Attolico to Anfuso, 11 July 1939, ASMAE, UC 8 (*DDI,* 8th ser., vol. 12, no. 535, 399–402).

67. Anfuso to Ciano, 14 July 1939, ASMAE, UC 8; Anfuso to Ciano, 12 July 1939, *DDI,* 8th ser., vol. 12, no. 540, 405; Attolico to Ciano, 13 July 1939, *DDI,* 8th ser., vol. 12, no. 540, 418; Pittalis (Munich) to Ciano, 13 July 1939, *DDI,* 8th ser., vol. 12, no. 540, 433.

68. Attolico to Ciano, 17 May 1939, *DDI,* 8th ser., vol. 12, no. 598, 449–50.

69. For rumors of Spanish approaches to France and its alleged estrangement from Italy, see Guariglia to Ciano, 22 June 1939, ASMAE, SAP—Francia, B 42; Viola to Ciano, 26 July 1939, ASMAE, SAP—Francia, B 42; Viola to Ciano, 24 June 1939, *DDI,* 8th ser., vol. 12, no. 333, 268–69.

70. For the text of the Duce's message, see Mussolini to Franco, 6 July 1939, *DDI,* 8th ser., vol. 12, no. 488, 368. The two leaders exchanged further messages of goodwill (Mussolini to Franco, 18 July 1939, *DDI,* 8th ser., vol. 12, no. 602, 452; Franco to Mussolini, 18 July 1939, *DDI,* 8th ser., vol. 12, no. 603, 452–53).

71. Colloquio del Conte Ciano col Generalissimo Franco, 19 July 1939, ASMAE, UC 47, UC 85 (*DDI,* 8th ser., vol. 12, no. 61, 458–62). For a published translation, see *CDP,* 290–95. For more in a similar vein, see Franco's conversa-

tion with Guido Viola, the Italian Ambassador, Viola to Ciano, 5 July 1939, *DDI,* 8th ser., vol. 12, no. 480, 362.

72. Admiral Canaris, Chief the Abwehr, provided an assessment of Spanish military problems to Italy's intelligence services (Lais to Cavagnari, 22 July 1939, ASMAE, UC 8 [*DDI,* 8th ser., vol. 12, no. 648, 485–57]). Canaris also indicated his belief that Hitler would make sure that there could be no peaceful solution of the Danzig crisis.

73. *CD,* 19 July 1939, 21 July 1939, 22 July 1939, 115–16, 116, 117.

74. Mussolini to Magistrati, 24 July 1939, ASMAE, UC 8 (*DDI,* 8th ser., vol. 12, no. 662, 497–500).

75. Mussolini provided the emphasis. (Mussolini to Magistrati, 24 July 1939, ASMAE, UC 8 [*DDI,* 8th ser., vol. 12, no. 662, 497–500]). For Ciano's instructions to Attolico, see Ciano to Attolico, 22 July 1939, *DDI,* 8th ser., vol. 12, no. 640, 481; Attolico to Ciano, 22 July 1939, *DDI,* 8th ser., vol. 12, no. 641, 481. For Attolico's account of the conversation, see Attolico to Ciano, 26 July 1939, ASMAE, UC 8 (*DDI,* 8th ser., vol. 12, no. 687, 517–22). For the German record, see Brücklmeier Memorandum, 25 July 1939, *DGFP,* ser. D, vol. 6, no. 718, 984–92. Late in 1942, the Italian Foreign Ministry inquired whether or not Attolico and Magistrati had left a written aide-memoire with von Ribbentrop or had only delivered the information orally. If Magistrati had left a written copy, then it would provide Germany with the only written evidence that Italy had promised to follow Germany's entrance into war (Nel riguardo la nota consegnata al Magistrati sul 24 maggio 1939, 2 October 1942, ASMAE, UC 8). Magistrati recalled that he had given a written copy to von Ribbentrop. Before leaving for Salzburg, Attolico had confirmed the lines of Mussolini's message in a discussion with von Weizsäcker (von Weizsäcker Memorandum, 24 July 1939, *DGFP,* ser. D, vol. 6, no. 711, 971–72; *CD,* 24 July 1939, 118).

76. Attolico to Ciano, 26 July 1939, ASMAE, UC 8 (Attolico to Ciano, *DDI,* 8th ser., vol. 12, no. 687, 517–22); Attolico to Ciano, 26 July 1939, *DDI,* 8th ser., vol. 12, no. 677, no. 678, 512–13, 513; see also Magistrati's cover letter for Attolico's report, Magistrati to Ciano, 27 July 1939, *DDI,* 8th ser., vol. 12, no. 702, 530; Brücklmeier Memorandum, 25 July 1939, *DGFP,* ser. D, vol. 6, 984–92. For the draft communiqué, see Draft communiqué, 22 July 1939, *DDI,* 8th ser., vol. 12, no. 647, 485.

77. Attolico to Ciano, 26 July 1939 (two correspondences), ASMAE, UC 8 (Attolico to Ciano, *DDI,* 8th ser., vol. 12, no. 687, no. 687, 517–22); *CD,* 26 July 1939, 27 July 1939, 28 July 1939, 118–19, 119, 119.

78. Attolico to Ciano, 28 July 1939, 1 August 1939, ASMAE, UC 8 (*DDI,* 8th ser., vol. 12, no. 717, no. 743, 536–38, 559–62);. Attolico to Ciano, 31 July 1939, *DDI,* 8th ser., vol. 12, no. 731, no. 732, 549, 549–50; *CD,* 28 July 1939, 30 July 1939, 2 August 1939, 119–20, 120, 120.

79. Magistrati to Ciano, *DDI,* 8th ser., vol. 12, no. 740, 555–56; *CD,* 3 August 1939, 120–21.

80. Roatta (Berlin) to Mussolini, 2 August 1939, 3 August 1939, ASMAE, UC 8; Attolico to Ciano, 4 August 1939, ASMAE, UC 8 (*DDI,* 8th ser., vol. 12, no. 750, no. 759, no. 767, 566–68, 572, 575).

81. Quoted in *CD,* 6 August 1939, 121–22.

82. For more on Italy's financial situation, see Catalano, *L'economia italiana di guerra,* 26–28.

83. *CD,* 6 August 1939, 7 August 1939, 9 August 1939, 121–22, 122; von Weizsäcker Memorandum, 7 August 1939, *DGFP,* ser. D, vol. 6, no. 777, 1073.

84. Crolla to Ciano, 30 June 1939, *DDI,* 8th ser., vol. 12, no. 408, 318.

85. Loraine pro-memoria, 7 July 1939, *DDI,* 8th ser., vol. 12, no. 463, 349–50.

86. Quoted in *CD,* 7 July 1939, 115.

87. Mussolini to Ciano, 7 July 1939, *DDI,* 8th ser., vol. 12, no. 505, 381–82.

88. Loraine to Halifax, 10 July 1939, FO 371 23818, R5652/399/22; Loraine to Halifax, 14 July 1939, FO 371 23786, R5788/1/22.

89. Attolico to Ciano, 13 July 1939, ASMAE, UC 8 (*DDI,* 8th ser., vol. 12, no. 562, 424–25).

90. Crolla to Ciano, 18 July 1939,ASMAE, SAP—Gran Bretagna, B 32.

91. Von Mackensen to von Ribbentrop, 13 May 1939, *DGFP,* ser. D, vol. 6, no. 377, 487–88.

92. Loraine to Halifax, Halifax to Loraine, 25 July 1939, FO 371 23786, R6049/1/22; Loraine to Halifax, 1 August 1939, FO 371 23786R6474.

93. Guariglia to Ciano, 25 July 1939, *DDI,* 8th ser., vol. 12, no. 673, 507.

94. Capranica (Paris) to Ciano, 1 August 1939, *DDI,* 8th ser., vol. 12, no. 745, 562; Margottini (Paris) to Ciano, 28 July 1939, *DDI,* 8th ser., vol. 12, no. 745, 563–64.

95. Auriti to Ciano, 24 June 1939, 26 June 1939, 29 June 1939, 3 July 1939, 4 July 1939, 10 July 1939, 11 July 1939, 24 July 1939, 25 July 1939, 28 July 1939, ASMAE, UC 71.

96. 9 August 1939, 10 August 1939, 11 August 1939, August 1939, ASMAE, UC 71 (*DDI,* 8th ser., vol. 12, no. 834, 619);. Ott to von Ribbentrop, 3 August 1939, *DGFP,* ser. D, vol. 6, no. 762, 1052; Ott to von Ribbentrop, 10 August 1939, *DGFP,* ser. D, vol. 7, no. 7, 6–7. On 9 August, Ambassador Shiratori told Ciano that the Japanese government was ready to sign the alliance. An openly skeptical Ciano questioned Shiratori's news, as he had received many false rumors in the past (*CD,* 9 August 1939, 123).

97. Vinci to Ciano, 20 June 1939, 26 June 1939 (two correspondences), 22 July 1939, *DDI,* 8th ser., vol. 12, no. 287, no. 350, no. 368, no. 643, 237–38, 280–82, 291–92, 482; Attolico to Ciano, 20 June 1939, *DDI,* 8th ser., vol. 12, no. 290, 241.

98. Attolico to Ciano, 1 July 1939, *DDI,* 8th ser., vol. 12, no. 426, 327–28; Ciano to Attolico, 7 July 1939, *DDI,* 8th ser., vol. 12, no. 506, 382; Vinci to Ciano, 13 July 1939, 15 July 1939, 419, *DDI,* 8th ser., vol. 12, no. 557, no. 582, 435–36.

99. Teleki to Mussolini, 24 July 1939, *DDI,* 8th ser., vol. 12, no. 663, no. 664, 500–1, 501.

100. Attolico to Ciano, 24 July 1939, 10 August 1939, *DDI*, 8th ser., vol. 12, no. 660, no. 827, 496–97, 615; De Paolis (Rome) to Ciano, 12 August 1939, *DDI*, 8th ser., vol.13, no. 3, 4. *CD*, 24 July 1939, 25 July 1939, 26 July 1939, 118–19; Attolico to von Weizsäcker, 29 July 1939, *DGFP*, ser. D, vol. 6, no. 739, 1018–19.

101. De Peppo (Ankara) to Ciano, 13 June 1939, *DDI*, 8th ser., vol. 12, no. 217, 187–88. Daneo (Sofia) to Ciano, 21 June 1939, *DDI*, 8th ser., vol. 12, no. 300, 248.

102. Attolico to Ciano, 6 July 1939, *DDI*, 8th ser., vol. 12, no. 490, 369–71; Talamo (Sofia) to Ciano, 8 July 1939, 12 July 1939, 13 July 1939, 3 August 1939, *DDI*, 8th ser., vol. 12, no. 510, no. 551, no. 559, 383–84, 414–17, 420–22, 573–74; Guidotti (Belgrade) to Ciano, 11 July 1939, 12 July 1939, *DDI*, 8th ser., vol. 12, no. 532, no. 548, 397–98; De Peppo (Ankara) to Ciano, 26 July 1939, 5 August 1939, *DDI*, 8th ser., vol. 12, no. 690, no. 782, 523–24, 584. *CD*, 28 July 1939, 119–20.

103. Indelli to Ciano, 12 June 1939, *DDI*, 8th ser., vol. 12, no. 196, 172–73; Ciano to Guidotti, 2 August 1939, *DDI*, 8th ser., vol. 12, no. 749, 566.

104. Gobbi to Anfuso, 22 June 1939, 26 June 1939, ASMAE, GAB 440 (Mussolini marked sections dealing with British pressure on Maček to reach an accord). Bombelles pro-memoria, 26 June 1939, ASMAE, GAB 440; Indelli (Belgrade) to Ciano, 22 June 1939, *DDI*, 8th ser., vol. 12, no. 313, 255; Gobbi (Zagreb) to Ciano, 1 July 1939, *DDI*, 8th ser., vol. 12, no. 738, 330–31; Guidotti (Belgrade) to Ciano, 1 August 1939, *DDI*, 8th ser., vol. 12, no. 738, 553; *CD*, 17 June 1939, 22 July 1939, 105, 117.

105. For the pessimistic appreciation of the Italian Naval Staff, see Mallett, *The Italian Navy and Fascist Expansionism*, 152–59.

106. Colloquio del Conte Ciano con il ministro degli affari esteri tedesco von Ribbentrop a Salzburg, 11 August 1939, ASMAE, UC 9, 85 (*DDI*, 8th ser., vol. 12, no. 1, 1–3). For a translation in English, see *CDP*, 297–299. *CD*, 11 August 1939, 124.

107. Primo colloquio con Hitler a Berchtesgaden, 12 August 1939, ASMAE, UC 9, 85 (*DDI*, 8th ser., vol. 13, no. 4, 4–7). For a translation in English, see *CDP*, 299–303. For the German record, see Schmidt Memorandum, 12 August 1939, *DGFP*, ser. D, vol. 7, no. 43, 39–49. Also see *CD*, 12 August 1939, 124–25.

108. Primo colloquio con Hitler a Berchtesgaden, 12 August 1939, ASMAE, UC 9, 85 (*DDI*, 8th ser., vol. 13, no. 4, 4–7). For a translation in English, see *CDP*, 299–303. For the German record, see Schmidt Memorandum, 12 August 1939, *DGFP*, ser. D, vol. 7, no. 43, 39–49. Also see *CD*, 12 August 1939, 124–25.

109. Secondo colloquio con Hitler a Berchtesgaden, 13 August 1939, ASMAE, UC 9, 85 (*DDI*, 8th ser., vol.13, no. 21, 19–20). For a translation in English, see *CDP*, 303–4. Also see *CD*, 13 August 1939, 125. For the German record, see Schmidt Memorandum, 13 August 1939, *DGFP*, ser. D, vol. 7, no. 47, 53–56.

110. *CD*, 13 August 1939, 125.

111. Colloquio del Conte Ciano con il ministro degli affari esteri tedesco von Ribbentrop a Salzburg, 11 August 1939, ASMAE, UC 9, 85 (*DDI,* 8th ser., vol. 12, no. 1, 1–3). For a translation in English, see *CDP,* 297–299. Progetto italiano di communicato per l'incontro di Salisburgo, 9 August 1939, *DDI,* 8th ser., vol. 12, no. 809, no. 810, 605–6, 606; German draft communiqué, n.d., *DDI,* 8th ser., vol. 13, no. 20, 18. *CD,* 11 August 1939, 124.

112. Emphasis in original. Attolico, 14 August 1939, ASMAE, UC 9; see also Magistrati's proposal on broadly similar lines and Ciano's response (Magistrati to Attolico, 15 August 1939, *DDI,* 8th ser., vol. 13, no. 47, 34–36; Ciano to Magistrati, 15 August 1939, ASMAE, UC 9).

113. Ciano to Attolico, 14 August 1939, ASMAE, UC 9; see also Mussolini appunto, 14 August 1939, *DDI,* 8th ser., vol. 13, no. 27, 22–23.

114. *CD,* 14 August 1939, 15 August 1939, 16 August 1939, 125–26, 126–27, 127; see also Minniti, *Fino alla guerra,* 195–97.

115. Pavelić pro-memoria, 13 July 1939, ASMAE, GAB 440, UC 49; Anfuso pro-memoria, 20 August 1939, ASMAE, UC 49; Bombelles to Anfuso, 17 July 1939, ASMAE, GAB 440; Anfuso to Gobbi (Zagreb), 6 August 1939, ASMAE, GAB 440; Anfuso appunto, 22 August 1939, ASMAE, GAB 440. After the Duce opted for neutrality in the coming war, he refused to carry out the risky undertaking of fomenting Croat secession (Anfuso appunto, 28 August 1939, ASMAE, GAB 440, on which Mussolini marked "no" in the margin of a request for funds to underwrite an Ustaša uprising).

116. *CD,* 17 August 1939, 127–28.

117. Nota sulla conversazione avvenuta al Castello di Fuschl il 18 agosto 1939, Pittalis (Munich) to Ciano, 19 August 1939, ASMAE, UC 9 (*DDI,* 8th ser., vol. 13, no. 102, no. 101, 68–71, 68).

118. Pittalis (Munich) to Ciano, 19 August 1939, ASMAE, UC 9 (*DDI,* 8th ser., vol. 13, no. 108, 73); Pittalis to Ciano, 20 August 1939, *DDI,* 8th ser., vol. 13, no. 116, 78–79. For a further conversation between Magistrati and von Weizsäcker, see von Weizsäcker Memorandum, 20 August 1939, *DGFP,* ser. D, vol. 7, no. 146, 160.

119. Roatta to Carboni (Rome), 18 August 1939, ASMAE, UC 9 (*DDI,* 8th ser., vol. 13, no. 95, 60–64).

120. Sullivan, "The Italian Armed Forces," 170–72, 191; Knox, *Common Destiny,* 120–21; Knox, *Mussolini Unleashed,* 30–33; Schreiber, "Political and Military Developments in the Mediterranean Area, 1939–40," 28–34. For the desperate state of Italy's finances, see also Catalano, *L'economia italiana di guerra,* 25–28, 37–38. For more detail on economic constraints and the Italian military, see Lucio Ceva, *Le forze armate* (Turin: UTET Libreria, 1981), and Minniti, "Le materie prime nella preparazione bellica dell'Italia, passim. Also see B.R. Mitchell, *European Historical Statistics, 1750–1975* (New York: Facts on File, 1975), 386–87, 421–22.

121. For more detailed consideration of Italian naval strategy, see Mallett, *The Italian Navy and Fascist Expansionism,* 152–55; Knox, *Common Destiny,* 121;

Knox, *Mussolini Unleashed,* 19–22; Schreiber, "Political and Military Developments in the Mediterranean Area, 1939–40," 86–89. For the belief that Britain and France would concentrate their naval power against Italy, see Signature illegible to Ciano, 1 August 1939, ASMAE, GAB 345.

122. Sullivan, "The Italian Armed Forces," 198–200; Knox, *Mussolini Unleashed,* 22–5; Lucio Ceva, "L'evoluzione dei materiali bellici in Italia," in *L'Italia e la politica di potenze in Europa (1938–40),* eds. Ennio Di Nolfo, Romain Rainero, and Brunello Vigezzi (Milan: Marzorati Editore, 1986), 359–79; Schreiber, "Political and Military Developments in the Mediterranean Area, 1939–40," 67, 78–85; For General Valle's assessment of the strategic position of the Italian air force, see von Mackensen to von Ribbentrop, 29 August 1939, *DGFP,* ser. D, vol. 7, no. 423, 417–18. In his conversation with von Mackensen, Valle emphasized that extremely limited fuel supplies would severely limit Italy's air capability.

123. John Sweet, *Iron Arm: The Mechanization of Mussolini's Army, 1920–1940* (Westport, Conn.: Greenwood Press, 1980), 132–51, 141–50, 159–61, 164, 182–83; Knox, *Mussolini Unleashed,* 25–29; Ceva, "L'evoluzione dei materiali bellici," 346–59; Schreiber, "Political and Military Developments in the Mediterranean Area, 1939–40," 66–78.

124. For Marshal Badoglio's assessment of the army's inability to carry out offensive operations, see the documentation in Emilio Faldella, *Revisione di giudizi: L'Italia e la seconda guerra mondiale,* 2d ed. (Bologna: Capelli, 1960), Badoglio to Mussolini, 17 August 1939, 31 August 1939, 132–33, 134.

125. Interestingly, the military situation was perhaps not as desperate as Mussolini's advisers thought. British strategists, for example, had determined that Anglo-French forces had very little chance of striking an early knockout blow against Italy. French troops would not attack toward Tripoli for at least two months after the outbreak of hostilities. In the meantime, Italian planes would be able to bomb Malta and perhaps Egypt. The Egyptian government feared the Axis threat and was willing to lift the treaty provision limiting the numbers of British forces available to defend the nominally independent country, but little likelihood existed of a dramatic blow against either Libya or Italy proper. In these circumstances, the British Committee of Imperial Defence argued that Italy's neutrality was preferable to its belligerence. The cabinet accepted this advice CAB 16/183a D.P. [P] [Revised], 24 July 1939; Mounsey Minute, 25 August 1939, FO 371 23786, R6812/1/22; Cadogan and Halifax Minutes, 23 August 1939, FO 371 23786, R6812/1/22; Pratt, *East of Malta, West of Suez: Britain's Mediterranean Crisis,* 185–87, 192–94). For the tendency of the Italian intelligence services and the General Staff to overestimate the power of enemy forces, see MacGregor Knox, "Fascist Italy Assesses its Enemies, 1935–1940," in *Knowing One's Enemies: Intelligence Assessment before the Two Wars,* ed. Ernest R. May (Princeton: Princeton University Press, 1984), 350–51, 358.

126. *CD,* 18 August 1939, 128–29. For Mussolini's consideration of the possible arrangement of forces in an attack on Yugoslavia, see Badoglio to Mussolini,

22 August 1939, *DDI,* 8th ser., vol. 13, no. 162, 107–8 and Mussolini to Badoglio, 23 August 1939, *DDI,* 8th ser., vol. 13, no. 162, 124. Badoglio ordered plans to be prepared urgently for possible attacks against Yugoslavia and Greece, depending on Mussolini's decisions. Schreiber, "Political and Military Developments in the Mediterranean Area, 1939–40," 53–54; Faldella, Badoglio letter to Valle, Cavagnari, Pariani, 122–23.

127. Anfuso to Ciano, 20 August 1939, *DDI,* 8th ser., vol. 13, no. 118, no. 119, 82; Jacomoni to Anfuso, 20 August 1939, *DDI,* 8th ser., vol. 13, no. 118, no. 120, 82.

128. Progetto di nota per il governo tedesco redatto il 20 agosto 1939, ASMAE, UC 9 (*DDI,* 8th ser., vol. 13, no. 123, 83); *CD,* 20 August 1939, 129–130.

129. Quoted in *CD,* 17 August 1939, 127–28; Ciano to Mussolini, 18 August 1939, *DDI,* 8th ser., vol. 13, no. 44, 54.

130. Loraine communicazione, 20 August 1939, ASMAE, UC 10.

131. *CD,* 20 August 1939, 129–30. Ciano received similar though less forceful and official notices from French sources (Magistrati to Ciano, 15 August 1939, 33, *DDI,* 8th ser., vol. 13 no. 45; Guargiglia to Ciano, 22 August 1939, *DDI,* 8th ser., vol. 13, no. 153, 103).

132. *CD,* 21 August 1939, 130–31; Weizsäcker to von Mackensen, 21 August 1939, *DGFP,* ser. D, vol. 7, no. 154, 165.

133. Vitetti Appunto, 21 August 1939, *DDI,* 8th ser., vol. 13, no. 129, no. 130, 85–89, 89–90. Ciano implied in his diary that he had written the document.

134. *CD,* 21 August 1939, 130–31.

135. Mussolini to Hitler, 21 August 1939, ASMAE, UC 9 (*DDI,* 8th ser., vol. 13, no. 136, 92); see also Mussolini to Vittorio Emmanuele III, 24 August 1939, *OO,* vol. 44, no. 17, where Mussolini conveyed this decision to the King.

136. *CD,* 21 August 1939, 22 August 1939, 130–31, 131–32.

137. Attolico to Ciano, 24 August 1939, *DDI,* 8th ser., vol. 13, no. 214, no. 218, 139, 141–44; *CD,* 23 August 1939, 132–33.

138. Ciano to Auriti, 23 August 1939, ASMAE, SAP—Germania, B 65 (*DDI,* 8th ser., vol. 13, no. 180, 120–11); Auriti to Ciano, 22 August 1939, 23 August 1939, *DDI,* 8th ser., vol. *XIII,* no. 156, no. 175, 105, 118–19.

139. Mussolini received proposals along these lines from Ciano, Attolico, and Magistrati. (Magistrati to Ciano, Mussolini Minute, 23 August 1939, ASMAE, UC 9 [*DDI,* 8th ser., vol. 13, no. 187, 124–26]; Attolico to Ciano, 24 August 1939, *DDI,* 8th ser., vol. 13, no. 218, 141–44; *CD,* 13 August 1939, 132–33; von Mackensen to von Weizsäcker, 23 August 1939, *DGFP,* ser. D, vol. 7, no. 227, 240–43).

140. Ciano to Attolico, 25 August 1939, *DDI,* 8th ser., vol. 13, no. 232, 155–56; Anfuso to Ciano, 24 August 1939, 25 August 1939, *DDI,* 8th ser., vol. 13, no. 208, no. 225, no. 234, 136, 152, 156; *CD,* 23 August 1939, 24 August 1939, 25 August 1939, 132–33, 133, 133–35; see also Attolico to Ciano, 25 August 1939, *DDI,* 8th ser., vol. 13, no. 258, no. 259, 168–69, 169.

141. Hitler to Mussolini, 25 August 1939, ASMAE, UC 87 (*DDI,* 8th ser., vol. 13, no. 245, 161–63); Hitler to Mussolini, 25 August 1939, *DGFP,* ser. D, vol. 7, no. 266, 281–83; Attolico to Ciano, 24 August 1939, *DDI,* 8th ser., vol. 13, no. 207, 136.

142. Mussolini to Hitler, 25 August 1939, ASMAE, UC 87 (*DDI,* 8th ser., vol. 13, no. 250, 164–65); Mussolini to Hitler, 25 August 1939, *DGFP,* ser. D, vol. 7, no. 266, 285–86 (emphasis in original).

143. For Hitler's views on the role that Fascist Italy would play, see Speeches by the Führer to the Commanders in Chief on August 22, 1939, *DGFP,* ser. D, vol. 7, no. 192, no. 193, 200–204. Interestingly, Hans von Mackensen, the German ambassador in Rome, had sent an extremely incisive report on the nature of Italian deliberations following the meeting in Salzburg. Italy would not obediently follow Germany to war, von Mackensen had warned, but Hitler and von Ribbentrop ignored this unwelcome counsel (von Mackensen to von Ribbentrop, 23 August 1939, *DGFP,* ser. D, vol. 7, no. 226, 240–43).

144. Attolico to Ciano, 25 August 1939, *DDI,* 8th ser., vol. 13, no. 266, 172; Anfuso to Ciano, 25 August 1939, *DDI,* 8th ser., vol. 13, no. 266, 173; *CD,* 25 August 1939, 133–35.

145. Hitler to Mussolini, ASMAE, UC 87 (*DDI,* 8th ser., vol. 13, no. 262, 170); Hitler to Mussolini, 25 August 1939, *DGFP,* ser. D, vol. 7, no. 277, 289; von Mackensen to von Ribbentrop, 25 August 1939, *DGFP,* ser. D, vol. 7, no. 280, 282, 291–93, 294.

146. *CD,* 25 August 1939, 133–35. Attolico also urged Ciano to make the demands as heavy as possible (Attolico to Ciano, 25 August 1939, *DDI,* 8th ser., vol. 13, no. 263, 171).

147. See, for example, Attolico to Ciano, 26 August 1939, *DDI,* 8th ser., vol. 13, no. 290, 188; Anfuso to Ciano, 26 August 1939, *DDI,* 8th ser., vol. 13, no. 290, 189; Unsigned appunto, 26 August 1939, *DDI,* 8th ser., vol. 13, no. 303, 195.

148. *CD,* 26 August 1939, 135–36.

149. Mussolini to Hitler, 26 August 1939, ASMAE, UC 87 (*DDI,* 8th ser., vol. 13, no. 293, 189–90); Hitler to Mussolini, 26 August 1939, ASMAE, UC 87 (*DDI,* 8th ser., vol. 13, no. 293, 192–93); Mussolini to Hitler, 26 August 1939, ASMAE, UC 87 (*DDI,* 8th ser., vol.13, no. 304, 195); *CD,* 26 August 1939, 135–36. Mussolini to Hitler, von Ribbentrop Minute, 26 August 1939, *DGFP,* ser. D, vol. 7, no. 301, 309–310; Hitler to Mussolini, 26 August 1939, *DGFP,* ser. D, vol. 7, no. 307, 313–15; Mussolini to Hitler, 26 August 1939, *DGFP,* ser. D, vol. 7, no. 317, 323; Attolico to Ciano, 26 August 1939, *DGFP,* ser. D, vol. 7, no. 299, no. 307, 193–94, 196–97; von Mackensen to von Ribbentrop, 26 August 1939, *DGFP,* ser. D, vol. 7, no. 308, 315–16; von Plessen Memorandum, 26 August 1939, *DGFP,* ser. D, vol. 7, no. 311, 319; von Mackensen Memoranda, 26 August 1939, *DGFP,* ser. D, vol. 7, no. 302, no. 316, 310–11, 322. The German ambassador noted the intense anguish that the decision to remain neutral had caused Mussolini (von Mackensen to von Ribbentrop, 26 August 1939, *DGFP,* ser. D, vol. 7, no. 320, 324–26).

150. *CD,* 26 August 1939, 135–36.

151. Hitler to Mussolini, 27 August 1939, ASMAE, UC 87 (*DDI,* 8th ser., vol. 13, no. 329, 211–12); Mussolini to Hitler, 27 August 1939, ASMAE, UC 87 (*DDI,* 8th ser., vol. 13, no. 348, 218); Hitler to Mussolini, 27 August 1939, *DGFP,* ser. D, vol. 7, no. 350, 346–47; Mussolini to Hitler, 27 August 1939, *DGFP,* ser. D, vol. 7, no. 350, 353–54; Attolico to Ciano, 27 August 1939, *DDI,* 8th ser., vol. 13, no. 331, 213; *CD,* 27 August 1939, 136–38. Von Mackensen Memoranda, 27 August 1939, *DGFP,* ser. D, vol. 7, no. 344, 348–49, 349; von Mackensen to von Ribbentrop, 27 August 1939, *DGFP,* ser. D, vol. 7, no. 345, 351–53. For a penetrating analysis of Mussolini's point of view, based on an informant's confidences, see von Mackensen to von Weizsäcker, 29 August 1939, *DGFP,* ser. D, vol. 7, no. 438, 430–33.

152. Ciano appunto, 27 August 1939, ASMAE, UC 10 (*DDI,* 8th ser., vol. 13, no. 333, 213–16); *CD,* 27 August 1939, 136–38. Weinberg, *Starting World War II,* 632–34, 642–43; Watt, *How War Came,* 488–89. For the cabinet discussion of the alliance proposal, see 24 August 1939, CAB 23/100 42(39).

153. Attolico to Ciano, 28 August 1939, 29 August 1939 (three correspondences), *DDI,* 8th ser., vol. 13, no. 375, no. 408, no. 414, no. 418, 234, 255–56, 258–59, 160–61; Magistrati to Ciano, 28 August 1939, *DDI,* 8th ser., vol. 13, no. 389, 241–44; *CD,* 27 August 1939, 29 August 1939, 130–32, 138–39; von Weizsäcker Memorandum, 28 August 1939, *DGFP,* ser. D, vol. 7, no. 395, 392; Mussolini to Hitler, 29 August 1939, *DGFP,* ser. D, vol. 7, no. 417, 410.

154. Loraine to Ciano, 30 August 1939 (three correspondences), ASMAE, UC 10 (*DDI,* 8th ser., vol. 13, no. 441, no. 449, no. 458, 275, 278–79, 282–83); *CD,* 30 August 1939, 139–40; von Mackensen to von Ribbentrop, 29 August 1939, *DGFP,* ser. D, vol. 7, no. 423, 417–18.

155. Attolico to Ciano, 31 August 1939, *DDI,* 8th ser., vol. 13, no. 487, 307; *CD,* 31 August 1939, 140–42.

156. Mussolini appunto, 31 August 1939, ASMAE, UC 9; Attolico to Ciano, 31 August 1939, *DDI,* 8th ser., vol. 13, no. 491, no. 504, no. 507, 308, 314, 315; von Weizsäcker Memorandum, 31 August 1939, *DGFP,* ser. D, vol. 7, no. 467, 456–57. Attolico had seized on the idea of direct negotiations between Germany and Poland and doggedly pursued the idea throughout 31 August (Attolico to Ciano, 31 August 1939, 1 September 1939, *DDI,* 8th ser., vol. 13, no. 510, no. 519, 317–18, 326; Schmidt Memoranda, 1 September 1939, *DGFP,* ser. D, vol. 7, no. 474, no. 478, 462, 465). For more detail on the extensive flurry of official and unofficial diplomatic maneuvers to avert the war, see Watt, *How War Came,* 498–528.

157. Hitler to Mussolini, 1 September 1939, ASMAE, UC 10 (*DDI,* 8th ser., vol. 13, no. 529, 330); Attolico to Ciano, 1 September 1939, *DDI,* 8th ser., vol. 13, no. 529, no. 536, 563, 330, 333, 344–45; *CD,* 31 August 1939, 1 September 1939, 140–42, 142–43; Hitler to Mussolini, 1 September 1939, *DGFP,* ser. D, vol. 7, no. 500, 483; von Weizsäcker Memorandum, 1 September 1939, *DGFP,* ser. D, vol. 7, no. 500, 486–87; von Mackensen to von Ribbentrop, 1 September 1939, *DGFP,*

ser. D, vol. 7, no. 500, 488–89. For a discussion of the British decision to accept Italian neutrality and to forego the chance for a preventive strike, see Pratt, *East of Malta, West of Suez: Britain's Mediterranean Crisis,* 181–97.

158. Guariglia to Ciano, 1 September 1939, ASMAE, UC 9 (*DDI,* 8th ser., vol. 13, no. 537, 333–34); Attolico to Ciano, 2 September 1939, ASMAE, UC 9 (*DDI,* 8th ser., vol. 13, no. 572, 352–53); Loraine aide-memoire, 2 September 1939, ASMAE, UC 10. *CD,* 2 September 1939, 143; Ciano Appunto, 2 September 1939, *DDI,* 8th ser., vol. 13, no. 571, 352; Attolico to Ciano, 2 September 1939, *DDI,* 8th ser., vol. 13, no. 555, no. 592, 358, 360; Ciano to Attolico, 2 September 1939, *DDI,* 8th ser., vol. 13, no. 359; Guariglia to Ciano, 2 September 1939, *DDI,* 8th ser., vol. 13, no. 368–70, appendix 1, 413; Schmidt Memorandum, 2 September 1939, *DGFP,* ser. D, vol. 7, no. 539, 512–13; Brücklmeier Memorandum, 2 September 1939, *DGFP,* ser. D, vol. 7, no. 544, 524–25.

159. Hitler to Mussolini, 3 September 1939, ASMAE, UC 10 (*DDI,* 8th ser., vol. 13, no. 639, 385–86); von Ribbentrop to von Mackensen, 3 September 1939, *DGFP,* ser. D, vol. 8, no. 565, 538–39; *CD,* 3 4 September 1939, 4 September 1939, 143–44, 144–45. For more detail on the wider context of the last-ditch struggle of diplomats to halt Hitler's war, see Watt, *How War Came,* 530–604.

Dénouement and Conclusion

Following the Anglo-French declarations of war, Ciano and Mussolini largely continued their disagreement about Italian policy. Ciano wanted to draw closer to the Western democracies; he had become convinced that their latent strength would overcome Germany's immediate advantage. He hoped to establish more productive trade with Britain and France, and he maintained his disapproval of Hitler's diplomatic tactics. Within strict limits, Ciano hoped to create tension within the Axis alliance, although he would not place his position as the Duce's allegedly faithful subordinate in jeopardy. At the same time, however, Ciano expected to profit from neutrality, and his attempts to further Italian influence in the Balkans carried the risk of provoking a wider conflict. Mussolini, for his part, initially hoped to arrange an armistice, primarily to restore his prestige. In his view, Italian nonbelligerency had stained his reputation as a warrior. If Italy brokered a peace deal that ensured German gains, then he could in part restore his status as a great European strongman. He also sought to secure Italy's status as Germany's primary ally in spite of the increasingly close relationship between Moscow and Berlin. As always, Mussolini would only be able to create his new empire with substantial German support. Finally, the Duce aimed to continue the expansion of Italian influence in the Balkans: attempting to create an Italian-dominated bloc of neutrals and to intimidate Greece to limit its association with Britain. He also ordered the *Regio Esercito* to prepare to attack Yugoslavia if Italian attempts to spark Croat unrest bore fruit. Above all, Mussolini took steps to organize the military to take part in a general war. He maintained the belief that Italy would have to escape its Mediterranean prison; he needed to be ready to capitalize on the potential opportunity to expand the Italian empire, whatever the outcome of the war between Germany and the West.[1]

Still, British attempts to appease Mussolini did not end with the outbreak of war. During the first months of the war, the Chamberlain government sought to arrange tighter economic ties with Italy. Foreign Office officials maintained the hope that patient diplomacy combined with economic concessions could win Mussolini back to the West and could prevent Italy from trading with Germany and thereby assisting the German war effort. British negotiators offered to supply Italy with the entire amount of its needs for imported coal. In exchange, Britain would purchase twenty million pounds of Italian manufactured goods, raw materials, and weapons. In essence, this proposal would serve to reorient Italy sharply away from its increased economic and military ties to Germany and would go a long way to render an Italian war against the West impossible. In spite of Ciano's fears of a harsh British reaction if Mussolini rejected the offer, the Duce rejected it, as he remained loyal to the broad lines of the Pact of Steel. Mussolini said, "Governments, like individuals, must follow a line of honour." As Ciano surmised, the British government reacted by interdicting German seaborne shipments to Italy, deepening the severe crisis in Italian industry owing to the shortage of coal.[2]

In the spring of 1940, Mussolini continued to reject any real association with the West. Although not without the occasional vacillation, he focused instead on the idea of a parallel war—fighting alongside Germany against Britain and France but seeking to achieve purely Italian ends.[3] When von Ribbentrop arrived in March 1940 with Hitler's promise to smash France and to liberate Italy from the tyranny of the belatedly established British economic blockade, Mussolini could no longer resist temptation; he promised to enter the war at "the appropriate moment," and argued that to achieve their destiny the populous nations would have to crush the plutodemocratic powers. It was either that, or as Hitler had warned, Italy would find itself returned to the ranks of second-rate powers.[4] At their meeting at the Brenner Pass a few days later, Mussolini promised Hitler that Italy would enter the war as soon as the German invasion of France had created a new balance of power in the West.[5]

On 31 March, Mussolini drafted a memorandum that indicated his social Darwinist *mentalité*. He thought that a negotiated peace remained an unlikely prospect, although he believed that the demographic weakness of the Western democracies, and the concomitant unwillingness to risk incurring casualties, meant that Anglo-French forces were unlikely to launch a major offensive against Germany's Western defenses. Despite the possible development of a long, stationary war of blockade, Mussolini said that it was "absurd and impossible" to think that Italy could long remain outside the conflict. Fascist Italy needed to break the walls of its Mediterranean prison, seizing Corsica, Tunisia, Malta, Gibraltar, and Suez. The Duce well recognized that Italy had insufficient funds to fight a long war and that a suitable delay would help Italy to continue its rearmament program. Nevertheless, he thought that if Italian forces did not seize the opportunity of a destabilized Europe to secure his new Roman Empire, then Italy would eventually be reduced to the status of Switzerland—a neutered power, albeit one ten times the size of the lowly Swiss. Mussolini, influenced by the insistent advice of Marshal Badoglio, believed that the army was too unprepared and too outnumbered to be able to take effective action outside of East Africa, at least in the initial stages of the war. Accordingly, he allotted the task of destroying British Naval power in the Mediterranean to the navy, with the air force to provide support for its sister services.[6]

Mussolini's determination to enter the war increased throughout April and May. Approaches from the Western democracies seeking to ensure Italian neutrality only whet his appetite for battle, and he contemptuously rejected overtures from Prime Minister Reynaud of France, Neville Chamberlain, and President Roosevelt.[7] Even the hesitations of his military commanders did not deflect the Duce from his path. He fully mobilized the *Regia Marina* in early April 1940, foreshadowing Italy's challenge to Anglo-French naval hegemony that imprisoned Italy in the Mediterranean. That summer, Mussolini expected two new and two refitted battleships to join the fleet. As well, the *Regia Aeronautica* had almost quadrupled the number of reasonably modern aircraft that it had available the previous September. After the initial reports of the *Wehrmacht's* successes in France, and even before the outcome of the battle was clear, Mussolini decided that the time had come to act; he could not stand aside indefinitely. Skillfully maneuvering to outflank the King, who retained the constitutional prerogative to declare war, Mussolini secured the right to command the armed forces during wartime. He promised his generals that the decisive German victory over France would mean that Italy could fight a short, successful war. The Duce planned for the army to remain on the defensive in the initial stages, while the fleet and air force would carry the battle against English bases in the Mediterranean in order to establish a secure Italian empire free of British tutelage. Mussolini hoped to be able to drive British forces from the Mediterranean, and he refused to share his service chiefs' beliefs about the inability of Italy's military to carry the battle to the enemy. Italian commanders' caution would blunt the effectiveness of any offensive action, but their bleak predictions of military defeat could not restrain the Duce's martial ardor.[8] On 10 June 1940, Ciano, resplendent in his *Regia Aeronautica* uniform, presented the British and French ambassadors with Italy's declaration of war. Mussolini explained the causes of the war to the Italian people.

Our enormous struggle is only a phase of the logical development of our revolution; it is the struggle of the numerous and poor peoples against the avaricious who ferociously hold the monopoly of all the riches and all the gold of the earth; it is the struggle of the fertile and young against the sterile and enfeebled; it is the struggle of two centuries and two ideas.[9]

The Duce had committed Italy to the fray.

* * * * *

The declaration of war in 1940 was the culmination of a long process. From the beginning of the Fascist movement, Mussolini had nourished extravagant ambitions, marrying nationalist ideology to a brand of revolutionary syndicalism. During the first decade of Mussolini's rule, he consolidated power both domestically, and, to some extent, internationally. Internally, he made compromises with the monarchy, landowners, the church, and the armed forces, diluting much of the reforming zeal that more ardent revolutionaries might have had. Mussolini made these essential compromises in order to secure support and freedom to pursue his major goal—conquering Italian *spazio vitale* in the Mediterranean. By the mid-1930s, Mussolini had established the expansion of Fascist Italy's borders as the central motivating principle of his regime. Subordinating most issues to his vision of national and state power, Mussolini sought to harness the demographic and, he believed, concomitant military power of the Italian people. Fueled by an intense social Darwinist belief system, he thought it necessary that Italy replace plutodemocratic France and Britain, supposedly weakened by Jewish and Masonic conspiracies, as the great North African imperial powers. For the Duce, only a young, vital, demographically vibrant country such as Italy had the power and energy to rule with a sufficiently firm imperial hand, keeping the fecund yet backward black African population cowed.

Although a rational planner in hindsight would see that the means for carrying out this planned expansion lay in a modern, well-equipped, highly trained military, Mussolini did not. He was hardly a rational thinker, and on this issue he believed that demographic power was more important than industrial power and that industrial cities, with their lower birthrates, sapped a nation's strength. He also had squandered Italian military strength in his wars in Ethiopia and Spain while seeking to expand Italy's ability to challenge the Western democracies. He sent hundreds of thousands of troops to Ethiopia, and despite the capture of Addis Ababa, revolts in Gojjam, the Amhara, and throughout the country kept occupation troops stretched beyond their capabilities. Mussolini had hoped that this venture would allow him to supplant Ethiopians with Italian settlers, but he was never able to realize his grandiose plans. Instead, Ethiopia became yet another sinkhole for precious Italian capital that he could have invested in modernization of his military or industrial plant.

Similarly, he maintained an army of up to 50,000 troops in Spain for almost three years and sent billions of lira in precious military supplies to Franco. This continuing commitment not only consumed enormous quantities of small arms ammunition, creating chronic shortages in the *Regio Esercito,* but it also helped to squander Italy's budget surplus, and Mussolini would be able to recoup little of this vast expenditure before his planned conflict with France and Britain. Nor did Franco prove as tractable an ally as the Duce had hoped. Far from a servile quasi-Fascist military ally against France, Franco turned his gaze toward reconstruction of Spain and continued destruction of his domestic foes rather than involving himself in Mussolini's or Hitler's wars. In spite of enormous expenditures on the military from 1926 onward, Mussolini's dubious battles from 1935 to 1939 limited his preparations for the greater war that he eventually planned to fight.

Nevertheless, Mussolini did understand that his dream of an African empire would require allies; Italy's putative eight million bayonets did not have the power to defeat France alone, never mind France supported by Great Britain. In 1936, in the aftermath of the Ethiopian war, Mussolini began to recruit possible partners in Europe. His initial approaches to Germany essentially traded Austrian independence for German recognition of the Ethiopian conquest and for possible German support of Italian expansion in the Mediterranean and the Balkans. Their combined though initially sporadic intervention in the Spanish Civil War, where Italian and German officials had begun tight cooperation on military and technical matters, furthered the process of bringing the two regimes closer together. Mussolini's relations with his Axis partner were not always entirely placid, but the relationship flourished, in spite of Hitler's cavalier treatment of Mussolini during the Anschluss, the occupation of Prague, the Nazi-Soviet Pact, and the invasion of Poland a full three years before Mussolini claimed Italy would be ready for war. The Duce became increasingly dependent on his German partner in order to establish the conditions necessary to build a new Fascist empire. Similarly, he tried to recruit the seemingly virile Japanese empire to help to intimidate Britain into abandoning its sometime French ally. That plan did not work, precisely because Mussolini and von Ribbentrop insisted that an Italo-German-Japanese alliance would have to be directed primarily against Great Britain.

When Hitler attacked Poland, Mussolini faced a premature war, and the Duce belatedly recognized a bitter truth; Fascist Italy was woefully unprepared for battle. Even Mussolini reluctantly had to admit that the Italian air force flew largely obsolete aircraft and that the Italian army could not muster eight million bayonets, never mind the regime's inability to equip its soldiers with modern artillery or tanks. Mussolini's devotion to warfare over the previous five years had paradoxically stripped Italy of the ability to fight the future wars that he contemplated. And although he declared his nonbelligerency in September 1939, his nature would not allow him to remain on the sidelines for long. As the German *Wehrmacht* crushed France in May and June 1940, Mussolini saw the opportunity to realize his ambition of creating a new Roman Empire in Africa. German force of arms had accomplished what the Duce's diplomacy could not—splitting France from Britain. Unfortunately for Mussolini, Fascist Italy proved incapable of defeating even one Great Power in North Africa, and his war brought not a vast empire but defeat after ignominious defeat.

Ultimately, the Duce's machinations led him down an ill-fated path. The strength of the German *Wehrmacht* could not save Italy from the industrial might of the Western allies and their democratic crusade against the dictatorships; the Western democracies proved to be far from the decadent, effete powers that Mussolini had assumed. In retrospect, we also know that Mussolini utterly failed to prepare his nation to fight the Second World War. Ironically, his *mentalité* drove him toward successive military confrontations, battles that bled Italy of the resources necessary to secure his long-term goals. Mussolini's fiery march ended with the devastation of Italy, and as Hitler had often forecast before the war, the two Fascist dictators shared a common destiny.

NOTES

1. "Rapporto ai Gerarchi di Genova," 30 September 1939, *OO,* vol. 29, 315–17. For accounts of Italian policy from September 1939 to the declaration of

war, see Knox, *Mussolini Unleashed,* 44–133; Schreiber, "Political and Military Developments in the Mediterranean Area, 1939–40," 8–125; C. J. Lowe and F. Marzari, *Italian Foreign Policy, 1870–1940* (London: Routledge & Kegan Paul, 1975), 337–70; Burgwyn, *Italian Foreign Policy in the Interwar Period, 1918–1940,* 207–16; Ennio Di Nolfo, "Mussolini e la decisione italiana di entrare nella seconda guerra mondiale," in *L'Italia e la politica di potenze in Europa (1938–40),* eds. Ennio Di Nolfo, Romain Rainero, e Brunello Vigezzi, (Milano: Marzorati Editore, 1986), 19–38; and, for a different, highly tendentious version, see Quartararo, "Inghiltera e Italia. Dal Patto di Pasqua a Monaco," 519ff.

2. Quoted in *CD,* 7 February 1939, 204–5; Giannini to Ciano, 16 January 1940, *DDI,* 9th ser., vol. 3, no. 146, 126–29; Loraine to Ciano, 13 February 1940, *DDI,* 9th ser., vol. 3, no. 300, 254–63; *CD,* 7–9 February 1939, 18 February 1939, 204–6, 209. For more on these negotiations, see Robert Mallett, "The Anglo-Italian War Trade Negotiations, Contraband Control, and the Failure to Appease Mussolini, 1939–1940," *Diplomacy & Statecraft* 8, no. 1 (1997): 137–67.

3. See, for example, *CD,* 22 January 1940, 23 January 1940, 31 January 1940, 1 February 1940, 4 March 1940, 8 March 1940, 199–200, 200, 203, 203, 215, 217–18, among many others.

4. Hitler to Mussolini, 8 March 1940, *DDI,* 9th ser., vol. 3, no. 493, 415–23; Mussolini colloquio con von Ribbentrop, 10 March 1940, *DDI,* 9th ser., vol. 3, no. 512, 435–44; Hitler to Mussolini, 8 March 1940, *DGFP,* ser. D, vol. 8, no. 663, 871–80; *CD,* 11 March 1940, 219.

5. Mussolini colloquio con Hitler, 18 March 1989, *DDI,* 9th ser., vol. 3, no. 578, 503–7; *CD,* 18 March 1940, 223.

6. Mussolini to Vittorio Emmanuele III, Ciano, Badoglio, Graziani and Pricolo, 31 March 1931, *DDI,* 9th ser., vol. 3, no. 669, 576–79. For Badoglio's response that the forces were preparing to meet these tasks, see Badoglio to Mussolini, 6 April 1939, *DDI,* 9th ser., vol. 3, no. 716, 618.

7. See, for example, Guariglia to Ciano, 22 April 1940, *DDI,* 9th ser., vol. 3, no. 165, 134–35; Reynaud to Mussolini, 22 April 1940, *DDI,* 9th ser., vol. 3, no. 166, 135–36; Ciano to Colonna (Washington), 1 May 1940, *DDI,* 9th ser., vol. 3, no. 263, 213–14; *CD,* 24 April 1940, 26 April 1940, 1 May 1940, 238–39, 239–40, 241–42.

8. Riunione presso il Capo del Governo, Mussolini, 29 May 1940, *DDI,* 9th ser., vol. 3, no. 642, 495–97; Faldella, Verbale della riunione dei Capi di Stato Maggiore, 30 May 1940, 5 June 1940, *DDI,* 9th ser., vol. 3, no. 642, 739–42, 743–46. For the grim assessment of Italy's strategic situation, see Mallett, *The Italian Navy and Fascist Expansionism,* 178–81, and Minniti, *Fino alla guerra.* Minniti's extensive coverage of Italian strategists' hesitations leads his analysis down a blind alley. Mussolini ultimately declared war in spite of Italy's military weakness, which nevertheless constrained the Duce's ability to drive his generals to carry out an offensive ground war (Minniti, *Fino alla guerra,* 225–27). While it is true that Mussolini had not decided among various possible plans, the fall of France freed him to pursue an offensive against Egypt and Greece, although with

disastrous results. Furthermore, Minniti well recognized that Mussolini was no rational military planner, suggesting that the approach to understand Italian foreign policy through studying the military plans of the Duce's subordinates is in itself a fundamentally flawed methodology.

9. "Al popolo italiano," 10 June 1940, *OO,* vol. 29, 403–5.

Appendix

Pact of Friendship and Alliance between Germany and Italy*

The German Chancellor

And

His Majesty the King of Italy and Albania,
Emperor of Ethiopia

deem that the time has come to strengthen the close relationship of friendship and homogeneity, existing between National Socialist Germany and Fascist Italy, by a solemn Pact.

Now that a safe bridge of mutual aid and assistance has been established by the common frontier between Germany and Italy fixed for all time, both Governments reaffirm the policy, the principles and the objectives of which have already been agreed upon by them, and which has proved successful, both for promoting the interests of the two countries and also for safeguarding the peace in Europe.

Firmly united by the inner affinity between their ideologies and the comprehensive solidarity of their interests, the German and Italian nations are resolved in the future also to act side by side with united forces to secure their living space and to maintain peace.

Following this path, marked out for them by history, Germany and Italy intend, in the midst of a world of unrest and disintegration, to serve the task of safeguarding European civilization.

---

*Pact of Friendship and Alliance between Germany and Italy, *DGFP,* ser. D, vol. 6, no. 426, 561–64.

In order to lay down these principles in a pact there have been appointed plenipotentiaries:

By the German Reich Chancellor:

The Reich Minister for Foreign Affairs,

Herr Joachim von Ribbentrop;

By His Majesty the King of Italy and Albania, Emperor of Ethiopia:

The Minister for Foreign Affairs,

Count Galeazzo Ciano di Cortellazzo;

who having exchanged their full powers, found to be in good and due form, have agreed on the following terms.

ARTICLE I

The High Contracting Parties will remain in continuous contact with each other in order to reach an understanding on all questions affecting their common interests or the general European situation.

ARTICLE II

Should the common interests of the High Contracting Parties be endangered by international events of any kind whatsoever, they will immediately enter into consultations on the measures to be taken for the protection of those interests.

Should the security or other vital interests of one of the High Contracting Parties be threatened from without, the other High Contracting Party will afford the threatened Party full political and diplomatic support in order to remove this threat.

ARTICLE III

If, contrary to the wishes and hopes of the High Contracting Parties, it should happen that one of them becomes involved in warlike complications with another Power or Powers, the other High Contracting Party would immediately come to its assistance as an ally and support it with all its military forces on land, at sea and in the air.

ARTICLE IV

In order to ensure in specific cases the speedy execution of the obligations of alliance undertaken under Article III, the Governments of the

High Contracting Parties will further intensify their collaboration in the military field, and in the field of war economy.

In the same way the two Governments will remain in continuous consultation also on other measures necessary for the practical execution for the provisions of this Pact.

For the purposes indicated in paragraphs 1 and 2 above, the two Governments will set up commissions which will be under the direction of the Two Foreign Ministers.

ARTICLE V

The High Contracting Parties undertake even now that, in the event of war waged jointly, they will conclude an armistice and peace only in full agreement with each other.

ARTICLE VI

The two High Contracting Parties are aware of the significance that attaches to their common relations with Powers friendly to them. They are resolved to maintain these relations in the future also and together to shape them in accordance with the common interests which form the bonds between them and these Powers.

ARTICLE VII

This Pact shall enter into force immediately upon signature. The two High Contracting Parties are agreed in laying down that its first term of validity shall be for ten years. In good time before the expiry of this period, they will reach agreement on the extension and validity of the Pact.

In witness whereof the Plenipotentiaries have signed this Pact and affixed to their seals.

Done in duplicate in the German and Italian languages, both texts being equally authoritative.
Berlin, May 22, 1939, in the XVIIth year of the Fascist Era.
Joachim V. Ribbentrop   Galeazzo Ciano

Secret Additional Protocol to the Pact of Friendship and Alliance between Germany and Italy

At the time of signature of the Pact of Friendship and Alliance, both Parties have reached agreement on the following points:

1. The two Foreign Ministers will reach agreement as soon as possible on the organization, headquarters and working methods of the commissions for military questions and questions of war economy to be set up under their direction as provided for in Article IV of the Pact.

2. In execution of Article IV, paragraph 2, of the Pact the two Foreign Ministers will as quickly as possible take all necessary steps to ensure continuous collaboration in the fields of the press, information and propaganda in accordance with the spirit and aims of the Pact.

For this purpose each of the two Foreign Ministers will assign to his country's Embassy, in the capital of the other, one or more specially qualified experts, who, in direct collaboration with the Foreign Ministry there, will continually consult on the steps which are suitable for promoting the policy of the Axis and counteracting the policy of opposing Powers in the fields of the press, information and propaganda.

Berlin, May 22, 1939, in the XVIIth year of the Fascist Era.

Joachim V. Ribbentrop   Galeazzo Ciano

Selected Bibliography

ARCHIVAL DOCUMENTS

Archivio Storico del Ministero degli Affari Esteri, Rome

Carte Grandi
Carte Lancelotti, Archivio di Gabinetto
Carte Lancelotti, Ufficio di Coordinamento
Carte Lancelotti, Ufficio di Spagna
Serie Affari Politiche:
      Cina
      Francia
      Germania
      Giappone
      Gran Bretagna
      Romania
      Spagna
      Ungheria
      Yemen

Archivio Centrale dello Stato, Rome

Carte Graziani
Segretaria Particolare del Duce, Carteggio Riservato

Public Record Office (Kew, U.K.)

Cabinet 23, 27
Foreign Office 371, 800, 954
Prime Ministers' Series 1

National Archive and Records Administration (Washington, D.C.)

Microfilm Series T586

University of Birmingham Library

Avon Papers
Neville Chamberlain Papers

PUBLISHED DOCUMENTS

I documenti diplomatici italiani, ottava serie, 13 vols. [*progetato*]. Rome: Istituto poligrafico e zecca dello stato, 1952.
I documenti diplomatici italiani, nona serie, vols. 1–4. Rome: Istituto poligrafico e zecca dello stato, 1952–53.
Documents diplomatiques français, 2d ser, 19 vols. Paris: Imprimerie nationale, 1963–1979.
Documents on British Foreign Policy, 2d ser., 21 vols. London: His Majesty's Stationery Office, 1948–1984.
Documents on British Foreign Policy, 3d ser., 10 vols. London: His Majesty's Stationery Office, 1949–1961.
Documents on German Foreign Policy, ser. C, 6 vols. London: Her Majesty's Stationery Office, 1957–1983.
Documents on German Foreign Policy, ser. D, 13 vols. London: Her Majesty's Stationery Office, 1949–1964.
Susmel, Edoardo e Duilio, ed. *Opera Omnia di Benito Mussolini.* 36 vols. Firenze: La Fenice, 1951–63.
Susmel, Edoardo e Duilio, ed. *Opera Omnia di Benito Mussolini.* 9 vols. Rome: G. Volpe, 1978–80.

MEMOIRS AND DIARIES

Anfuso, Filippo. *Da Palazzo Venezia al Lago di Garda (1936–1945).* Bologna: Capelli, 1957.
Bastianini, Guiseppe. *Uomini, cose, fatti.* Milan: Vitigliano, 1959.

Bottai, Giuseppe. *Diario, 1935–1944.* Edited by Giordano Bruno Guerri. Milan: Rizoli, 1982.

Cantalupo, Roberto. *Fu la Spagna: Ambasciata presso Franco, febbraio-aprile 1937.* Milan: Mondadori, 1948.

Ciano, Edda Mussolini. *My Truth.* Translated by Eileen Finsletter. New York: Morrow, 1977.

Ciano, Galeazzo. *The Ciano Diaries, 1939–1943.* Edited by Hugh Gibson. New York: Doubleday, 1946.

Ciano, Galleazo. *Ciano's Diplomatic Papers.* Edited by Malcolm Muggeridge. London: Odhams Press, 1948.

Ciano, Galeazzo. *Ciano's Hidden Diary 1937–1938.* Edited and translated by Andreas Mayor. New York: E. P. Dutton, 1953.

Dilks, David, ed. *The Diaries of Sir Alexander Cadogan.* New York: G. P. Putnam's Sons, 1974.

Donosti, Mario (Luciolli). *Mussolini e l'Europa: La politica estera fascista.* Rome: Leonardo, 1945.

Grandi, Dino. *Il mio paese: ricordi autobiografici.* Edited by Renzo De Felice. Bologna: Il Mulino, 1985.

Guariglia, Raffaele. *Ricordi 1922–1946.* Naples: E.S.I., 1950.

Hassell, Ulrich von. *Vom anderen Deutschland aus den nachgelassenen Tagebüchern, 1938–1944.* Zurich: Atlantis, 1948.

Jacomoni di San Savino, Francesco. *La politica dell'Italia in Albania.* Rocca San Casciano: Cappelli, 1965.

Evans, Trevor, ed. *The Killearn Diaries, 1934–46: The Diplomatic and Personal Record of Lord Killearn (Sir Miles Lampson).* London: Sidgwick and Jackson, 1972.

Magistrati, Massimo. *Il prologo del dramma: Berlino, 1934–1937.* Milan: U. Mursia, 1971.

Magistrati, Massimo. *L' Italia a Berlino, 1937–1939.* Verona: Arnaldo Mondadori, 1956.

Weizsäcker, Ernst von. *Erinnerungen.* Munich: Paul List, 1950.

BOOKS

Adamthwaite, Anthony. *France and the Coming of the Second World War, 1936–1939.* London: Frank Cass, 1977.

Adamthwaite, Anthony. *Grandeur and Misery: France's Bid for Power in Europe, 1914–1940.* London: Arnold, 1995.

Baer, G. W. *Test Case: Italy, Ethiopia and the League of Nations.* Stanford: Hoover Institution, 1976.

Bargoni, Franco. *L'impegno navale italiano durante la guerra civile spagnola.* Rome: Ufficio Storico della Marina Militare, 1992.

Barker, A. J. *The Civilizing Mission: The Italo-Ethiopian War, 1935–6*. London: Cassell, 1968.

Bolech Cecchi, Donatella. *Non bruciare i ponti con Roma: Le relazioni fra L'italia, la Gran Bretagna e la Francia dall'accordo di Monaco allo scoppio della seconda guerra mondiale*. Milan: Giuffrè Editore, 1986.

Bosworth, R. J. B. *The Italian Dictatorship: Problems and perspectives in the interpretation of Mussolini and fascism*. London: Arnold, 1998.

Brundu Olla, Paola. *L'equilibrio difficile: Gran Bretagna, Italia e Francia nel mediterraneo*. Milan: Giuffrè Editore, 1980.

Burgwyn, H. James. *Italian Foreign Policy in the Interwar Period, 1918–1940*. Westport, Conn.: Praeger, 1997.

Cannistraro, Philip, and Brian R. Sullivan. *Il Duce's Other Woman*. New York: Morrow, 1993.

Carlton, David. *Anthony Eden: A Biography*. London: A. Lane, 1981.

Cassels, Alan. *Fascism*. Arlington Heights, Ill.: Harlan Davidson, 1975.

Cassels, Alan. *Fascist Italy*. 2d ed. Arlington Heights, Ill.: Harlan Davidson, 1985.

Cassels, Alan. *Mussolini's Early Diplomacy*. Princeton: Princeton University Press, 1970.

Catalano, Franco. *L'economia italiana di guerra: La politica economico-finanziaria del fascismo dalla guerra d'Etiopia alla caduta del regime, 1935–1943*. Milan: Istituto Nazionale per la Storia del Movimento di Liberazione, 1969.

Cattell, David T. *Soviet Diplomacy and the Spanish Civil War*. Berkeley: University of California Press, 1957.

Ceva, Lucio. *Le forze armate*. Turin: UTET Libreria, 1981.

Ceva, Lucio. *Storia delle forze armate in Italia*. Turin: Libreria UTET, 1999.

Ceva, Lucio, and Andrea Curami. *Industria bellica anni trenta: Commesse militari, l'Ansaldo ed altri*. Milan: Franco Angeli, 1992.

Clarke, J. Calvitt. *Russia and Italy against Hitler: The Bolshevik-Fascist Rapprochement of the 1930s*. Westport, Conn.: Greenwood, 1991.

Coverdale, John F. *Italian Intervention in the Spanish Civil War*. Princeton: Princeton University Press, 1975.

Croce, Benedetto. *Philosophy, Poetry, History: An Anthology*. London: Oxford University Press, 1966.

De Felice, Renzo. *Il fascismo e l'Oriente: Arabi, ebrei, e indiani nella politica di Mussolini*. Bologna: Il Mulino, 1988.

De Felice, Renzo. *Mussolini: Parte I, Il rivoluzionario, 1883–1920; parte II, Il fascsita, volume I, La conquista di potere, 1921–1925, volume II, L'organizzazione dello Stato fascista, 1925–1928; parte III, Il duce, volume I, Gli anni del consenso, 1929–1936, volume II, Lo Stato totalitario, 1936–1940; parte IV, L'alleato, volume I (1), Dalla guerra 'breve' alla guerra lunga, I (2), Crisi e agonia del regime, volume II, La guerra civile, 1943–1945*. Turin: Einaudi, 1965–96.

Del Boca, Angelo. *L'africa nella coscienza degli italiani: Miti, memorie, errori, sconfitte.* Milan: Mondadori, 2002.

Di Nolfo, Ennio. *Mussolini e la politica estera italiana, 1919–1933.* Padua: Facoltà di scienze politiche dell'Università di Padova, 1960.

Duroselle, Jean-Baptiste. *La Décadence, 1932–1939.* Paris: Imprimerie nationale, 1979.

Faldella, Emilio. *Revisione di giudizi: L'Italia e la seconda guerra mondiale.* 2d ed. Bologna: Capelli, 1960.

Ferretti, Valdo. *Il Giappone e la politica estera Italiana, 1935–41.* Milan: Giuffrè Editore, 1983.

Funke, Manfred. *Sanktionen und Kanonen: Hitler, Mussolini und der internationale Abessienenkonflikt 1934–36.* Düsseldorf: Droste Verlag, 1971.

Gehl, Jürgen. *Austria, Germany and the Anschluss, 1931–1938.* London: Oxford University Press, 1963.

Guerri, Giordano Bruno. *Galeazzo Ciano: una vita.* Milan: Bompani, 1979.

Haslam, Jonathan. *The Soviet Union and the Struggle for Collective Security in Europe, 1933–39.* New York: St. Martin's Press, 1984.

Ipsen, Carl. *Dictating demography: the problem of population in fascist Italy.* Cambridge, U.K.: Cambridge University Press, 1996.

Iriye, Akira. *The Origins of the Second World War in Asia and the Pacific.* London: Longman, 1987.

Jackson, Julian. *The Politics of Depression in France, 1932–1936.* Cambridge, U.K.: Cambridge University Press, 1985.

Jackson, Julian. *The Popular Front in France: Defending Democracy, 1934–1938.* Cambridge, U.K.: Cambridge University Press, 1988.

Jäckl, Eberhard. *Hitler's Weltanschauung: A Blueprint for Power.* Middleton, Conn.: Wesleyan University Press, 1972.

Jordan, Nicole. *The Popular Front and Central Europe: The Dilemmas of French Impotence, 1918–1940.* Cambridge, U.K.: Cambridge University Press, 1992.

Kallis, Aristotle A. *Fascist Ideology: Territory and Expansionism in Italy and Germany, 1922–1945.* London: Routledge, 2000.

Knox, MacGregor. *Common Destiny: Dictatorship, Foreign Policy, and War in Fascist Italy and Nazi Germany.* Cambridge. U.K.: Cambridge University Press, 2000.

Knox, MacGregor. *Mussolini Unleashed, 1939–1941: Politics and Strategy in Fascist Italy's Last War.* Cambridge. U.K.: Cambridge University Press, 1982.

Koon, Tracy H. *Believe, Obey Fight: Political Socialization of Youth in Fascist Italy, 1922–1943.* Chapel Hill, N.C.: University of North Carolina Press, 1985.

Lamb, Richard. *Mussolini and the British.* London: John Murray, 1997.

Latour, Conrad, *Südtirol und die Asche Berlin-Rom, 1938–1945.* Stuttgart: Deutsche Verlags-Anstalt, 1962.

Lowe, C.J., and F. Marzari. *Italian Foreign Policy, 1870–1940.* London: Routledge & Kegan Paul, 1975.

Lyttelton, Adrian. *Italian Fascisms from Pareto to Gentile.* New York: Harper and Row, 1973.

Lyttelton, Adrian. *The Seizure of Power: Fascism in Italy, 1919–1929.* London: Weidenfeld and Nicolson, 1973.

Mack Smith, Denis. *Mussolini.* London: Weidenfeld and Nicolson, 1981.

Mack Smith, Denis. *Mussolini's Roman Empire.* London: Penguin, 1976.

Mallett, Robert. *The Italian Navy and Fascist Expansion 1935–1940.* London: Frank Cass, 1998.

McGaw Smyth, Howard. *Secrets of the Fascist Era: How Uncle Sam Obtained Some of the Top-Level Documents of Mussolini's Period.* Carbondale, Ill.: Southern Illinois University Press, 1975.

Michaelis, Meir. *Mussolini and the Jews: German-Italian Relations and the Jewish Question in Italy, 1922–1945.* Oxford. U.K.: Clarendon Press, 1978.

Minniti, Fortunato. *Fino alla guerra: Strategie e conflitto nella politica di potenza di Mussolini, 1923–1940.* Naples: E.S.I., 2000.

Mitchell, B.R. *European Historical Statistics, 1750–1975.* New York: Facts on File, 1975.

Morewood, Steven S. *The British Defence of Egypt. Crisis and Conflict in the Eastern Mediterranean, 1935–1940.* London: Frank Cass, 2003.

Moseley, Ray. *Mussolini's Shadow: The Double Life of Count Galeazzo Ciano.* New Haven. Conn.: Yale University Press, 1999.

Nello, Paolo. *Un fedele indisubbidiente: Dino Grandi da Palazzo Chigi al 25 luglio.* Bologna: Il Mulino, 1993.

Ovendale, Ritchie. *'Appeasement' and the English Speaking World: Britain, the United States, the Dominions, and the Policy of 'Appeasement', 1937–1939.* Cardiff, U.K.: University of Wales Press, 1975.

Peters, A.R., *Anthony Eden at the Foreign Office, 1931–1938.* New York: St. Martin's, 1986.

Pettracchi, Giorgio. *La Russia rivoluzionare nella politica italiana: Le relazioni italo-sovietiche 1917–1925.* Bari: Laterza, 1982.

Post, Gaines, Jr. *Dilemmas of Appeasement: British Deterrence and Defense, 1934–1937.* Ithaca, N.Y.: Cornell University Press, 1993.

Pratt, Lawrence. *East of Malta, West of Suez: Britain's Mediterranean Crisis.* Cambridge, U.K.: Cambridge University Press, 1975.

Preti, Luigi. *Impero fascista, africani ed ebrei.* Milan: Mursia, 1968.

Preston, Paul. *Franco: A Biography.* London: HarperCollins, 1993.

Proctor, Raymond L. *Hitler's Luftwaffe in the Spanish Civil War.* Westport, Conn.: Greenwood Press, 1983.

Quartararo, Rosaria. *Roma tra Londra e Berlino: La politica estera fascista dal 1930 al 1940.* Rome: Bonacci, 1980.

Richardson, R. Dan. *Comintern Army: The International Brigades and the Spanish Civil War.* Lexington, Ky.: The University Press of Kentucky, 1982.

Robertson, Esmonde M. *Mussolini as Empire Builder: Europe and Africa 1932–36*. London: MacMillan, 1977.

Rothschild, Joseph. *East Central Europe between the Two World Wars*. Seattle: University of Washington Press, 1974.

Rumi, Giorgio. *L'imperialismo fascista*. Milan: Mursia, 1974.

Sadkovich, James Joseph. *Italian Support for Croatian Separatism, 1927–1937*. Madison, Wisc.: University of Wisconsin Press, 1982.

Salerno, Eric, *Genocidio in Libia*. Milan: Sugarco, 1979.

Salerno, Reynolds. *Vital Crossroads: Mediterranean Origins of the Second World War, 1935–1940*. Ithaca, NY: Cornell University Press, 2002.

Salvatorelli, Luigi, and Giovani Mira. *Storia d'Italia nel periodo fascista*. Turin: Einaudi, 1956.

Salvatorelli, Luigi. *Storia del fascismo: l'Italia dal 1919 al 1945*. Rome: Edizioni di Novissima, 1952.

Salvemini, Gaetano. *The Fascist Dictatorship in Italy*. New York: Howard Fertig, 1967.

Salvemini, Gaetano. *Italian Fascism*. London: Victor Gollancz, 1938.

Salvemini, Gaetano. *Prelude to World War II*. London: Victor Gollancz, 1953.

Salvemini, Gaetano. *Under the Axe of Fascism*. London: Victor Gollancz, 1936.

Shorrock, William I. *From Ally to Enemy: The Enigma of Fascist Italy in French Diplomacy, 1920–1940*. Kent, Ohio: Kent State University Press, 1988.

Sternhell, Ze'ev, et al. *The Birth of a Fascist Ideology: From Cultural Rebellion to Political Revolution*. Princeton: Princeton University Press, 1994.

Taylor, A.J.P. *The Origins of the Second World War*. London: Hamilton, 1961.

Thomas, Martin. *Britain, France, and Appeasement: Anglo-French Relations in the Popular Front Era*. Oxford, U.K.: Berg, 1996.

Toscano, Mario. *Alto Adige-South Tyrol: Italy's Frontier with the German World*. Baltimore: John Hopkins University Press, 1975.

Toscano, Mario. *Designs in Diplomacy: Pages from European Diplomatic History in the Twentieth Century*. Baltimore: John Hopkins University Press, 1970.

Toscano, Mario. *The Origins of the Pact of Steel*. Baltimore: John Hopkins University Press, 1967.

Vergani, Orio. *Ciano: Una lunga confessione*. Milan: Longanesi, 1974.

Waley, Daniel. *British Public Opinion and the Abyssinian War, 1935–6*. London: Temple Smith, 1975.

Waterfield, Gordon. *Professional Diplomat: Sir Percy Loraine of Kinharle Bt., 1880–1961*. London: John Murray, 1973.

Watt, Donald Cameron. *How War Came: The Immediate Origins of the Second World War, 1938–1939*. London: Heinemann, 1989.

Weinberg, Gerhard L. Vol. 1, *The Foreign Policy of Hitler's Germany: Diplomatic Revolution in Europe 1933–36*. Vol. 2, *Starting World War II, 1937–1939*. Chicago: The University of Chicago Press, 1970–1980.

Whealey, Robert H. *Hitler and Spain: The Nazi Role in the Spanish Civil War, 1936–1939.* Lexington, Ky.: The University Press of Kentucky, 1989.

Wiskemann, Elizabeth. *The Rome-Berlin Axis: A History of the Relations between Hitler and Mussolini.* London: Oxford University Press, 1949.

Young, Robert J. *In Command of France: French Foreign Policy and Civil Military Relations, 1933–1940.* Cambridge, Mass.: Harvard University Press, 1978.

Zucotti, Susan. *The Italians and the Holocaust: Persecution, Rescue, and Survival.* New York, Basic Books, 1987.

Zunino, Pier Giorgio. *L'ideologia del fascismo: Miti, credenze e valori nella stabilizazione del regime.* Bologna: Il Mulino, 1985.

COLLECTED WORKS

Alexander, Martin S., and Helen Graham, eds. *The French and Spanish Popular Fronts: Comparitive Perspectives.* Cambridge, U.K.: Cambridge University Press, 1989.

Andrew, Christopher, and David Dilks. *The Missing Dimension: Governments and Intelligence Communities in the Twentieth Century.* London: Macmillan, 1984.

Aquarone, Alberto, and Maurizio Vernassa, eds. *Il regime fascista.* Bologna: Il Mulino, 1974.

Bosworth, Richard, and Patricia Dogliani, eds. *Italian Fascism.* London: MacMillan, 1999.

Bosworth, Richard, and Sergio Romano, eds. *La politica estera italiana (1960–1985).* Bologna: Il Mulino, 1993.

Cervi, Mario, ed. *Mussolini: Album di una vita.* Milan: Rizzoli, 1992.

Cohen, Michael J., and Martin Kohinsky, eds. *Britain and the Middle East in the 1930s: Security Problems, 1935–39.* New York: St. Martin's, 1992.

Craig, Gordon A., and Felix Gilbert, eds. *The Diplomats.* Vol. 1, *1919–1930: The Twenties.* Vol. 2, *1919–1939: The Thirties.* New York: Atheneum, 1953.

De Felice, Renzo, ed. *L'Italia fra tedeschi e alleati: La politica estera fascista e la seconda guerra mondiale.* Bologna: Il Mulino, 1973.

Del Boca, Angelo, ed. *Le Guerre coloniali del fascismo.* Rome: Laterza, 1991.

Diest, Wilhelm, et al., eds. *Germany and the Second World War.* Vol. 3, *The Mediterranean, South-east Europe and North Africa, 1939–1941.* Oxford, U.K.: Clarendon, 1995.

Di Nolfo, Ennio, Romain Rainero, and Brunello Vigezzi, ed. *L'Italia e la politica di potenze in Europa (1938–40).* Milan: Marzorati Editore, 1986.

Dilks, David, and Christopher Andrew, eds. *The Missing Dimension: Governments and Intelligence Communities in the Twentieth Century.* Chicago: University of Illinois Press, 1984.

Dilks, David, ed. *Retreat from Power.* Vol. 1, *1906–1939.* London: MacMillan, 1981.

Duroselle, J. B., and E. Serra, ed. *Italia, Francia e Mediterraneo.* Milan: Franco Angeli, 1990.

Friedman, Saul S., ed. *Holocaust Literature: A Handbook of Critical, Historical, and Literary Writings.* Westport, Conn.: Greenwood Press, 1993.

Gatzke, Hans, ed. *European Diplomacy between Two Wars, 1919–1939.* Chicago: Quadrangle, 1972.

Ion, A. Hamish, ed. *Great Powers and Little Wars: The Limits of Power.* Westport, Conn.: Praeger, 1993, 167–201.

Lukes, Igor, and Erik Goldstein, eds. *The Munich Crisis, 1938: Prelude to World War II.* London: Frank Cass, 1999.

Martel, Gordon, ed. *The Origins of the Second World War Reconsidered: A. J. P. Taylor and the Historians.* 2d ed. London: Routledge, 1999.

Martel, Gordon, ed. *The Origins of the Second World War Reconsidered: The A. J. P. Taylor Debate after Twenty-Five Years.* Boston: Allen and Unwin, 1986.

May, Ernest R., ed. *Knowing One's Enemies: Intelligence Assessment before the Two World Wars.* Princeton: Princeton University Press, 1984.

McKercher, B. J. C., and Roch Legault, eds. *Military Planning and the Origins of the Second World War in Europe.* Westport, Conn.: Praeger, 2001.

McKercher, B. J. C., and Michael L. Roi, eds. *Appeasement: Rethinking the Policy and the Policy-makers.* Cambridge, U.K.: Cambridge University Press, in press.

Michel, Henri. *Les Relations Franco-Britanniques de 1935 à 1939.* Paris: Éditions du Centre National de la Recherche Scientifique, 1975.

Migliazza, Alessandro, and Enrico Decleva, ed. *Diplomazia e storia delle relazioni internazionali.* Milan: Giuffrè Editore, 1991.

Millett, Alan R., and Williamson Murray, eds. *Military Effectiveness.* Vol. 2, *The Interwar Period.* Boston: Unwin Hyman, 1988.

Mommsen, Wofgang, and Lothar Kettenacher, eds. *The Fascist Challenge and the Policy of Appeasement.* London: George Allen and Unwin, 1983.

Morley, James William, ed. *Deterrent Diplomacy: Japan, Germany, and the USSR, 1935–1940.* New York: Columbia University Press, 1976.

Preston, Adrian, ed. *General Staffs and Diplomacy before the Second World War.* London: Croom Helm, 1978.

Richardson, Dick, and Glyn Stone, eds. *Decisions and Diplomacy: Essays in Twentieth-Century International History.* London: Routledge, 1995.

Sarti, Roland, ed. *The Ax Within: Italian Fascism in Action.* New York: New Viewpoints, 1974.

Serra, Enrico, and C. Seton-Watson, eds. *Italia e Inghilterra nell' età dell' imperialismo.* Milan: Angeli, 1990.

ARTICLES

Ádám, Magda. "The Munich Crisis and Hungary: The Fall of the Versailles Settlement in Central Europe." *Diplomacy & Statecraft.* 10. no. 2/3 (1999): 82–121.

Alegi, Gregory. "Balbo e il riarmo clandestino tedesco. Un episodio segreto della collaborazione italo-tedesco." *Storia contemporanea* 23, no. 2 (April 1992): 305–17.

Askew, William. "Italian Intervention in Spain: The Agreements of March 31, 1934, with the Spanish Monarchist Parties," *Journal of Modern History* 24, no. 2 (1952): 181–83.

Azzi, Stephen Corrado. "The Historiography of Fascist Foreign Policy," *Historical Journal* 36, no. 1 (March 1993): 187–203.

Baudouin, Paul. "Un voyage à Rome (fevrier 1939)." *Revue des deux mondes* (1 May 1962): 69–85.

Beck, Peter. "Politicians versus Historians: Lord Avon's Appeasement Battle against 'Lamentably Appeasement-Minded' Historians," *Twentieth Century British History* 9, no. 3 (1998): 396–419.

Bernardini, Gene. "The Origins and Development of Racial Antisemitism in Fascist Italy," *Journal of Modern History* 49, no. 3 (September 1977): 431–53.

Buccianti, G. "Hitler, Mussolini e il conflitto italo-etiopico," *Il Politico* 37 (1972): 415–28.

Cannistraro, P. V., and Wynot, F. D., Jr. "On the Dynamics of Anti-Communism as a Function of Fascist Foreign Policy, 1933–43," *Il Politico* 38 (1973): 645–81.

Carlton, David. "Eden, Blum and the Origins of Non-intervention," *Journal of Contemporary History* 6, no. 3 (1971): 44–55.

Cassels, Alan. "Deux Empires face a face: La chimère d'un rapprochement anglo-italien (1936–1940)," *Guerres Mondiales* 161, no. 1 (1991): 68–96.

Cassels, Alan. "Was there a Fascist Foreign Policy? Tradition and Novelty," *International History Review* 5, no. 2 (May 1983): 255–68.

Ceva, Lucio. "Altre notizie sulle conversazioni militari italo-tedesche alla vigilia della seconda guerra mondiale (aprile–giugno 1939)," *Il Risorgimento* 30, no. 1 (1978): 151–82.

Ceva, Lucio, "Appunti per una storia dello Stato Maggiore generale fino alla vigilia della non-belligerenza (giugno 1925–luglio 1939)," *Storia Contemporanea* 10, no. 2 (1976): 207–52.

De Felice, Renzo. "Alle origini dell patto d'acciaio: l'incontro e gli accordi tra Bocchini e Himmler del Marzo–Aprile 1936," *La Cultura* 1 (1963): 524–38.

Dutter, Gordon, "Doing Business with the Fascists: French Economic Relations with Italy under the Popular Front," *French History* 4, no. 2 (June 1990): 199–223.

Ferretti, Valdo. "La politica estera giapponese e i rapporti con l'Italia e la Germania (1935–1939)," *Storia contemporanea* 7, no. 4 (December 1976): 783–824.

Ferretti, Valdo. "La politica estera italiana e il Giappone imperiale (gennaio 1934–giugno 1937)," *Storia contemporanea* 10, no. 4/5 (July–October 1979): 873–923.

Funke, Manfred. "Le relazioni italo-tedesche al momento del conflitto etiopico e dello sanzioni della società della nazioni," *Storia contemporanea* 2, no. 3 (1971): 475–493.

Gallagher, M. D. "Leon Blum and the Spanish Civil War," *Journal of Contemporary History* 6, no. 3 (1971): 56–64.

Godley, Michael R. "Fascismo e nazionalismo cinese, 1931–1938. Note preliminari allo studio dei rapporti italo-cinese durante il periodo fascista," *Storia contemporanea* 4, no. 4 (December 1973): 739–777.

Goglia, Luigi. "Note sul razzismo coloniale fascista," *Storia contemporanea* 19 (1988): 1223–66.

Grange, D. "La Propagande arabe de Radio Bari," *Relations internationales* 5 (1976): 65–103.

Gretton, Vice Admiral Sir P. "The Nyon Conference—The Naval Aspect," *European History Review* 90 (1975): 103–12.

Knox, MacGregor. "Conquest, Foreign and Domestic, in Fascist Italy and Nazi Germany," *Journal of Modern History* 56, no. 1 (1984): 1–57.

Knox, MacGregor. "The Fascist Regime, its Foreign Policy and its Wars: An 'Anti-Anti-Fascist' Orthodoxy?" *Contemporary European History* 4, no. 3 (1995): 347–65.

Leoncini, Francesco. "Italia e Cecoslovakia, 1919–1939," *Rivista di studi politici internazionali* 45 (1979): 357–72.

MacDonald, C. A. "Radio Bari: Italian Wireless Propaganda in the Middle East and British Counter-measures, 1934–38," *Middle Eastern Studies* 13, no. 2 (May 1977): 195–207.

Mallett, Robert. "Fascist Foreign Policy and Official Italian Views of Anthony Eden in the 1930s," *Historical Journal* 43, no. 1 (2000): 157–87.

Marder, Arthur. "The Royal Navy and the Ethiopian Crisis," *American Historical Review* 75, no. 5 (1970): 1327–56.

Mazzetti, Massimo. "I contatti del governo italiano con I conspiratori militari spagnoli prima del luglio 1936," *Storia contemporanea* 10, no. 4 (December 1979): 1181–94.

Michaelis, Meir. "The Attitude of the Fascist Regime to the Jews in Italy," *Yad Vashem Studies* 4 (1975): 7–41.

Michaelis, Meir. "Il conte Ciano di Cortellazzo quale antesignago dell'Asse Roma-Berlino, del 1934 al 1936 alla lucidi alcuni documenti indeti," *Rivisti storica italiana* 61 (1997): 116–49.

Mills, William C. "The Chamberlain-Grandi Conversations of July–August 1937 and the Appeasement of Italy," *International History Review* 19, no. 3 (August 1997): 594–619.

Mills, William C. "The Nyon Conference: Neville Chamberlain, Anthony Eden, and the Appeasement of Italy in 1937," *International History Review* 15, no. 1 (February 1993): 1–22.

Minniti, Fortunato. "Le materie prime nella preparazione bellica dell'Italia, 1935–1943, parte prima" *Storia contemporanea* 17, no. 1 (1986): 5–40.

Minniti, Fortunato. "Le materie prime nella preparazione bellica dell'Italia, 1935–1943, parte seconda, " *Storia contemporanea* 17, no. 2 (1986): 245–276.

Minniti, Fortunato. "Il problema degli armamenti nella preparazione militare italiana dal 1935 al 1943," *Storia contemporanea* 9, no. 1 (1978): 5–61.

Morewood, Steven S. "Appeasement from strength: The making of the Anglo-Egyptian Treaty of Friendship and Alliance of 1936," *Diplomacy & Statecraft* 7, no. 3 (1996): 530–62.

Murray, Williamson. "Munich 1938: The Military Confrontation," *Journal of Strategic Studies* 2, no. 3 (1979): 282–302.

Parker, R. A. C. "Great Britain, France and the Ethiopian Crisis of 1935–1936," *English Historical Review* 85, no. 351 (1974): 293–332.

Pastorelli, Pietro. "L'Italia e l'accordo austro-tedesco dell'11 luglio 1936," *Annali dell'istituto storico italo-germanico in Trento* 15 (1989): 395–410.

Quartararo, Rosaria. "Inghilterra e Italia: Dal Patto di Pasqua a Monaco (con un appendice sul 'canale segreto' italo-inglese)," *Storia contemporanea* 7, no. 5/6 (October–December 1976): 607–716.

Quartararo, Rosaria. "L'Italia e lo Yemen: Uno studio sulla politica di espansione italiana nel Mar Rosso, 1933–1937," *Storia contemporanea* 10, no. 4/5 (July–October 1979): 811–872.

Robertson, Esmonde. "Race as a Factor in Mussolini's Policy in Africa and Europe," *Journal of Contemporary History* 23, no. 1 (January 1988): 37–58.

Rochat, Giorgio. "Ancora sul 'Mussolini' di Renzo De Felice," *Italia contemporanea* 33 (1981): 5–10.

Rochat, Giorgio. "L'attentato a Graziani e la repressione italiana in Etiopia nel 1936–1937," *Italia contemporanea* 26 (1975): 3–38.

Rochat, Giorgio. "L'ultimo Mussolini secondo De Felice," *Italia contemporanea* 43 (1991):111–119.

Sakmyster, Thomas L. "The Hungarian State Visit to Germany of August 1938: Some new Evidence on Hungary's Pre-Munich Policy," *Canadian Slavic Studies* 3, no. 4 (winter 1969): 677–91.

Salerno, Reynolds. "The French Navy and the Appeasement of Italy, 1937–9," *English Historical Review* 112, no. 1 (February 1997): 66–104.

Stafford, Paul. "The Chamberlain-Halifax Visit to Rome: A Reappraisal," *English Historical Review* 98, no. 1 (1983): 61–100.

Steurer, Leopold. "Die Südtirolfrage und die deutsch-italienischen Beziehungen vom Anschluss (1919) bis zu den Optionen (1939)," *Annali dell'Istituto Storico italo-germanico in Trento* 4 (1978): 387–419.

Strang, G. Bruce. "Imperial Dreams: the Mussolini-Laval Accords of January 1935," *Historical Journal* 44, no. 3 (September 2001): 709–809.

Strang, G. Bruce. "War and Peace: Mussolini's Road to Munich," *Diplomacy & Statecraft* 10, no. 2/3 (1999): 160–90.

Tedeschini Alli, Mario. "La propaganda araba del fascismo e l'Egitto," *Storia contemporanea* 7, no. 4 (1976): 717–49.

Vannoni, Gianni. "Su alcuni momenti salienti del rapporto fascismo-massoneria," *Storia contemporanea* 6, no. 4 (1975): 619–673.

Visser, Romke. "Fascist Doctrine and the Cult of the Romanità," *Journal of Contemporary History* 27, no. 1 (January 1992): 5–22.

Watt, Donald Cameron. "An Earlier Model for the Pact of Steel: The Draft Treaties Exchanged between Germany and Italy during Hitler's visit to Rome in May 1938," *International Affairs* 3, no. 2 (April 1957): 185–97.

Young, Robert J. "French Military Intelligence and the Franco-Italian Alliance, 1933–1939," *Historical Journal* 28, no. 1 (1985): 143–68.

Index

About the Author

G. BRUCE STRANG is Assistant Professor of History at Lakehead University.

Recent Titles in International History